# Chancellorsville

# Chancellorsville

By

John Bigelow, Jr.

SMITHMARK

This edition published in 1995 by SMITHMARK Publishers, Inc.
16 East 32nd Street, New York, NY 10016.

SMITHMARK books are available for bulk purchase for sales
promotion and premium use. For details write or call the
manager of special sales, SMITHMARK Publishers, Inc.,
16 East 32nd Street, New York, NY 10016; (212) 532-6600.

This edition published by arrangement with
W. S. Konecky Associates, Inc.

ISBN: 0-8317-1431-X

Printed in the United States of America

10 9 8 7 6 5 4 3 2 1

# CONTENTS

## PART I

### PERIOD OF PREPARATION

## PART II

### PERIOD OF EXECUTION

# PART I

PERIOD OF PREPARATION

# THE CAMPAIGN
# OF CHANCELLORSVILLE

## CHAPTER I

BY the end of the year 1862 our Civil War had lasted a year and nearly nine months.  In this time the North had wrested from the South the border states of Kentucky and Tennessee, and secured the possession of the Mississippi River.  But while these advantages were gained in the West no corresponding progress was made by the Federal forces in the East.  The Army of the Potomac, under General Burnside, lay checkmated by the Army of Northern Virginia, under General Lee, on the bank of the Rappahannock, not a good day's march across the frontier formed by the Potomac River.  The Federal navy had the whole seacoast of the Confederacy under blockade, but on the high seas the Confederate cruisers were making havoc of the Northern merchant marine; and beyond the seas the agents of the Confederate government had anticipated the North in enlisting the sympathies of the ruling and influential classes of European countries.  At the same time a formidable anti-war or peace party in the North was causing serious embarrassment to the Federal administration.  Such was the situation when, on the 1st of January, 1863, Abraham Lincoln, as commander-in-chief of the army and navy of the United States, issued his Proclamation of Emancipation, giving freedom to the slaves of secession masters.  Although officially a war measure, this act was generally hailed in Europe and in America as a philanthropic one, and made for the President and his administration a small number of enemies or critics and myriads of friends.  Its influence abroad was decisive in turning the tide of sympathy from South to North.

In the prosecution of the war each section had both a political and a military end to attain.  Secession being an accomplished fact, the political object of the South was the vindication of its sovereignty, or the securing of recognition as a nation; that of the North was the restoration of the Union. The military object of the South was the defence of its territory, and that of the North the conquest of the South. The South, and perhaps the North, did not realize what a blow at European recognition was struck by the Emancipation Proclamation. The popular sympathy which it awakened for the North made it practically impossible for any European government openly to side with the South. But there was danger of individuals, with the connivance perhaps of their governments, fitting out and manning Confederate vessels of war, and subscribing to Confederate loans. During the month of January the Confederate government conceived the plan of supplying means of carrying on the war by floating a European loan of about $15,000,000. This plan depended for its success upon the military prestige of the Confederacy.

Burnside's bloody repulse at Fredericksburg and the criticism which it evoked led him to tender his resignation as commander of the Army of the Potomac. The President accepted it, and charged himself with the task of appointing as Burnside's successor a commander who should retrieve the disaster of Fredericksburg, and give confidence to people both at home and abroad whose hearts were with the North. After carefully considering all the eligible officers and thoroughly discussing, with his cabinet, their military and political records, he settled upon one of them as apparently the best qualified to meet these requirements; on the 25th of January, 1863, a general order from the War Department announced to the armies of the United States that Major-General A. E. Burnside was, at his own request, relieved from command of the Army of the Potomac, and Major-General "J. Hooker" appointed in his stead.

Joseph Hooker was born of old Puritan stock in Hadley, Mass., on the 13th of November, 1814. His youth gave no indications of a military destiny. It is said that he was intended for the church. Graduating from the U. S. Military Academy at West Point in 1837, he became a commissioned officer in the artillery. He served with distinction in the Mexican War from 1846 to 1848. For a period of about two years (1850, 1851) he was in California as assistant adjutant-general of the Pacific Division. He afterward received a two years' leave of absence; at the end of that time, or in 1853, being unable to reconcile his energetic and ambitious nature to inactive service and slow promotion, and experiencing perhaps an attack of the "California fever," he resigned his commission as an officer of the army, purchased a mile of land in Sonoma County, improved it by substantial inclosures, and tilled the soil, laboring with his own hands. In this enterprise he was not very successful. The living that he made by it was a precarious one. In 1853 he was appointed road overseer of the county, and for two years he held the office of superintendent of military roads in Oregon. In 1859, expecting the war cloud soon to burst, he became the colonel of a regiment of California militia. When in 1861 his expectation of war was realized, he found himself pecuniarily involved through his indorsement of notes for friends, and reduced to such poverty that he could not pay his way to the Atlantic coast. As he expressed an earnest desire to resume his connection with the army, his friends subscribed the necessary funds, to the amount of $1000, and sent him to Washington.

Hooker was no politician and was addicted to criticizing his military superiors. This propensity had nearly caused his dismissal from the Military Academy at West Point. In the Mexican War he had allowed himself to criticize General Winfield Scott, which brought upon him that general's lifelong enmity. Scott being now in command of the army, Hooker was allowed to kick his heels in the anterooms of the War Department.

He witnessed the first battle of Bull Run without participating in it. In an interview which he had soon afterward with President Lincoln, having been presented to him as Captain Hooker, he said:

"Mr. President, I am not 'Captain' Hooker, but was once Lieutenant-Colonel Hooker of the regular army. I was lately a farmer in California, but since the Rebellion broke out I have been here trying to get into the service, and I find that I am not wanted. I am about to return home, but before going I was anxious to pay my respects to you, and to express my wishes for your personal welfare and success in quelling this Rebellion. And I want to say one word more," seeing that the President was about to speak. "I was at Bull Run the other day, Mr. President, and it is no vanity in me to say that I am a d—— sight better general than any you had on that field."

Hooker was at once made a brigadier-general of volunteers. He was one of the first appointments to that grade, his commission dating from May 17, 1861. In 1862 he was given the command of the Second Division, III Army Corps, Army of the Potomac. He fought as division commander through the Peninsula campaign; as corps commander, in the Antietam campaign; and as commander of the Center Grand Division, constituting about one third of the Army of the Potomac, in the Fredericksburg campaign.[1]

In person Hooker was about six feet tall, well proportioned, and soldierly in bearing. His features were clear cut, and handsome, but for a rather weak chin. He had a slight fringe of side whiskers, a rosy complexion, as delicate as a woman's, abundant blond or sandy hair, and great speaking gray or steel-blue eyes. He was spoken of as the handsomest man in the army.[2] Though of Puritan stock, he had

[1] *San Francisco Chronicle,* Nov. 1, 1879; *Appletons' Cyclopædia of American Biography; Circular No. 16, 1903, Thirteenth Mass. Regiment Assoc.*

[2] *Memoirs of Henry Villard,* I, 347, 348; *Obituary of J. W. de Peyster,* by "Anchor," New York, 1881; *General Hancock,* by General Francis A. Walker, p. 73.

in his temperament more of the cavalier than of the roundhead.  He at times precipitated an engagement when he should not have done so, and had not the great qualities necessary to lead or direct an army of over 100,000 men.  Up to a certain point of responsibility which he had not yet reached, he was capable of brilliant achievement, but at that point, if he reached it, he would break down.  He was more mortified than gratified at being known both in and out of the army as Fighting Joe Hooker.  "It sounds to me like Fighting Fool," he once said. "People," he used to say, "will think I am a highwayman or a bandit."[1] How he came by this distasteful sobriquet is thus told by one of the chief actors in the incident, the proof-reader of the New York *Courier and Enquirer*:

It was three o'clock in the morning . . . McClellan had come to grips with the Confederate forces, and was pressing them back upon Richmond.  Every two or three hours through the night had come from the Associated Press Reporters' Agency sheets of manifold, that is, tissue paper upon which a dozen sheets (by the use of carbon sheets interleaved) could be written at once—one for each newspaper.  These sheets told of desperate fighting all along McClellan's line. Among his Corps Commanders was General Hooker, whose command had been perhaps too gravely engaged.

Just as the forms—indeed the last form, was being locked, that is, the type firmly held together in a great frame that the impression might be taken for printing, came another dispatch from the reporters with the Union army.  It was a continuation of the report of the fighting in which General Hooker's Corps had been so gravely involved.  At the top was written "Fighting—Joe Hooker."  I knew that this was so written to indicate that it should be added to what we had had before.  The compositor (typesetter) who had set it up (put it in type) had known nothing about the previous matter, however, and had set it up as a heading, "FIGHTING JOE HOOKER."

I rapidly considered what to do; as if it were yesterday I can remember the responsibility I felt and how the thing struck me.  Well, I said to myself, it makes a good heading—let it go.  I fully realized that if a few other proof-readers beside myself acted as I did it would mean that Hooker would thenceforth live and die as "Fighting Joe Hooker."  Some did and some did not, but enough did as I did to do the business.  (Sidney V. Lowell, Brooklyn, N. Y.)[2]

Hooker's reputation for courage and his soldierly appearance made him more or less of a hero to the rank and file, but among the higher officers who had grown up in the service with him, and judged him critically, he was not generally admired.  He had bitterly denounced Lincoln as an incompetent, and suggested that the safety of the government required a military dictator, and he was accused of having failed

---

[1] *Circular No. 16, 1903, Thirteenth Mass. Reg. Assoc.; Men and Things I Saw in Civil War Days*, by J. F. Rusling, p. 54; Hooker's Comments on Chancellorsville, *B.* and L.*, III, 217. This and other incidents of Hooker's career will be found in *Harper's Monthly*, Vol. 31, pp. 639–645.

[2] Manuscript in possession of the author.

to give Burnside honest support in the Fredericksburg campaign.[1]  His appointment was not received with enthusiasm except by the men of his old division.[2]  The day before his appointment his predecessor recommended him to the President for dismissal from the army on the grounds set forth in the following draft of an order to be issued from the headquarters of the Army of the Potomac:

General Joseph Hooker, major-general of volunteers and brigadier-general U. S. Army, having been guilty of unjust and unnecessary criticism of the actions of his superior officers, and of the authorities, and having by the general tone of his conversation endeavored to create distrust in the minds of officers who have associated with him, and having, by omissions and otherwise, made reports and statements which were calculated to create incorrect impressions, and for habitually speaking in disparaging terms of other officers, is hereby dismissed the service of the United States as a man unfit to hold an important commission during a crisis like the present, when so much patience, charity, confidence, consideration, and patriotism are due from every soldier in the field.  This order is issued subject to the approval of the President of the United States.

The remainder of the order disposes in an equally summary manner of a number of other officers of high rank who, in Burnside's judgment, had proved themselves unworthy of the honor of being officers in the army of the United States or had outlived their usefulness in the Army of the Potomac.  Burnside was competent to issue this order on his own responsibility, and would doubtless have done so, but for the judicious advice of his associates to submit it to the President for approval.  The President disapproved of it.  His selection of Hooker to succeed Burnside was due not so much to his estimate of Hooker's military qualities as to the preference of his cabinet for Hooker as the only eligible general who was free from political aspirations, and therefore not a possible rival candidate for the Presidency.[3]  The President had his misgivings as to the consequences of the appointment.  So accompanying the order making it, or close on its heels, went the following dispatch from Halleck, General-in-Chief, to the new commander of the Army of the Potomac.  It was dated January 25:

The President directs me to say that he wishes an interview with you at the Executive Mansion as early as possible.

In compliance with this request Hooker repaired on the following day to Washington.  But before doing so he formally assumed his new command.

It may interest the reader to observe how Burnside acquitted himself

[1] *Recollections of Half a Century,* by A. K. McClure, p. 347.
[2] *The 20th Regt. of Mass. Vol. Infantry,* by G. A. Bruce, p. 229.

[3] For details of Burnside's removal see B. and L., III, 239; *Mag. of American History,* XV, 52–54.

of the delicate task of saying something appropriate to the army that he was about to leave, which in its two years of campaigning had known nothing but failure except when defending its own soil, and which was now to be commanded by an officer whom Burnside deemed unworthy of holding a commission in the army of the United States.

> Headquarters Army of the Potomac,
> Camp near Falmouth, Va., January 26, 1863.

General Orders, No. 9:

By direction of the President of the United States, the commanding general this day transfers the command of this army to Maj. Gen. Joseph Hooker.

The short time that he has directed your movements has not been fruitful of victory, or any considerable advancement of our lines, but it has again demonstrated an amount of courage, patience, and endurance that under more favorable circumstances would have accomplished great results. Continue to exercise these virtues; be true to your country, and the principles you have sworn to maintain; *give to the brave and skilful general who has so long been identified with your organization, and who is now to command you, your full and cordial support and coöperation, and you will deserve success.*[1]

In taking an affectionate leave of the entire army, from which he separates with so much regret, he may be pardoned if he bids an especial farewell to his long-tried associates of the Ninth Corps.[2]

His prayers are that God may be with you and grant you continual success until the rebellion is crushed.

> By command of Major-General BURNSIDE:
> LEWIS RICHMOND,
> Assistant Adjutant-General.

Hooker replied, with his first order:

By direction of the President of the United States, the undersigned assumes command of the Army of the Potomac. He enters upon the discharge of the duties imposed by this trust with a just appreciation of their responsibility. Since the formation of this army he has been identified with its history. He has shared with you its glories and reverses with no other desire than that these relations might remain unchanged until its destiny should be accomplished. In the record of your achievements there is much to be proud of, and with the blessing of God, we will contribute something to the renown of our arms and the success of our cause. To secure these ends, your commander will require the cheerful and zealous coöperation of every officer and soldier in this army.

In equipment, intelligence, and valor the enemy is our inferior; let us never hesitate to give him battle wherever we can find him.

*The undersigned only gives expression to the feelings of this army when he conveys to our late commander, Major-General Burnside, the most cordial good wishes for his future.*[3]

My staff will be announced as soon as organized.

[1] The italics are mine. J. B. Jr.        [2] Burnside's former command.
[3] The italics are mine. J. B. Jr.

Burnside tells the army how it may deserve success under its new commander, but does not promise its realization; and Hooker says nothing about Burnside's efforts in the past, but wishes him success in the future.

On the morning of the 27th, Hooker reported in person to the Secretary of War and the President. In the meantime the following letter from the general commanding the defences of Washington had been received at the headquarters of the army:

### Heintzelman to Halleck, January 26

There does not appear to be much connection between the Army of the Potomac and the troops for the defence of Washington. Scarcely an order issued from the headquarters of the Army of the Potomac applies here. On the contrary the commander acts under orders from the General-in-Chief or from the War Department. The duties being so different, cannot the defences be made into a separate department, with such limits as may be convenient?

Hooker was asked by the Secretary of War whether he desired to have command of the troops in and about Washington, and declined, assigning as his reason that it would require all his time to place the Army of the Potomac in proper condition for field service before the coming of spring.

His experience the previous winter under Burnside had satisfied him that a winter campaign would be unwise and more likely to be ruinous to himself than to the enemy. Accordingly on the 2d of February the garrison of Washington with its dependencies was constituted a separate department and designated the Department of Washington, with Major-General S. P. Heintzelman in command.

In his interview with the President, Hooker said that he hoped to succeed, provided the President would stand between him and Halleck, the commanding general of the army. He stated that he deemed this necessary for various reasons. The commanding general had, to a limited extent, been identified with the army of the West and seemed to think that there was no other army in the republic. He wrote and spoke freely of the army he had commanded at the expense of one he had never seen. His disparaging comparisons and reflections had been communicated to the Army of the Potomac, and neither it, nor its commander, expected justice at his hands. Besides, he continued, he had been reliably informed that Halleck had opposed his appointment to the command of the army on two occasions when the removal of Major-General McClellan from command was in contemplation, and again on the removal of General Burnside.[1]

What the President said to all this is not known. But it appears that

[1] *Rep. of Com.*, IV, 112.

Hooker went away satisfied that he would be fully supported by the President and the War Department, including the general-in-chief. On his return to the Army of the Potomac he received from the President an expression of his mind in the form of the following characteristic letter:

> Executive Mansion, Washington, D. C.,
> January 26, 1863.

MAJOR-GENERAL HOOKER.

*General:*

I have placed you at the head of the Army of the Potomac. Of course I have done this upon what appear to me to be sufficient reasons, and yet I think it best for you to know that there are some things in regard to which I am not quite satisfied with you. I believe you to be a brave and skilful soldier, which, of course, I like. I also believe you do not mix politics with your profession, in which you are right. You have confidence in yourself, which is a valuable, if not an indispensable, quality. You are ambitious, which, within reasonable bounds, does good rather than harm; but I think that during General Burnside's command of the army you have taken counsel of your ambition, and thwarted him as much as you could, in which you did a great wrong to the country and to a most meritorious and honorable brother officer. I have heard, in such a way as to believe it, of your recently saying that both the Army and the Government needed a dictator. Of course it is not for this, but in spite of it, that I have given you the command. Only those generals who gain successes can set up dictators. What I now ask of you is military success, and I will risk the dictatorship. The government will support you to the utmost of its ability, which is neither more nor less than it has done and will do for all commanders. I much fear that the spirit which you have aided to infuse into the army, of criticizing their commander and withholding confidence from him, will now turn upon you. I shall assist you as far as I can to put it down. Neither you nor Napoleon, if he were alive again, could get any good out of an army while such a spirit prevails in it. And now beware of rashness. Beware of rashness, but with energy and sleepless vigilance, go forward and give us victories.

> Yours very truly,
>
> A. LINCOLN.

Hooker was deeply impressed by the tone and spirit of this communication. To a group of officers who were with him when he read it, he said,—"He talks to me like a father. I shall not answer this letter until I have won him a great victory."[1]

His choice for chief of staff was General Charles P. Stone, one of the few officers in the U. S. Army who were well qualified to perform the duties of that office.

Charles Pomeroy Stone was a graduate of West Point with a record of varied and efficient service as a staff officer. In 1861 he was appointed Colonel and Inspector-General of the District of Columbia

[1] *Abraham Lincoln,* by Nicolay and Hay, VII, 88.

Militia, and later, Colonel of the 14 U. S. Infantry, and given charge
of the outposts and defences of Washington. Being ordered by General
McClellan to make a feint of crossing the Potomac at Ball's Bluff, he
naturally caused a part of his command to cross. This fraction was attacked in force, and pushed into the river with great loss. Among the
killed was Colonel Baker, who had been an influential member of Congress. On the 9th of February, 1862, Colonel Stone was suddenly arrested, and without trial or charges, confined in Fort Lafayette, where
he was kept until the 16th of August. He was then released, and placed
on waiting orders, in which status he remained until the campaign of
Chancellorsville was practically over.[1] The simple justice of an investigation by a court of inquiry was denied him on grounds of political
expediency. Secretary of War Stanton, who doubted General Stone's
loyalty, was strongly opposed to his being Chief of Staff of the Army of
the Potomac. So Hooker took as his second choice Major-General
Daniel Butterfield, then commanding the V Army Corps. Butterfield
was not a graduate of West Point, nor had he, like Stone, studied the art
of war in Europe, but he had done good service before and during the
Civil War. Entering the militia early, he obtained the command of a
regiment at the age of twenty-eight. His regiment was among the first
to enlist for three months; at the expiration of this term of service he
was appointed a lieutenant-colonel in the regular army and a brigadier-
general of volunteers. In 1862 he was made a major-general of volunteers. He took part in the Peninsula campaign, the second Bull Run
campaign, and the campaign of Fredericksburg, in which he commanded the V Corps. Hooker's entire staff was announced to the army
in his second general order, dated January 29:

Maj. Gen. Daniel Butterfield, chief of staff.
Brig. Gen. Seth Williams,[2] assistant adjutant-general.
Lieut. Col. Joseph Dickinson, assistant adjutant-general.
Brig. Gen. James A. Hardie, judge-advocate-general.
Brig. Gen. Henry J. Hunt, chief of artillery.
Brig. Gen. M. R. Patrick, provost-marshal-general.
Col. Rufus Ingalls, chief quartermaster.
Lieut. Col. F. Myers, deputy chief quartermaster.
Col. H. F. Clarke, chief commissary.
Surg. Jonathan Letterman, medical director.
Capt. Samuel T. Cushing, chief signal officer.
Lieut. D. W. Flagler, chief ordnance officer.
Maj. William H. Lawrence,
Capt. William L. Candler,
Capt. Alexander Moore,        } aides-de-camp.
Capt. Harry Russell,

[1] *Appletons' Cyclopædia of American Biography.*
[2] Adjutant-General of the Army of the Potomac.

There was an officer practically holding a very important position on Hooker's staff who is not named in the foregoing order. This was Brigadier-General Herman Haupt, Chief of Construction and Transportation, U. S. Military Railroads, who was nominally in charge of all the military railroads of the United States, but really only of those used by the Army of the Potomac. He wrote to Hooker on the 27th of January:

... It will be my effort, so far as the Department of Military Railroads is concerned, to coöperate efficiently in your movements, and I am well aware that the success or failure of a movement is often a question of prompt supply.

.   .   .   .   .   .   .   .   .   .   .   .

The existing organization and arrangements work very satisfactorily. J. H. Devereux is Superintendent of the Orange and Alexandria Railroad; William W. Wright, Superintendent of the Fredericksburg Railroad; Adna Anderson, engineer of construction on both roads. I have directed Mr. Anderson, who is a very efficient and experienced civil engineer, to report to you and keep you advised of his whereabouts, so that in the event of any movement, you can communicate with him. Colonel McCallum attends to the routine and red tape business of the Department.

For myself I am generally present when active operations are in progress, organizing and directing where my presence seems essential.

I may be absent for some weeks during the present session of the Massachusetts Legislature, but my arrangements are such that nothing will suffer in my absence. In everything pertaining to railroad transportation consult with or direct Mr. Wright, and in all that pertains to construction, Mr. Anderson.[1]

In Robert E. Lee, Hooker had as opponent one of the world's great military leaders. McClellan, Pope, and Burnside had in turn recoiled from him in failure or defeat. No other commander, North or South, at this or any later stage of the war, had such a creditable military record as his. Lee was seven years older than Hooker. If he had not as fresh a complexion as the latter, he had equally regular, handsome features, not only free from every suggestion of weakness, but telling unmistakably of strength. An erect, muscular figure, and a graceful, dignified bearing, united with his noble countenance to give him a pleasing, distinguished, and commanding appearance.

He was graduated from the U. S. Military Academy second in his class, in 1829. During his whole four years' course he never received a demerit mark for any breach of rules or neglect of duty.[2] But in those days the rules of the Military Academy were less numerous and exacting than they have been of late years. This is said not in derogation, but in vindication of Lee's military character. "Throughout his whole life he never used tobacco, and though in rare cases he would drink a

---

[1] *Reminiscences of General Herman Haupt*, pp. 184, 185.
[2] *Memoirs of Robert E. Lee*, by A. L. Long, p. 29.

glass of wine, he strictly avoided whisky or brandy, and did his utmost to favor temperance in others. The intemperate habits of many of the persons under his command were always a source of pain to him.''[1]

Upon graduation he was appointed a lieutenant in the U. S. Corps of Engineers. He served on the staff of General Wool and of General Scott in Mexico, distinguishing himself especially by his daring and skilful reconnaissances. Perhaps his most notable performance was his determination and preparation of the line of march by which Scott turned the position of Cerro Gordo.

In 1852 he was appointed superintendent of the U. S. Military Academy. He filled this position with eminent success for three years, when under the law of that day he was forced to relinquish it by accepting an appointment in the line. He became lieutenant-colonel of the newly created 2d regiment of cavalry, of which Albert Sidney Johnston was colonel, and joining it in 1856, spent, with intervals of leave and detached service, five years in the rough practical school of frontier service, pursuing and fighting Apaches, Comanches, and kindred tribes of Indians in northern Texas. In 1859, being in Washington on leave of absence, he was designated to arrest John Brown and his fellow agitators, which he accomplished with the assistance of Lieutenant (later Major-General) J. E. B. Stuart.

He was opposed to secession, but also to the coercion of the Southern states. He refused to allow his name to be proposed for appointment to the command of the Northern armies, and the first call of the North for troops determined him to resign his commission. Had his own state not seceded, and been permitted to remain neutral, he would probably have remained neutral himself. On his resignation he wrote to his sister,—'' . . . save in the defence of my native state, with the sincere hope that my poor services may never be needed, I hope I may never be called on to draw my sword.'' But if it came to the defence of his native state, he was resolved to take part in it. A month before the people of Virginia ratified the ordinance of secession that was passed by its convention, Lee had accepted from the governor a commission as major-general and commander-in-chief of the naval and military forces of the state. In this capacity he superintended the organization, equipment, and instruction of the first levies of Virginia soldiery, and sent some 50,000 more or less trained troops to the front. This force, known as the Virginia State Line, was still nominally in existence in the spring of 1863. But the Confederacy having passed a conscription law, it became advisable for Virginia to transfer her state army to the Confederacy, that she might be credited with it in the determination of her quota for future drafts. This transfer was effected by an act of the Virginia legislature passed February 28, 1863.

[1] *Memoirs of Robert E. Lee*, by A. L. Long, p. 29.

On the 25th of May, 1861, Lee was appointed a brigadier-general in the army of the Confederate States and assigned to the command of the Department of Virginia. In this position he conducted an unsuccessful campaign against Rosecrans. He was afterward transferred to the Department of South Carolina, Georgia, and Florida, in which he directed the construction of the coast defences.

About the middle of March, 1862, he repaired under orders to Richmond, where he remained as military adviser to the President until the 1st of June, when, by order of the President, he assumed command of the Army of Northern Virginia. In the few months between this date and that of Hooker's appointment as army commander he had caused McClellan's withdrawal from the Peninsula, defeated Pope's army at Bull Run, and repulsed Burnside's at Fredericksburg.

The principal officers on Lee's staff were the following:

Colonel R. H. Chilton, assistant adjutant and inspector general, chief of staff.
Lieutenant-Colonel E. Murray, assistant adjutant and inspector general.
Major H. E. Peyton, assistant adjutant and inspector general.
Major W. E. Taylor,[1] assistant adjutant and inspector general.
Captain H. E. Young, assistant adjutant and inspector general.
Captain A. P. Mason, assistant adjutant and inspector general.
Brigadier-General W. N. Pendleton, chief of artillery.
Lieutenant-Colonel B. G. Baldwin, chief of ordnance.
Lieutenant-Colonel J. L. Corley, chief quartermaster.
Lieutenant-Colonel R. G. Cole, chief commissary of subsistence.
Surgeon L. Guild, medical director.
Lieutenant-Colonel W. P. Smith, engineer officer.
Captain S. R. Johnston, engineer officer.
Colonel A. L. Long, military secretary.
Major T. M. R. Talcott,
Major Charles Marshall, } aides-de-camp.
Major C. S. Venable,

[1] Adjutant-General of the Army of Northern Virginia.

# CHAPTER II

## ORGANIZATION AND EQUIPMENT

BOTH in the North and in the South there was a regular or standing army, and a temporary army, or army for the war only. The latter was called in the North the Volunteer Army, or Volunteers, and this designation was retained throughout the war, although many of the men composing it were drafted into it, and in the latter part of the war most of those who volunteered did so only to escape being drafted. The Confederates avoided this anomaly by designating their temporary establishment as the Provisional Army.

The Confederate army was, on the whole, better organized than the Federal. Judicious appointments of officers were made early in the war, and at the same time rigorous conscription laws put in force. As a consequence the Army of Northern Virginia was made up of seasoned soldiers and competent officers, welded together by a common experience of hard marching and desperate fighting. The Army of the Potomac, on the other hand, had suffered repeated and radical changes in its organization and *personnel*. It depended for recruits upon volunteering. Men served in it for comparatively short periods. The officers had not so firm a hold of their men, nor so perfect a grasp of their duties as the Confederate officers. With the Confederates, military instruction was perhaps as little of an art as it was with the Federals. But the Confederates did not stand so much in need of it. They came into the army with more of the qualifications of officers and soldiers than the Federals.

The relative amount of military spirit in the North and in the South appears in the comparative attendance at the national Military Academy at West Point. Between the foundation of the Military Academy in 1802 and the outbreak of the Civil War in 1861, the number of cadets admitted from the South was from two and one half to three times as great in proportion to the white male population of the South as the number admitted from the North in proportion to the white male population of the North.

It should not be inferred therefrom that the proportion of West Point graduates in the Northern and Southern armies bore any such relation to each other. One hundred and sixty-two—nearly half—of the Southern graduates in the U. S. Army in 1861 remained loyal to the North.  Only nineteen of the Northern graduates went with the South. The proportion of West Pointers among the officers of the Northern armies was from once and a half to twice as great as among the officers of the Southern armies.  In the Army of the Potomac and in the Army of Northern Virginia, the commanding general, the chief of artillery, chief of cavalry, chief quartermaster, chief commissary, and chief engineer officer were West Pointers.

In the Army of the Potomac the adjutant-general and the chief of ordnance were West Pointers; in the Army of Northern Virginia they were not, but they were both graduates of the Virginia Military Institute, appropriately called the West Point of the South.  Among the corps, division, and brigade commanders the proportion of West Pointers was as follows:

|  | ARMY OF THE POTOMAC | ARMY OF NORTHERN VIRGINIA |
|---|---|---|
| Corps commanders . . . . | 71% | 100% |
| Division commanders . . . | 63% | 83% |
| Brigade commanders . . . | 32% | 18% |
| Corps, division, and brigade commanders . . . . . | 42% | 31% |

The advantage of the South in respect to officers was due only indirectly to the national Academy at West Point.  It was due directly to its own institutions, particularly its military schools and militia.  Disregarding West Point and Annapolis, the military schools in the United States in 1860 were distributed as follows:[1]

| NORTH | | SOUTH | |
|---|---|---|---|
| Vermont . . . . . . . . | 1 | Alabama . . . . . . . . | 1 |
| | | Kentucky . . . . . . . | 1 |
| | | Louisiana . . . . . . . | 1 |
| | | Mississippi . . . . . . . | 1 |
| | | South Carolina . . . . . . | 2 |
| | | Tennessee . . . . . . . | 1 |
| | | Virginia . . . . . . . . | 2 |
| | | | 9 |

The South, as the originator of secession, had an earlier and clearer apprehension of the "irrepressible conflict" than the North.  In this conception, and the fear of an uprising among the blacks, it had two potent stimuli to the organization and training of its militia that were almost totally lacking in the North.  As a consequence the militia of the

[1] Census of 1860, Miscellaneous Statistics, p. 510.

South was in a higher state of efficiency, and, in proportion to the population, more numerous than that of the North.

The South had a military advantage in the comparative homogeneousness of its population. The census of 1890 divides the surviving white soldiers and sailors of the Civil War into native-born (of native or of foreign parents) and foreign-born, as follows:

| FEDERAL | | CONFEDERATE | |
|---|---|---|---|
| Native | 82% | Native | 97% |
| Foreign | 18% | Foreign | 3% |

According to this indication the proportion of foreigners in the Federal army was about six times as great as it was in the Confederate.

The moving spirit of each army was loyalty to the section of country in which it grew up, and with which its destiny was cast. Each side considered the other as the aggressor. The North looked upon the South as a political renegade, aiming or working directly or indirectly for the destruction of the Union; the South looked upon the North as a military invader and would-be conqueror and oppressor.

Now that the North and the South, having fought their fight and shaken hands, know each other again as friends and brothers, it is hardly possible to realize the animosity with which they then clutched and held each other by the throat. Each side believed in the perfect justice of its cause, and could hardly find terms opprobrious enough with which to express its abhorrence of that of the other, and its hatred of those who upheld and defended it. It was *Yankees, hirelings,* and *mudsills* on one side, and *rebels, traitors,* and *slave-drivers* on the other.

The political and the military situations combined to relieve the South of the responsibility of the initiative and impose it upon the North. To secure recognition and preserve its territory, with the possible exception of strips along the border actually occupied by Federal troops, all that the Confederacy had to do was to hold its own. Every day that passed without a military success for the North was an encouragement to the friends of secession abroad, and a discouragement to the war party in the North.

While the Federals were still dependent for recruits upon volunteering, the Confederates were enforcing a conscription law, so stringent that it necessarily provided for the exemption of a portion of the military population for work in certain important industries, such as mining, railroading, farming, etc. These *details,* as such exemptions were called, gave rise to differences of opinion between the civil and military authorities, and between the administrative and combatant branches of the military establishment. A case in point is the following communication from Seddon to Lee, dated February 10:

The applications for details sent you through the Department have been rarely allowed, but on the contrary have been generally returned disapproved. . . . Such applications are not transmitted incautiously, but are sent by me reluctantly and stintingly, and only when, on large considerations of public interest, the requirements of the general service, in my judgment, demand them. I have preferred, instead of exercising the privilege of the Department to order such details, to submit them in the first instance to the consideration of the military authorities in the field. This course I wish to continue, and [I] feel satisfied that on this frank exposition of the course and views of the Department, its judgment will hereafter have more consideration and deference on the part of the officers . . .

In reply Lee expressed himself on the 21st as follows:

I know and feel the necessity of keeping up to the highest point of excellence and efficiency all the various works which furnish the army with material, clothing, and transportation. But there is an equal and absolute necessity for every man liable to military duty to be held in the army, for, as you know, the odds against us are very great. I have hoped, therefore, that persons having government contracts, or employed in government agencies, would endeavor to find fit workmen and agents among the thousands who in town and country are for one cause or another exempted from military service, or among those who, though liable to military service, contrive in some way to keep out of the army. . . .

All details which the Department may order from this army will be made at once, but if referred to my judgment, I fear I will be unable to recommend them, unless compatible with my views of the necessities of the service, both here and elsewhere.

The Army of the Potomac was organized as follows:

*Right Grand Division* (Major-General Couch):
   II Corps (Major-General Howard).
   IX Corps (Major-General Sedgwick).
   Two brigades of cavalry, with a battery of horse artillery (Brigadier-General Pleasonton).
*Center Grand Division* (Major-General Meade):
   III Corps (Brigadier-General Sickles).
   V Corps (Major-General Sykes).
   Six regiments of cavalry, with a battery of horse artillery (Colonel Kerr).
*Left Grand Division* (Major-General Smith):
   I Corps (Major-General Reynolds).
   VI Corps (Brigadier-General Newton).
   Five regiments and one company of cavalry, with one battery of horse artillery (Brigadier-General Gregg).
*Grand Reserve Division* (Major-General Sigel):
   XI Corps (Brigadier-General Stahel).[1]
   XII Corps (Major-General Slocum).[2]

[1] Five regiments of cavalry were included in this corps.
[2] Four companies of cavalry were included in this corps.

*General Artillery Reserve.*
*Signal Corps.*
*Engineers.*
*Ordnance Detachment.*
*Provost Guard.*
*Defences of Washington.*

These forces, exclusive of the defences of Washington, aggregated, on the 31st of January, about 149,000 officers and men present for duty. The grand divisions averaged about 35,900 officers and men present for duty.

Following is the organization of the Army of Northern Virginia:

> *First Army Corps* (Longstreet):
> > Anderson's division.
> > McLaws' division.
> > Pickett's division.
> > Hood's division.
> *Second Army Corps* (Jackson):
> > A. P. Hill's division.
> > D. H. Hill's division.
> > Early's division.
> > Trimble's division.
> *General Artillery Reserve* (Pendleton).
> *Cavalry Division* (Stuart).

In each army the Signal Corps used electric as well as visual signaling. For electric telegraphy the Army of the Potomac relied principally upon the U. S. Military Telegraph Service, which was entirely independent of the Signal Corps. The Military Telegraph Corps was nominally a branch of the quartermaster's department. About a dozen quartermasters were included in it for the receipt and disbursement of funds, but it was practically a separate organization. It reported directly to, and received orders directly from, the Secretary of War, and was not generally considered as an integral part of the U. S. Army. It comprised all the telegraph lines and officers in the United States. Men of loyalty and executive ability in whom Stanton, the Secretary of War, had implicit confidence, were in control of the whole system, inventing and using a cipher code which the Confederates were never able to unlock, and which the operators and translators never betrayed. Its chief was Major T. T. Eckert. By means of this corps the War Department was placed in direct communication with every arsenal, general military depot, military prison, barracks, rendezvous, camp, and fort in the Union, and, by Stanton's order, every message to, from, and between them passed through the department and was therein deciphered. A recorded duplicate was in every case placed upon the Secretary's desk.

President Lincoln visited the War Department frequently to get the latest news from the front. His tall form could be seen crossing the lawn between the White House and the War Department regularly morning, noon, and evening. He often walked around among the cipher operators, looking over their shoulders, as they translated from or into cipher, and asking questions about the messages.[1]

The Federal Signal Corps was a part of the regular army. For service in the field, signal troops were formed into parties usually of four officers and eight men, one such party being assigned to a division of infantry. The code was given to the officers only, and when they had memorized the characters it was destroyed. A soldier worked the flag while an officer called the numbers indicating the letters. There was a cipher disk by means of which all messages were sent in cipher. The countersign, or the cipher, was changed daily, sometimes oftener. In sending a long message it would be changed a number of times.

Lines of flag and torch communication were often gotten up from one part of an army to another 20 or 30 miles long, and maintained day and night for months, except during a fog, when neither flag nor torch could be seen. Usually a line longer than 10 miles had repeating-stations by which messages were received and transmitted. Regular reliefs were taken at the telescope by the officers and men watching the next stations, and two minutes would not pass without an eye at the glass.

The Army of the Potomac made use of three stationary balloons for purposes of observation. Under each one was a detail of men who had charge of the cables that held the balloon in position, and a number of couriers, all under the command of an officer. Written messages from a balloon were dropped, with a stone or other weight wrapped up in them, to the officer below, who sent them on to their destinations.

The Confederate War Department had an Engineer Bureau, and there were engineer officers in the several Confederate armies, but among these officers there was a lack of training in field work and of the organization and direction necessary to the efficient coördination of effort. On the 27th of March Lee wrote to the Chief Engineer, C. S. A.: "If I had an experienced engineer capable of conducting the professional operations of that department in this army, young officers could be advantageously employed, but as I am now situated, they give no assistance. . . ."

In the Army of Northern Virginia there was no battalion or corresponding organization of engineers at general headquarters. The duties of such troops were performed by staff officers at the various other headquarters and by officers and men detailed from the line, and

[1] *E. M. Stanton*, by F. A. Flower, pp. 216, 217; *Lincoln in the Telegraph Office*, by D. H. Bates, in the *Century*, May, 1907.

civilian labor hired or impressed.  In the Army of the Potomac the engineer force was divided into three parts, all attached to the head-quarters of the army: the Topographical Engineers; the Engineers, including the Engineer Battalion (a regular force); and the Engineer Brigade (a volunteer force).  The Chief of Topographical Engineers was Brigadier-General Gouverneur K. Warren, U. S. Volunteers.  The Engineers were commanded by Lieutenant (later Captain) Cyrus B. Comstock, U. S. Engineers; and the Engineer Brigade, by Brigadier-General D. P. Woodbury, U. S. Volunteers.  These separate branches had no common head.  General Warren, in his report of the campaign, says that he was placed in charge of the Topographical Engineers on the 2d of February.[1]  It appears, however, that he was not announced to the army as serving on Hooker's staff until the 30th of March.[2]  In the Federal, as well as in the Confederate army, the work of pioneers of the ordnance department, Signal Corps, train guards, and ambulance corps was done largely by troops of the line serving with their regi-ments or attached to higher headquarters.  As a rule each regiment had its corps of pioneers or axemen, whose work it was to open up and corduroy roads, to clear or "slash" the front of a position, to construct or repair bridges, barricades, log works, etc.

The Army of Northern Virginia numbered 62,800 officers and men present for duty.  An army corps numbered about 30,000 officers and men present for duty.

It will be observed that in the Federal army the cavalry was assigned to grand divisions or army corps.  There was no independent cavalry.  In the Confederate army the cavalry was all independent, constituting Stuart's cavalry division.

In the Confederate army the grade of commander might be said to be commensurate with his responsibility.  Lee had the rank of general; his corps commanders, of lieutenant-general; his division commanders, of major-general; and his brigade commanders, of brigadier-general.  In the Federal army there was no grade above that of major-general.  *Three army corps and thirteen divisions were commanded by brigadier-generals.*

In each army the artillery was assigned for the greater part to divi-sions.  In the Army of the Potomac two batteries were assigned, as a corps reserve or corps artillery, to the II Corps; the remainder of the artillery was organized as a general artillery reserve for the army.  In the Army of Northern Virginia there was no corps artillery.  Bat-teries not assigned to divisions constituted a sort of general artillery reserve without being regularly organized as such.  This force was officially referred to as "artillery in the rear."[3]

[1] *W. R.*, 39, p. 194.        [2] *Ib.*, 40, p. 167.
[3] *Ib.*, 40, pp. 602, 650.

In the Army of the Potomac the senior artillery officer of each corps was required by law, "in addition to his other duties," to act "as chief of artillery and ordnance at the headquarters of the corps."[1] This required a captain to command his battery while acting as chief of artillery and ordnance, a practical impossibility, which was not attempted. By order or custom, the senior artillery officers of divisions acted as chiefs of artillery and ordnance for their divisions.

The General Artillery Reserve was commanded, in the Army of Northern Virginia, by the chief of artillery of the army, Brigadier-General William N. Pendleton, and in the Army of the Potomac by a special chief.[2] The artillery had practically no regimental organization in either army. The pieces were muzzle-loading, and made of wrought or cast iron or brass. There was not a steel or a breech-loading piece in either army.[3]

The principal varieties used are given in the following table:

| DESCRIPTION OF PIECE | RANGE IN YARDS | USED IN |
|---|---|---|
| *Rifles* | | |
| 20-pounder Parrott gun . | 4,500 | Both armies |
| 10-pounder Parrott gun . | 6,200 | Both armies |
| 3-inch ordnance gun . . | 4,180 | Both armies |
| *Smooth-bores* | | |
| 12-pounder gun . . . . | 1,660 | Army of the Potomac |
| Light 12-pounder gun | | |
| (Napoleon) . . . . | 1,300 | Both armies |
| 6-pounder gun . . . . | 1,525 | Army of Northern Virginia |
| 12-pounder howitzer . . | 1,070 | Army of Northern Virginia |

In addition to the guns above mentioned there were in the Army of the Potomac a few 4½-inch "ordnance" guns, and in the Army of Northern Virginia a few Whitworth guns.

The proportion of rifles to smooth-bores was in the Army of the Potomac about as 7 to 3 and in the Army of Northern Virginia about as 2 to 3. To fully appreciate the consequent advantage of the Federal artillery, one must consider, not only that the effective range of a rifle was from twice to three times that of a smooth-bore, but also that the Federal smooth-bore artillery was more homogeneous, and on an average heavier, than the Confederate (see foregoing table). The Confederate ammunition, moreover, was largely defective, while that of the Federals was generally good. In *personnel* the Federals had an advantage in the superiority of their men as artisans or mechanics.

---

[1] Act of July 17, 1862.

[2] In Vol. 40 of the *War Records* this chief is given on page 15 as Captain G. A. de Russy, and on page 16 as Brigadier-General William Hays.

[3] At this time the Prussian artillery was partially armed with breech-loading rifled steel pieces of Krupp's manufacture.

"Whilst the South had at the beginning of the war a better raw material for infantry and cavalry, the North had the best for artillery. It has been well said that 'a battery carries with it all that goes to make up civilization.' It requires many mechanics with their tools and stores, and also what are called 'handy men,' intelligent and self-reliant, for no two men at a gun do the same work. No country furnishes better men for the artillery proper than our Northern, and particularly our New England States, and if, as in other armies, the best fitted for this service were assigned to it, we would lead the world in this arm."[1]

The principal projectiles used were the solid shot—which has been discarded in recent years by field artillery—percussion shell, shrapnel, and canister. The time shell was used with rifled pieces. A piece could be loaded and fired from twice to three times a minute. The 3-inch field-piece in the U. S. Army to-day has fired fifteen aimed shots a minute.

In the formation of cavalry from raw material, the North and the South had each its peculiar advantages and disadvantages. The North was rich in men, money, and draft-horses, but comparatively poor in riding-horses, riders, and marksmen. During the first year of the war the Confederate cavalry surpassed the Federal in nearly everything that went to make good soldiers. The Confederate cavalrymen came mostly from the best families in the South, were nearly all accomplished horsemen, and more or less accustomed to the use of firearms. It took but little drilling to convert the Confederate cavalry recruit into an efficient trooper. The Federal cavalry was recruited from offices, mines, and workshops, many of the men having never been on a horse or handled a firearm. The Confederate cavalry was mounted for the greater part on well-bred horses, well broken to the saddle; the Federal, on indifferent horses imperfectly broken. Time worked a change in both of the opposing services which brought them in the course of the war to a practical equality. But as late as January 15, 1863, General Ingalls, Chief Quartermaster of the Army of the Potomac, wrote to General Meigs, Quartermaster-General:

The cavalry and artillery horses are in fair condition, considering that the quality of the animals never was first-rate. First-class horses have never yet found their way into this army. Many of them have been "doctored up" by contractors, and sold into our hands, and the first service has discovered their unfitness.[2]

While the horses of the Confederate cavalry were generally better blooded than those of the Federal, they began early in the war to fall behind the latter in number and condition.

[1] *Our Experience in Artillery Administration*, by Brevet Major-General Henry J. Hunt, in *Journal of Military Service Institution*, XII, 214.

[2] *W. R.*, 31, p. 983.

At the beginning of the war, the Confederate government, charged as it was with the creation of an army and of war material of all kinds, felt itself unable to provide horses for the numerous cavalry companies which offered their services, especially from the state of Virginia. Many companies organized as cavalry were rejected. With those that were enrolled the government entered into a contract, the substance of which was that the cavalrymen should supply and own their horses, which would be mustered into service at a fair valuation; that the government should provide feed, shoes, and a smith to do the shoeing, and should pay the men a *per diem* of forty cents for the use of their horses. Should a horse be *killed in action,* the government agreed to pay to the owner the muster valuation. Should the horse be captured in battle, worn out or disabled by any of the many other causes which were incident to the service, the loss fell upon the owner, who was compelled to furnish another horse under the same conditions, or be transferred to some other arm of the service.

"That the government should have adopted such a policy at the beginning of the war was a misfortune; that it should have adhered to it to the very end was a calamity against which no amount of zeal or patriotism could successfully contend."[1]

In no case was the sum paid for a horse killed in action sufficient to replace it, for the price of horses constantly advanced as the demand for them increased. To replace a horse that was only wounded or otherwise disabled without losing the disabled one, it was usually necessary to get the latter home, for only one horse could be kept by a soldier at the public expense. Taking a horse home involved the rider's leading it there from the point where his regiment might be stationed, not unfrequently a hundred miles or more, at his own expense. Many Confederate troopers mortgaged their land on account of their horses. Not uncommonly it appeared to the men that their only chance of supplying themselves with horses lay in taking them from the enemy, and instead of getting a furlough, they obtained permission to scout. If a stray picket or straggler could then be captured, it was done. This accounts for much of the small war carried on by the Confederate cavalry against the Federal outposts.

Each Confederate trooper had to take care of the horse which he hired to the government, and in case the soldier was disabled, unless some friend looked after the riderless horse, the chances were that it would fall a victim to starvation and want of care, or become a total loss to the owner.[2]

[1] *Campaigns of Stuart's Cavalry,* by H. B. McClellan, late Major and Chief of Staff of the Cavalry Corps, Army of Northern Virginia, pp. 257, 258.

[2] These particulars of the service in the Confederate cavalry are drawn from an article by Thomas T. Munford, Esq., of Lynchburg, Va., late colonel 2 Va. Cavalry, in the *Journal of the U. S. Cavalry Association* for June, 1891.

The Federal cavalry was generally armed with the Smith's and the Sharp's carbines, both breech-loading, the Colt's revolver, and the saber. The Confederate cavalry had tried, but unsuccessfully, to provide itself with the same arms. It was generally armed with the pistol, many troopers carrying two or three. Not so large a proportion had a carbine in addition to a pistol. The carbines and pistols were not of uniform pattern as in the Federal service. Many troopers for lack of a carbine carried an infantry rifle or musket. A small number only were armed with a pistol, carbine, and saber. The Colt's revolver held its place to the end of the war, and although seldom used as a charging weapon was invaluable in the mêlée, and as a defensive arm for patrols and couriers. The confidence which the regulars had long felt in the saber was shared by the volunteers as soon as some training and experience in its use had rendered its grasp familiar.[1]

In connection with the cavalry, notice should be taken of the irregular mounted troops of the Confederacy, which were generally called Partisan Rangers. The several Partisan bands were recruited mainly among men who could not be compelled or induced to serve in the line. They were attracted to the Partisan service chiefly by the reward in money guaranteed them for whatever plunder they might secure. It was practically the application of the prize principle of nautical warfare to war on land. The Partisan Ranger Act, which was passed April 21, 1862, contained the following provisions:

289. That the President be and he is hereby authorized to commission such officers as he may deem proper, with authority to form bands of partisan rangers in companies, battalions, or regiments, either as infantry or [as] cavalry, the companies, battalions, or regiments to be composed each of such numbers as the President may approve.

290. That such partisan rangers, after being regularly received into service, shall be entitled to the same pay, rations, and quarters during their term of service, and be subject to the same regulations, as other soldiers.

291. That for any arms and munitions of war captured from the enemy by any body of partisan rangers, and delivered to any quartermaster at such place or places as may be designated by a commanding general, the rangers shall be paid their full value in such manner as the Secretary of War may prescribe.

Prize money, varied and exciting service, comparative freedom from the restraints of discipline, frequent and lengthy sojourns at home, these advantages could not but attract men already enlisted in the cavalry of the line. They caused considerable dissatisfaction, leading to more or less desertion among Stuart's troops. Stuart, while

[1] Captain Moses Harris, U. S. A., in *War Papers of Commandery of Wisc.,*
*Mil. Order Loyal Legion,* I, 354.

wishing success to the Partisans, was anxious to put a stop to their evil influence upon his command. The problem in his mind was to take from the Partisan service as many as possible of the attractions which it possessed for men of the line without depriving it of the attractions necessary for its recruitment among men not available for the line. Both Lee and Stuart wanted the Partisans to remain continuously in service, going into camp instead of disbanding and returning to their homes between operations; in other words, they wanted the so-called Partisans to cease being guerillas and be Partisans. But this they were never able to bring about.

When General Hunt was appointed the first Chief of Artillery of the Army of the Potomac, General Stoneman was appointed the first Chief of Cavalry; the functions of each at that time were purely administrative.[1]

Under General Pope and General Burnside, however, Hunt had been intrusted with the command as well as with the administration of the artillery.

The Federal infantry was armed generally with the Springfield muzzle-loading rifled musket, caliber 59; with here and there a regiment with breech-loaders, and more rarely one with smooth-bores. The Confederate infantry was armed in a heterogeneous fashion. Many of the men had smooth-bore muskets, caliber 69. Others had rifled muskets, caliber 54; and others still the Springfield rifled musket of the Federals. The latter could be loaded and fired from once to twice a minute. In 1863 the Prussian infantry was armed throughout with the breech-loading needle-gun, firing six aimed shots a minute. The rifle with which the U. S. infantry is armed to-day will fire thirty-three aimed shots a minute.[2]

In the Army of Northern Virginia the brigades were formed, as a rule, of regiments of the same state. In the Army of the Potomac there were a number of brigades similarly formed, or state brigades—for instance, Phelps', Revere's, O'Rorke's, and Greene's New York; Rowley's, Stone's, Owen's, Graham's, Tyler's, Allabach's, and Kane's Pennsylvania. But, as a rule, the brigades were formed of regiments of different states. In the Army of Northern Virginia the infantry of every

---

[1] "Headquarters Army of the Potomac,
          "March 26, 1862.
"General Orders, No. 110.
    "1. The duties of the chief of artillery and [chief of] cavalry are exclusively administrative, and these officers will be attached to the headquarters of the Army of the Potomac. They will be required to inspect the artillery and cavalry whenever it may be necessary, and will be responsible that they are properly equipped and supplied. They will not exercise command of the troops of their arms unless specially ordered by the commanding general, but they will, when practicable, be selected to communicate the orders of the general to their respective corps. . . ."

[2] The U. S. infantry was not armed throughout with breech-loaders until 1869.

division comprised brigades of different states; in the Army of the Potomac there were two divisions in which the infantry was all of one state. These were Doubleday's and Humphreys' of Pennsylvania. Sykes' division, which was known as the regular division, consisted of two regular brigades (parts of ten regular regiments) and two batteries (one regular and one volunteer).

The Fourth Division of the VI Corps (Burnham's) consisted of one brigade of five regiments of infantry and one battery of artillery.[1] With this exception, the Federal divisions consisted on an average of three brigades of infantry with from two to four batteries of artillery. In this narrative the batteries will be designated generally by the names of their respective commanders at the beginning of the campaign.

In both armies the infantry regiments were formed of ten companies and the cavalry regiments generally of ten or twelve companies.[2] The average regiment of infantry numbered in the Army of the Potomac about 433 and in the Army of Northern Virginia about 409 officers and men present for duty equipped, or effectives.[3] The average brigade of infantry consisted in the Army of the Potomac of about 4.7 regiments, aggregating about 2000 effectives, and in the Army of Northern Virginia of about 4.5 regiments, aggregating about 1850 effectives. In the latter army each brigade of infantry and cavalry had its battalion of sharpshooters. In the Army of the Potomac there was a brigade of sharpshooters named after its commander "Berdan's sharpshooters"; a company known as the "1st Company, Massachusetts Sharpshooters," attached to Gibbon's division; and other organizations of the kind. But the Federal sharpshooters were not so regularly organized as the Confederate. The average Federal division comprised about 6200 and the average Confederate division about 8700 infantry. In the Army of the Potomac the average corps, numbering about 16,000, was about equivalent to two Confederate divisions.

The reader may need to be informed or reminded of the difference in power between the firearms of 1861–1865 and those of the present day. Modern field artillery has a maximum effective range of 6000 yards; it will rarely seek a shorter range than 1500 yards, except in accompany-

[1] On the 3d of February, 1863, the 61 Pa. was chosen, together with four other regiments, the 31 and 43 N. Y., 6 Me., 5 Wisc., and Harn's light battery, 3 N. Y., to form the Light Division of the VI Corps, organized for special service, and designed to act in emergencies with great celerity (*History of Pennsylvania Volunteers*, by S. P. Bates, II, 410). After the campaign this division, greatly crippled, was broken up, and its regiments were distributed among other organizations.

In the Confederate army A. P. Hill's division ($\frac{1}{11}$) was known as the Light Division.

[2] A number of the Federal regiments were formed of squadrons of two companies each, others were formed of battalions of four companies each.

[3] These and the following figures of strength are based upon the returns for March and April, 1863 (see Chapter X, *post,* and *W. R.,* 40, pp. 696, 320).

ing victorious infantry or pursuing a beaten enemy. In our Civil War the greatest effective range of field artillery was about 2500 yards, and this was attained only with rifled pieces. For smooth-bores the maximum effective range was about 1500 yards, or the minimum artillery range of the present day. Solid shot was used from 350 yards out; shrapnel from 500 yards to 1000 yards out, and canister from 500 yards in.

Modern infantry fire is annoying at 2000 yards, effective at 1200, and decisive at 600. In our Civil War the fire of lines of battle usually commenced at a range of about 300 yards, although skirmishers and sharpshooters would not uncommonly try their skill at 500 and even 1000 yards.

# CHAPTER III

## THE MILITARY SITUATION

THE Army of the Potomac was at this time substantially in the position it occupied before and immediately after the battle of Fredericksburg—on the Stafford Heights, on the left bank of the Rappahannock, opposite Fredericksburg (Map 1, sheet A). The railroad to Aquia Creek Station, together with the Potomac River between that point and Washington, constituted its main line of communication. Its supplies came mainly from Washington. At Alexandria the loaded cars were run on floats, which carried them to Aquia Creek Station, where they took the tracks on which they proceeded to Falmouth.[1] The army communicated with Washington overland by the Telegraph Road, which went through Stafford Court-House, Aquia, Dumfries, Occoquan, and Alexandria. Its advance depots were at Falmouth, Brooke's Station, Stafford Court-House, Aquia Creek Station, Belle Plain, and Dumfries; its headquarters were at Falmouth.

The Army of Northern Virginia confronted the Army of the Potomac, as it did at the battle of Fredericksburg, on the heights back of that town. Lee's line of supply was the Richmond, Fredericksburg and Potomac Railroad, together with the Virginia Central Railroad. The latter, running almost across the theater of operations, constituted a sort of advanced base. Lee might retire upon it practically at any point, and find or procure supplies. But there were only two points on this base from which he could further retire and keep on a line of railroad connecting him with the interior of the Confederacy. These two points were Hanover Junction and Gordonsville. If compelled to retreat he must fall back, if possible, upon the former in order to cover Richmond, which the Confederate government was determined to hold to the last extremity. In this case the North and South Anna Rivers were to be used as lines of defence. Should he be severed from Richmond he would make for Gordonsville. He had advanced depots at Hamilton's Crossing and Guiney's Station. His headquarters were about three miles below Fredericksburg.

A Confederate force under Brigadier-General W. E. Jones occupied

[1] *Reminiscences of General Herman Haupt,* pp. 165, 179, 180.

the upper part of the Shenandoah Valley, known as the Valley District, with headquarters at Newmarket (Map 1, sheet B); and a Federal force under Brigadier-General R. H. Milroy held the lower part, with headquarters at Winchester.  Brigadier-General B. F. Kelley commanded the defences of the Upper Potomac, with headquarters at Harper's Ferry.  He and Milroy reported to Major-General R. C. Schenck, commanding the Middle Department, with headquarters at Baltimore. West of the Shenandoah Valley, the Confederates held a section of country designated as the Department of Northwestern Virginia, which was commanded by Brigadier-General J. D. Imboden, with headquarters at Staunton, Va., on the Virginia Central Railroad (Map 1, sheet B). Brigadier-Generals Imboden and W. E. Jones reported to Major-General Samuel Jones, commanding the Trans-Alleghany Department, or Department of Western Virginia, with headquarters at Dublin, Va., on the Virginia and Tennessee Railroad.  The Federals constituted West Virginia a district in the Department of the Ohio, and gave the command of this district to Brigadier-General J. D. Cox, whose headquarters were at Marietta, O., on the Baltimore and Ohio Railroad and the Ohio River.

On the 17th of March West Virginia was transferred from the Department of the Ohio to the Middle Department, Schenck's; and on the 28th this state was announced by the department commander to constitute a separate district of the department under the command of Brigadier-General B. S. Roberts.  The first headquarters of the new district were established at Clarksburg.[1]

The Federals commanded the whole line of the Potomac River and the sea.  The approaches to Hooker's army by water were guarded by the Potomac Flotilla, under direction of Commodore A. A. Harwood, commanding the Washington Navy Yard.  The flotilla consisted of two divisions.  The first division, commanded by Lieutenant-Commander Magaw, was stationed in the Potomac River off Aquia Creek.  The second, commanded by Lieutenant-Commander McCrea, was stationed at the mouth of the Rappahannock River (*Appendix 1*).  The Potomac is navigable to Washington; the Rappahannock, to Fredericksburg; the York, which is formed by the junction of the Pamunkey and the Mattapony, is navigable to West Point, whence vessels proceed under exceptional conditions up the Pamunkey to White House.  The James is navigable to Richmond, which is connected by the James River Canal with Buchanan, on the James River, about 40 miles above Lynchburg.

The Federals had posts at Fort Monroe, Norfolk, Suffolk, Yorktown, Gloucester, and Williamsburg.

*Fort Monroe* was regarded as the Gibraltar of the Chesapeake, the key to the bay and its tributaries.

[1] *W. R.*, 40, pp. 159, 163.

*Norfolk* was held chiefly to keep the enemy from using it as a naval base.

*Suffolk* was held to cover Norfolk, insure the inland communication to Albemarle Sound, and to keep the enemy at a distance.[1]

*Yorktown* gave control of the Peninsula up to that point, keeping the enemy at a distance from Fort Monroe, and commanded the York River in case it were needed for the movement of troops.

*Gloucester,* though commanded by Yorktown, might in the hands of an enemy have proved an annoyance to that post or to vessels on the river. It was regarded as auxiliary to Yorktown in controlling the navigation of the river.

*Williamsburg* was an advance post for watching movements of the enemy up the Peninsula. Though 13 miles from Yorktown, it was used as an outpost of the latter.

Fort Monroe was connected by cable with Sewell's Point, on the south shore of the James River, and with Cape Charles, on the north shore of Chesapeake Bay. All the Federal troops in this quarter were under the command of Major-General John A. Dix, commanding the Department of Virginia, with headquarters at Fort Monroe. The adjacent waters were guarded by the North Atlantic blockading squadron, under the command of Acting Rear-Admiral S. P. Lee, whose flag-ship was in Hampton Roads.

Generals Dix, Schenck, and Hooker reported to Major-General W. H. Halleck, General-in-Chief, whose headquarters were at Washington. The relations between Hooker and Halleck grew so unpleasant that Hooker ceased to consult Halleck regarding plans of operation, and conferred on them almost exclusively with the President.[2] The Confederates had no general-in-chief, but all the troops in Virginia and North Carolina were under the command of General Robert E. Lee. In both armies the commander-in-chief was the President. The Federal Secretary of War was E. M. Stanton; the Confederate was J. S. Seddon.

The plateau of the Stafford Heights is broken by numerous gullies in which streams, called by the people of the country *runs,* make their way on one side toward the Potomac and on the other toward the Rappahannock. By one of these gullies the railroad from Aquia ascends to

[1] Situated at the head of the Nansemond River, with the railroads to Petersburg and Weldon, Suffolk was regarded as the key to all the approaches to the mouth of the James River on the north of the Dismal Swamp (*W. R.*, 26, p. 275).

[2] Testifying, March 11, 1865, before the Committee on the Conduct of the War, Hooker stated as his conviction that if the general-in-chief had been in the rebel interest, it would have been impossible for him to have added to the embarrassment he caused Hooker from the moment he took command of the Army of the Potomac to the time when he surrendered it. "It was often remarked," he said, "that it was no use for me to make a request, as that of itself would be sufficient cause for General Halleck to refuse it." See also Halleck to Stanton, *W. R.*, 39, p. 156, and 40, pp. 506, 516; and to Dix, *ib.*, 26, pp. 730, 731.

Falmouth, and by another a road descends from that point to the river, where it appears at a ford, to reappear on the opposite side leading to Fredericksburg.

This place, at the head of tide-water as well as of the navigation of the Rappahannock, was once the shipping-point of a considerable coasting trade, but had been gradually reduced to comparative inactivity by railroads diverting its trade to Richmond. Its genteel colonial houses, with their shining white door-steps, suggested Philadelphia and Baltimore to persons acquainted with these cities. It had been almost abandoned by its population since the Federals in 1862 threatened to bombard it.

The site of the city of Fredericksburg rises but slightly near the river, but a mile south of it there are considerable heights, forming a curve like the arc of a circle, with the river as a chord. The intervening lowland, about a mile wide and two miles long, was traversed by several highways, the Richmond Railroad, and three streams, of which the Massaponax, the farthest down the Rappahannock, was the largest.

The Stafford Heights command the hills back of Fredericksburg as well as the low ground between them and the river. But here and there they stand so close to the river that the Federal guns on their crest can not be sufficiently depressed to fire into the water.

The position of the Army of the Potomac on these heights was considered impregnable.[1] That of the Army of Northern Virginia was hardly inferior to it in natural and artificial strength. But Lee was compelled by the proximity of his powerful opponent to maintain a defensive line about 25 miles long and correspondingly thin. His I Corps (Longstreet's) held a range of hills back of Fredericksburg and one below as far as Hamilton's Crossing, also the crossings above at Banks' Ford and United States Ford. His II Corps (Jackson's) occupied a position extending from Hamilton's Crossing to Port Royal. Above the United States Ford the crossings of the Rappahannock were watched by cavalry. On the day on which Hooker assumed command of the Army of the Potomac, orders were issued in Longstreet's corps for Pickett's division to take position at Salem Church, about 6 miles back of Fredericksburg, and intrench itself. Pickett was to form a position on which the troops along the river might rally in case of their being forced to abandon that line. A position was prepared facing Fredericksburg, on what was destined to be the battle-field of Salem Church.[2] The winter, although the inhabitants called it mild, proved to the Southern soldiers, and even to the Northern, quite severe. Until the latter part of January the cold was not particularly intense, nor

---

[1] The topography is shown in its main features on Map 2. The position of the troops at this time is indicated approximately on Map 1 (sheet A).

[2] W. R., 108, pp. 673, 674.

was snow or rain frequent, but at that time the snow fell often and once or twice to the depth of a foot. The rains became continual and heavy. The Confederates were generally quartered in log huts daubed with mud. Most of these were too close to one another and damp. As the spring set in they were ventilated by knocking out the daubing. The clothing of Lee's soldiers was insufficient in quantity and poor in quality. Men would rub out a jacket in two or three months—a pair of trousers in one. Sometimes even cotton trousers were offered them in midwinter. Scarcely a particle of flannel was to be had. Shoes were scarce, blankets were curiosities and overcoats phenomena.

In the Confederate army there was little drilling, and that was done carelessly. Picket duty was light.

Amusements were rare in number and of very mild quality. The principal one was snow fighting between regiments and brigades.[1]

The condition of the Confederate commissariat may be judged from the following correspondence:

### Lee to Seddon, Secretary of War, January 26

*Sir:*

. . . As far as I can learn, we have now about one week's supply, four days' fresh beef and four days' salt meat, of the reduced ration.[2] After that is exhausted, I know not whence further supplies can be drawn. The question of provisioning the army is becoming one of greater difficulty every day. The country north of us is pretty well drained of everything the people are willing to part with, except some grain and hay in Loudon [County],[3] nor can impressment be resorted to with advantage, inasmuch as any provisions retained for domestic use are concealed. A resort to impressment would, in my opinion, in this region, produce aggravation and suffering among the people without much benefit to the army. But I think if the citizens in the whole county were appealed to, they would be willing to restrict themselves and furnish what they have to the army.

I am more than usually anxious about the supplies of the army, as it will be impossible to keep it together without food.

### Indorsement on Lee to Seddon, January 26

Subsistence Department, January 28, 1863.

Fifteen months ago this Bureau foresaw that the supply of cattle in Virginia would be exhausted. . . . The meat has held out longer than was expected. . . . Last winter the Commissary-General of Subsistence urged that the necks and shanks of beeves, usually excluded by regulations, should be used so as to make the most of what was obtained. . . . The order of the War Department, dated April 28, reducing the rations [*sic*] of meat and increasing that of flour, as above referred to, has not been observed in the Army of [Northern] Virginia for a

---

[1] *History of McGowan's Brigade*, by J. F. J. Caldwell, p. 71.
[2] ¼ pound. Lee to Seddon, April 17, 1863.
[3] Between Lee's position and the Shenandoah Valley.

period of between three and four months, by order of General Lee, and the use
of the whole beef (necks and shanks included), which was attempted to be instituted by the Commissary-General of Subsistence, has not been observed in that
army, the discontent and other obstacles being urged as insurmountable in the
field. . . . Supplies can not be gathered in the country southwest of General
Lee's army. It has been or is being drained already. Nor can they be had on
the south side of James River. That country is held tributary in commissary
supplies to Petersburg [Map 1, sheet A] and the south (except in hogs), and
even if they were there (as they are not) in quantity to feed General Lee's army
they could not be had; neither time nor transportation will allow it. All the
transportation that can be begged will be needed to get wheat to be converted
into flour for the same army that now wants meat. General Lee's suggestion that
an appeal be made to the citizens to forward supplies is noted by this Bureau,
and is not approved. . . .

Respectfully,

L. B. NORTHROP,

Commissary-General of Subsistence. [1]

The Federals, while in many respects better off than the Confederates, had also to endure discomforts and privation. Uncertainty as
to how long the army would remain inactive prevented the troops from
being properly protected from the inclemencies of the weather. The
army was considered as in the field, and not as in winter quarters.
The only shelter provided by the government was the shelter tent.[2] The
men were left to burrow and shelter themselves as well as they were
able. In some cases they occupied the log huts constructed by the
enemy when he held and occupied the site of the camp; in others they
excavated the earth from six to eighteen inches, built a pen of logs two
or three feet high, and on this inclosure as the walls, set up their
shelter tents as roofs, or built roofs of brush and dirt. Many regimental commanders took little interest in the welfare of their men.

As the weather in the latter part of the winter turned cold, the timber,
which had been abundant, became scarce and difficult to obtain by reason of the sea of mud and mire with which the camp was surrounded.
On the 22d of February Major James F. Rusling, Assistant Quartermaster, of the Second Division of Sickles' (III) corps, wrote home
from Falmouth:

This morning there was a foot of snow everywhere. It has snowed ever since;
and as I write, 2 p.m., the storm still continues. Woke up this morning with my
blanket covered with snow that had drifted in under my tent, and altogether felt
rather blue. . . .

It is a gay "Washington's birthday" here. We would have had a great time

---

[1] *W. R.*, 108, pp. 674, 675.

[2] In general form the same as is used in the army to-day. Each man carries a half of
one in his kit. Two men combine to make and occupy a tent.

had it not snowed so savagely. His "Farewell Address" was to have been read at the heads of the regiments, and salutes fired at noon. The salutes were duly fired, the hoarse voice of the cannon roaring in all directions. But the reading of the "Address" will have to be postponed until another year.

Washington's birthday was celebrated also in the Army of Northern Virginia. General Lee wrote to his wife:

[The snow] was nearly up to my knees as I stepped out this morning [22d], and our poor horses were enveloped. We have dug them out, and opened our avenues a little, but it will be terrible, and the roads impassable. No cars from Richmond yesterday. I fear our short rations for man and horse will have to be curtailed.

The subsistence of the Army of the Potomac was not deficient in quantity, but it was in quality. The soldier regularly received a full field ration, which was more than he could eat. The portion not consumed was wasted or went to form a regimental fund.[1] But there was suffering among the officers as well as among the men for lack of fresh food and sufficient variety. The law provided for variety as well as quantity, but it was not carried out.[2]

Supplies that belonged to the regiments were disposed of to cash customers and itinerant purchasers, and the money thus obtained was appropriated by the commissaries. The system enriched many a "captain and assistant commissary" for the rest of his life.[3]

During the latter part of January diarrhœa and a fever of a typhoid type prevailed to a greater extent than was warranted by the situation of the army. Symptoms of scurvy also began to appear. The patients, moreover, did not recover as rapidly as the medical director of the army thought that they should. The low vitality of the army was caused, in his opinion, by the want of fresh vegetables. Large quantities of potatoes issued at the principal depot of commissary supplies for the army were not drawn by the corps commissaries.

In both armies there was a dearth of forage, due mainly to bad roads and broken-down or inefficient transportation, and, as a result, the horses and mules were generally poor.[4]

A considerable portion of the Federal army was dissatisfied with President Lincoln's proclamation emancipating the slaves in Southern

---

[1] About a year later the ration was reduced on the ground that it was greater than was necessary.

[2] Section 13 of "An act for the better organization of the military establishment," approved August 3, 1861.

[3] *History of the 9 Mass. Vol. Inf.*, by D. G. Macnamara, p. 276.

[4] "The roads are in so bad a condition that hay can not be procured. The mules are suffering badly. They will eat the hair off each other, and devour paper and rags" (Letter of Nathan Haywood, M.D., Surgeon 20 Mass. Volunteers, manuscript, Mil. Hist. Soc. of Mass.).

territory, issued January 1, 1863. The Army of the Potomac had not been paid for six months. Men who had enlisted under the conviction that their pay would enable them to support their families were daily receiving letters from the latter representing their destitution and distress. Friends and relatives of these men sent them packages of civilian clothing and did everything else that they could to assist them in escaping from the service and returning to their homes. The troops were deserting at an alarming rate.

On the 15th of February Hooker wrote to Army Headquarters, Washington, inclosing a statement of the absentees based upon the returns rendered him under his general order No. 3, copies of which he inclosed:

I would respectfully request that these returns may be placed in the hands of some bureau at Washington, with a view of informing the provost-marshals of the different states, or the proper authorities, of the names of all parties absent, and where they are likely to be found, in order that they may be returned to duty.

This return shows a total of 85,123 officers and men absent from this command when first placed in my charge.

The inclosure has never been published, but is on file in the War Department. The totals show that about one man in every ten on the rolls was in desertion or absent without leave.[1] The several corps, arranged inversely to their ratios of desertion, made the following showing. The commanders are those of January 31.

| | CORPS | | DESERTERS PER 1000 |
|---|---|---|---|
| 1. | XI Corps (Stahel) | . . . . . . . . . . . . . . . . . | 43 |
| 2. | II " (Howard) | . . . . . . . . . . . . . . . . | 90 |
| 3. | V " (Sykes) | . . . . . . . . . . . . . . . . | 91 |
| 4. | I " (Reynolds) | . . . . . . . . . . . . . . . | 108 |
| 5. | III " (Sickles) | . . . . . . . . . . . . . . . | 119 |
| 6. | VI " (Newton) | . . . . . . . . . . . . . . . | 122 |
| 7. | XII " (Slocum) | . . . . . . . . . . . . . . . | 136 |

Unauthorized intercourse between the pickets of the opposing armies had grown into a "custom of the service." Soldiers would cross the river to visit one another and trade, the usual exchange being Federal coffee for Confederate tobacco, or Northern for Southern newspapers. Such transactions were carried on, too, without crossing in person. The men would keep boats that they had fitted with square-rigged sails, and having loaded them, would head them for the opposite shore, and let them make their voyages alone.

---

[1] Hooker testified before the Committee on the Conduct of the War: "At the time the army was turned over to me desertions were at the rate of about 200 a day" (*Rep. of Com.*, IV, 112).

On the 20th of January the Richmond *Enquirer* published the following epistle as received by a Confederate picket:

January 17, 1863.

*Gents on Confederate States duty:*

We had the pleasure to receive your letter, and were very glad to find you in
good spirits.  We are sorry not to have any newspapers on hand, but will get
some as soon as possible.  We send you coffee whenever the wind permits us to
do so.  Can't one of you come over this evening in that little boat you have there?
—we will not keep you.  In the hope that Jeff Davis and Abe Lincoln will soon
give us peace, we send best respects.

Co. A, 46TH REG'T, N. Y. S. V.

It may be that between armies as between nations trade is productive
of mutual good will, and that messages more or less friendly passed
between the opposing pickets, but the genuineness of this one is open
to doubt for the reason that there was no such regiment in the Army of
the Potomac as the 46th New York Volunteers.

A typical instance of how the racial kinship of the armies responded
to touches of nature is here presented in the poetic form in which it has
been happily commemorated:

### MUSIC IN CAMP (DECEMBER 15–31, 1862)

.    .    .    .    .    .    .    .

A Federal band, which eve and morn
　Played measures brave and nimble,
Had just struck up with flute and horn
　And lively clash of cymbal.

Down flocked the soldiers to the bank,
　Till margined by its pebbles
One wooded shore was blue with "Yanks,"
　And one was gray with "Rebels."

Then all was still; and then the band,
　With movements light and tricksy,
Made stream and forest, hill and strand,
　Reverberate with "Dixie."

The conscious stream, with burnished glow,
　Went proudly o'er its pebbles,
But thrilled throughout its deepest flow
　With yelling of the Rebels.

Again a pause, and then again
　The trumpet pealed sonorous,
And "Yankee Doodle" was the strain
　To which the shore gave chorus.

The laughing ripple shoreward flew
  To kiss the shining pebbles—
Loud shrieked the crowding Boys in Blue
  Defiance to the Rebels.

And yet once more the bugle sang
  Above the stormy riot;
No shout upon the evening rang,
  There reigned a holy quiet.

The sad, lone stream its noiseless tread
  Spread o'er the glistening pebbles;
All silent now the Yankees stood;
  All silent stood the Rebels:

For each responsive soul had heard
  That plaintive note's appealing,
So deeply "Home, Sweet Home" had stirred
  The hidden founts of feeling.[1]

.    .    .    .    .    .    .    .    .

[1] *Poems of American Patriotism*, chosen by J. Brander Matthews, p. 211.

# CHAPTER IV

CHANGES IN THE ARMY OF THE POTOMAC. THE ABOLITION OF GRAND DIVI-
SIONS. THE INTRODUCTION OF PACK-TRAINS. THE FORMATION OF ARTIL-
LERY BATTALIONS IN THE ARMY OF NORTHERN VIRGINIA. DISCIPLINE IN
BOTH ARMIES. ADOPTION OF CORPS BADGES. SIGEL RELIEVED

HOOKER and his chief of staff applied themselves energetically to
the improvement of the army in organization, equipment, and
*morale;* they commenced by altering its organization as indicated in the
following order issued February 5:

I. The division of the army into grand divisions, impeding rather than facili-
tating the dispatch of its current business; and the character of the service it is
liable to be called upon to perform being adverse to the movement and operations
of heavy columns, it is discontinued, and the corps organization is adopted in its
stead. They will be commanded as follows:[1]

> First Corps, Major-General John F. Reynolds.
> Second Corps, Major-General D. N. Couch.
> Third Corps, Brigadier-General D. E. Sickles (temporarily).
> Fifth Corps, Major-General George G. Meade.
> Sixth Corps, Major-General John Sedgwick.
> Eleventh Corps, Major-General Franz Sigel.
> Twelfth Corps, Major-General H. W. Slocum.

II. Hereafter the corps will be considered as a unit for the organization of the
artillery, and no transfers of batteries will be made from one corps or division to
others except for purposes of equalization, and then only under the authority of
the chief of artillery.

III. The cavalry of the army will be consolidated into one corps, under the
command of Brigadier-General Stoneman, who will make the necessary assignments for detached duty.

The most noteworthy of these changes was the multiplication of the
strategic or grand tactical units, the substitution of seven corps (eight,
including the cavalry corps) for four grand divisions. If rightly viewed
and interpreted, it augured ill for Hooker's generalship. The two reasons which he assigns for the change may be distinguished as adminis-

---

[1] These assignments to the command of the several corps were, by law, subject to approval
by the President, and had yet to receive such approval.

trative and tactical. The administrative reason would have been a good one if administration were alone to be considered in the organization of an army, which it never is. Administration should not be permitted seriously to interfere with tactics. When administrative convenience and tactical efficiency conflict, administrative convenience should give way. Hooker's tactical reason for the change was an excellent one for not making it. The smaller the columns, the larger must be their number, and the greater the need of grouping them and having them directed by the group commanders rather than directly by the army commander. While Hooker's army was to be resolved into seven corps, Lee's comprised but two. It was but half as numerous as Hooker's, yet one of its corps was about twice as numerous as one of Hooker's.[1] One of the first principles of strategy and tactics as well as of drawing, painting, sculpture, etc., of the military art as well as of the fine arts, is to secure the effect of masses. This simple, fundamental truth is easy to grasp, but hard to apply. With great soldiers, and perhaps with great men generally, it is an instinct, or second nature. Grant and Lee and Jackson showed that they possessed it in a high degree. When Grant in the spring of 1864 joined the Army of the Potomac as Commander of all the armies of the United States, one of his first official acts was to reduce the number of his army corps by consolidating the five corps of the Army of the Potomac into three, which increased their average strength from 15,646 to 26,077 officers and men present for duty equipped, or "available for the line of battle." The average grand division numbered about 35,000 men, or, deducting cavalry, about 31,800 men present for duty equipped. Grant's annihilation of two historic organizations, with all their prestige and *esprit de corps,* would have been unnecessary had the grand divisions been preserved. It may be doubted whether the reason given in Hooker's order was the real, or the whole reason, for his abolition of them. He probably distrusted the ability of their commanders, and was unable to replace them by better ones or indisposed to offend them by so doing.

Major-General Franz Sigel, who had commanded the Grand Reserve Division, and on its abolition was given the command of the XI Corps, lately a part of that grand division, was not satisfied with the size of his command. He tried to have the XI Corps made larger, and not succeeding, asked on the 12th of February to be relieved from the command of it, expressing, however, a desire to remain in the service of the United States. He fought in the German revolution in 1848 and 1849, commanding bodies of volunteers varying in numbers from 4000 to

---

[1] Further particulars as to the strength and composition of the opposing armies will be found in Chapter X.

15,000. In 1852 he came to the United States, and became a teacher and the editor of a military magazine, first in New York and then in St. Louis.

At the outbreak of the war he was the rallying-point of the Germans of Missouri and the Northwest, raising the first German regiment. He was commissioned a brigadier-general in 1861, and major-general in 1862; participated in the fighting for the possession and control of Missouri, and commanded a corps under Pope in the second Bull Run campaign.[1]

General Sigel was popular, not only in the large German element of the XI Corps and of the Army of the Potomac, but among Germans in all the armies and throughout the country. "I fights mit Sigel" was a shibboleth of German-Americans.

Hooker indorsed Sigel's request with the remarks:

Respectfully forwarded and reluctantly approved, as Major-General Sigel requests it. This officer is my senior, and feels that he should have the largest corps to command. In breaking up the grand divisions, I preserved the corps organizations, for in that seemed to be strength. The officers knew the men, and the men their officers.

The Major-General commanding the Eleventh Corps desires that the action of the proper authorities may be telegraphed as soon as made.

On the 19th this paper was referred by Halleck to the Secretary of War, and submitted by him to the President. His action thereon was telegraphed to Hooker in the form of the statement: "He has given General Sigel as good a command as he can, and desires him to do the best he can with it."[2] Sigel was not satisfied. He left the army on leave, and the command of his corps devolved temporarily upon Brigadier-General Julius Stahel, who had held it under him in the grand division.

The assignment of Brigadier-General Sickles, though "temporarily," to the command of the III Corps, gave offence to Major-General Howard, who commanded the Second Division of the II Corps. He wrote to Hooker requesting that he be assigned to command according to his rank. Sickles and Howard were both commissioned as major-generals on the 29th of November, 1862. Howard accepted his commission, thus becoming a major-general on that date; Sickles did not accept his, and so did not become a major-general until March 29, 1863. Not wishing to relieve Sickles, Hooker telegraphed on the 20th to the Secretary of War:

Has the resignation of Major-General Sigel been accepted, or is that officer to be removed from command of the XI Corps? I desire to ascertain in order that.

[1] *Appletons' Cyclopædia of American Biography.*
[2] *W. R.*, 40, pp. 70, 71.

if so, Major-General Howard, the highest in rank in this army for advancement to corps commander, may be assigned to it.

General Howard is an officer of uncommon merit, is favorably known to this army, and is fully identified with its history. It is highly important that the commander of the XI Corps should be named and that he should be on duty with it.

This inquiry had not been answered when, on the 31st of March, Hooker issued the following order:

II. Maj. Gen. O. O. Howard, U. S. Volunteers, being the senior major-general not in command of a corps, is temporarily assigned to the command of the Eleventh Corps, and will assume the duties pertaining to it without delay.

Oliver Otis Howard was born in Leeds, Me., on the 8th of November, 1830, and graduated from West Point in 1854. He commanded a brigade at the first battle of Bull Run, and for gallantry in that engagement was made brigadier-general of volunteers; he was twice wounded at Fair Oaks, where he lost an arm; he participated in the battle of Antietam; and as brigadier-general, commanded the Second Division of the II Corps at the battle of Fredericksburg.[1] Though his military record was better than Sigel's, he was to the XI Corps *persona non grata,* principally because he was thought to have displaced their countryman and favorite. The Germans regarded Howard's appointment as a blow at their nationality, a reflection on German generalship. They "knew little and cared less about Howard's reputation as a great Biblical soldier, the Havelock of the army, as he was called, owing to his having studied for the ministry in the Presbyterian Church."[2]

Having learned that the recommendations of the corps commanders for appointments on their respective staffs, authorized by law, could not be favorably considered by the President until the corps commanders themselves had been designated by the President, Hooker wrote on the 10th of April to the Adjutant-General of the Army, requesting that his selections of corps commanders be confirmed with as little delay as practicable. These, including Howard, were accordingly published from the War Department on the 15th of April, as assignments made by the President.[3]

Couch, Sickles, Slocum, and Stoneman were born in the state of New York; Sedgwick in Connecticut; Reynolds in Pennsylvania, where he was to die on the field of Gettysburg; Meade, who was to command the Army of the Potomac on that field and to the end of the war, was born at Cadiz, Spain. The oldest corps commander was Sedgwick, number-

---

[1] *Appletons' Cyclopædia of American Biography.*
[2] *Chancellorsville and Gettysburg,* by Abner Doubleday, p. 3.
[3] *W. R.,* 40, pp. 195, 211, 212.

ing fifty years, one year more than Hooker; the youngest was Howard, numbering but thirty-three. All were graduates of West Point, except Sickles, who was a well-known Democratic politician and member of Congress from New York. No two of these West Pointers were classmates, but Sedgwick was a classmate of Hooker's. Reynolds, Couch, Meade, and Sedgwick had served in the war with Mexico, and fought Indians either in Florida or on the Plains. Sickles, Howard, and Slocum had not the advantage of such experience. Stoneman was not in the Mexican War, but had served in the field against Indians. As commanding officer of Fort Brown, on the Lower Rio Grande, he refused to obey the order of his department commander, General Twiggs, to surrender the government property to the secessionists. He evacuated the fort, and went to New York by steamer. Meade, Couch, and Slocum had resigned from the army. Meade returned to it, however, in 1842. At the outbreak of the war Couch had been in civil life six years, and Slocum five. All were in the military service of the United States or came into it in 1861, and had participated in various campaigns of the Civil War.[1]

Lee's two corps commanders, Jackson and Longstreet, were both graduates of West Point, and both served with distinction in the Mexican War. Longstreet served on the Plains before and after the Mexican War. Jackson had no such experience. In 1851, after a few years of garrison duty in the East, Jackson resigned from the army to accept a professorship of Natural and Experimental Philosophy, or Physics, at the Virginia Military Institute. He filled this position until 1861, when he exchanged it for a colonelcy in the Virginia State Line. The same year he was appointed a brigadier-general in the Provisional Army of the Confederacy. For distinguished service at the first Bull Run, where he won the name of Stonewall, he was promoted to major-general and given the independent command of the Valley District, comprising the Shenandoah Valley. His brilliant operations in this region, his masterly march from the Valley to the railroad north of Richmond and from the Rappahannock to the rear of Pope's army, and his able handling of a wing of Lee's army in the campaign of Antietam, brought him in October, 1862, promotion to lieutenant-general and appointment to the command of the II Army Corps. With this command he held the right of Lee's line at Fredericksburg. At the beginning of the Civil War he had less military experience than most, if not all, of the commanders on either side who had served in the "old army." But there were few, if any, who had mastered so much of the theory of war, and so perfectly disciplined their minds by the study of military and mathematical problems. By 1863 he had gained more war ex-

[1] *Appletons' Cyclopædia of American Biography.*

perience than any of them, with the single exception of R. E. Lee, and was second only to the latter in the hearts of the people and the soldiers of the South.

Longstreet, on resigning from the army in 1861, was appointed a brigadier-general in the Provisional Army of the Confederacy. He commanded a brigade at the first Bull Run. In 1862 he was made major-general. He commanded a division in the Peninsula campaign, a wing of Lee's army—Jackson commanding the other—in the second Bull Run campaign, and in the Antietam campaign. He was promoted to lieutenant-general and given command of a corps at the same time as Jackson, and with his corps held the left of Lee's line at Fredericksburg. In 1863 Longstreet was forty-two and Jackson thirty-nine years of age.

J. E. B. Stuart, Lee's chief of cavalry, was at this time but thirty years of age. Graduating from West Point six years after the Mexican War, he had no experience in regular warfare, but had served on the Plains and been wounded in an encounter with Indians. Resigning when his native state, Virginia, passed its ordinance of secession, he was appointed a lieutenant-colonel of infantry in the Virginia State Line. In July, 1861, he was appointed a colonel of cavalry in the Provisional Army of the Confederacy, and in September of the same year, a brigadier-general of cavalry. In July, 1862, he was promoted to major-general of cavalry. He had proved himself a master of the art of screening and reconnoitering, and had distinguished himself especially in two raids, one on the Peninsula, the Chickahominy raid, and one in Pennsylvania, the Chambersburg raid, in each of which he marched completely around McClellan's army.

General Hooker was the first commander of the Army of the Potomac, and the last one, to substitute pack-mules for army wagons extensively in that army. The coming of the pack-mule was announced by a special order, March 19, providing for the distribution of 2000 pack-saddles (*Appendix 2*). It made no mention of the cavalry corps or the artillery reserve, from which it was inferred that these commands were not to march with the army.

As compared with wagons, pack-mules require more men, and more animals to a given freight, take up more room on a road (if kept on it), and by leakage and drainage waste more of the freight. At every halt, wagon-mules can rest without being unharnessed or even unhitched—not perfectly, but far better than pack-mules can without being un-packed. To unpack a train of mules and afterward repack them, consumes so much time that it does not pay in halts of less than an hour's duration. It is harder on pack-mules to make the ordinary halts of five or ten minutes per hour than to keep going. Pack-trains are capable of traveling faster than wagon-trains, but to do this for any length of time without hardship they must be allowed to travel their own gait;

the troops must conform to the movements of the train or allow the train to travel independently, which in active campaigning is often inconvenient or unsafe. In a country covered with woods and underbrush, pack-mules straying off the roads will rub their loads loose and the packers exhaust themselves running after them. To obviate this, the mules in this campaign were tied together in strings of two or three, and led. Thus secured, they did not stray away, but instead of rubbing against trees, they rubbed against each other, with about the same effect upon the loads, and a worse effect upon their poor bodies. This arrangement must have been a cause of many of the sore backs engendered during the campaign.[1] The abolition of the grand divisions was unfortunate, but perhaps necessary. The introduction of the pack-trains was unfortunate and unnecessary, or ill advised. Another change made by Hooker to the detriment of the efficiency of his army was to strip his chief of artillery of all executive functions and so reduce him to his original purely administrative usefulness. He was not to take command of the troops, or to give any orders to the artillery, unless specially authorized to do so, and all such authority would "expire with the occasion."[2]

In the Army of Northern Virginia the only material change of organization took place in the artillery. The batteries were grouped into battalions generally of four batteries each, and these battalions assigned to corps. It was provided that all the artillery in both corps should "be superintended by, and report to, the general chief of artillery."[3]

There was no express provision for a general reserve of artillery, but one was formed of the batteries not assigned to an army corps or to the cavalry division.

The chiefs of artillery of the several corps assigned battalions to the divisions and to the reserves of the corps; that is, they determined the composition of the divisional artillery and corps artillery, and could change it by the transfer of battalions at their discretion. They had tactical as well as administrative control of the artillery; in the absence of specific instructions from the army commander, or their corps commanders, they were in action to direct the posting and firing of their batteries or battalions, as well as at all times to keep them properly supplied and instructed, and generally serviceable and efficient.

The Federals had no unit corresponding exactly to the artillery battalion of the Confederates, but the groups of batteries attached to the Federal corps and divisions served the purpose of battalions. They were, however, considerably weaker than the latter. The corps and divisional groups (including the single divisional batteries) of the Army

---

[1] For a full discussion of the transportation of the Army of the Potomac, the reader is referred to W. R., 40, pp. 544–563.

[2] Hunt's testimony, Rep. of Com., IV, 91–93.

[3] W. R., 40, p. 625.

of the Potomac numbered, on an average, but two batteries, or twelve pieces.

In the Army of Northern Virginia each corps had its reserve, or corps artillery; in the Army of the Potomac, corps artillery existed only in the II and XI Corps. The Federal drill regulations for artillery issued March 1, 1863, contained the following statement: "The *artillery reserve* is commanded by a superior officer of artillery, and constitutes a distinct arm of battle under the immediate orders of the general commanding." This artillery was to be kept in rear of the infantry until the enemy's force had been fully developed, then to be brought up and its fire concentrated upon the point selected for the decisive attack.

In the cavalry the Smith's carbines were condemned at this time, and replaced by the Sharp's. The latter had not the range and penetration of the infantry rifle, nor the rapidity of fire of the Spencer repeating carbine, which was later to take its place, but its fire was so much more rapid than that of the infantry rifle that the Federal cavalry dismounted would confidently withstand the attacks of much more numerous forces of infantry.

Under Hooker the inspector-general's department was not so much reorganized as created.[1] Vacancies were filled by competent officers, and the corps increased so as liberally to provide inspectors for all arms. Colonel E. Schriner was announced as inspector-general and Lieutenant-Colonel N. H. Davis as assistant inspector-general. There were inspectors of infantry, inspectors of cavalry, and inspectors of artillery. Each brigade had an inspector, and the inspectors themselves were organized thoroughly under the head of the inspector-general of the Army of the Potomac. There were frequent formal inspections of the regiments, and these inspections were extended to the outposts and pickets, which up to this time had been under the supervision simply of the officers commanding the troops (*Appendix 3*).

A proclamation of President Lincoln issued on the 10th of March held out a promise of complete amnesty to all absentees who should rejoin their regiments before the 1st of April. The President had relinquished his right to review the sentences of courts-martial. It was with his approval that Hooker, on the 14th of March, issued the following order:

III. Officers reviewing the proceedings of court-martial will hereafter withhold their approval from sentences which cannot be carried into effect within the limits of this army. When such [sentences] are awarded the court will be directed to reconsider its action.[2]

There were no more delays in the execution of military law, no more appeals to Washington, which Lincoln's humanity always terminated

[1] *History of the II Army Corps*, by F. A. Walker, pp. 202, 203.
[2] *W. R.*, 40, p. 137.

by a commutation of penalty. Deserters were arrested, and promptly tried, sentenced, and punished accordingly. The spectacle of a few of them shot to death in the presence of the troops produced a most salutary effect.[1]

Capital punishment was at this time familiar also to the Army of Northern Virginia. General Paxton, commanding the "Stonewall" brigade, wrote home on the 15th:

To-day I had a visit from the father and mother of a poor fellow who has been tried by a court-martial for cowardice. She was in great distress and said it would be bad enough to have her boy shot by the enemy, but she did not think she could survive his being shot by our own men. . . . I have about twenty of my men in close confinement, whose sentences have not been published, many of whom are condemned to death. It is for General Lee to determine what shall be done with them.[2]

A creation of Hooker's hardly less important than the inspector-general's department was his service of information.

When General Hooker assumed command of the army there was not a record or document of any kind at headquarters of the army that gave any information at all in regard to the enemy. There was no means, no organization, and no apparent effort, to obtain such information. And we were almost as ignorant of the enemy in our immediate front as if they had been in China. An efficient organization for that purpose was established, by which we were soon enabled to get correct and proper information of the enemy, their strength, and their movements. . . . I called Colonel [G. H.] Sharpe, commanding a regiment of New York troops [120th], to headquarters, and put him in charge of that bureau [Military Information] as a separate and special bureau.[3]

Colonel Sharpe was appointed deputy provost-marshal-general. This appointment, together with a number of others, was published to the army in a general order on the 30th of March.

Flags were prescribed for the designation of army-corps headquarters, and badges to be worn on the caps of officers and soldiers to indicate the corps and division to which they belonged (*Appendix 4*).

The provision regarding flags to designate corps headquarters was not generally carried out, but the badges became popular among both officers and men. They may be said to have originated with General Kearney on the Peninsula in 1862. That officer, experiencing the disadvantage of not being able readily to recognize the men and officers of his corps, required them to wear for their identification a patch of red cloth

[1] *History of the Civil War in America,* by Comte de Paris, III, 3, 4; *Mag. of Am. Hist.,* XV, 193.
[2] *Memoir and Memorials of Brigadier-* General E. F. Paxton, by his son J. G. Paxton, pp. 92, 93.
[3] *Rep. of Com.,* IV, 74.

on their caps, which came to be known as "Kearney's patch." The idea of corps badges to be worn throughout the army was suggested to Hooker by Butterfield, who devised the badges in detail.

How the vitally important problem of supplying ammunition was to be solved was prescribed in an order issued on the 25th of March.[1] We shall see that it did not prove an effective solution.

The evils of discomfort and disease among the men, due largely to neglect and ignorance on the part of their regimental officers, were remedied pursuant to recommendations made by the medical director.[2]

On the 7th of February the following order was issued at the request of the chief commissary:

Flour or soft bread will be issued at the depots to commissaries for at least four issues per week to the troops. Fresh potatoes or onions, if practicable, for two issues per week. Desiccated mixed vegetables or potatoes for one issue per week.

Commanders of army corps, divisions, brigades, and separate commands will require any commissary under their orders who fails to issue the above-named stores to the command to which he is attached, and as often as stated, to produce written statement of his supplies to the effect that they were not on hand at the depot for issue to him, or otherwise to satisfactorily account for his failure.

The soldiers' fare was further improved by an act of Congress providing for the supervision of the cooking by both medical and line officers; for the detailing of privates as cooks, and the enlistment, in each company, of "two under-cooks of African descent," who should receive for their compensation ten dollars per month and one ration per day. The same act provided for the issue of pepper in the proportion of four ounces to every hundred rations.[3]

By these measures and others the health of the army was improved (*Appendix 5*).

[1] *W. R.*, 40, pp. 156 *et seq.* Extracts from this order will be found in foot-note, pp. 375, 376, *post.*

[2] *Letterman to Hooker, March 9*

"I have the honor to invite the attention of the Commanding General to a practice quite prevalent in this army: that of excavating the earth, building a hut over the hole, and covering it over with brush and dirt or canvas. This system is exceedingly pernicious and must have a deleterious effect upon the health of the troops occupying these abominable habitations. They are hotbeds for low forms of fever, and when not productive of such diseases, the health of the men is undermined, even if they are not compelled to report sick. I strongly recommend that all troops that are using such huts be directed at once to discontinue their use, and that they be moved to new ground, and either build new huts or live in tents. I also recommend that, in huts covered by canvas, the covering be removed at least twice a week, if the weather will permit, and that the men throughout the Army be compelled to hang their bedding in the open air every clear day" (*Medical Recollections of the Army of the Potomac*, pp. 103, 104).

[3] "An act to improve the efficiency of the corps of engineers and of the ordnance department, and for other purposes, approved March 3, 1863," Sections 8–11.

Tobacco, the soldier's solace, was regularly issued, and an occasional issue of whisky was made upon return from severe exposure on picket or fatigue duty. The clothing, often before of shoddy material, was carefully inspected and furnished of better quality.[1]

The general state of the opposing armies as to numbers and efficiency at the end of the first month of spring is shown in the following table:[2]

*State of the Army of the Potomac and of the Army of Northern Virginia, Officers and Men, March 31, 1863*

### PRESENT

|  | FOR DUTY | SPECIAL EXTRA OR DAILY DUTY | SICK | IN ARREST OR CONFINEMENT | AGGRE- GATE |
|---|---|---|---|---|---|
| Army of the Potomac | 136,724 | 13,000 | 11,936 | 1,345 | 163,005 |
| Army of Northern Virginia | 64,799 | 5,050 | 6,308 | 1,222 | 77,379 |

### ABSENT

|  | DETACHED SERVICE | WITH LEAVE | SICK | WITHOUT LEAVE | AGGRE- GATE |
|---|---|---|---|---|---|
| Army of the Potomac | 20,188 | 3,058 | 26,575 | 1,941 | 51,762 |
| Army of Northern Virginia | 6,251 | 4,140 | 16,136 | 5,953 | 32,480 |

PRESENT AND ABSENT

| | |
|---|---|
| Army of the Potomac | 214,767 |
| Army of Northern Virginia | 109,859 |

The figures for the Army of Northern Virginia include Hampton's brigade, which was absent recruiting and remounting, and Jones' troops in the Valley District. They do not include the artillery of Jackson's corps,[3] but on the whole they are somewhat larger than they should be for the army confronting Hooker. They show, however, that the ratio of sickness, the ratio of absence (with and without leave), and the ratio of punishment were smaller in the Federal army than in the Confederate.

One of the most potent causes of desertion in the Army of the Potomac was the scarcity of furloughs and leaves of absence. Hooker, under some difficulties, did much to satisfy the natural desire of officers and men for such privileges (*Appendix 6*).

One of his chief measures for reforming the Army of the Potomac was the institution of regular theoretical and practical instruction. Both seem, however, to have been conducted on narrow lines, the theoretical instruction being limited to recitations on the drill regulations, or tactics, as they were then called; and the practical instruction, to drills in the school of the company, battalion, regiment, and brigade.[4] Field exercises, it seems, were few and far between, and on

[1] *Mag. of Am. Hist.*, XV, 190.
[2] Unpublished record of the War Department.
[3] *W. R.*, 39, p. 695.
[4] *Reminiscences of Service in the 1 R. I. Cavalry*, by G. N. Bliss, p. 14.

a small scale. There was practically nothing done for the training of corps and division commanders and their staffs under conditions of battle; no manœuvering of large units in the presence of a marked or represented enemy. The author can find nothing corroborative of Hooker's testimony on this point before the Committee on the Conduct of the War:

Believing idleness to be the great evil of all armies, every effort was made to keep the troops employed; and whenever the weather would permit it, they were engaged in field exercises, and whenever the state of the roads and the river would admit of a movement, expeditions were fitted out to attack the enemy's pickets and outposts, and gather supplies from the country in their possession; my object being to encourage and stimulate in the breasts of our men, by successes, however small, a feeling of superiority over our adversaries.

Both Hooker and Lee attended to fostering and developing the martial spirit of their armies by the bestowing of medals, the inscription of the names of battles on the flags, etc. (*Appendix 7*).

A weak point of the Army of the Potomac, to which Hooker and his chief of staff gave special attention, was the performance of outpost duty. Its improvement was slow and difficult of achievement (*Appendix 8*).

The boundary line between Maryland and Virginia, commencing on the seacoast, divides a peninsula into two parts, known as the "Eastern Shore" of Maryland and the "Eastern Shore" of Virginia. The latter region, which would seem geographically to belong to Maryland, was included in the act of secession by which Virginia joined the Confederacy. A portion of its population carried on regular traffic in contraband goods with people of the mainland of Virginia. By a system of daily communication between the Confederate commanders and their allies in Baltimore, full information was obtained of the disposition and movement of the Federal forces and the designs of the Federal government. To put a stop to these practices a Federal force marched into the Eastern Shore of Virginia in 1861. Though the country was occupied by Federal troops from that time on, it was not so controlled but that the Confederates whom it continued to harbor could ply their hostile vocation, as the following correspondence shows:

*Haupt to Wells, Secretary of the Navy, January 31*

I am informed that an extensive smuggling business is done near the mouth of the Potomac, opposite St. George's Island, in small boats, which are secreted in the creeks or drawn up in the bushes and used at night; that in this way mails are carried and many wagon-loads of shoes and other necessaries transported to Richmond. The trade could be broken up, or seriously interfered with, by searching for and seizing all the boats and by the establishment of an efficient river patrol.[1]

### Butterfield to Magaw, February 1

General Hooker desires that you should use every exertion to stop the passage of small boats conveying deserters from the army across the Potomac. It is believed that large numbers cross the Potomac in small boats above and below Aquia Creek. Any person detected in this occupation by your efforts, he requests be turned over to the provost-marshal at Aquia Creek, with written memoranda of the circumstances attending their capture.

I believe that spies and contraband information are conveyed across the Rappahannock below the lines of our army.

[1] *Naval W. R.*, Series I, Vol. V, p. 226.

# CHAPTER V

MOVEMENT OF A DETACHMENT TO RAPPAHANNOCK BRIDGE. THE IX CORPS AND HOOD'S AND PICKETT'S DIVISIONS DETACHED. LEE'S AND HOOKER'S CONJECTURES

ON the 5th of February a Federal force of three regiments of cavalry and a battery of artillery, supported by a division of infantry (altogether about 15,800 men), started from Falmouth under orders to go up the river and destroy the Rappahannock Bridge. The purpose of this destruction was probably a twofold one—to check the enterprises of the Confederate cavalry against the Federal outposts, and to sever one of the lines of communication between Lee's army and the Shenandoah Valley. The bridge had been destroyed by Federal troops the summer before and been rebuilt by the enemy.

The weather was exceedingly bad. Snow, hail, and rain succeeded one another all day and all night, and half of the next day. The expedition camped the first night at Grove Church in a rain which froze as it fell.

The following day, while the infantry and artillery guarded the lower fords, the cavalry pushed on to the bridge. A vigorous fire was opened on the enemy in rifle-pits on the south side of the river. Under cover of this fire and of a stone pier near the north side, a party got under the bridge and cut a number of the posts. Its attempt to fire the bridge failed on account of the dampness of the timber, together with the fact that the troops were not provided with combustibles, or incendiary material. To make a success it was necessary to drive the enemy away from his position on the south bank and gain at least temporary possession of the bridge. This was more than the cavalry alone was equal to, and it was not attempted. The work of destruction having been thus imperfectly accomplished, the whole expedition returned to Falmouth, where it arrived on the 8th. The causes of its failure were the bad weather, the lack of combustibles, and the resistance offered or threatened at the crossing by Wade Hampton's brigade of cavalry, which the Federals thought to be two brigades and to number about 4800 men.[1] The little damage done to the bridge was soon repaired.

[1] For reports, see *W. R.*, 39, pp. 7–9; for orders and correspondence, *ib.*, 40, pp. 45–49.

The Confederate horsemen continued to prowl about the Federal outposts and made occasional dashes at them, but the progress which Hooker made in the instruction of his army and the improvement of its *morale* caused a diminution in the frequency and effectiveness of such enterprises. General Lee found increasing difficulty in keeping himself posted as to what was going on in the Federal camp.

When Burnside resigned his position as army commander he went North on leave of absence. The following order was issued February 4:

II. The Ninth Corps, under Major-General William F. Smith, will embark for Fort Monroe without delay. . . . On arriving at Fort Monroe, Major-General Smith will report to Major-General Dix for further orders. . . .

It was not until after the movement was well under way that Dix received the following communication from Halleck, dated the 9th instant:

The Ninth Army Corps, ordered to your command, will be used as you may deem proper. It, however, should be kept together as much as possible. A portion of it may be ordered farther south immediately.

By the 11th most of the corps, numbering about 15,000 men, arrived and disembarked at Newport News. Lee wrote as follows:

### To Seddon, February 14

This evening I received information from scouts on the enemy's right up to the 12th instant. Two report that the Ninth Army Corps of General Hooker's army had embarked at Belle Plain, and sailed for Suffolk; that a large fleet of transports was at Aquia Creek, and there was other evidence of a general move. I have directed General Pickett's division[1] to march to-morrow for Richmond, and General Hood's division[2] to be held in readiness. One of the scouts reported that it was the Second Army Corps which had embarked for Suffolk. Although it is stated that their destination is Suffolk [Virginia], should no other troops follow, I think it probable that this corps is intended to reënforce their army in South Carolina. . . .

### February 15

. . . demonstrations by the enemy upon points of our communications through North Carolina are to be expected, to prevent reënforcements reaching Charleston [South Carolina].[3]

It seems to me to be the policy of the enemy now to apply his whole strength to take Charleston, and it is proper for us to expect him to do what he ought to do. Unless therefore his conduct enables us to draw a different conclusion, we ought, if possible, to be prepared for him there.[4]

[1] Longstreet's corps.
[2] *Ib.*
[3] The principal port of entry of Confederate blockade-runners.

[4] The Federals were in fact preparing an operation against Charleston to be executed by Admiral Dupont. It was afterward known as the Dupont expedition.

On the 15th he ordered Hood's division to follow Pickett's, and wrote to Stuart that, if on his arrival at Culpeper he should find that the opportunity of striking a damaging blow was greater on the Potomac than in the Shenandoah Valley, he should "give precedence to the former, and take measures accordingly."

The movement of the Federal IX Corps south had, perhaps naturally, given more apprehension to Davis than to Lee. It was only to comply with Davis' wish expressed in a letter from Seddon dated and received to-day that Lee ordered the movement of Hood's division.[1] While Lee was responsible for detaching one of his divisions at this time, Davis was responsible for his detaching two.

Following is the composition and organization of these detachments as given in field returns of March 9 and 10.[2] The numbers stand for officers and men Present for Duty.

Hood's division ($\frac{4}{1}$) . . . . . . . . . . . . . . . . 6,965
Pickett's division ($\frac{3}{1}$) . . . . . . . . . . . . . . 6,169
Lane's battery, unattached . . . . . . . . . . . . 133
Grand total . . . . . . . . . . . . . . . . 13,267

Thus the departure of the IX Corps from the Army of the Potomac had caused the departure of about an equal force, but a considerably larger portion, from the Army of Northern Virginia. Would the IX Corps keep this detachment from rejoining Lee's army? It was too soon for Hooker to be forming conjectures in this regard, as he had not yet learned that the detachment was made.

The serious question in Lee's mind was how much, if any, of the remainder of Hooker's army was to withdraw from his front. Was the IX Corps only an advance-guard to be followed by the main body of the Army of the Potomac, or was the remainder of the army to go elsewhere? On these points he kept up an active correspondence with the authorities in Richmond.

It appears therefrom that both Lee and Seddon were in doubt as to how much of Hooker's army was in front of Lee, and what it was doing or preparing to do (*Appendix 9*). Reconnoitering below Fredericksburg was obstructed by the broad Rappahannock and the Federal vessels that occasionally patrolled it. On the 21st Brigadier-General W. H. F. Lee, with his brigade of cavalry, appeared opposite a couple of gunboats and cannonaded them with two pieces of horse artillery. One of the vessels was hit twice and injured beyond repair outside of a navy yard.[3] But the affair yielded no information of any value to General

[1] Lee to Seddon and to Davis, February 16, 1863, *W. R.*, 40, p. 627.
[2] *Ib.*, 26, pp. 915, 916.

[3] *Naval W. R.*, Series I, Vol. V, p. 235; *Mag. of Am. Hist.*, XV, 193; *W. R.*, 39, p. 20.

Lee. An attempt made to force the Federal picket at United States Ford with the cavalry posted opposite to it failed. Spies did not furnish the information wanted; there was nothing left but to make a vigorous dash through the Federal outposts. This operation was intrusted to General Fitzhugh Lee. His execution of it, which will be described under the title *The Skirmish at Hartwood Church,* was so far successful that it satisfied Lee as to the presence of Hooker's army in his front and the general disposition of its masses, but it did not set him right as to the force that had been detached.[1]

On the 26th of February, Lee heard unofficially of the result of Fitzhugh Lee's reconnaissance and wrote to President Davis:

. . . I have only learned positively of three army corps of the enemy having descended the Potomac. . . . Franklin's former grand division, detached to Newport News, is probably intended for Burnside, and I see it announced in Northern papers that he is to repair immediately to his new command without stating where. I think the scene of his operations will be south of James River. . . . I believe for the present the purpose on the part of Hooker of crossing the Rappahannock is abandoned, and that the late storms or other causes have suspended the movements recently in progress down the river. The disposition I have described may be intended to continue the remainder of the winter, or until their conscript law becomes operative.[2]

With better information, he wrote on the 28th to the Secretary of War:

One of my scouts, who has been on the Potomac for the past ten days, reports on the 26th that everything has been quiet on the river for the past week, only three or four steamers passing up and down during the day. A great many sail-vessels and a great deal of hay descending. From the number of transports and their capacity, he estimates that 15,000 or 20,000 troops have passed down since the 9th.[3] I think it probable this is Burnside's command, with which he will endeavor to advance south of James River, while General Hooker pursues this route. The army in front of us at present is certainly very large. . . .

The design, which Lee attributes to Burnside, of pushing into Virginia to the south of the James River, does not appear to have been entertained by any Federal commander. Hooker knew that the Army of Northern Virginia had been weakened by detachments, but was deceived as to the strength and purposes of the detachments, and as to the

[1] Only the IX Corps had been detached. It had been reported to Lee that, in addition to Burnside's corps, Franklin's former grand division, which consisted of the I and VI Corps, had moved down the Potomac. Burnside had no command at this time.

[2] Lee refers here doubtless to the draft, the law for which was not passed until March 3, and did not go into effect until October 17.

[3] The IX Corps actually numbered about 15,000 men (*W. R.,* 40, p. 538).

impression made upon Lee by the transfer of the IX Corps. He tele-graphed

*To Kelton, about 2:30 p.m., February 25*

Information from deserters, contraband, and citizens, received within the past two or three days, when compared and collated, seems to corroborate the following statement: That the enemy have decreased their forces in our front; that two or more divisions of Longstreet's corps have gone to Tennessee and South Carolina; that the enemy are under the impression that we are evacuating from Aquia, leaving a sufficient force to keep Lee's army in front of us. . . . Jackson's corps is left to guard the passage of the river. Ransom's division, of Long-street's corps, is one mentioned as gone to Tennessee or South Carolina.[1] Pickett's division is one gone to Charleston, commencing their departure Feb-ruary 17.[2] . . .

Lee had now a fairly correct estimate of the detachment made from Hooker's army and knew where the detachment was. Hooker had greatly overestimated the detachment made from Lee's army, and had very erroneous ideas as to its location or distribution. But neither Lee nor Hooker doubted that he would have to do with his opponent's main force on the Rappahannock.

The officers and men present for duty at this time in the Southern Section of the theater of war were disposed as follows:[3]

### FEDERAL

*Department of Virginia,* under Dix, headquarters Fort Monroe, Va. . .   35,187
*Department of North Carolina,* under Foster, headquarters New Berne,
   N. C. . . . . . . . . . . . . . . . . . . . . . . . . . .   15,808

                                                   50,995

### CONFEDERATE

*Department of Virginia and North Carolina,* under Longstreet, headquarters Petersburg, Va. . . . . . . . . . . . . . . . . . .   43,239

While 50,995 Federals were divided between two separate depart-ments, powerless to move from one to the other without permission or orders from Washington, the 43,239 Confederates were included in a single department, within which the department commander could move them at his discretion.

On the 1st of April the command of Lieutenant-General Longstreet was reorganized as three departments, all under the supervision and general direction of General Lee: the Department of Richmond, under

---

[1] Ransom's division was in North Carolina.
[2] Pickett's division and Hood's were in front of Suffolk, Va., under Longstreet.
[3] *W. R.,* 26, pp. 546, 547, 898, 900, 901, 915, 916.

Major-General Elzey, headquarters Richmond; the Department of Southern Virginia, under Major-General French, headquarters at some central point near Blackwater; and the Department of North Carolina, under Major-General D. H. Hill, headquarters Goldsboro.[1]

General Longstreet was authorized to transfer troops from any one of these new departments to another.

Lee's conviction as to the location of the IX Corps was probably not disturbed until he received the following communication from Longstreet, dated March 17:

The force at Newport News is reported to-day as moving to reënforce Suffolk. I fear that the real object is to join Foster at New Berne. If this is the intention I shall be obliged to move all of Pickett's division down to Goldsboro.

At this time the First and Second Divisions of the IX Corps were at Newport News, and the Third Division had been sent by General Dix to Suffolk.[2] The divisions at Newport News were ordered to move to the Department of the Ohio, to the command of which General Burnside was assigned on the 16th.

On the 30th Lee wrote to Longstreet:

One of our scouts reports, under date of 29th instant, that he was in Washington and Baltimore the first of last week, and that Burnside's corps left Newport News at that time for the West. . . . The New York *Times* of the 25th and the Washington *Chronicle* of the 26th state that Burnside was in Cincinnati on the 24th and is charged with the defence of Kentucky, but do not mention his troops. Can you not ascertain definitely whether these statements are correct?[3]

Longstreet replied the same day:

The troops have left Newport News; embarked on Friday and Saturday [27th and 28th]; supposed to have gone to North Carolina. My informant says they sailed for North Carolina.[4]

Longstreet's informant was mistaken; there was no such movement. Lee seems to have known it, for he wrote to Davis on the 2d of April:

I believe General Burnside with his corps has gone to Kentucky.[5]

On the 4th Longstreet wrote to Lee:

All my information is to the effect that half at least of Burnside's command is still at Suffolk.[6]

[1] *W. R.*, 26, p. 953.
[2] *Ib.*, 26, pp. 558, 562.
[3] *Ib.*, 26, pp. 949, 950.
[4] *Ib.*, 26, p. 948.
[5] Burnside was at this time in command of the Department of the Ohio, which comprised, besides the state of Ohio, the states of Indiana, Illinois, and Michigan, eastern Kentucky, and so much of eastern Tennessee as the Federals had possession of. Two divisions of his corps were moving from Newport News, Va., to serve under him. His headquarters were at Cincinnati, O.
[6] *W. R.*, 26, pp. 959, 960.

Lee replied on the 6th:

I think you will find none of Burnside's corps opposed to you. . . . . Burnside's corps has certainly gone west.[1]

Here Longstreet was nearer right than Lee, as one of Burnside's divisions was still in Virginia, in front of Longstreet.

[1] *W. R.*, 26, pp. 966, 967.

# CHAPTER VI

THIS chapter is devoted for the greater part to an affair of outposts, which had no effect upon either army as a whole, but which throws light upon the *morale* and the tactical efficiency of the cavalry in each one.  For this reason the operation is described in some detail.

On the 23d of February Lee telegraphed to Fitzhugh Lee at Culpeper Court-House to take his brigade and break through the Federal outposts on the Falmouth Road, and ascertain what was occurring behind them (Map 2).  The Federal outposts were of extra strength.  On the right and rear a double cordon, formed of an inner one of infantry and an outer one of cavalry, extended from west of Dumfries to west of Falmouth; along the front a cordon of infantry connected the double cordon on the right with another double cordon on the left; the latter covered the left flank of the army from the Rappahannock to the Potomac.  Each cordon was formed in three lines.  The outer or picket line consisted of sentinels or videttes (mounted sentinels) backed up at a distance of a few hundred yards by picket posts or picket reliefs.  The sentinels or videttes were commonly spoken of as pickets.  The second or middle line, stationed one to two miles in rear of the picket line, consisted of the main reserves, called supports, or line of resistance.  The third line was formed of the Grand or General Reserve, now called the Reserve.  The pickets were changed every three days, or, including a day for going and coming, every four days.  The sentinels were posted mounted—in other words, as videttes—and relieved every two hours, being two hours on post and four hours off.  The posts were single or double.  The videttes were instructed to keep their revolvers or carbines always in hand, prepared to fire instantly, if necessary.  The officers of the picket visited the line frequently by day and by night, and a visiting patrol passed up and down the line every hour.  The supports were posted in deep hollows or other concealed places where fires were allowed, the men remaining dismounted, with the privilege of making themselves as comfortable as possible, but always keeping themselves ready for action.  The horses were not allowed to be unsaddled except a few at a time, for the purpose of being cleaned, and when this was done the saddles were at once replaced.

59

The general cordon of outposts was divided into sections and assigned by section to particular commands to guard.  The cavalry outposts were assigned by General Stoneman to divisions as follows:

From the Occoquan River and Cedar Run (Map 1, sheet A) to Aquia Creek, to the First Division (Pleasonton).

From Aquia Creek to the vicinity of Falmouth, to the Second Division (Averell).

From Corbin, on the Rappahannock, to the Potomac, to the Third Division (Gregg).[1]

These division sections were subdivided into minor sections which were assigned to brigades.

Describing the cavalry outposts, Captain Frank W. Hess, 3 Artillery, U. S. Army, formerly first lieutenant, 3 Pa. Cavalry, says:

> Much of this line was through a densely wooded country.  These forests had once been cultivated land, but had been abandoned as such, and were now thickly studded with a dense growth of small pines, the foliage of which was so dense as to prevent one from seeing for more than a rod or two through them, and they were threaded by innumerable paths.  The enemy's cavalry was on the opposite bank of the Rappahannock—right bank—which in the low stage of the water could be forded in many places.  From these camps it was an easy matter for him to detach commands of from two to five hundred men, send them across the river at various places; and, by the hidden roads which his men knew so well, concentrate on any given point on the line, and drive in or capture our pickets.  These forays were numerous during the winter and very annoying to our people.  Every inhabitant in this country was in full sympathy with the enemy, and no matter how frequently the posts of our videttes were changed and the reserves moved, it was but a short time until the precise location was known at the headquarters on the other side of the river.  Women and children as well as men took a patriotic pride in giving information as to our movements, and vied with each other in schemes and ruses by which to discover and convey to the enemy facts which we strove to conceal.  On the other hand, information of the enemy's position and intentions could be procured by us only by personal observation, and for this purpose frequent reconnaissances were made in considerable force, before which he always gave way, retiring to his own side of the river.[2]

In compliance with his instructions, Fitzhugh Lee set out at 9 a.m. on the 24th with detachments of the 1st, 2d, and 3d regiments of Virginia Cavalry, numbering together about 400 men, provided with three days' rations and as much corn as the men could well carry on their horses, marched through Stevensburg, and crossed the Rappahannock at Kelley's Ford.[3]

---

[1] W. R., 40, pp. 62, 72, 79, 91, 96, 97.

[2] First Maine Bugle, 1893.

[3] The strength given above of Fitzhugh Lee's command is taken from his report to R. E. Lee (W. R., 39, p. 25).

At least one other regiment of his brigade (4 Va.) probably supported the brigade by covering its flank or rear.  One of the companies of this regiment (the Black Horse Cavalry) participated in the attack which

The river was so high as to swim low horses; the ground covered with about fifteen inches of snow; and the roads almost impassable. But there was no opposition. Confederate scouts pushed on to the Federal outposts. About noon there was some firing between them and the Federal pickets. The commander of the outpost near Hartwood Church, Lieutenant-Colonel Jones of the 3 Pa. Cavalry, reported to Averell at brigade headquarters that he felt satisfied that the enemy would attack at some point on his line (some 10 or 11 miles long) and asked for reënforcements. Averell's reply was: "If the enemy attack, whip him." Jones directed the utmost care and vigilance to be observed during the night, and only lay down himself two or three hours, giving orders that he be waked before daylight.[1] Fitzhugh Lee bivouacked at Morrisville. About 8 a.m. on the 25th he resumed his march by the Warrenton Post Road. About 9:30 four of his troopers were seen at the Federal outposts and fired on.[2] After the usual breakfast hour at Jones' headquarters a report was brought to him, probably in the vicinity of Berea Church, that the left of his line had been attacked[3] and had repulsed the attacking force. He detailed a party of 2 officers and 20 men of the support to go out beyond the picket line, follow the enemy, and bring back a report of what his force was. The party came upon a company of the enemy and had a slight skirmish with him in a ravine. It narrowly escaped being surrounded and captured, but slipped away and returned toward the support. On the way, marching by file along a narrow path through mud and snow, it fell in with six companies of the 4 Va. Cavalry, and was captured to a man.

Lieutenant-Colonel Jones, after detaching this party, ordered the support to form line, standing to horse, and await developments. With one or two orderlies he rode out toward Hartwood Church.

Lee's column, approaching by the Warrenton Post Road, passed Grove Church and Hartwood Church without incident worth mentioning. About 11:30 a.m., not far from Hartwood Church, his advance came upon three of Jones' videttes (probably forming what is now called a Cossack post). Three of his own men, wearing Federal overcoats, approached them without being required to dismount. Immediately these videttes were themselves made to dismount and march off as prisoners.[4] This was all done without the discharge of a firearm. Through the opening thus quietly made the column dashed down the road, past or over the picket reserve, or picket post, without drawing its fire.

Jones was in the vicinity of Hamet when he was met by an officer

was made on the Federal outposts (Letter of Lieutenant-Colonel Carter in McClellan's *Campaigns of Stuart's Cavalry*, p. 205).

[1] *History of the 3 Pa. Cav.*, by Committee, pp. 189, 190.

[2] *Sabres and Spurs,* by Chaplain Frederic Denison, p. 204.

[3] *History of the 3 Pa. Cav.*, by Committee, p. 190.

[4] *Ib.*

shouting that the enemy was charging down the road. Immediately a squad came toward him at full speed, filling the road, and commenced firing at him.

It was now about noon. The outpost was about to be changed. The new detail was with the General Reserve. Portions were being told off for the supports, when firing was heard in the direction of Hartwood Church, and Lieutenant-Colonel Jones came in from the front with the report that his line was being driven in.

Lee's command was pushing on in two columns after the fleeing pickets: one column, consisting of the 1 and part of the 2 Va., by the Ridge Road; the other, consisting of the 3 Va. and the remainder of the 2, by the Warrenton Road. The new detail for this part of the Federal outpost consisted of six squadrons of various regiments, numbering about 600 men, under Lieutenant-Colonel Thompson of the 1 R. I. The colonel at once forwarded a squadron, about 100 men, to the relief of the old pickets. With the remainder of his force he moved forward about half a mile by the Ridge Road and rapidly formed line. He had hardly done so when Lee's right column was heard charging with loud yells past his left. Seeing his rear thus threatened, he detached two squadrons, about 200 men, by the Warrenton Road, against the charging column, retaining in hand three squadrons, one of the 4 N. Y. and two of the 16 Pa., altogether about 300 men. The two squadrons which he last detached had hardly gotten under way when Lee's left column came dashing upon his (Thompson's) three squadrons.

Two of the squadrons [those of the 16 Pa.] had never been under fire; the other [the 4 N. Y., a German regiment] had been, but had not been known to stay long under such circumstances; and the present occasion did not seem to be the one upon which to vary the rule. Accordingly, with the greatest alacrity, they [of the 4 N. Y.] broke by individuals to run to the rear. The other two squadrons [16 Pa.], after firing a few shots from their carbines, instead of obeying Lieutenant-Colonel Thompson's order to charge, followed the example of the departed squadron, and, considering the condition of the roads, made very good time to the rear.[1]

The two squadrons detached to the Warrenton Road were also driven back. Lee penetrated with his right column to a point about a mile beyond Hamet, where he was repulsed by the infantry outpost of the III Corps; and with his left as far as Wallace, where he was checked by a dismounted party of the 3 Pa. Cavalry.[2] Thereupon, finding himself assailed by mounted troops and apprehending an attack in force, he rallied his columns and commenced retiring by echelon, making occasional

[1] *Sabres and Spurs*, by F. Denison, p. 202.

[2] McClellan, in his *Campaigns of Stuart's Cavalry* (p. 204), says that Fitzhugh Lee came in sight of the camp of the V Corps.

Fitzhugh Lee's memorandum of the information which he obtained, inclosed in his report to Robert E. Lee, can not be found (*W. R.*, 39, p. 25).

counter-attacks upon his pursuers. About 7 p.m., having shaken off the Federal cavalry, he took up the march for Morrisville.

About 3 o'clock in the afternoon Averell received a report that the enemy was in force in front of his line of videttes, and in the vicinity of Hartwood Church. *Boots and saddles* was immediately sounded in his camp. He transmitted the report by courier to Stoneman, with the statement that he had sent to find out what was happening, and would let him know the result. He also reported by telegraph to Williams, Hooker's adjutant-general, and in reply was instructed to send a brigade to the point attacked. At 3:30 his 2d brigade was on the march for Hartwood Church.[1]

Stoneman forwarded the report which he received to Williams by courier, and before he heard from Averell as to "the result of his investigation," was called to Hooker's headquarters. When he arrived there Hooker had received further information, among which was the following from Sickles, commanding the III Corps:

About 2 o'clock [this p.m.] the enemy's cavalry in force drove in our videttes and approached within twenty yards of my infantry sentinels. Lieutenant-Colonel Cummins, 124 New York, opened fire on the assailants, and drove them back with loss. The attack was not renewed. Considerable firing was heard on the right of Colonel Bailey [general officer of Sickles' outposts]. It was reported that a considerable detachment of our cavalry, estimated from 60 to 100, was cut off by the enemy and made prisoners.

General Whipple, commanding 3 Division, III Corps, informs me that Colonel Bailey has taken a prisoner who states that he belongs to Fitzhugh Lee's cavalry, five regiments of which crossed the river this morning and made this attack. This man will be sent immediately to headquarters as soon as he arrives. Shall I go out with a brigade or so, to support my line?[2]

The reports received at general headquarters created the impression that the enemy was not confining his operations to the vicinity of Hartwood Church; that he was aiming, and perhaps more seriously, at Stafford Court-House and Dumfries. Averell was directed to assemble his division at Hartwood Church, and the following exaggerated statement with accompanying instructions was sent to Williams, commanding the XII Corps, at Stafford Court-House:

Telegraphic advices report three brigades of the enemy's cavalry moving in the vicinity of your front. Advise the force at Dumfries to be vigilant. Our infantry there can whip the cavalry if they come.

The cautioning of the force at Dumfries was hardly necessary, judging from a communication of this date from the commanding officer at Dumfries to the Adjutant-General of the XII Corps.[3]

[1] *History of the 3 Pa. Cav.*, by Committee, p. 165.

[2] *W. R.*, 39, p. 21.

[3] "Our scout brought in information this evening that he was told by a citizen that the enemy's cavalry intend making a raid

Hooker telegraphed to Heintzelman at 6:30 p.m.:

A large cavalry force has made its appearance in front of our right, said now to be moving toward Stafford Court-House. We send out up the river to try and get between them and the Rappahannock. Can you send out from Catlett's and Rappahannock Stations to intercept them if they move that way? . . .

There were no troops at this time at Catlett's or Rappahannock Station.

To the Commander of the II Corps Butterfield wrote at 7:30 p.m.:

. . . send a good brigade of infantry up to Berea Church. The enemy have a force of cavalry in front of our picket lines on the right. General Stoneman will endeavor to capture them. Averell is following them up, and a cavalry force from here will move to get between them and the river.

By Hooker's direction, Stoneman directed Pleasonton to hold his command in readiness at daylight to move from his camp, and sent for Captain Cram, commanding the reserve brigade, in order to issue the same instructions to him. Before the latter arrived, Stoneman was directed to have his whole available force (Pleasonton's and Averell's divisions and Cram's reserve brigade) in readiness to move at 1 a.m. Further instructions were issued to Averell on Potomac Run at 7:45 p.m., as follows:

The commanding general directs that you follow the enemy's force; that you do not come in until the force which General Stoneman is directed to send out at 1 a.m. gets up with the enemy, and you have captured him or found it utterly impossible to do so. Stoneman will endeavor to get between them and the river.

Shortly afterward, on the receipt, it would seem, of a dispatch from Stafford Court-House transmitting the forequoted message from the commanding officer at Dumfries, the order to Stoneman was changed to "Move at once."

Stoneman telegraphed to Pleasonton, commanding First Division:

Move with the whole of your division, and be in position on the Telegraph road, near Aquia Church, as soon as you can. . . .

Inform General Butterfield the hour you will be in the position indicated. . . .

This dispatch was duly received. Captain Cram was directed by Stoneman in person to push his brigade on to Hartwood Church.

on this place, to capture the commissary stores, etc., supposing that the new picket line established last Saturday was simply a ruse, and supposing that we have left this [place]. . . . We will be on the alert, and are able to repel any attack from their cavalry."

Butterfield telegraphed to Averell:

*8 p.m.*

Stoneman has been instructed to move the forces from here at once. Pleasonton to be in position at Aquia Church to coöperate, or execute any order.

*About 8 p.m.*

. . . General Hooker says that a major-general's commission is staring somebody in the face in this affair, and that the enemy should not be allowed to get away from us.[1]

Hooker telegraphed to Stanton:

. . . The rebels have a cavalry force on this side of the river outside of my exterior line of pickets, which I hope to hive before morning.

This dispatch was received at 9 p.m. At this hour Butterfield transmitted to Heintzelman information received from Dumfries, through Stafford Court-House, and added:

We are pushing our forces from here up the Rappahannock and toward Warrenton. Answer what coöperation we may expect from above.

Before this dispatch was received Heintzelman telegraphed to Butterfield in reply to Hooker's dispatch of 6:30:

I have sent out a force of cavalry 2000 strong, toward Catlett's and Rappahannock Stations, by the way of Fairfax [Court-House] to intercept the enemy. This force will leave by 8 o'clock [a.m.] February 26; if possible, sooner. . . .

The necessity of concentrating somewhat scattered forces accounts for the tardiness of the hour (8 a.m. on the 26th) when the promised movement was to commence.

Averell arrived with his division near Hartwood Church and went into bivouac about 9 p.m.[2] Butterfield telegraphed to the commander of the XII Corps:

*9 p.m.*

Dispatch from Colonel Creighton [Dumfries] received. Inform General Pleasonton of its contents. Averell has gone up with a division of cavalry toward Hartwood. The division [brigade] of Regulars will go up the river road. Pleasonton will be in position within a few hours at Aquia Church. A brigade of infantry has gone up to Berea Church.[3] Inform Pleasonton of all these arrangements. . . . Send a brigade of infantry to Aquia Church to support Pleasonton, if desired.

[1] Copies of this dispatch were furnished to General Pleasonton and Captain Cram.

[2] *Sabres and Spurs*, by Chaplain F. Denison, p. 205.

[3] This movement had not commenced. The order prescribing it had not come down through corps and division headquarters to brigade headquarters.

*9:10 p.m.*

. . . Prisoners captured and brought in report the force as Fitzhugh Lee's and Hampton's brigades.[1] Marched from 12 miles the other side of the Rappahannock last night, made a long circuit to-day, and horses very tired. We ought to capture every one of them. . . .

The 2d brigade, Second Division, II Corps (Couch's) got under arms at 9:30 p.m., and started for Berea Church at 10 p.m. It had just about 2½ miles to march, but, owing to the darkness of the night and the bad condition of the roads, did not reach its destination until about 11:15, nor complete its dispositions for holding the cross-roads until about 12 p.m. Guards were placed over the surrounding houses to prevent communication with the enemy; an escort of cavalry which was attached to the brigade was used for patrolling the roads and establishing and maintaining communication with the main body and the outposts.[2]

After these measures were taken, Stoneman left Hooker's headquarters for Hartford Church. At Falmouth he overtook the rear of the reserve brigade and sent forward to direct Captain Cram to push on as fast as the state of the roads would permit, getting through, if possible, to Hartwood Church before daylight, and if Stoneman should not be there, to report to General Averell. By daylight Averell was to be up the river as far possibly as Deep Run—thus, it was thought, effectually cutting off the enemy's retreat by the way that he had come by, and rendering his escape very difficult, if not impossible; Pleasonton was to be on the enemy's trail.

Learning that Averell had arrived with his division at Hartwood Church, Stoneman, at 11 p.m., wrote and telegraphed to Pleasonton:

. . . It is very possible the enemy is making for Dumfries. Get off at once, and if you can find out where the enemy is, push him to the utmost of your ability wherever he may go. Be sure to get between the enemy and the river.

Pleasonton had not yet started for Aquia Church. This dispatch was probably carried there, and from there back to Hooker's headquarters. At any rate, it was not delivered to Pleasonton. Soon apprehending that it would be too late on the following day for Heintzelman's cavalry to coöperate to any purpose, Butterfield telegraphed to Heintzelman at 11:15 p.m.:

The force is F. Lee's and Hampton's brigades. . . . Their horses are well tired. We are pushing all out to-night. Can not you push out to-night and push this side of the railroad and Rappahannock Station? . . .

[1] Hampton's brigade was south of the James River, recruiting. It did not return during the campaign.
[2] Report of brigade commander, *W. R.*, 107, p. 175.

This dispatch was received at midnight.[1] At this time Pleasonton's adjutant-general wrote to the commander of the XII Corps declining the support of a brigade of infantry and stating:

This division has been ordered to move at daylight to Aquia Church, by the Telegraph road. . . .

While these preparations were going on for the interception and *hiving* of Fitzhugh Lee, that chieftain, with his exultant troopers and a string of about 150 prisoners, marched back to Morrisville, and again went into camp there for the night. He left behind him 14 killed, wounded, and missing, and a surgeon to take care of his wounded. The Federals lost 36 killed, wounded, and missing.

About midnight, Butterfield telegraphed to Couch:

1

. . . The enemy are supposed to be lying around the vicinity of Hartwood. . . .

2

General Stoneman will be at Hartwood at daylight. Let the commanding officer [of the brigade at Berea Church] communicate with him and take his orders from him. . . .

At 3 a.m. on the 26th Pleasonton wrote to Butterfield:

General Stoneman directed me to inform you when I should leave for Aquia Church.[2] I have therefore the honor to report that the Second Brigade left its camp at 2:30 this morning and the First is about leaving. I shall move with the latter. One regiment of the Second is already at the Church, which is some 8 miles from here by the road which can now be traveled. . . . I shall not move beyond Aquia Church until I hear further concerning the rebel movements. I have requested General Williams to keep me informed.

This dispatch, it seems, was not received. The reserve cavalry brigade commenced passing through Berea Church about 3:30 a.m. The head of the column arrived at a point in the vicinity of Hartwood, where Averell was in bivouac, about 4:30. The rear was closed up about 6. Soon afterward Averell started out with his division and the greater part of the reserve brigade in search of the enemy. Stoneman himself remained at Hartwood Church with the remainder of the reserve brigade. About 7 a.m. he ordered the infantry brigade at Berea Church to march about 2 miles further up the Warrenton Road and take a position at that point, which it did. The rain which commenced falling about midnight, and continued all night, was coming down in torrents.

Stoneman sent a squadron to Richards Ferry and learned that a

[1] *Rep. of Com.*, IV, 196.
[2] He was directed to report, not when he would leave for Aquia Church, but when he would be there, or "in position on the Telegraph Road, near Aquia Church" (see Stoneman's first order to Pleasonton).

party of the enemy had crossed there by swimming. This party was
perhaps the scouts that had felt the left of Averell's line on the morning
of the 25th. Another squadron was sent out on the road to Warrenton
to see whether any parties had gone directly from Kelley's Ford
toward Dumfries. Having gone beyond Spotted Tavern, it returned
without finding any trail, which it would easily have found had any
troops passed that way, the ground being covered with snow. Having
learned from undoubted authority that the enemy had recrossed the
river and that the river was swimming and rising fast, Stoneman decided to abandon the pursuit. He sent out three officers with small
parties to intercept Pleasonton and order him to return to his camp,
supposing that he had received and acted on the orders sent him last
night. At this time the following dispatch of 10:15 to-day from Butterfield to Stoneman was probably on its way:

The accompanying dispatch just received from Pleasonton. His brilliant dash
and rapid movements will undoubtedly immortalize him.

*"8 a.m. In position at Aquia Church."*

It is fair to presume that he failed to receive your orders to push on, otherwise
I cannot account for his movements at all. I sent him a dispatch, of which I
inclose a copy [following]. General Couch has been ordered to withdraw his
infantry.

*Inclosure*

*Butterfield to Pleasonton, Aquia Church, February 26, 10:15 a.m.*

I don't know what you are doing there. Orders were sent you at 11 p.m. last
night, by telegraph and orderlies, to push for the enemy without delay, and to
communicate with General Stoneman at Hartwood. The enemy have recrossed
the river, at Kelley's Ford probably, and Averell is pursuing them. Get your
orders from Stoneman.

Stoneman intended, with General Hooker's permission, to resort to
the miserable protective measure of destroying the Rappahannock
Railroad Bridge. He sent to General Couch, commanding the II Corps,
for axes, which were promptly forwarded, but before they arrived, he
received the following order from Butterfield, dated 6:30 a.m.:

. . . in the event of your inability to cut off the enemy's cavalry, you will
follow them to their camp and destroy them.[1]

He moved with all the force that he had at Hartwood, except 500 men,
to the vicinity of Kelley's Ford, determined to cross the river, if possible, the following morning. On the march he learned from Pleasonton
that he and Averell were at Morrisville with their divisions. About
4:45 he was freed of the unpleasant prospect of a morning swim in the
Rappahannock by the receipt of the following order dated 12:30 p.m.:

[1] *W. R.*, 39, p. 23.

The major-general commanding directs that in case the enemy has recrossed the Rappahannock and are [*sic*] on the other side, you will return with all your command to camp.[1]

He communicated this order to Pleasonton and Averell, with instructions to carry it into effect after it had been ascertained beyond a doubt that "the enemy had recrossed the river and was on the other side." On receiving a note from Pleasonton assuring him that there was no doubt on that point, he ordered all the troops to return at once to camp.

A correspondent of the New York *Herald* wrote from Falmouth with reference to these operations:

. . . enough is known, Feb. 26, to establish the opinion that it was the determination of General Stuart to make his way to Potomac Creek, and destroy the expensive railroad bridge over which the supplies of this army are now conveyed in most part.

In this he was successfully foiled, and his retreat across the river was accomplished just in time to save his force from destruction, inasmuch as the rain of last night had caused a rise in the stream, rendering it impossible to ford.

Whether or not such a view was generally held in the Army of the Potomac, it does not appear to have been justified. Fitzhugh Lee's object was to locate the masses of Hooker's troops. In this he seems to have been successful.

The following dispatch of 12 m. from the commander of the III Corps to the Adjutant-General of the Army of the Potomac throws an interesting light on the fight made by the Federal outposts:

Colonel Bailey, commanding outposts, reports that after examining the dragoons whom he arrested yesterday for shamefully passing through his lines to the rear when attacked by the enemy, and finding some of them hurt by falling from their horses and one wounded, he let them go. The orders received last night will be strictly observed in the case of other stampeders who fall into Colonel Bailey's hands.[2]

Probably before daylight Butterfield was in receipt of the following dispatch from Heintzelman:

I have ordered the cavalry at Fairfax Court-House, about 600 strong, to leave camp immediately for Rappahannock Station, to be supported by the force leaving camp to-morrow [8 a.m., 26th].

What this cavalry, 600 strong, did is not known. The main force of 2000, which was to start this morning, consumed the day getting together at Centreville and rebuilding a bridge across Bull Run.[3] This

[1] *W. R.*, 39, p. 24.
[2] *Ib.*, 107, p. 988.
[3] Scout from Centreville to Falmouth,

Va., *W. R.*, 39, pp. 38–40; *Historic Records of the 5 N. Y. Cavalry*, by Rev. L. N. Boudrye, p. 51.

force, which was placed under the command of Colonel Wyndham, started from Centreville (Map 1, sheet A) about 6 a.m. on the 27th, or about twenty-four hours after Fitzhugh Lee recrossed the Rappahannock. Wyndham was ordered "to move toward Catlett's and Rappahannock Stations for the purpose of intercepting the enemy."[1] He followed the Warrenton Road across Bull Run and then halted until 10 o'clock to await the arrival of the remainder of his force. On account of the flooded state of the country he kept on by the Warrenton Road, a much better one than any leading to the railroad. He arrived at Warrenton about 3:30 p.m., and met a small squad of the enemy's cavalry, who dispersed after exchanging a few shots with his advance. Taking the Falmouth Stage Road, he pushed on to the Orange and Alexandria Railroad, and turning to the right, followed the railroad for about a mile, which brought him to Licking Creek (Map 6). This stream being too deep to be forded, he went into camp for the night, and shortly afterward noticed squads and videttes of the enemy on the opposite side of it. In the course of the night he heard that there was a force of the enemy at Elkton and Spotted Tavern, but did not learn that Fitzhugh Lee had recrossed the Rappahannock. So at 6 o'clock on the morning of the 28th he took up the march for Elkton. On the way there he learned "that the main force of the enemy had already crossed the Rappahannock, taking with them 100 prisoners,"[2] and that therefore the accomplishment of the object prescribed to him, the interception of the enemy, was impossible. He did not think, it would seem, of following the enemy across the Rappahannock. His forage had given out, a portion of his command not having brought any with it. So instead of returning directly to Fairfax Court-House, he continued his march to Falmouth, where he arrived about 2 p.m., having marched about 90 miles over roads heavy with mud and snow.[3] Later in the day the following report of his movements and intentions was telegraphed by Butterfield to Heintzelman:

Colonel Wyndham arrived here this morning with his force, *via* Warrenton, Rappahannock Station, and the Post road. Reports his command in good condition. Has a few prisoners—a corporal and 6 privates. Lost 1 horse only, by accident. He has been provided with rations and forage. Proposes to rest tomorrow, and return on Monday [March 2]. Please inform General Hooker, if he is still in Washington.[4]

With reference to certain statements in this dispatch, it may be remarked that Wyndham did not go within 7 miles of Rappahannock

[1] *W. R.*, 107, p. 988.
[2] *Ib.*, 39, p. 38.
[3] Wyndham's report, and report of Colonel Gray, 6 Mich. Cavalry, *W. R.*, 39, pp. 39, 40.
[4] Hooker went to Washington on the 27th.

Station, and that when he reached Falmouth, his command could not have been "in good condition."

On the 1st of March he sent the following report to Heintzelman's adjutant-general from Falmouth:

Having marched 90 miles in less than 48 hours[1] in endeavoring to accomplish the object for which I was sent out, it would be advisable to let my command rest for the day, where they have plenty of forage, at Falmouth Station. Will march at 6 o'clock to-morrow. If absolutely necessary can start immediately. If so, please telegraph. Roads very bad.[2]

About 7:30 a.m. on the 2d the command started on the return march. It proceeded through Stafford Court-House and halted for the night about 4 miles south of Wolf Shoals (Map 1, sheet A).

The next day, March 3, Wyndham crossed the Occoquan at Wolf Shoals, and returned to his camp, having broken down many horses and accomplished nothing.

This dash of Confederate cavalry, designated in the *War Records* as the Skirmish at Hartwood Church, and the manner in which it was met, are interesting evidence as to the relative efficiency of the two opposing cavalries. They show that Hooker's and Heintzelman's horsemen, and their commanders, had something to learn before they would be up to the standard of Lee's. It is plain that the country beyond the Federal outposts was not adequately patrolled, and that the troops were not proficient in turning out suddenly and promptly and getting on the march. There appeared, too, to be something wrong about the ways and means of transmitting orders and intelligence. This circumstance accounts for the issuing of the following order:

Headquarters Army of the Potomac,
Camp near Falmouth, Va., March 3, 1863.

General Orders, No. 18:

III. Citizens, non-residents, will not be allowed to remain within the lines of this army without a permit from the provost-marshal-general.

.    .    .    .    .    .    .    .    .    .

XIII. Important information from the outposts or advices regarding movements of the enemy must not be delayed in transmission. All reports of this character must be marked upon the envelope "important," and exertions made to hasten their arrival at headquarters. While the telegraph must be made use

[1] In his final report, Wyndham gives the distance marched as 80 miles and the time as 31 hours (*W. R.*, 39, p. 39). Colonel Gray, 6 Mich. Cavalry, says regarding this part of the operation: "During the march from Centreville to Falmouth Station, we made frequent deviations from the direct road. The distance thus marched was said to be 96 miles. The time occupied was less than 30 hours, allowing for the halt at Bull Run, Friday morning (27th), and including about 12 hours' halt on the Orange and Alexandria Railroad, Friday night. . . . On Saturday morning (28th) we marched 25 miles without any halt."

[2] *W. R.*, 107, p. 988.

of to transmit such intelligence, dispatching duplicates by couriers must not be omitted where the slightest possible doubt exists as to certain and correct transmission by telegraph.

The recent operations elicited from Stoneman on the 28th the following representation and suggestion to the Adjutant-General of the Army of the Potomac:

There are now in the cavalry corps about 12,000 men and 13,000 horses present for duty. The last return showed 11,955 enlisted men and 13,875 horses. The line this force has to guard is but little less than 100 miles. One third on duty at one time gives 40 men to the mile on post at one time, and one third of these gives 13 to the mile on post at one time. Considering the condition of the roads, it is a good day's march to get out to the line and another to return, so that actually the horses are out one half the time or more. Added to this the fact that frequently the whole cavalry force is in the saddle for several days together, and it will be perceived that but little more than one third of the time is allowed the horses in which to recruit.

I consider it my duty to call these facts to the attention of the general commanding for his information, which I should have done before, perhaps, but for the thought that I might possibly be considered as complaining.

The above communication brought about changes in the cavalry outposts. A new line was taken up, as indicated in the following letters, which, it will be seen, provide for a more frequent use of exploring or reconnoitering patrols:

### Stoneman to Averell, March 2

Your picket line will, until further orders, be as follows: Its left commencing with the infantry pickets on the Rappahannock River, and extending up the river to a point near Rocky Pen Creek; thence in front of Berea Church to Guy's Old Tavern, and thence to a point near the headwaters of Accakeek Creek, where you will connect with the left of the First Division.

. . . Patrols, mounted on the best horses, will be sent out on all the main approaches sufficiently often to keep you well informed of what is going on in your front. These patrols will not only watch all the main approaches, but will examine and thoroughly inspect the intervening country between these approaches.

### To Pleasonton

. . . Your left will connect with the right of the Second Division at a point near the headwaters of Accakeek Creek, and from thence northward to some point some 2 or 3 miles in front of the outposts of the force at Dumfries, and as much farther northward as you may think safety requires. . . .

Stoneman was called upon for an exact report of the forces engaged and the losses sustained in the recent operations; of the movements in full of each portion of the command, "and the delay of any portion to execute promptly and completely the part assigned it, together with the reasons therefor."[1]  In compliance with these instructions he submitted a report on the 4th of March, inclosing a report by General Averell, which has disappeared from the official records.  Stoneman says:

The movements of General Averell, until I found him near Hartwood Church, were made in accordance with instructions received from headquarters, and I presumed there was no delay.

The movements of Captain Cram, commanding Reserve Brigade, were extremely prompt and satisfactory.  Those of General Pleasonton were delayed, as he reports, by the non-arrival of the telegram directing him to push forward, though the two previous telegrams reached him with dispatch.[2]

Fitzhugh Lee and Averell had been at West Point together three years and were warm personal friends.  When Lee withdrew he left with his surgeon a note to Averell, which the surgeon, as he recrossed the Federal lines, delivered to a picket.  It read about as follows:

I wish you would put up your sword, leave my state, and go home.  You ride a good horse, I ride a better.  Yours can beat mine running.[3]  If you won't go home, return my visit, and bring me a sack of coffee.[4]

Fitzhugh Lee's note was promptly delivered, and General Averell determined to answer it at the first opportunity.  Hooker heard of this note being sent to Averell, and rode over to the latter's headquarters to pay him a visit.  The conversation turned upon the dash made by the enemy's cavalry against Hartwood Church, and Averell, somewhat nettled by it, asked Hooker for an order to cross the river and settle accounts with Fitzhugh Lee.  Hooker realized that no system of outposts would prove efficient protection against an aggressive and enterprising enemy who was determined to penetrate them, and that the only way to put a stop to the harassing of his pickets, and alarming of his camps, was to retaliate by vigorously attacking the enemy's cavalry.  He assured Averell that his request would be granted, and that very soon.  How far Hooker sympathized with Averell's impatience to get even with Fitzhugh Lee, and how much he desired on his own part to settle the question of relative prowess and efficiency between his newly created cavalry corps and Stuart's veteran cavalry division, or to inform himself regarding the terrain and the enemy south of the Upper Rappahannock, are debatable questions.  It may be asserted, however, that not one of these objects was viewed by Hooker as an end in itself, and that so far as he considered any of them he regarded them as means to giving rest to his pickets and security to his army.

[1] *W. R.*, 39, p. 22.          [2] *Ib.*, 39, p. 24.
[3] Referring to the speed with which the Federal pickets gave way when attacked.
[4] *Glimpses of the Nation's Struggle,* 2d Series, pp. 38–44.

It was on the occasion of this interview between Averell and Hooker that Hooker made the remark which was reported and circulated as "Who ever saw a dead cavalryman?" What he said was something to the effect that there had not been many dead cavalrymen lying around lately, and that if Averell should meet and defeat Lee there would be. He did not mean to cast any reflection on the cavalry nor to give rise to a standing joke on that arm of the service.

# CHAPTER VII

MOSBY AND HIS MEN. CAPTURE OF GENERAL STOUGHTON. TRANSFER OF
GENERAL STAHEL

IN the minor operations attending the preparation for a general
movement no one played a more prominent part than John S.
Mosby, who came upon the theater of war as a commander a few weeks
before Hooker. At the commencement of the war Mosby was a prac-
tising lawyer. He entered the army as a private of cavalry, and rose
to the position of adjutant of his regiment. Being thrown out of that
office by the reorganization of the regiment, he was selected by J. E.
B. Stuart as an independent scout. He was the first Confederate to
make the circuit of McClellan's army while in front of Richmond, and
by the information thus acquired he enabled Stuart to make his celebrated Chickahominy raid, accompanying him as a guide.

The independent scout of the American Civil War had no counter-
part in European warfare. He seems to have done most of the service
which in European armies devolved, and still devolves, upon the
officers' patrol. He was not uncommonly dressed in the uniform of
the enemy, and consequently when caught plying his vocation, a spy
to all intents and purposes.[1] Mosby says in his *War Reminiscences*
(p. 24) that he always wore the Confederate uniform with the insignia
of his rank. If such was the case, he wore that uniform when he was
not entitled to wear it.

During the autumn of 1862, not holding any commission in the
Confederate service, he asked Stuart from time to time to let him have
a few men with whom to operate against the enemy's communications.
His request was not granted until Stuart was about going into winter
quarters after the campaign of Fredericksburg, when he gave him
nine troopers. To these Mosby afterward added three or four civilian
volunteers. This mongrel squad (a guerilla chief, a few guerilla followers, and nine soldiers) commenced on the 10th of January operating
against the outposts of Washington. In a few days it succeeded in
making a capture of half a dozen men and sixteen horses. These were

[1] "Scouts or single soldiers, if disguised in the dress of the country, or in the uniform of the army hostile to their own, employed in obtaining information, if found within, or lurking about, the lines of the captor, are treated as spies, and suffer death" (General Orders, No. 100, War Department, Washington, April 24, 1863).

sent to General Fitzhugh Lee, who was stationed with his brigade at Culpeper Court-House. Mosby then reported to Stuart in the vicinity of Fredericksburg, and obtained from him a detail of 15 men, with whom and a few guerillas he started again on the 15th of January to harry the Federal pickets. He succeeded again in taking a number of prisoners, and caused the commander of the outposts, Colonel Percy Wyndham, to advance with 200 men against him before he retired.[1]

Hereafter Mosby's men were habitually recruited by himself from the country. They wore as uniform when on duty "something gray,"[2] but when off duty they lived at or near their homes, wearing usually the dress of the country or a semi-uniform that could hardly be distinguished from it. Their homes were known to Mosby, and generally to one another. When a meet was desired that had not been appointed at the last disbanding, word of the time and place was sent to one house, and the men who were there would bear it to others. In this way a hundred men could be gathered together in a few hours.

As to arms, each of Mosby's men habitually carried two Colt's revolvers. None carried a carbine, and very few a saber. They were expert pistol-shots, but had practically no training in the use of the saber. They naturally had the greatest confidence in the former weapon, and little or none in the latter. Their expertness with the pistol gave them, especially in the early part of the war, a great advantage over their enemies. Their irregular tactics, too, had peculiar advantages. "During the twelve months of my service," writes a Mosby veteran, "I learned but four commands—fall in and count off by fours, march, close up, and charge. There was another movement which we were not altogether unfamiliar with, an order technically known as the 'skedaddle,' but I never heard the command given. The rangers seemed to know instinctively when that movement was appropriate; . . . when the Yankees broke they would always run in a bunch, and all we had to do was to follow and pick them up. . . . But when we found it necessary to leave the scene of action, each man found his own salvation, and 'struck for home and fireside' by his own particular path."[3] When Mosby's men were routed they would dissolve, leaving nothing to follow.

On his last expedition, Mosby had a number of men who had accompanied him on his first raid and in the meantime had lived as peaceful

---

[1] For Wyndham's and Mosby's reports, see *W. R.*, 39, p. 5. Wyndham says that he captured 24 of Mosby's men. Mosby says that he lost but 3. According to Mosby, he inflicted a loss on Wyndham of 1 killed and 12 captured. Wyndham gives his loss as 1 wounded and 9 captured. In *Historical Records of the 5 N. Y. Cavalry* (p. 50) Chaplain L. N. Boudrye gives the number of Federals captured as 11, and the number of Confederates as 25.

[2] *Reminiscences of a Mosby Guerilla*, by J. W. Munson, p. 25.

[3] *Mosby's Men*, by John H. Alexander, pp. 19, 20.

citizens at their homes. Such combatants are not Partisans, but guerillas. Mosby himself, not holding any commission from the Confederate government, nor being enrolled in any Confederate army, had no right, if captured, to the treatment due to a prisoner of war.[1]

Against a mode of warfare such as he was instituting there was no defence but devastation; and the Federal commander, Colonel Wyndham, naturally, and properly, threatened to resort to it. As a consequence, a number of prominent Southern citizens united in presenting to Mosby a petition requesting him to depart from their section of country, but it only drew from him the following reply:

Fauquier County, February 4, 1863.

*Gentlemen:*

I have just received your petition requesting me to discontinue my warfare on the Yankees, because they have threatened to burn your town and destroy your property in retaliation for my acts. Not being prepared for any such degrading compromise with the Yankees, I unhesitatingly refuse to comply. My attacks on scouts, patrols, and pickets, which have provoked this threat, are sanctioned both by the custom of war and the practice of the enemy, and you are at liberty to inform them that no such clamors shall deter me from employing whatever legitimate weapon I can most efficiently use for their annoyance.[2]

There was no sanction either in a "custom of war" or in a "practice of the enemy" for disbanding to live in the guise of civilians between operations or for serving without a commission. But Wyndham did not carry his threat into execution, and Mosby pursued his career with impunity.

About 4 o'clock on the morning of the 26th of February, with 27 men, he drove in a Federal outpost at Thompson's Corner, about 5 miles from Fairfax Court-House (Map 1, sheet A), capturing about 50 men. He was driven off and pursued as far as Middleburg, but not punished.[3]

---

[1] "81. Partisans are soldiers armed and wearing the uniform of their army, but belonging to a corps which acts detached from the main body for the purpose of making inroads into the territory occupied by the enemy. If captured, they are entitled to all the privileges of the prisoners of war.

"Men or squads of men who commit hostilities, whether by fighting or inroads for destruction or plunder, or by raids of any kind, without commission, without being part and portion of the organized hostile army, and without sharing continuously in the war, but who do so with intermitting returns to their homes and avocations or with the occasional assumption of the semblance of peaceful pursuits, divesting themselves of the character or appearance of soldiers—such men or squads of men are not public enemies, and therefore, if captured, are not entitled to the privilege of prisoners of war, but shall be treated summarily as highway robbers or pirates" (General Orders, No. 100, War Department, Washington, April 24, 1863).

[2] *Partisan Life with Colonel John S. Mosby*, by Major John Scott, p. 27. This letter is not published in the *War Records*, but is apparently referred to along with other documents in Mosby's report, *W. R.*, 39, p. 5.

[3] *W. R.*, 39, p. 37; *Partisan Life with Colonel John S. Mosby*, by Major John Scott, p. 35; *Camp and Field Life of the 5 N. Y. Volunteer Infantry, Duryee Zouaves*, by Alfred Davenport, p. 371.

On the 2d of March two companies of the 1 Vermont Cavalry, which had gone in search of Mosby, were surprised by their intended captive at Aldie while they were feeding their horses. The captains of both companies and about 200 horses and men were captured.[1] Mosby relieved himself of his prisoners and booty by sending them to Culpeper Court-House, where they were turned over to Fitzhugh Lee, and then proceeded to an enterprise which was to prove the most remarkable foray of the war.

Between Centreville and Fairfax Court-House was a brigade of Federal infantry, with artillery and cavalry. At Centreville was the extreme outpost of Washington. From this point the line extended to the right by Frying Pan and Dranesville to the Potomac, and to the left to Union Mills and Fairfax Station. The force manning and supporting it was under the command of Brigadier-General Henry E. Stoughton, U. S. Volunteers. This officer was not twenty-five years old. He graduated from West Point in 1859 and served in the 6 U. S. Infantry until 1861, when he resigned from the regular army and became colonel of the 4 Vt. Volunteers. He won his brigadier-generalcy in the Peninsula campaign. His appointment dated from the 5th of November, 1862, but not being confirmed by the Senate, it was to expire by constitutional limitation on the 4th of March. His headquarters were at Fairfax Station, his quarters at Fairfax Court-House. Both were about 2 miles in rear of the main body of his command and about 8 miles in rear of his outer line of sentinels, or pickets. The line of the Federal pickets was not continuous. As if under a presentiment of what was going to happen, Stoughton wrote to Heintzelman's adjutant-general March 1:

I have discovered that our cavalry pickets do not keep up a connected line on our right. Thus, the right picket of Colonel Wyndham's right rests on the Ox road; then there is an opening of a mile or two before reaching the left picket of the command at Dranesville. This should be remedied, as it gives free ingress and egress to any wishing to give intelligence to the enemy. If anything transpires I will inform you. Last night about 9 o'clock, while I was at headquarters, at the station, a man, undoubtedly a spy, was at the court-house, dressed as a captain. He interrogated all my servants minutely respecting the troops in the vicinity, asking if I kept my horse saddled in the night, and other suspicious questions.

And again at 9:55 p.m. the same day:

. . . it is absolutely essential to the entire security of the commands in this vicinity that the women and other irresponsible persons in this neighborhood be compelled to take the oath, or placed outside the lines. I cannot fix upon any person or persons who are culpable, yet I am perfectly satisfied that there are

[1] W. R., 39, pp. 41, 42, 1121.

those here who, by means known to themselves, keep the enemy informed of all our movements. Soldiers in the Southern service have even gone so far as to pay their families in the vicinity visits, for a week at a time, without its being discovered; and the few Union people there fear to give the intelligence they would like to, lest the rebels should be informed of it, should they again get possession of this country, by their neighbors, who are watchful spies, notwithstanding they have subscribed to the oath.

No attention, it seems, was paid to these representations; at any rate, the changes which they suggested, or called for, were not made. Stoughton was perhaps imprudent under the circumstances in not taking quarters further within his lines.

On the 8th of March Mosby was joined at Aldie, his appointed rendezvous, by 29 men, and with this force he started late in the afternoon and in a drizzling rain for Fairfax Court-House. He had as guide a deserter by the name of Ames, lately a sergeant in the 5 N. Y. Cavalry, stationed at Fairfax Court-House. Having followed the turnpike about 8 miles, he halted to await the approach of night. When he resumed his march, darkness, combined with rain, furnished him an impenetrable screen, and a melting snow deadened the sound of his horses' hoofs. About 3 miles from Chantilly he turned off the turnpike to the right, slipped through the opening in the outer picket line of the cavalry, and gained the Warrenton Turnpike about half-way between Centreville and Fairfax Court-House. Here he cut the telegraph wires by which the force at Centreville might communicate with its support at Fairfax Court-House. He had no difficulty in pursuing his way. Nowhere did he meet with resistance. In the inky darkness it was impossible to tell from their appearance to which side his men belonged. The names of the cavalry regiments stationed along the line were known to him. Whenever he was challenged the answer was, "Fifth New York Cavalry," and it was all right. There was no countersign out.[1] Proceeding a short distance toward the court-house, he turned off to the right, passed around to the left of a corps directly in his front, continued past the town, and came into the latter by the eastern or near entrance about 2 o'clock in the morning. He had intended to reach the court-house at 12 o'clock, but in the darkness of the night a portion of his command had become separated from him and caused him a loss of two hours before he could reunite with it.

On reaching the court-house square the men were detailed in squads which were sent, some to the stables to collect the horses which were known to be there, others to the different quarters of the officers. Mosby was particularly anxious to capture Colonel Wyndham. He says:

[1] Report of Lieutenant D. L. O'Connor, Provost-Marshal, published in *Mosby's Rangers*, by J. J. Williamson, pp. 46, 47.

The commander of the Union cavalry at that time was Colonel Percy Wyndham, an English adventurer, who, it was said, had served with Garibaldi. He had been greatly exasperated by my midnight forays on his outposts and mortified at his own unsuccessful attempts at reprisal. In consequence he had sent me many insulting messages. I thought I would put a stop to his talk by gobbling him up in bed and sending him off to Richmond.[1]

It was found that Colonel Wyndham had gone to Washington that evening by the railroad, and so was not to be caught. The irony of fate made Ames the captor of his former commander (Captain Barker of the 5 N. Y. Cavalry). Brigadier-General Stoughton was found asleep in his bed, and required to get up and dress himself and go along. After spending about an hour making captures, Mosby started with his prisoners and booty toward Fairfax Station to deceive his pursuers. Having gone about half a mile, he turned off at right angles, and made for the pike leading from the court-house to Centreville (the Warrenton Pike), cutting telegraph wires as he went. He reached the pike about 4 miles from Centreville, and followed it at a fast trot about 3½ miles, when he came upon the smouldering camp-fire of a Federal picket abandoned a short time before. Dawn was just beginning to break. He passed the deserted picket, turned off the pike to his right, and proceeded past Centreville, leaving that place on his left. The camps were all quiet; there was no sign of alarm; his men could see the cannon bristling through the embrasures of the redoubts not more than two or three hundred yards away, and heard a sentinel on the parapet call them to halt, but paid no attention to him. As Mosby's prisoners outnumbered his own men, and he was coming from the direction of the cavalry camp, the sentinels doubtless mistook his column for a body of Federal cavalry going out on a scout.[2]

Soon after he had passed out of the Federal lines he came upon Cub Run, which was so swollen by the melting snow and rain that he was compelled to swim it. Proceeding through Sudley Springs, he came back into the Warrenton Turnpike at Groveton, and followed it to Warrenton.

Early this morning an expedition was fitted out by the Federals to capture Mosby by stratagem. Four men from each of the ten companies of the 42 Pa. Volunteers (Bucktails) were detailed for this service. They were formed in four squads and placed in four army wagons, in which they were concealed by the canvas sheets. The train of wagons was escorted by a plainly insufficient detachment of cavalry (1 R. I.).

[1] Mosby's account published in the *Belford Magazine* (no longer extant), 1892, and quoted at length in *Mosby's Rangers*, by J. J. Williamson. None of the "insulting messages" have come under my eye, but I surmise that their offensiveness lay in a just characterization of Mosby's methods as those of a guerilla and bushwhacker. J. B. Jr.

[2] Mosby's account.

Proceeding down the pike under the guidance of a civilian Unionist called "Yankee" Davidson, everything went peacefully; the party put up for the night in a barn. Hardly, however, was the expedition under way the next morning (March 10) when the cavalry in the advance ran into some of Mosby's men, and immediately retreated upon the wagons. The Bucktails, lying in their places of concealment, heard the cavalry come racing back, and naturally judged that the guerillas were in full pursuit. Leaping to their feet, they threw back the curtains of the wagons and blazed away. Instantly the Confederates realized the trap set for them, and not being too near, wheeled about and escaped. The hook having been seen, it was not to be expected that the prey would bite a second time, so this attempt to catch it was given up. The wagons, with their disappointed passengers and escort, returned to Fairfax Court-House.[1]

The same day Mosby reported with his command, and prisoners, and booty, to Fitzhugh Lee at Culpeper Court-House, where Stuart arrived in the course of the day from Fredericksburg. Some of his prisoners had escaped. He turned over to Fitzhugh Lee, besides Stoughton, 1 captain and 30 privates.[2] It is probable that at the time of his capture Stoughton had not received notification of his non-confirmation, and so was still practically a brigadier-general. The vacant colonelcy in the 4 Vt. had been filled.[3] Referring to the capture of Stoughton, Mosby says:

I was never able to duplicate this adventure; it was one of those things a man can do only once in a lifetime. The Northern cavalry got too smart to allow the repetition. My calculation of success was based upon the theory that, to all appearances, it was impossible. It was charged at the time that citizens of the place were in collusion with me, and had given the information on which I had acted. It was not true; I had had no communication with any one there.[4]

At Fairfax Court-House there resided a Mr. Ford, with whom several of Stoughton's staff officers boarded. Mr. Ford had a young, good-looking daughter. Whether this had anything to do with the patronage of Mr. Ford's board by the officers must be left to conjecture. At any rate, Miss Ford made herself very agreeable to her guests, impressing them as a loyal Union woman. She was permitted to visit a lady cousin outside of the Federal lines; and this cousin was permitted to visit her at Fairfax Court-House. On one of these visits, the cousin made a diagram of the house in which Stoughton was quartered and the surroundings, showing the positions of the troops, and this diagram, it seems, she gave to Mosby.

[1] *History of the Bucktails*, by O. K. Thomson and W. R. Ranch, pp. 247, 248.
[2] *W. R.*, 39, p. 44.
[3] Editorial foot-note, *History of the Civil War in America*, by Comte de Paris, III, 12.
[4] *Belford Magazine*, 1892; and *Mosby's Rangers*, by J. J. Williamson, p. 46.

Miss Ford was arrested on suspicion by the Federal Detective Police, and sent North. On her person or at her residence were found a number of private letters from officers and other persons in the Confederate service, eighty-seven dollars in Confederate bank-bills, and a commission as honorary aide-de-camp to General Stuart.[1]

Stoughton was taken South and confined in Libby Prison. He was released several weeks afterward, but the ridicule excited by his capture had destroyed his military prospects. He resigned from the army, and entered upon the practice of law in New York City, where he died in 1868.

The showing made by the Federals in this affair mortified both the army and the public. The New York *Times,* in its issue of March 16, commented on it as follows:

The capture of General Stoughton in his bed by a party of rebel cavalry at Fairfax Court-House is another of those utterly disgraceful incidents with which this war has abounded. . . . Colonel Johnson,[2] the cavalry officer in command of the post, was himself in bed, and undressed, and escaped in his shirt[3] by taking refuge in the roof of a barn. . . .

We believe that in the regular army of any other country such a thing as a cavalry officer in command of an outpost undressing and going to bed at night is unknown; we believe, moreover, that there are but few military men in any well-ordered service who ever think under such circumstances of doing more than taking their coats off.

One can at least understand Lincoln's remarking when informed that Mosby carried off a number of horses:

Well, I am sorry for that, for I can make brigadier-generals, but I can't make horses.[4]

This exploit of Mosby's elicited from General J. E. B. Stuart the following complimentary notice:

Headquarters Cavalry Division, March 12, 1863.
General Orders, No. 7:

Captain John S. Mosby[5] has for a long time attracted the attention of his generals by his boldness, skill, and success, so signally displayed in his numerous

---

[1] *History of the U. S. Secret Service,* by General L. C. Baker, pp. 170 *et seq.; History of the Army of the Potomac,* by J. H. Stine, p. 316.

[2] Lieutenant-Colonel Johnstone, commanding cavalry brigade.

[3] The report of Provost-Marshal O'Connor says, "in a nude state" (*W. R.,* 39, p. 43). The Comte de Paris says, "without

clothes under a stack of hay" (*History of the Civil War in America,* III, 13).

[4] *History of the U. S. Secret Service,* by General L. C. Baker, p. 170.

[5] The title is purely honorary. Mosby held no commission at this time. He had been offered by Governor Letcher a captaincy in the Provisional Army of Virginia, an organization which had practically

forays upon the invaders of his native state.  None know his daring enterprise and dashing heroism better than those foul invaders, though strangers themselves to such noble traits.

His late brilliant exploit, the capture of Brigadier-General Stoughton, U. S. Army, 2 captains,[1] 30 other prisoners, together with arms, equipments, and 58 horses, justifies this recognition in general orders.  The feat, unparalleled in the war, was performed, in the midst of the enemy's troops at Fairfax Court-House, without loss or injury.

The gallant band of Captain Mosby share the glory, as they did the danger, of this enterprise, and are worthy of such a leader.[2]

In order to strengthen his command for another foray Mosby proposed to take the dismounted men of Fitzhugh Lee's brigade, promising to mount and equip them in return for a short term of service. His proposition was declined, and the dismounted men were sent under charge of one of their own officers to get horses and equipments from the enemy.  The result was that they were all captured.[3]

On the 20th of March Major-General Stahel, promoted from Brigadier-General on the 17th, was relieved from duty with the Army of the Potomac, and ordered to report to Major-General Heintzelman, commanding the Department of Washington.  He was temporarily succeeded in the command of the XI Corps by Major-General Carl Schurz, lately commanding its Third Division.  On the 25th the three brigades of cavalry in the Department of Washington were organized as a division, which, together with the outposts lately commanded by Stoughton, was placed under the command of General Stahel. Colonel Wyndham was transferred to the Cavalry Corps of the Army of the Potomac.

Mosby was not content to rest on his laurels.  On the 16th he wrote to Stuart from near Middleburg, Va.:

I start with my command to-day, to go down in the neighborhood of Dranesville.  I expect to flush some game before returning.  I have received several more recruits.

Public sentiment seems now entirely changed, and I think it is the universal desire here for me to remain.

Accordingly on the 16th, with about 50 men, he attacked a Federal outpost between Middleburg and Dranesville.  The pickets gave the alarm, which brought up about 200 of their supporting cavalry.  Mosby was driven off and pursued about 2 miles.  Being then suitably

---

ceased to exist, and this empty honor he had declined (*Partisan Life with Colonel John S. Mosby,* by Major John Scott, p. 51).

[1] Fitzhugh Lee said *one.*

[2] *W. R.,* 40, p. 856.  For Federal reports, see *ib.,* 39, p. 43, and *Mosby's Rangers,*

by J. J. Williamson, p. 47.  For Confederate reports, see *W. R.,* 39, pp. 44, 1121; and 40, p. 667.

[3] *Partisan Life with Colonel John S. Mosby,* by Major John Scott, p. 53.

situated, he halted and prepared an ambush. His pursuers ran into it, were fired upon from front and flank, charged, and routed, with a loss according to Mosby of 5 killed, a considerable number wounded, and 1 lieutenant and 35 men captured.[1]

On the 17th he made a dash at Herndon Station on the Loudon and Hampton Railroad, surprised a picket of 1 officer and 25 men, and captured the whole of it, with 3 officers who happened to be visiting the post.[2] Before this exploit came to the knowledge of President Davis, the latter had appointed him a Captain of Partisan Rangers in the Provisional Army of the Confederate States.

Lee, hearing unofficially of this appointment, wrote to Davis on the 21st, inclosing Mosby's report of the affair at Herndon Station:

You will, I know, be gratified to learn by the inclosed dispatch that the appointment you conferred a few days since on Capt. J. S. Mosby was not unworthily bestowed. . . . I wish I could receive his appointment, or some official notification of it, that I might announce it to him.

A few days later Mosby received the following communications:

### From the Adjutant-General, Army of Northern Virginia, March 23

. . . the President has appointed you captain of Partisan Rangers. . . . it is desired that you proceed at once to organize your company, with the understanding that it is to be placed on a footing with all troops of the line, and to be mustered unconditionally into the Confederate service for and during the war.

Though you are to be its captain, the men will have the privilege of selecting the lieutenants so soon as its numbers reach the legal standard. You will report your progress from time to time, and when the requisite number of men are enrolled, an officer will be designated to muster the company into the service.[3]

### From Stuart, March 25, 1863

. . . you will be continued in your present sphere of conduct and enterprise, and already a captain, you will proceed to organize a band of permanent followers for the war, but by all means ignore the term "Partisan Rangers." It is in bad repute. Call your command "Mosby's Regulars," and it will give it a tone of meaning and solid worth which all the world will soon recognize, and you will inscribe that name of a fearless band of heroes on the pages of our country's history, and enshrine it in the hearts of a grateful people. Let "Mosby's Regulars" be a name of pride with friends and respectful trepidation with enemies.

You will have to be very much on your guard against incorporating in your command deserters from other branches of the service. Insist upon the most unequivocal evidence of honorable discharge in all cases. Non-conscripts under and over age will be very advantageous. Their entry into service must be unconditional, excepting that you are their captain, and their lieutenants to be chosen by the men, provided no unworthy man be so chosen. As there is no time within which

[1] *W. R.*, 39, p. 72.        [2] *Ib.*, 39, pp. 65, 66.        [3] *Ib.*, 40, pp. 856, 857.

you are required to raise this command, you ought to be very fastidious in choosing your men, and make them always stand the test of battle and temptation to neglect duty before acceptance.

I was greatly obliged to you for the saddle of Stoughton. I wish you would send me whatever evidence you may be able to furnish of Miss Ford's innocence of the charge of having guided you in your exploit at Fairfax, so that I can insist upon her unconditional release.

We must have that unprincipled scoundrel Wyndham. Can you catch him? Do not get caught.

. . . . . . . . . .

Be vigilant about your own safety, and do not have any established headquarters anywhere but "in the saddle."

. . . . . . . .

Your praise is on every lip, and the compliment the President has paid you is as marked as it is deserved.

Mosby was quite willing to have the title and commission of Captain of Partisan Rangers, provided it would not prevent his being a guerilla, but nothing was further from his thoughts than being a Partisan—say nothing of being a regular. He knew that if he discarded the character of a guerilla he would greatly diminish, perhaps wholly stop, recruiting for his command; and that the numerous cavalry of the enemy would soon capture it. He wrote to Stuart:

I have received from the War Office a notice of my appointment as Captain of Partisan Rangers. The letter of Captain Taylor [Adjutant-General] says that they are to be organized with the understanding that they are to be on the same footing with other cavalry. The men who have joined me have done so under the impression that they are to be entitled to the privileges allowed in the Partisan Ranger Act. If they are to be denied them, I can not accept the appointment. Please let me know.[1]

This letter was forwarded to Lee.

On the 16th Pleasonton reported to Hooker the capture, between Dumfries and Occoquan, of a Federal cavalry patrol consisting of a corporal and 6 privates. "It is recommended," he wrote, "that the rebel partisans and bushwhackers be cleared out from the vicinity of Occoquan and Brentsville by a command from this division. One brigade and a couple of guns would be sufficient." Referring to this occurrence, General Stoneman wrote Hooker on the 17th:

These annoyances will continue until some stringent measures are taken to clear that section of country of every male inhabitant, either by shooting, hanging, banishment, or incarceration. I had a party organized some time ago to do this, but the commanding general did not at that time think it advisable to send it out. A great portion of the country is of such a nature that it is impossible for

---

[1] *Partisan Life with Colonel John S. Mosby*, by Major John Scott, p. 76.

cavalry to operate in it, and to perform the duty properly will require the coöperation of an infantry force. The country is infested by a set of bushwhacking thieves and smugglers who should be eradicated root and branch.

Regarding these recommendations Hooker, on the 26th, wrote to Pleasonton:

If there are any of the male portion of the community operating as bushwhackers or guerillas against our troops, and the facts can be proven, let them be arrested and brought in. The commanding general can not understand why our cavalry can not operate where the enemy's cavalry prove so active.[1]

In the meantime a blow had been struck by the Federal cavalry which brought some relief to Hooker's vexed and troubled outposts. This was the battle of Kelley's Ford, to be described in the next chapter.

On the 23d of March Mosby was again on the war-path. He had learned on his raid to Fairfax Court-House that the Federals had a force of infantry, artillery, and cavalry, about 3000 strong, posted at Ox Hill (Map 1, sheet A), with outposts at Frying Pan and Chantilly, each composed of about 100 men of the 5 N. Y. Cavalry. The force at Ox Hill was the General Reserve; the forces at Frying Pan and Chantilly were the main reserves, or what we now call the supports. The latter were covered by pickets. Mosby's object was to surprise the posts at Frying Pan and Chantilly. Starting from Rector's Cross-Roads, he followed the turnpike in the direction of Chantilly to within 6 miles of that point, and there turned off the road to the right. Proceeding across country to within about a mile of Chantilly, he surprised a picket of 10 men, killing 1 and capturing 7. Perceiving that the enemy was turning out to attack him, he withdrew precipitately, as if really retreating, to a point between the Toll Gate and Cub Run, where the Federals had closed the turnpike with a barricade. Here he halted and formed a portion of his force dismounted behind the obstruction, and the remainder mounted in the woods lining the road. He was hotly pursued by the 5 N. Y. Cavalry. As the column, strung out along the road, approached the barricade, it was arrested by a fire of carbines and pistols in front and flank. It wavered and the next moment was charged and broken. Its fragments were chased about 3 miles, when they were reënforced by a reserve from Frying Pan, and Mosby was in turn put to flight. He was pursued about 8 miles, but not overtaken.[2]

[1] W. R., 39, pp. 45, 46.

[2] A historian of the 5 N. Y. Cavalry says with reference to that organization in this affair: "For some reason the regiment never acted with so little concert, and was never so badly beaten by so small a force, supposed to be about 80 strong. Every one felt mortified at the result of this day's work, and resolved to retrieve our fortunes on some more fortunate occasion."

For Federal and Confederate reports, see W. R., 39, pp. 70–73. The affair is desig-

For this affair Mosby was rewarded with the following commendation sent him by Stuart on the 27th:

*Captain:*

Your telegram announcing your brilliant achievement near Chantilly was duly received and forwarded to General Lee. He exclaimed upon reading it,—''Hurrah for Mosby! I wish I had a hundred like him.''[1]

At the instance of General Lee he was appointed a major. He had not yet accepted his captain's commission, as he had not received any answer to the letter he had addressed to Stuart and which the latter had forwarded to Lee. The answer came in the form of the following indorsement by Lee:

No authority has been given Major Mosby to raise partisan troops, nor has it been so intended. He was commissioned as such [major] to give him rank, pay, and command, until he could organize companies that could be mustered regularly into the service. He was so informed when his commission was sent him, to prevent mistake. His commission was limited to himself, and did not extend to his troops.[2]

Not satisfied with Lee's view of the matter, Mosby appealed to the Secretary of War, who decided that Mosby's commission entitled him to recruit a command for the Partisan service.[3] Mosby thereupon accepted his commission as captain. He did not receive his commission as major.[4]

On the 31st of March, returning from a scouting expedition, he arrived with 65 men at Miskell's Farm, near Dranesville. It was 10 o'clock at night. Having ridden over 40 miles through snow and mud, his men and horses were exhausted. They went into a barn-yard surrounded by a high board fence, outside of which was another board fence encircling the farm. The men tumbled in upon the hay and under the eaves outside of the barn and fell asleep. None of the horses were saddled or bridled. No precautions were taken against surprise. There must have been some friend of the Federals, perhaps a negro, about the place, for that night Mosby's location and numbers were

---

nated as *Skirmish on the Little River Turnpike near Chantilly, Va.*

[1] *Partisan Life with Colonel John S. Mosby,* by Major John Scott, p. 62.

[2] *Ib.,* p. 76.

[3] *Ib.,* pp. 76, 77.

[4] The evils of Partisan service led to the repeal of the Partisan Ranger Act on the 17th of February, 1864. But the repealing act assured the maintenance of Mosby's command and one or more similar bodies by the following provision:

"294. The Secretary of War shall be authorized, if he deems proper, for a time or permanently, to exempt from the operation of this act such companies as are serving within the lines of the enemy, and under such conditions as he may prescribe."

Mosby continued a guerilla under the name of Partisan to the end of the war. For the purpose of surrender, his command was recognized by the Federals as a part of the Army of Northern Virginia, although it was never so regarded by the Confederates.

reported to Major Taggart, commanding the Federal outpost at Union Church, who immediately dispatched Captain Flint, with 150 men of the 1 Vt. Cavalry, to rout or capture Mosby and his force.

Early the following morning one of Mosby's men, who had been out looking around on his own account, came dashing into the barn-yard at Miskell's Farm, yelling: "Mount your horses! the Yankees are coming!" Before most of the sleepers had raised their weary heads Captain Flint with his men tore through the farm gate, and opened fire upon them with carbines. The fire, it seems, was delivered mounted; at any rate it was ineffective, and Flint, perceiving the fact, ordered a charge. When this was checked by the fence inclosing the barn-yard, Mosby opened upon the disordered Federals with pistols, and pouring out of the gate of the barn-yard charged them with the Mosby yell. The Federals were panic-struck, and ran for the farm fence through which they had entered. The Confederates followed, shooting and yelling. They poured a murderous fire into the struggling, howling mob jammed in the narrow farm gate, and followed its fleeing fragments 7 or 8 miles down the pike. Captain Flint was killed and a lieutenant mortally wounded. Mosby says that he left 25 killed and wounded on the field and brought off 82 prisoners. General Stahel, reporting the affair, says: "In comparison to the number engaged, our loss was very heavy." He also says: "I regret to be obliged to inform the commanding general that the forces sent out by Major Taggart missed so good an opportunity of capturing this rebel guerilla. It is only to be ascribed to the bad management on the part of the officers and the cowardice of the men." In reporting the affair to President Davis, General Lee said: "I had the pleasure to send by return courier to Major Mosby his commission of major of Partisan Rangers. . . ."

# CHAPTER VIII

## THE BATTLE OF KELLEY'S FORD

ABOUT the 14th of March, Hooker gave Averell an order to take 3000 cavalry and six pieces of artillery, and with that force to attack and rout or destroy "the cavalry forces of the enemy reported to be in the vicinity of Culpeper Court-House."[1]

The 17th of March, 1863, was a red-letter day for the cavalry of the Army of the Potomac; for on this day was fought at Kelley's Ford the first purely cavalry fight east of the Mississippi River in which more than one battalion was engaged on each side. In preparation for the event, Averell, the Federal commander, had instructed his men to have their sabers sharpened, and to use them. He promised them a victory.[2] Pursuant to Hooker's order, he left the main body of the army about 8 a.m. on the 16th of March with portions of the 1st and 2d brigades of his division and of the reserve brigade, aggregating about 3000 men, and provided with four days' rations and one day's forage. About dark he arrived at Morrisville, 16 miles from camp. Here he bivouacked for the night, and, about 11 p.m., was joined by Martin's 6-gun battery of horse artillery, commanded by Lieutenant Browne, from the artillery camp near Aquia Creek.

His orders were accompanied by reports of operations of the Confederate cavalry in the vicinity of Brentsville, in which the number of the enemy was represented as from 250 to 1000 men. As a precaution he requested that a regiment of cavalry be sent to Catlett's Station (Map 1, sheet A), which he regarded as the key-point to the "middle" fords of the Rappahannock, to throw out pickets in the direction of Warrenton, Greenwich, and Brentsville; but as this request was not granted, he detailed the 1 Mass. and the greater part of the 4 Pa., together about 900 men, to guard the fords and observe the enemy on the north side of the Rappahannock. It is hard to justify this weakening of his active force. He had no train or depot between himself and the Army

---

[1] The text of the order can not be found. The gist of it is given as above in Averell's report of March 20 (*W. R.*, 39, p. 47) and in Hooker's letter of May 13, transmitting it to Kelton (*ib.*, p. 1073).

[2] Captain D. M. Gilmore, 3 Pa. Cavalry, in *Glimpses of the Nation's Struggle*, 2d Series, pp. 38–44.

of the Potomac. There was nothing to be guarded in his rear except his line of retreat, and that he should have been able to open, if any force which the enemy could spare from his front had presumed to close it. He may have apprehended a movement in some force against his rear from the direction of the Shenandoah Valley. In that case he should, it seems, have contented himself with communicating his apprehensions to Hooker, leaving it to him to provide such protection as might be necessary.

Captain Hart of the 4 N. Y., with 100 picked men taken partly from that regiment and partly from the 5 U. S. Regulars, was ordered to proceed to Kelley's Ford as an advance-guard, and at the first glimpse of dawn on the 17th to dash across the river and capture the pickets on the south bank. His command was to be supported by the remainder of the 4 N. Y. In the course of the evening this regiment and the detachment of the 5 U. S. took position near the river. The advance was thus formed almost wholly of the 4 N. Y. (first New York German regiment). The reader may ask why Averell selected for so dangerous, difficult, and important a service, a command which bore, to say the least, an unenviable reputation as to fighting, and which disgraced itself in the action at Hartwood Church only about three weeks before.

About 11 a.m. on the 16th, Fitzhugh Lee, at Culpeper Court-House, received a telegram from R. E. Lee informing him that "a large body of cavalry had left the Federal army, and was marching up the Rappahannock."[1] By 6 p.m. his scouts had located this force at Morrisville, and reported the fact to him, but they left him in doubt as to whether the Federals would cross at Kelley's Ford or at Rappahannock Ford, or pursue their march toward Warrenton. He reënforced his picket of 20 sharpshooters at Kelley's Ford with 40 more, and ordered the remainder of his sharpshooters to be stationed at daylight where the road to the ford leaves the railroad and held ready to move to either crossing. About 4 a.m. on the 17th Averell started from Morrisville with the following command:

|  | MEN |
|---|---|
| 1st brigade, Second Division (4 N. Y., 6 O., 1 R. I.), Colonel Duffié | 775 |
| 2d brigade, Second Division (3 Pa., two squadrons of the 4 Pa., 16 Pa.), Colonel McIntosh | 565 |
| Reserve brigade (1 U. S. and three squadrons of 5 U. S.[2]), Captain Reno[3] | 760 |
| 6 N. Y. Battery, First Division, Lieutenant Browne (6 pieces) | 100 |
| Total | 2,200 |

. The force left behind—1 Mass. and four squadrons of the 4 Pa.— took post along the railroad between Bealeton and Catlett's Stations,

---

[1] Fitzhugh Lee's report, *W. R.*, 39, p. 61.
[2] Companies C, E, G, H, I, K.
[3] Who commanded a detachment of the 7 U. S. Cavalry at the Custer massacre, 1876.

with a reserve at Morrisville, and pickets at the fords and beyond the railroad.

The Confederate force available to oppose Averell's consisted of Fitzhugh Lee's brigade of cavalry and Breathed's battery of horse artillery (4 pieces). The brigade comprised at this time the 1st, 2d, 3d, 4th, and 5th regiments of Virginia Cavalry. There were thus 5 regiments to oppose to Averell's 6⅔ regiments; and 4 pieces to oppose to his 6. The Confederate regiments, however, were not as strong as the Federal. The author hesitates to state the numerical strength of the Confederates, there being a wide disagreement among authorities who have expressed themselves regarding it. Fitzhugh Lee does not give it in his official report, but in his *Chancellorsville Address* he says that he had less than 800 men in the saddle, and "less than 800" is the expression used by Stuart in his report to R. E. Lee for the number of men in action.[1] The Comte de Paris says that Fitzhugh Lee could not put more than 1000 sabers in line.[2] Major D. A. Grimsley, 6 Va. Cavalry, says, "Lee's brigade numbered perhaps 1200 in all," but he refers to it as occupying Culpeper Court-House and encamped in the vicinity of Brandy Station and Stevensburg, and does not state how much of it was assembled for this engagement.[3] Major Frank W. Hess, 3 Artillery, who was a captain in the 3 Pa. Cavalry, calculates Fitzhugh Lee's force as about 1500 sabers.[4] Rev. Frederic Denison, the historian of the 1 R. I. Cavalry, says that Lee's five regiments and horse artillery must have given him about 3000 effective men.[5] D. M. Gilmore, late captain of the 3 Pa. Cavalry and a participant in the action, says: "The forces were nearly equal, about 3500 men and a battery on each side."[6] The correct number will probably be found between that of the Comte de Paris and that of Major Grimsley. Let us assume that, including the artillery (which did not arrive until the action was about half over) and the men at the ford, Fitzhugh Lee's force aggregated 1100, or half as many as Averell's.

Averell selected Kelley's Ford as the place of crossing because the country beyond it was better known to him than that beyond any other crossing, and it afforded the shortest route to the enemy's camp. When his column arrived near the ford, the cracking of carbines told that the passage of the river by the advance under Hart had not been effected. The head of the main column reached the ford about 6 a.m.[7] The river at this point was about 100 yards wide, four feet deep, and running

---

[1] *W. R.*, 39, p. 59.

[2] *History of the Civil War in America*, V, 25, 26.

[3] *Battles in Culpeper County, Virginia*, by D. A. Grimsley, p. 7.

[4] *The First Battle of Kelley's Ford*, *First Maine Bugle*, 1893.

[5] *Sabres and Spurs*, by F. Denison, p. 213.

[6] *Glimpses of the Nation's Struggle*, 2d Series, p. 42.

[7] Averell gives the hour as 8 a.m. (*W. R.*, 39, p. 48); Lieutenant Browne as 6:30 a.m.; Colonel McIntosh as 6 a.m.; General Fitz-

swiftly.  The approach on both banks was obstructed by abatis.  The southern bank was manned by the detachment of Fitzhugh Lee's sharpshooters under Captain Breckinridge of the 2 Va. Cavalry and Company K of the 4 Va. Cavalry, commanded by Captain Moss, the latter having come up this morning.[1]  These troops were in rifle-pits or in a dry mill-race, which in the present instance may be regarded and referred to as a rifle-pit.  Deduction being made for horse-holders, Captain Breckinridge's command numbered about 45 and Captain Moss' about 85 men, or the two together about 130 men.

Averell was indignant at finding that the surprise of the enemy's picket had not been attempted.  The left bank of the river was traversed here for a short distance by a road which had been worn down to the depth of about three feet by long usage.  Under cover afforded by this road, Hart's command was firing at Moss' men in the rifle-pits.

On catching sight of the Federal column, Captain Breckinridge, commanding the remainder of the Confederate force, had mounted his men, and marched them to the rear to place his horses in a safe place.  The first thing that suggested itself to Averell was to detach a small force to steal a passage above or below the ford, and take the enemy in rear. This he accordingly did, directing the movement below the ford.  Major Chamberlain of the 1 Mass. Cavalry, his chief of staff, dashed down in the meantime to Captain Hart's command, and ordered it, including the main body of the 4 N. Y., to mount, form in column of fours, and follow him across the river.  On reaching the river's bank he was arrested by the abatis and his command overwhelmed with fire.  His horse was shot in three places and he himself in the face.  His men recoiled and retreated rapidly up the bank.  Sending to Averell for pioneers, he obtained 20 men of the 16 Pa. with axes, whom he put to work cutting away the abatis.  Two dismounted squadrons were placed by Averell in the sunken road to cover the axemen with their fire.  By this time a couple of field-pieces were unlimbered, and it would have been easy with their fire to demolish the enemy's defences and drive him beyond the range of his carbines.  But to do this would have been to announce the point of crossing and the magnitude of the expedition to Fitzhugh Lee.  So Averell contented himself with keeping up the fire of his two squadrons, numbering 100 men, with a view to preventing the enemy from rising to take aim.  Under cover of this fire Major Chamberlain

hugh Lee as about 5 a.m. (*W. R.*, 39, pp. 48–61), and Frederic Denison as about daylight (*Sabres and Spurs*, p. 208).

[1] General Fitzhugh Lee in his official report (*W. R.*, 39, p. 61) makes no mention of Captain Moss' company, and says regarding Breckinridge's men: "Only about 11 or 12 of them got into the rifle-pits in time for the attack of the enemy (owing to an unnecessary delay in carrying their horses to the rear), which commenced about 5 a.m."  But see the letter of Captain Moss in *The Battle of Kelley's Ford*, by J. B. Cooke, published by the Soldiers' and Sailors' Historical Society of Rhode Island.

again ordered the 4 N. Y. to follow him, and dashed at the river. The trees had been only partially removed, for the fire from the sunken road had not sufficed to protect the Federal axemen; and the fire from the enemy's rifle-pits had driven them from their work. It proved too hot for the men of the 4 N. Y., and they returned at breakneck speed.

General Averell had placed himself on a little knoll to the left of the approach to the ford, and from this point overlooked and directed operations. His division stood in column of fours stretched out along the road, eagerly and anxiously looking for a chance to "mix in." The force detached to try a crossing below the ford had returned baffled by the depth and swiftness of the water and the precipitous character of the banks. There was nothing left to do but to force a crossing in the face of the enemy at the ford.

It was impossible to get into or out of the river until the abatis was removed, and the work of cutting it away had to be done under the fire of the enemy's carbines or rifles at the very short range of from 50 to 100 yards.

Major Chamberlain again showed himself the man for the occasion. Giving his valuables to a staff officer, he rode up to the main column and called for volunteers to carry the crossing, offering the first opportunity to the regiment at the head of the column, the 1 R. I. The whole regiment replied by moving to the front. The nearest platoon, which was commanded by Lieutenant S. A. Browne, was selected and made ready for the dash. The fire from the sunken road was now keeping down that from the pits, and under its protection the axemen resumed their work, and made some progress toward opening the approach to the ford. They now ceased working and formed mounted in rear of Browne's platoon. The main body of the 1 R. I. and the 6 O. were moved up in support. The first dash was to be made by Browne with his 18 troopers. Major Chamberlain placed himself at the post of danger and honor in front of Browne. The signal was given, and away they went. As soon as they entered the road they were subjected to a withering fire. Browne's men broke, and came back in confusion. Major Chamberlain's horse was mortally wounded just as it reached the water, and at the same moment the major himself received a second wound. A ball struck him in the left cheek and ranged down through the neck, the shock throwing him from his horse. He was dragged up the bank by the pioneers. There, sitting on the ground partially blinded with blood, he emptied the chambers of his revolver, firing first, it is said, at the fleeing Rhode Islanders, and then at the enemy on the opposite side of the river. The men, however, were soon rallied and brought back. With a cheer they went forward again, and dashed into the ice-cold water. Close behind them went the mounted axemen. The latter had left their carbines behind, and had their sabers fastened to their saddles to facilitate mounting and dismounting. As they pushed forward, intermingling with Browne's men, their axes shining and glittering above their heads, the ford and its passengers presented a singularly picturesque scene suggestive of mediæval men-at-arms with their battle-axes. This party was followed by the remainder of the 1 R. I. and the 6 O.

Fortunately for Browne, the enemy was not altogether ready for him. Breckinridge had gone with his 60 men so far to the rear that he could not get more than about a dozen of them back into the rifle-pits by the time the assailants took to the water. His handful of men, being short of ammunition, did not fire. Moss' 85 carbines divided their fire between Browne's little band and the two dismounted squadrons in the sunken road. As soon as Browne's men and the pioneers began to approach the south shore the Federal fire from the sunken road had to be suspended, which gave the enemy an opportunity to increase his. Captain Moss directed all the fire he could upon the gray horse ridden by the gallant young Federal commander whom he saw plowing the surging waters at the head of his column. The horse was a larger mark than its rider, and he knew that the horse being disabled, the rider would be also. Besides, the rider had won his admiration by his courageous bearing. The axemen, on arriving about in the middle of the stream, inclined to the right, going up-stream, some of their horses swimming. They landed above the road, and coming down to it, went to work with a will at the obstruction. Of the 18 men of Browne's platoon who entered the ford with him, but 3 came out with him on the enemy's side, all the rest being either killed or wounded or having their horses disabled. The actual loss amounted to 2 men killed, 3 officers and 5 men wounded, and 15 horses killed or rendered permanently unserviceable.[1] The axemen suffered little. The loss fell principally upon Browne's horses. Browne rode up the bank and fired a shot among the enemy in the rifle-pits now below him. Then turning toward the ford, he waved his sword to the main body of his regiment, and called on it to come on. A few of the leading men arrived, and broke through or over the obstructions. In the meantime the enemy in the rifle-pit, perceiving their inability to hold their position, commenced retiring toward their horses. Being afoot and pursued by mounted men, it was well for them that they started early. As it was, 25 of them were made prisoners. They were found to be armed with new English revolvers—Kerr's patent—and provided with ammunition recently made in Connecticut.[2]

The Federal advance formed close column of squadrons, throwing out pickets on the roads radiating from the ford. About two hours were

[1] *First Maine Bugle,* October, 1893, p. 13.
[2] *History of the 1 Mass. Cavalry,* by D. H. L. Gleason, p. 117.

spent in removing the obstructions on the south bank and getting the remainder of the force across. The ammunition for the artillery was taken out of the limbers and carried over by a squadron of cavalry in nose-bags, which was necessary in order to prevent its being wet. This precaution would be unnecessary with the fixed ammunition of the present day. The guns were dragged through the water, which came up to the tops of the limber-boxes. The division was formed up so as to meet the enemy in any direction. The horses were watered. On account of the narrowness of the ford this had to be done by squadrons, which caused considerable delay. In the meantime General Averell galloped to the front with a detachment, and made a hasty reconnaissance, which satisfied him that the proper place for the expected battle was an open field which he could see about ¾ of a mile from the river. From what he had learned about Lee's position, and what he knew of him personally, he was confident that he would not await an attack in his camp, but would come out and attack Averell wherever he might be. So, about 10:10 a.m., everything being ready, Averell put his whole command in motion toward the forementioned field. The column marched through the hamlet of Kelleysville, consisting of six houses and a grist-mill, which the Confederates kept constantly employed; and took the road leading northwestward past R. Dean's to the railroad (Map 3). The advance was formed of Duffié's brigade, the 6 O. being deployed as skirmishers, the 4 N. Y. and 1 R. I. following as supports. The movement was conducted with caution and as slowly as if made with infantry, the ground scouts dismounting to search the woods. A squadron was left at the ford as picket, or rear-guard.

While Averell was crossing the river, Fitzhugh Lee was at Culpeper Court-House, awaiting news from the front. A report of the attack at the ford was sent to him, but failed to reach him.[1] The first intimation he received of an attempt to cross was at 7:30 a.m., to the effect that the enemy had succeeded in crossing, capturing 25 of his men who were unable to reach their horses.[2] Fitzhugh Lee at once moved his brigade at a rapid trot to the road junction about a mile and a half

---

[1] This statement is made on the authority of Fitzhugh Lee, who makes it in his report (*W. R.*, 39, p. 61). It implies that the dispatch was delivered to the bearer or courier before the rifle-pits were abandoned. If this was the case and the courier started promptly on his mission, he could hardly have been captured. It can not be supposed that he lost his way, for the route which he had to travel must have been generally known and easy to find or ascertain. He must have been exceedingly derelict.

[2] "This occasion as well as many others demonstrated the fact that the horse-holders in a cavalry fight should be the coolest and bravest men in the company. 'Number Four' has no right to be exempt from the perils of the battle. He holds the horses of his comrades only in order that they may more efficiently fight on foot; and he should always be near at hand to give whatever aid the occasion demands. In the present instance several brave men were captured simply because their horses were so far distant" (*The Campaigns of Stuart's Cavalry*, by H. B. McClellan, pp. 207, 208).

northeast of Brandy Station, ordering his wagons and disabled horses back to Rapidan Station.

Some time having elapsed, and the enemy not appearing, he pushed on rapidly toward the ford. About 12 m., as the Federal skirmishers emerged from a belt of timber about a mile from the ford, they received a volley from a dismounted squadron which Lee, thinking he had to do only with an advance-guard, had posted behind a stone fence a short distance from the wood. Averell at once deployed the 4 N. Y. dismounted on the right of the road, the 4 Pa. on the left, placed a section of artillery between them, and ordered the line to advance "to the edge of the woods and use carbines." The two dismounted regiments exhibited some unsteadiness; it required the exertions of General Averell and his staff to bring them under the carbine fire which was now sweeping the woods. But they soon regained their firmness, and opened an effective fire in return.[1]

Averell ordered McIntosh to deploy his two regiments $\left(\frac{3 \text{ Pa., } 16 \text{ Pa.}}{2.2. \text{ C}}\right)$ on the right, and Reno to send three squadrons to act as reserve for the right wing (McIntosh's command), and one squadron up the road to support the left (4 N. Y., 4 Pa., and 1 R. I.); he also ordered a section of artillery to operate with the right wing. The remainder of Reno's command, consisting of the greater part of the 1 and 5 U. S., he retained as a general reserve (Map 3).

As the 4 N. Y. and 4 Pa. advanced with a cheer against the stone fence, about 100 dismounted men of the 16 Pa., who were smelling powder for the first time, double-timed through the woods on the right, and came in the rear of the stone fence, causing the force that occupied it to beat a hasty retreat. The 4 Pa. and the 4 N. Y. established themselves behind the stone fence. The Confederates were seen advancing covered by mounted skirmishers, whose fire soon made itself felt. But Lee was not going to content himself with mounted skirmishing. At the head of his main column was the 3 Va. This regiment threw down a rail fence about 100 yards below Brannin's House, and moved to near J. Brown's House to form. Here Lee ordered it to charge. It did so in column of fours, directing the movement against the stone fence. Underestimating Averell's force and the extent of his front, Lee meant that this regiment should gain the right flank or rear of the Federal line. The Confederate troopers, finding that they were heading into a line of men firing dismounted with carbines, veered to their left, across the front of the Federal line, looking in vain for an opening, discharging their pistols with little or no effect, and receiving a withering fire from the Federal carbines. As they came opposite the Federal right they were joined by the 5 Va. The two regiments tried to gain the

[1] W. R., 39, p. 49; Hist. of the 3 Pa. Cavalry, by the Regimental Association, p. 208.

cover of the Wheatley House (Wheatleyville) to strike from there against the Federal right and rear, and cut the force off from the ford. But McIntosh, commanding Averell's brigade, was too quick for them. He had the building occupied by dismounted men of the 16 Pa., who with their carbine fire compelled them to fall back. Among the losses sustained by the enemy was John Pelham, the "Boy Major," Stuart's young and capable chief of artillery, killed by a piece of shell.[1]

The 3 and 5 Va. were badly shaken up, and should have been charged as they retired, but General Averell had no troops in position from which an effective charge could be made; besides, Lee's strength had not yet been developed, and the charging force might, he thought, be exposed to a destructive counter-attack. About this time Colonel Duffié, on the Federal left, started on his own responsibility to lead his brigade out in front of Averell's line as an invitation to the enemy to advance. The colonel was a Frenchman, formerly an officer of the 4 Chasseurs d'Afrique. He was a good swordsman, believing in the efficacy of the saber and the mounted charge, and had imbued his command with his own dashing spirit. Duffié was hurrying his regiment (1 R. I.) "front into line" on the head of his column, when a line of sabers was seen flashing along the edge of the woods immediately in his front. It was the 1, 2, and 4 Va. regiments, which, requiring no invitation, were advancing in three lines under Lee at a trot. The Federals awaited at a halt their approach to within 50 or 100 yards, when the 1 R. I. dashed forward to the charge, followed on its right by the 6 O. and the two squadrons of the 4 Pa., and on its left by two squadrons of the 5 U. S. At the same time the 3 Pa., clearing the ground lately covered by the 3 and 5 Va., threatened to take Lee's lines in flank and rear. There were thus nearly 4 Federal regiments in action against the 3 Confederate. The former were not only numerically stronger and in better condition than the latter, but, with their broader front, had a better formation for attack. The Confederates, perceiving the hopeless disadvantage at which they were placed, fired a few shots with their pistols, wheeled rather irregularly by fours and platoons to the right, and immediately repeating the manœuver, made off in haste, pursued principally by the 1 R. I. Among the prisoners taken by the latter was Major Breckinridge, a cousin of the Vice-President of the Confederacy. A portion of the 1 R. I. carried the pursuit too far. A fresh squadron of the enemy being thrown into the running fight, 2 officers and 18 men of the Federals were captured.

[1] His body was borne to the rear on the bow of the saddle of a fleeing Confederate trooper (*The Life and Campaigns of Major J. E. B. Stuart*, by Major H. B. McClellan, p. 217). In his purse was found, folded away, a slip of paper on which was written by a Federal officer, once his companion and friend: "After long absence I write,— 'God bless you, dear Pelham; I am proud of your success'" (New York *Times*, May 3, 1863).

This squadron of the enemy was met by a charge of two squadrons of the 5 Regulars. Lieutenant Nathaniel Bowditch, of the 1 Mass. Cavalry, an assistant adjutant-general on Duffié's staff, was mortally wounded after having cut down three men. A squadron of the 3 Pa. on the right spontaneously rushed forward to join in the pursuit, but was promptly recalled. Averell then and there issued a very emphatic order, that troops once assigned a position in line should under no circumstances leave it without orders from himself or some one designated by him as competent to act for him. Such an order is prohibitive of effective cavalry action.

The 3 Pa. crossed the field in echelon of squadrons at a walk, annoying the retreating enemy with volleys from the saddle, and as it neared the next wood, formed "front into line" at the trot. The 16 Pa. accompanied this movement on the extreme right. The 1 U. S. was, for the greater part, still in reserve under Reno.

Prisoners taken in the last charge stated that Stuart himself, with his chief of artillery, was on the field, from which Averell apprehended that more than Fitzhugh Lee's brigade would soon be before him. Stuart's chief of artillery, as already stated, had fallen. Stuart was indeed on the field, but he had brought no troops with him. He and Pelham, happening to be at Culpeper Court-House on court-martial duty, had simply come out with Fitzhugh Lee to see the fight.

Being driven at every point, Lee withdrew about a mile, rallied his command, and formed line across the road on the north side of Carter's Run, with mounted skirmishers in front (Map 4). Behind his right wing stood a battery of four guns, which had not been able to come up in time to take part in the first encounter. Averell spent a half-hour or more preparing to advance. He marched in line of columns. His left, formed of the 1 R. I. and 6 O., rested its left on the road, the ground on the left of the road being impracticable. The scattered sections of artillery were assembled, and the battery advanced with the cavalry to the further edge of the next strip of wood, where it formed in battery to receive the enemy, who was expected to make a charge. Here two of the pieces were sent to the rear, their ammunition being nearly exhausted. After an appreciable delay the battery advanced in column of pieces, following and overtaking the cavalry. The latter in the meantime had come under the fire of the enemy's battery. Emerging from the strip of wood, and discovering the enemy, the Federal cavalry halted and formed line. The two lines were separated by an open field about 600 yards wide, sloping gently down from each side toward Carter's Run. The ground beyond the Federal left was now practicable, so it was necessary to extend the line in that direction. This was done by the 5 U. S. under a heavy fire of artillery and small arms (Map 4). In his present position Averell again waited to be attacked.

Again the enemy accommodated him. Lee ordered his whole brigade to charge. From his left, the 1, 3, and 5 Va. regiments steered for the center of the Federal right. Crossing Carter's Run and reforming, they directed their course on three squadrons of the 3 Pa. Cavalry, which had been posted on the outer edge of a small wood. In the Federal squadrons the front rank had advanced carbines, and the rear rank drawn sabers.[1] The enemy was impeded by the soft ground, and a scattering fire from several squadrons of the 16 Pa., on the right of the 3. He was not within 100 yards of his objective, but his line was commencing to sift to pieces. More than half of the men had halted or were proceeding in a half-hearted way. A few only of the most daring spirits on the best horses arrived within from 25 to 50 yards of the Federal line. The Sharp's breech-loading carbines in the front rank of the 3 Pa. were now brought to an aim, and volley after volley was delivered with effect. The assailants pulled up, turned about, and retired in small squads to reform on the ground whence they started. As soon as General Averell perceived that it was the purpose of the enemy to charge on this part of the line, he hurried up Reno's command, the 1 U. S. Cavalry, and placed it in position about 100 yards to the left and slightly in advance of the 3 Pa., with the intention of making a counter-charge on the right flank of the advancing line as soon as the latter had made contact with the 3 Pa. But as the charge terminated in the air, Reno could not execute this counter-attack, and he was prohibited by Averell's forementioned order from pursuing. The 3 Pa., too, was prevented by the same order from rushing at once on the disorganized enemy. But despite the order, individual officers and men rode out from both sides and engaged in hand-to-hand contests.[2] Not until after the shattered squadrons had in a measure recovered their spirits and formation did the order come for the 3 Pa. to charge. Carbines were dropped, and sabers drawn; the regiment dashed forward and drove the enemy from the field.

Lee's right, consisting of the 2 and 4 Va., made an attack on the Federal left, aiming apparently at the supports of the battery, the four pieces of which had just come into action. The Confederate formation was column of squadrons. Starting at a trot, and passing to a gallop, and then to a charge, the yelling and cheering lines, firing an occasional shot from a pistol or carbine, swept on toward the ranks of motionless figures with drawn sabers silently awaiting them. The battery opened

[1] The Federal cavalry was formed at that time, as most European cavalry is to-day, in double rank, which formation has been totally discarded in the U. S. cavalry since the war.

[2] "Since the crossing of the river there had been many personal encounters—single horsemen dashing at each other with full speed, and cutting and slashing with their sabers until one or the other was disabled. The wounds received by both friends and foes in these single combats were frightful —such as I trust never to see again" (New York *Times,* March 20, 1863).

on them with shell at 1500 yards, with shrapnel at about 1000 yards, and with double-shotted canister at about 400 yards. The leading squadron had begun to waver, files were breaking off from its right and left. Simultaneously with the first belch of canister rang out the command—"Charge!" The expectant horsemen, giving sudden vent to their pent-up feelings and energy, shot forward. The enemy could not stand up to the impending shock. The Federal force comprised the 1 R. I. and parts of the 5 U. S., 6 O., and 1 U. S.[1] Lee's dashing horsemen had again to give way before Averell's superior numbers. They broke and ran in disorder, leaving a number of dead, wounded, and prisoners. The pursuit was conducted by Reno. He did not return to the line, but halted about a mile in advance of it, or about on the ground vacated by the enemy, where he was joined by the rest of the Federal cavalry. The Confederate cavalry halted about half a mile in rear of their late position, where it was concealed for the greater part by woods or swells in the ground. The artillery on both sides remained in its late position (Map 5). For a considerable time there was not a formed body of Confederate cavalry on the field. The Confederate battery was engaged with the Federal battery. All that Averell had to do to rid the country of Fitzhugh Lee's cavalry was to launch his own after it, reckless of everything but speed, to pulverize the fragments of Lee's shattered regiments, and scatter the particles far and wide. But he did not attempt it. About this time he heard that infantry had been seen at a distance on his right moving toward his rear, and he himself heard cars running on the railroad in rear of the enemy, which he supposed were bringing reënforcements. As a matter of fact there was no infantry nearer his opponent than the Confederate army about Fredericksburg; and the cars which he heard were moving back and forth by Fitzhugh Lee's order to discourage the Federals, and perhaps to encourage his own men. Averell got the idea that the enemy's line was covered with earthworks; it had no protection but what was afforded by the terrain. He says in his report:

It was 5:30 p.m., and it was necessary to advance my cavalry upon their intrenched positions, to make a direct and desperate attack, or to withdraw across the river. Either operation would be attended with immediate hazard. My horses were very much exhausted. We had been successful thus far. I deemed it proper to withdraw.

Detachments of cavalry were deployed in front of the artillery, and the division commenced its return march. Captain Reno, with the 1 and 5 U. S., covered the rear. His task was anything but an easy one, the battery having almost exhausted its ammunition, and having there-

[1] *Battle of Kelley's Ford,* by J. B. Cooke, p. 28; *History of the 3 Pa. Cavalry,* by Committee, p. 213.

fore to fire very slowly. The enemy, taking advantage of this fact, followed it up with the fire of his battery. Once or twice Reno halted to allow him to come up, but the latter contented himself with long-range firing. The enemy's object was to drive away the cavalry escort with artillery fire, and then charge the battery. The Federal cavalry had therefore to stand this fire, and stay with the battery. To have left it would have been to surrender it to the enemy. The battery lost heavily in horses, but, under the protection of its gallant escort, brought off all its guns. The sound of the artillery firing reached the ears of the Federal troops celebrating St. Patrick's day in their camps about Falmouth.[1]

Among Averell's wounded were two officers who could not be removed and were consequently left at a farm-house with a surgeon and some medical supplies. The surgeon was intrusted with a part of a sack of coffee and a note hastily written in about the following words:

*Dear Fitz:*
Here's your coffee. Here's your visit. How do you like it? How's that horse?
                                                            AVERELL.[2]

A few weeks afterward Averell received from Fitzhugh Lee the following message:

Your two officers are well enough to go home, where they ought to be. Send an ambulance to Kelley's and you can have them.

This was done. The officers were sent across the river without being paroled, and went to their homes.

The Federal cavalry had crossed the river about 2200 strong, with supplies for four days and orders to rout or destroy an enemy about half as numerous as itself. About twelve hours later it returned; it had advanced but about 2½ miles (to R. Dean's Shop), or less than one fourth of the distance to the enemy's camp (Culpeper Court-House, Map 2), and had done him no serious injury.

Averell says in his report:

The principal result achieved by this expedition has been that our cavalry has been brought to feel their superiority in battle; they have learned the value of discipline and the use of their arms. At the first view I must confess that two regiments [4 N. Y., 4 Pa.] wavered, but they did not lose their senses, and a few energetic remarks brought them to a sense of their duty. After that the feeling

[1] New York *Times,* March 22, 1863.
[2] This letter is taken from the forementioned newspaper account in the library of the Massachusetts Historical Society. Following is the version of it given by Captain Hess, 3 Artillery: *"Dear Fitz:* Here's your coffee. How is your horse? AVERELL."

became stronger throughout the day that it was our fight, and the manœuvers were performed with a precision which the enemy did not fail to observe.

Averell's claim that the action elevated the *morale* of his command was undoubtedly well founded.[1]  But it was not for this that he had been given 3000 troopers and four days' rations and ordered across the Rappahannock.  He was to rout or destroy the enemy.  As it was, the gain of his force in *morale* was probably offset by that of the enemy.  For Fitzhugh Lee and his command felt that it was they and not the Federals who carried off the honors of the day.  And it could hardly have been otherwise, unless they had been driven to their camp and captured or at least run out of it.  The fight seems to have demonstrated that the Federal regiments were at least as well drilled and disciplined as the Confederate, but that Averell had not the aggressiveness essential to the effective command of cavalry.  His plan of action was based upon what he expected the enemy to do, rather than upon what he himself was ordered or determined to do.  When he met the enemy, instead of proceeding to attack him, he took up a position and awaited his attack.  This he did three times.  In his third position neither side attacked, and he decided to withdraw.  He did not make a single general attack.

To attain his object, he would have been justified in sacrificing half of his command.  How much of a loss did he incur?  According to his own report, 56 in killed and wounded, and 22 in captured and missing. Lee claims to have captured 29.  Accepting the latter number, we have a total of 85, which is less than four per cent. of the force with which he crossed the river.  Although on the offensive, he suffered less absolutely and proportionately than the enemy.  Fitzhugh Lee gives his killed and wounded as 99, and his loss by capture as 34.  Averell claims to have captured 47.  Accepting the latter number, we have for Lee's total loss 146, or more than eleven per cent. of his force.

Averell's order depriving his subordinates of all initiative appears to have been caused by injudicious aggression on the part of Duffié and other officers, which would show that the Federal officers were deficient in instruction and discipline.  While Averell erred from excess of caution, Fitzhugh Lee may be criticized for excess of daring.  His attacks were practically all directed against the enemy's front.  This was just what Averell expected and wanted.  Had Lee known Averell's tactical

---

[1] "The cavalry are in good spirits over their affair. . . . The enemy are not inclined to talk about it, and no slurs or insinuations come from their pickets" (New York *Herald*, March 20).  "Rebel officers who have since met our own under the flag of truce seem to be very sore about the affair, and express astonishment at the splendid fighting of our cavalry.  Fully one third of our wounded show marks of the saber, so close was the contest.  The effect of the fight upon the tone of our entire army has been admirable" (New York *Tribune*, March 21).

temperament as well as Averell knew his, or knowing it, taken advantage of it to make proper reconnaissances and execute flanking and turning movements, he might have struck Averell a disastrous blow. As it was, he did not strike an effective one. His every attack was followed, or might have been, by an advance of his adversary. It is hardly unjust to Lee or to Averell to say that Averell gave Lee a victory by retiring when he should not have done so.

The result of the contest was communicated to R. E. Lee by the following dispatches:

Headquarters, Two miles from Kelley's Ford,
March 17, 1863, 7 p.m.

*General R. E. Lee,* Richmond, Va.:

Enemy is retiring. We are after him. His dead men and horses strew the roads.

J. E. B. STUART,
Major-General.[1]

Headquarters, Culpeper, March 18, 1863.

*General R. E. Lee,* Richmond, Va.:

I telegraphed you last night enemy had retired [to] north bank of Rappahannock. From the best information it was Averell's division, 3000 in the saddle. Pork and hard bread packed in boxes. He was very badly hurt, and left a hospital on this side. It was undoubtedly intended as a great expedition, but, thanks to the superior conduct of General Fitzhugh Lee and his noble brigade, it has failed. . . .

J. E. B. STUART.[2]

The following congratulatory orders were issued from Stuart's and Fitzhugh Lee's headquarters:

### Stuart

The series of fierce contests in which Brig. Gen. Fitz Lee's brigade was engaged on the 17th instant, with an enemy greatly superior in numbers, resulting in entire success to us, reflects the highest credit on its commander, its officers, and its men. On no occasion have I seen more instances of individual prowess—never such heroic firmness in the presence of danger the most appalling. The enemy, afraid to contest the palm as cavalry, preferred to rely upon his artillery, ensconcing his cavalry, dismounted, behind stone fences and other barriers, which alone saved him from capture or annihilation, thus converting the long-vaunted raid, which was "to break the backbone of the rebellion" with preparations complete for an extensive expedition, into a feeble advance and a defensive operation.

### Fitzhugh Lee

The general commanding the brigade announces to his command his high gratification and proud appreciation of their heroic achievements upon the ever-

---

[1] *W. R.,* 108, p. 865. For similar dispatch see Richmond
*Enquirer,* March 19, 1863.
[2] *W. R.,* 108, p. 686.

memorable 17th instant. The enemy crossed the Rappahannock at Kelley's Ford with a force of certainly not less than 3000 cavalry and a battery of artillery. Confident in numbers and equipments, it was their purpose to penetrate the interior, to destroy our railroads, to burn, rob, and devastate, and to commit their customary depredations upon the property of our peaceful citizens. Soldiers of the brigade! you have been taught a lesson, and the enemy have also profited. . . . Rebel cavalry have been taught that a determined rush upon the foe is the part of sound policy as it is the part of true courage. Rebel cavalry have taught an insolent enemy that, notwithstanding they may possess advantages of chosen position, superiority in numbers and weapons, they cannot overwhelm soldiers fighting for the holiest cause that ever nerved the arm of a freeman or fired the breast of a patriot. . . . You have repeatedly charged an enemy sheltered by stone fences and impassable ditches, in the face of his artillery and volleys from thousands of his carbines. You checked his triumphant advance, and caused a precipitate retreat, with the legacy of his dead and wounded. . . .

Averell's congratulatory order, if he issued one, is not to be found. Colonel Duffié, whose brigade may be said to have decided the first encounter, congratulated his command as follows:

Again we have met the enemy, and beaten him at all points. . . . the enemy appeared in force, with their boasted 4 Virginia Cavalry in advance at a charge, supported in their flank and rear by three full regiments. Here was an opportunity—so long sought for—of meeting the rebel cavalry in a fair and square fight in an open field.

The Rhode Island squadron dashed at their column, broke the head of it in a moment, and sent the whole body back to their reserves, capturing nearly all the charging regiment with its commander. Again the enemy came thundering down, and these squadrons, nobly supported by the 6 Ohio, again showed the chivalrous sons of the "sacred soil" that on an open field they were no match for the hated Yankees. Although they were five to our one, a third time the lines were formed and this time by their famous Stuart, who had determined, if possible, to retrieve his evil fortune. On they came. And then took place that terrible hand-to-hand fight—man to man—horse to horse—saber to saber—which ended in their utter defeat, and our most glorious victory. . . .[1]

Butterfield wrote to the commanders of the I, XI, and XII Corps:

I send, for your information, the following synopsis of Averell's affair.

He sent in a large number of prisoners (about 80), including 1 major. Captain Moore, of General Hooker's staff, who accompanied him, reports it as a brilliant and splendid fight—the best cavalry fight of the war—lasting five hours, charging and recharging on both sides, our men using their sabers handsomely and with effect, driving the enemy 3 miles into cover of earthworks and heavy guns. Forces about equal.

Hooker's judgment of the affair was decidedly different. He remarked:

[1] *Sabres and Spurs,* by F. Denison, pp. 315, 316.

. . . After the brigadier-general commanding had permitted one third of his force to remain on the north bank of the Rappahannock, his passage of the river with the residue of his force appears to have been eminently soldierlike, and his dispositions for engaging and following the enemy, up to the time of his recrossing the river, were made with skill and judgment; and had he followed his instructions and persevered in his success, he could easily have routed the enemy, fallen upon his camp, and inflicted a severe blow upon him. The enemy was inferior to the command he had in hand in all respects. The reason assigned— that he heard cars arriving at Culpeper, and not knowing but that they might be bringing reënforcements to the enemy—is very unsatisfactory, and should have had no influence in determining the line of that officer's conduct. He was sent to perform a certain duty, and failed to accomplish it from imaginary apprehensions.[1]

That Averell's generalship on this occasion was satisfactory to the powers at Washington was forcibly, if not elegantly, attested by the following communication from Stanton:

*Major-General Hooker:*

I congratulate you upon the success of General Averell's expedition. It is good for the first lick. You have drawn the first blood, and I hope now soon to see "the boys up and at them." Give my compliments and thanks to Averell and his command.

How the conduct of Fitzhugh Lee's command was regarded by R. E. Lee is shown in the following letter of March 27 from Lee to Stuart:

. . . I am much gratified at the noble conduct of the officers and men in repulsing a greatly superior force of the enemy, and compelling him to give up the attempt to strike a blow at our line of communication. The reports have been forwarded for the information of the Department, and as an evidence of the merit and gallantry of Fitz Lee and his brigade. I regret with you the loss of our noble dead, and concur in your commendations of the living.

So it would seem that everybody was satisfied except Hooker, and he was perhaps too severe in his criticism of Averell.[2]

[1] *W. R.*, 39, p. 1073.
[2] For a defence of Averell's generalship, see *History of the 3 Pa. Cav.*, by Committee, pp. 216–225.

# CHAPTER IX

PREPARATIONS FOR A GENERAL MOVEMENT. PLANS OF OPERATION. BREAD
RIOT IN RICHMOND. THE JONES AND IMBODEN EXPEDITION

WHILE attending to the improvement of his army, Hooker be-
thought himself of what he should do to satisfy the President's
and the country's desire for a successful campaign. On this subject he
obtained the views of others but did not give his own. He "kept his
intentions an entire secret from every one, fearing that otherwise what
he intended to do might come to the knowledge of the enemy."[1] In the
letter from the President already cited, dated January 26, he had an
intimation that the administration wanted a victory and did not care in
what form. On the 31st of January he received a letter from General
Halleck expressing his views as follows:

In regard to the operations of your army, you can best judge when and where
it can move to the greatest advantage, keeping in view always the importance of
covering Washington and Harper's Ferry, either directly or by so operating as
to be able to punish any force of the enemy sent against them.

I inclose herewith a copy of my letter of the 7th instant to Major-General
Burnside. . . . That letter was submitted to the President and approved by
him. . . .

In the inclosure Halleck says to Burnside:

. . . When the attempt at Fredericksburg was abandoned, I advised you to
renew the attempt at some other point, either in whole or in part, to turn the
enemy's works, or to threaten their wings or communications; in other words, to
keep the enemy occupied until a favorable opportunity offered to strike a decisive
blow. I particularly advised you to use your cavalry and light artillery upon his
communications, and attempt to cut off his supplies, and engage him at an advantage. In all our interviews I have urged that our first object was not Richmond,
but the defeat or scattering of Lee's army, which threatened Washington and the
line of the upper Potomac.

I now recur to these things simply to remind you of the general views which I
have expressed, and which I still hold. The circumstances of the case, however,
have somewhat changed since the early part of November. The chances of an
extended line of operations[2] are now, on account of the advanced season, much

---

[1] Butterfield, *Rep. of Com.*, IV, 74.
[2] Of operating far from one's base. Halleck seems to refer especially to the execution
of wide turning movements. J. B. Jr.

less than then. But the chances are still in our favor to meet and defeat the enemy on the Rappahannock if we can effect a crossing in a position where we can meet the enemy on favorable or even equal terms. I therefore still advise a movement against him.

The character of that movement, however, must depend upon circumstances, which may change every day and almost every hour. . . . It will not do to keep your large army inactive. As you yourself admit, it devolves upon you to decide upon the time, place, and character of the crossing which you attempt. I can only advise that an early attempt be made and as early as possible.

This communication is made up of hints and suggestions, except for the two positive directions:

(1) That the Army of the Potomac shall assume the offensive without any unnecessary delay.

(2) That it shall not uncover Washington.

With these sole limitations, Hooker was free to plan and direct the operations of his army according to his own ideas.

On the 2d of February Lieutenant Comstock, Chief Engineer Officer, recommended to Hooker the fortification of his base at Aquia Creek Landing as a protection to his rear-guard in case of an embarkation, and to his depot against raiding parties in case of an advance. This recommendation was adopted; the construction of the necessary works commenced on the 8th of February and terminated on or before the 9th of March. On the 3d of February the same officer submitted to Butterfield a report on the topographical and tactical features of the following points of crossing (Map 2), commencing down-stream: Skinker's Neck, Hayfield's, Seddon's, Franklin's Crossing, Banks' Ford, and United States Ford, without recommending any of them.[1] On the 6th he wrote to Butterfield suggesting for consideration "the propriety of thoroughly preparing the approaches which would be needed if a crossing of the river were attempted either at United States Ford or at Seddon's."

On the 8th he submitted to Hooker a memorandum for bringing the material for a bridge from Baltimore by water to and up the Rappahannock and throwing the bridge at Seddon's or Skinker's Neck. Hooker was thinking at this time of turning Lee's right flank, and forcing it from the Richmond and Fredericksburg Railroad. He intended then to defeat his army in battle, and compel him to retreat toward Gordonsville, thus uncovering Richmond.[2]

He spent the 11th of March in Washington with the President, the Secretary of War, General Halleck, and the Committee on the Conduct of the War. What passed between him and the other members of this council is not known, but it may be assumed that he discussed with them

[1] *W. R.*, 107, pp. 980, 981.
[2] *Across the Continent with the 5 Cavalry*, by Captain G. F. Price, pp. 113, 114.

his plan for getting around Lee below Fredericksburg. On this visit, and on others of similar character, he exhibited great enthusiasm for his prospective campaign.

At Falmouth on the 19th he reviewed the XII Corps. Meeting the officers afterward at Slocum's headquarters, he expressed to them his reliance upon their assistance and hearty coöperation in the impending campaign, and his determination that, so far as he was concerned, there should be no more mistakes or doubtful results. "If the enemy does not run," he said, "God help them."[1]

Again on the 29th, he remarked to a party of officers whom he was entertaining in his tent: "I have the finest army the sun ever shone on. I can march this army to New Orleans. My plans are perfect, and when I start to carry them out, may God have mercy on General Lee, for I will have none."[2]

A few days later he received the following instigation to action:

Washington, D. C., March 27, 1863, 2:30 p.m.

*Maj. Gen. Joseph Hooker,* Falmouth, Va.:

Dispatches from Generals Dix, Foster,[3] and Hunter,[4] and from the west, indicate that the rebel troops formerly under Lee are now much scattered for supplies, and for operations elsewhere. It would seem, under these circumstances, advisable that a blow be struck by the Army of the Potomac as early as practicable. It is believed that during the next few days several conflicts will take place, both south and west, which may attract the enemy's attention particularly to those points.

H. W. HALLECK,
General-in-Chief.

Hooker was influenced, moreover, to initiate operations at an early date by the thought that he had in his army a number of regiments enlisted, some for two years and others for nine months, mostly from New York State, whose time would be up in the course of the spring. It was important that the services of these men should be utilized before the time when they would have to be sent home to be mustered out, for they were entitled to be mustered out at the place where they were mustered in.

Concerning a general plan of operations, he realized that it was impossible to assail the enemy in front. The mere passage of the river presented no serious difficulty, for Lee, adhering to his usual policy, invited rather than threatened that operation; but his line of intrenchments, stretching along the sides of the crest of the heights, was in

---

[1] New York *Tribune,* March 21, 1863.

[2] *War Talks in Kansas,* p. 194.

[3] Major-General J. G. Foster, commanding Department of North Carolina, headquarters New Berne.

[4] Major-General D. Hunter, commanding Department of the South, headquarters Port Royal.

plain view, and the hopelessness of attacking it was a conviction in the mind of even the privates in the ranks. The enemy could then be assailed only by turning his position. The river increased so rapidly in width that to cross it below Port Royal, where Lee's right rested (Map 1, sheet A), would require 1000 feet of bridging, and the pontoon trains and artillery must march 20 miles over a broken and wooded country by roads of clayey mud. The march of an army under such conditions would be extremely slow. Lee's spy system was so efficient that the movement could not be kept from him, and his intrenchments might be extended down the river to keep pace with it. Furthermore, a movement of the army in this direction would uncover Washington.

Above Fredericksburg the roads were comparatively firm and of easy grade, and the rivers narrower. A movement in this direction need not uncover Washington, unless, on account of the precautions taken by the enemy to prevent it, such a movement would have to be much more extensive than one below.

About 2½ miles above Fredericksburg, as one ascends the river, the bluffs on each side of the Rappahannock close in upon it. They rise about 150 feet above the water, the right bank attaining a somewhat greater height than the left. Their slopes are generally well wooded, very steep, and deeply cut by ravines. Good ground for approaching the river from either side first presents itself at Banks' Ford. Here a foothold on the opposite hills gives command of the enemy's line. This important point was guarded by Wilcox's brigade and Penick's battery of Anderson's division, and presumably could not be surprised. Owing to the bend in the river, it is twice as far from the Federal position as it is from the Confederate, and, moreover, is just now impassable.

The next point that offers a practicable approach is United States Ford. Here, also, the river was at this time unfordable; the approach, moreover, was covered by long lines of works, to be manned whenever necessary by troops of Mahone's and Posey's brigades of Anderson's division, camped near by. Just above United States Ford is the junction of the Rapidan with the Rappahannock. Any attempt to turn the enemy's left above this point involves the passage of both streams, each of which is from 200 to 300 feet in width.

General Haupt was summoned from Washington to confer with Hooker. Describing the interview, Haupt says:

[Hooker] handed me a paper to read, saying that it contained his plan of operations, but I must not on any consideration open my lips to any living soul; that even the members of his staff did not know what his plans were, and would not know until the time arrived for putting them in execution; he had left them under the impression that a very different movement was contemplated. He added that when he did move he expected to advance very rapidly, and as he would depend upon me for his supplies, I had a very important duty to perform; that upon its performance success or failure might depend, and he had concluded to advise me fully, so that I might make the necessary preparations.[1]

Having read the paper, Haupt said that he would be ready. With this in view, he issued the following instructions, a copy of which was forwarded to Hooker:

> War Department, U. S. Military Railroads,
> Washington, D. C., March 26, 1863.
> A. ANDERSON, ESQ., Chief Engineer Military Railroads of Virginia.
> Sir:
> You will take measures to have everything in readiness to meet the wishes and second the movements of the commander of the Army of the Potomac, sparing no labor or necessary expense to secure the most effective action when called upon, and to provide the materials and men necessary for the purpose.
> You will have a well-organized force of skilled men, complete in its appointments, and fully provided with every means and appliance to facilitate the work it may have to do. You will apply to the commander of the army for such details of soldiers as you may want, and to the chief quartermaster for transportation of all kinds and forage for animals.
> While endeavoring to consult a judicious economy in expenditures, avoid that false economy which is purchased at the expense of efficiency. When active forward operations are resumed, the all-important object will be to secure the reconstruction of roads and bridges and the reopening of communications in the shortest possible time.
>
> .    .    .    .    .    .    .    .    .    .
>
> Very respectfully,
> H. HAUPT,
> Chief of Construction and Transportation, U. S. Mil. R. R.

General Haupt had a profile of the line from Fredericksburg to Richmond, and knew the dimensions of all the bridges on it. He had a large number of bridge trusses prepared in spans of 60 feet to be transported on flat cars, hauled from the cars by oxen to the sites of the bridges, and hoisted bodily into position by suitable machinery.[2]

The prospect of active operations occasioned, too, the following communication of the 31st instant from Comstock to Butterfield:

In case a siege of Richmond is deemed among the possibilities of the coming campaign, I think the chief quartermaster should be notified that he may be called on to furnish on our arrival in front of Richmond 10,000 shovels, 5000 picks, 5000 axes, and 2000 shingling hatchets; that the Engineer Department should hold in readiness 30,000 sand-bags; and the secret service should, if possible, obtain authentic maps of the defences of Richmond, either through their agents or by the public offer of large rewards. Such maps would be of no less

[1] *Reminiscences of General Herman Haupt*, p. 193.          [2] *Ib.*, p. 178.

value in case of an assault than in case of a siege. In the first case they would save valuable time that would otherwise be spent in selecting the proper point of attack, or might indicate at once that point. Such maps are undoubtedly in existence. Copies or originals may perhaps be obtained. It is believed to be impossible to compile such maps here from information given by persons who enter our lines, so as to obtain with sufficient accuracy either the strength of the works or the character of the ground around them.[1]

The following day, April 2, Hooker wrote to Stanton:

I send you our last advices from Richmond. The papers contained but little news. Lieutenant-General Longstreet [himself] was on the opposite side of the river night before last. It is reported that his command is returning. . . . Why is not the Second Regiment New Hampshire Volunteers on its way back?[2]

It looked as if the IX Corps was not a sufficient attraction to keep Longstreet away from Lee. But the following letter from Peck, dated April 4, put a new face on the matter:

. . . My information from various sources has been that Longstreet had within 20 or 30 miles of this place [Suffolk] 15,000 [men], and 15,000 along the railway this side of Petersburg, which he could concentrate [at an intermediate point] in 12 hours, and I was advised from headquarters [Fort Monroe] a few days since that one of our spies had a list of the regiments and the strength, and they amounted to 28,000. . . .

Ever since my arrival the enemy has been impressed with the idea that an army [Federal] would attempt this route, and they have watched very closely.[3]

The expectations expressed in the following letter of Lieutenant Henry Ropes, 20 Mass. Volunteers,[4] dated March 31, were perhaps shared by a large portion of the Army of the Potomac:

. . . it appears likely that our corps [II] will remain to cover this front and conceal our movement from the enemy, in whatever direction the army goes. . . .

---

[1] *W. R.*, 107, p. 999

[2] The 2 N. H. had been furloughed to go home and carry an election for the Republican party. It did not return until after the campaign (*Hist. of the 2d Regiment of N. H. Vol. Infantry*, by M. A. Haynes, pp. 152, 153).

[3] The Richmond *Enquirer* of March 25, discussing the strategic deployment of the Federal armies, said: "Another great army is now threatening our communications, distributed between Suffolk in Virginia, and New Berne in North Carolina; it may amount in the whole to 60,000 men; and is intended to take possession of the railroad somewhere between Goldsboro and the Vir-

ginia line, thus cutting our communication with a great part of the Confederacy." Goldsboro and New Berne are south of Weldon and nearer the coast. They are not shown on the map.

[4] I shall take occasion again to quote from this young officer's letters home, using the manuscript copies deposited in the library of the Military Historical Society of Massachusetts, by John C. Ropes, Esq., of Boston, the founder of the society and distinguished military historian, and a brother of Lieutenant Ropes. The II Corps sustained a heavier loss than any other at the battle of Fredericksburg, December 13, 1862. J. B. Jr.

It seems to be the general opinion that he [Hooker] will move secretly down the river, cross, say, 40 miles below, under cover of the gunboats, and move on the enemy's communications with Richmond. . . .

The following representations were doubtless received at Hooker's headquarters in the course of the next few days:

### Keyes to Halleck, April 8

H. A. Gibbon, a deserter from the 57 Regiment North Carolina [2. 3. II], . . . states that Lee has collected large pontoon trains, and is ready to cross the Rappahannock;[1] that he will attack Hooker soon, if Hooker does not attack; that Lee's army is 80,000 strong, all well armed, and mostly with Enfield rifles. The men are in good condition, and feel entire confidence that they will beat Hooker. . . .

### Brigadier-General Pleasonton, First Cavalry Division, to Assistant Secretary of War, April 10

1. The rebel force on the Rappahannock has not been diminished. Two divisions of Longstreet's troops [Hood's and Pickett's] have returned to Fredericksburg.[2]

2. The rebels are fortifying the fords of the Rapidan [in the vicinity of Rapidan Station], and intend to fight on that stream [in that vicinity] and at Fredericksburg.

3. There are no works or troops on the railroad from Culpeper to within 3 miles of Richmond. All the heights around Richmond are fortified. . . .

.          .          .          .          .          .          .

5. . . . There is much suffering among the citizens in the south, but the soldiers are well supplied, and are in good health and spirits. Everybody has been conscripted. The troops have 22 ounces per day of flour, one-fourth pound of meat, with some sugar and rice occasionally.[3]

The strength attributed to Lee's army in the first of these dispatches was about 30 per cent. in excess of the actual number. A truer estimate of it was given in a project for a passage of the Rappahannock below Fredericksburg prepared by Captain Comstock, and presented to Hooker on the 12th: "It is assumed," said Comstock, "that the force of the enemy within 15 miles [a day's march] of Fredericksburg is probably 40,000 men, and does not exceed 60,000."[4]

Comstock's estimate of Lee's numbers, say 50,000, is from 15 to 20 per cent. too small. It may be assumed that, balancing the various estimates afforded him, Hooker had a pretty correct idea of the strength of Lee's army.

[1] This statement appears to be an error. The author can find no evidence of Lee's having the material for a pontoon bridge that would span the Rappahannock.

[2] These divisions had not returned. J. B. Jr.

[3] These particulars may have been true as to the other Confederate armies. In Lee's army the ration of flour was 18 ounces (Lee to Seddon, March 27, *ante*).

[4] *W. R.*, 107, p. 1003.

On the south side of the Rappahannock the planning for a general movement looked less to the offensive than to the defensive. In answer to two letters from General Trimble proposing an attempt in force on the Federal camp at Falmouth, Lee wrote on the 8th of March:

. . . I know the pleasure experienced in shaping campaigns and battles according to our wishes, and have enjoyed the ease with which obstacles to their accomplishment (in effigy) can be overcome. The movements you suggest in both letters have been at various times studied, canvassed with those who would be engaged in their execution, but no practicable solution of the difficulties to be overcome has yet been reasonably reached. The weather, roads, streams, provisions, transportation, etc., are all powerful elements in the calculation, as you know. . . . The idea of securing the provisions, wagons, guns, of the enemy, is truly tempting, and the desire has haunted me since December. Personally I would run any risk for their attainment, but I cannot jeopardize this army.

I consider it impossible to throw a trestle bridge over the Rappahannock below the Rapidan, with a view to a surprise. Our first appearance at any point would be the signal for the concentration of their army, and their superior artillery would render its accomplishment impossible without great loss of life. A bridge might be thrown over the Rapidan above the Germanna Mills, and has been contemplated. Our movements might be concealed until we crossed the Rappahannock, but the distance from there to Aquia is great; no forage in the country; everything would have to be hauled. The route by Orange and Alexandria Railroad is the most feasible. The bridge is passable at Rappahannock Station. We must talk about it some time.

### On the 12th he wrote to Stuart:

. . . I have written to W. H. F. Lee [commanding cavalry below Port Royal] to be prepared to move at short notice, and to select one regiment to remain in that section. . . . I will send Captain Johnson [of the Engineers] up to Rapidan Station [Map 1, sheet A] to see if rifle-pits can be constructed there to protect the bridge. I think it probable that a dash may be made at it to destroy it, in connection with other movements. What can you put there to guard it?

. . . . . . . . . . .

The information from Falmouth is that the enemy will, as soon as roads permit, cross at *United States Ford, Falmouth, and some point below*, the attempt at Falmouth to be a feint. . . .

I have told Johnson to throw up some works at Gordonsville, so that Major Boyle's men [posted there] might make a stand against cavalry.[1]

Under acts of the Virginia legislature, application was made by the chief of the Engineer Bureau at Richmond, to the Secretary of War, for 2832 slaves to labor on the fortifications and complete them ''within the time desired by General Lee.''[2]

[1] The italics are mine.  J. B. Jr.          [2] Gilmer to Seddon, March 4.

On the 16th of March, Lee wrote to Longstreet:

. . . I am led to believe that none of the army of General Hooker have left the vicinity of Aquia, except the corps of General Smith,[1] which went to Newport News.  It is also reported that it is General Hooker's intention to cross the river and advance as soon as the state of the roads will permit, and that in fact he has issued repeated orders to that effect.  I am not fully informed as to their apparent intentions, strength, etc., on the south side of the James River, but we should be prepared to concentrate to meet him wherever he should advance in force. From present indications it is fair to presume that we shall be called upon to engage him first on the Rappahannock, and I desire you to be prepared for this movement, and make endeavors to keep yourself advised of the disposition and preparations of the enemy on our front for moving the troops recently detached from the First Corps [Confederate], or such of them or others as may be necessary in that direction.[2]

Lee took the incursion of the Federal cavalry under Averell to be a preparation for a general advance of the Army of the Potomac; by a letter to Longstreet, dated 10:30 p.m. the 17th, he ordered Hood's and Pickett's divisions to return to Fredericksburg.  Longstreet replied under date of the 18th:

I do not think it would be well to draw off any portion of Pickett's division at present.  All of it can not well be taken from here as long as the enemy holds this force of his so near Richmond.[3]

On the same day Lee learned that the Federal cavalry had recrossed. He concluded that he had mistaken the character of the enemy's operation, and telegraphed the Adjutant-General at Richmond:

Please detain Hood's and Pickett's divisions until further notice.  No infantry of enemy reported to be crossing.  Cavalry retiring.  Stuart pursuing.  Divisions can either resume former or take more convenient positions.  No more troops needed here.

Mahone's and Posey's brigades of Anderson's division $\left(\frac{1.\ 2}{1.\ 1}\right)$, both under command of Mahone, were posted to dispute the passage of the Rappahannock.  At United States Ford a detail of 120 men was made from the two brigades to report to Captain Collins, Chief Engineer of General J. E. B. Stuart's staff, at Germanna Ford, on the Rapidan River, for the purpose of rebuilding a bridge across the river at that point.  The double object of this work was to improve the communication between Lee's army and Stuart's cavalry and horse artillery at

[1] IX Corps.  It left the Army of the Potomac for Newport News on the 10th of February, commanded by Major-General W. F. Smith.

[2] W. R., 26, pp. 921, 922.

[3] Ib., 26, p. 924.

Culpeper Court-House; and to facilitate a raid which Stuart was contemplating upon the Federal depots at Falmouth.[1]

On the 17th, the day of the battle of Kelley's Ford, Anderson wrote to Mahone:

*General:*

I wish you to place the forces under your command in the best position for checking any attempt of the enemy to cross at United States Ford, to examine the river above and below you for some distance, and to ascertain whether any practicable ford exists. I have been informed that there is one, called the Blind Ford,[2] just below the junction of the rivers.

If your position can be strengthened, have all needful work done. Have the road repaired. Learn all that you can about United States Ford. This may be effected by inducing one of the enemy's cavalry picket to come over to exchange papers or to trade.[3]

Let me have timely notice of any movement of the enemy. Keep up communication with our cavalry picket at Ely's Ford, on the Rapidan.

On the 17th Longstreet wrote to Lee:

. . . I shall be ready to join you with Hood's division at any moment, and trust to your being able to hold the force in your front in check until I can join you.[4]

One of the criticisms made since the war on the strategy of the Southern generals is that the Confederate armies did not generally withdraw from their frontiers so as to realize the advantage of prolonging the Federal, while shortening the Confederate lines of communication. Whatever might be said for this manœuver in an inland country, as illustrated, for instance, in the campaign of Atlanta, it offered no such advantage on the coast. As the Federals commanded the sea, their army would supply itself, as Grant's did during the Wilderness campaign, from its transports and its advanced bases established therefrom. Hence in the plea which Longstreet now enters for a withdrawal from the Rappahannock, and Lee's answer thereto, there is no reference to the Federal communications.

Longstreet wrote to Lee on the 19th of March:

. . . It seems to me to be a matter of prime necessity with us to keep the enemy out of North Carolina in order that we may draw all the supplies there, and if we give him ground at all it would be better to do so from the Rappahan-

---

[1] *Magazine of Am. Hist.*, XX, 378. This raid, it would seem, was to be made, as a sort of counter-offensive, when the Federal army should advance.

[2] There seems to have been a ford by this name just above the junction of the rivers, but none for some distance below. J. B. Jr.

[3] The following instruction was issued on the 27th of February, from Hooker's head-quarters, relative to communications under flags of truce:

"Newspapers may be received; but not exchanged except under special approval from these Headquarters."

[4] *W. R.*, 26, pp. 558, 562. Messages of similar import were sent on the 21st and 22d (*ib.*, 26, pp. 926, 927, 933).

nock.  It is right, as you say, to concentrate and crush him; but will it be better
to concentrate [first] upon his grand army rather than on his detachments, and
then make a grand concentration on the grand army?  If we draw off from the
front of his grand army we ought to be able to crush rapidly his detachments,
and at the same time hold the grand army in check as far back [from Richmond]
as South Anna at least, particularly while the roads are so very bad, then concentrate on the grand army and try and dispose of that.[1]

On the 24th he wrote informing Lee that certain counties of Virginia
and North Carolina, containing abundant supplies for the Confederate
armies, were within the Federal lines, and representing that he could
occupy these if he had another division of his corps.[2]

Lee replied on the 27th:

You have about 40,000 effective men; the enemy can bring out no more.[3]  I
feel sure that with equal numbers you can go where you choose.

The latter statement is striking evidence of Lee's belief in the superiority of the Confederate troops over the Federal, and is incompre-
hensible without an appreciation of his readiness to trust to sheer valor
for overcoming the advantages which inhere in the defensive.  He went
on to say:

If this army is further weakened we must retire to the line of the Annas,[4] and
trust to a battle near Richmond for the defence of the capital.  It throws open a
broad margin of our frontier and renders our railroad communications[5] more
hazardous and more difficult to secure.  Unless, therefore, a retrograde movement becomes necessary, I deem it advantageous to keep the enemy at a distance
and trust to striking him on his line of advance.

While not strong enough to attack Hooker in position, he might
strike him an effective blow on the march.  Recurring to Longstreet's
situation, he added:

A sudden, vigorous attack on Suffolk would doubtless give you that place.  Of
the propriety of this step, you can best judge. . . .  If operations in that quarter
should draw reënforcements from General Hooker, more troops could be spared
from this army.[6]

Longstreet wrote back on the 17th:

. . . I think it utterly impossible for the enemy to move against your position until the roads are sufficiently dry for him to move around you and turn

---

[1] W. R., 26, pp. 926, 927.
[2] Ib., 26, p. 944.
[3] The Federals present for duty numbered: in southern Virginia, under Dix,
24,031, and in North Carolina, under Foster, 14,671; total 38,702 (W. R., 26, pp.
573, 576).  Longstreet's command numbered

at the end of February (ante) 43,239 present for duty.
[4] North and South Anna Rivers.
[5] Virginia Central Railroad, Richmond
and Danville Railroad, and South Side
Railroad.
[6] W. R., 26, pp. 943, 944.

your position. By reënforcing here we might destroy the enemy and get our forces together again in time to resist him at the Rappahannock. But if we succeed in destroying him here and have to retire to the Annas before we can give him a general battle, we will accomplish a great deal and really have the enemy in a better position for our operations than the one he now occupies.[1]

By this time the information which Lee had acquired from the skirmish at Hartwood Church seemed no longer reliable. He was doubting again whether Hooker's army or only a fraction of it was in his front. On the 2d of April he wrote to President Davis:

. . . their lines are so closely guarded that it is difficult to penetrate them. Their pickets [mounted] are placed within sight of each other, with dismounted men in the intervals.[2] . . . I have apprehended, from the jealous manner of guarding their lines and the systematic propagation of reports of an intended advance of their armies on the Rappahannock and Blackwater [south of the James River], that their object is to deceive us, and that they may, while intending to act on the defensive, have reënforced other points for offensive operations, but I have no means of ascertaining the truth of my suspicions until we are able to make some aggressive movements. It was with this view that General Fitz Lee was ordered some time since to penetrate General Hooker's lines, and from his report I judge that his whole army was then in position.

Being on the defensive, Lee could afford to bide Hooker's time for commencing operations, but what if Hooker's objective were elsewhere? Lee must try to meet him or send aid to those who were to do so. Not knowing Hooker's designs, he replied to Longstreet on the 2d of April:

. . . unless General Hooker soon takes the aggressive I must endeavor to operate to draw him out.[3]

But he had another reason for thinking of taking the offensive, or wishing that he could do so. Foreshadowing the campaign of Gettysburg, he wrote on the 9th to the Secretary of War:

Should General Hooker's army assume the defensive, the readiest method of relieving the pressure upon General Johnston[4] and General Beauregard[5] would be for this army to cross into Maryland. This can not be done, however, in the present condition of the roads, nor unless I can obtain a certain amount of provisions and suitable transportation. But this is what I would recommend, if practicable.

[1] W. R., 26, p. 950.
[2] This is a mistake as to the pickets in general. J. B. Jr.
[3] W. R., 26, p. 954.
[4] Commanding the Department of the West, which included a portion of western North Carolina and northern Georgia, the states of Tennessee, Alabama, and Mississippi, and part of the state of Louisiana east of the Mississippi River (W. R., 36, pp. 202, 203, 213).
[5] Commanding Department of South Carolina.

Longstreet, returning to the subject of withdrawing from the Rappahannock, wrote on the 3d:

. . . I have thought since about January 23 last (when I made the same suggestion to you) that one army corps could hold the line of the Rappahannock while the other was operating elsewhere.

I cannot now appreciate the necessity of your retiring to the Annas in case you send off more troops from the Rappahannock. There you are fortified on the river and on the heights; on the Annas you would have neither. Besides, you would lose *morale* and encourage the enemy.[1]

On the other hand, according to Longstreet's message of the 30th ultimo, the Federals, on the Annas, would be in a better position for Lee's and Longstreet's operations than they were in on the Rappahannock. He added on the 4th:

I hope to be able to finish with the operations in this section in time to join you as soon as the roads are in condition for you to operate.[2]

Lee replied on the 6th:

. . . I cannot say whether General Hooker will advance or not, though, as before stated, all the information I receive from every source goes to show that it is his intention to do so, and that he is prepared. It may be a part of their general plan to deceive us while reënforcing their general armies; but as soon as I can move I will find out. In the meantime I do not think it prudent to weaken the force here.[3]

On the 7th Longstreet wrote to Lee:

I do not propose to do anything more than draw out the supplies from that country unless something very favorable should offer. . . . If I find that I can do no more than haul off supplies, I shall hurry one of my divisions [Hood's] back, so as to be within reach of you, unless the force is much stronger than you suppose it to be.[4]

The remark, "I do not propose to do anything more than draw out the supplies," etc., was thrown out to excuse a possible failure in offensive operations.[5] General Longstreet had set his heart upon the investment and capture of Suffolk, for which he had a qualified approval from Lee.[6]

The remark, "unless the force is much stronger than you suppose it

[1] *W. R.*, 26, p. 959.
[2] *Ib.*, 26, p. 960.
[3] *Ib.*, 26, p. 967.
[4] *Ib.*, 26, p. 970. For Longstreet to Seddon, April 6, see *ib.*, 26, p. 910.

[5] *The Siege of Suffolk*, by Brevet Brigadier-General Hagard Stevens (manuscript, Mil. Hist. Soc. of Mass.).
[6] Lee to Longstreet, March 27 (*ante*).

to be," seems intended to make Lee responsible for the siege which Longstreet was then carrying on. Lee had only sanctioned "a sudden vigorous attack on Suffolk," and that only at the discretion of General Longstreet.

On the 6th of April, Lee wrote to his chief of artillery at Chesterfield Station that as soon as the roads were sufficiently improved, he might, with advantage, post the artillery "in part, if not the whole, about 3 miles west of Guiney's Station, where it would be about equidistant from Port Royal, Fredericksburg, and United States Mine Ford, *embracing the limits of the Rappahannock within which an attempt to cross by the enemy may be expected.*"

The italics are the author's. It is important to note this evidence of Lee's expectations as to Hooker's movements. On account of the bad condition of the roads, the artillery remained in its winter quarters until the campaign was fairly begun.

The unsatisfactory manner in which outpost duty was still performed and the habitual deportment of the Army of the Potomac on the march, together with the prospect of an early resumption of operations, caused the following order to be issued on the 10th:

. . . . . . . . . .

II. . . . Officers of outposts are expected to inform themselves accurately of all events transpiring in their vicinity, and those whose fears magnify trifling squads into large bodies of the enemy as richly deserve death as the base wretch who deserts his country's flag, or his comrades in battle. It has been too much a practice, upon outposts and battle-fields, to send back reports and calls for reënforcements, founded upon imagination or the tales of a frightened or cowardly shirk. The fate of battle may be changed by such reports.

. . . . . . . . .

III. Upon the march straggling must not be permitted. Corps commanders will take effectual measures to prevent it. Officers who fail to prevent it in their respective commands must be relieved and sent to the rear, and their names and the number of their regiments forwarded for publication in orders. Leaves of absence and furloughs must also be withheld from regiments in which straggling is tolerated. Drumhead court-martial, if necessary, can be held for the punishment of this class of offenders.

IV. Corps and division commanders, and assistant inspectors-general, should watch the conduct and behavior of officers and men on the march as well as in battle. Regiments not moving promptly as ordered, permitting straggling, or where the officers show a lack of capacity and zeal in pushing forward and overcoming obstacles, must be specially reported for such neglect, in addition to other measures that may be taken by commanders in such cases for the enforcement of discipline.

Three days later the following order was issued by General Stonewall Jackson for the government of his corps:

II. Each division will move precisely at the time indicated in the order of march, and if a division or brigade is not ready to move at that time, the next will proceed and take its place, even if a division should be separated thereby.

III. On the march, the troops are to have a rest of ten minutes each hour. The rate of march is not to exceed 1 mile in twenty-five minutes, unless otherwise specially ordered. The time of each division commander will be taken from that of the corps commander. When the troops are halted for the purpose of resting, arms will be stacked and ranks broken, and in no case during the march will the troops be allowed to break ranks without previously stacking arms.

IV. When any part of a battery or train is disabled on a march, the officer in charge must have it removed immediately from the road, so that no part of the command be impeded upon its march.

Batteries or trains must not stop in the line of march to water; when any part of a battery or train, from any cause, loses its place in the column, it must not pass any part of the column in regaining its place.

Company commanders will march at the rear of their respective companies; officers must be habitually occupied in seeing that orders are strictly enforced; a day's march should be with them a day of labor; as much vigilance is required on the march as in camp.

.     .     .     .     .     .     .     .     .     .

V. All ambulances . . . will . . . follow in rear of their respective brigades. . . .

Any one leaving his appropriate duty, under pretext of taking care of the wounded, will be promptly arrested, and as soon as charges can be made out, they will be forwarded.


On the same day Hooker addressed the following circular to his corps commanders:

The major-general commanding directs that your command have packed in their knapsacks by to-morrow (Tuesday) night five days' rations of hard bread, coffee, sugar, and salt.

That you have in readiness, so that it may be issued and cooked at short notice, three days' rations of pork or bacon, with hard bread, coffee and sugar, to be placed in the haversacks.

That your command have drawn before Wednesday morning [15th], and ready for the movement, five days' fresh beef on the hoof, making complete eight days' rations to be carried with the troops.

That each officer, by the use of his servant and his haversack, provide himself with eight days' rations.

That the small-arm ammunition to be carried will be 150[1] rounds—60 rounds on the person—the full complement of the pack-train, and the balance to be in the [wagon] train, ready to start first when the wagon-trains move.

The supply-trains will be in readiness for such movements as may be ordered.[2] Each teamster must have with him the forage for his own team.

[1] Changed by circular of 14th to 140 rounds.
[2] It will be observed that the supplies to be loaded in these trains are not stated.

The batteries will carry eight days' subsistence for the troops and their full capacity of forage, at least six days' grain, as much as possible on the guns.

The general hospital for those unable to move will be designated by the medical director, who will give all the necessary directions in the premises.

The surplus clothing of the troops, beyond the extra shirt, pair of socks and drawers [which each soldier is to take with him], should be stored under the supervision of the quartermaster's department.

Corps commanders will require every serviceable man to march with the column.[1]

There was perhaps some encouragement for the Federal administration in a report which had reached Washington of a riot in Richmond. About 10 o'clock in the morning of April 2, a crowd of about 4000 women collected in a park in front of the Capitol, and clamorously demanded bread for their starving families. President Davis appeared on the steps of the Capitol, and made a speech promising them money. They declared it worthless and drowned his voice with cries of "Bread!" "The Union!" "No more starvation!" etc. The crowd then proceeded to the general commissary depot, broke into it, and carried off a large quantity of stores. Davis remarked that such disgraceful affairs were worse than Union victories.[2] At the Confederate War Department the affair was thought serious enough to call for the following communications:

Richmond, April 2, 1863.

To the Richmond Press.

*Gentlemen:*

The unfortunate disturbance which occurred to-day in this city is so liable to misconstruction and misrepresentation abroad that I am desired by the Secretary of War to make a special appeal to the editors and reporters of the press at Richmond and earnestly to request them to avoid all reference directly or indirectly to the affair. The reasons for this are so obvious that it is unnecessary to state them, and the Secretary indulges the hope that his own views in this connection will be approved by the press generally. Any other course must tend to embarrass our cause, and to encourage our enemies in their inhuman policy.

Very respectfully, etc.,

Jno. Withers,

Assistant Adjutant-General.[3]

---

[1] ". . . the articles of clothing which each man was to carry were minutely specified. It was evident that in the move about to be made wagon-trains were to be kept out of the way of capture. The soldiers likewise gained the impression that more attention was being paid to the details of their necessities, and that their commanders knew just how much ought to be expected of them" (Goss, *Recollections of a Private*). The event is to prove that the commanders miscalculated what their men would carry. J. B. Jr.

[2] *W. R.*, 107, p. 1002.

[3] *Ib.*, 26, p. 958.

Richmond, April 2, 1863.

*W. S. Morris, Esq.,*

President Telegraph Company:

I am desired by the Secretary of War to request that you will permit nothing relative to the unfortunate disturbance which occurred in the city to-day to be sent over the telegraph lines in any direction for any purpose.

Very respectfully, etc.,

JNO. WITHERS,

Assistant Adjutant-General.[1]

The Richmond *Enquirer* of the 4th made light of the affair with a zeal and vigor which betokened disingenuousness. It said in part:

A handful of prostitutes, professional thieves, Irish and Yankee hags, gallows-birds from all lands but our own, congregated in Richmond with a woman huckster at their head, who buys veal at the toll-gate for 100 and sells the same for 250 in the morning market, undertook the other day to put into private practice the principles of the commissary department. Swearing that they would have "goods at government prices," they broke open half a dozen shoe-stores, hat-stores, and tobacco-houses, and robbed them of everything but bread, which was just the thing they wanted least. . . .

On the 6th General Elzey said in a letter to Longstreet:

Owing to the continually threatened riots in Richmond, it would not do to move any of Rhett's command [garrisoning the city].[2]

### The Jones and Imboden Expedition

The Shenandoah Valley (Map 1, sheet A) was the great granary of Virginia, and it was the object of the Confederate forces to control as much of it as possible. The lower, or northern, portion of the Valley was connected with the open country east of it by the Manassas Gap Railroad, which joins the Orange and Alexandria Railroad at Manassas Junction. These two roads would have been most useful in transferring the produce of the Valley to Lee's army could the Confederate authorities have operated them. But this they were prevented from doing by the Federal troops defending Washington. The Orange and Alexandria Railroad was held by the Federals as far as Centreville. Between that point and the Rappahannock River the two roads were a sort of disputed territory which each army could keep the other from occupying, but could not occupy itself. The Confederate supplies going from Manassas Gap to Rappahannock Bridge would cut off the bend of

---

[1] *W. R.*, 26, p. 958.

[2] Referring to these disturbances, General Pleasonton wrote to the Assistant Secretary of War (dispatch of April 10 previously quoted): "The bread riots in Richmond were gotten up by Union men, of whom there are as many as ever."

the railroad by leaving the Manassas Gap Railroad at Salem and going by ordinary road over the mountain to Warrenton.

Referring to Milroy, Lee wrote to W. E. Jones in the Shenandoah Valley:

### February 2

I am very anxious to expel him from the Valley, and nothing but the immediate presence of General Burnside's large army (now commanded by General Hooker) and its threatened movements have prevented me from detaching a portion of the cavalry of this army to aid in effecting this object.

As I think it probable that General Hooker will not be able to move for some time, should the weather and roads not prevent, I wish now to carry this plan into effect. I wish you therefore to be prepared with all your available force to move at short notice against the enemy in front, while the forces from this side of the [Blue] Ridge will gain his rear and cut off his communications from Martinsburg and endeavor to destroy or capture the force in Winchester. I hope, therefore, you will be able to provide beforehand subsistence and forage for your troops, and, if possible, collect enough for 2000 men in addition, in case it should be required.

.    .    .    .    .    .    .    .    .    .

### February 13

. . . I have . . . directed General Stuart, with select detachments from Hampton's and Fitz Lee's brigades, to cross the Blue Ridge should no unforeseen circumstances prevent, and I desire you with your whole available force to be in readiness to join him. As I cannot now detach any infantry from this army, it is hoped, by a combination of the cavalry with your command, that the enemy's [Milroy's] communication with the railroad and his depot of supplies may be cut off, if not destroyed. . . .

On the 9th of February Fitzhugh Lee's brigade broke camp below Fredericksburg and moved toward Culpeper Court-House, where on the 12th it relieved Hampton's brigade, and assumed the duty of picketing the Upper Rappahannock. Hampton's brigade was detached to the south side of the James River to recruit.

On the 2d of March, General Imboden, commanding the Department of Northwestern Virginia, wrote to General Lee, setting forth a plan which he had formed for operations to be conducted by himself, with the double object, first, of destroying the bridges and trestling on the Baltimore and Ohio Railroad from Oakland to Grafton, and, second, of defeating and capturing the enemy's forces at Beverly, Philippi, and Buckhannon, enlisting in the Confederate army the young men of that section, and holding the country long enough, if possible, to overthrow the local government, of which four fifths of the people, he said, were heartily tired. "The movement," he remarked, "must be a dash from its commencement to its conclusion, and . . . can not be safely undertaken before about the 1st of April on account of the swollen streams."

Lee replied on the 11th:

I have received your letter of March 2, and approve the plan therein proposed. I think, if carried out with your energy and promptness, it will succeed. I will endeavor to give you the two regiments you ask, 25th and 31st [Va.], if I can replace them temporarily in this army, otherwise I shall not be able to spare them.[1] . . . I am expecting General Hooker's army to move against me as soon as the roads will permit, and I do not feel that I ought to diminish this army by a single man. By the 1st of April, or before that time, I expect this army to be engaged in active operations.

On the 26th of March he wrote to W. E. Jones, setting forth his plan for the raid. While Imboden dashed at the Baltimore and Ohio Railroad and destroyed it from Oakland to Grafton, W. E. Jones and Samuel Jones were to divert the attention of the Federal forces by demonstrating—the former to the right against Romney, New Creek, and Cumberland, and the latter to the left against the Little Kanawha Valley. He continued:

I think these operations will draw Milroy from Winchester and the Valley to the northwest; open up that country [the Shenandoah Valley and northwestern Virginia] for a time, at least, to us; enable us to drive out horses, cattle, etc.; and afford an opportunity to our citizens who wish to join us, and give relief to others now suffering under oppression and robbery.

He wrote also

### To Davis, April 2

When the roads permit of our moving, unless in the meantime General Hooker takes the aggressive, I propose to make a blow at Milroy, which, I think, will draw General Hooker out, or at least prevent further reënforcements being sent to the west. . . .

### To Seddon, April 4

. . . General W. H. F. Lee's cavalry brigade is now moving from our extreme right below Fredericksburg to the Upper Rappahannock . . . to enable me to throw forward Fitz Lee's brigade into Loudon [County[2]] with a view of collecting all the supplies possible.

On the 31st of March W. E. Jones wrote to Lee proposing that instead of his diverting Milroy's attention while Imboden destroyed the Baltimore and Ohio Railroad from Oakland to Grafton, both Jones and

---

[1] On the 9th of April, Lee ordered these regiments to report to Imboden; he was enabled to do so by receiving the 50 Va., a strong regiment of infantry, sent him as a substitute for the forementioned regiments by General Samuel Jones.

[2] Loudon County is east of the Blue Ridge, in the angle formed by the Blue Ridge and the Potomac, about half of it lying between the Blue Ridge and the line of the Bull Run and Catoctin Mountains. W. H. F. Lee's brigade $\frac{2}{6}$ took position at Culpeper Court-House, relieving Fitzhugh Lee's $\frac{1}{6}$, which moved to Sperryville.

Imboden should strike the railroad and apply themselves to its destruction at the same time, Jones at Oakland and Imboden at Grafton.[1]   In reply, Lee wrote on the 7th of April:

Two simultaneous attacks on the Baltimore and Ohio Railroad, at the points proposed [Oakland and Grafton], will certainly increase the probabilities of success, and facilitate a more complete destruction of the road.   I therefore agree to the arrangement, and assent to the part to be undertaken by you. . . .

About the time appointed for your departure, I will cause some demonstration to be made [by Stuart] east of the mountains, which may serve to fix his [Milroy's] attention upon his lines of communication, and thus give you time to make your blow.

I feel it unnecessary to advise you that your movement must be expeditious and bold, but that you must take every precaution against discovery and failure. . . . The utmost secrecy in regard to your expedition must be observed, and I consider that the collection of cattle, horses, and provisions will be of as much importance to us, and, under certain contingencies, even more, than the destruction of the railroad.   I hope, therefore, that what so primarily concerns us may not be neglected. . . .

At this time Jones was at Lacy Springs, and Imboden at Staunton, whence he moved to Shenandoah Mountain (Map 1, sheet B).  We will leave these officers and their commands thus located, while we follow the preparations and operations of the opposing armies.[2]

[1] W. R., 39, p. 119.
[2] The Jones-Imboden expedition will be described in Chapter XXIX.

# CHAPTER X

HOOKER wrote on the 23d of March to Kelton:

. . . I would respectfully suggest that hereafter the permits to visit this army be restricted to absolute positive necessity, and that the permission heretofore granted to females is denied.

It is advisable that these restrictions be gradually introduced within the next few days, and not upon the ground that anything is likely to occur here requiring such a course. It cannot be foreseen at what moment this army will move, and the action in respect to the stoppage of travel heretofore has invariably been such as to indicate to the country pretty nearly the precise time of a movement.

The Army of the Potomac was soon stripping for the march. How this was done is partially indicated in the following regimental order:

Headquarters Thirteenth Mass. Vols., April 1, 1863.

Company commanders, in accordance with previous orders, will turn in to the A. B. Q. M.,[1] on or before 11 a.m., April 2, all wall tents, flies, and poles, and all other surplus camp and garrison equipage.

One shelter tent will be furnished to each commissioned officer.[2] Transportation for line officers will be furnished for five-mess[3] kits only.

Rations, cooking utensils, and all other appurtenances of each mess must be properly packed in one case not larger than a hard-bread box.

Trunks will not be carried, neither blankets nor shelter tents, on wagons.

Company books and blanks will be well packed in strong boxes, and distinctly marked—the boxes to be of the size of company clothing books, and not over five inches deep in the clear.

The pack-mules will carry one shelter tent, two wool [blankets] and one rubber blanket for each officer, also (if possible) the officers' rations needed on the march.

Transportation will be furnished for all surplus private baggage, under charge of an officer detailed from the brigade.[4]

Lee issued the following orders:

*March 21*

With a view to a resumption of active operations by the 1st of April, the army will at once prepare for the approaching campaign.

---

[1] Acting Brigade Quartermaster.
[2] The officers had heretofore been allowed wall tents.
[3] Messes of five members.
[4] *Three Years in the Army*, by C. E. Davis, Jr., p. 197.

I. All surplus baggage, public and private, properly marked, will be sent to Richmond, under charge of a responsible officer from each brigade. . . .

II. No further leaves of absence will be given, to extend beyond the 31st instant, except on surgeon's certificate of disability, as prescribed in Regulations, or in cases of extraordinary urgency.

.        .        .        .        .        .        .        .        .        .

IV. It will be necessary to reduce the transportation of the army to the lowest limit. . . . The commanding general regrets the necessity for curtailing the comforts of an army which has evinced so much self-denial in the endurance of privations, but feels satisfied that ready acquiescence will be shown in all measures tending to secure success and the more speedy conclusion of the war, and appeals to officers and men to aid him in the accomplishment of this greatly desired object by the strict observance of orders and careful preservation of the property in their hands, daily becoming more valuable by the difficulty of replacing it.

On the 23d of March Lee issued an order for the observance of the 27th of March as Thanksgiving Day, in accordance with a proclamation by President Davis.[1]  The dinners promised to be short.  Supplies of all kinds were growing scarcer and consequently dearer.  Acts passed by the Confederate Congress March 26 and April 27, 1863, empowered the government to take whatever was necessary to the army, wherever it might find it, and pay for it whatever a joint board appointed by the President and the governor of the state should appraise it at.  The trials of the army and the people which led to the adoption of these drastic measures appear in the contemporary correspondence of General Lee (*Appendix 10*).

About the beginning of the month of April President Lincoln accepted an invitation from Hooker to visit the Army of the Potomac. His party comprised, besides himself and Mrs. Lincoln, his youngest son "Tad," Attorney-General Bates, Dr. A. G. Henry of Washington Territory, who was an old friend of Mr. Lincoln, and Noah Brooks.  It began to snow furiously soon after the President's little steamer, the

---

[1] "In obedience to the proclamation of the President of the Confederate States, setting apart Friday, the 27th of March, as a day of fasting and prayer for the nation, all duties will be suspended on that day in the Army of Northern Virginia, except such as are necessary for its safety and subsistence. Religious services appropriate to the occasion will be performed by the chaplains in their respective regiments.

"Soldiers! no portion of our people have greater cause to be thankful to Almighty God than yourselves.  He has preserved your lives amidst countless dangers; He has been with you in all your trials; He has given you fortitude under hardships, and courage in the shock of battle; He has cheered you by the example and by the deeds of your martyred comrades; He has enabled you to defend your country successfully against the assaults of a powerful oppressor.  Devoutly thankful for His signal mercies, let us bow before the Lord of Hosts, and join our hearts with millions in our land in prayer that He will continue His merciful protection over our cause; that He will scatter our enemies and set at naught their evil designs, and that He will graciously restore to our beloved country the blessings of peace and security."

*Carrie Martin,* left the Washington Navy Yard. Noah Brooks, describing the experience of the party, says:

So thick was the weather, and so difficult the navigation, that we were forced to anchor for the night in a little cove in the Potomac opposite Indian Head, where we remained until the following morning [April 5]. I could not help thinking that if the rebels had made a raid on the Potomac at that time, the capture of the chief magistrate of the United States would have been a very simple matter. So far as I could see, there were no guards on board the boat, and no precautions were taken against a surprise. After the rest of the party had retired for the night, the President, Dr. Henry, and I sat up until long after midnight, telling stories and discussing matters, political or military, in the most free and easy way. During the conversation, after Dr. Henry had left us, Mr. Lincoln, dropping his voice almost to a confidential whisper, said: "How many of our ironclads, do you suppose, are at the bottom of the Charleston harbor?" This was the first intimation I had had that the long-talked-of naval attack on Fort Sumter was to be made that day; and the President, who had been jocular and cheerful during the evening, began despondently to discuss the probabilities of defeat. . . .

Our landing-place, when *en route* for Falmouth, was at Aquia Creek, which we reached next morning [April 5], the untimely snow still falling. "The Creek," as it was called, was a village of hastily constructed warehouses, and its water-front was lined with transports and government steamers; enormous freight-trains were continually running from it to the army. . . .

The President and his party were provided with an ordinary freight-car fitted up with rough plank benches, and profusely decorated with flags and bunting. A great crowd of army people saluted the President with cheers when he landed from the steamer, and with "three times three" when his unpretentious railway carriage rolled away.[1]

The ravages of war were visible all the way from Aquia to Falmouth. In the frequent clearings where farming had been carried on, there was nothing to be seen but half-destroyed fences, and the ruins of dwellings and outhouses without any inhabitants. At Falmouth Station the party was met by two ambulances and an escort of 200 mounted officers. The honors were done by General Butterfield.

Lincoln was not a soldier. He could not critically inspect or test the great machine which he had come to see. Nor was it exhibited to him in a way to show its essential excellencies or deficiencies. One might suppose that the army would have shown itself off as in battle or on the march, that corps or divisions would have manœuvered against each other, displaying their proficiency in reconnoitering and deploying, in guarding and attacking and defending positions. Instead of that, it gave itself up to a kind of a "circus." The military exercises consisted chiefly of reviews. The 6th was cavalry day. The corps marched past under Stoneman at a walk and at a trot. Then the 6 Pa. (Rush's

---

[1] *Washington in Lincoln's Time,* by Noah Brooks, pp. 45–57.

Lancers) came alone on the ground in column of squadrons at a gallop, and elicited applause by its execution of the useless evolution of wheeling at a gallop into line and halting. This seems to have been the only organization that showed that it was capable of galloping. There was no charging, no dismounting to fight on foot, no firing. The 7th was devoted to a walk through the camps of several divisions and a collation at the headquarters of General Sickles, commanding the III Corps. The camps covered an undulating plain, with here and there a grove of trees in the green of an early Southern spring. Arches of evergreens decorated with flowers were thrown at intervals over the roadway. It did the army good to see the chief magistrate of the nation and commander-in-chief. Officers and men who came in contact with him were impressed by his earnest, care-worn, and kindly countenance, his rugged manliness and native dignity. As he passed through the camps the bands played, and the men gave cheer after cheer. Thousands of them crowded around his horse, hoping to touch his hand or hear his voice. These demonstrations affected the President deeply, awakening fresh life in his pale, anxious face. Wherever he went he had a hearty shake of the hand and a warm "God bless you" for the lowest in rank as well as the highest. In the camps of the Second Division of the V Corps, Sykes' regulars, the *orphans* of the army, beyond the pale of Sanitary Commission and spiritual salvation—for they had no chaplains—the President's visit and attentions were especially appreciated.[1] The President was escorted by the staff officers of the corps, and the division, brigade, regimental, and battery commanders, all mounted and in full uniform.

It was at the collation at General Sickles' that the Princess Salm-Salm, the beautiful wife of the colonel of a New York regiment, won a wager and a unique reputation by stealing a kiss from President Lincoln. Her example was quickly followed by a bevy of female companions. Mrs. Lincoln was not present, but of course she learned of it. The next day it was generally known in camp that the President had been subjected to an unhappy quarter of an hour for allowing the princess and other ladies to kiss him, and that General Sickles was quite out of favor with Mrs. Lincoln.

On this day, the 8th, came a joint review of four corps, the II, III, V, and VI, and the General Artillery Reserve. The President sat his small but handsome black horse with ease, his long legs hanging straight down, the feet nearly reaching to the ground. He was dressed in a suit of plain black clothes, with a much-worn black silk hat. His pale, sad face contrasted strongly with the florid countenance of General Hooker, who rode by his side.[2] The general's military seat and carriage, his

---

[1] *Mag. of Am. Hist.*, XV, 195.

[2] *Abraham Lincoln*, by W. H. Ward, D.D., p. 188; *History of the Tenth Regiment of Cavalry, N. Y. State Volunteers*, by N. D. Preston, p. 64.

glittering uniform and equipments, and shining white horse, combined to accentuate the plain, somber appearance of the President. The long and tiresome ceremony was followed by an exhibition given by the 5 N. Y. (Duryee Zouaves) in battalion drill, quick and double time, and the manual of arms, and bayonet exercise. In the course of the visit Hooker remarked to the President: "I have under my command the finest army on the planet." He gave a dinner-party to the President and Mrs. Lincoln, which was attended by all the corps commanders.

"I recall with sadness," says Noah Brooks, "the easy confidence and nonchalance which Hooker showed in all his conversations with the President and his little party while we were at headquarters. . . . One of his most frequent expressions when talking with the President was 'When I get to Richmond,' or 'After we have taken Richmond,' etc. The President, noting this, said to me confidentially, and with a sigh: 'That is the most depressing thing about Hooker. It seems to me that he is overconfident.' "[1]

On the day after the President's arrival, Hooker received the following communication from G. V. Fox, Assistant Secretary of the Navy. It was dated April 6, 8 p.m.

There is reasonable ground to expect important news hourly from Charleston *via* Richmond. Will you be on the *qui vive* for anything from the enemy opposite?[2]

On the 9th it was hallooed across the river to Couch's pickets: "You have taken Charleston." The news was sent to Hooker's headquarters. President Lincoln, hearing of it, invited Couch to come up and talk the matter over. Arriving at headquarters, Couch was ushered into a side tent in which there was no one but Hooker and the President. His entrance apparently interrupted a weighty conversation, for both were looking grave. The President's manner was kindly, while Hooker, usually courteous, forgot to be conventionally polite. The Charleston rumor having been briefly discussed, Lincoln remarked that it was time for him to leave. As he stepped toward Hooker, who had risen from his seat as well as Couch, he said: "I want to impress upon you two gentlemen—in your next fight"—and turning to Couch, he completed the sentence—"put in all your men."[3]

The report of the capture of Charleston was a canard. The defences were attacked on the 7th by Dupont's fleet of ironclads, but an hour's engagement sufficed to prove that vessels were no match for forts, that it was useless to try to carry the place without the coöperation of a land force. As no such coöperation was possible, the attack was abandoned. On the 9th the presidential party reviewed the I Corps, made a visit to the XI and XII Corps, and embarked for Washington.

[1] *Washington in Lincoln's Time*, by Noah Brooks, pp. 51, 52.
[2] *W. R.*, 107, p. 1001.
[3] General Couch in *Battles and Leaders of the Civil War*, III, 155.

The President had on the whole been favorably impressed. The bands and banners, the tramping columns, the precise wheels and alignments, the streets of tents, the general method and smartness pleased him. He was particularly impressed with the soldierly appearance of Schurz's division of the XI Corps.[1] He was delighted with the great and wonderful improvement in the *morale* of the army,[2] but he saw nothing that demonstrated the inurement of the troops to marching, their proficiency in the duties of advance and rear guards, nothing that showed how the army commander and his corps and division commanders would act in the presence of an enemy, how orders would be framed and transmitted, ammunition supplied, and sick and wounded cared for. His judgment of the tactical proficiency of the army, if he formed any, must have been based on its appearance at review, and the showing made by companies and regiments at drill. He had yet by bitter disappointment to learn that a collection of well-drilled regiments is not necessarily a well-trained army.

In the course of his stay with the army he had sent for General Averell and expressed great interest in the fight which had taken place at Kelley's Ford, inquiring particularly about the Confederate Commanders. Averell told him how the fight came to pass, and showed him the note which he received from General Fitzhugh Lee with reference to the Federal wounded. Lincoln put on his spectacles, and read it carefully, then he asked:

"Were you and General Lee friends?"

"Certainly," said Averell, "and always have been."

"What would happen should you meet on the battle-field?"

"One or both of us would be badly hurt, or killed."

After a pause Lincoln said, with emotion:

"Oh, my God, what a dreadful thing is a war like this, in which personal friends must slay each other, and die like fiends! General Averell, I wish you would give me this letter of Lee's."

It is said that for a long time afterward President Lincoln carried that note about with him, and would frequently take it out of his pocket and show it.

Hooker had intended to have Butterfield escort the presidential party back to Washington, but he changed his mind and charged Sickles with this act of courtesy in order that he might make his peace with Mrs. Lincoln. Sickles got along very well with the President, but do what he would, he could not soften the freezing look with which Mrs. Lincoln met his advances. At supper the President tried his capital story-telling to bring about a reconciliation, but without success. Turning finally to General Sickles, he said: "I never knew until last night that you were a very pious man." Sickles, taken aback, replied that he

---

[1] *Washington in Lincoln's Time*, by Noah Brooks, p. 51.

[2] *Mag. of Am. History*, XV, 195.

feared that the President had been misinformed. "Not at all," said the President, gravely; "Mother [Mrs. Lincoln] says you are the greatest Psalmist in the army. She says you are more than a Psalmist, you are a Salm-Salmist." Mrs. Lincoln joined in the hearty laughter about the table, and forgave the general.[1]

After the departure of the President the preparations for a general movement proceeded with increased vigor.

On the 13th of April the Medical Director of the Army of the Potomac ordered the establishment of division hospitals (formed of tents) for the II, III, V, and VI Corps near Potomac Creek Bridge;[2] for the XI and XII Corps near Brooke's Station; and for the I Corps, and the Cavalry Corps, on the Potomac River near the mouth of Aquia Creek. An officer of the line was detailed to act as quartermaster and commissary for all these hospitals.[3]

The commander of the Engineer Brigade was directed to have his command ready for a move in any direction at short notice.

The cavalry pickets, while retaining in general the lines that they had held, were reduced in strength about one half.

Before taking up Hooker's plan of operation, let us consider somewhat in detail the composition and strength of the opposing armies:

## THE ARMY OF NORTHERN VIRGINIA

### Effective Strength

| COMMANDS | INFANTRY OFFICERS AND MEN | ARTILLERY OFFICERS AND MEN | PIECES | CAVALRY OFFICERS AND MEN | TOTAL OFFICERS AND MEN |
|---|---|---|---|---|---|
| I Corps, Longstreet: | | | | | |
| 1 Division, Anderson { 1 Brigade, Mahone; 2 " Posey; 3 " Perry; 4 " Wilcox; 5 " Wright; Artillery, Hardaway[4] } | 8,050 | 320 | 16 | | 8,370 |
| 2 Division, McLaws { 1 Brigade, Kershaw; 2 " Semmes; 3 " Wofford; 4 " Barksdale; Artillery, Cabell[5] } | 8,345 | 320 | 16 | | 8,665 |
| Artillery Reserve (no chief) . . | | 720 | 36 | | 720 |
| Total . . . . . . . . . | 16,395 | 1,360 | 68 | | 17,755 |

[1] *A Biographical Memorial of General Daniel Butterfield,* edited by Julia L. Butterfield, pp. 161, 162.

[2] The railroad bridge across Potomac Creek.

[3] *Medical Recollections of the Army of the Potomac,* by Jonathan Letterman, pp. 113, 114.

[4] Commanded also by Garnett.

[5] Commanded also by Hamilton.

THE ARMY OF NORTHERN VIRGINIA—*Continued*

| COMMANDS | INFANTRY OFFICERS AND MEN | ARTILLERY OFFICERS AND MEN | PIECES | CAVALRY OFFICERS AND MEN | TOTAL OFFICERS AND MEN |
|---|---|---|---|---|---|
| **II Corps, Jackson:** | | | | | |
| 1 Division, A. P. Hill {1 Brigade, Heth[1]; 2 " Pender; 3 " McGowan; 4 " Lane; 5 " Archer; 6 " Thomas; Artillery, Walker[2]} | 11,351 | 400 | 20 | | 11,751 |
| 2 Division, Rodes[4] {1 Brigade, O'Neal[3]; 2 " Doles; 3 " Iverson; 4 " Colquitt; 5 " Ramseur; Artillery, Carter} | 9,663 | 400 | 20 | | 10,063 |
| 3 Division, Early {1 Brigade, Gordon; 2 " Hoke; 3 " Smith; 4 " Hays; Artillery, Andrews} | 8,276 | 320 | 16 | | 8,596 |
| 4 Division, Colston[7] {1 Brigade, Paxton; 2 " Jones[5]; 3 " Warren[6]; 4 " Nicholls[8]; Artillery, Jones} | 6,669 | 320 | 16 | | 6,989 |
| Artillery Reserve, Crutchfield[9] . | | 800 | 40 | | 800 |
| Total . . . . . . . . . | 35,959 | 2,240 | 112 | | 38,199 |
| General Artillery Reserve, Pendleton | | 480 | 24 | | 480 |
| Cavalry Division, Stuart {1 Brigade, Fitzhugh Lee; 2 " W. H. F. Lee; Artillery, Beckham} | | 320 | 16 | 4,138 | 4,458 |

[1] Commanded also by Brockenbrough.

[2] Commanded also by Pegram.

[3] In the absence of Rodes, permanent commander; commanded also by Hall.

[4] In the absence of D. H. Hill, permanent commander.

[5] Commanded also by Garnett and by Vandeventer.

[6] In the absence of Colston, permanent commander; commanded also by T. V. Williams and by Brown.

[7] In the absence of Trimble, permanent commander.

[8] Commanded also by J. M. Williams.

[9] Commanded also by Alexander.

THE ARMY OF NORTHERN VIRGINIA—*Continued*

| SUMMARY | INFANTRY | ARTILLERY | | CAVALRY | TOTAL |
|---|---|---|---|---|---|
| COMMANDS | OFFICERS AND MEN | OFFICERS AND MEN | PIECES | OFFICERS AND MEN | OFFICERS AND MEN |
| I Corps . . . . . . . . . . | 16,395 | 1,360 | 68 | | 17,755 |
| II Corps . . . . . . . . . | 35,959 | 2,240 | 112 | | 38,199 |
| General Artillery Reserve . . . . | | 480 | 24 | | 480 |
| Cavalry Division . . . . . . . | | 320 | 16 | 4,138 | 4,458 |
| Total . . . . . . . . . . | 52,354 | 4,400 | 220 | 4,138 | 60,892 |

This table is based mainly upon the return of the Army of Northern Virginia for the month of March, 1863.[1] There is no corresponding return for April, 1863. The figures stand for effective officers and men, and include about 1500 recruits supposed to have joined during the month of April.[2] The strength of the Confederate artillery can not be determined solely from the official records. The author has supplemented what information he could gather therefrom with the results of inquiry among ex-officers of the Confederate artillery regarding the number of pieces. Where the *personnel* was not otherwise to be determined, he computed it on the basis of 20 officers and men to a piece.[3] The author is assured by Mr. Kirkley, of the *War Records* office, that the numbers given in the abstract[4] for Stuart's cavalry division do not include Jones' brigade, in the Valley; that they stand for three brigades: Hampton's, which was absent recruiting, and W. H. F. Lee's, and Fitzhugh Lee's. Hampton's brigade numbered five regiments and those of the two Lees ten. The abstract gives Stuart but twelve pieces of artillery. During the campaign he had sixteen, as appears from the reports of various commanders.[5] Deducting 240 officers and men, for twelve pieces of artillery, from the 6967 officers and men present for duty in the division, as given in the abstract, and taking ⅔ of the result, we have 4138 officers and men for Stuart's two brigades of cavalry. It should be borne in mind that this is only the *personnel*. It does not represent the number of serviceable horses, or number of mounted men, or effectives. Three fourths of the number of men, or about 3000, would be a liberal estimate of the number of effective cavalrymen in Stuart's command on the Rappahannock. The Confederate brigades and divisions were generally designated solely by the names of their commanders. They are numbered in the foregoing table for convenience of reference and notation.

[1] W. R., 40, p. 696.

[2] This gain is given as about 3500 by General Alexander (*Memoirs*, p. 322), and as 4000 by Colonel Henderson (*Stonewall Jackson*, II, 508). General Longstreet gives it as possibly 1000 (*From Manassas to Appomattox*, p. 328).

[3] For official authority, see W. R., 39, p. 789 (Organization of the Army of Northern Virginia), also reports of chief of artillery and of artillery commanders, same volume.

[4] W. R., 40, p. 696.

[5] Ib., 39, p. 794.

The two divisions of Longstreet's corps (Anderson's and McLaws') were commanded directly by General Lee. Both Federal and Confederate returns commonly give in separate columns the officers and men *Present for Duty,* from whom men on *Extra Duty* (teamsters, etc.), the sick, and the officers and men in arrest or in confinement, are excluded. The Federal returns give, in addition to the *Present for Duty,* the officers and men *Present for Duty Equipped.* The Confederate returns give nothing that exactly corresponds to the latter, but give a column of *Total Effective Present.*

The statement of *Present for Duty,* being compiled in the same way in both of the opposing armies, is the best standard for their numerical comparison according to the records. But to get nearer to the fighting strength, I have obtained the figures resulting from the deduction of certain non-combatants. The term *Present for Duty Equipped* is defined to be "those officers and men who are actually available for the line of battle at the date of the regimental report,"[1] and the term *Total Effective Present,* or *Total Effective,* to be the "total enlisted men present, less sum of enlisted men sick and on extra duty."[2] The first of these definitions was not strictly observed, if indeed it was adopted, at the time of the campaign of Chancellorsville. In Hooker's tri-monthly return for April 30 we find the Provost Guard included in this category, while the Engineer Brigade and Signal Corps, to whom the definition would better apply, are not.

The *Aggregate* (officers and men) *Effective Present* can be obtained with practical accuracy by adding the officers *Present for Duty* to the *Total Effective.* According to the definition above given for *Total Effective,* the Confederates included in their effective strength the officers and men in arrest or confinement. They did not, nor did the Federals, include them in the *Present for Duty.* The return of the Army of Northern Virginia for March[3] gives the *Effective Total* as exactly equal to the *Men Present for Duty,* though the table given in Chapter IV of this volume shows 1222 officers and men *In Arrest or Confinement.* During the period covered by this narrative the number of *Present for Duty Equipped* was generally about ten per cent. less than the number of *Present for Duty,* and the *Effective* or *Effective Present* (officers and men) about equal to the *Present for Duty.* Henceforth in this work, numbers expressing the strength of bodies of troops in *personnel* stand for officers and men of infantry, cavalry, and artillery, *Effective* or *Present for Duty Equipped,* according as the forces are Confederate or Federal. In a statement like "5000 men with 16 pieces of artillery" the word *men* includes officers and men of artillery as well as of infantry and cavalry. To determine the latter without the artillery, deduct about 20 men for each piece.

[1] *W. R.,* 40, p. 320.          [2] *Ib.,* 45, p. 947.          [3] *Ib.,* 40, p. 696.

## THE ARMY OF THE POTOMAC

### Effective Strength (Present for Duty Equipped)

| COMMANDS | INFANTRY OFFICERS AND MEN | ARTILLERY OFFICERS AND MEN | PIECES | CAVALRY OFFICERS AND MEN | TOTAL OFFICERS AND MEN |
|---|---|---|---|---|---|
| I Corps, Longstreet: | | | | 60[1] | 60 |
| I Corps, Reynolds { 1 Division, Wadsworth / 2 " Robinson / 3 " Doubleday } | 15,782 | 1,061 | 51 | 65 | 16,908 |
| II Corps, Couch { 1 Division, Hancock / 2 " Gibbon / 3 " French / Artillery Reserve, Kirby } | 15,907 | 977 | 48 | 9 | 16,893 |
| III Corps, Sickles { 1 Division, Birney / 2 " Berry / 3 " Whipple } | 17,568 | 1,153 | 60 | | 18,721 |
| V Corps, Meade { 1 Division, Griffin / 2 " Sykes / 3 " Humphreys } | 14,867 | 857 | 42 | 100[2] | 15,824 |
| VI Corps, Sedgwick { 1 Division, Brooks / 2 " Howe / 3 " Newton / 4 " Burnham } | 22,427 | 1,136 | 54 | 104 | 23,667 |
| XI Corps, Howard { 1 Division, Devens / 2 " von Steinwehr / 3 " Schurz / Artillery Reserve, Schirmer } | 12,170 | 757 | 36 | 50 | 12,977 |
| XII Corps, Slocum { 1 Division, Williams / 2 " Geary } | 12,929 | 521 | 28 | | 13,450 |
| General Artillery Reserve, Graham | 320 | 1,290 | 56 | | 1,610 |
| Cavalry Corps, Stoneman { 1 Division, Pleasonton / 2 " Averell / 3 " Gregg / Reserve Brigade, Buford / Reserve Regiment (6 Pa.), Morris / Artillery Reserve, Robertson } | | 462 | 28 | 11,079[3] | 11,541 |
| Provost Guard, Patrick . . . . . . . | 1,868 | 254 | 10 | 95 | 2,217 |
| Total  .  .  .  .  .  .  .  .  .  .  .  . | 113,838 | 8,468 | 413 | 11,562 | 133,868 |

[1] In Hooker's return (*W. R.*, 40, p. 320) the cavalry attached to his headquarters as guards and orderlies, or escort, is not reported as *Present for Duty Equipped*, or "available for the line of battle," while that attached in the same capacity to the headquarters of his corps commanders is. I can see no good reason for this distinction, and have accordingly included Hooker's escort (Companies E and I, 6 Pa. Cav.) in my figures for the *Present for Duty Equipped* (see *History of Pennsylvania Volunteers*, by S. P. Bates, IV, 1002).

[2] *History of Pennsylvania Volunteers*, by S. P. Bates, IV, 1002.

[3] According to return of April 10, the latest available (*W. R.*, 40, p. 320).

This table is based upon the return of the Army of the Potomac for April, 1863.[1] The figures stand for officers and men *Present for Duty Equipped.*[2]

As in the table of the Army of Northern Virginia, the cavalry is given in number of men. The Federal cavalry could mount about 11,000 men.

The foregoing tables give with satisfactory accuracy the strength of the larger units of both armies at the beginning of operations. But as the operations proceed, deductions have to be made on account of losses. Unfortunately, the tables in the official records do not give the losses from day to day; they give them only for the whole campaign, which may be considered as lasting from the 28th of April to the 6th of May, both dates inclusive. The daily loss in killed, wounded, and missing may be gathered in a small number of cases from the reports of commanders. The data afforded by these cases the author has compiled into a table and used as a basis for the calculation or estimation of losses of the three classes mentioned from day to day (*Appendix 12*). But the killed, wounded, and missing are not all the losses that may deserve consideration. The effective strength of an army marching and fighting for seven days is diminished more or less by the loss or deterioration of arms and equipment, by sickness, and by straggling and skulking, detected as such and consequently not included in the missing, to say nothing of possible arrests and confinement for punishment, or of formal transfers from combatant to non-combatant branches of the service. The most reliable figures as to the numbers taken into action are reports based upon roll-calls, held immediately before the action, but such figures are very rare. Here and there in the official records commanding officers report the numbers that they took into action, but without indicating how the numbers were arrived at. These statements the author has tabulated as a basis for calculating or estimating the effective strength from day to day (*Appendix 13*). There are then two ways of determining the effective strength for a particular engagement. One is to take the figures from the returns,[3] and deduct the losses incurred between the dates of the returns and the engagement

---

[1] *W. R.*, 40, p. 320.

[2] For official authority see Organization of the Army of the Potomac (*W. R.*, 39, p. 156). I have taken the batteries as given in the forementioned statement, and determined—generally from official reports, but always from good authority—the number of pieces composing them. It will be seen that my total is somewhat greater than that given in the abstract of return on p. 320 of Vol. 40 of the *War Records*. Mine differs only by one piece from that given by General Hunt, the Chief of Artillery, in

his report (*ib.*, 39, p. 252). The considerable disparity between my total and that of the abstract of return may be attributed to the fact that the army return was compiled from regimental and battery returns made up some time before the compilation, while my total is determined from reports corresponding in date to the compilation. The composition of the units of artillery and their assignments in both armies are given in *Appendix 11*.

[3] *W. R.*, 40, pp. 320, 696.

(*Appendix 12*). This may be called the method by Return. Its inaccuracy is due chiefly to the following circumstances:

1. The returns are compiled weeks before the engagement.

2. The figures in the returns are for corps and divisions; those for smaller units have to be computed.

3. The losses are given in the records only for the whole campaign. Daily losses have to be estimated or computed.[1]

The other, which may be called the method by Report, is based upon the reports of regimental and higher commanders as to the number of men which they took into action (*Appendix 13*). Such reports being exceptional, the total or aggregate is obtained by generalization from particular and meager data. The inaccuracy of this method is due, not only to the process of generalization, but also to the disposition of commanding officers in their reports to minimize the numbers that they took into action. The most accurate figures obtainable are perhaps a mean between those furnished by these two methods. For the purpose of this study, however, the method by return is generally preferable, and is the one employed unless otherwise indicated.[2]

Regarding the general condition and efficiency of the Army of the Potomac, Hooker testified before the Committee on the Conduct of the War:

> During the time allowed us for the preparation, the army made **rapid strides** in discipline, instruction, and *morale*, and early in April was in a condition to inspire the highest expectations. Its ranks had been filled by the **return of** absentees. All were actuated by feelings of confidence and devotion to the **cause**, and I felt that it was a living army, and one well **worthy** of the republic.

President Lincoln's views of the strategic situation were substantially those expressed by Halleck to Burnside and to Hooker. They were recorded by the President himself on the 11th of April in the form of the following memorandum:

> My opinion is that, just now with the enemy directly ahead of us, there is *no* eligible route for us into Richmond; and consequently a question of preference

[1] *W. R.*, 39, pp. 172–192, 806–809.

[2] According to my calculations the regiments of infantry averaged in the larger units of the opposing armies the strength indicated in the following table (J. B. Jr.):

| Army of the Potomac | | | Army of Northern Virginia | | |
|---|---|---|---|---|---|
| I Corps | . . . . . . . . | 405 men | I Corps: | | |
| II " | . . . . . . . . | 350 " | 1 Division | . . . . . . | 383 men |
| III " | . . . . . . . . | 420 " | 2 " | . . . . . . | 452 " |
| V " | . . . . . . . . | 390 " | II Corps: | | |
| VI " | . . . . . . . . | 520 " | 1 Division | . . . . . . | 405 men |
| XI " | . . . . . . . . | 450 " | 2 " | . . . . . . | 439 " |
| XII " | . . . . . . . . | 440 " | 3 " | . . . . . . | 414 " |
| Army | . . . . . . . . . . | 433 " | 4 " | . . . . . . | 233 " |
| | | | Army | . . . . . . . . | 409 " |

between the Rappahannock route[1] and the James river route is a contest about nothing. Hence our primary object is the enemy's army in front of us, and is not with or about Richmond at all, unless it be incidental to the main object.

What then? The two armies are face to face, with a narrow river between them. Our communications are shorter and safer than are those of the enemy. For this reason we can with equal powers fret him more than he can us. I do not think that by raids toward Washington he can derange the Army of the Potomac at all. He has no distant operations which can call any of the Army of the Potomac away; we have such operations which may call him away, at least in part. While he remains intact, I do not think we should take the disadvantage of attacking him in his intrenchments, but we should continually harass and menace him, so that he shall have no leisure nor safety in sending away detachments. If he weakens himself then pitch into him.[2]

Assuming that the enemy did weaken himself, and that Hooker did "pitch into him," what was to be accomplished? What was Lincoln's "general idea"? It was simply to score a victory and thereby encourage the war party at home and discourage the intervention, or recognition, party abroad. Beyond that he did not pretend to look.

Though the roads were hardly practicable for artillery and wagons, Hooker believed that the time had come for operations to commence; that the army was in condition to march on the enemy.[3] His plan was communicated to the President in the following letter:

Camp near Falmouth, Va., April 11, 1863.

*His Excellency the President of the United States:*

After giving the subject my best reflection, I have concluded that I will have more chance of inflicting a heavier blow upon the enemy by turning his position to my right, and if practicable, to sever his communications with Richmond, with my dragoon force and such light batteries as it may be advisable to send with him. I am apprehensive that he will retire from before me the moment I should succeed in crossing the river, and over the shortest line to Richmond, and thus escape being seriously crippled. I hope that when the cavalry have established themselves on the line between him and Richmond, they will be able to hold him and check his retreat until I can fall on his rear, or, if not, that I will compel him to fall back by the way of Culpeper and Gordonsville, over a longer line than my own, with his supplies cut off. The cavalry will probably cross the river above the Rappahannock Bridge, thence to Culpeper and Gordonsville and across the Aquia [Richmond and Fredericksburg] Railroad, somewhere in the vicinity of Hanover Court-House. They will probably have a fight in the vicinity of Culpeper, but not one that should cause them much delay or embarrassment. I have given directions for the cavalry to be in readiness to commence the movement on Monday morning next [April 13]. While the cavalry are moving I shall threaten the passage of the river at various points, and after they have passed

---

[1] By water to Urbana, on the Lower Rappahannock, and thence overland to Richmond.

[2] *Abraham Lincoln,* by J. G. Nicolay and John Hay, VII, 90.

[3] Hooker, *Rep. of Com.,* IV, 113.

well to the enemy's rear, shall endeavor to effect the crossing. I hope, Mr. President, that this plan will receive your approval. It will obviate the necessity of detaching a force from Washington in the direction of Warrenton, while I think it will enhance my chances for inflicting a heavy blow upon the enemy's forces.

We have no news from over the river to-day, the enemy refusing to let us have the newspapers. . . .

It seems that the former or original plan was to cross with the greater part of the army below Fredericksburg and move against Lee's right flank and communications, while minor fractions of the army crossed or pretended to cross above Fredericksburg as far as United States Ford. Probably before any of these movements commenced, and to divert attention therefrom, a force was to advance from Washington toward Warrenton and thus threaten the Upper Shenandoah Valley. In the new plan the cavalry going up the river was to serve, instead of a force from Washington, as a diversion in the direction of the Valley.

While the cavalry, with a few light batteries, crossed the Rappahannock and proceeded as indicated in the foregoing letter, the remainder of the army was to cross below Fredericksburg, seize or threaten the Richmond and Potomac Railroad in the enemy's rear, and attack the enemy or pursue him, "as occasion might require." As he kept but a limited amount of stores at Fredericksburg, it was believed that he would have to abandon his defences immediately, and retire in the direction of Richmond or Gordonsville.[1]

The roads were not considered firm enough for the movement of infantry with trains up the river and around the enemy's flank. It was for this reason that the turning of the enemy in that direction was intrusted entirely to the cavalry, and the passage of the broad Lower Rappahannock, without a ford, projected for the infantry, artillery, and trains. Hooker knew that the passage of the river would be resisted, and perhaps defeated, if brought to the knowledge of the enemy. He accordingly took every precaution to keep it a secret, even to the officers of his staff, and would not intrust it to the mail.[2]

"As to whatever General Hooker's plans were," says his chief of topographical engineers, "they were kept perfectly secret from everybody until the movements themselves developed them. I did not know any of his plans until I saw them being carried into operation."[3] That they were not known to his chief engineer appears in the project previously mentioned, which that officer presented to Hooker on the 12th. According to that, the highest crossing was to be "at U. S. Ford or at Banks' Ford, if possible," by a force to consist of "cavalry with two or three brigades of infantry to clear the way."[4]

---

[1] Hooker, *Rep. of Com.*, IV, 115.
[2] *Ib.*, I, 43.
[3] Warren, *Rep. of Com.*, IV, 43.
[4] Comstock, *W. R.*, 107, p. 1003.

To deliver the foregoing letter to Lincoln, Butterfield was sent on a special mission to Washington. Incidents of the interview between the President and Hooker's chief of staff on this occasion are related in *A Biographical Memorial of General Daniel Butterfield,* edited by Julia Lorillard Butterfield, pp. 153 *et seq.*; and in the *History of the Army of the Potomac,* by J. H. Stine, pp. 329, 325. If they are correctly presented, Butterfield was at this time thoroughly informed as to Hooker's plan, and discussed it freely with Lincoln, but not in the presence of any one else. The President signified his approval of Hooker's plan by the following telegram of 12:10 a.m., April 12:

Your letter, by the hand of General Butterfield, is received, and will be conformed to. The thing you dispense with [detaching a force from Washington in the direction of Warrenton] would have been ready by midday to-morrow.

Hooker expected that if Lee was cut off from Richmond, or abandoned it, he would take that place himself. But why should not Lee, while Hooker was doing this, throw himself upon the latter's communications with the North? To provide for this contingency, Hooker was to have a million and a half rations, over ten days' supply for his army, on board lighters; these were to be towed by gunboats down the Potomac and up the Pamunkey, so that his advance should not be impeded by the loss of his land communications, nor by slowness in the movement of his trains.[1]

[1] Hooker to Colonel Ross, Feb. 28, 1864, in *B. and L.,* III, 223; *ib., Rep. of Com.,* IV, 145.

# CHAPTER XI

HOOKER'S cavalry prepared for active service in accordance with the following instructions of the 11th of April:

I. The effective force of this corps will be in readiness to move at daylight on Monday, April 13.

II. Each trooper will carry on his horse not less than three days' rations for himself and horse, and as much more as shall be judged practicable for him to take on short marches; and he will carry as much ammunition for the arms he bears as he can conveniently on his person, the amount not to be less in any case than 40 rounds of carbine and 20 rounds of pistol cartridge.

III. The pack-trains will be loaded with five days' rations for the men.  The supply-trains will be loaded with rations of grain and subsistence in such proportion that men and animals will be supplied to the same date.

IV. The headquarters of the corps will be designated at night during the campaign, either in bivouac or on the march, by a red lantern.[1]

On the same day Heintzelman, commanding the Department of Washington, issued an order for forty-six of his regiments, which probably aggregated about 18,000 men, to be immediately prepared to take the field, and be ready the morning of the 13th.[2]

Instructions for the employment of the cavalry corps were issued to General Stoneman on the 12th in the form of the following discursive letter from Williams, Adjutant-General:

. . . you will march at 7 a.m. on the 13th instant, with all your available force, except one brigade, for the purpose of turning the enemy's position on his left, and of throwing your command between him and Richmond, and isolating him from his supplies, checking his retreat, and inflicting on him every possible injury which will tend to his discomfiture and defeat.  To accomplish this, the general suggests that you ascend the Rappahannock by the different routes, keeping well out of the view of the enemy, and throwing out well to the front and flank small parties to mask your movement and to cut off all communications with the enemy by the people in their interests, living on this side of the

---

[1] *From Everglade to Canon with the 2 Dragoons*, by T. F. Rodenbough, Colonel and Brevet Brigadier-General, pp. 530, 531; and *W. R.*, 40, p. 198.
[2] *W. R.*, 107, pp. 1002, 1003.

river. To divert suspicion it may not be amiss to have word given out that you are in pursuit of [W. E.] Jones' guerillas, as they are operating extensively in the Shenandoah Valley, in the direction of Winchester.

He further suggests that you select for your place of crossing the Rappahannock some point to the west of the Orange and Alexandria Railroad, which can only be determined by the circumstances as they are found on the arrival of your advance. In the vicinity of Culpeper you will be likely to come against Fitzhugh Lee's brigade of cavalry, consisting of about 2000 men, which it is expected that you will be able to disperse and destroy without delay to your advance or detriment to any considerable number of your command.

At Gordonsville the enemy had [has] a small provost guard of infantry, which it is expected you will destroy, if it can be done without delaying your forward movement. From there it is expected that you will be able to push forward to the Aquia and Richmond Railroad, somewhere in the vicinity of Saxton's [Hanover] Junction, destroying along your whole route the railroad bridges, trains, cars, depots of provisions, lines of telegraph communication, etc. The general directs that you go prepared with all the means necessary to accomplish this work effectually. As the line of the railroad from Aquia to Richmond presents the shortest one for the enemy to retire on, it is more than probable that the enemy may avail himself of it and the usually traveled highways on each side of it for this purpose, in which event you will select the strongest positions, such as banks of streams, commanding heights, etc., in order to check or prevent it, and, if unsuccessful, you will fall upon his flank, attack his artillery and trains, and harass and delay him until he is exhausted and out of supplies. Moments of delay will be hours and days to the army in pursuit. If the enemy should retire by Culpeper and Gordonsville, you will endeavor to hold your force in his front, and harass him night and day on the march and in camp unceasingly. If you can not cut off from his columns large slices, the general desires that you will not fail to take small ones. Let your watchword be, fight, fight, fight, bearing in mind that time is as valuable to the general as the rebel carcasses. It is not in the power of the rebels to oppose you with more than 5000 sabers, and those badly mounted, and—after they leave Culpeper—without forage or rations; keep them from Richmond, and, sooner or later, they must fall in our hands.

The general desires you to understand that he considers the primary object of your movement the cutting of the enemy's connections with Richmond by the Fredericksburg route, checking his retreat over those lines, and he wishes to make everything subservient to that object. He desires that you keep yourself informed of the enemy's whereabouts and attack him wherever you find him. If, in your operations, any opportunity should present itself for you to detach a force to Charlottesville, which is almost unguarded, and destroy the depot of supplies said to be there, or along the Aquia Railroad in the direction of Richmond, to destroy the bridges, etc., or the crossing of the Pamunkey in the direction of West Point, destroying the ferries, felling trees to prevent or check the crossing, they will all greatly contribute to our complete success. You may rely upon the general being in connection with you before your supplies are exhausted. Let him hear from you as often as necessary and practicable.

A brigade of infantry will march to-morrow morning at 8 o'clock for Kelley's Ford, with one battery and a regiment to the United States and Banks' Fords, to threaten and hold those places.

It devolves upon you, general, to take the initiative in the forward movement of this grand army, and on you and your noble command must depend in a great measure the extent and brilliancy of our success. Bear in mind that celerity, audacity, and resolution are everything in war, and especially is it the case with the command you have and the enterprise upon which you are about to embark.

The gist of all this is that the cavalry corps is to cross the Rappahannock above the railroad bridge, and operate against the communications and resources of the enemy, and against his marching columns. The instructions relative to the latter are based upon the expectation that the enemy will retreat as Stoneman proceeds with the destruction of the Richmond, Fredericksburg and Potomac Railroad, and will direct his march either toward Richmond or toward Gordonsville. If toward Richmond, Stoneman will be in position to oppose him in front; if toward Gordonsville, he is, if possible, to place himself across the enemy's front, and if not, to hang on his flank and rear. While in respect to time the work of demolition is expected to precede the operation of interception, in respect to importance demolition is subordinated to interception. "Keep them from Richmond," said Hooker, "and sooner or later they must fall in our hands." How was a cavalry corps that should not have been expected to muster more than 10,000 effectives to keep an army estimated at from 60,000 to 80,000 men from going where it chose to; and how was keeping the enemy from Richmond to make him fall into the hands of the Army of the Potomac? Hooker may have had answers to these questions, but it is hard to believe that, if he had, he would not have given expression to them.

Should Lee not retreat, Stoneman's operations would be a blow in the air or, at best, an effective raid.

The only provision made for communication between Stoneman and Hooker was the injunction: "Let him [Hooker] hear from you as often as necessary and practicable." What if it should not be practicable for Stoneman to get a message to Hooker? In that case he could not expect to be in communication with the latter until the army and the cavalry were reunited. "You may rely," says the letter, "upon the general being *in connection* with you before your supplies are exhausted." How soon was this to be? The order did not prescribe the amount of supplies to be carried. Stoneman's circular required the pack-trains to be loaded with five days' rations and each trooper to carry on his horse not less than three days' rations and "as much more as shall be judged practicable for him to take on short marches." It also provided that the animals should be rationed to the same date as the men. The expedition may therefore be considered as supplied for a period of from eight to ten days—a long time to be possibly without news or instructions from army headquarters.

Neither Hooker's order nor Stoneman's circular makes any reference to subsisting off the country. Stoneman was to decide for himself whether he should fraction his command or keep it united.

The following force of cavalry was to remain with the army:

Of the First Division—the commanding general (Pleasonton), the 2d brigade (Devin), and the battery (Martin).
Of the Third Division—the 1 Pa. of the 2d brigade.

As diminished by the deduction of this force and the dismounted men, the cavalry corps marched on the 13th to Morrisville (21 miles). It numbered 9895 cavalrymen and 22 guns manned by 427 artillerymen:[1]

CAVALRY CORPS—Stoneman

*First Division, 1st brigade* (8 Ill., 3 Ind., 8 and 9 N. Y.) —Davis.
*Second Division*—Averell.
  1st brigade (1 Mass., 4 N. Y., 6 O., 1 R. I.) —Sargent.
  2d brigade (3, 4, and 16 Pa.) —McIntosh.
  Battery A, 2 U. S. (horse artillery) —Tidball.
*Third Division*—Gregg.
  1st brigade (1 Me., 2 and 10 N. Y.) —Kilpatrick.
  2d brigade (12 Ill., 1 Md., 1 N. J.) —Wyndham.
*Reserve Brigade* (1, 2, 5, and 6 U. S.) —Buford.
*Reserve Regiment* (6 Pa. Lancers) —Rush.
*Corps Artillery* (horse) —Robertson.
  Battery B and L,[2] 2 U. S.—Vincent.
  Battery M, 2 U. S.—Clark.
  Battery E, 4 U. S.—Elder.

The command had with it six days' rations and five days' short forage, carried on the horses or on pack-mules or in a wagon-train which was to accompany the column during the first two days. An extra supply-train of 275 wagons, carrying three days' rations and three days' short forage, was sent by the chief quartermaster of the army (Lieutenant-Colonel Ingalls) to Bealeton. The command was thus provided with nine days' subsistence and eight days' short forage.

The only force available to oppose it was four regiments of W. H. F. Lee's cavalry brigade[3] and a portion of Stuart's horse artillery. The

[1] *W. R.*, 39, p. 1067.
[2] Formed by the consolidation of two depleted batteries.
[3] 2 N. Ca., 5, 9, and 13 Va. The 10 and 15 Va. of this brigade were detached; the former was near Beaver Dam, on the Virginia Central Railroad, and the latter on the Lower Rappahannock below Fredericksburg.

former numbered about 1200 men.  The latter consisted probably of two batteries, or eight pieces, manned by about 150 men.  This force was assembled about Culpeper Court-House, with outposts along the Rappahannock.  Fitzhugh Lee's brigade (1, 2, 3, and 4 Va.), with perhaps a battery of horse artillery, was at Sperryville (Map 1, sheet A).  It numbered about 1000 sabers.  Of Stuart's remaining battery one or two pieces were probably with the 15 Va. Cavalry below Fredericksburg, and the others detached between the Rapidan and the Virginia Central Railroad.

For the concealment and protection of the Federal movement, infantry was ordered to take post as intimated to Stoneman—the 91 Pa. (1. 3. V) at Banks' Ford, and Buschbeck's brigade $(\frac{1}{2.\,XI})$ at Kelley's Ford, each with instructions to prevent a crossing by the enemy or any communication across the river, and to keep as far as practicable from being seen.[1]

Stoneman issued the following order (Map 6):

Three[2] squadrons of Davis' brigade will cross the North Fork of the Rappahannock at Sulphur Springs about 12 o'clock to-night [13th], and follow down the south bank of this fork, and clear out any enemy's force met with between the point of crossing and Freeman's Ford, at which point Colonel Davis will be with the head of his brigade.  As soon as Colonel Davis opens up communication with these three squadrons, he will cross with the whole of his brigade, and turn Beverly Ford, where General Averell will be with the head of his division.

General Averell will cross with his division at Beverly Ford, followed by General Gregg with his division.  General Buford, with his Reserve Brigade, will cross at the ford in the vicinity of the Rappahannock railroad bridge simultaneously with General Averell.  As soon as General Averell and General Buford are across the river and both have formed their commands a short distance beyond the river, Averell will push on to Culpeper Court-House, keeping to the right of the railroad, if possible to transport his artillery, or if there is no road leading along the right and near the railroad, then by the nearest road.  Gregg will cross the river as soon after Averell as possible, and follow him well closed up on his rear.

If there should be a route practicable for artillery, and running parallel to the route pursued by Averell, Buford will follow it, provided it does not lead too far to the left.  If there is no such route, the artillery of Buford will be sent to the rear of Gregg, and the Reserve Brigade will march through the country, irrespective of roads, keeping at such distance from Averell as to give room for Averell to form his division front into line of battle.  Averell will move on in the direction of the enemy, who is supposed to be a mile or so this side of Culpeper Court-House.  In case Averell comes upon the enemy, Gregg will form his division at once, and hold it in readiness to move to the right of Averell's division, and Buford will act looking to the left, and Davis will endeavor to turn the

[1] *W. R.*, 40, p. 202.
[2] In the official publication this word reads *the;* it should evidently read *three.*  J. B. Jr.

enemy's left flank. If the enemy is encountered he will be attacked at once and with the utmost vigor, pouring in upon him every available man, excepting a limited reserve in each command.

Colonel Rush, commanding Lancers [6 Pa.], will report in person at daylight, April 15, to these headquarters, for special service.

The major-general commanding expects to be kept informed of all that may be deemed by commanding officers as important, and commanding officers will keep themselves posted as to what is transpiring on their right and left.

Corps headquarters will be, after to-night, with headquarters Gregg's division, until further orders.

The night of the 13th was quite cold. In spite of the heavy frost, Stoneman's cavalry bivouacked without fires, and consequently without sleep.

The following communication was addressed to-day (13th) to the commander of the XII Corps, and one of the same tenor to the commander of the III Corps:

A large portion of General Stoneman's cavalry force have gone in the direction of the Shenandoah Valley, and will be absent some days. Your infantry pickets must be vigilant and strong, as they will have no cavalry force of any account to rely upon.

It does not appear whether this dispatch was intended to be intercepted, but seems well adapted to deceive in case it should be. However this may have been, W. H. F. Lee, near Culpeper Court-House, received information in the course of the night from Lieutenant Payne—commanding the famous company of the 4 Va. Cavalry known as the Black Horse Cavalry—that the Federal cavalry and artillery, in heavy force, were moving up from Fredericksburg in the direction of Kelley's Ford.[1] Lee reënforced the picket at the ford with a company of sharpshooters and awaited developments.

The Federal movements for effecting a passage were then in progress. Davis took up the march for Sulphur Springs at 11 p.m., and marched on through the night. Buschbeck not having come up, Buford was sent with his brigade and a battery of horse artillery to Kelley's Ford, where he was to make a demonstration in the morning as a diversion in favor of Davis. It was contemplated that the 14th would be consumed by the movement of Davis' brigade down the river, and that the crossing of the remainder of the corps and the pack-train would take place on the morning of the 15th.

On the 14th, a clear, fine day, the cavalry proceeded to Bealeton, on the Orange and Alexandria Railroad, about 6 miles from Morrisville (Map 6). Here its wagons were unloaded and sent back to Morrisville.

---

[1] *W. R.*, 39, p. 85.

At daylight General Buford made a demonstration, as ordered, at Kelley's Ford, which had the desired effect of drawing the greater part of W. H. F. Lee's brigade from Culpeper to Kelley's Ford. Davis crossed the river at Sulphur Springs and Freeman's Ford, and marched for Beverly Ford. His brigade numbered about 1500 men. To avoid unnecessary delay in crossing the river, an attempt was made to-day to force it without the coöperation of Davis' brigade. Gregg's division went to the Rappahannock Bridge, leaving Averell's division and the artillery at Bealeton. The position at the river was examined, and it was found that a small body of the enemy was strongly posted on the opposite side to dispute the crossing, a part at the far end of the bridge, the remainder in a blockhouse and a line of rifle-pits beyond the bridge. While two companies forded the river below the bridge under a sharp fire, three companies charged across the bridge, and after a slight skirmish with the men in the blockhouse and line of rifle-pits, went back across the river. Gregg then examined Beverly Ford, and finding the south bank occupied by dismounted men, posted two squadrons opposite them on the north bank, and went into camp between Bealeton and Rappahannock Station.

A determined effort on the part of General Gregg's command could not have failed to secure the passage of his division at the railroad and at Beverly Ford; and success at these points would have caused the withdrawal of the Confederates at Kelley's Ford.[1]

Buschbeck's brigade, ordered to take post at Kelley's Ford, arrived there about 3 p.m. to-day. One of its regiments (29 N. Y.) was detached to Rappahannock Station to guard the bridge and the train which was thought to be at that point. The following letter from Stoneman's chief of staff was on its way to Buschbeck:

The major-general commanding desires that as soon as the cavalry shall have crossed the river to-morrow morning, you direct the regiment of your brigade now at the Rappahannock railroad bridge to rejoin you at Kelley's Ford. After it has joined you, you will send one regiment back to Morrisville, to guard your right and rear and protect the wagon-train which will be left at that point. At early dawn to-morrow morning [15th] the major-general commanding desires you to make a vigorous demonstration at Kelley's Ford, so as to induce the enemy to believe that you intend crossing at that point. Extend your pickets well down the river, so as to prevent the enemy crossing below and cutting you off.

At 4 p.m. Buford's brigade and battery withdrew from Kelley's Ford and went into camp probably near Gregg's division, between Bealeton Station and Rappahannock Bridge.

[1] *Campaigns of Stuart's Cavalry*, by McClellan, p. 222. See also *History of the 10th Regiment of Cavalry, N. Y. State Volunteers*, by N. D. Preston, pp. 68, 69.

The following dispatch was received in Washington at 10:20 a.m.:

Headquarters Army of the Potomac, April 14, 1863.

*Postmaster,* Washington, D. C.:

Major-General Hooker, commanding this army, would like to have the entire mails of to-day from his army detained twenty-four hours in your office, if you can do so with propriety. He has very urgent reasons for making this request, as you may readily imagine. Inform me whether or not you will comply.

RUFUS INGALLS,

Colonel and Quartermaster.[1]

At 9:20 p.m. on the 13th Hooker telegraphed to Halleck:

If it is deemed of importance to keep open the telegraph communication to this point, it will require that a regiment of cavalry be sent from Washington to patrol and guard the line *via* Occoquan to Dumfries. My cavalry have other duties that will prevent their attending to this. The force should be sent without delay.

This dispatch was received at 9:35 and answered at 10:45 as follows:[2]

I do not think that the safety of Washington depends upon the maintenance of communication with your army, but I think it is your duty to maintain your communications with Washington, and to keep the War Department advised of all your movements and intended movements. You therefore have my orders to keep up such communications.

At 7:30 a.m. on the 14th the Secretary of War received the following dispatch of the same day from Hooker:[3]

I have the honor to transmit herewith copies of my telegram to Major-General Halleck [9:20 p.m., April 13, and his reply thereto, 10:45 p.m., April 13]. I respectfully request that these be laid before the President of the United States without delay.

The President took the part of Hooker and caused Halleck to reply at 11 a.m.:[4]

[1] The author wrote to the Postmaster-General for information as to the action taken on this dispatch, and received the following answer:

". . . the Postmaster at Washington informs me that there are no records in his office to show that any reply was made to the dispatch mentioned, but he learns from employees who were in the office at the time, that such requests to hold mail were not infrequent. It is probable that the telegram was complied with without any record being made of the fact."

[2] The hours are taken from the *Report of the Committee on the Conduct of the War* (IV, 214). The dispatch, it seems, was repeated on the 14th (*ib.,* p. 215).

[3] The *War Records* give the hour as 7:50 p.m., which is in all probability erroneous. The hour is *a.m.* in the *Report of the Committee on the Conduct of the War* (IV, 214).

[4] The *War Records* give the hour as 11 p.m., which is in all probability erroneous. The hour is *a.m.* in the *Report of the Committee on the Conduct of the War* (IV, 215), from which the text is taken.

General Heintzelman has ordered a regiment of cavalry to scout south of Occoquan and Dumfries.

Hooker now expected that General Dix at Fort Monroe, with Peck at Suffolk, would detain Longstreet about Richmond while Stoneman carried out his instructions. He had reason to believe that the Federal movements on the Peninsula had caused a depletion of the garrison of Richmond, but he did not wish his cavalry to be led off by this circumstance from its prescribed task. Referring to a report from Peck, he wrote to Stoneman on the 14th:

. . . the enemy . . . must have withdrawn all his forces from Richmond, and you can have nothing to apprehend from there. This information must not delay or divert you from the main object of your expedition, as set forth in your instructions. The general is exceedingly anxious that you should be at your work [of destruction] on the Aquia and Richmond [Railroad] lines at the earliest practicable moment.

Peck, not being informed of Hooker's plans, was not unnaturally concerned for the safety of his post and garrison. He communicated his uneasiness to the President, and the latter at 5:30 p.m. telegraphed to Hooker:

Would like to have a letter from you as soon as convenient.

Hooker replied at 11 p.m.:

. . . As soon as Stoneman's designs are discovered to the enemy, Peck will be relieved. The enemy have not to exceed 30,000 men between Richmond and Suffolk, including both of those towns.

The enemy had actually about the following effective forces:

Garrison of Richmond (Elzey) . . . . . . . . . . . . . 5,100
Department of Southern Virginia (French) . . . . . . . 7,471
Hood's and Pickett's divisions (Longstreet) . . . . . . . . 11,050

23,621 [1]

On the morning of the 15th, Hooker added:

A letter from Major-General Stoneman, dated 1 p.m. yesterday, informs me that his command will be across the river before daylight this morning [15th]. It was his intention to cross at three points all above the Rappahannock Station. I sent him six days' rations for men and animals, by wagons, to be distributed just before his passage of the river.[2] The wagons are now on their return [to Falmouth].[3]

[1] W. R., 26, pp. 952, 978, 929, 916.

[2] It would appear herefrom, together with the promise conveyed in Williams' letter of the 12th, that six days was the longest time after passing the Rappahannock that Stoneman might have to wait to come again into communication with Hooker.

According to his official report Stoneman was assured that Hooker would "certainly communicate" with him within that time (W. R., 39, p. 1062).

[3] They probably arrived by nightfall. J. B. Jr.

From the Rappahannock, if he should meet with no unusual delay, he will strike the Aquia and Richmond Railroad on the night of the second day [17th].

Meanwhile I shall do what I can to keep the enemy up to their works in my front, and if they should fall back, shall pursue with all the vigor practicable.

Up to date last night the enemy appeared to have no suspicions of our designs. This morning I can see nothing from the storm.

I am rejoiced that Stoneman had two good days to go up the river, and was enabled to cross it before it had become too much swollen. If he can reach his position [on the Richmond and Fredericksburg Railroad], the storm and mud will not damage our prospects. . . .

Alas for these fond hopes and fair promises. The heavy rain, which set in about 2 o'clock in the morning, and the consequent rapid rise of the river, put a sudden end to the crossing. Rush's Lancers reported to the corps commander at daylight, and received their orders "for special service." This regiment was to cross the Rappahannock with the main command, and while the latter did the heavy work on Lee's communications, was to make a dash at Richmond, and by forced marches rejoin the main command at Suffolk or Fort Monroe. It marched down to the river, and finding it so swollen as to be impassable, returned to camp.[1] Buford was at Rappahannock Bridge with his brigade at 6:30 a.m., ready to cross. He received orders to await further instructions. But no "further instructions" came, except to return to camp.

Buschbeck did not receive the order for him to make a demonstration until about 7:30 o'clock. Having heard no firing above, he judged that the cavalry had not attempted to cross, and that it would be useless to make a demonstration. So he made none. He dispatched his adjutant to the headquarters of General Stoneman at Bealeton "to examine into the state of affairs and to receive further orders," and received from Stoneman an order to remain at Kelley's Ford, and let the regiment at Rappahannock Station remain at that point to guard the bridge.

Davis' brigade, which was working its way down toward the bridge by the south bank, was recalled, and before it finished crossing, had to swim its horses. Its rear-guard was charged by about 50 cavalrymen. One lieutenant and 24 men were captured and several men and horses drowned in the rapid waters. The Confederates sustained a loss of 1 killed, 2 wounded, and 6 captured or missing. They also lost 20 horses, killed, wounded, and captured.[2] W. H. F. Lee explains this loss by the statement that the men "were separated some distance from their horses, and being partially surprised, they had to make their escape without their horses, as they were in great danger of themselves being captured."[3]

[1] *Annals of the 6 Pa. Cavalry*, by S. L. Gracey.
[2] *W. R.*, 39, pp. 85, 86, 88.          [3] *Ib.*, 39, p. 86.

The following communications went to Stoneman on the 15th:

### From Hooker's Chief of Staff

. . . The tenor of your dispatches might indicate that you were manœuvering your whole force against the command of Fitz Lee, numbering not over 2000 men. The commanding general does not expect, nor do your instructions indicate, that you are to act from any base or depot. . . .

### From Hooker's Adjutant-General

. . . As you state in your communication of yesterday that you would be over the river with your command at daylight this morning, it was so communicated to Washington, and it was hoped that the crossing had been made in advance of the rise in the river. If your artillery is your only hindrance to your advance, the major-general commanding directs that you order it to return, and proceed to the execution of your orders without it. It is but reasonable to suppose that if you can not make use of that arm of the service, the enemy can not. If it is practicable to carry into execution the general instructions communicated to you on the 12th instant, the major-general commanding expects you to make use of such means as will, in your opinion, enable you to accomplish them, and that as speedily as possible. This army is now awaiting your movement. I am directed to add that, in view of the swollen condition of the streams, it is not probable, in the event of your being able to advance, that you will be troubled by the infantry of the enemy.

Regarding Stoneman's movements Hooker telegraphed to President Lincoln at 8 p.m.:

Just heard from General Stoneman. His artillery has been brought to a halt by the mud, one division only having crossed the river.[1] If practicable, he will proceed without it. All the streams are swimming.

He received the following reply, same date:

It is now 10:15 p.m. An hour ago I received your letter of this morning, and a few moments later your dispatch of this evening. The latter gives me considerable uneasiness. The rain and mud, of course, were to be calculated upon. General S. is not moving rapidly enough to make the expedition come to anything. He has now been out three days, two of which were unusually fair weather, and all three without hindrance from the enemy, and yet he is not 25 miles from where he started. To reach his point [on the Richmond and Fredericksburg Railroad] he still has 60 miles to go, another river (the Rapidan) to cross, and will be hindered by the enemy. By arithmetic, how many days will it take him to do it? I do not know that any better can be done, but I greatly fear it is another failure already. Write me often; I am very anxious.

Even had Gregg's division remained across, and cleared the south bank of the river, Stoneman could not have begun a general movement until about midnight, as it took until then to get the wagons unloaded

---

[1] The troops that crossed were Gregg's division and Davis' brigade. J. B. Jr.

and their contents issued. By this time Davis with his brigade was within striking distance of Beverly Ford. But his coöperation could perhaps not be counted upon before the morning of the 15th. A crossing might have been made, however, without assistance from Davis. It should again have been attempted. Stoneman must have known from indications in the sky that a storm was brewing, and before it could break and cause the river to rise, he might have forced the position of Beverly Ford or Rappahannock Bridge, and got his whole command across the river. No delay was caused by, or involved in, Davis' wide turning movement, as it was accomplished by the time the main force was ready to advance, which, under the circumstances, could hardly have been earlier than it was—the morning of the 15th. The cause of Stoneman's tardiness is to be found, not in the elements, nor in any one's failing him under fire or on the march, but in his having handicapped himself with a column of wagons the contents of which had to be transferred to pack-mules before he could cross the river. He should have packed his mules before leaving Morrisville, and have crossed the river with his whole force on the 15th, ascending it, if necessary, still further for a practicable crossing. He might have dispensed with the supplies that he put on his pack-mules, and carried such supplies as he could in saddle-pockets, trusting to the enemy's country for the remainder.

At the same time that Stoneman was to cross the Rappahannock, Jones and Imboden were to start on their raid to the Baltimore and Ohio Railroad.[1] Imboden, who had moved to Shenandoah Mountain, was to proceed from there on the 15th; W. E. Jones was to take up the march from Lacy Spring about the same time. Thus, as Hooker was coming out of his winter quarters of his own accord, these commanders were starting to "draw him out."

With a view to the demonstration which was to fix Milroy's attention upon his communications while W. E. Jones and Imboden struck at the Baltimore and Ohio Railroad, Fitzhugh Lee put his brigade in motion (14th) from Sperryville toward Salem, on the Manassas Gap Railroad; but hearing that a large force of "Yankee" cavalry was at Morrisville, preparing to cross at Kelley's Ford and attack W. H. F. Lee, he abandoned this movement and marched back to Amissville, where he encamped for the night.[2]

W. E. Jones received the following dispatches of this day from R. E. Lee:

1

I learn enemy's cavalry are moving against you in Shenandoah Valley; will attack Fitz Lee in passing. They have crossed at Rappahannock Station. Gen-

---

[1] Lee to W. E. Jones, March 25 and April 7.
[2] *Campaigns of Stuart's Cavalry*, by H. B. McClellan, p. 220.

eral Stuart, with two brigades, will attend [to] them.  Collect your forces and be on your guard.

2

The dispatch I sent you is confirmed; main body of enemy's cavalry is moving *via* Liberty [north of Bealeton Station, Map 6] toward Warrenton, with the intention to march into Shenandoah Valley against you.  General Stuart, at Rappahannock Bridge, is apprised; directed to join you.  Be prepared.

The Jones-Imboden expedition was consequently suspended.  S. Jones wrote to W. E. Jones:

I countermand the movement of troops.  Meet an advance of Hooker's cavalry into the Valley; will detain me here for the present.

The late attempt of the Army of the Potomac to advance was to have been supported by its naval auxiliary.  On the 13th of April Hooker requested Magaw, commanding the first division of the Potomac Flotilla, to send two of his gunboats up the Rappahannock as far as Port Royal and further if possible, having reason to believe that the Confederate batteries below Port Royal had been withdrawn.  "It is desired," he said, "that your demonstrations shall hold the enemy in that vicinity, and keep them from retiring.  If the batteries are there, the purposes for which you go would be favored by exchanging a few shots with them. It is hoped that this movement will be made as soon as possible."[1]

On the 14th Magaw wrote to Harwood, commanding the Potomac Flotilla:

I shall make an effort to reach Port Royal by to-morrow night (15th). . . . If we had some transports with [even] raw troops on board, the enemy's attention might be attracted, but without a coöperating force, I fear "General W. P. [W. H. F.] Lee" will laugh at us.[2]

On the 15th the U. S. ships *Anacostia* and *Dragon* went up the Rappahannock as far as Briscoe Mines, a distance of 110 miles, without receiving any shots.  Arriving too late in the day to proceed with safety, they anchored for the night.  From reports received, the commander believed "that the enemy were in strong force and with heavy batteries from Port Tobacco to Fredericksburg."  He consequently renounced the idea of reaching Port Royal, and to prevent being cut off, dropped down during the night below Leedsburg.  He did not advance again. "I am convinced," he said in his report, "that squads of the enemy's cavalry cross the river above and below Briscoe Mines almost daily."[3]

[1] *Naval W. R.*, Series I, Vol. V, pp. 255, 256.
[2] *Ib.*, p. 256.
[3] *Ib.*, pp. 258, 259.

The line of cavalry outposts from Falmouth westward and northward was now dispensed with. Devin's brigade $(\frac{2}{1.\text{ C}})$ remained in camp resting up. The brigade of the XII Corps at Dumfries $(\frac{1}{2.\text{ XII}})$ was relieved by dismounted cavalry. The 1 Pa. Cavalry, with headquarters at King George Court-House, picketed the Rappahannock from Falmouth down to Port Conway, and thence across country at right angles with the river a distance of about 3 miles, making occasional reconnaissances beyond the picket line.[1]

The withdrawal of the old line of cavalry on the 13th was noticed by the residents on the north side, and probably by those on the south side, of the Rappahannock when they rose the following morning, as they had the pickets and some of the reserves in full view. On the 14th a Confederate picket called over: "You need not be so still; we know all about it; you have got orders to move." Lieutenant Ropes, 20 Mass., wrote home:

We have every reason to expect an immediate move, but in what direction, no one can tell.

The correspondents of the Richmond *Whig* and Richmond *Examiner* wrote from Fredericksburg:

1

Report says that the enemy have been massing troops in the vicinity of U. S. Ford for several days past. Yesterday and to-day considerable bodies of cavalry and immense wagon-trains were moving up the river. . . .

2

. . . It is hoped that Hooker will advance. His coming is anxiously awaited by the Army of Northern Virginia, who now regard the destruction of the Army of the Potomac as a military necessity; and believing that the war is near its termination, they desire to give it a brilliant *coup de grâce*. . . .

It was now understood in both armies that Hooker was about to move, but whether he would try to cross the Rappahannock, and if so where, were still matters of conjecture. In Lee's army it was generally supposed that, if he attempted a crossing, it would be at or near United States Ford. There was not a suspicion of Hooker's purpose of placing the cavalry corps on Lee's line of retreat. As has been shown, the Federal cavalry was believed to be aiming at the Shenandoah Valley.

On the night of the 15th the following conversation was carried on across the river:

*Confederate:* "Any signs of a move?"
*Federal:* "Yes, we have got eight days' rations, and expect to move in a few days. We have three days' rations in our haversacks and five in our knapsacks."

[1] *History of the First Reg't Pa. Reserve Cav.*, by W. P. Lloyd, p. 45.

*Confederate:* ''Where is the move to be?''
*Federal:* ''Up to the right.''[1]

General Longstreet says:

Long and close study of the field from the Potomac to the James River, and the experiences of former campaigns, made it clear that the Army of the Potomac had been drawn into a false position, and it became manifest that there were but two moves left open for its spring campaign: first, by crossing the upper fords of the Rappahannock; secondly, by detaching forces to the south side of the James, and by that route moving against Richmond.

To guard against the former, I laid out lines for field works and rifle-pits covering all approaches by the upper fords *as far as the road leading from United States Ford.* From that point the line broke to the rear, crossing the Plank Road and extending back half a mile to command the road from Chancellorsville to Spottsylvania Court-House.[2]

By ''upper fords'' Longstreet meant the fords between Fredericksburg and the United States Ford. The lines that he mentions can not be located with any accuracy, but, on careful consideration, seem to have extended from the vicinity of Banks' Ford westward to the old Mine Road in the vicinity of Childs, thence southwestward to some point between Chandler's and Chancellorsville, on the road to Ely's Ford, and thence southward toward the Plank Road. These lines, be it observed, were not intrenched; they were only ''laid out.''

[1] *W. R.*, 40, p. 219.
[2] *From Manassas to Appomattox*, pp. 323, 324. The italics are mine. J. B. Jr.

# CHAPTER XII

## HOOKER'S THIRD PLAN OF OPERATION

THE rain continued with short intervals, making the river impassable, for about two weeks. The Federal cavalry remained near Warrenton Junction, confronted on the south side of the river by W. H. F. Lee's cavalry brigade and Beckham's horse artillery, and on the north side by Fitzhugh Lee's brigade, Mosby's guerillas, the Black Horse Cavalry, and a portion of the 2 N. Ca. Cavalry.

W. E. Jones wrote to Imboden:

There is no sign of the enemy in the Valley. News has reached me from Sperryville just now, but no tidings of the move anticipated [into the Valley]. . . . My opinion is, the attack on the Valley has been abandoned, if ever entertained, by the enemy. . . .

R. E. Lee wrote

### To President Davis, April 16

The last dispatches from General Stuart, dated yesterday, report the enemy's cavalry north of the Rappahannock, massed opposite Kelley's and Beverly Fords and Rappahannock Bridge. Prisoners report they were rationed for eight days. The cavalry were accompanied by artillery and wagons. General Stuart thinks the movement a feint to cover other operations. He can learn of no force moving toward the Blue Ridge, but thinks from the reports of his scouts that General Hooker intends to transfer his army to White House, on the Pamunkey, or to the south side of James River. My own impression has been that the movement was intended to draw us to the Upper Rappahannock, that Fredericksburg might be seized, and the bridges across the river rebuilt. I do not think General Hooker will venture to uncover Washington City by transferring his army to James River, unless the force in front of Alexandria is greater than I suppose, or unless he believes this army incapable of advancing to the Potomac. My only anxiety arises from the present immobility of the army [of Northern Virginia], owing to the condition of our horses and the scarcity of forage and provisions. I think it all-important that we should assume the aggressive by the 1st of May, when we may expect General Hooker's army to be weakened by the expiration of the term of service of many of his regiments, and before new recruits can be received. If we could be placed in a condition to make a vigorous advance at that time, I think the Valley [of the Shenandoah] could be swept of Milroy, and the army opposite me be thrown north of the Potomac. . . .

P.S. A dispatch from General Stuart, dated 9 p.m. yesterday, just received, states that the heavy rains and swollen streams have entirely arrested military operations on the Upper Rappahannock.

### To Cooper, April 16

. . . I doubt whether General Hooker will be quiescent. There is some movement in agitation now not yet developed. By the last report he was drawing rations for 90,000 men. . . . Making a liberal deduction, I should think this would give from 65,000 to 70,000 effectives.[1]

### To Seddon, April 17

I am informed by the chief commissary of the army [of Northern Virginia] that he has been unable to issue the sugar ration to the troops for the last ten days. Their ration consequently consists of $\frac{1}{4}$ pound of bacon, 18 ounces of flour, 10 pounds of rice to each 100 men about every third day, with some few peas and a small amount of dried fruit occasionally, as they can be obtained. This may give existence to the troops while idle, but will certainly cause them to break down when called upon for exertion. . . . The time has come when it is necessary the men should have full rations. Their health is failing, scurvy and typhus fever are making their appearance, and it is necessary for them to have a more generous diet.

Lieutenant Ropes wrote home on the 16th:

. . . The river has risen tremendously, say 12 feet. Roads muddy, of course. We do not in the least know what to expect. . . . Hooker seems to be about a great thing now, if the impossible order to carry eight days' rations means anything. If this is often repeated, we shall lose half the army by sickness; but it may be only for a great march and a great strike and then a rest.

Hooker wrote to President Lincoln on the 17th:

His [Stoneman's] failure to accomplish speedily the objects of his expedition is a source of deep regret to me, but I can find nothing in his conduct of it requiring my animadversion or censure. We can not control the elements. . . .

While a commander can not control the elements, he can, within limits, regulate his movements by them. It is rather surprising after reading Hooker's defence of Stoneman in this letter to find his adjutant-general writing to him on the same day:

. . . it was not expected that you would embarrass yourself with wagons in your present expedition. It was supposed that your pack-mules would furnish a sufficient amount of transportation for your purpose.

---

[1] This is about the strength at which Hooker estimated Lee's army (Halleck to Stanton, *W. R.*, 40, p. 505). It seems that throughout the operations to be described Lee underestimated the strength of Hooker's army, and Hooker overestimated that of Lee's.

The general fears that your artillery is so strong that it will detract from the rapidity of your movements. He desires that you will use your discretion in returning to camp such portions of it as will embarrass you.

These comments should have been made when Stoneman was starting from Falmouth with his wagons and artillery.

Hooker's adjutant-general wrote to Stoneman at 9 a.m. on the 18th:

No evidence exists here that the enemy has made any change in the disposition of his forces from the United States Ford down the river in consequence of your movement. Your delay in consequence of the storm may enable him to bring up a small force to dispute the passage of the river. It can only be a small one, and must be knocked out of the way.

The major-general commanding directs that you bear in mind that a part of your route lies along the line over which the enemy receives his supplies, and it may be with reason expected that some portion of them will fall into your hands. From the character of your movement, it should not be expected that you will be provided with full rations every hour in the day. Such never has been and never will be the case.

If, from your delay, Culpeper or Gordonsville should be found to have been reënforced with infantry of considerable number, he suggests that you go around them.

The same day Lee wrote to W. E. Jones:

I wish you to keep General J. E. B. Stuart informed of all movements of importance of the enemy in the Valley, while he [Stuart] is operating on your right flank. He is now near Culpeper Court-House.

The Special Correspondent of the Richmond *Whig* wrote from Fredericksburg:

The improving condition of the roads and thoroughfares, rendering military operations practicable, and particularly the demonstrations of the cavalry recently, warranted the expectation that Hooker would ere this have attempted a passage of the Rappahannock at one or more points simultaneously. . . . If we may form an opinion from appearances, the enemy have been moving up the river for several days. . . .

Lieutenant Ropes wrote home:

I incline to think the movement is for the present given up, or at any rate is to be altered. The Rebels know all about it now, and are shouting to our pickets in a derisive manner about the eight days' rations they are to carry.

On the 19th Lee wrote to Stuart:

. . . It appears to me that he [Hooker] is rather fearful of an attack from us than preparing to attack. His operations in front of you look rather to prevent your moving against his right or getting in his rear.

. . . I am aware that from the superior strength of the enemy he will be able to overpower you at any one point, but believe by your good management, boldness, and discretion, you will be able to baffle his designs. I do not think the enemy's infantry extend as high as Kelley's Ford. They have a picket at the United States Mine Ford and a strong reserve about Hartwood Church. They may extend to a higher point.[1]

. . . Save your horses all you can. Put yourself in communication with the commanding officer in the Valley, and desire him to keep you informed of all matters of importance.

Hooker's adjutant-general wrote to Stoneman:

. . . you have two small brigades of cavalry opposed to you, numbering between 4000 and 5000 sabers. The prisoners from there state that they are wretchedly mounted, as we know they must be. Your force of cavalry and artillery is more than double that of the enemy.

The two brigades referred to were Fitzhugh Lee's and W. H. F. Lee's, which numbered, including detached regiments, about 3000 men.

The 29 N. Y. returned on the 18th to its brigade at Kelley's Ford and was replaced on the 20th by 230 men of the 73 Pa. of the same brigade.

Correspondence between the Army of the Potomac and the Potomac Flotilla was resumed with the following telegram of the 20th from Butterfield to Magaw, commanding first division Potomac Flotilla:

The major-general commanding desires to be informed of the number of boats in the Potomac Flotilla, what orders you have, and where the boats are. He has been advised by the President that they will act under his orders. He desires that none should go away without his knowledge. He desires the same information with regard to the fleet of Commander McCrea [second division Potomac Flotilla]. Please answer.

The substance of this dispatch was referred by telegraph to Commodore Harwood, who replied the same day that all the available steam force of the Potomac Flotilla, not under repair, had been already detached to coöperate with the army, either off Aquia Creek or in the Nansemond River; and that two vessels were detailed to convoy General Hooker's transports.[2]

The situation on and near the Peninsula occasioned the following correspondence:

*Halleck to Dix, April 17*

. . . I think that Lee's main army will be massed between Richmond and the Rappahannock. This would of course give you an opportunity to operate in the

[1] They extended to Rappahannock Bridge, 4 miles above Kelley's Ford.
[2] The composition and disposition of the Potomac Flotilla at this time are given in *Appendix 1.*

direction of Hicksford or Weldon, to destroy the railroads connecting with the south. But would that be a safe operation? . . . Would it not be more in accordance with principles for you and Hooker to act as nearly together as possible, and at the same time to secure your smaller force from the enemy's heavy blows? Suppose, while General Hooker operates against the enemy's front, you threaten his flank and rear by the Pamunkey and Mattapony in such a way as to secure your own retreat, would there not be greater chance of success? It seems to me that West Point furnishes you a most excellent base for such an operation. . . .

*Dix to Halleck, April 18, about 1:30 p.m.*

. . . I have long been in favor of occupying the point referred to [West Point].[1]

*Peck to Hooker, April 21*

. . . I hold everything yet. How do you get along?

*Hooker to Peck, 10 p.m.*

I am glad to hear good tidings from you. You must be patient with me. I must play with these devils before I can spring. Remember that my army is at the bottom of a well, and the enemy holds the top.

On the 21st Hooker wrote to President Lincoln:

. . . As I can only cross the river by stratagem, without great loss, which I wish to avoid, it may be a few days before I make it. I must threaten several points, and be in readiness to spring when a suitable opportunity presents itself.

Deserters inform me that the talk in the rebel camp is that when we cross the river it is their intention to fall in our rear and attack our depot at Aquia. The recent arrival of a pontoon train at Hamilton's Crossing lends plausibility to these reports.[2]

The sanguine temperament of the commander of the Army of the Potomac stood him in good stead through the trying period of boggy roads and swollen streams and consequent inaction. At perhaps its darkest moment he expressed himself as follows:

Camp near Falmouth, Va., April 21, 1863, 9 a.m.

*His Excellency the President of the United States:*

My latest advices from Major-General Stoneman were up to 9 o'clock yesterday morning. At that time his command was moving to ascertain whether or not the fords were practicable. If he had crossed, I can not but feel that I should have been informed of it ere this. . . .

The weather appears to continue averse to the execution of my plans as first formed, as, in fact, for all others; but if these do not admit of speedy solution, I feel that I must modify them to conform to the condition of things as they are.

---

[1] *W. R.*, 26, p. 1002.

[2] This is probably a reference to a pontoon train reported by Couch, which had no existence (*Appendix 8*). At any rate, there is no evidence of the presence of a pontoon train at Hamilton's Crossing at this time. J. B. Jr.

I was attached to the movement as first projected, as it promised unusual success; but if it fails, I will project a movement which I trust will secure us success, but not to so great an extent, and one in the execution of which I shall be able to exercise personal supervision.

Very respectfully, etc.,

JOSEPH HOOKER,

Major-General Commanding.

The last sentence shows Hooker's characteristic distrust of his subordinates. His concern for the secrecy of his plan had received a rude shock. A letter of April 4 from his medical director (*Appendix 5*) was published in full in the Washington *Morning Chronicle* of the 17th. It contained the statements: "*The paper marked A shows the whole number of sick in this army to be on the 28th of March ultimo 10,777,*" and "*The ratio of sick for the whole army is 67.64 per 1000.*" From these it was easy, by simple proportion, to determine the strength of the whole army in officers and men present as 159,329. Such calculation is alluded to by Lee in a letter to Davis dated April 27 and in one to Seddon dated May 10.[1] According to the consolidated morning report the aggregate present on the 31st of March was 163,005. Lee was getting near the truth, but not quite as near as these figures would indicate. He discounted them too much on account of non-effectives. On the 7th of May he wrote to President Davis:

> The strength of the enemy seems to be greater than I had estimated, as from various sources it is stated that they crossed the Rappahannock with 120,000 men.

If from Hooker's effective strength we deduct for the cavalry and horse artillery left behind 2400 men, for the 20 Me. Infantry 400 men, for the General Artillery Reserve, less Brooker's battery, 1500 men, and for the Provost Guard 2200 men, we get as about the force which, first and last, crossed the Rappahannock 127,460. On the 21st Hooker wrote to his friend in Washington, the Secretary of War, inviting his attention to the newspaper article and remarking:

> Already all the arithmeticians in the army have figured up the strength of the sick and well, as shown in this published extract, as belonging to the army. Its complete organization is given, and in the case of two corps [I, VI] the number of regiments. The chief of my secret service department would have willingly paid $1000 for such information in regard to the enemy at the commencement of his operations, and even now would give that sum for it to verify the statements which he has been at great trouble to collect and systematize.

On the 21st the pickets of Devin's brigade of cavalry were ordered in, and at 3 p.m. the three regiments proceeded to Potomac Bridge.[2]

---

[1] *W. R.*, 40, pp. 752, 790.

[2] *The Cavalry at Chancellorsville*, by J. E. Carpenter, in Philadelphia *Weekly Times*.

On the 22d Stoneman received another set of long, rambling instructions in which the following points are to be observed (*Appendix 14*):

1. He is to be ready to move on short notice.

2. He may subdivide his force, but if he does, he must have the several parts come together at some point in the enemy's country which he is to designate.

3. He is, if necessary, to subsist off the country.

They contain nothing about intercepting the enemy's retreat upon Richmond, which in the instructions issued on the 12th was made the "primary object" of Stoneman's movement. True, those instructions had not been revoked, but those of the 22d, not referring to this object, and dwelling upon certain other objects, might give the impression that the latter had been substituted for the former.[1]

To confuse the enemy as much as possible Hooker made demonstrations as if to attack at both ends of his line. On the 19th Doubleday's division of the I Corps marched to Port Conway (Map 2), 21 miles below Fredericksburg, where it made a pretence of crossing, and at night built fires in every direction to make the impression of a large force. It returned on the 22d.[2] On the 20th the cavalry corps moved toward the Rappahannock to ascertain whether it was fordable; and about this time the small infantry force ordered to Rappahannock Ford and Beverly Ford showed itself at both points.

On the 23d Lee wrote to General Jackson:

. . . I think that, if a real attempt is made to cross the river, it will be above Fredericksburg.[3]

On the same day he wrote to the Adjutant and Inspector General:

As regards the reported movement of General Hooker toward Richmond, I know of no direct route which he can take, shorter than the line which we now

---

[1] Writing from Warrenton Junction, Stoneman reported his situation as follows. It should be premised that the enemy had evacuated Warrenton, and that Stoneman was drawing his supplies from Alexandria:

"*April 22*

"Averell's division and Davis' brigade are on the railroad, half-way between Warrenton and the Junction. Gregg's division and Buford's brigade are at the Junction. All are on the railroad. As we have not, nor, by being there, do we require, wagons to transport our supplies, I shall make arrangements to keep on hand two days' rations of long, and six of short forage, and eight of subsistence stores. I patrol the road to Bristoe Station, and have telegraphed the commanding officer of Alexandria of the fact, and requested that the force at Washington be sent out as far as Bristoe, where I will connect with it by patrol from Cedar Run. I am sorry to say that the horses have suffered considerably for want of forage and from exposure to rain and wind. A few days, I hope, will bring them up again. The railroad is in good order up to the Rappahannock railroad bridge and to Warrenton. The construction train is now at the bridge. Three trains have arrived with stores.

"*April 23*

"The command is now separated [divided?] by impassable streams, and I am unable to communicate with the different portions of it, owing to the small streams being swimming. The pickets are cut off by high water."

[2] Itinerary of the I Army Corps, *W. R.*, 39, p. 256.

[3] *W. R.*, 40, p. 859.

occupy, and should he attempt such a movement when the army is able to operate, I think he will find it very difficult to reach his destination.

On the 22d another demonstration was made below Fredericksburg. Two regiments of infantry $(\frac{24}{4.1.1}, \frac{84'}{1.1.1})$ left their camp near Belle Plain at 1:30 p.m., and about 10 p.m. bivouacked about half a mile in rear of the village of Port Conway. About 3 a.m. on the 23d, the 24 Mich. was under arms and marched into the village. Twenty men were picked from each company to set up canvas boats and cross the river to Port Royal. Owing to a heavy rain, and the entire ignorance of the men as to the manner of constructing the boats, the work was not completed and the crossing effected until nearly 6 a.m. At that hour, thirteen boats crossed the Rappahannock without opposition. Parties were sent in different directions through the village of Port Royal. A wagon-train was captured and destroyed, several prisoners taken, and a mail seized. The boats returned to Port Conway about 9 a.m.[2] The expedition commenced its march toward camp about 11 a.m. and arrived there about 7:30 p.m. It rained all day, and the roads were almost impassable.[3]

"It seems," said Captain Candler, an aide on Hooker's staff, writing home on the 24th, "as though it were never to stop raining; the longer it rains the harder it seems to come down. I can see no prospects of any clearing up. . . . Our entire plan may have to be changed, and unless fortune favors us our chances for complete victory will not be very high. Could you come into Headquarters at any time during the day you would see that something was wrong; every one is moving around in an aimless, nervous way, looking at the clouds and then at the ground, and in knots trying to convince themselves that it is going to clear off and they will be able to move day after to-morrow."

The 25th dawned bright and springlike, with a good stiff breeze, which dried the mud rapidly. The day promised a spell of good weather and held out a prospect of an early move. The country was gay with fresh shrubs and flowers. Peach-trees were in full bloom. Bulbs and hyacinths abounded in the gardens of the deserted houses, and the Plymouth Mayflowers in the woods.

Howard was instructed to send knapsacks and other supplies to Buschbeck's brigade at Kelley's Ford, and informed confidentially that his whole corps would "probably move in that direction as early as Monday a.m., 27th."[4]

---

[1] 14 N. Y. Militia.

[2] The record, as published, gives this hour as 9 *p.m.*, manifestly an error.

[3] *W. R.*, 39, pp. 137, 256.

[4] The brigade had marched from its camp without knapsacks (*Autobiography of O. O. Howard*, I, 350).

The 91 Pa. (1. 3. V) was relieved from duty at United States Ford and Banks' Ford by the 155 Pa. (2. 3. III).

Hooker's feints, while they did not deceive the enemy, deceived his own army. Lieutenant Ropes wrote home on the 25th:

I hear from undoubted authority something which I tell you, and do not wish to have go further at present, viz., that it was, and probably still is, Hooker's plan to attack Fredericksburg again *in front* to accomplish what Burnside failed to do. The recent storm stopped it, but a few days ago the bridges were actually moved down and ready to be thrown across in the same places again. . . . Another thing, Macy [commanding 20 Mass.] has been asked if he will volunteer his regiment to lead in a desperate assault, and has of course accepted. So you may hear of another Fredericksburg any day, and the 20th will probably be ahead. Do not, of course, speak of this, for it must not get round. Nothing would so demoralize the army, and destroy the little confidence they feel in Hooker, as to know that he intended to repeat Burnside's move.

But he added on the 26th:

I heard from a staff officer last night that the projected move across the river here is given up. Couch told me so. . . . The rebels appear to be fitting up their works and increasing them. The river has now gone down to about its normal size. Weather fine.

Under date of April 25, 1 a.m., Lee wrote to Stuart:

I think it probable that among the considerations that prevent Stoneman from crossing the Blue Ridge is the apprehension that you will plunge into the rear of their army and cut up their line of communications. Should he cross into the Valley, nothing would call him back sooner than such a move on your part, and it is worthy of your consideration how you could, in that event, most damage him. Should you determine to follow him, Mosby and the Black Horse [Cavalry] might be let loose on his rear, which would, perhaps, produce similar consternation, though not so much harm.

Stoneman never thought of crossing the Blue Ridge. Lee's deception on this point was to prove, as we shall see, a potent and unexpected factor of success in the execution of Hooker's grand manœuvre.

Stuart's adjutant-general wrote on the 25th to Mosby that the general was extremely anxious to know what was going on behind Centreville, and whether Hooker was moving any troops up in that vicinity.[1]

[1] *W. R.*, 40, p. 860. Stuart wrote to Mosby on the 26th: "There is now a splendid opportunity to strike the enemy in rear of Warrenton Junction. The trains are running regularly to that point (it may be by the time that you get this, the opportunity may have gone). Capture a train and interrupt the operation of the railroad.

*April 26*

On the 26th a detachment of the 1 Pa. Cavalry went from King George Court-House down the Neck, the peninsula between the Rappahannock and the Potomac, for the purpose of capturing mails or small parties of Confederate troops, of breaking up contraband trade, seizing or destroying supplies intended for the enemy, stopping the Confederate conscription, and arresting any citizens that might appear to be actively hostile to the United States. It reached Leedsburg (Map 1, sheet A) and returned the same day with a dozen prisoners, having destroyed several boats and a considerable amount of contraband property.[1]

By this time a material change was made in the Federal plan of operation. The new plan was stated and discussed by Hooker and his chief of staff about a year later as follows:

### Hooker

. . . as the season was now more advanced, and the roads firmer, with a prospect that the rainy season had ended, I concluded to change my plan and strike for the whole rebel army, instead of forcing it back on its line of retreat, which was as much as I could hope to accomplish in executing my first design.

As modified, the problem was to throw a sufficient infantry force to cross at Kelley's Ford, descend the Rappahannock, and knock away the enemy's forces holding the U. S. and Banks' Fords by attacking them in rear, and as soon as these fords were open to reënforce the marching column sufficiently for them to continue the march upon the flank of the rebel army until the whole force was routed; and if successful his retreat intercepted. Simultaneously with this movement on the right, the left were [*sic*] to cross the Rappahannock below Fredericksburg, and threaten the enemy in that quarter, including his depot of supplies, to prevent his dispatching an overwhelming force to his left.[2]

What I wanted was Lee's army; with that Richmond would have been ours, and indeed all of Virginia; and it was with this view that instructions were given General Stoneman.[3]. . . I not only expected a victory, but I expected to get the whole army. I had reason to expect it, and I struck for that object.[4]

### Butterfield

General Hooker finally determined upon a plan of campaign the intent and purpose of which was to destroy the army of General Lee where it then was,

Stoneman's main body of cavalry is located near Warrenton Junction, Bealeton, and Warrenton Springs. Keep far enough from a brigade camp to give you time to get off your plunder and prisoners. Information of the movements of large bodies is of the greatest importance to us just now. The marching or transportation of divisions will often indicate the plan of a campaign. Be sure to give dates and numbers and names as far as possible."

[1] *W. R.*, 40, p. 249; *History of the First Reg't Pa. Reserve Cav.*, by W. P. Lloyd, pp. 45–47.

[2] *Rep. of Com.*, IV, 116.

[3] *Ib.*, 139.

[4] *Ib.*, 145.

not merely to fight a battle and gain possession of the battle-ground, and have the enemy fall back on Richmond, but to destroy him there; for General Hooker believed that we could better afford to fight the enemy nearer Washington than Richmond.[1]

The new plan lent itself, by turning the enemy's left, to forcing him off his communications and up against the impassable obstacles of the Atlantic seaboard, but Hooker had no thought of such strenuous tactics. His general idea, as it appears in the foregoing statements, was to "march upon" the enemy's left flank, to "threaten" his right flank, and at the same time to intercept his retreat. It was apparently expected that the enemy would retreat, or attempt to, at the slightest pressure on a flank. He was then, if possible, to be intercepted and captured on the heights of Fredericksburg, or if that was not possible, to be followed and harassed till he brought up against the Federal cavalry, and then to be crushed between that force holding him in front and Hooker's army falling on his rear.

The following instructions went to Stoneman at 9:10 a.m.:

. . . you will use all possible means of obtaining information in regard to the different routes leading from the Rappahannock Station into the interior and leaving Culpeper and Gordonsville to the right, the best place of crossing the Rapidan, the best roads, etc. . . . Also what information, if any, of the forces at Culpeper and Gordonsville. . . .

In the course of the day Hooker received a report from Stoneman that the people of the enemy's country were expecting an advance of Hooker's army on Gordonsville *via* Culpeper, that it was rumored that pontoon bridges had been thrown across the Upper Rappahannock for that purpose, and that there was probably a large force in front of Hooker at Fredericksburg.

He stated in reply:

. . . We know the strength of the enemy in front, and he is looking for us to advance in this vicinity.

He received the following telegram from Peck:

Longstreet is still here. Heavy artillery is coming to him from Petersburg. The storm has ceased; mud drying up. Advise me in cipher of as much as you deem proper of your operations.

To which he replied:

. . . I have communicated to no one what my intentions are. If you were here, I could properly and willingly impart them to you. So much is found

---

[1] *Rep. of Com.*, IV, 74, 75.

out by the enemy in my front with regard to movements, that I have concealed my designs from my own staff, and I dare not intrust them to the wires, knowing as I do that they are so often tapped.

Reference has already been made to the two years' and the nine months' men in Hooker's army whose time was to expire in the spring. These men, like all the volunteers, enlisted originally as state troops, and were subsequently mustered into the service of the United States. They were given to believe, it seems, that their period of service would be reckoned from the time when they enlisted as state troops; in other words, that they would be discharged the service of the United States two years after their enlistment in state regiments. On the 19th Hooker repaired to Washington to consult with the authorities on this question, and satisfied himself that they were not entitled to their discharge until two years from the time of their being mustered into the service of the United States. The men of the 5 N. Y. Volunteers, Duryee Zouaves, enlisted in the service of the state of New York April 23, 1861, and were mustered into the service of the United States May 9, 1861. They believed themselves entitled to their discharge from the service of the United States on the 23d of April, 1863. But on that day their colonel assembled them in a square, and read to them an order of Hooker's informing them that they would be held to service until May 9.[1] They took it in very bad grace. There were three years' men, too, in these two-year regiments who had been deceived, or had deceived themselves, into believing that they would be discharged with their regiments. They felt greatly aggrieved when notified that they would be transferred to other regiments to serve out their time. Many of the men thus disappointed resolved that they would not go into another battle.

About the 19th President Lincoln, Secretary Stanton, and General Halleck visited the army and spent a couple of days with it. Their presence in the camp was interpreted to mean an early move. It was intended to have, and doubtless did have, a favorable effect upon the dissatisfied men. Speeches were made which it was hoped would cause large numbers of the two years' and the nine months' men to decide to reënlist on the expiration of their terms of enlistment, but this hope was disappointed. On the 22d Hooker wrote to the Adjutant-General, U. S. Army, Washington, inclosing a list of the nine months' men and two years' men who were soon to be discharged by expiration of enlistment. Referring to them, he said:

. . . I have reason to believe but few, if any, will reënlist at this time. They appear to be of opinion that they will be under less restraint to retire from service before incurring new obligations, and that if they should conclude to re-

[1] G. O. No. 44, headquarters Army of the Potomac, April 20, 1863. See G. O. No. 85 for bounties offered in case of reënlistment (*W. R.*, 40, pp. 233, 234).

turn, they will be able to realize a larger bounty as substitutes for conscripts than is provided by law. The large bounties heretofore paid by the State and Federal Governments seem to be uppermost in their minds, and they will be likely to hold back for their recurrence. At all events, they are unwilling to reënlist now.

On the 24th of April, a general order from the Adjutant-General's office, Washington, directed that volunteer regiments about to be discharged be returned at the expiration of their terms of service to the states in which they were raised, and that they "turn over their arms and equipments" before leaving the army in which they served. The latter requirement caused dissatisfaction, as it deprived these troops of the privilege of parading on their way home with the arms which they had carried in the field.[1] This grievance was removed by an order issued from the headquarters of the Army of the Potomac on the 1st of May, when the army was engaged in active operations.[2]

[1] For the case of the 7 and 8 N. Y., which, on their return from two years of service in the Army of the Potomac, paraded in New York City without arms, see New York *Times*, April 29, 1863.

[2] "Pursuant to instructions which have been received from the War Department, hereafter regiments of volunteers leaving the field on account of expiration of term of service will be permitted to take their arms and accoutrements to the place of discharge, to be delivered to the governor of the state or to the officers appointed by him to receive them."

# PART II

PERIOD OF EXECUTION

# CHAPTER XIII

## Right Wing

THE following orders were issued for the grand turning movement:

### To Commanding Officers, XI and XII Corps, April 26

. . . the Eleventh and Twelfth Corps, in the order named, will begin their march at sunrise to-morrow morning, the former to encamp as near Kelley's Ford as practicable, without discovering itself to the enemy, and the latter as nearly in its rear as circumstances will permit. They will be established in their camps on or before 4 p.m. on Tuesday, the 28th instant. Corps commanders will be held responsible that the men are kept in camp and do not go to the river. . . .

### To Commanding Officer, V Corps, April 27, 1 a.m.

. . . your corps is to march to-morrow [to-day] so as to reach the vicinity of Kelley's Ford by Tuesday [28th] at 4 p.m. The corps of Generals Slocum [XII] and Howard [XI] take the same direction (and will be on the same route probably) from Hartwood.[1]

### To Commanding Officer, II Corps

The major-general commanding directs that you move at sunrise to-morrow morning two divisions of your corps to encamp as near as practicable to Banks' Ford without exposing your camps to the view of the enemy; that one brigade and one battery of one of these two divisions take position at United States Ford; the movement to be made quietly; the officers and men restrained from exhibiting themselves or making any show or appearance upon the river beyond the necessary picket duty. The division left in camp should be the one whose camps are most exposed to the view of the enemy. . . . [It] will be directed to keep up the picket line on the river and [to keep] in readiness to repel any attempt that may be made by the enemy to cross the river. Should the demonstration of the enemy prove of sufficient strength to indicate such a purpose, the Third Corps will be available for support. The division left in camp, as well as the divisions at Banks' and United States Fords, will be held in readiness to follow up any successful movements without delay. In moving from camp or breaking

---

[1] It had been originally proposed that General Meade with the V Corps should cross at United States Ford, as the XI and XII Corps moved down the river on the south bank. This idea was abandoned on the representation by Meade of difficulties likely to ensue.

camp, the practice of [making] large fires and burning camp rubbish will not be permitted.

The Rappahannock at Kelley's Ford was about 100 yards wide, and not fordable for infantry. For its passage bridges would be necessary. If these were brought up with the troops from the vicinity of Falmouth, the fact might become known to the enemy and betray the purpose of the march. This was probably why it was decided to have the bridge train brought by a better-concealed route. Captain Ludley of the 15 N. Y. Engineers was sent to-day to Washington with orders to get a canvas pontoon train and take it to Alexandria, and thence by rail to Bealeton, so as to arrive there by 10:30 a.m. to-morrow, the 28th.

No effort was to be made to lay the bridges at Banks' Ford until the night of the 29th, but they were to be held in readiness to be thrown across the river as soon as the enemy should leave the opposite bank.

Two ambulances only and the pack-train of small-arm ammunition were to accompany each division, except that the II Corps, having no pack-train, was allowed wagons for the transportation of small-arm ammunition. With this exception the wagon transportation was limited to "a small number" or "a few" to each corps to carry forage for the animals. The heavy trains of these divisions remained in rear of Falmouth.

While stealing a march to cross at Kelley's Ford, Hooker tried to appear to be preparing to cross at Banks' Ford and United States Ford. He wanted the enemy to learn of the movement of troops to the latter points. His precautions against the unnecessary exposure of these troops to the enemy's view were merely a trick to give the movement an air of seriousness, or a blind. These troops, which may be considered for the present as the center of Hooker's army, were intended to withdraw attention from the Federal right wing, but not from the left. They were to appear to the enemy as constituting about half of the Federal army and seeking by a demonstration or turning movement to facilitate the advance of the remainder directly against the lines of Fredericksburg.

The commanders of the V, XI, and XII Corps were enjoined to consider the information imparted to them regarding their respective destinations as "strictly confidential." No such injunction was placed upon the commander of the II Corps.

The V, XI, and XII Corps were limited in artillery to one battery per division; the portion of the II Corps directed up the river was to take with it "all the artillery attached to the two divisions" (two batteries per division), and the corps artillery, consisting of two batteries.

The artillery left behind, including the corps artillery of the XI Corps, was to be forwarded to the several corps after the successful execution of the turning movement.

The best road from Falmouth to United States Ford, and one that Hooker would naturally take, having regard to concealment, is the one through Hartwood Church. The V, XI, and XII Corps were assembled in the course of the day at this point (Map 7).

Medical Director Letterman, learning that only two ambulances per division were to accompany the troops, ordered all the other ambulances, and all the medicine and hospital wagons, to be taken to United States Ford and parked on the north side of the river.

The troops carried on their persons, as required by Hooker's circular of the 13th, eight days' field rations, except the beef for five days, which was driven along. The usual load of their haversacks had been three days' rations. They had carried five, but never more. Of the eight which they were now required to carry, they put five in their haversacks and three in their knapsacks. The men were stiff from their long encampment, and had not the strength and hardiness that might have been acquired from practice marches. The weight of the packs, as determined by certain quartermasters after the campaign, was about 45 pounds.[1] But these officers ignored all those personal belongings which a soldier thinks as important as many of the articles which he holds in trust for the government. No account was taken, for instance, of his towel or pocket-handkerchief, knife, pencil, pipe or tobacco, Bible or pack of cards, etc., or of the water or coffee in his canteen. The quartermaster of the VI Corps estimates the load of the soldier at from 56 to 60 pounds.[2] Swinton gives it as 60 pounds.[3]

The day was gloomy, rainy, and cold; the roads were in places almost impassable. The men made the short march to Hartwood Church in excellent spirits, but lining the road with overcoats and other articles thrown away as too heavy or cumbersome to be borne.[4] General Hooker passed through the camp late in the afternoon and was greeted with deafening cheers. The soldiers sang "Hooker is our Leader":

> The Union boys are moving on the left and on the right,
> The bugle-call is sounding, our shelters we must strike;
> Joe Hooker is our leader, he takes his whisky strong,
> So our knapsacks we will sling, and go marching along.[5]

The XI Corps was accompanied by 58 wagons, about twice as many as accompanied either of the other corps. A number of them were loaded with the knapsacks of Buschbeck's brigade at Kelley's Ford. Others carried extra rations. This corps had provided itself with ten

[1] *W. R.*, 40, p. 545.     [2] *Ib.*, 40, p. 554.
[3] *Campaigns of the Army of the Potomac*, p. 272.
[4] *Papers read before Illinois Commandery, Loyal Legion*, IV, 177.

[5] The whole song will be found in the *History of the Corn Exchange Regiment* (118 Pa. Vols.), by the Survivors' Assoc., p. 166.

days' supplies, or two days more than it was required or authorized to carry.[1]

It was expected that at the end of eight days, if not before, the troops would be joined by the main trains. These were loaded on an average with field rations for five days and grain for two, making, with the supplies accompanying the troops, subsistence for thirteen days and grain for eight. They contained also medical supplies and reserve ammunition for artillery and infantry. Besides the ammunition carried in the limbers and caissons, the artillery had from 100 to 150 rounds per piece in wagons of the main trains. The train of the V Corps remained at Stoneman's Switch. That of the XII Corps marched to the vicinity of Banks' Ford. That of the XI, which was required by order to do likewise, was parked at a road junction about a mile east of Berea Church by order of the corps commander.[2]

The 140 rounds of infantry ammunition prescribed by Hooker's circulars to be provided per man were carried as follows: 60 on the person (40 in cartridge-boxes, 20 in pockets of clothing), 20 on pack-mules, 60 in wagons of main trains.

Pursuant to instructions from Hooker, General Hunt, his chief of artillery, made a reconnaissance of the enemy's position at Banks' Ford, and determined upon the number and position of the guns to be placed there "to enfilade the enemy's rifle-pits; to crush the fire of his work on the hill overlooking the river; to cover the throwing of the bridges at that ford; and to protect the crossing of the troops."[3] The necessary instructions for placing the pieces, preparing cover for them, and taking command of the artillery at this point were given by Hunt to his inspector of artillery, Major A. Doul. Two batteries of position from the General Reserve (Brooker's four 4½-inch guns and von Blücher's four 20-pounders), and the batteries left behind by the II, XI, and XII Corps, were posted accordingly by the major.

One regiment of the V Corps $\left(\frac{20}{3.\ 1.\ V}\right)$ was left in camp at Falmouth on account of its having the smallpox.[4]

---

[1] Report of chief quartermaster, XI Corps, *W. R.*, 40, p. 555. Howard says in his *Autobiography* (I, 353):

"Our orders were very strict to keep down the trains to the smallest number for ammunition and forage only. I found that on that march several of my subordinate commanders had been very careless in not carrying out these instructions to the letter. General Hooker and his staff passed my trains during the march and said to me: 'General Meade has done better than you.' Of course I had issued the orders, but field officers would here and there slip in an extra wagon till there were many; for where were they to get their meals, if ration wagons were all left behind? This condition I quickly corrected, but it was my first mortification in this campaign. Some of the American officers were as careless as some of the foreign in the matter of orders —glorious in eye-service, but conscienceless when out of sight."

There is good reason, as we shall see, for questioning the assertion that the trains were quickly reduced to proper size.

[2] *W. R.*, 39, p. 632, and 40, pp. 557, 558.
[3] *Ib.*, 39, p. 246.    [4] *Ib.*, 39, p. 519.

In compliance with instructions from Halleck, General Stahel, with the 2d and 3d brigades of his cavalry division and a battery of four guns, marched from Fairfax Court-House to 2 miles beyond Middleburg. This movement, which the enemy might take for a reconnaissance to clear the way for Stoneman's cavalry into the Shenandoah Valley, was intended to hold in check the Confederate troops remaining in the Valley. Federal troops were being sent from the Valley westward to meet Jones and Imboden.

Stoneman forwarded to headquarters the result of the "inquiries and investigations into the character and nature of the country lying south of the Rappahannock and east of the Orange and Alexandria Railroad." He reported in part:

The roads leading out from Kelley's, Kemper's, and Barnett's Fords are country roads, and tolerably good in dry weather. There is a very good road leading from Culpeper Court-House to Germanna Mills [or Ford], on the Rapidan River, *via* Stevensburg, and another from the Court-House to Raccoon Ford, on the same river. The fords over the Rapidan River are numerous, and their practicability depends entirely upon the stage of water in the streams. The banks are generally rolling, open, and well cultivated, and the whole of it, as far north as Culpeper Court-House, is overlooked and in plain view from the top of Clark's mountain, on the top of which mountain the enemy has a telegraph station (signal).[1] . . .

The inhabitants of Culpeper Court-House have been leaving for the Shenandoah Valley. These fleeing inhabitants, as also the prisoners which have fallen into our hands, would lead us to suppose that the enemy expected an attack from this direction, but I am assured by yourself that such is not the case.

If Hooker meant that the enemy was not looking for an advance upon Gordonsville, he was mistaken. A correspondent in the field wrote as follows:

The rebels seem to regard Hooker's designs against Gordonsville as impolitic, and likely to result disastrously, saying that the "Confederates are making Gordonsville stronger than Fredericksburg was, and that we will discover [that] it is not the easiest way of getting to Richmond." . . . The blacks, as a general rule, come voluntarily forward, and disclose such facts as they deem to our advantage to be apprised of, oftentimes at much personal risk to themselves, for their masters threaten them with summary vengeance for all such acts. The owners regard their slaves with marked distrust.

Stoneman's reconnaissances have cleared up the country as far as the Rapidan. Beyond that line its most notable feature is a dense tangled forest of pine and oak interspersed with black-jack and other scrub growths, known as the Wilderness. A single good road, the Plank Road, leads from Fredericksburg westward, leaving comparatively open

[1] A station for flag or torch signaling.

country behind it, and enters the Wilderness at a place called Salem Church. About a mile beyond this point, or a half-mile from Tabernacle Church, it divides into two branches. The southern branch is the continuation of the Plank Road, and retains its name; the northern branch is known as the Turnpike. These two roads come together at Chancellorsville, about 4 miles from Tabernacle Church, or 10 miles from Fredericksburg. They continue one road to a point about 3 miles distant called Wilderness Church, where they separate as before, forming the two roads which connect this region with Orange Court-House, on the Orange and Alexandria Railroad.

Chancellorsville consists of a single brick dwelling, and owes its importance to the meeting here of several roads. Around this house is an irregular cleared space of about 100 acres, or extending about 200 or 300 yards in every direction. A road of inferior quality, known as the River Road, runs from Fredericksburg along the river to the vicinity of Mineral Spring Run, and thence to Chancellorsville.

### Left Wing

Instructions sent to Sedgwick, commanding the I, III, and VI Corps (left wing), were received about 6 p.m.

The three corps were to be in position to cross the river as follows:

I and VI Corps, at or before 3:30 a.m. the 29th—the former at Fitzhugh's Crossing, the latter at Franklin's Crossing.

III Corps, as a support, at or before 4:30 a.m. the 29th—at either of the forementioned crossings. The ambulances and trains to be parked in the rear, and concealed behind the range of hills that was visible to the enemy, and to be ready to move when desired. The troops, as far as possible, to be concealed until they executed the demonstration which was to follow. The necessary batteries of the corps and of the General Artillery Reserve to be placed in position under direction of General Hunt to cover the crossing. . . . Two bridges to be laid at each crossing under the supervision of General Benham before 3:30 a.m. the 29th. Any troops needed to assist the Engineer Brigade in the performance of this duty to be furnished to General Benham, under the direction of General Sedgwick. A demonstration in full force to be made on the morning of the 29th with a view to securing the Telegraph Road and barring that route to Richmond. In the event of the enemy detaching any considerable part of his force against the troops operating toward Chancellorsville, Sedgwick was to attack and carry the works in his front at all hazards, and establish his force on the Telegraph Road to prevent the enemy's turning his position on that road and gaining the route to Richmond. In case the enemy should succeed in doing this or should previously fall back on Richmond, Sedgwick was to pursue him with the utmost vigor.

It was suggested that, in case the enemy retired, a force be thrown on the Bowling Green Road and pursuit be made both on that road and on the Telegraph Road.

The 155 Pa. at Banks' and United States Fords was replaced by troops of the "Irish brigade," commanded by General Meagher. Two regiments $\left(\frac{69, 116}{2. 1. II}\right)$ were posted at United States Ford and two $\left(\frac{63, 88}{2. 1. II}\right)$ at Banks' Ford. The remaining regiment (28 Mass.) camped at Hartwood Church *en route* to United States Ford. Detachments of these regiments were distributed among the houses through the country, with instructions to keep the inhabitants from leaving their vicinity, and so prevent their giving information to the enemy.

In preparation for supporting the II Corps, if necessary, the following dispatch was sent to the commander of the III Corps:

The commanding general directs that you have your command in readiness to move early to-morrow [28th] with the subsistence (eight days) and ammunition prescribed by existing orders for the march. Further instructions will be sent to you later in the day.

This corps was reviewed to-day by a number of distinguished visitors who were received at Hooker's headquarters yesterday. The reviewing party consisted of Secretary Seward; the Swedish minister; the secretary of the Swedish legation; the Prussian minister; Mr. Peale, examiner of patents; Mr. French, second auditor of the Treasury; Mr. F. W. Seward, Assistant Secretary of State; the Governor of Maine; the Governor of New Jersey; General Hooker and staff, and a large body of civilians. The line was formed at 10 o'clock, the regiments having only company front. The artillery was formed in the rear, and the transportation in another part of the field. Notwithstanding this contracted formation, the infantry alone presented a mile and a half of army blue, gaily relieved by the regimental colors and the designating flags of brigades and divisions. Secretary Seward and the Swedish secretary rode on horseback with General Hooker and staff. The rest of the party were in two carriages, drawn by four horses each.

The troops appeared in heavy marching order, with knapsacks and haversacks packed. For nearly an hour, as the solid column filed by, General Hooker was enabled to entertain his foreign visitors with accounts of the exploits of its organizations.

A noticeable feature of the review was the excellent appearance of the transportation of the corps, embracing over 400 wagons, with a long string of pack-animals. After the review and a lunch at General Hooker's headquarters the visitors returned to Washington.

At 3:30 p.m. Lincoln telegraphed to Hooker:

How does it look now?

Hooker replied at 5 p.m.:

I am not sufficiently advanced to give an opinion. We are busy. Will tell you all as soon as I can, and will have it satisfactory.

Lee wrote to President Davis:

I feel by no means strong, and from the condition of our horses and the amount of our supplies, I am unable even to act on the defensive as vigorously as circumstances may require. A report sent me last night by Major Norris of the signal corps at Richmond, and which probably may have been submitted to you, states the strength of General Hooker's army to be from 150,000 to 160,000,[1] and that reënforcements had been sent him from Baltimore, Washington, Alexandria, and Harper's Ferry. Though bodies of troops heretofore retained in Maryland to keep that state in subjection, I believe, have been forwarded to General Hooker, still I think his numbers much exaggerated. But this report, said to be brought by a special scout from Washington, corroborates all previous intelligence showing that troops from the rear have been moved to the Rappahannock. This would indicate a forward movement of the Federal Army.

A dispatch last night from General Stuart, dated 2 p.m., 26th instant, states that General Stoneman is encamped at Warrenton Springs.

A brigade of infantry (Federal) is guarding Rappahannock Bridge and Beverly and Kelley's Fords, and trains over the Orange and Alexandria Railroad were arriving hourly without bringing troops, so far as known. He may intend to push his cavalry along by that route [toward Culpeper Court-House and Gordonsville], while his infantry attempt to seize this.

And to Longstreet:

Can you give me any idea when your operations will be completed and whether any of the troops you have in North Carolina can be spared from there?[2]

Major Norris, Chief Signal Officer, C. S. A., telegraphed to Longstreet and doubtless to Lee:

Washington is almost stripped of its garrison. Mules with pack-saddles for ammunition have been sent to him [Hooker]. Hooker is going to cross the river at three points—two above and one below [Fredericksburg].[3]

The Chief Signal Officer of the Army of the Potomac, Captain S. T. Cushing, was directed by the Chief of Staff to extend the telegraph line from headquarters to Banks' Ford and to Franklin's Crossing. Beyond this no intimation was given him as to any projected movement. He asked for information as to the general course of operations, but

---

[1] Doubtless the estimate referred to by Hooker in his letter to the Secretary of War, April 21 (page 162 *ante*).

[2] *W. R.*, 26, pp. 1024, 1025.

[3] Banks' Ford and United States Ford above, and probably Franklin's Crossing below. J. B. Jr.

none was granted him. He was simply informed that the work ordered should be accomplished by night. The line that was to extend to Franklin's Crossing went *via* Phillips House to Tyler's Hill, where Sedgwick had his headquarters. The station at Tyler's Hill was ready for operation at 4:30 p.m., but was not operated to-day. The line to Banks' Ford was arrested by the Federal pickets at a point near England, about 2 miles from Banks' Ford. It was ready for operation by night. Imagining that a portion of the army would cross at or near Banks' Ford, Captain Cushing directed Captain B. H. Fisher of the Signal Corps to be at Banks' Ford at dawn on the 28th, and take charge of all signal operations with the right wing of the army. Signal stations (flag and torch) were now established watching the movements of the enemy from the England House, the Phillips House, the Seddon House, and opposite Buckner's Neck. Only the latter two, it seems, communicated with each other. The one at the Phillips House was equipped with a powerful telescope.

The departure of the V, XI, and XII Corps from their winter quarters may have been known this evening throughout the Army of the Potomac. But where they were going, and when the remainder of the army would move, and in what direction, were generally a mystery. Hooker's orders to his corps and wing commanders did not divulge his general plan. His messages to commanders in the right wing contained, so far as known, no reference to the orders issued for the left wing, and *vice versa.*

To-night Hooker sent for Couch, and explained to him, as next in rank, his plan of campaign. He informed Couch that, under certain contingencies, the right wing would be placed under his command.[1]

Lee's dispositions were the same as they had been during the winter (Map 2), except that Early's division of Jackson's corps $\left(\frac{3}{11}\right)$ had moved up the Rappahannock to the lines of Fredericksburg, and W. H. F. Lee's brigade of cavalry had gone up to Brandy Station, leaving only the 15 Va. in the vicinity of Port Royal.

What would Lee have done, had he at this time known the plan of operation which Hooker was starting to execute? During the last three months he must have spent many hours in thinking of manœuvers that Hooker might attempt against him, but the one that was now under way had never, it would seem, suggested itself to him; nor apparently did he ever express himself as to how, had it done so, he would have planned to meet it. On the latter point some speculation may not be unprofitable. Lee could hardly undertake to oppose Hooker in force at Kelley's Ford without exposing his depots and the Richmond and Fredericksburg Railroad to capture and destruction, or the fractions of his army, one at Fredericksburg and one at Kelley's Ford, to

[1] *B. and L., III, 157.*

separate attack and defeat.  It seems probable that he would have left a minor portion of his army in the lines of Fredericksburg to oppose Sedgwick, and established the major portion somewhere between Chancellorsville and the Rapidan to meet and repel the Federal right wing under Hooker.

It may be assumed that Hooker's chief concern for the present is:

1. That his columns may reach the Rapidan before Lee can take position to oppose its passage.

2. That he may strike a decisive blow before Longstreet can be brought up to Lee's assistance.

# CHAPTER XIV

## Right Wing

BUTTERFIELD wrote to Stoneman at Warrenton Junction:

One of Colonel Sharpe's[1] men just in from Kelley's Ford says, in his opinion, no large body of infantry there. Held mostly by cavalry and artillery. Rebel sympathizers on this side believe enemy have fallen back beyond Rapidan, meaning to make that their line of defence. . . . They think our cavalry move a feint, and that the crossing will be made at United States Ford, where they are still at work.

The cavalry brigade left with Pleasonton (Devin's) marched this morning to Grove Church, whence at 5 a.m. its commander wrote to Pleasonton:

We arrived here at 4 a.m.[2] . . . made a reconnaissance in person (after halting and feeding horses and men) to Ellis' Ford. Woke up their infantry, who came down into the rifle-pits and drew bead on us. . . . Picketed near Ellis', Kemper's, and Field's, and communicated on the right with a brigade of Howard's, between Kelley's and Rappahannock. Found no [Confederate] picket at the fords between Richards' and Kelley's. . . . The report among contrabands [negroes] here is that at the fords the water has been filled with iron wirework, calculated to entangle the feet of horses, while the sharpshooters pop them off. They say they have things fixed for our cavalry now. . . .

A battalion of the 2 N. Y. Cavalry (1. 3. C) reconnoitered from Warrenton Junction northeastward as far as Brentsville (Map 1, sheet A), capturing several guerillas;[3] and Stahel's division marched from Middleburg to Rectortown, Salem, White Plains, and back, taking a number of prisoners, mostly from Mosby.

The First and Third Divisions of the II Corps, with two ambulances per division, three batteries of divisional artillery,[4] and the two batteries of corps artillery, marched to the vicinity of Banks' Ford.

---

[1] Colonel G. H. Sharpe, Deputy Provost-Marshal-General, Chief of Secret Service.

[2] Official publication reads *p.m.*, evidently an error. J. B. Jr.

[3] *Three Years in the Federal Cavalry,* by Willard Glazier, p. 175.

[4] Thomas' and Pettit's (1. II), Arnold's (2. II). According to Hooker's orders,

The 5 N. H. and 81 Pa. (1. 1. II) were sent out, under Colonel Cross of the former regiment, to picket houses and roads to United States Ford, in order to prevent information from going to the enemy. The two regiments occupied 41 dwelling-houses and a number of roads. They found the occupants of the houses full of suppressed hostility, but civil.[1]

The troops carried, on their persons or on the hoof, rations as pre-scribed, for eight days. The small-arm ammunition was carried in a train of 70 wagons. A supply-train of 45 wagons carried forage for six days and hospital stores, though the orders limited the forage to a sup-ply for four or five days, and precluded the carrying of hospital stores in wagons. The remainder of the trains, containing five days' field rations and two days' grain, was parked in rear of Falmouth. The con-tents of all the trains, with what the troops had on their backs and on the hoof, would supply the command with subsistence for thirteen days and with forage for eight. Carroll's brigade $(\frac{1}{3.\,\text{II}})$, Ames' battery $(\frac{1}{3.\,\text{II}})$, and the train for two bridges near Falmouth went to United States Ford; Meagher's brigade $(\frac{2}{1.\,\text{II}})$ assembled at Banks' Ford. While a pretence of crossing was made at this point by throwing up works, etc.,[2] large working parties were employed repairing the road to United States Ford. The Second Division (Gibbon's) remained in position opposite Fredericksburg with two batteries.[3]

The III Corps remained with the left wing under Sedgwick. The "further instructions" which were to have been sent yesterday "later in the day," to the commander of this corps, were not sent—proba-bly to avoid drawing forces of the enemy toward Banks' or United States Ford. Hooker expected that the arrival of his right wing on the Rapidan would cause the enemy to withdraw his troops from United States Ford and that the further advance of that wing, reënforced by his center, would dispose in like manner of the enemy at Banks' Ford. He repaired to Morrisville to superintend in person the passage of the Rappahannock at Kelley's Ford. About 2 p.m. he there issued the fol-lowing instructions:

### To Slocum, commanding XI and XII Corps

. . . so long as the Eleventh and Twelfth Corps are operating on the same line, you will exercise the command of both.

The general directs that the Eleventh Corps cross to the opposite side of the river to-night, and that the Twelfth Corps commence crossing at daylight to-morrow morning, and to be thrown over with all possible rapidity, and both corps marched by the most direct route without delay and seize the bridge, if

---

each division was to be accompanied by its own artillery. Arnold's battery for some reason took the place of Adams' battery of the Third Division.

[1] *History of the 5th Regiment N. H. Vol-unteers,* by William Child, pp. 179, 181.
[2] *W. R.,* 39, p. 306.
[3] Brown's (2. II), Adams' (3. II).

standing, and the ford, at Germanna Mills. He suggests that you make use of a cavalry regiment and three or four smart marching [infantry] regiments to execute this duty and that you cross both of your corps over the Rapidan River to-morrow. You will find guides in General Pleasonton's cavalry.

Major-General Meade will move on almost a parallel line at the same time, and will be in easy communication with you. He will cross [the Rapidan] at Ely's Ford. If his passage should be disputed, as you will probably be able to learn from the firing, or through your communication with that officer, the general directs that you dispatch a corps along the south bank of the Rapidan, to knock away the enemy, to enable him to cross, and when the Fifth Corps is across, that you push on with both of your corps to Chancellorsville, at which point the three corps will come together and you will command by virtue of your seniority.

The enemy have a brigade[1] holding the United States Ford, which they will abandon as soon as they hear of your approach. This will open the United States Ford to us, when bridges will at once be thrown across the river, and will afford you a direct communication with headquarters. Telegraphic communication is established from that point [United States Ford to headquarters].[2] If your cavalry is well advanced from Chancellorsville, you will be able to ascertain whether or not the enemy is detaching forces from behind Fredericksburg to resist your advance. If [he is] not [doing so] in any considerable force, the general desires that you will endeavor to advance at all hazards, securing a position on the Plank road, and uncovering Banks' Ford, which is also defended by a brigade of the rebel infantry $\left(\frac{4}{1.1}\right)$ and a battery $\left(\frac{2}{1.1}\right)$. If the enemy should be greatly reënforced you will then select a strong position, and compel him to attack you on your ground. You will have nearly 40,000 men, which is more than he can spare to send against you.[3] Every incident of your advance you will communicate to the general as soon as communication is established by the United States Ford. Two aides-de-camp are sent to report to you for this service. You are already advised of the operations going on below Fredericksburg.

The general desires that not a moment be lost until our troops are established at or near Chancellorsville. From that moment all will be ours. A copy of this will be furnished Major-General Meade.

It will be much easier to replenish batteries, ammunition, etc., by Banks' Ford than by the United States Ford, if you should succeed in uncovering it.

Here we see the first reference in a communication to an officer of the right wing to what is going on in the left wing, and Hooker's first reference to the possibility of the enemy's assuming the offensive. If the enemy advanced in force, Slocum was to renounce the offensive, take up a strong position, and compel the enemy to attack him on his own ground. How was he to effect such compulsion? He could only do it, if at all, by cutting every line by which Lee might retreat. "The general desires," says the order, "that not a moment be lost until our

[1] Two brigades and a battery. J. B. Jr.
[2] This was a mistake.
[3] Testifying about a year later before the Committee on the Conduct of the War,

Hooker gave the strength of the three corps as probably not exceeding 36,000 men. Adding 1000 for the cavalry would give for the whole command about 37,000.

troops are established at or near Chancellorsville. *From that moment all will be ours.''* The possession of Chancellorsville would give him Lee's shortest line of retreat to Gordonsville, but unless the neighboring roads by which Chancellorsville might be turned under cover of the surrounding forest were watched and guarded, this would not cut Lee off from Gordonsville. Moreover, assuming that it did, it would leave him his line of retreat to Richmond. Hooker had no designs apparently against the latter. He supposed that his occupation of Chancellorsville would compel Lee to attack him.

In case the enemy did not advance in force, he would proceed beyond Chancellorsville for the immediate purpose of opening communication by Banks' Ford and taking up a position across the Plank Road. What he meant to do afterward he neither states nor intimates. The following dispatches were sent about this time:

### To Comstock, Chief Engineer

. . . as soon as the Fifth Corps have crossed the bridge [at Kelley's Ford], you will call on Major-General Meade for the necessary details to enable you to take it up and prepare it for land transportation, and have it accompany the column of that officer for service at the Rapidan, if required. After that, and as soon as the United States Ford is uncovered, he desires it to be thrown across the Rappahannock at that point, in order to open a short communication with headquarters, and also to enable Couch's [II] Corps to cross should circumstances render it expedient.[1]

### To Meade, commanding Fifth Corps

. . . you will exercise all your accustomed zeal and devotion in hastening the passage of the troops across the Rappahannock. He feels assured that you will.

It is a great object to effect the passage of the Rapidan to-morrow, as you well know; and in so doing the United States Ford will be uncovered, and our line of communication established with the left wing of the army.

I inclose herewith copies of instructions to Major-General Slocum, Brigadier-General Pleasonton, and Captain Comstock, and also reports of the strength of the enemy's forces holding fords on the Rappahannock above its junction with the Rapidan. I hope that you will be able to pick up some of them. Use your cavalry freely, and send them well out, to bring you timely information. Would it not be well to detach a division to seize the ford [Ely's]? From the most reliable information in our possession, the ford must be a good one now. The cavalry can ascertain.

The general will join you as soon as he can—probably not until the United States Ford is opened. A portion of Couch's corps [II] now hold it on our side. The general will direct two aides-de-camp to report to you to furnish him with information. Use them freely. . . .

[1] The support of the II Corps might not be deemed necessary to carry the right wing from the Rapidan to the rear of Fredericksburg, where it would open up Banks' Ford. In that case this corps might be sent back to Banks' Ford to cross there, as that point is nearer United States Ford by the north than by the south bank.

The right wing, with the XI Corps in front, the XII next, and the V last, marched to the vicinity of Mount Holly Church, about 2 miles from Kelley's Ford. It rained almost all day, making the roads difficult and the packs heavy. Advantage was taken of every halt to throw away overcoats, knapsacks, or other articles of equipment that had become intolerable.[1] The XI Corps, which started at 4 a.m., was formed up in camp at 4 p.m. The V Corps did not all get in until after 10 o'clock. The distance marched was about 17 miles.

Every house along the route that might possibly harbor a disloyal man or woman was put under guard. So there was reason to believe that the movement had not been observed by the enemy. The men of Buschbeck's brigade, at Kelley's Ford, welcomed the arriving troops, and encouraged them with the prospect of an easy passage in the morning.

Slocum, who commanded the XI and XII Corps, issued the following instructions to Howard, commanding the XI:

. . . you will cross the river at Kelley's Ford at the earliest possible moment to-night. You will report to me as soon as your troops commence crossing, and also immediately after the crossing is effected. As soon as you have effected a crossing, you will take a defensive position, and await the crossing of the Twelfth Corps, which will precede you on the road to Germanna Bridge [Ford]. You will hold your command in readiness, and follow immediately in their rear. Keep your column well closed, with all your baggage-wagons in rear of your entire corps, except your rear-guards. Have two batteries accompany your leading brigades [in your several columns?].

Pleasonton received the following order:

. . . report with your command of cavalry [Devin's brigade] to Major-General Slocum, for service with his command. A portion of your force will accompany his command; and a portion will be sent to report for duty with the Fifth Corps, and will report to Major-General Meade.

Having reported to Slocum and received his orders, Pleasonton ordered Devin at Grove Church to send the 17 Pa. to report to Howard, to draw in his pickets, and concentrate the rest of his brigade in the neighborhood of Mount Holly Church; also to furnish guides acquainted with the country to Generals Howard and Meade.

The bridge train of canvas boats (advance-guard train) coming from Washington arrived at 5:30. At 7 p.m. the 15 N. Y. Engineers, assisted by men of the XI Corps, commenced laying it under the direction of Captain Comstock of the Engineer Corps. General Hooker was also present superintending this work. About 400 men of Buschbeck's brigade of the XI Corps manned a number of boats concealed in Marsh

---

[1] *History of the 22 Mass. Infantry,* by J. L. Parker, p. 284.

Run, crossed the river in them below the ford, and cleared the opposite bank. At 10 p.m. the troops commenced crossing, the XI Corps taking the lead.[1] The 17 Pa. Cavalry, accompanying the advance, was ordered to send scouts and patrols up the different roads, and picket the front. At midnight Schurz's division and part of Devens' (3, 1) had crossed.[2] Pleasonton's order to Devin had been carried out except that the 8 Pa. Cavalry and brigade headquarters had not arrived at Holly Church.

The Confederate pickets at Kelley's Ford were captured. The men in support, being stationed further back, made their escape; but their communication with the lower pickets was cut off, and so they could not give them the alarm.

W. H. F. Lee's brigade (except the 10 and 15 Va.) was at Brandy Station; Fitzhugh Lee's brigade (except one regiment at Stevensburg) and the horse artillery were at Culpeper Court-House. W. H. F. Lee sent forward the 13 Va. to meet the advancing infantry. By 9 o'clock p.m. Stuart at Culpeper Court-House (Map 8) received a report that Federal troops were making preparations to cross at Kelley's Ford, but their number was concealed by darkness, and he would not leave his position to determine it, for fear of exposing the country in his rear, especially the railroads, to depredations by Federal cavalry. So far as he could observe, the crossing at Kelley's Ford might be but a diversion in favor of such operations. He accordingly ordered the enemy to be enveloped with pickets to observe the direction which he took, and ordered the concentration of his command at Brandy Station by daylight.

The following order was sent to Stoneman:

. . . the instructions communicated for your government on the 12th instant are so far modified as to require you to cross the Rappahannock at such points as you may determine between Kelley's and Rappahannock Fords, and including them, and for a portion of your force to move in the direction of the Raccoon Ford and Louisa Court-House, while the remainder is engaged in carrying into execution that part of your original instructions which relates to the enemy's force and [in?] position on the line of the Orange and Alexandria Railroad and the line itself, the operations of this column to be considered as masking the column which is directed to move by forced marches to strike and destroy the line of the Aquia and Richmond Railroad.

You are further directed to determine on some point for the columns to unite, and it is recommended that it be on the Pamunkey and near that line, as you will

---

[1] According to Howard the bridge was not completed before 10 p.m. (W. R., 39, p. 627). According to Benham it was completed at 7:45 p.m. (ib., p. 215). It is inadvertently omitted from Maps 8 and 9.

[2] This statement is based upon vague and meager data. I have found no statement of the order in which the divisions crossed.

Schurz says that the XI Corps "crossed before midnight" (Reminiscences, II, 408). A historian of the 26 Wisc., 2d brigade, Schurz's division, says that his regiment crossed "at midnight" (Wisconsin in the War of the Rebellion, by W. De Love, p. 397). According to two joint historians of the 153 Pa., 1st brigade, Devens' division,

there be in position with your full force to cut off the retreat of the enemy by his shortest line. In all other respects your instructions as before referred to will remain the same.

You will direct all your force to cross to-night, or, if that should not be practicable, to be brought to the river, and have it all thrown over before 8 o'clock to-morrow morning. If the fords should be too deep for your pack-animals and artillery, they will be crossed over the bridge at Kelley's Ford. You will please furnish the officers in command of these two columns with a copy of this and of your original instructions.[1]

Under this order Stoneman's latitude in the selection of a point of crossing was restricted to certain definite limits between Kelley's and Rappahannock Fords; he was required to be across by 8 o'clock in the morning, to divide his command into two columns, and to determine on some point for the columns, after the destruction of the Richmond, Fredericksburg and Potomac Railroad, to unite at and intercept the retreat of Lee's army.[2]

The cavalry corps was accordingly formed in two columns. One consisted of Averell's division, Davis' brigade of Pleasonton's division, and Tidball's battery of horse artillery. This column numbered about 3400 sabers and 6 guns, and was commanded by Averell. The other consisted of Gregg's division, Buford's reserve brigade, to which the 6 Pa. had been attached, and a provisional battery of horse artillery under Captain Robertson. It numbered about 4200 sabers and 6 guns, and was commanded directly by Stoneman. The provisional battery was formed by taking a section from Elder's, Clarke's, and Vincent's batteries. The remaining sections of these batteries were sent back to Falmouth.

The foregoing order was given to Stoneman at Hooker's headquarters at 5:45 p.m.

From Morrisville to where the cavalry corps lay was 13 miles, from there to where some of the extreme pickets were was 13 more, so that it was quite late at night before the command was all assembled and ready to start.

The head of Stoneman's column started, however, at 5 p.m., and the head of Averell's at 10 p.m.;[3] the former directed upon Kelley's Ford,

this regiment completed its crossing by midnight, following Schurz's division (*The Volunteer's Manual,* by W. Simmers and P. Bachschmied, p. 20). Devens says that his division crossed "at 1 a.m. on the morning of April 29." J. B. Jr.

[1] *W. R.,* 39, p. 1065.

[2] "I concluded to divide the cavalry into two columns, each one outnumbering the entire cavalry force of the enemy between the Rappahannock and James Rivers. They were to cross the Rappahannock the same day with the infantry, the 29th, and one column was to move directly to its destination, while the other was threatening Culpeper and Gordonsville, and as soon as one had passed, the other was to follow and join it. . . . The object was to have no time lost in severing Lee's communications with Richmond" (Hooker, *Rep. of Com.,* IV, 137).

[3] *W. R.,* 39, pp. 1058, 1081, 1074. The following statement of the experience of one

the latter upon Rappahannock Ford.  Averell was to cross on his arrival at the ford, and await orders.  At midnight most of the corps was
resting at or near Bealeton.

Meade, who was to take the road to Ely's Ford, issued the following
order to his corps, the V:

The order of march for to-morrow, 29th instant, will be, first, Griffin's division; second, Sykes' division; third, Humphreys' division.  Brigadier-General
Griffin will be prepared to move at 7 a.m.  He will send a staff officer at daylight
to communicate with Major-General Slocum, in order to ascertain the earliest
moment at which the road to Kelley's Ford will be open.  Major-General Sykes
will move at 7 a.m. and close up on Griffin's division.  He will place his battery
in front of his column, prepared to move forward, to report to General Griffin
in case its services are required.  Brigadier-General Humphreys will move immediately after General Sykes.  He will furnish the necessary details to Captain
Comstock to take up the pontoon bridge.  When taken up he will place the
pontoon train in his own train between his brigades, and so dispose his artillery
as to cover to the best advantage the rear of the column, the protection of which
he has the especial charge [of].  All officers are earnestly enjoined to keep their
commands well closed, and prevent all straggling.  Under instructions of the
commanding general, this command will be called on to-morrow to make a long
and rapid march.  The major-general commanding the corps fully relies upon
every man cheerfully submitting to the exertions he will be called upon to make
for the purpose of securing the success which it is earnestly hoped and believed
will attend the movement.[1]

## Left Wing

The left wing (I, III, VI Corps) was to break camp this morning, but
on account of the rain no movement was made until noon, when the
I Corps took up the march.  The VI Corps followed about 3 p.m., and
the III about 5 p.m.  On this march as well as on that to Kelley's Ford,
the roads were lined at every halt with equipments thrown away.  The
I Corps halted at Fitzhugh's Crossing about 5:30 p.m., and the VI
Corps at Franklin's Crossing about 9 p.m., and the III Corps between
these two corps and somewhat in rear of them, also about 9 p.m.  The
trains of the I and VI Corps were parked about a mile in rear of their
respective corps.  The train of the III Corps remained to-day parked
near Falmouth.

Sedgwick received the following communications:

of Stoneman's regiments may be applicable
to others: "About 5 o'clock in the evening
of the 28th, 5 days' rations and 3 days' forage were issued, and orders to hold the
regiment in readiness to move at a moment's notice.  Tents were immediately
struck, wagons loaded, horses saddled, and
the whole command ordered to stand to
horse, and await orders.  Hour after hour

passed, finding us in the same position;
midnight, and we were still impatiently
waiting, and wondering why we did not
move.  Near midnight rain began to fall,
and continued with increased severity as
the day dawned" (*Annals of the 6 Pa. Cavalry*, by Rev. S. L. Gracey, Chaplain of the
Regiment, p. 136).

[1] *W. R.*, 107, p. 1014.

*From Butterfield*

The major-general commanding has left for the scene of operation above. . . .

Signal officers have been directed to be vigilant and watchful and to report everything. I shall keep you fully advised of everything that is reported here at Falmouth. Have you any wishes or commands? . . .

The night before last, April 26, Rodes' (D. H. Hill's) division had not moved. A. P. Hill's and Trimble's[1] also, and there are no signs of a move. This from deserters who have just come in.[2]

*From Williams, Adjutant-General*

. . . your operations for to-morrow are for a demonstration only, to hold the forces of the enemy while the operations are carried on above, unless the enemy should leave the position, or should weaken his force materially by detachments.

As long as the enemy remained in position back of Fredericksburg, Sedgwick was to demonstrate to deter him, if possible, from moving, but not to attack. Should the enemy retreat, Sedgwick was to pursue. Should the enemy turn against the right wing, Sedgwick was to attack and establish himself on the Telegraph Road, and the right wing was to be reënforced with troops from the left. But the left wing might draw the main force of the enemy upon itself. It must try to anticipate this, and not expose itself to a serious attack. Under some apprehension on this score, Hooker wrote to Butterfield from Morrisville at 3 p.m.:

Considering the [backward] state of affairs here, it will be advisable to suspend the crossing of the troops under Sedgwick and Reynolds until further orders, except the number necessary to protect the bridges after they are thrown, which will be [thrown] as already directed. Be pleased to have it [this] communicated.

The dispatch was transmitted to Sedgwick at 11:45 p.m. Brooks' division ($\frac{1}{VI}$) had already been selected by Sedgwick to protect the bridges of the VI Corps, and the following order to Brooks, commanding First Division, was probably issued about as the corps went into bivouac:

. . . you will have your division in the immediate vicinity of Franklin's Crossing at 11 p.m., ready to cross in boats and hold the ground on the opposite side until the bridges are completed. You will not move from the heights on this side of the river until you have the cover of the darkness. The crossing in the boats must be effected with the utmost celerity and in the strictest silence. General Benham will indicate to you the exact time and place of crossing.[3]

From the top of the ridge on which Sedgwick's lines were formed the ground sloped abruptly to the river, gullied here and there by ravines

---

[1] Commanded by Colston.          [2] *W. R.*, 107, p. 1015.          [3] *Ib.*

running obliquely to the base of the ridge. Through several of these ravines roads had been built which enabled the Federal artillery and pontoon trains to reach the comparatively level ground adjacent to the river. About dusk the pontoon trains halted on the level ground at the edge of a piece of timber about two thirds of a mile from the water. At 10 o'clock Brooks' division was roused and prepared for crossing. The 3d brigade, Russell's, which was to take the lead, began to rehearse its part. It fixed and unfixed bayonets so deftly that the men could hardly hear themselves do it, deployed as skirmishers, and charged through the dark at an imaginary foe in invisible rifle-pits. Four men of the 15 N. Y. Engineers were assigned to each boat as oarsmen. The boats were to go and return until the whole of Russell's brigade had reached the opposite shore, when the bridge was to be laid.

Similar preparations were made in Wadsworth's division ($\frac{1}{I}$), designated by Reynolds to cover the bridges in his corps. General Benham, commanding the Engineer Brigade, who was charged by Hooker with the laying of the bridges, understood that General Brooks and General Wadsworth, commanding the details for covering the operation, were subject to his orders. General Brooks and General Wadsworth did not so understand. The consequence was friction and delay.[1]

In each corps the boats were to be carried to the river on men's shoulders, lest the rumbling of pontoon trucks should give the enemy notice of the intended crossing. It was calculated that if they left their place of concealment by 11:30 they would be in the water by 12:30, and that if the crossing commenced at once, it would be accomplished by 1:30, leaving an hour and a half for the construction of the bridge. Orders were accordingly issued for the boats to be taken down to the river at 11:30. It was nearly midnight before Brooks' men had taken a boat from its place of concealment. Reynolds' men went to work promptly, but had only gotten a number of boats part of the way to the river when Reynolds ordered them put on the trucks and all to be taken down by teams.

Telegraphic communication was opened this morning between Sedgwick's and Hooker's headquarters.[2] The line, which was in operation to England, was extended to within 2 miles of United States Ford, but, owing to an accident to one of the instruments, could not be operated to-day. The heavy rain and lack of signalmen prevented the establishment of communication by flag or torch.

Lieutenant Ropes wrote home:

. . . The great movement has commenced, and our division [Gibbon's $\frac{2}{II}$] is, I believe, to be left to cover this front for the present. We are under marching orders. I also hear that the real attack is to be made in front, here, and that the

---

[1] *W. R.*, 39, p. 211, and *ib.*, 45, p. 63.          [2] The former was on Tyler's Hill.

movements up the river are feints.  I can hardly believe this; it seems like stark madness.  You may hear exciting news very soon.  I sometimes think the entire thing may be a great feint, but it is generally thought that we are on the eve of a great battle. . . .

In the course of the day Lee was informed by Stuart that "a large body of infantry and artillery was passing up the river."[1]  This vague item seems to have been the only information that Lee possessed regarding Hooker's movement.  The Federal force, it would seem, might be anything from a division to an army.  Its destination might be the Shenandoah Valley or Gordonsville.

[1] *W. R.*, 39, p. 796.

# CHAPTER XV

## Right Wing, Forenoon

DEVIN, with the 8 Pa. Cavalry, started from Grove Church about 3 a.m., marched to Kelley's Ford, and on arriving, crossed the river. His brigade comprised the following units:

| ORGANIZATIONS | AGGREGATE STRENGTH |
|---|---|
| 7 troops of the 6 N. Y. . . . . . . . . . . . . . . . . . . . . . . . | 267[1] |
| 17 Pa., except 2 troops attached to the headquarters of the V Corps . . . | 500[2] |
| 8 Pa. . . . . . . . . . . . . . . . . . . . . . . . . . . . . . | 350[3] |
| 1 troop (Company L) of the 1 Mich. . . . . . . . . . . . . . . | 40[4] |
| | 1,157 |

The 6 N. Y. was assigned to the XII Corps. It started about 4 a.m., and marched on the road to Germanna Ford so as to cover the right and front of the column; General Pleasonton accompanied this regiment and directed its operations. The 17 Pa. was assigned to the XI Corps and took position to cover the right of that corps (Map 9). The 8 Pa. and Company L of the 1 Mich. were to cover the front and left of the V Corps, and accordingly took the road to Ely's Ford. Colonel Devin marched with this force and took general charge of it. In rear of the cavalry came Ruger's brigade ($\frac{3}{1, XII}$) of five regiments accompanied by two pieces of artillery from Battery M, 1 N. Y. This command moved out on the Germanna Ford Road about 4:30 a.m. as support and reserve for the cavalry at the head of the column. The main body of the XII Corps followed at a distance of about 2½ miles. The XI Corps cleared the bridge a little before daylight, or the time fixed for the XII Corps to come upon it.

Stuart captured an officer on the staff of General Carl Schurz, "who

---

[1] *History of the 6 N. Y. Cavalry,* by Committee, p. 101. The number is given as 254, but does not include officers. This statement is made on the authority of Lieutenant F. A. Easton, who compiled the work. To include the officers I increased the number 5 per cent.

[2] *Onward* for February, 1870, p. 164.

[3] The strength of the 8 Pa. is given by J. W. de Peyster as 200 (*Onward,* February, 1870, p. 164), by Major Huey and Captain Wells as 300 (*Charge of the 8 Pa. Cav. at Chancellorsville,* pp. 42, 49, 65), and by General Pleasonton as between 400 and 500 (*Rep. of Com.,* IV, 28).

[4] Estimated.

represented that the Eleventh Corps was certainly across; how much more was to follow, he could not tell; but thought that the force altogether in this column was about 20,000."[1] In the light of this and other evidence, Stuart telegraphed to Lee at an early hour that Howard had crossed at Kelley's Ford with a "division" of about 14,000 men, 6 pieces of artillery, and some cavalry.[2] Expecting an advance toward Gordonsville, W. H. F. Lee had taken position between Brandy Station and Kelley's Ford, with the 13 Va. pushed out toward the ford. Fitzhugh Lee was held in reserve at Brandy Station, with a regiment at Stevensburg.[3] Orders were telegraphed to the 10 Va. Cavalry near Beaver Dam Station (Map 1, sheet A) to move at once to hold and occupy the fords on the Rapidan, but it was doubted whether this would be done with sufficient promptness.[4]

The V Corps commenced to cross as soon as the XII had cleared the bridge. This was about 10:30 a.m., or three hours and a half after the time designated by Meade for his corps to be ready to start. At the same time the XI Corps took up the march in rear of the XII.

The weather was damp and misty. A threatening sky lowered impressively over masses of troops crouching in close columns near the river. The long, thin column that wound serpentlike down to them from an amphitheater of hills deployed here and there to ward off a possible attack. General Hooker came over from his headquarters at Morrisville to superintend the movement, and as he passed through the lines, was cheered to the echo.

About noon the First and Second Divisions of the V Corps had completed their crossing. The cavalry in advance of the XII Corps encountered the 13 Va. Cavalry about 2½ miles from Kelley's Ford, and skirmished with it until within about 3 miles of Germanna Ford.

It was about 10 a.m. when the Confederates at Germanna Ford first received reliable information of the crossing of the Federals at Kelley's Ford. The bridge-builders had three spans completed. All the men of the detail were quartered in an old mill on the south side of the river. About 50, who were engaged in the work of construction, were on the north side. On receipt of the forementioned information the Confederate commander put a picket of 10 men out on the road in his front, and had fifty who were working at the bridge go to their quarters, get their guns, and return.

About 11 a.m., when the infantry advance-guard under Ruger reached a point about 2 miles from Germanna Ford, its commander received the report that there was a detachment of about 150 men at the ford engaged in building a bridge. Soon afterward he learned that the Federal

---

[1] *W. R.*, 39, p. 1046; *Reminiscences of Carl Schurz*, II, 408.
[2] *W. R.*, 39, pp. 796, 1045, 1046; *ib.*, 40, p. 758.
[3] *Ib.*, 39, p. 1046.　　　　　[4] *Ib.*

cavalry was checked. It was reported that the enemy occupied the rifle-pits on the right (west) of the road and on the north side of the river. About noon, having reached a point about ¾ of a mile from the ford, he received orders to deploy skirmishers on both sides of the road and advance rapidly. He had one regiment form on the right and one on the left of the road (Plan 1). Each of these regiments took up about a mile of front,[1] which gave a density of about 1 man to every 3 or 4 yards. One regiment, in column of fours, kept on the road, followed by a section of artillery. The remainder of the advance-guard, consisting of the 13 N. J. and 107 N. Y., followed the deployed regiments as supports in line of columns of fours.

The approaches to the Rapidan ran through dense thickets of scrub-oak, up to the immediate bluff overlooking the river, which spreads out for a few hundred yards into a comparatively easy plain. Upon the south bank (the Confederate side) were steep hills rising somewhat precipitously from the very edge of the river, which forms a decided bow at the ford, the bend being northward in such a shape that all the approaches to the ford on the south bank were completely covered by a cross-fire from those who should occupy the north bank. Ruger's long skirmish line stealthily, and rapidly, enveloped this bag. The first notice that the Confederate picket had of the Federal operation was the sound of firing in its rear. Under cover of the undergrowth it made its way unobserved some distance up the river, and was fortunate enough to find a boat in which to cross. The 50 men working on the bridge near the north bank were all captured. The Federal line swept across the river, firing a few shots as a warning rather than to start a fight, and completed their capture. The number of prisoners made on both banks aggregated 103, of whom 7 were officers. On their way to the rear they gave frequent vent to their astonishment at the thousands of men that they passed, showing that the Federal movement had been executed without the knowledge of the enemy.

Averell arrived at Rappahannock Bridge about 5 a.m. and found the ford impassable "without imminent hazard of drowning." At 6:25 a.m. he received a copy of Hooker's instructions to Stoneman of April 12 (Chapter XI) and of those of April 28, modifying these (Chapter XIV), but no instructions addressed directly to him except a message from Stoneman to the effect that, if the ford was impracticable, he should be guided by his own judgment as to the place of crossing.[2] Pursuant to the latter, he marched to Kelley's Ford, where Stoneman's column had arrived at 8 a.m. Stoneman was not authorized to use the bridge except for pack-animals and artillery. But on account of his having but one ford, he assumed the responsibility of crossing half of

---

[1] The usual density of a line of skirmishers was one to every 5 or 10 yards.
[2] W. R., 39, p. 1077.

his troopers by the bridge. On the north side of the Rappahannock at Kelley's Ford was a slough, or swamp, which could not be crossed except by a trestle bridge, constructed for that purpose. Neither the ford nor pontoon bridge, therefore, could be used by the cavalry until the infantry of the V Corps (First and Second Divisions) had cleared the trestle bridge. The cavalry commenced crossing by both the ford and the pontoon bridge about noon. The Third Division of the V Corps (Humphreys') was detailed about this time to remain behind to cover the passage of the trains and bring up the bridge.

## Right Wing, Afternoon

The detachments of Confederate cavalry that observed and followed the Federal columns (contact detachments) were careless, it seems, about reporting what they saw. It was about 1 p.m. when Stuart learned from his pickets about Madden that a large force of Federal infantry was moving in that direction. Assembling his two brigades, he marched to that point and there pierced the Federal column, taking prisoners from the V, XI, and XII Corps.[1] The rear of the XI Corps was shelled by a couple of light pieces. The only way to stop this annoyance was to attack and defeat Stuart's cavalry. But for this Pleasonton's cavalry was not sufficiently strong, Stuart's outnumbering it two to one. So the shelling had to be endured until about 3:30 in the afternoon, when a portion of Stoneman's force came up and drove the enemy away. When Stuart learned that the right column was marching upon Germanna Ford, it was too late for him to warn the Confederate detachment at that point; the Federals were in possession of the ford.[2] As already stated, this party had warning, hours before, of the Federal passage of Kelley's Ford, but they did not suspect, it seems, that it seriously concerned them.

The handful of Confederates that escaped from Germanna Ford retreated under cover of the woods to the vicinity of Wilderness Tavern, where they halted about 4 p.m. to await instructions from General Mahone or spend the night.[3] The sound of firing at the ford brought

[1] These circumstances are deduced from conflicting statements in the official reports. Meade did not march in the same column with Slocum and Howard. The men of the corps who were captured by Stuart's first dash at Madden were perhaps flankers or connecting patrols (*W. R.*, 39, pp. 519, 796, 1046).

[2] Stuart says in his report: "Couriers had been, by direction, sent to Ely's and Germanna [Fords] to notify our parties there of the enemy's advance, but were captured; consequently the parties at those

points received no notice" (*W. R.*, 39, p. 1046).

[3] Writing in 1888 for the *Century Magazine*, Pleasonton stated:

"In the afternoon (29th) at Germanna Ford, I surprised and captured a picket of some fifty of Stuart's cavalry soldiers. With them was an engineer officer belonging to Stuart's staff. On searching the party, as is done with all prisoners, I found on this engineer officer a very bulky volume, which proved to be a diary which he had been keeping throughout the war. I

General Slocum to the front. When the affair was over, he gave orders for the immediate crossing of the river. The cavalry and Ruger's and Knipe's brigades, with Battery M, 1 N. Y., crossed accordingly by the ford, the infantry wading almost to the armpits, with bayonets fixed, their cartridge-boxes and haversacks hanging on their bayonets. The music-boys were carried over on the shoulders of stalwart men. Numbers of men were swept down the river, and only rescued from drowning by cavalrymen mounted on the largest, heaviest horses, and boatmen, stationed in the stream a short distance below the crossing. As the guns of the battery were hauled out on the farther shore, the water poured in streams from the muzzles. By the time the forementioned troops had crossed, the bridge built on the piers of the burnt bridge had been completed far enough to permit the rest of the infantry to use it. The artillery, cavalry, and trains continued to use the ford. Men relieved the pack-mules of their burdens by carrying the ammunition over the bridge while the little animals swam the stream to resume their loads on the other side. As night fell, huge bonfires were kindled on the banks. The light of the fires danced with the moonbeams on the bayonets and the water, and wrought fantastic shapes on the hillside, while the long dark column streamed down from the woods into the gleaming current and the gorge beyond. The jubilant soldiers made the still night ring with their jokes and laughter. Communication across the river was maintained by signal stations established on both banks. The XII Corps completed its crossing about 11 p.m., when the XI Corps commenced to cross. At midnight it was still crossing (Map 10).

At the intersection of the River Road with that to Culpeper, Colonel Devin, commanding the cavalry with the V Corps, sent a party to the right to communicate with General Slocum's column, also a squadron to Barnett's Ford, to ascertain whether the enemy was still at that point. Having established communication with Slocum's column, but not heard from the squadron sent to Barnett's Ford, he moved on to Richardsville. Here he dispatched Major Keenan with two squadrons to Richards' Ford, with instructions to drive the enemy, if possible, from that point, and establish communication with the Federal pickets opposite it, and then rejoin the command at Ely's Ford, which left him one squadron and one company.[1] This done, he awaited the arrival of

spent the greater part of the night in reading it in hopes of finding something that would be of advantage to us, nor was I disappointed. This diary stated that in the first week of March a council of war had been held at General Stuart's headquarters, which had been attended by Generals Jackson, A. P. Hill, Ewell, and Stuart. They were in conference over five hours, and came to the decision that the next battle would be at or near Chancellorsville, and that that position must be prepared" (*B. and L.*, III, 176). I have been unable to find this diary or a copy, or any trace of it. J. B. Jr.

[1] Devin's report, *W. R.*, 39, p. 779. Ac-

General Meade. At the head of the infantry was the 1st brigade of the First Division, under General Barnes, marching at top speed. Word was sent ahead to its commander that the men were falling out in squads, unable to keep up. Barnes sent back word that it was necessary to preserve a rapid gait, in order to seize the bluffs upon the opposite bank before the enemy, and thus prevent a battle. The roads were strewn with knapsacks and superfluous clothing thrown away by the men.[1] Straggling and desertion gave employment to the provost guards. But the men in general, stimulated by the sound of cannon in the direction of Fredericksburg, responded heartily and effectively to the appeal made to them by their corps commander in his order of the day before.

When General Meade, who rode between his infantry and his cavalry, reached Richardsville, the dispositions made by his cavalry were approved, and its commander, Colonel Devin, was ordered to go to Ely's Ford and ascertain and report the state of affairs there. Devin resumed his march accordingly. On reaching Ely's Ford he found a picket of 10 mounted men on the opposite side, who made no motion to retire. He sent to General Meade for instructions, as he understood that the general did not wish to cross until he heard from Slocum's column at Germanna Ford. General Meade wanted to see the place of crossing himself, and to have troops at hand to support the cavalry before ordering it to cross. So Devin had to wait for Meade's arrival.

The river at Ely's Ford was three or four feet deep, and running with a swift current. Meade reached it with the head of his First Division about 4:30 p.m. He did not consider the depth of the water sufficient to warrant waiting for the pontoon train and the laying of a bridge.[2] So the cavalry was at once put across. The Confederate horsemen on the south bank stood their ground until the Federals had nearly reached the shore, when they scampered away, taking the road to Chancellorsville. The Federal cavalry was promptly followed by the First Division of infantry. As opposition was expected, orders were

cording to Huey's report, *ib.*, p. 783, Devin had no cavalry in reserve.

[1] When the command started in the morning, the 5 N. Y. left in its camp at Kelley's Ford 20 rifles belonging to as many three-year men who had taken advantage of darkness to desert rather than be consolidated with the 146 N. Y., to serve out the remainder of their term (*Camp and Field Life of the 5 N. Y. Vol. Infantry, Duryee Zouaves*, by A. Davenport, p. 379).

[2] Meade had perhaps heard by this time from Slocum. "While Slocum was sitting on his horse intently watching his men who were struggling so manfully in the river, an officer rode up and, presenting the compliments of General Meade, announced that the V Corps had just arrived at Ely's Ford, the next ford below. He informed Slocum that the water there was very deep, up to a man's hips; said something about pontoons, and seemed to be asking for instructions. Slocum replied somewhat curtly that his men were fording through swift water breast-deep, and that the V Corps must cross without further delay" (*Slocum and his Men*, by Committee, p. 159).

issued that no clothing should be removed. The men arranged their cartridge-boxes, haversacks, knapsacks, blankets, and valuables about their heads and necks, or secured them to the ends of their fixed bayonets, and plunged into the cold water. Some were swept away as at Germanna Ford, to be picked up by cavalry stationed below. The Second Division followed the First across after dark. The river was lighted by large fires on the farther bank, the sight of which cheered the troops forward. Out of the chilly water they climbed the slippery hillside—for it was then raining—and went to hunting fire-wood in the darkness, building fires, cooking suppers, pitching shelter tents, drying clothes and shoes as best they could, and finally rolling up in blankets, feet to the fire, for a comfortless night.[1]

Devin sent a squadron to scour the country to the right toward Germanna and the road leading from that point into the Wilderness. He also picketed the roads about Ely's Ford. In the meantime the Federal squadron sent to Barnett's Ford, having found no enemy, joined the two squadrons under Keenan, and all three marched to Richards' Ford, where they surprised the enemy in his rifle-pits, captured 28 men and 1 commissioned officer, and forwarded dispatches to Hooker. These were not received, it would seem, before night.

Butterfield wrote to Slocum from Falmouth:

. . . the bridges are all across here.[2] The demonstration here is a very strong one. Fifty or 60 prisoners taken in the enemy's rifle-pits report Jackson's whole force here. The enemy are in position, anticipating our main attack at Franklin's Crossing. The general directs that you move as high up as Chancellorsville; establish your right strongly on the Plank road; look out for your left, too. The map indicates that from Chancellorsville to the Rappahannock is a very strong position. You must have that, and move to command the Plank road, which is the line of the enemy's retreat. As soon as you uncover United States Ford, you will be reënforced by C. [Couch] (two divisions), and then probably by S.'s [Sickles'] entire command. The general will be up to-morrow. The bearer, if he succeeds in reaching you, may be able to return with a dispatch from you.

It will be observed that no reference is made in this communication to uncovering Banks' Ford. The idea is to secure a defensive position based upon United States Ford and cutting off Lee's retreat, thus compelling him to attack. That this will result in his defeat and loss of Fredericksburg, is a fixed idea in Hooker's mind. It is his intention that as soon as he has possession of Fredericksburg, the railroad bridge at that point, which has been destroyed, shall be reconstructed, and that as fast as the army advances along the railroad toward Richmond, the road shall be put in working order by his construction corps. From the following letter of Lieutenant Ropes, dated to-day, it would seem that

---

[1] *Mag. of Am. Hist.*, XX, 378.          [2] Five pontoon bridges below. J. B. Jr.

at least a part of the Army of the Potomac was still ignorant of the new plan of campaign:

As far as I can make it out, the whole of the army, except the II Corps, has gone down [the river] to make a grand attack on the enemy's right. . . . I understand the troops are in good spirits, and I am sure I hope for success, but I do not see how it can be decisive, for the enemy have a perfect line of retreat, unless Hooker crosses so far below as to be able to get between them and Richmond, while the bulk of their force is gathered to resist the feigned attack on their left. . . .

Using the ford and the pontoon bridge at Kelley's Ford, Stoneman managed "by dint of great exertion" to get all his cavalry over by 3 and his trains by 5 p.m. He camped with his column for the night at Madden. No fire or noise was allowed. The horses remained saddled, the men in each set of fours taking turns in holding the four horses by the bridles while the other three men slept. The night was rendered still more uncomfortable by the cold, drizzly rain.[1]

Here [says Stoneman in his report] I assembled the division and brigade commanders, spread our maps, and had a thorough understanding of what we were to do, and where we were each to go. Averell ... was to push on in the direction of Culpeper Court-House, and myself [with the main column] . . . to push on toward Stevensburg. It was expected that Averell would be able to reach Brandy Station that night, driving whatever enemy was there before him, and I was to communicate with him at that point.[2]

What orders he issued are not given verbatim in the official records, and appear to have been communicated verbally. Averell reports:

I was directed to proceed in the direction of Brandy Station, reach there, if possible, that night [29th], and communicate with Buford, who would be at Stevensburg. On the day following I was to proceed to Culpeper Court-House and Rapidan Station, attacking the cavalry of the enemy and keep him occupied while Buford proceeded with the major-general commanding the corps to execute that portion of the original instructions which referred to operations in rear of the enemy's main body.[3]

It would seem from the two reports that Averell was ordered to be at Brandy Station on the night of the 29th, "if possible"; and was to govern his movements beyond that point by orders which he was to receive from time to time from Stoneman and to carry out conformably to such general instructions as he might have received; also that he understood that the active operations on Lee's communications were to be executed by the reserve brigade under Buford, accompanied and directed by Stoneman. What Gregg was to do, can only be conjectured.

---

[1] *History of the First Maine Cavalry, 1861–1865*, by E. P. Tobie, p. 134.
[2] *W. R.*, 39, p. 1058.  [3] *Ib.*, 39, p. 1074.

It was perhaps to follow the left column as a sort of general reserve. From these circumstances and others to develop later, it appears that the understanding which Stoneman had at this time with his division and brigade commanders as to what they were to do and where they were to go was not in any proper sense a "thorough" one.

Only Buford's brigade went to Stevensburg. From there two squadrons were sent on to Brandy Station to communicate with Averell. Near midnight Stoneman learned from a staff officer of Averell's that Averell had gone into camp not far from Kelley's Ford. He at once sent an officer of his staff with a platoon to recall the two squadrons. These had reached Brandy Station and found there the 13 Va. Cavalry and a battery of artillery, but no sign of Averell. A messenger sent back to Stevensburg with a report to this effect was either killed or captured on the way. After waiting for some time at Brandy Station, the squadrons returned to Stevensburg and thence with the brigade to Madden, arriving there soon after midnight.

Averell had been led to believe by deserters and intercepted dispatches that Stuart with his entire force, reported as four brigades and fifteen pieces of artillery, was at Brandy Station awaiting his approach. He had consequently suspended his advance.

The following dispatch was picked up on the march, delivered to him, and forwarded by him to Stoneman, who, however, was not to receive it to-day:

*Important*

Headquarters Cavalry Division,
Near Brandy Station, Va., April 29, 1863.
COLONEL CHAMBLISS, Thirteenth Virginia Cavalry.
*Colonel:*

The major-general commanding directs me to say that he wishes you to get a man posted so as to have a view of the road leading down on the other side of Kelley's Ford, and find out what kind of troops marched down behind the wagons.[1] The enemy have made a demonstration toward Stevensburg, but so far it amounts to nothing. The general is very anxious to know where to look for Stoneman, as we have heard nothing from him.

Most respectfully, your obedient servant,

R. CHANNING PRICE,
Assistant Adjutant-General. [2]

After the Federal cavalry and its trains had cleared the bridge at Kelley's Ford, a few remaining troops of the XI and XII Corps were allowed to cross. Then came the trains of these corps, which were fol-

---

[1] Referring, it would seem, to wagons which accompanied the right wing to the vicinity of Kelley's Ford and were probably escorted by troops that were to remain behind.

[2] *W. R.*, 39, p. 1059. The subsequent operations of Stoneman's cavalry, being independent of those of the army, are described separately in Chapter XXVIII.

lowed by those of the V Corps.[1]  Finally Humphreys crossed with his division, and about 7 p.m. the Engineers commenced taking up the bridge.[2]  About this time Humphreys received a communication from his corps commander advising him of the importance, as he supposed, of having the pontoon train at Ely's Ford at the earliest possible moment.  It was about 11:30 when the bridge train was ready to move, and Humphreys' division accompanied by it was put in motion through the darkness.  At midnight this column was about 2 miles on its way from Kelley's to Ely's Ford.

Stahel marched this afternoon with his division of cavalry from Fairfax Court-House westward to the vicinity of Aldie and returned after dark.

## Center and Left Wing

The two divisions of the II Corps completed the road to United States Ford.  Excepting the two regiments under Colonel Cross $\left(\frac{5.81}{1.1.11}\right)$, they took up the march at 2 p.m. in compliance with the following instructions addressed to the "Commanding Officer, II Corps, Banks' Ford":

1

The commanding general directs that you encamp with your two divisions to-night at the United States Ford, leaving a company at Banks' Ford, and that you keep the road you have been repairing clear of wagons.  The wagons must take the fields on the right and left of the road.  Please acknowledge.

2

The commanding general does not care about your movement to the United States Ford being kept secret from the enemy.  He wishes you to march to-day, and by the best road.  He also desires to know what road you have repaired.

The two divisions, with the forementioned exception, bivouacked at United States Ford.  The supply-train hauled two days' rations to them, and the wagons, after being reloaded at the depot at Falmouth, returned to the park.  The trains for two bridges were also sent from Banks' Ford to United States Ford.

It was late in the afternoon when two cavalry videttes galloped up to General Mahone's headquarters, and reported the Federals to be advancing in force on the road from Ely's Ford.  A little later information came to him of another column marching east by the Plank Road from Germanna Ford.  In a few moments couriers were dashing off with orders, and within an hour the winter quarters were abandoned, wagons and *impedimenta* of all sorts were started to the rear, and the

---

[1] Humphreys, in his report, mentions a train consisting of at least 125 wagons and 55 spring wagons and ambulances belonging chiefly, almost entirely, as reported to him, to the XI Corps (*W. R.*, 39, p. 550).

[2] *Ib.*, 39, p. 215.

two brigades were posted to meet the advancing Federals—Mahone's to the north of Chancellorsville, covering the approaches from Ely's Ford and United States Ford; and Posey's to the west of it, covering the approach from Germanna Ford, with two guns of Grandy's battery $(\frac{1}{1.1})$ on each road. A regiment and a half, about 600 men, were left at United States Ford to hold the position as long as possible.[1]

It was nearly sunset when a courier from General Mahone reached the party at Wilderness Tavern with an order to make a reconnaissance toward Germanna Ford. This was done, and developed the fact that there was a large force of Federals at the ford. At midnight the reconnoitering party was on its way back to Wilderness Tavern.[2]

Sometime after 6:30 p.m. the following order was sent to Couch at United States Ford:

General Hooker directs that you establish communication with General Meade, at Ely's Ford, Rapidan, or vicinity, to-night. Use a pontoon boat or raft across the Rappahannock. Swim a horse if necessary above its junction with Rapidan. Send following to Generals Meade and Slocum [V and XII Corps]:
"General Hooker learns that pontoon bridge has been made use of for crossing cavalry. He prefers that no dragoons should have crossed the Rappahannock. If Fords at Germanna and Ely's should be impracticable for artillery, cross infantry without waiting for artillery (infantry can raise cartridge-boxes) or trains, and drive enemy from before United States Ford." . . .

Hooker no longer trusted to the movement upon Chancellorsville for opening the United States Ford. He now required, as he should have done in the first instance, that a force move upon the ford. Couch, it seems, did not receive this message. At any rate, he failed to communicate with Meade; and neither Meade nor Slocum took any action toward compelling the hostile detachment at United States Ford to retire.

How is it now with the passage of the river by the left wing below Fredericksburg? Brooks' boats were not in the water until about 1:30 a.m., and then it was found impossible to get a crossing party. General Russell thought that the movement could not succeed in the dark, and would not let his brigade embark before daylight. Benham ordered him into arrest, but he paid no attention to the order. The situation was reported to Brooks and to Sedgwick, but the night wore away without bringing any material change in it. At 4:20 a.m. boats pushed from the shore, each containing 45 men and a quota of officers. These 1215 men were the 95 and 119 Pa., who had been chosen to surprise the enemy's pickets. The boats were soon lost in the fog. The river is not more than 80 or 100 yards wide at this point, but the

---

[1] The 12 Va. of Mahone's brigade and five companies of the 19 Miss. of Posey's brigade (Posey's report, *W. R.*, 39, p. 871).
[2] *War Talks of Confederate Veterans*, by G. S. Bernard, pp. 49 *et seq.*

progress of the boats, owing probably to the necessity of silence, was unusually slow. Suddenly there rang out on the misty air the unmistakable sound "Fire," and about 200 yards of the opposite bank were lit up with musketry. The men crowded together in the boats could not reply. Their comrades on shore, peering after them through the impenetrable fog, held their breath. But soon a loud cheer followed by another, and then another, told that the opposite bank was reached and held. The boats made another trip, bringing over the remainder of Russell's brigade. A bridge was immediately and rapidly laid, being commenced at 5:50 and completed at 7 a.m. A second bridge was laid between 6 and 7:30; and a third between 7 and 9:45. In the meantime the remainder of the division crossed in boats with perhaps a dozen casualties.

Wadsworth did not have his boats in the water until about 4:30, and then no men were at hand to enter them. The crossing in boats at this point did not commence until about 9 o'clock. It was completed about 10. The work of laying two bridges commenced about 10:15. It was completed, and the troops commenced crossing on the bridges about 12 m. Russell's line of skirmishers drove the skirmishers opposing it out of two lines of rifle-pits, and established itself about 100 yards from the enemy and about 300 yards from the river. It was prolonged to the left until it connected with Wadsworth's line. It was known that troops up the river were executing an offensive movement, and it was thought that at any moment a sound of firing might come from them that would be a signal for the left wing to advance.

Benham received the following communication of this day from Hooker's adjutant-general:

Your attention is called to the following extract from orders issued yesterday, of which you were furnished a copy:

"The bridges, two at each crossing, to be laid complete before 3:30 a.m. on the 29th, under the supervision of General Benham, who is charged with the responsibility thereof."

The major-general commanding is informed that, agreeably to your request, General Sedgwick placed at your disposal a brigade of infantry, and he desires to know why these orders were not complied with, and those bridges laid at the hour specified.[1]

Benham replied in the course of the day with a lengthy report,[2] which seems to have cleared him of all responsibility for the delay. Whether or not the responsibility was ever officially fixed upon any one, the author is unable to state. Russell, in his report, accounted for the delay by the bare and simple statement: "The arrangements for crossing were not perfected till 4:20 o'clock on the morning of Wednesday, April 29."

[1] W. R., 39, pp. 204, 205.  [2] Ib., 39, p. 205; ib., 45, p. 63.

The two divisions covering Sedgwick's five bridges were themselves covered by groups of guns on the north bank posted under the direction of the Chief of Artillery of the Army of the Potomac. At Franklin's Crossing was a line of forty-six pieces $\left(\frac{21.\ 6^2}{A}, \frac{3.\ 4}{1.\ VI}, \frac{1}{2.\ VI}, \frac{1}{3.\ VI}, 4.\ VI, \frac{4}{2.\ III}\right)$, commanded by Colonel Tompkins, Chief of Artillery of the VI Corps, and at Pollock's Mill, a line of thirty-four pieces of the I Corps $\left(\frac{1.\ 2}{1.\ I}, \frac{1.\ 3.\ 4}{2.\ I}, \frac{1.\ 2.\ 3}{3.\ I}\right)$, commanded by Colonel Wainwright, Chief of Artillery of that corps. Still further down the river, near Traveller's Rest, was a battery of sixteen pieces of the General Reserve under Colonel Warner, Inspector of Artillery of the Army of the Potomac.[3] This battery was to command the bridge over the Massaponax and the valley of that stream, and so prevent the enemy from attacking Sedgwick's left flank after he had crossed. In addition to these groups of guns, five batteries of Napoleons (brass smooth-bore 12-pounders), numbering twenty-six pieces, were stationed near Falmouth, in readiness for service when and wherever they might be required.[4] The batteries of the I, III, and VI Corps, not mentioned, were likewise available for action. There still remain to be accounted for two batteries attached to the Provost Guard, numbering ten pieces. These were probably on the line of communication between Falmouth and Aquia Creek.

About daybreak the officers at Jackson's headquarters were aroused with the stirring news that Federal troops were crossing the Rappahannock in pontoons under cover of a heavy fog. Jackson, who had spent the night at a house near by, was at once informed of the fact, and promptly issued orders for his divisions to prepare for action. As the long roll resounded through his camp, an officer of his staff rode over to army headquarters, and gave the news to General Lee, who expressed no surprise, but remarked in playful tones:

Well, I thought I heard firing, and was beginning to think it was time some of you young fellows were coming to tell me what it was all about. Tell your good general that I am sure he knows what to do. I will meet him at the front very soon.[5]

After going out and personally observing the enemy, he telegraphed to the Adjutant-General and to President Davis:

The enemy is crossing below Deep Run, about the same place as before [in the Fredericksburg campaign]. The fog has been so thick during the night and morning that we can only see a few yards.[6] Taken with the reports received

---

[1] Four 4½-inch guns.

[2] Six 20-pounder guns.

[3] Taft's 5 N. Y., four 20-pounders; Hart's 15 N. Y., six 3-inch guns; and Gaston's 32 N. Y., six 3-inch guns.

[4] $\frac{2}{1.\ III}, \frac{3}{2.\ III}, \frac{1}{3.\ III}, \frac{10.\ 11}{A}$.

[5] *B. and L.*, III, 203; for a slightly different version see *Life and Letters of R. E. Lee, Soldier and Man*, by J. W. Jones, p. 241.

[6] The Rappahannock is usually covered with fog early in the morning.

from our left, it looks like a general advance; but where his main effort will be made, can not say. Troops not wanted south of James River had better be moved in this direction, and all other necessary preparations made.

About 5 a.m. a courier dashed into Fredericksburg with the intelligence that the Federals were crossing the Rappahannock a short distance below. Immediately the Episcopal Church bell, the ringing of which had been agreed upon as a signal, sounded the alarm, and the streets presented a spectacle of military preparation, and women and children leaving the town.

By 10 a.m. Lee received Stuart's report of Howard's passage of the Rappahannock yesterday at Kelley's Ford. The fog having then lifted, he observed that more Federal troops had crossed in his front. He telegraphed to the Adjutant-General at Richmond:

The enemy is in large force on north bank of Rappahannock, opposite railroad at Hamilton's Crossing. He is crossing troops below the point at which he crossed in December, and extends lower down the river.[1] I have discovered nothing lower than the mouth of Massaponax Creek. He is certainly crossing in large force here, and it looks as if he were in earnest. I hear of no other point at which he is crossing, except below Kelley's Ford, where General Howard has crossed with his division, said to be 14,000, six pieces of artillery, and some cavalry. Stoneman will probably cross about the Warrenton Springs, and I fear will make for Gordonsville, and may destroy our roads. I have nothing to oppose to all that force up there except the two weak brigades of cavalry under General Stuart. All available troops had better be sent as rapidly as possible by rail and otherwise.

Lee was inclining to believe that the main force of the Federals was crossing, after all, below Fredericksburg. But what, he asked himself, was Howard's objective? Apparently it was Gordonsville, but his ''division'' might be the advance of a force directed upon Richmond or Lee's communications or his army. Lee may have been misled by a subsequent report from Stuart. At any rate, he telegraphed also to the Adjutant-General somewhat later:

If any troops can be sent by rail to Gordonsville, under a good officer, I recommend it. Longstreet's division[s], if available, had better come to me; and the troops for Gordonsville and the protection of the railroads [be forwarded] from Richmond and North Carolina, if practicable. General Howard of the enemy's forces making toward Gordonsville. . . .

He contracted his main line by moving Jackson's corps into the space between the Massaponax Creek and Deep Run; placed Wright's brigade $(\frac{5}{1.1})$ within supporting distance of Early's left; formed Kershaw's brigade $(\frac{1}{2.1})$ on Early's left; and placed the half of Semmes' brigade

[1] The battle of Fredericksburg was fought on the 13th of December, 1862.

$\left(\frac{2}{2.1}\right)$ that was near the Plank Road in rear of Wofford $\left(\frac{3}{2.1}\right)$ as reserve. The trains of Hill's division, and probably of the other divisions of Jackson's corps, were assembled in the vicinity of Hamilton's Crossing.[1]

Lee sent the following dispatch to the commander of the 15 Va. Cavalry:

You had better draw up your pickets below Port Royal as high as the enemy's lowest picket, keeping well below their [infantry?] picket; and replace the infantry picket [on our side] above Port Royal, where they are withdrawn. Station your men to the best advantage at points where they can observe their [own] line, so that the number [of our pickets] may be diminished as much as possible with safety. Caution your men to be very much on the alert, as a great deal depends upon their watchfulness and coolness.[2]

Jackson proposed to Lee to attack the troops under Sedgwick that had crossed the river. In reply Lee said: "It will be hard to get at the enemy, and harder still to get away, if we succeed in driving him to the river. But, General, if you think you can effect anything, I will give orders for the attack."

Jackson asked for time for a careful reconnaissance, and having made it, reported that, upon closer examination, he concurred with Lee in the opinion that such an attack would accomplish nothing.[3]

Between 6:30 and 6:45 p.m.[4] couriers and stray cavalrymen from the Rapidan reported to Lee that Federal cavalry crossed the river at Germanna Ford and Ely's Ford about 1:30 p.m.[5] and that there was infantry with the cavalry that crossed at Germanna Ford.[6] This was Lee's first information of a Federal movement toward the Rapidan. It came too late to enable him to take up, say nothing of intrenching, the line that Longstreet had laid out. Together with the fact that he had not heard from Stuart since before noon, it satisfied him that the enemy was marching in force upon Germanna and Ely's Fords, and had cut Stuart off from him, but it left him presumably in doubt as to whether Howard was really marching toward Gordonsville or was with this force on the

[1] The author has been unable to get satisfactory information regarding the movements of the Confederate trains. The only published data that he has found refer to the trains of Hill's division, and appeared in a paper of the Southern Hist. Soc. by Captain R. E. Park (Vol. XXXIII).

[2] W. R., 108, pp. 698, 699.

[3] Papers of the Mil. Hist. Soc. of Mass., Vol. 3, p. 145.

[4] Lee to McLaws and to Anderson, W. R., 40, p. 759.

[5] Dispatch from Lee to McLaws says 1 p.m.; dispatch from Lee to Davis says 2 p.m.

[6] In both of the opposing armies the cavalry was trained to fight both on foot and on horseback. It was never necessary to attach infantry to cavalry for the protection of the latter. The practice which obtained in Europe as late as the Franco-German War, of moving infantry in wagons beyond supporting distance of the army, was uncalled for and practically unknown in our war. Hence the presence of infantry, however few, indicated the proximity of a large force.

Rapidan. The circumstance that after crossing this river the routes followed by the Federal columns converged toward Chancellorsville, suggested this point as the immediate, and Lee's army as the final, objective of the Federal force, but it did not preclude a movement by at least one of the Federal columns upon his line of retreat to Richmond. If the Federals wanted to close with his army, he would give them the opportunity; this meant for him an essentially defensive fight with his communications with Richmond intact. But if they were trying to cut him off from Richmond, he meant to get ahead of them by retiring. He would not commit himself to the tactical offensive with his supplies cut off. He telegraphed to Pendleton, his chief of artillery at Chesterfield Station, to come up with all the artillery. Most of the artillery of the II Corps was at Bowling Green. Its chief, Colonel Crutchfield, was promptly communicated with, and probably had all his artillery up before midnight. Of the artillery of the I Corps, Alexander's battalion, Manly's and McCarthy's batteries of Cabell's battalion (2. I), and Moore's battery of Hardaway's battalion (1. I) took up the march from near Chesterfield for Fredericksburg that afternoon. Wright's brigade $\left(\frac{5}{1.1}\right)$ was ordered to report to Anderson, whose headquarters were near the point occupied by Perry's brigade $\left(\frac{3}{1.1}\right)$, and the latter sent to relieve the half of Semmes' brigade in front of Falmouth. This half brigade reported to its brigade commander near Lee's Hill. Anderson was ordered to withdraw the brigades of Mahone and Posey from near United States Ford, where they were liable to be turned, and post these troops and Wright's brigade $\left(\frac{5}{1.1}\right)$ at Chancellorsville, so as to cover the roads to Fredericksburg, taking the strongest line he could, and holding it to the best advantage. He was directed to go forward himself to attend to this matter. "See," said Lee, "if you can find where Colonel Davis' cavalry [10 Va.] is, and collect all the mounted men you can in your front."

Anderson received this order at 9 p.m. He proceeded to carry it out, sending an order to Wright to march with his brigade to Chancellorsville. Wright received this order in bivouac near Tabernacle Church at midnight, at which hour Anderson arrived at Chancellorsville. General McLaws, commanding at Fredericksburg, was ordered to communicate to General Jackson and General Anderson all movements of the enemy affecting them, and if they asked for reënforcements, to furnish what he could. Lee was anxious about his cavalry, for he depended upon it for information enabling him to anticipate or counteract the enemy's operations. In his dispatches to Anderson and McLaws he observed:

We may be obliged to change our position in consequence of the enemy's having come between us and General Stuart. Make your preparatory arrangements to-night to secure all your property.

In a dispatch to President Davis he said with reference to Meade and Slocum:

Their intention, I presume, is to turn our left, and probably to get into our rear.

Our scattered condition favors their operations.[1]   I hope if any reënforcements can be sent, they may be forwarded immediately.

The bridges over the [North and South] Annas ought to be guarded, if possible.

And with reference to Sedgwick:

The day has [by reason of the fog] been favorable for his operations, and to-night he will probably get over the remainder of his forces.

It was late in the afternoon when Stuart learned that the Federal columns were marching, one upon Germanna Ford, and one upon Ely's Ford.  The intelligence, with as much detail as practicable, was telegraphed to General Lee from Culpeper Court-House.[2]  Lee was now satisfied that Howard was not marching on Gordonsville, but was with the Federal force on the Rapidan.  On the other hand, he had learned, it seems, of Stoneman's passage of the Rappahannock.  He directed Stuart to make arrangements for the protection of the public property along the railroads, and then to swing around so as to join the left wing of Lee's army, endeavoring at the same time to impede the progress of the Federal column marching by way of Germanna Ford.[3]  Stuart detached W. H. F. Lee, with the 9 and 13 Va. and half of the available artillery (about 1000 men and 6 guns), to go by Culpeper Court-House toward Gordonsville; the other column was to be watched by the 10 Va. Cavalry, expected from Beaver Dam.  With the remainder of his force, consisting of Fitzhugh Lee's brigade and the 5 Va. and 6 guns (about 1600 men), he marched for Raccoon Ford, where he arrived about midnight, crossed, and halted for a few hours' rest.  Colonel Owen with the 3 Va. went on without stopping, to get in front, if possible, of the Federal column at Germanna Ford.  Owing to the darkness of the night and the fatigue of his men, three squadrons became separated from him, leaving him only two squadrons.  The former marched under the command of Lieutenant-Colonel Carter to rejoin the brigade under Stuart and Fitzhugh Lee.  At midnight Owen with his two squadrons reached Locust Grove.[4]

Two signal stations (flag and torch) were established at United States Ford to watch for the Federal column coming down the river, but the

---

[1] Referring especially to the absence of Longstreet with two mixed divisions and of Hampton with a brigade of cavalry.

[2] *So. Hist. Soc. Papers*, VIII, 252.  The author says: "It was nearly night before the Federal movements became fully enough developed to make it certain that they were directed upon Germanna and Ely's Fords."

[3] *W. R.*, 39, pp. 796, 1046.

[4] *So. Hist. Soc. Papers*, VIII, 252.

observers did not catch sight of it to-day. The telegraph line was extended from England to United States Ford, but this extension was not in successful operation until 9 p.m. In the meantime communication between England and United States Ford was maintained by courier.

A flag and torch station was established at the Fitzhugh House, near Reynolds' headquarters, and Tyler's Hill near Sedgwick's, whence there was already telegraphic communication with Butterfield (old general headquarters). There was now a continuous line of flag and torch communication from opposite Buckner's Neck, through Seddon's, the Fitzhugh House, and Tyler's Hill, to the Phillips House. A flag and torch line of the Signal Corps connected Reynolds' with Sedgwick's headquarters.

Hooker received the following dispatch of this day from Peck:

I think I can hold Longstreet here [at Suffolk] for some time, which will favor your operations very materially. When he retires it will only be to his two railroads, where he can go to Lee or strike at me, according to circumstances. You and I will have plenty of work.

He telegraphed to "Major-General Peck or Dix":

I have fully commenced my operations here. The result may be to draw troops from your front, and afford you an opportunity to push or hold them.

The following dispatch sent to-day was probably received in the course of the night:

### Davis to Lee

One half of Colonel Rhett's command (600 men and one battery) leave to-night by rail for Gordonsville. The remainder to-morrow morning.[1] Generals Longstreet, French,[2] and D. H. Hill [3] have been telegraphed to on the subject of reënforcements, but have not yet been heard from. Three regiments of cavalry from Western Virginia supposed to be *en route* to join you, but have not been heard from; neither has anything been heard from the two cavalry regiments in North Carolina.[4]

In consequence of Jackson's movement, numerous messages were forwarded to-day from the Federal signal stations below Fredericksburg to the Federal headquarters, reporting infantry, artillery, and trains, of the enemy, in motion up the river. But these reports did not give a definite idea of the numbers of the troops that had moved or of the distance they had covered. The following dispatch from Butterfield to Sedgwick was sent from Falmouth probably after dark:

If the enemy are massing troops in front of Brooks $(\frac{1}{VI})$ it will suit the general's purposes.

[1] Total force, 1400. Letter of May 1 from Cooper to Lee, *W. R.*, 39, p. 763.
[2] At Petersburg, Va.     [3] At Goldsboro, N. Ca.     [4] *W. R.*, 108, p. 698.

. . . The moment news arrives with regard to the progress made to-day by the right wing, plans for to-morrow will issue. *The manœuvers now in progress, the general hopes, will compel the enemy to fight him on his, Hooker's, own ground. He has no desire to make the general engagement where you are, in front of Brooks or Wadsworth.*

The italics are the author's. It appears therefrom that Hooker was thinking more of the defensive than he was of the offensive, and that he contemplated renouncing the initiative and relying for successful achievement upon the enemy's doing what he wanted him to do; that is, attacking him "on his own ground." By the phrase "on his own ground" he meant in a position of his own choice, and against such part only of his line as should be suited and prepared to receive an attack.

With a view to the reënforcement of the right wing, Sickles, commanding the III Corps, was ordered to hold his command "well in hand and all in readiness to march at a moment's notice."

The battery of Pleasonton's division (1. C) marched to-day from its camp near Potomac Bridge to Hartwood Church under orders from General Pleasonton to report to him at United States Ford.

The six batteries of the XI and XII Corps left on the north side of the river marched toward United States Ford, halting for the night probably at Hartwood Church.

A correspondent wrote to the New York *Herald:*

It is rumored that the enemy are falling back toward Richmond, but a fight to-morrow seems more than probable. We expect it, and we also expect to be victorious.

# CHAPTER XVI

APRIL 30 (MAP 11) . . . ARRIVAL OF THE ARMY OF THE POTOMAC AT CHAN-
CELLORSVILLE. DEMONSTRATION BY LEFT WING ORDERED AND SUSPENDED.
LINE OF DEFENCE AT CHANCELLORSVILLE. III CORPS IN MOTION. ADVANCE
FROM CHANCELLORSVILLE COUNTERMANDED. HOOKER'S CONGRATULATORY
ORDER. AVERELL MARCHES TO RAPIDAN STATION. STUART INTERCEPTED AT
TODD'S TAVERN

## *Right Wing, Forenoon*

ABOUT 1 a.m. the Confederate party returning from Germanna Ford reached Wilderness Tavern, and delivered its report to a courier of General Mahone's. Between 4 and 5 a.m. its commander received an order from Mahone to fall back at once to Chancellorsville.

Anderson decided to move back from Chancellorsville with Posey's and Mahone's brigades, and take up a position across the Turnpike and Plank Road between Zion Church and Tabernacle Church. Before he began this movement the Federal cavalry had commenced clearing the ground in front of Meade. Three squadrons of the 8 Pa. (Arrow-smith's, McCallum's, and Wickersham's) started from Ely's Ford under Major Huey, commanding the regiment, to reach United States Ford, and open communication with the Federal forces on the opposite bank of the Rappahannock. Their advance-guard, favored by the fog and the mat of wet leaves which covered the ground, surprised and captured a picket of Mahone's consisting of Company H of the 12 Va. This party had taken possession of an old school-house which stood in a convenient position in the center of the road where it forked, and occupied it for shelter. The dash upon it was so sudden and unex-pected that those who were inside had no opportunity to see, or judge of, the strength of the attacking force, which numbered only 8 men. While the Confederate sentries and videttes outside were being cared for, the door of the school-house was guarded, and each man was obliged to deliver his arms as he passed out. The 22 men and 3 commissioned officers who were thus taken were much chagrined when they saw the handful of men to whom they had surrendered, but it was then too late to make resistance.[1]

[1] J. E. Carpenter, late Captain 8 Pa. Cavalry, in Philadelphia *Weekly Times*. See also *War Talks of Confederate Veterans*, p. 50, and Huey's report, W. R., 39, p. 783.

Arrowsmith's squadron proceeded toward United States Ford, and McCallum's toward Chancellorsville. McCallum found a force of the enemy intrenched near the point where the road from Chancellorsville branched toward Ely's Ford and United States Ford, and became sharply engaged. Wickersham's squadron was sent to his assistance, and finally the whole of the 8 Pa. became engaged. Colonel Devin sent word to General Meade that he had driven in the enemy's pickets on the United States Ford Road, and having pursued them for several miles, had encountered the enemy drawn up in line of battle to the number, he thought, of at least a brigade. Meade received this message just as his main column was about to move. Concluding that the enemy was preparing to dispute the opening of the United States Ford, he ordered his leading division (Sykes') to proceed at once to that ford, and with Griffin's division took up the march for Chancellorsville. After crossing Hunting Run, he halted to await the development of Sykes' movement. By this time Devin had disposed of the enemy in Meade's immediate front and pursued him to the vicinity of Chancellorsville. Halting there, he sent a request to Meade—"that the point, from its evident importance, be occupied in force." Wright arrived with his brigade $\left(\frac{5}{1.1}\right)$ at Chancellorsville and reported to Anderson at daybreak. About 6 a.m. the whole command took up the march for the vicinity of Zion Church, Mahone's brigade $\left(\frac{1}{1.1}\right)$ by the Turnpike, Wright's and Posey's $\left(\frac{5}{1.1}, \frac{2}{1.1}\right)$ by the Plank Road. Anderson in person took the Plank Road. An advance detachment of the 8 Pa. Cavalry also took this road in pursuit. On reaching the open ground about Magee (A),[1] it made a bold attack upon Mahone's rear-guard, consisting of the 12 Va. Infantry. The latter deployed in two lines of skirmishers, one in rear of the other, which retired alternately, uniting for combined fire when pressed. The Federal cavalry was so effectually repulsed that it desisted from further attempt to interfere with the enemy's retreat, contenting itself with following and observing him in small bodies. The main body remained in the vicinity of Chancellorsville.[2] Anderson, with Mahone's brigade, reached his new position about 9 a.m. Wright arrived with his about 8 a.m. Here Anderson was met by the chief engineer of the Army of Northern Virginia and another engineer officer, who were sent to him by General Lee to assist him in selecting a defensive position. Mahone's brigade $\left(\frac{1}{1.1}\right)$ was established on the Turnpike; Posey's $\left(\frac{2}{1.1}\right)$ between the Turnpike and the Plank Road; and Wright's $\left(\frac{5}{1.1}\right)$ between the Plank Road and the unfinished railroad. Anderson

---

[1] The affixes (A) and (B) are the author's, to prevent confusion between the name *Magee* and that of *McGee* beyond Mott Run.

[2] *War Talks of Confederate Veterans,* by G. S. Bernard, p. 50; *W. R.*, 39, pp. 850, 862, 783; *The Charge of the 8 Pa. Cav. at Chancellorsville*, by Pennock Huey, p. 26.

wrote to Lee requesting that Semmes' brigade $(\frac{2}{2.1})$ be sent to him as reënforcement. His line being selected, the work of intrenching it commenced. Alexander's battalion of artillery (24 pieces) arrived at Anderson's position about 10 a.m., and Moore's battery (4 pieces 1. I) somewhat later in the forenoon. At noon the General Artillery Reserve and the Washington Artillery, advancing from Chesterfield depot by the Telegraph Road, were perhaps in the vicinity of Chilesburg (Map 10).

About 1 o'clock this morning Captain Comstock, on the march with Humphreys from Kelley's Ford, received a message from the headquarters of the Army of the Potomac urging him to hurry up the bridge train. It was evidently sent under the impression that a bridge would be needed for the passage of the Rapidan. The train was in rear of the troops, and could not move faster than they, but kept well closed up on them. At 3 o'clock the whole column was brought to a halt by the darkness. As soon as it was light enough to see, the bridge train was sent ahead under escort of two regiments, and the column resumed its march. At 7 a.m. Humphreys received the following dispatch from corps headquarters:

.    .    .    .    .    .    .    .    .

The major-general commanding is of the opinion that, in consequence of the force we have across the river, there is no necessity for keeping the whole of your command with the train. He thinks one regiment ought to suffice. You are desired, therefore, to push forward with all speed possible with the rest of your command, in order to join the column. . . .[1]

Early this morning General Warren at United States Ford reconnoitered the approach to the river, and finding it impracticable, procured 500 men from General Couch, and put them to work improving it. The mist so obscured his view of the opposite bank that he could not tell whether the enemy had withdrawn from it until about 9 o'clock, when the appearance of a number of Meade's cavalrymen showed it to be in possession of the Federals.

At 9:40 Humphreys received the following dispatch sent at 8:15:

The major-general commanding (V Corps) . . . has gone on to Hunting Run, at the head of General Griffin's column. You will follow on at once. The order of march this morning is, Sykes first, then Griffin, on the road to Chancellorsville.[2]

The Confederate scouting party falling back from Wilderness Tavern on Chancellorsville reached the latter point just as Devin's cavalry emerged from the woods into an open field immediately north of the Chancellor House. The Confederates quickened their steps to escape

---

[1] *W. R.*, 107, p. 1017.          [2] *Ib.*, 107, p. 1018.

capture, and a moment or two afterward came upon Mahone's rear-guard, retreating toward Zion Church, and joined it.[1]

Meade, still on Hunting Run, received Devin's report, and concluding therefrom that there was no enemy at United States Ford, proceeded with Griffin's division ($\frac{4}{V}$) to Chancellorsville. He arrived about 11 a.m.[2] The Federals found the house occupied. On an upper veranda were four ladies in light, attractive spring costumes, who, neither abashed nor intimidated, scolded audibly and criticized severely. They seriously condemned the stoppage, and urged a more expeditious movement, representing General Lee as just ahead, and anxiously awaiting an opportunity to dispense the "hospitality of the country." They little suspected the terrors that were in store for them as participants in that bountiful hospitality. General officers with their staffs, as the troops approached, gathered about the house and occupied the porches.[3]

On Meade's arrival Griffin directed Colonel Devin to send out a strong picket on the Plank Road, and a reconnoitering patrol toward Banks' Ford. At noon these parties were still out. Sykes' and Humphreys' divisions were marching up from the Rapidan. The former ($\frac{2}{V}$) was about 2 miles, and the latter ($\frac{3}{V}$) about 4 miles from Chancellorsville.

According to the instructions given Slocum on the 28th, the right wing was to advance from Chancellorsville to a point that should give it command of Banks' Ford. Once there, it could be reënforced by Gibbon's division ($\frac{2}{II}$) and soon afterward by the III Corps, assuming that the latter started from below Fredericksburg about the same time as the right wing from Chancellorsville. But it was decided this morning at Hooker's headquarters that the right wing should wait to-day at Chancellorsville for the enemy to attack it. Butterfield wrote to Warren at 9:30 a.m.:

I have not received a word from United States Ford this morning. Do send me by the bearer all the news. He is directed to run his horse.

I have sent up additional details from the Engineer brigade to assist at the bridges [at United States Ford]. When they are thrown across, I desire you to report to the commanding officer at Chancellorsville, to assist him, and give him the benefit of your advice in establishing a line of defence at that place or vicinity. The maps indicate that a formidable position can be taken there. Please show this to General Slocum, and to General Couch when he comes up.

I am informed that the enemy continues in full force in front of General Sedgwick. At all events, we want to hold the strongest position that section

[1] W. C. Smith in *War Talks of Confederate Veterans*, pp. 307–311.

[2] Barnes, commanding the leading brigade, says that his brigade "reached Chancellorsville at noon" (*W. R.*, 39, p. 514). Griffin's division had but one of its four batteries with it. The other three were to join it by way of United States Ford. As previously stated, one of its regiments ($\frac{20}{3.\,1.\,V}$) was left at Falmouth.

[3] *History of the Corn Exchange Regiment*, by the Survivors' Assoc., p. 171; *Marginalia*, by "Personne," p. 53.

[about Chancellorsville] affords to-night, and be in readiness to take the initiative in the morning.

Until Banks' Ford is uncovered, the route by the United States Ford must be understood as our line of operations. The weather is favorable for securing our positions, and, after all is over [across], the Rapidan is no advantage to the enemy over ourselves.

Colonel Owen upon halting with his two squadrons at Locust Grove, or soon after 12 p.m. the 29th, sent out scouting parties to Germanna and Ely's Fords with instructions to get as close to the enemy as possible and ascertain his strength and position. At 3 a.m. he received a dispatch from Fitzhugh Lee directing him to move forward, get in front of the enemy, and delay him, giving all attainable information to General Lee. He marched to Wilderness Tavern, turned up the road to Germanna Ford, and sent forward another scouting party. Between 6 and 7 a.m. his scouts from Germanna Ford reported a column of from 15,000 to 20,000 infantry across the Rapidan, with a considerable advance-guard of cavalry, mounted and forming to march. At 8 a.m. his scouts reported back from the direction of Ely's Ford.[1] About the same time a detachment of the 6 N. Y. Cavalry at the head of Slocum's column came into view. This was soon followed by skirmishing and charging for the possession of the cross-road, in which the Confederates had some success, until the odds against them became too great. One of their best-mounted troopers was sent westward with a dispatch for Fitzhugh Lee reporting what had been learned as to the force at Germanna Ford, also that a heavy wagon-train and artillery-train were across at Ely's, and under escort of a large force of infantry moving toward Chancellorsville. This man was captured by Federal cavalry in the woods before he had gone a mile. Couriers returning from Chancellorsville to the vicinity of Wilderness Tavern reported that they had been unable to communicate with the Confederate troops who were falling back; and that the Federals were already at Chancellorsville, and sending out scouting detachments. It was now nearly 9 a.m. Owen wheeled about and went toward Chancellorsville, but finding a strong force in his front, he turned to the right toward Todd's Tavern. As his column moved on, he started a courier with a dispatch to Major Taylor, R. E. Lee's adjutant-general, giving him all the information that he had of the two columns moving from Germanna and Ely's Fords. This man was cut off by the Federal cavalry at Chancellorsville, and thus compelled to go around that place, but he reached the general sometime between 11 a.m. and 1 p.m., bringing him the first intelligence that he received that day from the direction of the Rapidan.[2] It

[1] *So. Hist. Soc. Papers,* VIII, 252.

[2] Testifying a year later before the Committee on the Conduct of the War, Pleas-

onton said: "At a place called the Wilderness [Tavern] I captured a courier from General Lee with a dispatch in Lee's own

amounted to little more than a confirmation of the information last received by telegraph from Stuart. At noon Owen was at Todd's Tavern resting and feeding his horses.

Slocum resumed his march between 6 and 7 a.m.,[1] the XII Corps leading, with Geary's (2d) division in front. About 10 a.m., or soon after Owen's departure with his two squadrons of the 3 Va., Stuart with the remainder of Fitzhugh Lee's brigade, including the three squadrons of the 3 Va. under Carter, arrived in the vicinity of Wilderness Tavern, and, with three or four regiments and two pieces of artillery, attacked the 28 Pa., covering the right of Geary's division. Two regiments of infantry went out, and about noon drove him away. In the meantime the

handwriting. It was dated at 12 o'clock that day [30th], and I captured it at 1 o'clock, only one hour from his, Lee's hands. It was addressed to General Anderson, and read: 'I have just received reliable information that the enemy have crossed the [Rappahannock] river in force. Why have you not kept me informed? I wish to see you at my headquarters as soon as possible.'

"As soon as I got that dispatch I went to General Slocum and showed it to him, and told him that the rebel army had not moved from Fredericksburg and did not know the crossing of the three corps at the Rapidan, and I advised him then to send one of his corps, the 11th, as that was the nearest one, immediately to Spottsylvania Court-House, and to take up a position there and intrench. General Slocum said that he was ordered to concentrate his three corps at Chancellorsville. I told him that General Hooker never dreamed of getting three corps across that river in that position and Lee not know it, and without a fight, and that it gave us such an advantage that he ought to take the responsibility of putting that corps in that position. But he declined to do so and concentrated his three corps at Chancellorsville.

"I think it was about 5 or 6 o'clock in the evening that General Hooker arrived there and I saw him. I mentioned this fact to him of the importance of the position at Spottsylvania Court-House, and told him what I had recommended to General Slocum, and urged him by all means to put a corps there that night. General Hooker, however, said that he did not think it was necessary; that he had the rebel army, and it could not get away" (*Rep. of Com.*, IV, 27).

Writing for the *Century Magazine*,

Pleasonton stated that the dispatch was addressed to Major-General McLaws, and continued: "At 2 o'clock p.m., one hour later, I reported to General Hooker at Chancellorsville, and submitted to him the diary [of an engineer officer captured the day before] and General Lee's dispatch, both of which he retained, and I suggested that we had evidently surprised General Lee by our rapid movements, and, as Lee had prepared for a battle at Chancellorsville, he had better anticipate him by moving on toward Fredericksburg. . . . Every instinct induced me to suggest to General Hooker—to relieve ourselves from our embarrassment—to send the Eleventh Corps to Spottsylvania Court-House by the Jack Shop road, and make the line of battle from Chancellorsville to Spottsylvania. This proposition was not approved" (*B. and L.*, III, 173).

Pleasonton thus contradicts himself, stating that the dispatch was addressed to Anderson, and that it was addressed to McLaws; that Hooker, he thinks, arrived at Chancellorsville about 5 or 6 p.m., and that he arrived at or before 2 p.m. In neither of his official reports (one to Sickles, and one to Hooker) does he mention any such incident as the capture of a dispatch from Lee. The document referred to is not among the records of the War Department.

[1] Slocum says at *daylight* (*W. R.*, 39, p. 669), which would have been by 5 a.m. Geary, whose division led the column, says *early* (*ib.*, p. 728). His subordinates (*ib.*, pp. 743, 748, 750, 755, 764) give the hour as 8 a.m. Howard, who followed Slocum, says 7 a.m. (*Autobiography*, I, 355). It is probable that the cavalry started an hour or two before the infantry.

Federal main body continued its march.[1] Learning that the Federals were in possession of Chancellorsville, Stuart took up the march with Fitzhugh Lee's brigade toward Todd's Tavern. He meant to proceed thence by way of Spottsylvania Court-House to join the army under Lee.

### Right Wing, Afternoon to 4 O'clock

With reference to the reënforcement of the right wing the following instructions were issued to Couch:

. . . You will have the bridges laid without delay as soon as the enemy leaves. Don't let a small force keep you back. Establish rapid communication [by signal or courier] with the telegraph at Banks' Ford and with Meade and Slocum, as the telegraph from Banks' to United States Ford works so slow. You will move to support Slocum. Be careful that no trains [not even fighting trains] cross at United States Ford until further orders, as they will only be in the way. Meade's ammunition wagons may have to cross. [Until orders authorize the passage of trains at United States Ford,] the trains should cross at some point to be designated [by you].

The general directs me to add,—in moving in support of Slocum, move toward the heaviest firing, in the event of his advance being disputed. The general wishes you to be up with him to-night.

At 1 p.m. Sykes' division $(\frac{2}{V})$ joined Griffin's $(\frac{1}{V})$ at Chancellorsville.

The II Corps, it will be remembered, was to have crossed the Rappahannock at 7 a.m. By 1 p.m. there was a practicable approach to the United States Ford. At 2 the laying of the two bridges commenced; at 3:30 the work was completed, and the band of the Engineer Brigade crossed playing "In Dixie's land I'll take my stand." It was followed by the II Corps. The advance was taken by Carroll's brigade $(\frac{1}{3. \text{ II}})$, which formed line of battle on the south side, and skirmished through the woods, finding no enemy, but catching reports of artillery that came rumbling through the forest from the left. A road had to be made up the river-bank; this was soon done, whereupon the whole force pushed on past the enemy's abandoned defences, elated with the prospect of meeting him in the open field. The two divisions of the II Corps were accompanied by six ambulances,[2] or two more than they were allowed.[3] They left on the north side of the river the two regiments under Cross $(\frac{5. \ 81}{1. \ 1. \ \text{II}})$ and the 88 N. Y. of Meagher's "Irish" brigade $(\frac{2}{1. \ \text{II}})$.

Humphreys reached Ely's Ford with his division between 12 m. and 1 p.m., but his troops being greatly fatigued, he proceeded only as far

---

[1] W. R., 39, p. 669. Stuart, who was deceived by appearances, thought that he delayed the main body (ib., 39, p. 1047).

[2] Ib., 39, p. 549.          [3] Ib., 39, pp. 266, 267.

as Hunting Run, and halted for the night. He received the following dispatch sent at 2 p.m.:

> Bring your command on as far as you can without destroying entirely their efficiency. We are going into camp near this place [Chancellorsville], and I [Meade] would like you to get up as far at least as the crossing of Hunting Creek by the road from Ely's Ford. Report where and when you go into camp.[1]

Colonel Owen, after feeding his horses at Todd's Tavern, marched toward Fredericksburg. Before 4 p.m. he joined General Wright at Tabernacle Church, where he bivouacked in rear of the infantry, throwing out pickets to the front and upon each flank of Anderson's position.[2]

At 4 p.m. Stuart, marching toward Todd's Tavern, was probably in the vicinity of Poplar Run. The 6 N. Y. Cavalry reached Chancellorsville about 1 p.m. By order of General Pleasonton, its commander, Lieutenant-Colonel McVicar, reported his arrival to General Slocum, who was about 3 miles back. He received the following verbal order:

> You will proceed with your command to Spottsylvania Court-House, where you will be joined by others of our troops. Should you meet the enemy in force and offering resistance, you will gradually fall back and report to me by couriers. Meeting no resistance, you will continue the march.[3]

After repeating the order to insure that he understood it, he saluted and retired. He had not gone far toward his regiment when it occurred to him that he had no instructions or intimation as to whom he should report to at Spottsylvania Court-House upon the arrival of other troops at that point. He remarked to his adjutant, who was with him,—"I wish for more definite information as to the troops we shall meet at Spottsylvania, and to whom I shall report." Riding back to Slocum, he began his inquiry and was interrupted with the statement,—"You have your orders, sir; go." As he went away he remarked that the order indicated a "dusty job with results uncertain and perilous." Upon rejoining his regiment he put it in motion toward Spottsylvania Court-House (Map 11). He followed the Plank Road to Aldrich, turning off there on the road that led by Piney Branch Church, and at 4 p.m. was probably not far from the latter point. Meade heard from Devin that he had driven in the enemy's pickets on the Banks' Ford Road, and pursued them until he could see their line of battle, and that from the wagons visible he concluded they were about to evacuate the position. He sent him Barnes' brigade of infantry[4] ($\frac{1}{1.1}$).

[1] W. R., 107, p. 1018.

[2] So. Hist. Soc. Papers, VIII, 254; W. R., 39, p. 850.

[3] History of the Sixth New York Cavalry, by Committee, pp. 102, 103.

[4] Meade in his report gives the time when this took place as 3 p.m. (W. R., 39, p. 506). Barnes gives it as 1 p.m. (ib., p. 514). J. L. Parker, in his History of the 22 Mass., gives it as 1:30 p.m. It was probably about 1:15 p.m.

Slocum's column, after passing Wilderness Tavern, kept on the Germanna Plank Road to Wolfrey, and then followed the Orange Plank Road northeastward to the Turnpike (Map 11).[1]

The head of the XII Corps reached Chancellorsville about 2 p.m. Before he arrived there, Slocum received the following order, copies of which were sent to Couch and Meade:

> Headquarters Army of the Potomac, April 30, 1863, 2:15 p.m.
>
> *Captain Comstock:*
>
> The general directs that no advance be made from Chancellorsville until the columns [II, III, V, XI, and XII Corps] are concentrated.  He expects to be at Chancellorsville to-night.
>
> > DANL. BUTTERFIELD,
> >
> > Major-General, Chief of Staff.

Meade could not have received his copy of the foregoing order, for he greeted Slocum with the words: "This is splendid, Slocum; hurrah for old Joe; we are on Lee's flank, and he does not know it.  You take the Plank Road toward Fredericksburg, and I 'll take the Pike, or *vice versa*, as you prefer, and we will get out of this Wilderness."  His anticipations were at once dampened by the reply: "My orders are to assume command on arriving at this point, and to take up a line of battle here, and not to move forward without further orders."[2]

Howard reached the vicinity of Dowdall's Tavern with the head of his corps by 4 p.m.  While his corps closed up and went into bivouac he rode over to Slocum's headquarters at Chancellorsville and reported for orders.  Slocum told him that Hooker's orders were for Howard to cover the right of the general line, posting his command near Hunting Creek.[3]  Pointing to the place on the map marked *Mill,* he said,—"Establish your right there."[4]  He gave Howard to understand that he would himself take care of the entire front from Chancellorsville to Howard's left, the latter to be in the vicinity of Dowdall's Tavern, but afterward one of his division commanders sent Howard word that he would have to cover about three fourths of a mile of the Plank Road east of Dowdall's Tavern in order to connect with Slocum.  Howard gave the right of his line to his First Division (Devens').  Of the two brigades of this division the 2d (McLean's) was posted near Taylor, facing southward; and the 1st (von Gilsa's), about half a mile to the right of the 2d, facing westward, with half a regiment deployed as skirmishers in the interval to keep up connection between them.  In rear of the First Division, on the open ground about Hawkins' Farm,

---

[1] Map 6, Plate CXXXV, Atlas, *W. R.*

[2] *Life of General G. G. Meade,* by R. M. Bache, p. 260.

[3] *W. R.,* 39, p. 628.  In *Battles and Leaders* (III, 191) he says "near Dowdall's Tavern."

[4] Howard says there was no mill at this point, but the point was definitely located (*W. R.,* 39, p. 268; *B. and L.,* III, 191).

he placed the Third Division (Schurz's), facing westward. The Second Division extended in a single thin line a mile long to the vicinity of the Old School-House. The XI Corps was apparently considered by Hooker, Slocum, and Howard as a sort of flank detachment to secure the army against an attack from the west.[1] As such it was too much scattered and did not extend far enough to the rear. Howard says in his report that his right "rested in the vicinity of the point marked *Mill* on the map." But his own map, as well as Schurz's, shows that he had not a battalion within half a mile of that point. On the other hand, pickets were placed out in front on the Brock Road a considerable distance beyond the general line of outposts.[2]

The XII Corps formed a curve projecting southward and extending from the Old School-House eastward beyond the Plank Road. In the angle between this road and the Turnpike two batteries supported by two regiments were posted to command both roads. Further to the left and near Chancellorsville were the two divisions of the V Corps.

Some intrenchments and abatis were constructed along the fronts of the XI and XII Corps. It does not appear that any intrenching was done to-day in the V Corps.

About 4 p.m. Meade heard from Barnes that his brigade was in the presence of a superior force of the enemy, and would require support if it was to maintain its position. Meade now learned to his surprise that the scene of action was not on the Banks' Ford Road, but on the Turnpike. Devin, who chased the Confederate cavalry up the Turnpike, had been brought to a halt in front of an outpost of Anderson's on an eminence to the east of Mott Run (McGee, Map 11). McQuade's brigade of Griffin's division $(\frac{2}{1.\,V})$ now went to the support of Barnes, but Griffin had orders not to bring on an engagement.

"After several hours of impatient waiting, in buoyant expectancy of a promised success, the whole force was withdrawn to the rifle-pits near the Chancellorsville House, over which they had charged the enemy in the morning. There they remained in bivouac for the night. The soldiers were as discomfited as if they had been checked by a serious repulse. . . .

"Both General Griffin and [General] Barnes were much chagrined at the peremptory order to stop. . . . Griffin, filled with soldierly enthusiasm, and justly confident of his ability to take and hold the eminence, offered to surrender his commission if his attempt should prove a failure."[3]

---

[1] The commanding officer of the 145 N. Y. (1. XII) says in his report: "Our position at this time was about the center of the XII Corps, which occupied the right flank of the army" (*W. R.*, 39, p. 706).

[2] Devens says in his report at a distance of 3 miles from the position taken by his division (*W. R.*, 39, p. 633). They probably did not remain out that far.

[3] *History of the Corn Exchange Regiment* (118 Pa. Volunteers), by the Survivors' Assoc., pp. 173, 174.

At 4 p.m. Lee's General Artillery Reserve, under Pendleton, had arrived or was arriving at Massaponax Church (Map 10). The Washington Artillery was still in rear.[1]

### Right Wing, 4 p.m. to 12 p.m.

Hooker, with a portion of his staff, started from Falmouth for Chancellorsville about 4 p.m. His aide, Captain Candler, who was in the saddle from 6 p.m. yesterday till 5:30 a.m. to-day, wrote home:

We are off. Have some 30 miles to ride. Fight to-morrow. We have outwitted the Rebels so far. God grant us good fortune.

The distance to Chancellorsville was little over 20 miles. Hooker arrived there between 5 and 6, and presumably received in due time the following message signaled to him by Butterfield at 6:45:

Considerable cannonading in front of Sedgwick. Nothing from him yet. I have received no orders for Gibbon. He is held in readiness to move in accordance with your last instructions. . . . Comstock is here, pretty well used up; gone to bed; reports his train in bad condition; not fit for crossing trains, only for infantry, possibly for cavalry. Have directed him to United States Ford very early to-morrow a.m. in case nothing from you,—to take his train again.

All quiet here [Falmouth] now. No apparent diminution in enemy's strength in front of Sedgwick, and no movement reported.

By this time the following congratulatory order had been published to the troops under Sedgwick and to the II Corps. It was published in the right wing in the course of the evening and the following morning:

Headquarters Army of the Potomac,
Camp near Falmouth, Va., April 30, 1863.

General Orders, No. 47:

It is with heartfelt satisfaction the commanding general announces to the army that the operations of the last three days have determined that our enemy must either ingloriously fly or come out from behind his intrenchments and give us battle on our own ground, where certain destruction awaits him.

The operations of the 5th, 11th, and 12th Corps have been a succession of splendid achievements.

By order of Major-General HOOKER:

S. WILLIAMS,

Assistant Adjutant-General.[2]

Here, then, is Hooker's answer to the question: What was to be done in case the enemy would not attack him on his own ground? In this case the enemy would "ingloriously fly," and there would be nothing for the Army of the Potomac to do but to pursue him.

[1] According to Pendleton it was on the march, but had lost its way (*W. R.*, 39, p. 810).
[2] *Ib.*, 39, p. 171.

The two divisions of the II Corps, with the batteries already mentioned accompanying them, commenced arriving at the Chandler House about 10 p.m. and were closed up, and went into bivouac there about midnight. The two regiments under Cross ($\frac{5.\ 81}{1.\ 1.\ II}$) marched from the vicinity of Banks' Ford to United States Ford, where they were joined by the 88 N. Y. of Meagher's brigade ($\frac{2}{1.\ II}$). These three regiments were here formed into a provisional brigade which was commanded by Colonel Cross throughout the campaign. It will be considered as the 5th brigade of Hancock's division.[1] In addition to this infantry on the north bank, the 116 Pa. of Meagher's brigade was left in the vicinity of United States Ford, on the south bank. Meagher's brigade, with the exception of the 88 N. Y. and 116 Pa., took post in the vicinity of Scott's Dam. The two divisions of the II Corps were accompanied by the corps ammunition-train (wagon) and six ambulances,[2] or two more ambulances than they were required or authorized to take.[3]

The 17 Pa. Cavalry, attached to the XI Corps, picketed the roads to the right and rear.

The V, XI, and XII Corps had each marched with one battery per division. The XII was joined by one of its remaining batteries, F, Pa., Second Division. The other two ($\frac{1.\ 3}{1.\ XII}$) were on the south bank of the Rappahannock near United States Ford. The five batteries of the V Corps that were left on the north bank marched to-day to Hartwood Church. Those of the XI Corps (corps artillery) crossed the river at United States Ford, but did not join the corps.[4] Brooker's Battery B, 1 Conn. (four 4½-inch guns), of the General Artillery Reserve, from Banks' Ford, crossed also at United States Ford, and remained near the river.

The following order was sent to Humphreys ($\frac{3}{V}$) at 9:30 p.m.:

. . . come forward to this place to-morrow morning. You will march by early daylight, as it is all-important that you report with your command at the earliest possible moment. Headquarters are at Mrs. Chancellor's house at this place. . . . The orderly who brings this will remain with you to-night to communicate with the commanding general.

The Federal cavalry in this part of the field, consisting of the 8 Pa., bivouacked without unsaddling on the west side of Mott Run, with one squadron picketing the Turnpike beyond it. Hooker had available for action between the Rapidan and Chancellorsville about 50,000 men and

---

[1] *A History of the 5th Regiment N. H. Volunteers,* by William Child, pp. 179, 182; W. R., 39, p. 159.

[2] Batchelder's report, *W. R.,* 40, p. 549.

[3] Williams to commanding officer II

Corps, April 27 and 30, *W. R.,* 40, pp. 266, 267, 304.

[4] It is assumed that they bivouacked on the south bank in the vicinity of United States Ford.

108 pieces of artillery.[1]  With this force he barred Lee's line of retreat to Gordonsville, and, together with Sedgwick below Fredericksburg, threatened to cut him off from Richmond.  His confident expectation of victory was shared by the army.  It was generally expected that on the morrow it would advance to attack the enemy if he should stand; to pursue him if he should flee.  Hooker's congratulatory order should have disabused all minds of the idea that he intended to attack.  But understood, or misunderstood, as it was, the order was received with wild demonstrations of enthusiasm.  In every direction as it was read, regiments could be seen cheering and tossing their hats in the air, while bands discoursed national music.  But here and there an old soldier went on smoking his pipe in silence, and when reproached for his seeming apathy would reply to the effect that Lee had never been known to ingloriously fly, that it would be better to wait until after the battle to do one's cheering.[2]

Colonel McVicar, with the 6 N. Y. Cavalry, followed the road from Aldrich (Map 10) past Piney Branch Church to the first road on his left, and proceeded thereby to the road that led from Todd's Tavern to Spottsylvania Court-House, which he reached at the junction from half to three quarters of a mile northwest of H. Alsop.  The road from Chancellorsville to this point was scarcely wide enough for a column of fours, and lined with woods nearly the entire distance.  Night was falling.  The moon was between half and full.  Detachments commanded by officers were sent out, one toward Spottsylvania Court-House, one toward Fredericksburg, and one to the right, perhaps on a wood road or path.  The main body closed up in column, and dismounted to await developments.

At nightfall Stuart halted at Todd's Tavern, intending that his troops should bivouac here, and he with his staff ride on through Spottsylvania Court-House to army headquarters and receive instructions. He had not gone far beyond the Tavern when he found himself confronted by a detachment of the 6 N. Y. numbering about 30 men.  Fired upon and charged by these men, he beat a hasty retreat for some distance, and then the pursuit ceasing, he halted and sent on to Todd's Tavern for aid.  About as this firing was heard at the head of the

| [1] ORGANIZATIONS | INFANTRY | CAVALRY | ARTILLERY | AGGREGATE | PIECES |
|---|---|---|---|---|---|
| $\frac{1.\ 3}{II}$  . . . . . | 7,414 | 9 | 733 | 8,156 | 36 |
| V  . . . . . | 14,477 | 100 | 286 | 14,863 | 14 |
| XI  . . . . . | 12,170 | 50 | 757 | 12,977 | 36 |
| XII  . . . . | 12,929 | | 335 | 13,264 | 18 |
| General Artillery Reserve  . . | | | 92 | 92 | 4 |
| Pleasonton  . . . . | | 1,150 | | 1,150 | |
| | 46,990 | 1,309 | 2,203 | 50,502 | 108 |

[2] *Slocum and his Men,* by Committee, p. 161.

Federal column, the officer sent out to Spottsylvania Court-House returned with the report that hostile troops blocked the way to that point,[1] and another came in with the report,—"The road is full of rebs."[2] Men mounted without orders. "We must have room to fight," they said. "Down with that gate! Forward!" and the regiment dashed through the opening made for itself into a field between the two roads that part at this point and meet about a mile further on, the Alsop Field. Here the command was formed in line facing the gate through which it had entered, or toward its late rear. Stuart's brigade had not yet dismounted. The 5 Va., being the nearest regiment, was launched at once toward Spottsylvania Court-House. Driving the Federal detachments before it, it dashed in column of fours at the opening into the Alsop Field, but was driven back with considerable loss by the concentrated carbine fire of the Federal horsemen delivered from the saddle. The rest of the command having come up, Stuart now ordered his next regiment, the 3 Va. (three squadrons under Carter), to renew the attack. It attempted, like the 5th, to charge through the entrance, but, like the former, was hurled back with the fire of carbines from the saddle. Colonel McVicar, perceiving that he was heavily outnumbered, concluded that he was in danger of being surrounded and captured with his whole force. So forming column of fours with sabers drawn, and rising in his stirrups, he called out: "Sixth New York follow me. *Charge!*" The bugles sounded, the men cheered, and the column darted at the gate. About 70 feet from it McVicar fell, shot through the heart. The charge nevertheless continued through the gate to the right on the road to Spottsylvania, and then again to the right back by the lower road, driving fragments of the enemy's regiments before it, aiming at the junction where the road branches off toward Piney Branch Church and Chancellorsville. The 2 Va. was now ordered to take the road, and open the way, if possible, to Spottsylvania Court-House. Stuart informed Colonel Munford, its commander, of the importance of his reporting in person to R. E. Lee, and stated that if he could not get through by Alsop's he would have to take some other route to the Court-House.[3] The 2 Va., with a yell which is said to have had more effect than sabers or pistols,[4] broke through the column of the 6 N. Y., cutting off the rear portion, and opened the way for Stuart. The latter

---

[1] *Hist. of the 6 N. Y. Cav.*, by Committee, p. 103. According to another authority, this report was that there was a heavy force at Spottsylvania Court-House (*Journal U. S. Cav. Assoc.*, June, 1891, p. 110). Stuart says in his report,—"Artillery as well as trains were passing Spottsylvania unprotected at the time" (*W. R.*, 39, p. 1046).

[2] Verbal statement of Lieutenant F. A. Easton, 6 N. Y. Cav.

[3] Letters from Colonel T. T. Munford and Sergeant C. E. Adams, 2 Va. Cavalry.

[4] Letters of Corporal M. T. Rucker and Sergeant C. E. Adams, 2 Va. Cavalry.

pushed on with the brigade toward Spottsylvania Court-House, and the unintercepted portion of the 6 N. Y. went back by way of Piney Branch Church toward Chancellorsville. This was about midnight. The Federal loss in killed, wounded, and missing was 51 officers and men.[1] The Confederate loss is not reported. The Federals took a number of prisoners, but seem to have lost them afterward. Major McClellan, in his *Campaigns of Stuart's Cavalry* (p. 231), mentions but one Confederate casualty. As result of the contest the 6 N. Y. was prevented from reaching Spottsylvania Court-House, and Stuart was delayed some twelve hours in communicating with R. E. Lee.

The train of led horses, mules, etc., from Stoneman's cavalry, went by way of Germanna Ford to Chancellorsville, and thence to United States Ford, yielding the main road to troops going to the front. The rear portion of the column was cut off by the enemy at or near Chancellorsville. At United States Ford, after waiting for the troops that were crossing to clear the bridge, the train crossed the river to the north side and went into camp near the ford.[2]

Early this morning (April 30) Averell received the following order from Stoneman's adjutant-general:[3]

. . . we did not get off this morning as soon as was anticipated, but will endeavor to carry out our original instructions in the next twenty-four hours, Keep your communications open with your infantry support. Our pack-train with Eleventh Corps.[4]

By "infantry support" Averell not unnaturally understood the division of the V Corps left at Kelley's Ford. It was intended, it seems, to mean the nearest portion of the right wing at the front (XI and XII Corps). W. H. F. Lee fell back through Culpeper Court-House to Rapidan Station, leaving a squadron at Culpeper Court-House. Averell's movement to the latter point was made in extended order. For miles to right and left lines of mounted skirmishers steadily advanced in excellent order, driving back the enemy's skirmishers. Immediately in rear marched their support of squadrons in line about ⅛ of a mile apart. Then came the main body of the division, in columns of regiments with squadron front, about ¾ of a mile apart, each regiment with a squadron as special advance-guard. The horse artillery was distributed between the regiments. The whole as it moved to the sound of cracking carbines over the beautiful open country formed a grand and imposing spectacle. About noon it contracted its front, and

---

[1] *W. R.*, 39, p. 192.

[2] *History of the 10th Regiment of Cavalry, New York State Volunteers*, by N. D. Preston, pp. 70, 77.

[3] Averell gives the hour of receipt both as 7 a.m. and as 8:05 a.m. (*W. R.*, 39, pp. 1075 and 1078).

[4] *Ib.*, 39, p. 1075.

marched through Culpeper Court-House toward Rapidan Station, meeting with some resistance from Lee's squadron.[1]

At 4 p.m. he halted for rest on the battle-field of Cedar Mountain (1862), recognizable at this time by a number of open trenches filled with human bones. At 6:30 p.m., being again on the march, he received the following dispatch:

> The major-general commanding [General Stoneman] directs me to say that we have been delayed by high water, etc., and that he desires you to push the enemy as vigorously as possible, keeping him fully occupied, and if possible, drive him in the direction of Rapidan Station. He turns the enemy over to you.[2]

He understood from these instructions that he was not expected to rejoin the cavalry corps for an indefinite time. The intention was that he should disperse W. H. F. Lee's brigade at once, and march without delay to join the force under Stoneman. Between 7:30 and 8 p.m. he arrived at Rapidan Station, and found himself confronted by W. H. F. Lee on the opposite side of the river. All the information that he had been able to gather from a mail captured at Culpeper Court-House, prisoners, and other sources, went to show that the enemy believed the Army of the Potomac to be advancing behind him, and that Stonewall Jackson was at Gordonsville with 25,000 men to resist it. This information, strange to say, was "deemed reliable and important" and was sent to General Hooker at 11 p.m.[3]

### Left Wing, Forenoon

The following message was probably received at Hooker's headquarters early this morning:

F Signal Station, April 30, 1863, 7 a.m.

Captain Samuel T. Cushing,
    Act'g Chief Signal Officer, Hqrs. Army of the Potomac:
    The enemy have occupied the cut of the River road from the city to near Hamilton's Crossing, the stone wall in front of Marye's, the ditches near Hazel Run, at the foot of the hill back of Hoblison's [Howison's] house [Map 12]; also on the top of the hill. See but two batteries in position yet. No force above the city other than pickets.

JAS. S. HALL,
Captain and Signal Officer.

The enemy seemed then to be remaining in position, but if he was, would he continue to do so? To obtain an answer to this question,

---

[1] *History of a Cavalry Company* (A, 4 Pa.), by Captain William Hyndman, p. 89; and *History of the 3 Pa. Cavalry,* by Committee.
[2] *W. R.,* 39, p. 1075.          [3] *Ib.,* 39, p. 1078.

Hooker had the following instructions sent at 8:30 a.m. to the commander of the left wing:

. . . make a demonstration on the enemy's lines in the direction of Hamilton's Crossing at 1 o'clock, the object being simply to ascertain whether or not the enemy continues to hug his defences in full force; and if he should have abandoned them, to take possession of his works and the commanding ground in their vicinity. . . .

If you are certain that the enemy is in full force in your front . . . the demonstration herein directed will not be made. The general must know the position of affairs and be advised fully; also as to what you do, at once.

The enemy have a pontoon train at Hamilton's.[1] The general expects that you will not permit them to cross the river.

Sedgwick wrote to Butterfield probably about 11 a.m.:

General Reynolds is satisfied that the enemy have not weakened their forces either in infantry or artillery; and that a demonstration will bring on a general engagement on the left. General Brooks thinks the infantry force in his front is undiminished and strong. He can see nothing of their batteries.

This intimation of a possible movement of artillery from in front of Brooks seems to have been the only cause for apprehending any transfer of troops toward Chancellorsville.

In answer to the foregoing note Butterfield wrote at 11:30 a.m.:

Let the demonstration be suspended until further orders.

### Left Wing, Afternoon

Having renounced the idea of a movement beyond Chancellorsville to-day, Hooker wanted to secure every possible advantage for the one to be undertaken to-morrow. Among these was early communication by way of Fredericksburg and Banks' Ford, and the reënforcement of the right wing,—whence the following instructions:

*To Haupt* (12 m.): To be ready to commence work on the Richmond and Fredericksburg Railroad on the 2d.

*To Benham:* To have two bridges, one at Franklin's and one at Fitzhugh's Crossing, taken up during the night and placed in position to be laid at Banks' Ford before daylight. Nothing to be done before dark, the movement to be concealed from the enemy.

*To Sickles* (12:30 p.m.): To march with his corps to United States Ford and cross by 7 a.m. to-morrow.[2]

---

[1] There was no pontoon train with Lee's army. J. B. Jr.

[2] *Butterfield to Sickles, 12:30 p.m.:* "Upon the receipt of this order you will proceed with your corps [III] without de-

lay, by the shortest road, concealed from view of the enemy, to the United States Ford. The batteries taken from your command, placed in position to cover the crossing [below Fredericksburg], will be re-

*To Sedgwick:* In case of the enemy's exposing a weak point, to attack and destroy him; in case of his appearing to fall back, to advance in pursuit by the Bowling Green Road and Telegraph Road.

*To Gibbon* (about 5:30 p.m.): To be ready to move with his division at daylight to-morrow to join his corps.

In Hooker's instructions to Sedgwick there was much stress laid upon attacking, striking, destroying, capturing, etc., but all to be done by Sedgwick. There was no promise in them of any such action on the part of Hooker. The right wing was apparently intended to serve as a sort of anvil on which Sedgwick was to crush Lee's army. The instructions required him to throw his whole force on the Bowling Green Road and at the same time to have a column advance on the Telegraph Road.[1] Sedgwick telegraphed for an explanation of this contradiction (*Appendix 15*).

Reports from Fredericksburg indicated to Hooker that Lee was being reënforced from Richmond, but they gave him apparently no serious concern.[2]

Butterfield wrote to Sedgwick:

The general in speaking privately to me about the order No. 47, in which the movements of the Fifth, Eleventh, and Twelfth Corps were commended, said he had been informed that there was some little feeling down on the left that they

lieved, it is expected, in time to join you. It is desired that, in marching, your troops and your trains entire should be concealed from the sight of the enemy, that they may not be aware of your movement. Your pack-mules, small-arm ammunition-train, and two ambulances to a division, to accompany you. Forage for animals for two days from to-day. The greatest promptness in executing this movement and arriving at your destination is expected of you. As much of your corps as can cross on the bridge at United States Ford to cross to-night, and all to cross by 7 a.m. to-morrow. "General Couch precedes you, and the batteries left by General Meade also. After crossing, you will take up your line of march toward Chancellorsville. . . . "

[1] *Butterfield to Sedgwick:* ". . . [Hooker's] Headquarters will be at Chancellorsville to-night. It is proposed that the army now at that point [V, XI, and XII Corps] will assume the initiative to-morrow morning, and will advance along the line of the Plank road, uncovering what is called Banks' Ford, where bridges will be at once thrown across the river, which route will then become the shortest line of communication between the two wings of the army.

. . . It is not known, of course, what effect the advance [of the right wing] will have upon the enemy, and the general commanding directs that you observe his movements with the utmost vigilance, and should he expose a weak point, attack him in full force and destroy him. If he should show any symptoms of falling back, *the general directs that you throw your whole force on the Bowling Green road,* and pursue him with the utmost vigor, turning his fortified positions by the numerous by-roads which you can make use of for that purpose. If any portion of his organized forces should pass off to the east of the railroad, you will by detachments pursue until you destroy or capture him. *Simultaneously with the advance of your column on the Bowling Green road, if at all, a column will also advance on the Telegraph road,* and between you [your two columns] will sweep the country between the two highways and the railroad [between the Bowling Green road and railroad on one hand and the railroad and Telegraph road on the other]. . . . when you strike, let it be done to destroy. . . . "

The italics are mine. J. B. Jr.

[2] *Reynolds to Hooker, 2:20 p.m.:* "I think that movements indicate that they

were not counted in. He said that would all come right. He expected when he left there, if he met with no serious opposition, to be on the heights west of Fredericksburg to-morrow noon or shortly after, and if opposed strongly, to-morrow night. . . .

The departure of Brooker's battery had left at Banks' Ford only von Blücher's light battery of the General Reserve and perhaps a detachment of engineers and provost guard.

Hooker's order for the III Corps to come up to Chancellorsville by United States Ford was received at 1 p.m. By 1:30 the corps was under way. Orders had been issued to the chief commissary to replace the rations that had been consumed. This was generally done, but there were instances in which the troops refused to burden themselves with the new rations, and left them lying on the ground. The brigade commissaries remained behind, gathered up these stores, and replaced them in the supply-wagons. The corps marched in three parallel columns, well concealed from the enemy, to Hamet, where it went into bivouac about 11:30 p.m. The train, left below Fredericksburg, broke camp about 5 p.m. It was formed of the supply section, carrying subsistence stores; the baggage section, carrying camp and garrison equipage; and the ammunition section, carrying ammunition. Each section carried eight days' rations of grain for itself. As the train proceeded in the wake of the troops it passed many places where knapsacks had been emptied of their contents, or slung into the bushes. When it reached Falmouth, the officer in charge was ordered to park the baggage and supply sections and push forward the ammunition section at all hazards. The ammunition section accordingly went on. The baggage and supply sections did not leave Falmouth again during the campaign, though portions of the supply section were detached and sent to the front as occasion required. The ammunition section kept close behind the troops.

Martin's horse battery (1. C), ordered to report to Pleasonton, marched to United States Ford, and camped on the north side.

Lee's expectation that more Federal troops would cross in front of Fredericksburg was not realized. The troops under Sedgwick and under Early remained quiet to-day, except for some long-range artillery dueling,—a bit of the "Song of the Rappahannock," interesting to the spectators, and more or less impressive to every one within range of its

are passing troops up to our right [toward Chancellorsville]. . . . The railroad seems to be busy to-day. . . ."

*Butterfield to Reynolds:* "What did the locomotives draw? Could it be transportation trains [transportation of troops]?"

*Reynolds to Butterfield:* "The trains they ran were passenger and platform cars."

*Sedgwick to Butterfield* (3:45 p.m.): "General Reynolds sends word in regard to movement of troops of the enemy on his front as follows: 'I think it must be troops from Richmond.'"

*Butterfield to Sedgwick:* "General Hooker hopes they are from Richmond, as the greater will be our success."

far reverberations, but not of any tactical effect. The men, for the greater part, continued their usual games of ball and quoits, played cards, cut hair, and slept. Officers sat under their little shelter tents as deeply buried in a novel as in the days of drills, parades, and reviews.

Lee was undecided during most of the day as to whether he should abandon his position near Fredericksburg or fight to retain it. He wrote at 2:30 p.m. to Anderson, at Tabernacle Church:

> Set all your spades to work as vigorously as possible. I hope to send you additional troops. . . . Keep two days' rations cooked that the men can carry on their persons, and give orders that everything be prepared to pack your trains and move off at any moment when ordered. All your baggage, camp equipage, including your headquarters, etc., must be immediately reduced in order to accomplish this.
>
> General Stuart writes that the Third Virginia Cavalry, Colonel Owen, and Second North Carolina [Cavalry], Colonel Payne, have been ordered to report to me. They are probably on the Plank road; direct them to keep in your front, and to keep you advised of all movements of the enemy, and to delay his progress as much as possible.

The concentration of troops at Chancellorsville, together with the inactivity of those at Franklin's Crossing, satisfied him later in the day that the enemy's main effort was being made upon his left flank and rear. Expecting that Hooker would push on from Chancellorsville to attack him, he determined to leave a sufficient force in his lines to hold them, and to move out with the main body of his army to give battle to the advancing columns. He issued the following order:

> I. Major-General McLaws will designate a brigade of his division to hold the lines in rear of Fredericksburg, the commander of which will report to the major-general left in charge [division commander: see paragraph II]. With the rest of his division [three brigades and artillery] General McLaws will move as soon as possible to reënforce General Anderson at the Tabernacle Church, on the Plank road to Orange Court-House.
>
> II. General Jackson will designate a division to hold the lines in front of the enemy on Pratt's and Bernard's farms. The commander of the division will establish such pickets as may be necessary. With the remainder of his corps General Jackson, at daylight to-morrow morning, will proceed to Tabernacle Church, and make arrangements to repulse the enemy.
>
> III. The troops will be provided with two days' cooked provisions. The trains of all the divisions will be packed with their equipage, and [will] move to the rear under the direction of the chief quartermaster of the army. The reserve ammunition-trains will be under the charge of the chief of ordnance [at the rear]. The regimental ordnance wagons, ambulances, and medical wagons will accompany the troops.
>
> IV. The chief of artillery will superintend the service of the batteries in position on the lines, and take charge of those not required to operate with the troops.

McLaws designated Barksdale's brigade ($\frac{4}{2.1}$), and Jackson, Early's division ($\frac{3}{11}$), to remain in the lines of Fredericksburg. Wilcox with his brigade and two batteries was to hold Banks' Ford.

At 6 p.m. Semmes' brigade ($\frac{2}{2.1}$), by General Lee's order, left its position in rear of Howison's, and marched toward Anderson's at Zion Church. At midnight it was probably within a mile of its destination[1] (Map 12).

Lee wrote to Lieutenant-Colonel Critcher, commanding the 15 Va. Cavalry:

You will close your cavalry pickets up to the infantry on the Rappahannock. I have sent you orders by a courier, but have heard nothing from you.[2]

This officer, it seems, had crossed the river, and been captured by men of Reynolds' corps.[3]

Longstreet was ordered to move with his command to Richmond "to effect a junction with General Lee."[4]

Hooker's canvas bridge train brought down from Kelley's Ford recrossed the Rappahannock at United States Ford, and was not laid again during the campaign. His telegraph line was extended across United States Ford and a station established at the Red House. The line between England and United States Ford was not working well, but flag and torch stations were established connecting these points; on the left the telegraph was extended from Sedgwick's to Reynolds' headquarters, but communication was not opened to-day. At 3 p.m. the flag and torch station opposite Buckner's Neck was broken up.

In compliance with a request of the United States Senate, this day was designated by President Lincoln, in a proclamation, to be set apart for the expression of national humiliation, and the invocation of divine blessing. Little could be done in observance of it. Here and there, out of the immediate presence of the enemy, a chaplain succeeded, with the aid of more or less coercion, in getting an audience, and held forth on the crisis through which the nation was passing, the seriousness of life, and the solemnity of death.

---

[1] Semmes' report, *W. R.*, 39, p. 833. McLaws erroneously reports that it took up the march toward Anderson's position at 12:30 a.m. on the 1st of May (*ib.*, p. 824).

[2] *Ib.*, 108, p. 699.

[3] On the 25th of May Captain Lytle, Provost-Marshal, Army of the Potomac, wrote to Colonel Hoffman, Commissary-General of Prisoners:

"Colonel Critcher has undoubtedly been detailed to remain on the north side of the Rappahannock to organize bushwhacking parties, and to furnish information of our movements to the enemy. One dispatch from him to General Lee was intercepted, which led to his capture. There is not sufficient evidence to hold him as a spy, but it is requested that every impediment possible be thrown in the way to prevent his exchange for some time to come" (*W. R.*, 118, p. 706).

[4] *Ib.*, 26, p. 1032.

Butterfield wrote to Heintzelman asking that the cavalry of his command extend its patrols to the vicinity of Rappahannock Station.

As a protection against the indiscreet publications of the press an order was issued from the headquarters of the Army of the Potomac requiring all newspaper correspondents "to publish their communications over their own signatures," under penalty of being excluded from, and having the circulation of their papers suppressed within, the lines of the army.  The following dispatches remain to be noticed:

### Dix to Hooker

. . . A successful movement on your part, for which we are all most anxious, will be of great service to us by preventing Longstreet from being further reënforced, and may compel him to withdraw.

### Hooker to Dix, 12:30 p.m.

The enemy has need of every man here.  He has his hands full.  Rely on this. I can say no more.

#### COMMENTS

Hooker erred in consigning Sedgwick to inaction.  To keep up the semblance of an offensive operation it is necessary to do something. Sedgwick should at least have thrown additional troops across the river.

Hooker's passage of the Rappahannock, and march to the rear of Lee's army, is classed among the most brilliant manœuvers in military history.  What was the main secret of its success?  It certainly was not punctuality of movement.  On the 28th the right wing, which was to cross at Kelley's Ford "at the earliest possible moment," did not commence crossing until six hours after it was formed up in the vicinity of the ford; the left wing, which was to have left its bivouacs early in the morning, did not leave them until about the middle of the afternoon. On the 29th the bridges which should have been laid below Fredericksburg by 3:30 a.m. were not all down until noon; the cavalry corps, which was to have crossed the Rappahannock by 8 a.m., did not get over until 5 p.m.  On the 30th the two divisions of the II Corps that should have crossed at United States Ford at 7 a.m. crossed at 3:30 p.m.  Nor was the success due to concealment.  The plan had been kept a secret, but the movement, once started, was not long unobserved.  It was executed, for the greater part, under the eye of the enemy.  Its success must be attributed in the main to the circuitous and eccentric direction of the preliminary marches,—including perhaps the movements of Stahel's division of cavalry from Fairfax Court-House, which led the enemy to believe that the movement was directed not against him, but against the Shenandoah Valley or the remote railroad center of Gordonsville.  It caused Stuart to post his cavalry so that the Federal columns cut it from its proper field of operation—the Federal front—

and prevented him from warning his pickets along the Rappahannock. For this error of judgment Stuart is hardly to be criticized. "Show me the commander who has never made a mistake, and I will show you one who has never made war."

Had Hooker been imbued with the true offensive spirit he would not have allowed his whole force to camp in the vicinity of Chancellorsville, but would have pushed at least a portion of it down the Rappahannock and gained possession of Banks' Ford. All necessary arrangements should have been made beforehand for proceeding by rapid marches from the time the general movement commenced until Banks' Ford was secured. These arrangements in fact were made, and the movement went on with every promise of success until Hooker conceived the idea of receiving an attack at Chancellorsville.

A year later he was asked by the Committee on the Conduct of the War: "What was your reason for leaving so large a reserve force under Sedgwick at or near Falmouth?" He answered: "I left Sedgwick's corps and Gibbon's division there for this reason in part: they were encamped in sight of the enemy, and to have moved their camp would have betrayed our movement. I knew I could not cross the river in the presence of Lee's army, if he was informed of my movement. The great difficulty I apprehended was in crossing the river. I apprehended no serious trouble after I had crossed. At the time I had to leave a force at Falmouth to keep the rebel force there. I did not want the enemy to throw a force to meet me on the Rapidan; and, besides, I was informed that they had a pontoon bridge at Hamilton's Crossing, and did not want them to cross the river while I was away, as that would enable them to strike at my depots. Mine were large and full, and the enemy would have willingly exchanged theirs for them; for theirs were comparatively empty."[1]

This is only half an answer. It does not account for Reynolds and Sickles as part of Sedgwick's command. If they were not necessary for Sedgwick, one at least should have been with Hooker from the start; at any rate, if one of them was necessary to Hooker, and could not have been furnished him without entailing a delay in his advance, the plan of campaign was radically defective, and should not have been adopted.

Any advance that Hooker might make with the right wing was to have one of two objects: the pursuit of a fleeing enemy, or the taking up of a new defensive position. He had no intention apparently of looking up the enemy and attacking him. Now Lee was not retreating,—was he going to retreat? Suppose he should march on Chancellorsville. Would Hooker, after waiting for Sickles to join him, have time to anticipate Lee at a position commanding Banks' Ford or otherwise preferable to Chancellorsville? Misgivings in this regard prevented his issuing

[1] *Rep. of Com.*, IV, 145.

orders to-day for a movement to-morrow. His indecision, which was more or less apparent and disquieting to visitors at headquarters, did not in the least abate his confidence of victory. In his mind Lee was doomed to destruction. It was only a question as to how and where he should meet his ignominious fate. He said in the hearing of at least one newspaper correspondent:

The rebel army is now the legitimate property of the Army of the Potomac. They may as well pack up their haversacks and make for Richmond. I shall be after them.[1]

Without the boastful speeches of which this is a sample, or the vainglorious order No. 47, Hooker was under peculiar and heavy bonds to gain a victory. His severe and open criticisms of his predecessors in the command of the army warranted a general expectation of something brilliant and decisive from him.[2]

[1] Swinton's *Campaigns of the Army of the Potomac*, p. 275.

[2] The state of the public mind was reflected in an editorial of the New York *Herald* of this day:

"The army of General Hooker is in motion and has been for several days past. . . . He must win or his fall will be, like that of Lucifer, never to rise again. His published testimony before the Congressional Committee on the Conduct of the War [given December 20, 1862, and March 11, 1863] places him in a position of extraordinary responsibility. . . . General Hooker has now no alternative before him but victory or death—death in the field or death to his reputation as a military leader. He has voluntarily set himself up as the superior of McClellan and Burnside, and he must make his pretensions good or sink into irretrievable public disgrace. . . . We have no doubt that General Hooker is aware of all this, and that with his magnificent army he goes forward with his plans so carefully considered, and in such resolution to succeed, that he can not fail. . . ."

Another paper said:

"He enters upon the momentous task before him with everything supplied him, essential to success, by the government and the people, except those essential qualities of unfailing skill, promptitude in action, and vigilant discretion, which he is expected himself to supply, and which we trust he will supply as the leader to the magnificent army which he commands. We await the next intelligence of his advance, therefore, with confidence that it will give us the best assurance of a victorious campaign."

# CHAPTER XVII

### Right Wing until 11 a.m.

IN the course of the night the 6 N. Y. Cavalry arrived in the vicinity of Chancellorsville and took position with the Federal pickets on the Plank Road.[1] Its scattered fragments were here reformed and brought together during the day.[2]

On the morning of the 1st of May, there existed much anxiety and apprehension among nearly all, if not all, the corps, division, and other commanders [of the Federal army]. It was of current report that General Hooker, the night before, had said that God Almighty could not prevent his destroying the rebel army, which created great uneasiness—even to the most irreligious. Doubtless the absence of plan and preparation for combat contributed largely to disturbing the minds of many; still the blasphemy (no one hesitating to call it that) produced a profound impression.[3]

It was a beautiful day. A fresh soft breeze stole through the forest, rustling the banners uncased to dry. Warren had gone out bright and early toward Fredericksburg on a reconnaissance. Hooker was waiting to hear from him and from the III Corps. A calm like that of an old-time Sabbath rested upon the camps. The corps commanders, impelled by impatience and curiosity, drifted over to Chancellorsville, and gathered encouragement from conferring with the army commander or members of his staff. Hooker showed in his countenance and speech the complete confidence which he felt that a decisive victory was about to crown his brilliant manœuver.

At 7:30 a.m. the III Corps commenced crossing the Rappahannock at United States Ford and massing on the south side. At 9 o'clock Sickles, in advance of his corps, reported to Hooker at Chancellorsville. At 10 Warren returned from his reconnaissance, having gone a little over 3½ miles, and taken a look at the enemy's lines.[4] Generals were

[1] *W. R.*, 39, p. 779.
[2] *Journal U. S. Cavalry Assoc.*, June, 1891; *The Campaigns of Stuart's Cavalry*, by H. B. McClellan, pp. 230, 231.
[3] E. S. Pittman in *Papers of Michigan*

*Commandery, Loyal Legion*, I, 77; *History of the 27 Indiana Vol. Inf.*, by a member of Company C, p. 313.
[4] *W. R.*, 39, p. 198.

dispatching their aides in every direction for orders. It was evident that the morning's programme had been arranged. A newspaper correspondent asked of Lieutenant-Colonel Dickinson, of Hooker's staff, how matters were progressing.

"Everything," he answered, "is going on splendidly, just as the general wants it."

"Any news from General Stoneman?" an officer asked of another member of the staff.

"Best news in the world," was the reply; "he has cut the enemy's railroad communication."

Stoneman had done nothing of the kind. But the effect of the speech was just as good as if he had. With Stoneman tearing up his communications, Lee would soon be in retreat, and there was therefore no serious opposition to be expected on the way to Fredericksburg. While Hooker had been wasting precious hours in waiting for reënforcements, Lee, through his trusty lieutenant, had proceeded to the execution of his plan. Jackson with his corps, except Early's division, took up the march for Tabernacle Church at about 3 a.m. At 5:30 a.m., after he had traveled with the head of his column about 5 miles, Butterfield wrote to Hooker:

From deserter just in, learn that Jackson's whole corps is opposite Franklin's Crossing. Camp rumor that Longstreet had gone to Culpeper [from the south side of the James]; that Lee had said it was the only time he should fight equal numbers; that we had about 80,000. Some of Trimble's division [commanded by Colston] told him [the deserter] they had to march to Culpeper to-morrow. They all knew that we had crossed 40,000 men above.

This deserter came into the lines of Reynolds' corps last night, and was sent to Butterfield this morning.[1] By "to-morrow" he may have meant this day, the 1st. Whatever he said or meant, Butterfield believed, it seems, that Jackson's whole corps was still in front of Sedgwick. It is not improbable that this deserter was an emissary of Jackson's. Longstreet's corps had not moved from the south side of the James.

Reynolds wrote to Sedgwick:

The enemy appear to remain in their position, and as far as we can learn, have not changed. . . . The fog is so thick we can do little but be ready to meet an attack. . . .

Butterfield wrote to Hooker at 8:30 a.m.:

. . . Your dispatch[2] is dated May 1, and says Patrick and Gibbon are to cross to-morrow, which would be May 2. Is this right? . . . I have endeavored to send

---

[1] Reynolds to Sedgwick, *W. R.*, 40, pp. 336, 337.
[2] Not found.

this dispatch by telegraph, but the line works very badly, and I send by orderly. I hope to have the new line constructed by night and in working order, with a party to work across [to you] from Banks' Ford the moment the bridge is laid. Please leave directions there [at Banks' Ford as to] where they will carry the telegraph to on the other side.

The questions here raised were partly anticipated by the following dispatch from Hooker, which was not delivered until 11:30 a.m.:

### To Butterfield, 7 a.m.

Hurry over the provost-marshal-general and his cavalry. Major-General Sedgwick was directed [in to-day's dispatch] to throw his whole force on the Bowling Green road, and no other.

Sedgwick's movement seems now intended as a manœuver against the enemy's communications. With Sedgwick threatening one line of supply and Hooker astride of the other, Lee would have to choose at once between taking to flight and closing with Hooker.

Butterfield, still in doubt as to Hooker's intentions regarding Gibbon, sent the following dispatches:

### To Gibbon, 9:25 a.m.

I have received a dispatch from the general directing you to cross at Banks' Ford to-morrow at 9 a.m.[1] This dispatch is dated May 1. I have strong reason to apprehend that it was intended that you should cross to-day at 9 a.m. I am momentarily expecting a telegram. I wish you would send a staff officer to Banks' Ford to read all telegraphic dispatches there. Hold your command in readiness to spring,—in case this should prove an error, and it is intended you should cross to-day at 9 o'clock,—to move to that point as rapidly as possible, to cross. . . .

### To Hooker, 10:13 a.m.

Is the order still effective for General Gibbon to move to Banks' Ford to-day with his whole division, or is he to wait until it is uncovered?

About 6 a.m. Martin's six-gun battery of horse artillery (6 Independent N. Y.) arrived at Chancellorsville, and reported to Pleasonton for duty with the cavalry. At the same time the two batteries of the First Division of the XII Corps ($\frac{1.3}{1. \text{XII}}$) arrived from United States Ford and joined their division. The XII Corps now had all its artillery. At 7 a.m. Humphreys' division ($\frac{3}{V}$) joined its corps on the left of Chancellorsville. Probably about the same time the 17 Pa. Cavalry, which had been attached to the XI Corps, reported at brigade headquarters near Hunting Run, leaving two squadrons to picket the right and front of the XI Corps and observe the country toward Orange Court-House and Spott-

[1] Butterfield seems to refer here to the dispatch referred to in his of 8:30 a.m. to Hooker.

sylvania Court-House.[1]  The XI Corps was still short of its corps artillery, which was probably between United States Ford and Chancellorsville.  Between 9 and 10 a.m. Cross's brigade crossed the Rappahannock and proceeded toward Chancellorsville.  It was not to arrive until 4 p.m.[2]

Between 11:30 last night and 7 this morning two pontoon bridges were brought up to Banks' Ford from below Fredericksburg—one from Franklin's Crossing, and one from Fitzhugh's Crossing.  This left three bridges below Fredericksburg.  The two at Banks' Ford were held ready to be laid as soon as the ford was uncovered.

Including the forementioned reënforcements, Hooker's available force numbered about 70,000 men,[3] with 184 pieces of artillery (32 batteries).

The general movement for to-day was prescribed in detail as follows:

Circular:                    Chancellorsville, Va., May 1, 1863, 11 a.m.

The Fifth Corps, including three batteries,[4] will be thrown on the River road by [the] most direct route, the head of it advanced to near midway between Mott's and Colin Runs, the movement to be completed at 2 o'clock.

The Twelfth Corps, including its [5] batteries, will be massed below the Plank road, the head of it resting near Tabernacle Church, and masked from the view of the enemy by small advanced parties, and the movement to be completed at 12 o'clock to enable the Eleventh Corps to take its position.

The Eleventh Corps, with its [6] batteries, will be masked on the Plank road, about 1 mile in rear of the Twelfth.  This movement to be completed at 2 o'clock.

One division of the Second Corps, with one battery, will take a position at Todd's Tavern, and will throw out strong detachments on the approaches in the direction of the enemy.

The other division and batteries[5] of the corps will be massed out of the road near Chancellorsville, these dispositions to be made at once.

The Third Corps will be massed as fast as it arrives about 1 mile from Chancellorsville, on the United States Ford road,[6] excepting one brigade with a battery, which will take position at Dowdall's Tavern.

General Pleasonton will hold his command, excepting those otherwise engaged, at Chancellorsville.

After the movement commences, headquarters will be at Tabernacle Church.

By command of Major-General HOOKER:

WM. L. CANDLER,

Captain and Aide-de-Camp.

[1] At 9:30 a.m. Hooker issued the following circular: "Corps commanders will hold their corps in hand, and wherever their commands may find themselves night or day, they will keep pickets well thrown out on all the approaches to their positions.  The safety of this army depends upon this being rigidly executed. . . ."

[2] *History of the 5th Regt. N. H. Volunteers*, by William Child, p. 179.

[3] Infantry 65,188; cavalry 1309; artillery 3641.

[4] Of the eight batteries belonging to this corps only three had crossed the river $\left(\frac{3}{1.\,V},\ \frac{2}{2.\,V},\ \frac{2\varsigma}{3.\,V}\right)$.  These aggregated 14 pieces.

[5] Of the eight batteries of this corps only six had crossed the river.

[6] At the junction of this road with the Ely's Ford Road.

This order appears to be incorrectly timed. It was probably issued, in substance, verbally or in writing, formally or informally, at an earlier hour than it purports to have been. According to J. Watts de Peyster, orders for the V Corps to advance on the River Road were given verbally to Captain Paine of Hooker's staff about 10:30, and orders for the XII Corps were issued in printed form upon the return of Captain Paine from the V Corps.[1] Warren says that on returning from his reconnaissance, about 10 a.m., he found that an advance had been ordered.[2] Captain Waterman, commanding a battery ($\frac{3}{1.V}$), says:

> Broke camp at 10 a.m. . . . and marched on the road to . . . Fredericksburg.[3]

According to Humphreys he received instructions from Meade not long, it would seem, after 7 a.m.[4] It can hardly be doubted that the hour of starting was nearer 10 than 11.

Regarding the text of the forequoted 11 a.m. order, there was no reference in it to attacking. Hooker testified before the Committee on the Conduct of the War:

> As soon as Couch's divisions and Sickles' corps came up, I directed an advance for the purpose, in the first instance, of driving the enemy away from Banks' Ford, which was six miles down the river, in order that we might be in closer communication with the left wing of the army.[5]

The movements prescribed are only a transfer of the army from one defensive position to another. Besides uncovering Banks' Ford it would take the army out of the Wilderness to ground on which its artillery would be able to act and its general preponderance to tell. So much for Hooker's purpose "in the first instance." What was it in the second instance? What, if anything, did Hooker mean to do after he had placed his army in its new position? When asked by the Committee: "What action was taken on the 1st of May?" he answered: "I went out to attack the enemy."[6] There is reason to believe that he contemplated advancing at 2 p.m. from the position of Tabernacle Church against a force supposed to be on a line of hills between Salem Church and Banks' Ford.[7] But in the light of subsequent events it seems more probable that, when the time had come, he would have decided to await an attack. However that may have been, his immediate

---

[1] *John Watts de Peyster,* by Frank Allaben, p. 113.

[2] *W. R.,* 39, p. 198.

[3] *Ib.,* 39, p. 524.

[4] *Ib.,* 39, p. 546.

[5] *Rep. of Com.,* IV, 124. See also Hooker's Comments on Chancellorsville, *B. and L.,* III, 218.

[6] *Rep. of Com.,* IV, 140. In a dispatch to Butterfield received at 8:45 p.m., he said: "The attack was ordered at 2 p.m.," but no such order can be found in the records.

[7] Warren and Meade, *W. R.,* 39, pp. 198, 506; Warren, *Rep. of Com.,* IV, 44; *John Watts de Peyster,* by Frank Allaben, p. 113.

object was to take up a new defensive position. His main line was to be covered in rear by a division at Todd's Tavern, a brigade at Dowdall's Tavern, a corps (with the exception of a brigade) near Chandler's, and the cavalry at Chancellorsville.

A signal station was established in a tree about a mile and a half east of Chancellorsville, in the vicinity of Newton, under Captain Fisher, and one about a mile and a half east of Howard's headquarters under Captain Castle. The former was to be used as an observation station and the latter to connect Howard's headquarters with Hooker's.

Semmes' brigade ($\frac{2}{2.1}$) reported to Anderson, and, about 1 a.m., went into position with its left resting on the right of Mahone's brigade ($\frac{1}{1.1}$), the left of the latter resting on the Turnpike. Between midnight and 12:30 a.m., Kershaw's and Wofford's brigades of McLaws' division ($\frac{1.3}{2.1}$) took up the march, by General Lee's order, for Anderson's position, where, on arrival, they formed up to the right and left about Smith's Hill, their left connecting with Semmes' right.[1] About 8 a.m. Jackson, in advance of his column, arrived at Tabernacle Church, and assumed command. By this time Anderson, with the help of Lee's engineers, had strongly intrenched the whole front. The flanks were more or less protected, on the right by Mott's Run and the Rappahannock, and on the left by Massaponax Creek. For the defence of this line, about 3 miles in length, there were to be available about 40,000 infantry, which would furnish from 7 to 8 men to the yard, but the force at present on the ground did not number more than about 13,000 men with 44 pieces of artillery[2] (Map 12). Stuart and Fitzhugh Lee's brigade went on from Alsop's to Spottsylvania Court-House and about daylight proceeded thence toward Anderson's position at Zion Church. Stuart started from Spottsylvania Court-House about daylight, followed by Fitzhugh Lee's brigade. By 11 o'clock he had probably communicated with Lee or Jackson and directed his march northward toward Chancellorsville. About this time he was joined by the 10 Va. and parts, at least, of the 15 Va. and 2 N. Ca. Allowing for casualties, he must now have had a force of about 2000 sabers,[3] or about twice as many as Pleasonton had. The Confederate cavalry presented about the same anomaly as an organization that the Federal did. It consisted in the main of a brigade commanded by a major-general and a brigadier-general (Stuart and Fitzhugh Lee). Lee's instructions to Jackson were to "proceed to Tabernacle Church and make arrangements to re-

---

[1] W. R., 39, pp. 824, 830, 833.

[2]
| Mahone | . . . . | 1,915 | Infantry | . . . . | .11,695 |
| Semmes and Wofford | 4,068 | | Artillery (44 pieces) | . | 880 |
| Kershaw | . . . | 2,712 | Cavalry (4 Va. and | | |
| Wright and Posey | . 3,000 | | part of 3) | . . . | 500 |
| Infantry | . . . | 11,695 | Total | . . . . | 13,075 |

[3] 1, 2, 3, 4, 5, 10, and part of the 15 Va. and 2 N. Ca., and 8 guns (*Chancellorsville*, by Hotchkiss and Allan, p. 151; *W. R.*, 39, pp. 794, 1049, 1051; *So. Hist. Soc. Papers*, VIII, 249).

pulse the enemy." They did not require him to go beyond Tabernacle Church. On the other hand, they did not prohibit it. That was enough for Jackson. With only about 10,000 Confederates between him and Sedgwick, he thought with dread of Federal guns thundering in his rear. For this reason as well as to secure, if possible, the advantage of the initiative, which he knew so well how to utilize, he ordered the work on the intrenchments to cease and the troops to prepare to advance. But he had first to wait for his own column and other reënforcements. About 10:30 a.m. his advanced troops moved out, Mahone's brigade on the Turnpike and Posey's on the Plank Road.[1] His reënforcements were still 2 or 3 miles off, but the sight of them approaching, as it seemed, from every direction, was restoring the spirit of the troops, somewhat dampened by the recent retrograde movement.

The Federals were now pursuing their way eastward in columns well closed up, by the two roads that fork at Chancellorsville. Arriving opposite the house, they halt by brigade, load their pieces, and move on.

### Right Wing, 11 a.m. to 2 p.m.

The V Corps with three batteries, and the XII with two batteries,[2] altogether about 28,000 men and 28 guns, formed three columns (Map 12). The V Corps had two roads, the River Road and Turnpike. Griffin's and Humphreys' divisions $(\frac{1.3}{V})$ under Meade took the River Road, and Sykes' division $(\frac{2}{V})$, the Turnpike. Humphreys' division was to hold itself ready to reënforce Griffin's or Sykes', as exigencies might require.[3] The XII Corps marched on the Plank Road. After crossing Mott's Run Sykes' division was to turn to the left, deploy and open communication with Griffin's on its left and Slocum's corps on its right. The two corps were to take up a position extending from Tabernacle Church on the right to near Banks' Ford on the left, a distance of about 2½ miles—the position actually held by Anderson. Together with the XI Corps, which was to support the movement, the forces thus set in motion aggregated about 40,000 men and 62 guns. Two batteries $(\frac{2}{2.V}, \frac{2}{3.V})$ went with Sykes, one battery $(\frac{3}{1.V})$ with Meade. The other five batteries of the V Corps were on the march from Hartwood Church.

---

[1] Authorities differ considerably as to the hour when the movement commenced. Semmes, Kershaw, and Wright give it as about noon (*W. R.*, 39, pp. 833, 829, 865). Lee and McLaws give it as 11 (*ib.*, pp. 794, 849, 824), and Posey gives it as 9. Mahone's leading regiment was the 12 Va. Lieutenant Keiley of this regiment wrote on the 7th of May, 1863, "About 10 we moved to the front" (*War Talks of Confederate Veterans*, p. 62).

[2] $\frac{2}{1.\text{XII}}, \frac{1}{2.\text{XII}}$ (*W. R.*, 39, p. 674). The author can not state why this corps was not accompanied by its five batteries as required by Hooker's order of 11 a.m.

[3] Meade's report, *W. R.*, 39, p. 506. Humphreys was originally directed to follow Sykes, but his instructions were subsequently modified so as to require him to follow Griffin (*ib.*, 39, p. 546). This change, it will be seen, proved unfortunate.

General Warren, Hooker's chief of topographical engineers, accompanied Sykes' column.

The woodiness of the country would considerably restrict the use of artillery, but would not altogether prevent it. There were straight stretches of road where a single gun might bring a hostile column to a halt or compel it to take to the woods. There were openings, too, affording positions for lines of guns.

About 11 a.m. Sickles' corps commenced arriving from United States Ford at the junction of Ely's and United States Ford roads, and being massed there by Hooker's order. It left at United States Ford, on the south bank, as guard to the bridge, Mott's brigade of six regiments ($\frac{3}{2.\text{ III}}$) and Jastram's and Seeley's batteries ($\frac{2}{1.\text{ III}}$, $\frac{4}{2.\text{ III}}$); and on the north bank, the ambulances.[1] Colonel Ingalls, chief quartermaster of the army, forbade the crossing of trains until further orders.[2] The engineer battalion, numbering 300 men, was also at the ford on the south side of the river.[3] Meagher's brigade ($\frac{2}{1.\text{ II}}$) at Scott's Dam was joined by the 116 Pa. from United States Ford.

The following instructions were issued to the left wing:

Chancellorsville, May 1, 1863, 11:30 a.m.

*General Butterfield:*

Direct Major-General Sedgwick to threaten an attack in full force at 1 o'clock, and to continue in that attitude until further orders. Let the demonstration be as severe as can be, but not an attack.

JOSEPH HOOKER,<br>Major-General Commanding.

That Sedgwick's attack was to be a pretended and not a real one shows that Hooker was not aware of the transference of most of Lee's army from the lines of Fredericksburg toward Chancellorsville.

As Hooker outwitted Lee by massing his right wing at Chancellorsville, so Lee outwitted Hooker by concentrating his army at Zion Church. The first point in the game was made yesterday by Hooker; the second, which, as we shall see, neutralized the first, was made to-day by Lee. Sedgwick, by his demonstration at 1 o'clock, was to prevent the now consummated reënforcement of Anderson.

Jackson's force marched in two columns. On the Turnpike went Mahone's brigade ($\frac{1}{1.\text{ I}}$) and McLaws' three brigades ($\frac{1.2.3}{2.\text{ I}}$), with six batteries of artillery ($\frac{1.2.4}{1.\text{ I}}$, $\frac{3.4}{2.\text{ I}}$, $\frac{2}{\text{I}}$), numbering 24 pieces, all under the command of McLaws. This force was covered by Owen's two squadrons of the 3 Va. Cavalry and Jordan's battery of 4 guns (included in the 24 above mentioned), and followed by Wilcox's brigade

---

[1] *History of Battery E, 1 R. I. Light Artillery*, by George Lewis, p. 157; W. R., 39, pp. 384, 421.

[2] *W. R.*, 39, pp. 399, 401, 411, 493.					[3] *Ib.*, 39, pp. 384, 216.

$(\frac{4}{1.\,\overline{1}})$ from Banks' Ford, and Perry's brigade $(\frac{3}{1.\,\overline{1}})$ from the vicinity of Falmouth.

On the Plank Road the column was headed by Posey's and Wright's brigades $(\frac{2.\,5}{1.\,\overline{1}})$, together with Alexander's battalion of artillery of the I Corps, numbering 14 pieces.[1] The main body of this column consisted of Rodes' and A. P. Hill's divisions $(\frac{2.\,1}{\overline{11}})$. Its left flank was covered by the 4 Va. Cavalry (Colonel Wickham), detached by General Stuart this morning. The right column, including Wilcox's and Perry's brigades, numbered about 12,000 men with 24 pieces of artillery; the left column (including Jackson's leading and next division), commanded directly by Jackson, about 28,000 men with 54 pieces of artillery. These columns aggregated, it would seem, to a man the same strength as the forementioned Federal columns (40,000 men), but comprised 78 pieces of artillery, or 16 more than the Federal columns. They were followed by Colston's division $(\frac{4}{\overline{11}})$ and Jackson's corps artillery, numbering together about 7800 men with 56 pieces, which were too far behind to come up before the afternoon was well spent, but might be counted on as a reserve to be used before night. On both sides the movements at this time were somewhat disjointed. The units were separated by excessive distances—on the side of the Federals, to right and left, and on the side of the Confederates, to front and rear.

Stuart's cavalry was divided into two parts, each with its particular function to perform. One, under Fitzhugh Lee, was to preserve contact with Hooker's army, and furnish information regarding it; the other, under Stuart, was to keep in touch with Lee's army, and protect it from annoyance and as far as possible from observation. Of Stuart's artillery, 6 pieces were detached with W. H. F. Lee. Two pieces, under Breathed, accompanied Fitzhugh Lee; 8 pieces, under Beckham, were with Stuart.

Jackson's columns are hardly in motion when the Federals become aware of the fact. About 11:15 the pickets of the 8 Pa. Cavalry in front of Mott's Run are attacked by McLaws' skirmishers, consisting of the 12 Va. The 8 Pa. comes to the support of its pickets, and succeeds in retarding the enemy's progress, but not in checking it. While it is giving way the head of Sykes' division, with Watson's battery of four pieces $(\frac{2}{2.\,\overline{V}})$, comes up. The only artillery opposing the Federal battery is a piece of Jordan's battery $(\frac{2}{\overline{1}})$ and a piece of Grandy's $(\frac{1}{1.\,\overline{1}})$.[2] As a shell is seen bursting over the woods, a captain in the XII Corps, looking at his watch, remarks: "Twenty minutes past eleven; the first gun of the battle of Chancellorsville."

---

[1] The number left after deducting for Jordan's battery on the Turnpike and Rhett's battery and two pieces of Parkers at Fredericksburg.

[2] *W. R.*, 39, pp. 525, 883; *War Talks of Confederate Veterans*, p. 69. The Confederate artillery was subsequently reënforced to 4 pieces (*ib.*).

The rumbling of the guns traveling on to Fredericksburg informs Lee that Jackson has met and engaged the enemy, and assures Sedgwick, so far as he may need to be assured, of the success, thus far, of Hooker's turning movement. Sykes, advancing still at double time, drives the Confederate skirmishers back, and about 12 o'clock[1] occupies a ridge with open ground in its front, about 2½ miles from Chancellorsville or about half-way from Chancellorsville to Anderson's late position at Zion Church[2] (Map 13). Sykes' position is not the open ground that Hooker has been aiming at outside of the Wilderness, but an open space within the Wilderness. His formation is in two lines. In his first line, Burbank with the 2d brigade and Watson's battery forms the right and center; and Ayres with the 1st brigade, the left. His second line is formed of the 3d brigade.

McLaws sends word to Jackson that the enemy is in force in his (McLaws') immediate front and is advancing, and that a large force can be seen along the heights about a mile or more to the rear (↑), and that the country is favorable for an attack from the Plank Road upon the Federal right flank. Jackson in reply tells McLaws to hold his position; that he is advancing his artillery; and that if this does not succeed, he will try to gain the enemy's rear. About this time Jackson receives the following dispatch:

*General:*                    Headquarters Cavalry Division, 12 m., May 1, 1863.

I am on a road running from Spottsylvania C. H. to Silvers, which is on Plank Road, three miles below Chancellorsville. General Fitz Lee is still further to the left and extends scouts to Plank Road (Orange), and has Turnpike watched beyond to see if any large movement takes place that way. I will close in on the flank and help all I can when the ball opens. I will communicate through Wickham and Owen to you.

May God grant us victory.        Yours truly,

                                          J. E. B. STUART,
                                          Major-General.

Upon the back of this dispatch Jackson wrote:

MAJOR-GENERAL J. E. B. STUART.                    12½ p.m., May 1, '63.
    *General:*

    I trust that God will grant us a great victory. Keep closed on Chancellorsville.

                              Yours very truly,
                                          T. J. JACKSON,
                                          Lieut. General.[3]

Precisely where Fitzhugh Lee was at this time, is not known. He was perhaps near the junction of the Brook Road and Brock Road (Map 15). Stuart was probably not far from Welford's Furnace.

---

[1] *W. R.*, 39, p. 198.          [3] These two communications are taken
[2] *Ib.*                              from the *So. Hist. Soc. Papers*, XI, 137, 138.

About noon Colonel Owen of the 3 Va. reported to McLaws that a Federal column was advancing by the Mine Road. This was probably a flanking detachment of Meade's. McLaws kept the four brigades of Mahone, Wofford, Semmes, and Kershaw (about 8700 men) in his front to oppose Sykes, and sent the two brigades of Wilcox and Perry, as they arrived, out to his right to cover his flank and rear against a movement by the Duerson's Mill Road and Mine Road (Map 13). McLaws' main force now maintained a defensive attitude. His skirmishers, however, especially on his flanks, kept up a vigorous demonstration.

Sykes heard no sound of cannon from the direction of Meade or Slocum. He was totally isolated. He had a good field of fire in his front, and his flanks rested upon woods, but these were not impassable to the Confederate skirmishers, who were threatening to envelop both of his flanks and gain his rear. Colonel O'Rorke, commanding his second line, sent out six companies of the 146 N. Y. as skirmishers to protect the right flank, and the whole of the 5 N. Y. (Duryee Zouaves) also as skirmishers to protect the left flank (Map 14). A detachment of the 8 Pa. Cavalry sent to the left to connect with the column on the River Road failed to do so. An aide of General Warren's who attempted to communicate with General Slocum ran into the enemy's skirmishers and narrowly escaped capture. A similar effort by one of General Sykes' aides was foiled in the same way.[1] About 1 p.m. Sykes reported his situation to Hooker. Soon afterward he received an order to retire in the direction of Chancellorsville. Arnold's battery $(_2{}^1\text{II})$ was sent to report to him, and later Couch was ordered to support him with a division. Couch went himself with the available infantry of Hancock's division $(\frac{1\ 3.\ 4}{\text{II}})$, about 3800 men.[2] Before this infantry arrived, probably soon after 1:30 p.m., Sykes commenced retiring, covered by Arnold's and Watson's batteries $(_2{}^1\text{II}, \ _2{}^2\text{V})$. The 8 Pa. Cavalry retired to the vicinity of Chancellorsville, where it stood to horse the rest of the day.[3] By 2 p.m. Hooker had probably received the following dispatch of 12:30 from Butterfield:

*Butterfield to Hooker, 12:30 p.m.*

Patrick [provost-marshal-general] ordered from Banks' to United States Ford, and cavalry[4] ordered there from Hartwood. Balloon and signal reports

---

[1] *W. R.*, 39, pp. 198, 199.

[2] Couch says he gave his order to Arnold at 1 p.m.; Arnold says it was given at 2 p.m. (*W. R.*, 39, pp. 306, 360). Couch says in a report of May 9 that he went with Hancock's division at 1 p.m. (*ib.*, 39, p. 305); and in a report of May 20, that instructions for him to do this were given him soon after 1 p.m. (*ib.*, 39, p.

311). It is probable that Arnold moved out a little before 1:15 and Hancock a little later.

[3] *The Charge of the 8 Pa. Cavalry at Chancellorsville*, by Pennock Huey, p. 77.

[4] About 140 of Patrick's cavalry. About 40 of these went on to Chancellorsville to keep the communications open.

to this moment all sent you. The enemy will meet you between Chancellorsville and Hamilton's Crossing. He can not, I judge from all reports, have detached over 10,000 or 15,000 men from Sedgwick's front since sun cleared fog. . . . I will have telegraph to Banks' Ford shortly. Shall I keep party waiting there to cross, or build line from United States Ford to Chancellorsville?

It was long after the time for Sedgwick's demonstration ordered this morning, and there were no signs of its being made. Hooker could not count on Sedgwick's coöperation, and feared that without it, and perhaps with it, he would be unable to deploy outside of the Wilderness; that the heads of his columns would be crushed, and his forces beaten in detail. We will leave him now to his disquieting reflections, and take a look at the Federal column on the right.

The XII Corps took up the march as ordered on the Plank Road about 10:30 a.m. Having advanced about a mile, it came upon the skirmishers of the enemy with one howitzer[1] in the vicinity of Decker (A). The advance-guard deployed in line of skirmishers, and pushed on, driving the enemy before it. The main body deployed on either side of the road; Geary's division $\left(\frac{2}{\text{XII}}\right)$ on the right, Williams' $\left(\frac{1}{\text{XII}}\right)$ on the left, each division with two brigades in the first line and one in the second. The brigades in the first line were formed each in two lines; and those in reserve in double column. This triple line of battle was a long time in forming. It did not advance until about 1 p.m., or about the time when Sykes, barely holding his own on the Turnpike, sent a report of his situation to Hooker.[2]

Jackson reënforced his advance under Anderson with Ramseur's brigade $\left(\frac{5}{2.\text{II}}\right)$. The three brigades, Posey's on the right, Ramseur's in the center, and Wright's on the left, pushed back Slocum's advance upon his main line (Map 14). The artillery of the head of Jackson's column (14 pieces) went into action and was opposed by Atwell's battery $\left(\frac{1}{2.\text{XII}}\right)$ of 6 pieces; Winegar's battery $\left(\frac{2}{1.\text{XII}}\right)$ was put into position to add its fire to that of Atwell's; and Crosby's battery $\left(\frac{3}{1.\text{XII}}\right)$ was brought up from Chancellorsville and posted near Atwell's. Neither Winegar nor Crosby had opened fire, and Atwell had fired but about sixty rounds,[3] when, about 1:30 p.m., Slocum received an order from Hooker directing him to return to the position which he occupied the night before.[4] Consequently before the artillery duel was decided or his reserve brigades were brought into line, he broke off the engagement, and put his force in retreat. He was followed by the three brigades under Anderson, a part of Stuart's cavalry, Alexander's battalion of artillery, and McGraw's battery of A. P. Hill's division

[1] W. R., 39, p. 821.
[2] Ib., 39, p. 728, first line.
[3] Ib., 39, pp. 723, 771.

[4] Slocum errs, it seems, in stating that this order was received at 1 p.m. (W. R., 39, p. 670).

$(\frac{4}{1.\,\text{II}})$.[1] Rodes' artillery, it seems, was not engaged at all. Rodes deployed his four remaining brigades $(\frac{1.2.3.4}{2.\,\text{II}})$ between the Plank Road and the Turnpike. A. P. Hill's division $(\frac{}{\text{h}})$ formed line of columns on both sides of the Plank Road.

Howard received an order at 12 o'clock to place his corps a mile in rear of the XII, but he had hardly started from camp when it was countermanded.[2] The corps resumed its former positions, except that the Third Division, which had been at Hawkins' Farm, facing westward, was placed in the line between the First and Second Divisions, facing southward, leaving the 82 O. (not brigaded) at Hawkins' Farm (Map 15). When the corps started forward Captain Castle's signal station was broken up. It was not reëstablished.

The V Corps marched, as ordered, by the River Road. An order was issued for its recall probably about 1 p.m., but at 2 p.m. it had not been received. About 1 p.m. Graham's brigade $(\frac{1}{1.\,\text{III}})$[3] and Turnbull's battery $(\frac{3}{1.\,\text{III}})$ took up the march from the junction of the Ely's Ford and United States Ford Roads by way of Chancellorsville for Dowdall's Tavern, pursuant to a provision of Hooker's order of 11 a.m. Whether it was before or after the issue of this order can not be stated, but by midday Hooker had an apprehension that a force of Confederate cavalry was demonstrating against his right and rear, which was probably caused by patrols of Fitzhugh Lee's looking for Federal troops on the Germanna Plank Road. As a consequence Graham was directed to picket well out to the right and rear, connecting on his right with Whipple $(\frac{3}{\text{III}})$, who was to connect his right with Berry $(\frac{2}{\text{III}})$.[4] On arriving at Dowdall's Tavern Graham halted by order of General Howard to await further orders.[5] Whipple on the left and Berry on the right

---

[1] *W. R.*, 39, pp. 821, 937.

[2] Howard's report, *ib.*, 39, p. 628. Howard says in his *Autobiography* (I, 361) that his corps had "gone out two miles." Captain Castle, Howard's signal officer, says in his report that the corps was turned back at Chancellorsville (*W. R.*, 39, p. 231).

[3] Except the 105 Pa., which had not come up from United States Ford.

[4] *W. R.*, 39, p. 384.

[5] "Howard met Graham half-way from Chancellorsville[?] to Dowdall's Tavern. 'Where are you going?' Howard asked Graham. 'To Dowdall's Tavern.' 'Perhaps you mean Todd's Tavern?' 'No, Dowdall's.' 'That can not be; there must be some mistake about this. My headquarters are there.' 'I do not know anything about that,' replied Graham; 'such are my orders. Perhaps they are afraid of an attack, and I am sent to support you.' 'That can not be,' replied Howard. 'I would send my compliments to the whole rebel army, and invite them to attack me, in my present position; and if it was not out of compliment to General Sickles, I would order you back.' To this Graham, having observed that he would not be justified in obeying such an order, turned to Briscoe (attached to Birney's staff as engineer) and said to him: 'There seems to be some misunderstanding here; you had better go back with Bullard [his aide] to General Birney, and find out.' Graham then proceeded on to Dowdall's Tavern, where he found General Carl Schurz and a number of officers of the XI Corps; while Howard kept on to Chancellorsville to see General Hooker" (*Chancellorsville*, by J. Watts de Peyster; *Onward*, December, 1869. See *Report of Committee on Con-*

established a line of outposts extending from the Plank Road to the United States Ford.[1]

In the meantime General French with his division ($\frac{3}{11}$) and Pettit's battery ($\frac{1}{11}$) got under way for Todd's Tavern. After he had made about 1½ miles the XII Corps, coming up the Plank Road, intersected his column, and compelled him to halt until it had passed, when he received orders to return to his original position. He turned back about the same time as Howard.[2]

### Right Wing, 2 p.m. to 6 p.m.

A little after 2 p.m. Couch with Hancock's division met Sykes with his in the vicinity of Newton. At this moment Couch received the following order:

Headquarters Army of the Potomac, May 1, 1863.

General Sykes will retire to his position of last night, and take up a line connecting his right with General Slocum [XII Corps], making his line as strong as he can by felling trees, etc. General Couch will then retire to his position of last night.                              Major-General HOOKER.[3]

Hancock deployed to cover Sykes' withdrawal. "General Couch, while preparing to obey the order, so far as concerned Hancock's division, determined at least to delay its execution until he could communicate to the commanding general his own earnest belief that the position which had been reached should be held, and he accordingly dispatched Major Burt, his senior aide, to headquarters, with urgent representations as to the admirable nature of the ground he held, and his ability to 'stand off' any enemy on his front, if Meade and Slocum could keep their place on his flanks. Major Burt returned with a peremptory order to retire."[4]

At 2 o'clock Hooker telegraphed to Butterfield:

From character of information have suspended attack. The enemy may attack me—I will try it. Tell Sedgwick to keep a sharp lookout, and attack if [he] can succeed.

Probably about the same time he wrote:

. . . Hope the enemy will be emboldened to attack me. I did feel certain of success. If his communications are cut [by Stoneman] he must attack me. I

duct of the War, 1865, I, xlv, 4, 6, 34, etc.; Chancellorsville, by Hotchkiss and Allan, 48, 50; W. R., 39, pp. 412, 413).

[1] W. R., 39, pp. 385, 448.

[2] French in his report says that he received the order to move to Todd's Tavern at 8 a.m. and implies that he started about that time. But his report, read in connection with the reports of Captain Pettit,

Colonel Powers, commanding his leading brigade, General Slocum, and General Howard, seems to show that he could not have started much before noon (W. R., 39, pp. 362, 375, 628, 669).

[3] History of the II Army Corps, by Francis A. Walker, p. 221.

[4] Ib.

have a strong position. . . . All the enemy's cavalry are on my flanks, which leads me to suppose that our dragoons will meet with no obstacles in cutting their communications.

The "information" to which Hooker referred in his telegram does not admit, unfortunately, of specification. But it probably consisted in substance of the items that 15,000 men or more had moved from about Fredericksburg toward Chancellorsville; and that the total in the former position did not appear to have been diminished, from which Hooker naturally inferred that Confederate reënforcements had arrived from Richmond. This view of the situation was probably confirmed by the receipt of the following dispatch from Butterfield:

*2:05 p.m.*

I have two deserters just from Hays' brigade, Early's division. They report A. P. Hill left here this morning to move up to our right [Chancellorsville]. Hood's division arrived yesterday from Richmond. The deserter was from New York State originally; an intelligent man. He said he knew it was Hood's division, for he asked the troops as they passed along. He reports D. H. Hill, Early, and Trimble in front of Sedgwick. Anderson, McLaws, A. P. Hill, and Hood would therefore be in your front.[1]

Hooker's reckoning with the cavalry involved three erroneous ideas:

1. That all of Stuart's cavalry was with Lee,
2. That all of Stoneman's cavalry was with Stoneman,
3. That Stoneman was carrying out Hooker's orders.

Reynolds wrote to Sedgwick:

If they have not detached more than A. P. Hill's division from our front, they have been keeping up appearances [of detaching more], showing weakness [here], with a view of delaying Hooker.

Reynolds, it seems, was now satisfied that the enemy's forces had for the greater part been withdrawn from their old lines, but was in doubt as to whether they had gone on to Chancellorsville or lay concealed in rear of Fredericksburg.

About this time Slocum, falling back before Jackson, made a stand on the Welford's Furnace and Newton Road, but there was no communication between Slocum and Couch.

---

[1] D. H. Hill was in North Carolina; his division, commanded by R. E. Rodes, was with Jackson; Trimble's division, commanded by Colston, was also with Jackson; Hood was still south of the James River. This dispatch represented the force opposing Sedgwick as nearly three times as strong as it was, and that opposing Hooker as about four fifths as strong as it was.

At 2:30 p.m. the following dispatch was sent from Jackson's head-quarters to McLaws:

> The lieutenant-general commanding directs me to say that he is pressing on up the Plank road; also that you will press on up the turnpike toward Chancellorsville, as the enemy is falling back.
>
> Keep your skirmishers and flanking parties well out, to guard against ambuscade.

About 3 p.m. General Heth of A. P. Hill's division was detached with three brigades $\left(\frac{1.3.4}{1.\,\text{II}}\right)$ to go over to the Turnpike, and having reached it, to feel his way, and advance in the direction of Chancellorsville; and General Wright of Anderson's division was ordered to move his brigade $\left(\frac{5}{1.\,\text{I}}\right)$ "across and to the left of the Plank Road, and bearing well off from the road, endeavor to get upon the enemy's right flank and rear."[1] Slocum, having resumed his retreat, was pressed in rear and on his right rear by Posey's brigade $\left(\frac{2}{1.\,\text{I}}\right)$, supported by Alexander's artillery and Jackson's leading division (Rodes'). His command was thrown into some disorder, but got back without much loss to its original position about 4 p.m. His artillery, numbering twenty-eight pieces, was disposed in two batteries of equal strength, "for defence against the probable following enemy"—one at the junction of the Plank Road and Turnpike east of Chancellorsville, commanding both approaches; and the other on the height of Fairview, west of Chancellorsville, facing south. Wright took the line of the unfinished railroad, followed it rapidly to the Welford's Furnace Road, and proceeded by the latter toward the Furnace. He apparently intended to go on from the Furnace to the elevation of Hazel Grove and there place himself in an advantageous position on the flank and rear, as he thought, of the Federal line. He arrived at the Furnace about 4:30 p.m.[2] Here he found Stuart with his staff, and Beckham, commanding the horse artillery, with six guns.[3] From Stuart he learned that the Federals occupied the woods north of the Furnace. His brigade comprised three regiments of about 380 men each and one battalion numbering, say, 150 men. He deployed two of his regiments, keeping one regiment and the battalion in reserve. The former were ordered, he says, "to move cautiously forward through the almost impenetrable forest, and finding the enemy, to press him vigorously." They advanced rapidly, and were soon engaged with two regiments on the outposts of Williams' division, the 3 Wisc. and 123 N. Y. $\left(\frac{3}{3.\,1.\,\text{XII}},\ \frac{123}{2.\,1.\,\text{XII}}\right)$. Colonel Hawley of the 3 Wisc. says that he saw three Confederate regiments, so Wright's third regiment was probably put into action. At any rate, Wright

---

[1] W. R., 39, p. 866.

[2] This is about an hour and a half earlier than the hour given by Wright (W. R., 39, p. 866), but is based upon a careful study of all the reports, Federal and Confederate.

[3] W. R., 39, pp. 1048, 1049.

forced the Federals back to the Farm-House, whereupon he ordered a halt and called upon Stuart for a portion of his artillery. Beckham was sent forward with four guns, under the supposition that the Federals had little or no artillery at this point. Owing to the character of the ground and the bad condition of the roads, it was about 5:30 when the Confederate guns came into position and opened fire. The immediate effect of the fire was to compel the Federal regiments to fall back to the intrenchments on the northern edge of Hazel Grove. A third regiment, the 27 Ind. (3. 1. XII), which had come to their support, was ordered back with the others before it had time to deploy. This was no sooner accomplished, however, than Beckham's four pieces were fired upon by eight pieces of artillery at Fairview.[1] Soon afterward they became the target also of two pieces at Hazel Grove, the latter supported by a regiment of infantry (Sketch 1). While this action was in progress, General Jackson with his staff came galloping up from the Plank Road. Going forward with the artillery, he came under the heavy fire to which it was subjected. The danger of the situation elicited from Stuart the remark: "General Jackson, we must move from here." Before they could turn, Stuart's adjutant-general was mortally wounded.

Fitzhugh Lee, with his brigade of cavalry and two pieces of Breathed's battery of horse artillery, had been feeling the Federal outposts about a mile and a half further west. Soon after 4 p.m. his two pieces of artillery opened fire on Carpenter's Farm. A regiment was sent out from Howard's line (1. 3. XI) and drove them back, silencing their fire.

Probably about 4 p.m. Wilcox, coming over with his brigade $\left(\frac{4}{1.\,1}\right)$ from the Turnpike, took position on the right of Perry's brigade, occupying part of a line of rifle-pits running from Banks' Ford to within a few hundred yards of the Mine Road (Maps 13, 14).

McLaws received Jackson's order of 2:30 at 4 p.m. and proceeded accordingly with his whole force "to press on up the Turnpike toward Chancellorsville." He left Wilcox, however, in the position just described, and Perry in his position on the Mine Road (Map 14). The latter moved forward about 5 p.m., following the Mine Road.

Heth passed between Rodes and McLaws, and came out on the Turnpike about half a mile in advance of McLaws, Couch having fallen back from Newton. Heth's skirmishers became engaged with Hancock's.

It may have been in answer to an inquiry from Hooker that Butterfield wired the latter at 2:45 p.m.:

All passage of troops from enemy's right to his left ceased about 11:30 o'clock. Nothing apparently going now except small detachments. . . .

[1] Winegar's battery $\left(\frac{2}{1.\,\mathrm{XII}}\right)$ and one section of Crosby's $\left(\frac{3}{1.\,\mathrm{XII}}\right)$.

At any rate, the receipt of this message or some other circumstance seems to have revived Hooker's spirits. After Sykes, in compliance with Hooker's order to retire, had passed through Hancock's line, Hancock commenced withdrawing his division. When all but two of his regiments had retired (about 4:30 p.m.) the following order was delivered to Couch:

Headquarters Army of the Potomac, May 1, 1863.

*General Couch:*

Hold on to your position till 5 p.m., and extend your skirmishers on each flank, so as to secure yourself against being surrounded. General Slocum will hold a position on the Plank road equally advanced.

By command of Major-General HOOKER:

WILLIAM L. CANDLER, Captain,

Aide-de-Camp.[1]

But what might have been done a couple of hours before was now no longer possible. Couch replied with warmth to the bearer: "Tell General Hooker he is too late; the enemy are on my right and rear. I am in full retreat," and proceeded accordingly. Fisher's signal party fell back from their observation station. The position thus abandoned (Newton) was high ground, more or less open in front, over which an army might move, and artillery be used advantageously. General Meade is said to have remarked: " . . . if we can't hold the top of a hill, we certainly can't hold the bottom of it." Hancock, with his division, stood across the main road to Fredericksburg, with two pieces of artillery on the Turnpike, and one on a wood road nearly parallel to it about 200 yards to the left.

The following answer to Hooker's telegram of 2 p.m. went to him from Butterfield at 4 p.m.:

. . . copy announcing suspension of your attack sent Sedgwick. He and Reynolds remain quiet. They consider that to attack before you have accomplished some success, in view of the strong position and numbers in their front, might fail to dislodge the enemy and render them [Sedgwick and Reynolds] unserviceable at the proper time. They are anxious to hear from you. . . .

Hooker was waiting for Sedgwick to do something, and Sedgwick was waiting for Hooker to do something.

When Hooker ordered a return to Chancellorsville, Meade was still advancing; and Couch and Slocum felt able to hold their positions. The latter expected to be adequately supported, and resume the advance. Hooker saw that to advance in the face of the attack which had developed or seemed impending meant his making a general attack with his somewhat scattered forces. He was more or less unnerved by the unex-

---

[1] *History of the II Army Corps,* by Francis A. Walker, p. 222.

pected aggression of the enemy. He wanted the enemy to attack him, but not then or there. He had started out to fight a battle, but he wanted to fight it in a position of his own choice. But here he was between his position of the night before, which he had but partially abandoned, and his contemplated new position, which he could not reach without fighting an offensive battle. He had remained at Chancellorsville in order, no doubt, to be as near as possible to the terminus of his telegraph line, which was broken or out of order most of the day. Not being at the front, he did not know the ground on which his troops were fighting. He had not uncovered Banks' Ford, and therefore could not expect any reënforcement from the north side of the river. He felt that he must choose between attacking in full force and retreating. At this critical moment he perhaps recalled the President's earnest warning: "Beware of rashness."

General Francis A. Walker in his interesting biography of General Hancock says: "Various explanations have been given of Hooker's actions on the afternoon of the 1st of May. The writer has always believed that they were due partly to lack of that firm moral stamina which is so often found to accompany a spirit of arrogance and boastfulness, but chiefly to a nervous collapse occasioned by the excitement and fatigue of the four preceding days. Drunkenness, once alleged, certainly was not any part of the cause."[1] It has indeed been asserted that Hooker was suffering at this time from the need of a stimulant.[2]

About 3 p.m. the V Corps, on the River Road, had reached Decker (B), about two miles from Banks' Ford and in sight of that point, when it received orders to turn back. Humphreys' division proceeded to execute the order at double time. Griffin did not receive the order, it would seem, until sometime between 5 and 6 o'clock, when his division took the back track at a killing pace.

[1] The report that Hooker was drunk at Chancellorsville is denied or discredited by Sickles, Birney, Wadsworth, and Pleasonton, before the Committee on the Conduct of the War (IV, 15, 37, 73, 31), by the Committee itself (IV, p. xlix), and finally by Hooker himself, testifying before the same (IV, 149). "The truth seems to be that Hooker was accustomed to drink a large amount of whisky daily without being prevented from attending to his round of duties; but when he started on this campaign, or, at all events, on the day that he reached Chancellorsville, from motives which do him honor, he stopped drinking entirely" (Rhodes' *History of the United States*, IV, 264, foot-note).

[2] Letter from Brooks to Hooker in *Army and Navy Journal*, III, 27; Couch's article in *Battles and Leaders of the Civil War*, III, 170; *Military Miscellanies*, by James B. Fry, p. 432; and *The Campaign of Chancellorsville*, by T. A. Dodge, pp. 268, 269.

# CHAPTER XVIII

### Right Wing, 6 p.m. to 12 p.m.

HETH kept up his pressure on Hancock until the latter, in obedience to an order from Hooker, took position on Sykes' left (Map 15). O'Rorke's (3d) brigade of Sykes' division was then between these commands and the enemy. About 6 p.m. Heth was forced by the Federal fire and approaching darkness to withdraw. To make room for McLaws, who was approaching from the rear, he moved to the left and went into bivouac near the right of the Plank Road.[1] McLaws halted at dark and bivouacked along the heights between Newton and R. McGee, Jr.

Lee wanted to attack from his right, and cut Hooker off from United States Ford. He went forward himself to examine the ground and receive reports from officers charged with reconnoitering and feeling the enemy. About 6:30 p.m. Wilcox moved with his brigade ($\frac{4}{1.1}$) to Duerson's Mill. From there he sent out a patrol of two companies "with the view of ascertaining whether or not the enemy occupied the River Road near Decker's house," and, if not, to communicate with the Confederate pickets left near Banks' Ford. The patrol did not catch sight of Meade's column, but captured three Federal soldiers, making their way, they said, to the United States Ford. Perry's and Wofford's brigades ($\frac{3}{1.1}$, $\frac{3}{2.1}$) moved up the Mine Road—Wofford on the left and losing connection with the line on *his* left. The 4 Va. Cavalry was transferred to the right, and coöperated with the two squadrons of the 3 Va. under Owen. But no suitable point of attack was found. Posey ($\frac{4}{1.1}$), between the Turnpike and the Plank Road, brought up about this time in Big Meadow Swamp, where he was arrested by the difficulty of the ground and a rapid shelling. On Posey's left, Ramseur ($\frac{5}{2.11}$) charged up the Plank Road. Receiving the fire of eight pieces of artillery, he withdrew, and, night approaching, went into bivouac. Off to their left and front Beckham's four pieces of artillery pluckily held out against the ten pieces of Best's for about three quarters of an hour, and then,

---

[1] *W. R.,* pp. 890, 894.

together with the infantry, went back, by order of General Wright, to the Furnace.

Wright's operation failed not only as a flank manœuver, but also as a reconnaissance. Neither Wright nor Fitzhugh Lee, so far as can be learned, penetrated the Federal outposts far enough to see the main line.

General Howard says in his *Autobiography:*

During the confusion of the changes of troops at Dowdall's Tavern some female members of a family there, taking a basket of provisions with them, escaped from our lines and informed some Confederate officer of the situation, carrying accurate information of how we occupied that position.[1]

On what authority this statement is made is not known. The author is convinced, however, that the information thus carried into the Confederate lines did not serve to locate the Federal right flank.

Lee, who had followed Jackson's advance from Zion Church, was puzzled by the feebleness of the resistance which it met with. To clear this matter up, he dispatched the following message to Stuart:

Plank Road, 2 miles from Chancellorsville,
May 1, 1863, 4 o'clock.

*General:*

The captured prisoners agree in stating that this is Meade's [V] corps with which we are now engaged, and that Howard's [XI] corps preceded them across the Rapidan, and has taken some other road. This is the only column that we can find in this direction. What has become of the other two [Howard's and Slocum's XI and XII Corps]?

Meade appears to be falling back.

I am, very respectfully yours, etc.,
R. E. LEE,
General.

Lee apparently was not aware that the III Corps and two divisions of the II Corps had joined the Federal right wing, and was uncertain as to whether the XI and XII Corps were still with it. At the close of the day he had a fairly correct idea of the position of Hooker's left, his line from the Plank Road around northward to the Rappahannock; but as to his right wing, he was quite in the dark. He not improbably supposed it to extend from near Slocum's right over the Vista of Hazel Grove south of west through the woods between Carpenter's Farm and the Orange Plank Road. Apprehending, it would seem, that a considerable fraction of Hooker's army was marching upon Gordonsville, he ordered W. H. F. Lee at Rapidan Station to destroy the bridge over the Rapidan at that point.

[1] See also *B. and L.,* III, 194.

In the Army of the Potomac two general plans of operation were now considered. One was to select a line of defence and intrench it; the other, to select a point of attack and advance upon it.[1] The former plan was adopted. The line chosen was the one actually held, except that the right was to be thrown back to a better position. At 4 p.m. Sickles was directed to bring up his whole corps except Mott's brigade ($\frac{3}{2. \text{ III}}$) and Seeley's battery ($\frac{4}{2. \text{ III}}$), still guarding the United States Ford, and get it rapidly into position parallel to the Plank Road at Chancellorsville. This he proceeded to do, recalling Graham's brigade of Birney's division from Dowdall's Tavern. Instructions for the adjustment and strengthening of the lines were issued in the following form:

*4:20 p.m.* Commanders of the Second, Fifth, Eleventh, and Twelfth Corps will at once have their commands established on the lines assigned them last night, and have them put in condition of defence without a moment's delay. The major-general commanding trusts that a suspension in the attack to-day will embolden the enemy to attack him. . . .

Chancellorsville, Va., May 1, 1863, 4:45 p.m.

*Major-General Slocum:*

Let the right of your line [XI and XII Corps] fall back and rest at the sawmill ruin on Hunting Run, or in that direction, and have everything passed to the rear of it.

By command of Major-General HOOKER:

WM. L. CANDLER,

Captain and Aide-de-Camp.

*6 p.m.* Corps commanders will set their pioneers at work in their fronts to make abatis, and clearing for artillery. The pioneers will be kept at work during the night.

A copy of the second dispatch was sent directly to Howard. Both Slocum and Howard protested against the refusal of the right wing. They believed that the forest about them was impenetrable to troops except on the roads, and represented that they were abundantly able to hold their position against any force which the nature of the ground in their front would enable the enemy to bring against them, and that to fall back would have some of the demoralizing effect of a retreat. It was consequently decided not to change the position of the right wing, but to strengthen it with breastwork and abatis, for which the timber and brushwood afforded an abundance of useful material. The line was strengthened as rapidly as possible "by each division, brigade, or regiment, according to its own idea of military engineering."[2] The art of field fortification was not so well understood nor the advantage of it so highly appreciated, in either army, as it was to be later in the

---

[1] *W. R.*, 39, p. 199.

[2] *Ib.*, 39, p. 199; *Journal of the Mil. Serv. Inst. of the U. S.*, XII, 285.

war. The intrenchments constructed in the XI Corps were weak even for this time, and decidedly inferior to those constructed in the XII, V, and II Corps. Where the line had not been intrenched, it was generally covered with abatis. It was commanded in several places, but Hooker preferred retaining it to changing it in the presence of the enemy. The work of fortifying it went on here and there through the night. It does not appear that there was any fortifying in Lee's army until after midnight.

Did Hooker consider that the passive defence, if good for himself, might be good for his opponent; and think of what he should do, should Lee now renounce the offensive, leaving the initiative again to Hooker? What was there in this case for Hooker to do, but to attack; and would it not be harder for him to advance from his present position than it was to continue advancing from the one that he had abandoned? No, he did not worry himself with any such questions; his all-absorbing thought was hurling back the enemy's decimated ranks, trusting that Lee's easy success thus far had made him bold enough to attack the Federal intrenchments in front.

When Couch after the fight went to Hooker and made his report on it, Hooker remarked: "It is all right, Couch; I have got Lee just where I want him; he must fight me on my own ground." "The retrograde movement," says Couch, "had prepared me for something of the kind, but to hear from his own lips that the advantages gained by the successful marches of his lieutenants were to culminate in fighting a defensive battle in that nest of thickets was too much, and I retired from his presence with the belief that my commanding general was a whipped man."

In the course of the afternoon, probably between 2 and 4 p.m., Devin's cavalry brigade with its battery of artillery was assembled in camp on Little Hunting Run to feed and rest, having left the 8 Pa. near Chancellorsville and two squadrons of the 17 Pa. with General Howard, "charged with the duty of picketing to his right and front, and observing the country toward Orange and Spottsylvania Court-House."[1] Companies D and H of the 33 Mass. (2. 2. XI) were placed in observation on a road leading to Ely's Ford (Map 15). The infantry picket line extending from the Plank Road on Howard's right to United States Ford was withdrawn.

Hancock's division $\left(\frac{1}{II}\right)$ bivouacked about on the ground taken up early this morning in three lines of battle supported on its right and rear by Sykes' division $\left(\frac{2}{V}\right)$, which formed parallel to the Turnpike, facing south. About dusk Humphreys' division $\left(\frac{3}{V}\right)$ arrived on its return from Decker's. Meade now received orders to occupy a line from Chancellorsville to the river. He at once sent Humphreys with his divi-

[1] W. R., 39, p. 778.

sion $(\frac{3}{V})$ to take the extreme left of this line on the river-bank near Childs and hold the approach to the United States Ford by the River Road. The woods through which the column wound its way to the new position were on fire. Their light was taken by the enemy for that of camp-fires, and this, together with the rattling of canteens, drew upon it a brisk fire of musketry. Griffin's division $(\frac{1}{V})$, on its return from Decker's, was halted some distance from Chancellorsville and put in position on Hancock's left (Map 15). The V Corps was reënforced this evening by its five batteries from the north bank of the river (28 pieces); and the II Corps by the three regiments which it left at United States Ford $(\frac{5}{1.\,1.\,II}, \frac{81}{1.\,1.\,II},$ and $\frac{84}{2.\,1.\,II})$.

Of the batteries which had been in action on the Turnpike, Arnold's $(\frac{1.}{2.\,II})$ returned to the artillery camp at Chandler's, Watson's $(\frac{2}{2.}v)$ bivouacked near Chancellorsville, Randol's $(\frac{3}{3.}v)$ rejoined its division under Humphreys on the left. Of Waterman's battery $(\frac{1}{1.}v)$, which had accompanied Humphreys on the River Road, two pieces took position about midway between Chandler's and Childs; the other four bivouacked near Chancellorsville.

The artillery of the XII Corps was formed, as stated, in two batteries: one near Chancellorsville, commanding the Plank Road from Fredericksburg; the other on the height of Fairview, facing south. Each numbered fourteen pieces. These were the only masses, or considerable groups, formed by the artillery of the right wing, which (including Seeley's and Jastram's batteries at United States Ford) numbered 183 pieces.

Hooker had dispensed with the services of his chief of artillery, and there was no one to make proper disposition of the batteries.[1]

French's division $(\frac{3}{II})$ was held massed near Chandler's until about sunset, when the 1st and 2d brigades were deployed on the skirts of a wood between Chandler's and the position held by the XII Corps. The 3d brigade remained near Chandler's. The III Corps, moving in accordance with Hooker's order of 4 o'clock, arrived in the vicinity of Chancellorsville while the Confederates were pressing Slocum in front and on his right. Graham's brigade, after receiving several orders and counter-orders, took position in close column of regiments in rear of Best's batteries at Fairview, ready to support them or to advance to the aid of Williams' division, then engaged in repelling Wright's attack. The brigade was immediately ordered to lie down to escape the fire of Beckham's artillery, to which it was subjected, and from which it lost 1 man killed and 5 wounded.

About sunset Birney's division $(\frac{1}{III})$, except Graham's brigade $(\frac{1}{1.III})$ and Jastram's battery $(\frac{1}{1.III})$, was moved up the Plank Road to the right

---

[1] *Journal of the Mil. Serv. Inst. of the U. S., XII, 285.*

of the XII Corps, and bivouacked near the interval between the XI and XII Corps. Two regiments and three pieces of this division took a forward position near two regiments of the XII Corps (Map 15).[1] While this was being done the sound of skirmishing indicated that an enemy was near. Shells and bullets reached the troops as they came into position.

"To discover the enemy's movements five or six daring men had climbed to the tops of the highest trees, from which they had a view over the surrounding woods. The position was very dangerous, for they might become targets for the rebel sharpshooters. In order to guard against it as much as possible, they kept up a continual shaking of the trees in which they were; they could be seen thus swinging in the air more than 100 feet above the ground, braving the double danger of the enemy's bullets and a fall—death in either case."[2]

Jastram's battery $(\frac{2}{1. \text{III}})$ moved up from United States Ford, and about midnight bivouacked near Chandler's.[3]

Whipple's division $(\frac{3}{\text{III}})$ bivouacked in reserve at Chancellorsville, also the infantry of Berry's division $(\frac{2}{\text{III}})$, except Mott's brigade $(\frac{3}{2. \text{III}})$, left at United States Ford. Berry's artillery, except Seeley's battery $(\frac{4}{2. \text{III}})$, left at United States Ford, bivouacked near the junction of the United States Ford and Ely's Ford Roads, about a mile in rear of Chancellorsville.

With Hooker's approval, Sickles gave orders during the night to Birney to occupy at daybreak a portion of the front line between the XI and XII Corps, so as, to some extent, to relieve those corps, and enable them to strengthen their lines.

In the course of the day a line of shallow rifle-pits was constructed from the vicinity of Buschbeck's position northward past Dowdall's Tavern. This will be referred to hereafter as the Buschbeck line (Map 15).[4]

About nightfall, von Gilsa's brigade $(\frac{1}{1. \text{XI}})$ was drawn in, and the half a regiment by which it maintained connection with McLean's brigade on its left replaced by two regiments. The brigade now connected directly with McLean's. Two pieces of Dieckman's battery $(\frac{1}{\text{XI}})$ were placed in the angle on the Turnpike facing down the latter. The 8 Pa. joined the cavalry brigade on Hunting Run.[5]

During to-day's fighting in the Wilderness the wounded, who were not numerous, were taken to some houses near the scene of action,

[1] W. R., 39, pp. 408, 429, 442, 708.

[2] Four Years with the Army of the Potomac, by R. G. de Trobriand, p. 438.

[3] History of Battery E, 1 R. I. Light Artillery, by George Lewis, p. 159.

[4] Schurz's map, W. R., 39, p. 649.

[5] Pleasonton's report, W. R., 39, p. 774; Devin's report, ib., pp. 778, 781; Martin's report, ib., p. 786; Carpenter's letter in The Charge of the Eighth Penn. Cavalry at Chancellorsville, p. 77.

where they were promptly attended to. Authority was obtained to take a few ambulances to the front from United States Ford, by which, when the lines fell back, the wounded were removed to the field hospitals. After urgent representation permission was obtained to order a few medicine-wagons to the field; not enough, however, to supply the wants of all the wounded. The defect was remedied by transporting the supplies in the ambulances and on horses and mules. In this way medical and surgical supplies in ample quantities were conveyed to the field hospitals.[1] The wounded of the V Corps were carried to the Chancellor House, part of which was turned into a hospital and the remainder used by General Hooker as his headquarters. The yard was occupied by wounded who could not be accommodated in the house. The ladies of the house, suppressing their feelings as hostiles to obey their kindly and tender instincts as women, came with their gentle ministrations to the assistance of the surgeons. A hospital for Hancock's division, which became the hospital of the II Corps, was established in the woods near Chandler's. Here the wounded were placed in rows upon blankets. Dry leaves gathered by attendants served as straw, which ordinarily took the place of mattresses. This evening, by order of the medical director, all the wounded were sent to the division hospitals prepared for them beyond Falmouth.

Anderson's division ($\frac{1}{I}$) bivouacked on or near the Turnpike, and Jackson's corps (II) on or near the Plank Road (Map 15). Jackson sent word to Lee that his advance was checked and that the enemy was in force at Chancellorsville. This brought Lee toward Jackson, who met him on his return from the Furnace, or about 7:30 p.m., at Decker (A). Lee had now more reason than Jackson had this morning to apprehend an advance on the part of Sedgwick against his rear. He knew Hooker's reputation as an aggressive fighter, even to the nickname that it had fastened upon him; and must have credited him with knowing that Longstreet had been detached from Lee's army. He had every reason to expect, and, as it seems, did expect, of his opponent a speedy resumption and a vigorous prosecution of the offensive. He felt that he could not himself remain inactive where he was. Before deciding to retire he wanted to try an attack. He believed that to succeed he must strike quickly. The question was, Where should he deliver his blow? Satisfied that it should not be in the direction of his right, he asked Jackson if he had found any suitable point for an attack by the left. Jackson replied with a description of Wright's unsuccessful attempt to advance from the Furnace. Major Talcott, an aide of General Lee's, and Captain Boswell, Jackson's chief engineer, were now sent out together to reconnoiter the enemy's front. During their absence

---

[1] *Medical Recollections of the Army of the Potomac,* by Jonathan Letterman, late Medical Director of the Army of the Potomac, pp. 124, 125.

Jackson spoke to Lee about what he had seen and heard during the advance, and commented upon the promptness with which the enemy had appeared to abandon his movements toward Fredericksburg when opposed, and the ease with which he had been driven back to Chancellorsville, and concluded by expressing the opinion very decidedly, and repeating it more than once, that the enemy would recross the Rappahannock before morning. He said in substance: "By to-morrow morning there will not be any of them this side of the river." General Lee expressed the hope that General Jackson's expectations might be realized, but said that he did not look for such a result; that he did not believe the enemy would abandon his attempt so easily; and expressed his conviction that the real move was to be made from Chancellorsville and not from Fredericksburg. On this point there was a great difference of opinion among the higher officers of his army, and Lee was the only one who seemed to have the absolute conviction that the real movement of the Federal army was the one he was then meeting. In this belief he never wavered from the first.

Talcott and Boswell returned about 10 p.m. and made a report that was unfavorable to an attack in front. According to Hooker's thinking, there was now no recourse for Lee but inglorious flight. But Lee did not think so. About this time he received a report from Fitzhugh Lee "describing," says Dabney,[1] "the position of the Federal army and the roads which he held with his cavalry leading to its rear." This description could not have been very accurate. The positions of the Federal troops were determined mainly, it would seem, by feeling the pickets. The positions of the latter can not now be determined. It would seem that they changed frequently, also that the pickets, patrols, and larger detachments kept the Confederate scouting parties at a good distance from the Federal lines.

Howard says: "The first distant symptoms occurred on the evening of May 1. Then was heard the sudden crack of rifle-shooting. It began with Steinwehr's skirmishers and then passed on to Schurz. Schimmelfennig pushed out a brigade[2] straight forward toward the southwest and received a sudden fire of artillery from the intruders. They left him and pushed on.

"It was a 'rolling' reconnaissance, evidently to determine for Lee's and Jackson's information the position of our flank."[3]

It may be safely asserted that not an officer or soldier of Lee's had seen the right flank of Hooker's army, and that the road which led to

---

[1] *Life of Jackson*, p. 673.

[2] Doubtless an erroneous reference to the regiment sent by Schimmelfennig to Carpenter's Farm (*W. R.*, 39, pp. 628, 650).

[3] *B. and L.*, III, 193, 194. According to Schurz, a negro brought in from Carpenter's Farm reported that he had seen Confederate troops moving westward, but the information which he gave was very indefinite (*W. R.*, 39, p. 650).

its rear, the Brock Road (Map 15), was not held by Confederate cavalry further north than the Orange Plank Road, if that far. It would seem that Fitzhugh Lee considered and represented the Federal right flank as resting somewhere in the angle formed by the Orange Plank Road and the Brook Road. Rev. Mr. Lacy, a chaplain in Jackson's corps, who was familiar with the country about Chancellorsville, and acquainted with the roads in that neighborhood, stated to Lee that troops could be conducted around Hooker's right by way of Wilderness Tavern.[1]  On the strength of the foregoing representations Lee and Jackson in consultation projected a turning movement against Hooker's rear.[2]  The execution of this movement was intrusted to Jackson. Lee indicated its principal features and said in conclusion: "General Stuart will cover your movement with his cavalry." General Jackson listened attentively, and his face lighted up with a smile while General Lee was speaking. Then rising and touching his cap, he said: "My troops will move at 4 o'clock." Lee remarked that before he moved, if he should have any doubt as to whether the enemy was still in position, he could send a couple of guns to a spot close by and open fire, which would speedily settle the question. This was after midnight.[3]  The general direction of his march being indicated by Lee, it was left to Jackson to decide upon the route that he would take. When Mr. Lacy pointed out to him on a map the road that he had in mind for him to follow, Jackson remarked: "That is too near; it goes within the line of the enemy's pickets. I wish to get around well to his rear without being observed. Do you know no other road?" It seems probable that the road proposed by the chaplain was the one running from Decker(A) past Welford's Furnace to the Brook Road (generally parallel to the Plank Road between Chancellorsville and Dowdall's Tavern) and that what Jackson objected to was the stretch from the Furnace to the Brook Road. To Jackson's question the chaplain replied that he had no perfect knowledge of any other road, but presumed that the one running from Welford's Furnace southward past Welford's House intersected the Brock Road, as the directions of the two roads were convergent. The needed information was soon obtained. It was found that the roads came together, affording a practicable route outside of the Federal outposts. This route Jackson decided to adopt. The bend in the road at the Furnace was held by the

---

[1] *Memoirs of R. E. Lee,* by A. L. Long, p. 252; *General Lee,* by Fitzhugh Lee, pp. 245, 246.

[2] Lee's report, W. R., 39, p. 798; Lee to Mrs. Jackson, Henderson's *Stonewall Jackson,* II, 582; W. R., 39, p. 940; and other Confederate reports.

[3] The details of the interview between Lee and Jackson are deduced from conflict-

ing accounts by a number of writers (*Life and Campaigns of Lieut.-Gen. T. J. Jackson,* Dabney, pp. 672, 673; *Chancellorsville,* Hotchkiss and Allan, pp. 41, 42; *Memoirs of Robert E. Lee,* Long, pp. 252, 254; *Stonewall Jackson and the American Civil War,* Henderson, II, 532; *So. Hist. Soc. Papers,* XXXIV, 1; Fitzhugh Lee's *Chancellorsville Address, ib.,* VII, 545).

main body of Stuart's cavalry and his horse artillery. The latter had probably been reënforced by midnight by the two detached pieces, making ten pieces. Wright's brigade, recalled by an order from Jackson, rejoined the force on the Plank Road at 11 p.m.

At this hour Posey received an order from Anderson to advance as far as he could. He succeeded in crossing the swamp, and pushed on to within "a short distance of the enemy's line of works."

Since the commencement of operations this morning both sides have been reënforced by artillery—the Federals by 28 pieces (560 men), and the Confederates by 2 pieces (40 men). The losses since the opening of the campaign have been slight on both sides, the Federal amounting to about 290 infantry, 80 artillery (4 pieces),[1] and 65 cavalry, the Confederate to about 100 infantry and 50 cavalry. The Federal loss in infantry fell wholly on Sykes' division, and the Confederate on Anderson's, McLaws', and Rodes' divisions. Adding the gains and deducting the losses, we get for the forces about Chancellorsville at the end of the day the following figures:

|  | INFANTRY | CAVALRY | ARTILLERY | AGGREGATE | PIECES |
|---|---|---|---|---|---|
| Federal . . . . . | 64,900 | 1,246 | 4,121 | 70,267 | 208 |
| Confederate . . . . | 42,170 | 1,953 | 2,880 | 47,626 | 144 |

Lee was still at a loss to estimate the numbers that confronted him. He had no knowledge of more than two corps. He probably believed 30,000 and apprehended as many as 45,000 Federals to be intrenched or intrenching about Chancellorsville.

### Federal Left Wing

Hooker's order of yesterday to Sedgwick regarding an attack or pursuit was received about 11:30 a.m. Sedgwick did not observe any "weak point" in the enemy or any symptom of his "falling back," so he continued inactive. Hooker's order of to-day for a demonstration at 1 p.m. did not reach Butterfield until 4:55 p.m., nor Sedgwick until about 5:45 p.m. A feeble demonstration was made by the I and VI Corps after 6 p.m. The light division of the VI Corps was sent across the river, its infantry relieving Russell's brigade $(\frac{3}{I, VI})$ at the front. At 9:05 p.m. Sedgwick received from Butterfield an order from Hooker countermanding the demonstration as too late.[2]

In the expectation that Sedgwick was soon to drive the defenders of Fredericksburg before him, Rufus Ingalls, Chief Quartermaster of the Army of the Potomac, still on the north side of the Rappahannock, wrote to W. W. Wright, railroad superintendent at Aquia:

Be prepared to lay the railroad bridge over the Rappahannock on short notice.

[1] 4½-inch battery returned to north side of river.
[2] W. R., 107, p. 1034.

On the completion of the telegraph line between Sedgwick's and Reynolds' headquarters, the flag and torch station at Fitzhugh House was broken up. Orders were issued for patrols on the telegraph lines to put to death instantly any person found tampering or interfering with them. Ten miles of telegraph wire were at Banks' Ford, with instruments, ready to cross there or be sent, if necessary, to United States Ford. The provost-marshal-general spent the day at United States Ford with 100 cavalry, engaged in keeping the communications open. He reported that the telegraph wire was broken by the carelessness of the artillery.[1]

The main train of the XII Corps moved to-day from Banks' Ford to United States Ford, where it connected with the troops.[2]

At 1:30 p.m. Hooker received copies of dispatches from Butterfield to Reynolds and Sedgwick, which, together perhaps with other reports, gave him the impression that one of the enemy's columns was threatening to gain possession or command of Banks' Ford. He ordered General Hunt, Chief of Artillery, to return to headquarters at Falmouth, collect the disposable artillery, move it to Banks' Ford, and prevent any attempt of the enemy to cross at that point. Hunt did not go to Falmouth. He went to United States Ford, which was then in telegraphic communication with Falmouth, and telegraphed to Butterfield to send to Banks' Ford the disposable batteries near headquarters. He ordered the 4½-inch battery which had crossed the Rappahannock to recross, and return to its position at Banks' Ford, and proceeded to that point himself. From there he sent von Blücher's battery of the General Reserve (four 20-pounders) down the river to relieve Hart's (six 3-inch guns), which he had called up from Traveller's Rest. While Hart's and von Blücher's batteries were changing posts, Hart's battery was replaced at Traveller's Rest by Amsden's ($\frac{3}{3.1}$) from Pollock's Mill.[3] Von Blücher's was placed in battery near the Fitzhugh House.

The following dispatches were sent this evening:

### Hunt to Hooker, 7:20 p.m.

Six guns are up here [at Banks' Ford], ten more will come certain, and more if General Sedgwick can send them. I have carefully examined the passes [crossings and approaches], and it is not practicable to prevent the passage of hostile troops, if a serious attempt is made, without infantry, at least a very strong division. General Benham has but 600 men [2. 2. II].

### Hooker to Butterfield, 8:45 p.m.

. . . Direct General Gibbon to send one brigade of his division to Banks' Ford, and have a suitable officer sent there to see that they are properly posted

---

[1] W. R., 40, p. 333, and 39, p. 219.
[2] Ib., 40, p. 558.
[3] Amsden says in his report: "Left this position [Pollock's Mill] at 4 p.m. May 1;

took position near Traveller's Rest, on Widow Gray's Farm, about 10 a.m." (W. R., 39, p. 304). He probably left Pollock's Mill at 4 a.m.

to prevent crossing. . . . If the absence of one brigade should weaken General Gibbon too much, which I hope will not be the case, he must call on General Sedgwick for assistance. . . . all the enemy's cavalry are in my immediate presence, which I trust will enable Stoneman to do a land-office business in the interior. I think the enemy in his desperation will be compelled to attack me on my own ground. . . . In half an hour more I shall probably have been engaged.[1]

### Butterfield to Hooker, 10 p.m.

There are now twenty-two guns of the Horse Artillery at Banks' Ford[2] and a brigade of infantry ordered there.[3] There will be in the neighborhood of thirty-four guns in all in the morning.[4]. . . Benham says if he had a full division from any troops, he should feel that he could defy them. If he could not defy them from the river with thirty-two pieces of artillery and a brigade of infantry, he ought to be pitched into the river himself. . . .

There was apparently a serious disagreement between Hunt and Benham on one side, and Hooker and Butterfield on the other, as to the amount of infantry needed at Banks' Ford.

Regarding the strength of the enemy, a Federal spy from Richmond reported 59,000 rations as issued to Lee's army, and gave the forces about Richmond at "8000 or 10,000 troops." Butterfield telegraphed to Peck (7:30 p.m.):

Hood's and Pickett's divisions of Longstreet's corps are in our front; so reported by deserters and prisoners captured to-day.

Peck replied:

There may be portions of Longstreet's troops with your opponents. If so, they are the first instalments. Deserters and contrabands who came in yesterday from Hood's and Pickett's divisions agree in all points with others that have fallen into our hands. . . .

Touching this matter the following dispatch of this date from Cooper to Lee was probably received to-day:

Orders were sent on Wednesday [April 29] to General Longstreet to move forward his command to reënforce you. He replied he would do so immediately, but expected to be a little delayed in gathering up his transportation train . . . General D. H. Hill, at Kinston, was also directed to send forward a brigade

---

[1] *W. R.*, 107, p. 1034.

[2] There were only 28 pieces of horse artillery altogether. Of these 6 were with Pleasonton, 6 with Stoneman, and 6 with Averell. There could not have been more than 10, therefore, at Banks' Ford. The additional force at that point was probably Graham's and Meinell's batteries of the General Reserve (12 pieces).

[3] $\frac{2}{2.\,\text{II}}$, except the picket details of the

several regiments. These were left in front of Fredericksburg. An additional regiment $\left(\frac{19}{1.\,2.\,\text{II}}\right)$ was ordered to Banks' Ford.

[4] The heavy battery from United States Ford (B. 1. Conn.) arrived and was posted after 7:30 p.m., making 26 guns in position. Hart's battery of 6 guns and Kinzie's of 4, both of the General Reserve, arrived during the night, but were not posted.

(Ransom's), and from his reply, it may be expected here to-night, when it will be immediately pushed forward. . . .

Early received an order this evening from Lee,—in case troops were withdrawn from his front, to post a guard in his position, and with the remainder of his force to join Lee. Pendleton observed heavy columns marching over the hills back of Falmouth toward the Federal right, but interpreted the movement as a feint, as no train was put in motion.[1] He probably did not report the fact to Early.

About 10:30 a.m. a signal message from Port Royal announced the presence of two gunboats shelling that place. This, together with Sedgwick's display of force in the afternoon, kept Early from detaching **any of his force, except that the report** from Port Royal caused him to send two batteries ($\frac{2.3}{A}$), numbering 8 pieces, to the river bluff near Port Royal. The remainder of his artillery, numbering 56 pieces, he disposed between Hamilton's Crossing and the Plank Road. At 11 p.m. he had 46 pieces in position on this line and the other 10 in reserve in rear of its center.[2] One battery $\left(\frac{3}{1.1}\right)$ of four pieces remained on the line of communication between Early's position and Chesterfield depot. There was considerable cheering along Early's front, induced, no doubt, by reports of the progress made by Jackson and Lee in the direction of Chancellorsville. The Federals endeavored to drown the Confederate voices with counter-cheering.

With a view to the moving of Hooker's supply-boats, the Federal Secretary of the Navy cabled to-day to Rear-Admiral Lee at Fort Monroe: "Dispatch two of the four tugs sent to you from the Potomac, to the mouth of the Rappahannock"; and Ingalls, about to leave for Chancellorsville, telegraphed to Rucker (5:40 p.m.): "Be prepared for transportation of forage and subsistence in light-draft vessels, if required."

Averell had been feebly engaged most of the day with W. H. F. Lee at Rapidan Station. He could distinctly hear the firing in the Wilderness, which seemed to come from the direction of Fredericksburg, where Hooker was supposed to be fighting Lee. Hooker, learning of Averell's position, had the following message sent to him at 6:30 p.m.:

*General:*

I am directed by the Major-general commanding to inform you that he does not understand what you are doing at Rapidan Station. If this finds you at

---

[1] Pendleton's report, *W. R.*, 39, p. 810. These columns must have been artillery, signal corps men, and provost guards, going to Banks' and United States Fords.

[2] In position: a section of Parker's battery, *2 pieces;* Fraser's battery, *4 pieces;* Rhett's battery, *4 pieces;* Carlton's battery, *4 pieces;* Nelson's battalion, *12 pieces;* 2 guns of the 2d battery and 2 of the 4th battery of the Washington Artillery, under Richardson, *4 pieces;* Andrews' battalion, *16 pieces.*

In reserve: the remainder of the Washington Artillery, *6 pieces;* Patterson's battery, *4 pieces.*

that place, you will immediately return to United States Ford, and remain there until further orders, and report in person.

.       .       .       .       .       .       .       .

P.S. If this reaches you at one o'clock in the morning you will start immediately.[1]

In compliance with the request sent yesterday from Hooker's head-quarters, the 3d brigade of Stahel's cavalry division was sent to-day from Fairfax Court-House to Bristoe Station. One regiment (5 N. Y.) reconnoitered from there to Rappahannock Station, and took post at Warrenton Junction.

## COMMENTS

In the advance from Chancellorsville, the connection that was to have been established after crossing Mott's Run was not effected. The Confederates formed but two columns. The smaller one under McLaws demonstrated against Hooker's front while the larger one under Jackson sought to overpower his right. The two commands were in constant communication with each other. While the Federals advanced in isolated columns, the Confederates came on practically in unbroken line of battle, and overlapped and turned their enemy wherever they met him.

The Federal cavalry did not prove itself as efficient as the Confederate. When Hooker marched out toward Tabernacle Church there was not a trooper in advance of his columns except the pickets of the 8 Pa. Cavalry. When this regiment was relieved by Sykes' division, it should have taken a post of observation on a flank of that division, or have occupied itself with establishing and maintaining connection with the adjoining columns. Instead of that, it went to the rear, leaving the two squadrons of Owen's 3 Va. Cavalry unopposed.

It was a capital mistake of Hooker's to detach the cavalry corps. Sending it ahead of the army as the latter ascended the Rappahannock served the important purpose, already pointed out, of deceiving the enemy as to Hooker's intentions. So far its employment was judicious, but after it crossed the Rappahannock it should have been used to screen and protect the turning columns and to keep Stuart from joining Lee. Especially after the right wing crossed the Rapidan was the cavalry needed to reconnoiter toward Chancellorsville and Fredericksburg, and to screen the army on the side of Spottsylvania and Richmond. In testifying before the Committee on the Conduct of the War, Hooker said:

From the place of crossing the river, Kelley's Ford, the infantry had about twenty-five miles to march to Chancellorsville; and the cavalry between fifty and sixty, to their post on the Aquia and Richmond railroad. Hence I concluded that they would reach their respective destinations about the same time.

[1] *W. R.*, 39, p. 1080. This dispatch was borne by Lieutenant Blunt of the 6 N. Y. Cavalry, with an escort of 4 men. The party passed through Stevensburg, where hostile patrols were encountered, going and coming (*ib.*, 39, p. 782).

He expected that the cavalry and the rest of the army would cross the Rappahannock by the morning of the 29th; and that by the night of the 30th Averell would have disposed of W. H. F. Lee and joined Stoneman near Hanover Junction. As it turned out, Averell on the night of the 30th had not become seriously engaged, and Stoneman had not gotten beyond the Rapidan. The infantry was at Chancellorsville; and the cavalry, not half-way to Hanover Junction. This backwardness of the cavalry was due primarily to Hooker's tardiness in issuing his orders for it to march from Warrenton Junction.

# CHAPTER XIX

## *Right Wing until 8 a.m.* (Map 16)

DURING the night of the 1st and 2d, Sykes' division ($\frac{2}{V}$) was withdrawn to the Mineral Spring Road near the Chandler House, where it intrenched itself. Griffin's division ($\frac{1}{V}$) fell back into the interval between Sykes' and Humphreys'. Hancock's ($\frac{1}{II}$) formed a new line of which the left crossed the Turnpike perpendicularly and the right ran obliquely thereto, connecting with Geary's left ($\frac{2}{XII}$) near the Plank Road.

At 1:55 a.m. Hooker wrote to Butterfield:

> Direct all the bridges to be taken up at Franklin's crossing and below before daylight, and for Reynolds' corps to march at once, with pack-train, to report to headquarters.

He intended, it seems, to place this corps and Averell's cavalry on Howard's right, so as to form a continuous line from the Rappahannock on the left to the Rapidan on the right.

While there was more or less discouragement, as already shown, in consequence of yesterday's retrograde movement, the army was generally buoyed up with the belief that it was about to fight a great and decisive battle. Captain Candler, aide-de-camp to Hooker, wrote home at 3 a.m.:

> . . . Were attacked by Johnny Reb yesterday. Fell back at first to draw him on, then took a position and gave him "fits." Expect the fight to commence again in half an hour. We are all right. They have reënforcements from Richmond, but we can whip them anyway, for they must come out of their works and attack us in our own position. To-day will tell a big tale. God grant we may be successful. Staff and general all sound as yet.

At or about daylight the following movements took place within the Federal lines: Graham's brigade ($\frac{1}{1.III}$) from the rear of Fairview to its division on the Plank Road; Arnold's battery ($\frac{1}{2.II}$) to Chandler's; one section of Pettit's battery ($\frac{1}{1.II}$) from Chandler's to the Irish brigade ($\frac{2}{1.II}$) at Scott's Ford, the remainder of this battery (4 pieces) taking position near Chandler's; Pleasonton's cavalry, with its battery, from

Hunting Run to Chancellorsville, leaving one squadron of the 6 N. Y. on picket at Ely's Ford. Between 7 and 8 a.m. Carroll's brigade $(\frac{1}{3.\ II})$ occupied the interval between Hancock and Sykes, where it intrenched itself in the course of the day. By request of General Meade (commanding V Corps) a regiment of Mott's brigade $(\frac{7}{3.\ 2.\ III})$ was ordered at 8 a.m. to report to General Humphreys, commanding Meade's third division. It was placed on Humphreys' extreme left to connect his line with the river. The Irish brigade $(\frac{2}{1.\ II})$ had probably withdrawn to a position in rear of Humphreys' division.

From Chancellorsville westward, the Federal line runs for the greater part along the crest of a ridge, constituting the watershed between the Rappahannock and Mattapony Rivers. About three fourths of a mile from Chancellorsville is an eminence known as Fairview, which commands Chancellorsville and the Plank Road east and west. About three fourths of a mile southwest of Fairview is another eminence, which, though clear but for a solitary clump of hazel-bushes, is called Hazel Grove. In the depression between these two eminences is a small brook with swampy banks running southward. On a swell of ground about a mile from Hazel Grove is Dowdall's Tavern, where Howard had his headquarters. About half a mile beyond this point is another rise of ground called Taylor after the farm-house situated on it. The Federal line passed by the south of Fairview and north of Hazel Grove, with a break where it crossed the creek, and extended westward beyond Taylor, its right resting in the depth of the forest. Taylor overlooks and commands the front of the XI Corps. The enemy in possession of it, and the whole position of that corps, would have to be abandoned. It is the key-point of this part of the line.

At sunrise Hooker, accompanied by Sickles, started from Chancellorsville on a tour of inspection along his line on the right. He found Birney with his three brigades on the crest of Hazel Grove between the XI and XII Corps, where he had taken position after consultation with Howard and in pursuance of Sickles' order. All along the line he was greeted by the troops with hearty and prolonged cheers.

Hooker had ordered his position to be intrenched in the hope that Lee and Jackson, following Burnside's example, would dash their divisions into fragments against them [sic], and thus become an easy prey. Lee, with a broader appreciation of the true tactical bearing of ditch and parapet, determined to employ them as a shelter for his own force until Jackson's movement was completed and the time had come for a general advance. Orders were at once sent to General McLaws to cover his front, extending across the pike and the Plank roads, with a line of breastworks; and long before daylight the soldiers of his division, with the scanty means at their disposal, were busy as beavers amongst the timber.[1]

---

[1] *Stonewall Jackson and the American Civil War*, by G. F. R. Henderson, **II, 530.**

As already stated, Lee decided to endeavor to turn the Federal right flank with a portion of his army under Jackson while demonstrating against the Federal left and front with the remainder.

To Jackson were assigned the infantry of his three divisions and the 8 S. Ca. of Kershaw's brigade of McLaws' division $(\frac{8}{1.2.1})$,[1] Stuart's three regiments of cavalry, and fractions of two others, the artillery of the II Corps (except Dance's and Hupp's batteries of the corps artillery, and the artillery of Early's division), Alexander's battalion of the corps artillery of the I Corps (except Rhett's and Jordan's batteries and 2 pieces of Parker's battery), and Stuart's 10 pieces of horse artillery, altogether about 31,700 men and 112 pieces of artillery (88 of the II Corps, 14 of the I Corps, and 10 of the cavalry). The following forces were to remain under Lee, confronting the Federal left and front: the infantry of Anderson's division $(\frac{1}{I})$ except Wilcox's brigade, —with Dance's and Hupp's batteries of the corps artillery of the II Corps (8 pieces); the infantry of McLaws' division $(\frac{2}{II})$ except Barksdale's brigade and the 8 S. Ca.,—with Manly's and McCarthy's batteries of McLaws' division, Grandy's battery of Anderson's division $(\frac{1}{I})$, and Jordan's, of the corps artillery of the I Corps, each numbering 4 pieces; the 4 and about half of the 3 Va. Cavalry; altogether about 13,000 men with 24 pieces of artillery. Lee thus assigned to his turning force about ⅔ of his infantry and ⅘ of his artillery—retaining for demonstration about ⅓ of his infantry and ⅕ of his artillery.[2]

The enemy was astir at an early hour. Between 2:30 a.m. and daylight Wilcox with his brigade and Moore's and Lewis' batteries $(\frac{2.4}{1.1})$ returned to Banks' Ford. Wofford moved to the left, establishing connection with the line in that direction. About daylight Iverson's brigade $(\frac{3}{2.II})$ relieved Ramseur's $(\frac{5}{2.II})$ at the front on the Plank Road. At 7 a.m. Thomas' brigade $(\frac{6}{1.II})$ relieved Posey's $(\frac{2}{1.I})$. The latter with Wright's $(\frac{5}{1.I})$ took position on the left of the Plank Road near Decker(A) (Map 16).

Major Pegram, commanding an artillery battalion of Jackson's corps, was directed to advance as many rifled guns on the road leading from the right of the Confederate line to Chancellorsville as could be used, "for the purpose of shelling the enemy's infantry in the woods." According to Major Pegram this was at 6:30 a.m. But Colonel B. T. Brockman of the 13 S. Ca. says, "the cannon firing opened at 5:16

[1] *W. R.*, 39, p. 832.

[2] The numbers in each fraction were about as follows:

|  | INFANTRY | CAVALRY | ARTILLERY | AGGREGATE | PIECES |
|---|---|---|---|---|---|
| Under Jackson . . . | 28,050 | 1,450 | 2,240 | 31,740 | 112 |
| " Lee . . . . . | 11,981 | 500 | 480 | 12,961 | 24 |
| Total . . . . . . . | 40,031 | 1,950 | 2,720 | 44,701 | 136 |

o'clock."[1]   The order was probably received about 5 o'clock.   Pursuant thereto Brunson's and McGraw's batteries ($\frac{1.4}{1.\text{II}}$) were posted between the Plank Road and Turnpike and afterward reënforced with 2 pieces, making a line of 10 pieces.   They drew upon themselves the fire of two Federal batteries (Atwell's ($\frac{1}{2.\text{XII}}$) and probably Hampton's ($\frac{2}{2.\text{XII}}$), say 12 pieces).   For about twenty minutes they kept up their cannonade, some of the guns shelling the woods while the others engaged the Federal batteries.[2]   A strong line of skirmishers advanced from McLaws' position,[3] which together with the fire of the artillery developed the fact that Hooker was still in the vicinity of Chancellorsville and ready at least to defend himself.

In consequence of these and other preliminaries Jackson did not make as early a start as he had intended to.   There was some delay in assembling his troops.[4]   Colquitt's brigade took up the march from the vicinity of Aldrich Tavern about 5:30 a.m., proceeded by the Plank Road to Decker(A), and thence, apparently after some further delay, pursued its way westward toward Welford's Furnace.   Colonel E. P. Alexander says: "Two hours after sunrise [about 7 a.m.] Lee, standing by the roadside, watched the head of the column march by, and exchanged with Jackson the last few words ever to pass between them."[5]   This was probably in the vicinity of Decker(A).

The infantry was preceded by the 2 Va. Cavalry, and protected on the right by the 1 and 5 Va. Cavalry and part of the 3.[6]   The 4th regiment and the other half of the 3d, under Wickham and Owen, remained behind watching the Federal left.   The main column was headed by the Second Division (Rodes'), of which the 4th brigade (Colquitt's) was in front.   Behind the Second Division came the Fourth (Colston's), and behind the Fourth the First (A. P. Hill's).   In each division the infantry was followed by the artillery and the fighting train, composed of ambulances and ammunition-wagons.[7]   The regimental and main trains went by roads further to the South directed upon Todd's Tavern.[8]   A detail of cavalry was attached to Jackson's staff as couriers: frequent reports were to be sent back to General Lee.[9]

*Right Wing from 8 a.m. to 2 p.m.* (Map 17)

About 8 a.m. the column commenced crossing the high open ground on the east side of Scott's Run, near Welford's Furnace, and descend-

---

[1] W. R., 39, pp. 937, 910.

[2] Ib., 39, pp. 937, 938, 890, 771.

[3] Ib., 39, p. 825.

[4] *Military Memoirs of a Confederate*, by E. P. Alexander, p. 333.

[5] Ib., p. 329.

[6] Letters of Colonel T. T. Munford, 2 Va. Cav., to the author.

[7] *Military Memoirs of a Confederate*, by E. P. Alexander, p. 330.

[8] *Papers of Mil. Hist. Soc. of Mass.*, V, 371.

[9] *Johnny Reb and Billy Yank*, by Alexander Hunter, p. 359; *Stonewall Jackson and the American Civil War*, by G. F. R. Henderson, II, 532.

ing therefrom to cross the creek. Here Colquitt, by order of General Jackson, detached from his brigade the 23 Ga. "with instructions to guard the flank of the column in motion against a surprise, and to call, if necessary, upon any officer whose command was passing, for reën-forcement."[1] Jackson crossed the Run at the head of his infantry, and declining a breakfast prepared for him at the Furnace, pushed on by the road leading southward. The procession of infantry, artillery, and wagons, rising into the clearing east of Scott's Run and sinking with a southward trend into the woods beyond, was soon observed from General Birney's lookouts in the tops of high trees about Hazel Grove.[2] Birney ordered up a section (two guns) of Sims' battery $\left(\frac{1}{1.\text{III}}\right)$ and about 10 a.m. had it open fire on the column at a distance of about a mile and a quarter, causing the troops to "double-quick" past the point fired at.[3] Sims brought up the rest of his battery and about 11 a.m. opened on a train which was then passing.[4] In the meantime Turnbull's battery $\left(\frac{3}{1.\text{II}}\right)$ was brought up to Hazel Grove and parked on the edge of the clearing, where it was joined probably about 11:30 by Jastram's battery $\left(\frac{2}{1.\text{III}}\right)$ from the vicinity of Chandler's.[5]

The peppering to which Sims subjected the enemy's column caused some hastening of its movement and perhaps a slight deflection of the line of march from the route over the high open ground to one concealed by the latter.

"Never can I forget," says Hunter McGuire, late medical director of Jackson's corps, "the eagerness and intensity of Jackson on that march to Hooker's rear. His face was pale, his eyes flashing. Out from his thin compressed lips came the terse command: 'Press forward, press forward!' In his eagerness as he rode, he leaned over on the neck of his horse, as if in that way the march might be hurried. 'See that the column is kept closed, and that there is no straggling,' he more than once ordered; and 'Press on, press on!' was repeated again and again. Every man in the ranks knew that we were engaged in some great flank movement, and they eagerly responded and pressed on at a rapid gait.'"[6]

Regimental commanders were ordered to march in rear of their regiments with a guard of strong men with fixed bayonets to prevent straggling.[7]

[1] W. R., 39, pp. 975, 979.

[2] There is reason for believing that it was seen also from one or more of the Federal balloons; but it is doubtful whether any report of the fact reached Hooker. A Federal balloon was visible to the Confederates as they marched over the open ground near the Furnace (Letter to the author from Captain Randolph Barton, Baltimore).

[3] W. R., 39, pp. 408, 443. "There would be a temporary break in the column, as though it had stopped or was going by some other route. Sometimes the men and teams would go on the run while passing. That was all. Shortly the column would be moving as before" (The 27 Indiana Vol. Infantry, by a member of Company C, p. 318).

[4] W. R., 39, pp. 404, 443.

[5] History of Battery E, 1 R. I. Light Artillery, by George Lewis, p. 159.

[6] Southern Hist. Soc. Papers, XXV, 110.

[7] Histories of the Several Regiments and Battalions from N. Ca. in the Great War

The roads were wet enough to be easy to the feet and free from dust. The weather was fine, but very warm, at least for a soldier in a marching column, shut in by dense wood on either side. There was suffering for want of water and food.[1]

Captain Smith, Jackson's assistant adjutant-general, after starting the last of the heavy trains on the road from Aldrich to Todd's Tavern, proceeded to join his chief at the head of the column. As he slowly and with difficulty forced his horse along the narrow, crowded road past the plodding infantry, he was the target for all the chaff at their command. "Say, here's one of Old Jack's little boys; let him by, boys! Have a good breakfast this morning, sonny? Better hurry up or you'll catch it for getting behind. Tell Old Jack we're all a-comin'. Don't let him begin the fuss till we get there!" and so on.[2]

At a little after 9 o'clock Hooker had completed the inspection of his lines. Returning to his headquarters, he found waiting there couriers from General Birney, who informed him that a column of the enemy was visible moving continuously across his front toward the right, accompanied by trains, guns, and ambulances, and had been visible since 8 o'clock. From his tent Hooker caught sight of one portion of Jackson's column after another coming up on the divide near the Brick House, saw it sink into the valley of Scott's Run, and reappear on high open ground, going southward down the Run. This southward turn was suggestive of a march on Richmond. However, after watching the movement awhile, he spread a map on his bed and carefully studied it, soliloquizing, says J. Watts de Peyster, somewhat thus: "It can't be retreat; retreat without a fight? That is not Lee. If not retreat, what is it? Lee is trying to flank me." For the first time, it seems, he considered the possibility of Lee's attacking him, not on his, but on Lee's own ground. His recent inspection had revealed to him that his position, though strong in front, was weak on the extreme right. To remedy this defect, he sent the following dispatch:

Headquarters Army of the Potomac, Saturday, May 2, 9:30 a.m., 1863.
To GENERAL HOWARD.

*General:*

I am directed by the Major-General commanding to say the disposition you have made of your corps has been with a view to a *front* attack by the enemy. If he should throw himself upon your flank, he wishes you to examine the ground, and determine upon the position you will take in that event, in order that you may be prepared for him in whatever direction he advances.

*1861–5,* by W. Clark, I, 191. According to Lieutenant-Colonel Henderson, "all stragglers were to be bayoneted" (*Stonewall Jackson and the American Civil War,* II, 532).

[1] "Many," says the colonel of the 27 Ga., "fell out of ranks exhausted, some fainting and having spasms; only a few had eaten anything since the morning before" (*W. R.,* 39, p. 981).

[2] J. P. Smith, in *B. and L.,* III, 205, 206.

He suggests that you have heavy reserves well in hand to meet this contingency.

J. H. VAN ALEN,

Brig. General and A. D. C.

We have good reason to suppose that the enemy is moving to our right. Please advance your pickets for purposes of observation as far as may be safe in order to obtain timely information of their approach.[1]

Hooker thus protected himself, as he thought, against an attack in flank. He did not know, as he should have known, that his right flank was more than 2 miles from the Rapidan, and that there was practically nothing in the interval to cover his communications. So he did nothing for the safety of the latter. His problem, as he now viewed it, was to meet an attack in front or flank or both. Had he risen to the occasion, he would have made Lee look to his own security. Rather than accept his present situation, he would have recognized the fault that he committed in assuming the defensive, and have put forth his whole strength offensively. At 9:30, when he sent his message to Howard, he wrote to Butterfield:

The General Commanding desires you to instruct General Sedgwick, if an opportunity presents itself with a reasonable expectation of success, to attack the enemy in his front. We have reliable information that all the divisions known to us as having belonged to the army at Fredericksburg except Ewell's [Early's] are in this vicinity. It is impossible for the general to determine here whether it is expedient for him [Sedgwick] to attack or not. It must be left to his discretion.

It is to be observed that Sedgwick's attack as above prescribed was to be a real, not a pretended one. Hooker was now aware that Sedg-

[1] I am indebted for the text of this document to H. M. Kellog, Esq., of Cortland, N. Y., who copied it from the original while on duty as clerk at Howard's headquarters on the 30th of June, 1863. Until then, nearly two months after the campaign of Chancellorsville, and forty-eight hours after the departure of General Hooker from the Army of the Potomac, no record of this order had been made in the *Letters Received* book of the XI Corps (Affidavit of H. M. Kellog, in *The Battles of Chancellorsville and Gettysburg*, by Captain A. H. Nelson, p. 36). The original has disappeared from the files of the War Department, and can not be found. A dispatch of the same import, but addressed: *"Major-Generals Howard and Slocum,"* is given in the *War Records* (40, p. 360). It is taken from Hooker's *Letters Sent* book, in which the order is annotated in red ink: "Copy furnished General Howard." An-

other document of the same import, but marked "Circular" and addressed: *"Major-General Slocum and Major-General Howard,"* is given in the *Report of the Committee on the Conduct of the War* (IV, 126). It is presumably this one that is given as addressed to *"Major-Generals Slocum and Howard,"* in *Battles and Leaders of the Civil War* (III, 219). Howard received two copies of this dispatch a short time apart. They made so little impression on him that he afterward denied having ever received them (Carl Schurz in *B. and L.*, III, 220, and in *McClure's Magazine*, June, 1907; and Howard in *B. and L.*, III, 196). In his *Autobiography* (1907) Howard neither denies nor admits having received this order. In 1874 Hooker wrote with reference to Howard: "His offence to me was forgotten when he acknowledged it" (Letter to General W. G. Le Duc, Feb. 24).

wick had failed to hold Lee in his position on the Rappahannock. Sedgwick was to force the position "in his front." In what direction he was to pursue was not stated. About 10 o'clock Manly's and McCarthy's batteries ($\frac{3.4}{2.I}$) opened fire from their position on the Turnpike. This demonstration may have drawn the attention of the Federal commander in this direction. At any rate, when General Sickles returned to headquarters Hooker ordered him to make a reconnaissance in front and to the left of Chancellorsville. "Two reliable regiments led by circumspect and intrepid commanders," the 11 Mass., Colonel Blaisdell, and the 26 Pa., Colonel Tilghman ($\frac{11.\ 26}{I.\ 2.\ III}$), were sent out, the former in front of Hancock, on the Turnpike, the latter on the Plank Road, each accompanied by a detachment of Berdan's sharpshooters from Whipple's division ($\frac{3}{III}$). The 26 Pa. took a few prisoners who reported that they had missed the road and that they were marching toward the Federal right.

Meanwhile Lee was calmly waiting for the accomplishment of Jackson's manœuver. Fully appreciating, and resolutely facing, the possibility of failure, he wrote to President Davis:

> I find the enemy in a strong position at Chancellorsville and in large force; his communications extend to the Rapidan at Germanna and Ely's Fords, and to the Rappahannock at United States Mine Ford. He seems determined to make the fight here, and, from what I learn from General Early, has sent up troops from his position opposite Fredericksburg.[1]
>
> . . . . . . . . . .
>
> It is plain that if the enemy is too strong for me here, I shall have to fall back and Fredericksburg must be abandoned. If successful here, Fredericksburg will be saved, and our communications retained. I may be forced back to the Orange and Alexandria or the Virginia Central road, but in either case I will be in position to contest the enemy's advance upon Richmond. I have no expectation that any reënforcements from Longstreet or North Carolina will join me in time to aid in the contest at this point, but they may be in time for a subsequent occasion.
>
> . . . . . . . . . .
>
> I am now swinging around to my left to come up in his [the enemy's] rear.
>
> I learn from prisoners taken that Heintzelman's troops from Washington are here[2] and the enemy seems to have concentrated his strength for this effort. If I had with me all my command, and could keep it supplied with provisions and forage, I should feel easy, but as far as I can judge the advantage of numbers and position is greatly in favor of the enemy.

Lee's artillery was disposed in two fractions of 12 pieces each: Grady's, McCarthy's, and Manly's batteries ($\frac{1}{I.\ I}$, $\frac{3.4}{2.I}$) with McLaws on

---

[1] Lee refers here to the movement of the III Corps.

[2] Heintzelman, commanding the defences of Washington, had not left his command. None of his troops had joined the Army of the Potomac.

the Turnpike; Jordan's, Dance's, and Hupp's ($\frac{2}{1}$, $\frac{2.4}{11}$) with Lee on the Plank Road.

McLaws had orders from Lee to "hold his position, as General Jackson would operate to the left and rear, . . . not to engage seriously, but to press strongly as soon as it was discovered that General Jackson had attacked."[1]  As the troops between Semmes' brigade and the Plank Road marched off to follow Jackson, Kershaw's brigade came into the front line and, together with Semmes' and the artillery, occupied the space between the Plank Road and the Turnpike.  Lee on the left and McLaws on the right, each had 8 pieces of artillery in position and 4 in reserve.  Lee's 8 were posted by Major Hardaway, Anderson's chief of artillery, as follows: 2 pieces on the Plank Road, 2 on a road further to the left leading into the Plank Road, and 4 distributed along the Welford's Furnace Road at intervals of about 400 yards to command the hollows leading into Scott's Run.  McLaws' 8 ($\frac{3.4}{2.1}$) were posted between Semmes' and Wofford's brigades on the left of the Turnpike.  His reserve battery ($\frac{1}{1.1}$) had been withdrawn on account of the pieces not having sufficient range.[2]

About 11 o'clock Sickles received several reports in quick succession from Birney to the effect that a column of the enemy was moving toward the Federal right.  He consequently, with Hooker's approval, joined Birney at Hazel Grove.  The movements of the enemy indicated to Sickles a retreat on Gordonsville or an attack upon the Federal right flank—perhaps both, for if the attack failed, the retreat might be carried out.  Sickles hastened to report the movement through staff officers to Hooker, and proposed that he use his whole corps in following up the enemy and attacking his columns.  He communicated the substance of this message to Howard on his right and to Slocum on his left, inviting their coöperation in case Hooker should accede to this proposition.  About noon Hooker sent him orders to "advance cautiously toward the road, followed by the enemy, and harass the movement as much as possible,"[3] with Birney's and Whipple's divisions ($\frac{1.3}{III}$), but refused to let him have Berry's ($\frac{2}{III}$).  Hooker's dispatch of 9:30 a.m. reached Howard a little after 12.  Howard in the meantime had sent the following dispatch, which reached Hooker about 11:30:

Headquarters 11th Corps, May 2, 10 m. to 11 o'k [10:50 a.m.].
MAJ. GEN. HOOKER, Com'd'g Army.

General:

From Gen. Devens' headquarters [Taylor] we can observe a column of infantry moving westward on a road parallel with this on a ridge about 1½ to 2 m. south of this.  I am taking measures to resist an attack from the west.

Respectfully,

O. O. HOWARD,
Maj. Gen.

[1] W. R., 39, pp. 825, 826.    [2] Ib., 39, p. 883.    [3] Ib., 39, p. 386.

The distance of the column referred to, from Devens' headquarters, was 2 miles or more.[1]  What these "measures to resist an attack from the west" consisted in, Hooker could only conjecture.  He probably conceived them to be a refusal of Howard's right, and pictured to himself a division or more of this corps thrown back and prolonged toward the Rapidan.  All that was done, so far as can be learned, was to place the reserve artillery, as it arrived, in position facing west (Map 17)[2] and to send Captain Castle of the Signal Corps toward the west to watch the movements of the enemy.[3]  This was about 11 o'clock.  The captain established a station in the vicinity of von Gilsa's line on the extreme right.  About noon Lieutenant Keen opened a signal station at Dowdall's Tavern (Howard's headquarters) to communicate with Castle.  These two stations were in communication with each other until about 6 o'clock this evening, when, as we shall see, the movements of the enemy broke them up.[4]

About noon the 26 Pa. was withdrawn from its forward position on the Plank Road and returned to its brigade $(\frac{1}{2.\ \text{III}})$, leaving the 11 Mass. of the same brigade on the Turnpike, coöperating with Hancock's advance skirmishers under Colonel Nelson A. Miles of the 61 N. Y. Volunteers.

At noon Sickles received Hooker's order for harassing the enemy. He brought up two battalions of sharpshooters under Colonel Berdan to be deployed as skirmishers and as flankers, so as to get all possible knowledge of the enemy's movements and of the approaches to his line of march; he communicated again with Slocum and Howard, and was assured of their prompt coöperation;[5] and hastily ordered Birney "to follow the enemy, pierce the column, and gain possession of the road over which it was passing."[6]  About 12:30 Hayman's brigade $(\frac{3}{1.\ \text{III}})$,[7] covered in front and on both flanks with skirmishers from Berdan's and his own, pushed across Scott's Run, heading for the point on the road which had been reached by the fire of the artillery.  Jackson's corps artillery, followed by its ammunition-train and other trains, was now passing the Furnace.  Orders were sent back for the rear portion of the column to take the road which turns south at a point east of the Furnace and joins the Furnace Road beyond the Welford House. Brooke's battery of four 12-pounder Napoleons $(\frac{1}{\text{II}})$ was taken out of the column.  One piece was hastily thrust out to the right with orders to fire one charge and retire, thus giving time for the other pieces to take position on a hill south of the railroad cut.  The single piece fired three rounds of canister, double-shotted, from the right of the road,

[1] W. R., 39, p. 386.
[2] Ib., 39, p. 651.
[3] Ib., 39, p. 231.
[4] Ib.

[5] Ib., 39, p. 386.
[6] Ib., 39, p. 408.
[7] Except the 37 N. Y., which remained between Birney's right and Howard's left.

and fell back to join the other three pieces, which in the meantime had taken position at Welford's House. This was about 2 p.m.

The 23 Ga. $(\frac{23}{4.\,2.\,II})$, covering the flank of Jackson's column, had not suffered from the Federal artillery, which had aimed only at the column; it was therefore quite fresh, but it was altogether too weak to resist the force directed upon the Furnace. Lee had directed Anderson to send a brigade to resist the further progress of the Federal column. Anderson about noon sent Posey's $(\frac{2}{1.\,I})$ with orders to dislodge the enemy.[1] About 1 p.m. its pickets were driven in. Its skirmishers, however, delivered such an effective fire that Birney had to order up Graham's brigade $(\frac{1}{1.\,III})$ to the support of Hayman's. At the same time Sickles ordered Whipple's division to come within supporting distance of Birney's. Best soon perceived that he was greatly outnumbered and would not be able to maintain his position. So, leaving about 40 men as rear-guard, he withdrew about 2 p.m. with the remainder of the regiment toward the cut of the unfinished railroad.

At the time of Birney's advance against the Furnace (12:30–1 p.m.) the fraction of the 3 Va. Cavalry under Lieutenant-Colonel Carter was on picket duty at the Furnace. Carter himself carried to the rear of Jackson's column a report that the train was attacked and in danger of being captured. A similar report was sent to Lee's headquarters. As a consequence the 14 Ga. of Thomas' brigade was sent back "to the assistance of the artillery-train,"[2] and Wright's brigade $(\frac{5}{1.\,I})$ started from the Plank Road toward the Furnace to support Posey. About the same time Ward's brigade $(\frac{2}{1.\,III})$ moved out to support Hayman's and Graham's brigades, and Whipple's division $(\frac{3}{III})$ commenced arriving at Hazel Grove as reserve.[3]

Jackson's column kept moving on. The cavalry guarding its right flank had here and there come in sight of Federal pickets and patrols, and generally maintained toward them an attitude of observation or defence. The advance-guard had not met a hostile soldier when about 1 p.m., as it approached the Orange Plank Road, the 2 Va. Cavalry, still leading the way, caught sight of a Federal vidette, who quickly disappeared. On reaching the Plank Road, the Confederate cavalry turned to the right and followed the road as far as Hickman's place, where it dismounted to rest.[4] Soon afterward one squadron went further down the road, and meeting a picket of Federal cavalry, dislodged it and pursued it some distance, returning thereupon to Hickman's. The officer commanding this detachment reported to Colonel Munford that

[1] *W. R.*, 39, pp. 798, 851, 871. This brigade left one regiment (48 Miss.) behind as skirmishers, which reduced it to three regiments.

[2] *Ib.*, 39, p. 913.

[3] Two pieces of Lewis' battery of this division remained, it seems, in the vicinity of Chancellorsville (*W. R.*, 39, p. 726).

[4] The name *Wolstry* on the map, near Hickman's, should read *Wolfrey*.

he had got a view of the right of the Federal line; this report was promptly forwarded to General Fitzhugh Lee. Soon afterward Jackson arrived with the head of the infantry, and went in person with Fitzhugh Lee to the high ground on which Burton's Farm is situated, to reconnoiter the Federal position. Here, only a few hundred yards from him, he saw a line of intrenchments extending along the Turnpike, with abatis in front, and stacked arms in rear, and back of these, soldiers in groups, laughing, chatting, and smoking. One can imagine his satisfaction at perceiving that the enemy was thus unconscious of his proximity. But one may reasonably believe, too, that this satisfaction was mingled with disappointment. He had expected to find the Orange Plank Road clear and to advance by it against the enemy's rear. He found that it was occupied by Federal pickets and that an advance by it would bring him obliquely against the Federal front. So far from being in the enemy's rear, he was not even on his flank. He saw that the enemy's line extended westward beyond the junction of the Turnpike and Orange Plank Road as far as the edge of the wood beyond Taylor; he may have learned from Fitzhugh Lee that the Turnpike was free from the enemy in the vicinity of Wilderness Tavern, but he could not tell how far the Federal line extended toward that point. It was plain, however, that to take it in rear he would have to extend his turning movement to the Turnpike. Having given about five minutes to observation and reflection, he turned toward his courier, saying: "Tell General Rodes to move across the Plank Road and halt when he gets to the old Turnpike. I will join him there."[1] One more look at the Federal line, and he rode rapidly down the hill. Lee was directed to manœuver his two squadrons at Burton as if preparing to charge the opposing cavalry.

About 2 p.m. the march was resumed along the Brock Road toward the Turnpike. At the same hour Archer turned back with the last two brigades, his own and Thomas' $(\frac{5.6}{1.\text{II}})$, to go to the protection of the trains, and Geary, in the Federal center, was ordered by Hooker to move out on the Plank Road with a portion of his command $(\frac{2}{\text{XII}})$ "for the purpose of cutting off the train of the enemy, who was supposed to be retreating toward Gordonsville."

The 12 Va. Infantry was detached from McGowan's brigade as a guard to trains and prisoners.[2]

### Right Wing, 2 p.m. to 5 p.m. (Map 17)

The 40 men of the 23 Ga. left at the Furnace were captured by Berdan's sharpshooters. The main body of the regiment fell back toward

---

[1] Fitzhugh Lee's *Chancellorsville Address.*

[2] *History of McGowan's Brigade*, by F. J. Caldwell, pp. 76, 77; *W. R.*, 39, p. 906.

Since the departure of Archer's and Thomas' brigades, McGowan's brigade was the rearmost one in Jackson's column.

the railroad cut, where it arrived and established itself about 2:30 p.m. It had in the meantime been joined by two companies of the 14 Tenn. and perhaps two companies of the 7 Tenn., which had been marching to overtake the columns and had turned back from some point southwest of Welford's House, before reaching the column, to assist in protecting the train.[1] About 3 p.m. the 14 Ga., marching back from Thomas' brigade, took position on the left of the main Furnace Road, at the point where a road comes into it from the north, to prevent the Federals from cutting off the rear of the column by that road. Hayman's and Graham's brigades ($\frac{3.1}{1.\text{III}}$) started to go past the Furnace in pursuit of the retiring 23 Ga., which brought them under a galling fire of musketry poured into their flanks by Posey's brigade, and the fire of Brooke's battery ($\frac{1}{\text{II}}$) at Welford's House. This caused them to halt and wait for artillery to engage that of the enemy. Birney ordered Sims' battery ($\frac{1}{1.\text{III}}$) to move to the Furnace. But the chief of artillery of the corps disapproved of moving it on account of its being already in position, and sent an order to the chief of artillery of the division to send one of the other two batteries to the front. Turnbull's battery ($\frac{3}{1.\text{III}}$) went forward with the guns and limbers only, the caissons being left behind.

About 3:30 p.m. the last regiment of Birney's division on Howard's left ($\frac{37}{3.1.\text{III}}$) moved out to join its brigade.

Wright's brigade, on arrival, took position on Posey's right; its place on the left of the Plank Road was taken by Mahone's brigade ($\frac{1}{1.7}$). While Turnbull's battery was coming up, the Federal skirmishers developed Best's position in the railroad cut.

About 2:45 p.m. Sickles sent word to Hooker that it was practicable to gain the road by which the enemy was marching and break his column, adding that, as he must expect to encounter a heavy force and stubborn resistance, and bearing in mind Hooker's admonition to move cautiously, he would not advance until the support from the XI and XII Corps closed up on Birney's right and left.[2] At the same time he wrote to Howard and to Slocum:

I am advancing a strong line of two brigades to ascertain whether the enemy is retreating. General Birney reports that he has reached a brigade of the enemy in rifle-pits, posted, as I think, to cover the retreating column. I will attack if the enemy is not stronger than the reports so far represent him, and occupy the road by which he is retreating.

Please support my advance.

This message was received by Howard at 3 p.m. Slocum received his at 3:30. The latter referred the matter to Hooker. Howard replied that he had no troops to spare.

[1] *W. R.*, 39, pp. 934, 929.     [2] *Ib.*, 39, pp. 386, 387.

Archer reached the Welford House and assumed command there about 3:30 p.m. By this time the train was virtually saved. No part of it was lost except a caisson taken at the Furnace.[1] But it was still necessary to hold the position for some time to enable the train to gain a safe distance. So General Archer, while he proceeded to withdraw and follow Jackson, ordered Colonel Best to hold his position until ordered by him to leave it. Best replied that he might hold it if his flanks were protected, especially his left.[2] This was about 4:45 p.m.

More or less of a demonstration had been kept up all along the line to the right of Posey. But about 3:15 p.m. a specially vigorous attack was made along the Turnpike by Wofford's brigade of McLaws' division against Hancock's advanced line held by Colonel Miles. It was kept up for about an hour. About 4 p.m. Perry's brigade, on the extreme right of the Confederate line, closed in to the left until it connected with McLaws' right.

While the Confederates on the Turnpike had pressed the Federal lines as already stated, the force on the Plank Road had been subjected to Federal aggression. General Geary had considered the movement prescribed for him about 2 p.m. of sufficient importance to be conducted by himself in person. Accordingly, with 2 regiments of his first brigade, his second brigade (together 7 regiments), and Atwell's 6-gun battery $(\frac{1}{2.\,XII})$ from Muhlenberg's line, he advanced about 500 yards, when he discovered the enemy drawn up and intrenched with a number of cannon. Only two pieces of his own artillery could come into action. They were soon crippled by a combined fire of infantry and artillery. Some of his infantry, too, was badly shaken. He was still facing these conditions when, about 4:30 p.m., he received an order to retire. In the meantime Atwell's battery had been replaced in Muhlenberg's line by Pettit's four pieces $(\frac{1}{1.\,II})$.[3] Muhlenberg picked up the two pieces of Lewis' battery $(\frac{1}{3.\,III})$ near Chancellorsville "not subject to any orders," and placed them "in position covering that occupied by the artillery of the First Division under Captain Best."[4] This section, and Atwell's battery on its return, gave Muhlenberg 20 pieces.

About 4 p.m. Pleasonton's cavalry, still waiting at Chancellorsville for something to do, was ordered forward to coöperate with the III Corps. It proceeded accordingly by way of Hazel Grove toward Sickles' line.[5] The 8 Pa. was placed in advance, and on the march Pleasonton posted its commander, Major Huey, as to the

---

[1] *W. R.*, 39, p. 980; *Berdan's U. S. Sharpshooters*, by C. A. Stevens, p. 251.

[2] *W. R.*, 39, p. 980.

[3] His other two pieces were with the Irish brigade.

[4] *W. R.*, 39, p. 726.

[5] This was the only time that the command operated together as a brigade, and the only time that it was under the direct command of General Pleasonton, from the passage of the Rappahannock to the end of the campaign. For the movements of the cavalry to-day, see the following authorities: Pleasonton, *W. R.*, 39, p. 774;

duties that were to devolve on him. He said that the impression was that the enemy was retreating, and that the cavalry was to charge through his lines, open communication with Sedgwick, and harass the rear of the enemy's column; that the 8 Pa. would take the advance, and he would follow with the remainder of the brigade, including Martin's horse battery.

About 4 p.m. Howard received an order from Hooker to send a brigade to the support of Sickles' corps. He at once went forward, accompanied by von Steinwehr with Barlow's brigade $(\frac{2}{1.\,XI})$, except the two companies of the 33 Mass., left on the road to Ely's Ford. The men left their knapsacks stacked in their camp.

Let us now look at Howard's dispositions in detail. His First Division, commanded by Devens, comprised two brigades, an unattached company of the 8 N. Y., and one battery of six guns. The 1st brigade (von Gilsa's) numbers four regiments, the 2d (McLean's) numbers five. Von Gilsa's brigade was on the right with two regiments, and two companies of another regiment, thrown back at right angles to the Pike, the men standing about three feet apart, or one to every five feet, and covered only by a slashing of small trees and bushes. In the angle on the road two guns were posted to enfilade the road, which here passed through dense wood. About 1000 yards out on the Turnpike was a picket formed of two bodies of sharpshooters, each of about the strength of a company, one on each side of the Turnpike,—the whole without support. On the left of the 1st brigade was the 2d, with three regiments in the front line and two, the 75 O. and 25 O., in support; the former regiment was well in rear of the 2d brigade, with instructions to act as reserve for the 1st brigade, if necessary.[1] On the left of the First Division, about half a mile from the two guns already mentioned, were the other four guns of the battery trained on the Plank Road. In the vicinity of the Taylor House, division headquarters, was the flag and torch station communicating with Howard's headquarters at Dowdall's Tavern. Next to the First Division was the Third, commanded by Schurz. It had the same organization as Devens'. The 1st brigade (five regiments) was in line connecting with Devens' left, with two regiments (82 Ill., 157 N. Y.) in second line. Of the other brigade (four regiments) one regiment (119 N. Y.) was in line somewhat in advance of the other regiments; one (75 Pa.) was on picket, and two (26 Wisc., 58 N. Y.) were on a road leading to Ely's Ford facing west, and covered, like von Gilsa's brigade, with slight abatis. An unattached regiment of this division (82 O.) stood in rear and to the left of these two regi-

Devin, *ib.*, p. 781; Martin, *ib.*, p. 786; Huey, *ib.*, p. 784, and *Charge of the 8 Pa. at Chancellorsville*, p. 12; *The Battle of Chancellorsville*, by A. C. Hamlin, p. 51; and *B. and L.*, III, 183–185.

[1] *Trials and Triumphs*, by Hartwell Osborn, p. 64.

ments, also facing west. The latter three regiments, 26 Wisc., 58 N. Y., and 82 O., were placed as above described by Schurz on his own responsibility. Schurz's battery was posted near the Wilderness Church to command the Plank Road and some open ground adjoining it. To the left and front of this division, and slightly overlapping it, was the line of von Steinwehr's division $(\frac{2}{XI})$, which was now formed of Buschbeck's brigade of four regiments $(\frac{1}{2.\,XI})$ and the divisional battery; the remainder of the division, Barlow's brigade, being detached.[1]

Howard's infantry regiments were stronger than those of any other corps. They averaged on the 30th of April about 450 men. His corps comprised more artillery in proportion to infantry than any other corps except the I. On the front facing south, about 2200 yards in length, he had 20 regiments (about 8600 infantry) and 16 guns. Facing west he had 5 regiments, about 2200 infantry and 3 batteries of corps artillery (18 guns). Exclusive of Barlow's brigade, the corps numbered about 10,500 effectives.[2] The corps artillery was near the edge of the wood in rear of the intrenchments running north and south. Buschbeck's brigade, being next to these intrenchments, might be considered as available for occupying the latter. It will be observed that there were three distinct, though feeble, lines of resistance facing west, which may be designated as von Gilsa's, Schurz's, and Buschbeck's. Between the left of the XI and the right of the XII Corps was a gap about a mile wide caused by the advance of Birney's division and Barlow's brigade. As the right did not rest upon any obstacle, the rear of the army was at the mercy of any respectable force that should march around that flank. "As we were situated," says Schurz, "an attack from the west or northwest could not be resisted without a complete change of front. . . . It was almost impossible to manœuver some of our regiments, hemmed in as they were on the old Turnpike by embankments and rifle-pits in front and thick woods in the rear, drawn out in long, deployed lines, giving just room enough for the stacks of arms and a narrow passage. This

---

[1] On the map accompanying Schurz's report all four regiments of Buschbeck's brigade (29 and 154 N. Y., 27 and 73 Pa.) are shown as in a line of rifle-pits south of the Plank Road, and von Steinwehr's battery as in rear of the regiment on the right. According to von Steinwehr's report the 29 N. Y. was sent from the line of rifle-pits south of the road to the north side of the road before the attack commenced, to fill the place vacated by Barlow's brigade $(\frac{2}{2.\,XI},$ W. R., 39, p. 645). The author has adopted for Buschbeck's brigade and two thirds of von Steinwehr's battery the disposition given by Hamlin in his minute account of the battle, especially of the part taken in it by the XI Corps,— according to which the 29 N. Y. was in reserve on the north side of the Plank Road and the battery was distributed in sections along the line. According to Schurz and to Wiedrich, commanding the battery, one section was kept in rear of the line (ib., 39, pp. 647, 651).

[2] These figures include the pickets, many of which were destined to be cut off from their regiments or prevented from joining them until after the impending action. Except for the Third Division, which furnished the 75 Pa., the picketing seems to have been done by regiment, each regiment sending out one or two companies.

Turnpike Road was at the same time the only line of communication we had between the different parts of our front.''[1]

The danger gathering about the Federal right flank should have been well known to Howard and to Hooker. Captain Castle, from his signal station on Howard's right, sighted the enemy's column, and reported the fact to Howard. He stated subsequently that his information was not credited, and that no attention was paid to it.[2] Between 11 and 12 o'clock there had been skirmishing along the line of McLean's brigade $\left(\frac{2}{1. \text{ XI}}\right)$ caused by aggressions of Confederate cavalry. The pickets of Devens' division $\left(\frac{1}{\text{XI}}\right)$ brought in two men who stated that they had been sent out from another portion of the line as scouts, and that the enemy was moving in great force upon the Federal right flank. They were immediately sent to corps headquarters, under charge of a trusty sergeant, with orders that, after reporting to General Howard, they should at once proceed to the headquarters of the major-general commanding the army.[3]

Several reconnaissances, made by a small body of cavalry placed at Devens' disposal, discovered early in the afternoon bodies of the enemy's cavalry moving upon his right. In one case the party was fired on, and the fact was immediately reported by its commanding officer to the corps commander.[4] General Schimmelfennig, commanding Schurz's 1st brigade, made several reconnaissances in his front and in front of General Devens' division, especially on the Plank Road and through the wooded country south of it. These reconnaissances made with infantry, in bodies not larger than a regiment, were necessarily confined to a narrow zone, but they brought the fact to light that there were hostile skirmishers at a distance of from 1½ to 2 miles in considerable number. The enemy's column which had been observed marching westward had disappeared, but reports from Hooker's headquarters indicated that it was harassed by Sickles in flank and rear. Sickles' artillery, too, was heard, but not for long, and when it ceased it seemed to Schurz and others that Sickles' operation had been checked or given up. But Devens and Howard continued to believe that it was progressing successfully. Devens was lying down resting at the Taylor House. About 1 o'clock, and again about 2, Colonel Lee, commanding the 55 O. of Devens' 2d brigade, came to his headquarters with a messenger from the picket line, who reported that the enemy was moving with infantry and artillery across the front of the division to its right flank. Devens said that he had no information to that effect from

[1] *McClure's Magazine*, June, 1907, p. 164.
[2] *W. R.*, 39, p. 231; *History of the Army of the Potomac*, by J. H. Stine, p. 350.
[3] *W. R.*, 39, p. 958.
[4] Devens' report, *ib.*, 39, p. 633. There

seems to be no reason to doubt that the two men sent by Devens to corps and army headquarters saw both Howard and Hooker.

corps headquarters, and that he certainly would have had if the reported movement were a fact. It is doubtful whether he sent the report to corps headquarters.[1] Colonel Friend, his officer of the day, came to him from the picket line and reported that a large force of the enemy was passing to his rear, but Devens refused to give credit to the report. Friend then went to the headquarters of the corps, where he was rebuked for his statement, and warned not to bring on a panic. He returned to the picket line, and again at 2 p.m. went to corps headquarters and was called a coward, and ordered to his regiment, with the remark that the enemy was retreating.[2] Von Gilsa, commanding the 1st brigade, and Schurz, commanding the Third Division, as well as many of the regimental commanders, apprehended danger. Acting Major Owen Rice of the 153 Pa., in command of von Gilsa's picket line, sent in the following message:

On Skirmish Line, on Culpeper Road, 2:45 p.m.
*Colonel L. von Gilsa*, Commanding 1st Brig., 1st Div., 11th Army Corps:

A large body of the enemy is massing in my front. For God's sake, make disposition to receive him!

OWEN RICE,
Act. Maj. 153 P. V.

Von Gilsa himself carried this dispatch to Howard, and was repulsed with taunts and the dictum that no force could penetrate the outlying thickets.[3]

At 3 p.m. Major Schleiter was sent with the 74 Pa. $\left(\frac{1}{3. \text{XI}}\right)$ on a reconnaissance up the Plank Road, with instructions from Howard's headquarters to avoid everything that might bring on an engagement. He returned with the information that the enemy was massed for an attack, and was sent by Schurz to report the same to Howard. He made his report to Howard's staff—Howard being absent—and was laughed at, and told not to be alarmed, for the corps commander had gone forward with Barlow's brigade to join Birney and capture some regiments.

Captain Dilger, commanding a battery in Howard's corps, went out with an orderly on the exposed flank to reconnoiter. He ran into Jackson's column advancing, and was pursued by some of his cavalry, narrowly escaping capture. Making his way by the rear of the XI Corps to Hooker's headquarters, he reported the result of his reconnaissance, and was told to go to his corps and tell his yarn there. At Howard's headquarters he was told that General Lee was in full retreat, and that

---

[1] *The Battle of Chancellorsville*, by A. C. Hamlin, pp. 58, 144; *Trials and Triumphs*, by Hartwell Osborn, p. 69.

[2] *The Battle of Chancellorsville*, by A. C. Hamlin, pp. 55, 145.

[3] *Publications of Loyal Legion, Ohio Commandery*, 1888, I, 379.

Barlow's brigade, accompanied by the corps commander, had gone out to fall upon his rear.[1]

As Jackson's column proceeded across the Orange Plank Road Paxton's (Stonewall) brigade $(\frac{1}{4.\ \text{II}})$ and Moody's and Parker's batteries of Alexander's battalion $(\frac{3.4}{\text{I}})$ were detached from it and posted at Hickman's under the command of Fitzhugh Lee to support the two squadrons of cavalry at Burton in covering the marching columns. With the exception of these two squadrons and the 2 Va., still at the head of Jackson's column, the brigade of cavalry was scattered along the line of march as flank guards.

By 2:30 p.m. Jackson's leading regiment of infantry, the 5 Ala., had reached the Turnpike, followed it eastward to the vicinity of Luckett, and proceeded to form for attack about 6 miles from its starting-point in the morning, having marched about 12 miles.

Hooker had quite recovered from his apprehension of the morning, and was bent upon following the retreating enemy. The following circular letter was sent to the corps commanders:

> Headquarters Army of the Potomac,
> May 2, 2:30 p.m., 1863.
>
> *General:*
>
> The Major-Gen. Com'g desires that you replenish your supplies of forage, provisions, and ammunition to be ready to start at an early hour to-morrow.
>
> Your obdt. servant,
>
> J. H. VAN ALEN,
>
> Brig. Genl. & A. D. C.[2]

---

[1] These particulars are deduced from statements some of which do not quite agree. See *The Battle of Chancellorsville,* by A. C. Hamlin, Chapter VI, and notes 7 and 8, pp. 143, 144; also Schurz's report, W. R., 39, p. 654.

An eminent authority says: "It is passing strange that in spite of incessant reports of Jackson's advance, and the fact that two deserters came in about 2 p.m. and were sent to General Howard's headquarters, who confirmed the reports of our scouts, and gave all details of the movement, Howard nevertheless left his command at 4 p.m. to accompany Barlow's brigade. Nor did he keep Hooker informed of the reports received. General Howard speaks in the *National Tribune* of the pickets he threw out, but in every case they seem to have been sent out by his subordinates without his knowledge; in other words, all knowledge of Jackson's movements was obtained by independent scouts.

When they reported to Howard, it would seem from regimental histories that he wholly disapproved of these expeditions. He said that he 'commanded the corps, and his subordinates were usurping his functions'" (Doubleday). See also *The 25 Ohio Volunteer Infantry,* by E. C. Culp, p. 63.

Howard's purpose in accompanying Barlow was "to examine the ground between his left and Sickles, thinking that if the battle became general in that quarter he might have to move his entire corps to the support of Sickles." Having attained this purpose, he returned at a gallop to his headquarters at Dowdall's Tavern (Captain Hartwell Osborn, *Military Order Loyal Legion, Commandery of Illinois,* IV).

[2] I am indebted for this document to Brevet Lieutenant-Colonel G. A. Bruce, author of *The 20th Regiment Mass. Vol. Infantry.*

As this message was going out Jackson arrived at Luckett's and sent the following dispatch to Lee:

Near 3 p.m., May 2, 1863.

*General:*

The enemy has made a stand at Chancellors [Dowdall's Tavern], which is about 2 miles from Chancellorsville. I hope as soon as practicable to attack.

I trust that an ever-kind Providence will bless us with great success.

Respectfully,

T. J. JACKSON,

Lt. Gen.

P.S. The leading division is up, and the next two appear to be well closed.

T. J. J.[1]

The wording of this dispatch can hardly be explained without the assumption of former dispatches sent back by Jackson to R. E. Lee, representing the Federals as falling back. It seems to confirm the intimation given in the preceding chapter that Jackson believed the Federal right flank to lie somewhere in the angle formed by the Orange Plank Road and the Brock Road.

About 4 p.m. the Confederate videttes showed themselves to von Gilsa's picket, and were fired on by the latter. This occurrence, which was signaled to Howard's headquarters, brought on a brief skirmish in which the two guns with von Gilsa's brigade participated by firing their two charges without orders.[2] Howard had no suspicion of danger.

The following message went to Butterfield at 4:10 p.m.:

The Major-General commanding directs that General Sedgwick cross the river as soon as indications will permit; capture Fredericksburg with everything in it, and vigorously pursue the enemy. We know that the enemy is fleeing, trying to save his trains. Two of Sickles' divisions are among them.

Again he does not say in what direction the enemy is to be pursued, from which we may infer that by pursuing the enemy he means marching on Hanover Junction, or Richmond. It would appear that he did not himself believe everything that he said in this dispatch, but felt justified in sending it as a means of hastening Sedgwick's movements. He could not have known that Sickles was among the enemy's trains, as Sickles never was among them. But he probably believed that the movement observed and reported by Sickles indicated the retreat of a portion of Lee's army, and hoped that by the time his dispatch would reach Sedgwick the retreat would be converted into a rout.[3] At this

---

[1] Dabney's *Life of Jackson*, p. 679; *B. and L.*, III, 206.

[2] These particulars are also deduced from conflicting statements. See report of Signal Officer, *W. R.*, 39, p. 231; reports of Generals Devens and Schurz, *ib.*, pp. 634, 654.

[3] Referring to a report from Sickles on

time "there was a general feeling in the army that Lee's army was running away."[1] Late in the afternoon, probably about 4:20, a party of cavalry went out on the Pike, but soon returned, and the captain in command reported to Devens at the Taylor House that he could go but "a little ways," as he met a large body of infantry. Devens replied impatiently: "I wish I could get some one who could make a reconnaissance for me." The captain replied: "General, I can go further, but I can not promise to return." The cavalry was ordered to bivouac.[2]

Jackson formed his available force in three lines perpendicular to the Turnpike and extending about a mile on each side of it. In the first line he deployed the Second Division, except Ramseur's brigade $\left(\frac{5}{2.\,\text{II}}\right)$, which was to form in the second line. He gave Colquitt $\left(\frac{4}{2.\,\text{II}}\right)$ the right, Iverson $\left(\frac{3}{2.\,\text{II}}\right)$ the left,[3] Doles $\left(\frac{2}{2.\,\text{II}}\right)$ the right center, and O'Neal $\left(\frac{1}{2.\,\text{II}}\right)$ the left center. This line was covered with sharpshooters deployed as skirmishers about 400 yards to the front, and charged with preventing communication with the enemy.[4] The second line was formed of the Fourth Division (Trimble's command by Colston), except Paxton's (1st) brigade, which had been detached, and Nicholls' (4th),[5] which formed by mistake in the third line. To the right of the second line Ramseur's brigade $\left(\frac{5}{2.\,\text{II}}\right)$ was formed in support of Colquitt's $\left(\frac{4}{2.\,\text{II}}\right)$, overlapping it by the front of one regiment.[6] To the left of the first and second lines the 23 N. Ca. of Iverson's brigade $\left(\frac{3}{2.\,\text{II}}\right)$ was formed as flankers in column of route, with skirmishers on its left.

which the dispatch was based, he testified a year later before the Committee on the Conduct of the War: "At the time this news [that the enemy was retreating] was received by me, I was of the impression that the general was mistaken, but nevertheless felt that no harm could follow from its transmission to General Sedgwick."

[1] Warren's testimony, *Rep. of Com.*, IV, 45.

[2] *The Battle of Chancellorsville*, by A. C. Hamlin, pp. 60, 145. The cavalry is called a squadron, and a few lines further on is referred to as a squad (p. 60). It was probably a small company.

[3] Iverson had left his skirmishers, say one regiment, behind when he started on the march in the morning, and was not rejoined by them until late at night (*W. R.*, 39, p. 984).

[4] "Jackson's orders were carried out so accurately by these men [on the skirmish line] that although over ten thousand men rested on their arms for two hours or more within a mile of the Army of the Potomac, not a man deserted or escaped to give warn-

ing of the coming storm" (*The Battle of Chancellorsville*, by A. C. Hamlin, p. 16).

[5] The distance of the second line from the first is given by Colston, commanding the second line, as about 200 yards; Colonel H. A. Brown, commanding a regiment in Colston's brigade $\left(\frac{3}{4.\,\text{II}}\right)$, and Brigadier-General Ramseur, commanding the brigade on the right of Colston's division, give it as about 100 yards (*W. R.*, 39, pp. 1004, 1032, 995).

Hamlin in his *Battle of Chancellorsville* (p. 16) gives it as about 100 *paces*. Hotchkiss and Allan give it as 200 *yards* (*Chancellorsville*, by H. and A., p. 47). It was probably about 150 yards.

[6] The distance of this brigade in rear of the first line is given by its commander, General Ramseur, as about 100 yards. According to Rodes, commanding the first line, Ramseur's brigade was formed about 100 yards from the first line and in continuation of the second. It may be assumed to be in the second line or about 150 yards in rear of the first.

In the third line Pender's brigade $(\frac{2}{1.\,II})$ was deployed in rear of Warren's $(\frac{3}{4.\,II})$, its right near the Turnpike. Nicholls' brigade $(\frac{4}{4.\,II})$ took position on a line with it beyond the left of the first line.[1] Heth's brigade $(\frac{1}{1.\,II})$ when it came up was ordered to form on the left of the second line, but before it did so, the second line advanced. It was then placed in the third line, on the left of Pender's brigade $(\frac{2}{1.\,II})$,[2] or between that brigade and Nicholls' $(\frac{4}{4.\,II})$. Lane's brigade $(\frac{4}{1.\,II})$ was in rear of these lines in column of route. On either side of Lane was a line of skirmishers to prevent straggling. Two pieces of Stuart's artillery were placed in the first line on the Turnpike and four others in rear, ready to relieve them (Breathed's battery and half of Moorman's). The width of the road did not allow of more than two pieces being in action at once. The 2 Va. Cavalry took position on the left of the infantry with orders to cover its flank and, when the advance commenced, to proceed to seize and hold the road to Ely's Ford. The object of this movement was apparently the interception of Federal detachments either retreating toward the ford or advancing therefrom.[3] The forces thus arrayed for attack aggregated about 26,500 men[4] and 6 guns. In addition thereto Carter's battalion of artillery (20 pieces, $\frac{2}{II}$) took position in an open field on the right of the road. The remainder of the artillery (except Brown's battalion, and two batteries of Alexander's battalion left with Paxton) formed in column of pieces on the road. When the lines advanced, Carter's battalion filed into the road at the head of this column of artillery. Brown's battalion (except Dance's and Hupp's batteries, left with Lee), McGowan's brigade except the 12 Va., Archer's and Thomas' brigades $(\frac{3.\,5.\,6}{1.\,II})$, and Iverson's skirmishers were also marching up from the rear. Paxton's brigade was at Hickman's.

The men took their positions in silence, orders were transmitted in a low voice, the bugles were still; the soldiers abstained from saluting their general with their usual cheers. Each brigade commander received positive instructions as to what he should do. Each line was to push

---

[1] In the official reports the position of Nicholls' brigade is variously given. Colonel Williams, who commanded the brigade, says that it was formed "in the rear, with the right resting near the Plank Road," meaning, it seems, as a fourth line, with its right on the Turnpike (*W. R.*, 39, p. 1037). According to Captain Willett, commanding the right regiment of the brigade, his regiment formed part of the "second line of battle," "in rear and to the left of Rodes' division" (*ib.*, p. 1038). Colston, commanding the Fourth Division, says that Nicholls' brigade was on the "extreme left"

of his line, second (*ib.*, p. 1004). Lieutenant Hinrichs, Colston's chief engineer, says: "General Nicholls on coming up formed on the left of General Pender's brigade $(\frac{1}{II})$ by mistake, which threw him in the rear of our line" (*ib.*, p. 1009).

[2] *Ib.*, 39, p. 890.

[3] *Memoirs of the Confederate War*, by H. von Borcke, II, 227; Letters from Colonel T. T. Munford (at the time commanding 2 Va. Cav.) to the author.

[4] 25,983 infantry, 400 cavalry, 120 artillery.

ahead, keeping the road for its guide. When any portion of the first
line needed reënforcements, the officer commanding this portion was to
call for, and receive, aid from the line in his rear without further instructions. Jackson expected to come upon positions at right angles to
Hooker's main line and to overlap them on both flanks. The position
at Taylor's House was to be carried at all hazards, as it commanded the
second position of the Federals at Dowdall's Tavern. If the Federals
showed a determined front at Dowdall's, the infantry was to halt until
the artillery could come up and dislodge them. Under no other circumstances was there to be any pause. Jackson intended that when he had
advanced far enough to establish connection with Lee, say to the vicinity
of the Old School-House, a portion of his force should be directed upon
Chandler's so as to take the elevation of Fairview and the whole position of Chancellorsville well in rear, and favor his purpose of severing
Hooker's communications with the fords of the Rapidan and Rappahannock and driving his routed army upon the latter river.

The sound of the firing on the Plank Road and on the Turnpike
reached the point where Jackson was watching the formation of his
lines. Captain Moorman of the horse artillery ventured to ask him
whose firing it was. Jackson asked: "How far do you suppose it is?"
"Five or six miles," was the answer. "I suppose," said Jackson, "it
is General Lee."[1]

While Geary was retiring up the Plank Road Slocum received
Hooker's consent to his sending assistance to Sickles. Consequently
about 4:30 p.m. Williams' division ($\frac{1}{XII}$) moved out to support Birney
on his left (Map 18). A considerable interval between Birney ($\frac{1}{III}$) and
Williams ($\frac{1}{XII}$) remaining unoccupied, Sickles sent Whipple with his
division ($\frac{3}{III}$) to occupy it. Williams was to proceed 2 or 3 miles
through the woods, so as to strike the rifle-pits and other temporary
works of the enemy (Anderson) on the flank and rear, and then, coming
around from the south, sweep both sides of the Plank Road toward
Chancellorsville. He arranged with Whipple to move well to the right,
in order to strike the enemy as far as possible from Chancellorsville,
and to connect closely with Whipple's left.[2] Williams and Whipple both
went forward without artillery, Williams having left his in the line of
the XII Corps, and Whipple his at Hazel Grove, with the exception of
one section (2 pieces) left in the vicinity of Chancellorsville,[3] besides
which Williams left the 28 N. Y.[4] (1. 1. XII) in his intrenchments and
the 13 N. J. (3. 1. XII) at Hazel Grove, and Whipple left the 110 Pa.
(2. 3. III) at Hazel Grove. Berry's division ($\frac{2}{III}$) was a good deal scat-

---

[1] *So. Hist. Soc. Papers*, XXX, 111.

[2] *W. R.*, 39, p. 678.

[3] A section of Lewis' 10 N. Y. Battery
(*W. R.*, 39, pp. 726, 1127, 162).

[4] Comprising but four companies, numbering about 107 men. The rest of this
regiment was detached as provost guard
and train guard.

tered.   The 11 Mass. (1st brigade) was still in position in front of Hancock.   Of the four batteries of this division, three were at the junction of the Ely's Ford and United States Ford Roads; the other battery $\left(\frac{4}{2.\,\mathrm{III}}\right)$ and one brigade $\left(\frac{3}{2.\,\mathrm{III}}\right)$ were at United States Ford.   The remainder of the division (two brigades except one regiment) was held in reserve at Chancellorsville.

About 5 p.m. Sickles received from Hooker an order to assail the enemy on his right flank and check his advance—accompanied with the notice that he must rely upon the force that he had, as Berry's division $\left(\frac{2}{\mathrm{III}}\right)$ could not be spared to reënforce him.   At the same time Barlow's brigade, accompanied by Howard and von Steinwehr, reached Birney's right wing $\left(\frac{1}{\mathrm{III}}\right)$, where it found the latter's sharpshooters engaged. Barlow at once reported to Birney that he had completed the connection between the latter's division and the XI Corps.[1]   At this time (5 p.m.) Turnbull's battery $\left(\frac{3}{1.\,\mathrm{III}}\right)$, ordered up from the rear, was at Welford's Furnace, firing upon Brooke's battery $\left(\frac{1}{\mathrm{II}}\right)$; and Pleasonton reported to Sickles near the Furnace with his three regiments of cavalry and battery of horse artillery.[2]

---

[1] Birney's report, *W. R.*, 39, p. 408; Howard's report, *ib.*, p. 630; von Steinwehr's report, *ib.*, p. 645.

[2] A squadron of the 6 N. Y. was left on picket at Ely's Ford.

# CHAPTER XX

### *5 to 6:10 p.m.* (Map 18)

AT 5 o'clock Jackson inquired of Rodes at the Luckett Farm: "Are you ready?" "Yes," Rodes replied, and nodded to Major Blackford, commanding his sharpshooters, or line of skirmishers.  The mass in rear of the skirmishers was soon in motion, the center following the Turnpike; but on account of the command not being promptly transmitted to the skirmishers on the left, these failed to advance, and the first line, coming up on them, caused some confusion.  This necessitated a general halt to straighten out the lines and allow the skirmishers to gain their distance to the front.[1]  About 5:15 the lines moved silently forward again, and buried themselves in the depth of the forest; in a moment—so close had they been to the enemy—their skirmishers were engaged by the sharpshooters of the XI Corps on the Turnpike.  Silence and secrecy were now discarded.  For a mile on either side of the Turnpike the bugles rang out clear and loud in the evening air, and a mighty roar of human voices shook the forest, starting the deer and other animals from their lairs.  As swiftly as the dense brushwood would permit, the first line pushed forward, followed by the second and third.  The men had their clothing almost torn from their bodies, but still the lines swept on in tolerable order and with great enthusiasm.  The Federal picket fell rapidly back, firing and giving the alarm to the forces in rear.  The two pieces of Stuart's artillery in the first line galloped well out to the front and fired two shots which went whizzing down the Pike and finally struck the ground in front of the Taylor House.  The guns that had fired were then passed by others ready to fire.  Breathed, commanding the artillery at the front, was directed to advance with the infantry, "keeping a few yards in rear of the line of skirmishers."

---

[1] Authorities differ as to the hour when Jackson advanced to the attack.  Rodes gives it as 5:15, Colston as "6 o'clock precisely," Hill as "about 6 p.m." (*W. R.*, 39, pp. 941, 1004, 885).  Colonel Vandeventer, commanding Jones' brigade $(\frac{2}{i,ii})$, gives it as 4 p.m.  The other brigade commanders of Jackson's corps who make any mention of it give it as 5 or 5:30.  Hotchkiss and Allan say, "Just before 6 o'clock."  Captain Poland, chief of staff of the Federal III Corps, gives it as about 3 p.m., and Colonel Brooke, commanding Hancock's 4th brigade, as about 4 p.m.  A. C. Hamlin gives it as about 5 p.m. (*Battle of Chancellorsville*, p. 65).

This he could not do, on account of the narrowness of the road and its obstruction by fallen trees and other obstacles. He was able, however, to keep up an almost continual fire from one or two guns.[1] Howard's troops with "stacked arms" were preparing their evening meal and making themselves comfortable for the night. They had time, however, to seize their guns, take their places in ranks, and occupy the positions assigned them.[2] Colonel Lee, commanding the 55 O., mounted his horse and galloped to the right, where he found von Gilsa ready to receive the attack, but not aware of the extent of Jackson's front. He rode thence to the Taylor House and found Devens mounted and uncertain as to what to do; and there was no one to tell him, his corps commander having just left Barlow's brigade, about 2 miles away, to return to the corps. Lee asked permission to change front with his regiment. "Not yet," was the reply, and he galloped to the right of his regiment, where he found it raked by the fire of the artillery and infantry coming down the Pike. The two regiments of von Gilsa in the road, exposed to the same fire, began to break. Lee again rode at the top of his speed to Devens, and asked permission to change front. After some time he was dismissed with a wave of the hand. The enemy marched steadily on, and Doles' brigade ($\frac{2}{2.\,\mathrm{II}}$) encountered von Gilsa's. The front which the latter presented facing the enemy was something of a surprise to him. From the Burton hilltop Jackson had observed Schurz's and von Steinwehr's divisions and part of Devens', but had not seen von Gilsa's little brigade, hidden by the trees, on the extreme right of the Federal line.[3] Two of Doles' regiments were detached: one by the right, against the two regiments parallel to the Turnpike; one by the left, against and around the outer flank of the face perpendicular to it. The other two regiments assailed the latter in front (Sketch 2). Von Gilsa's two pieces of artillery fired several times, and seeing that resistance was useless, tried to limber up and retreat. But before they could do so the horses were shot down and the pieces captured. The two regiments facing south, exposed to a withering fire in front, flank, and rear, broke up without firing a shot. About half of them formed in rear of the two regiments facing down the Pike. The joint force of about three regiments stood its ground long enough to fire three rounds and went to pieces. Having run about 400 yards, they came upon the 75 O., which had changed front and moved up to von Gilsa's assistance. A few attached themselves to this regiment, which now confronted two brigades of the enemy and Stuart's two guns on the Pike, the latter playing upon it with canister. For ten minutes this single regiment with its few rallied supports attempted to breast the fiery tide. Its colonel was killed, its adjutant wounded, and 150 of its rank and file struck down.

[1] W. R., 39, p. 1050.        [2] J. Watts de Peyster, A. C. Hamlin.
[3] A. C. Hamlin in Stories of Our Soldiers, collected by the Boston Journal, pp. 34, 38.

The survivors retreated to a new line formed by the 25, 55, and 107 O., supported by the 17 Conn., in the vicinity of the Taylor House. This position was soon enveloped by three brigades of the enemy and subjected to a rapid fire of canister at short range.

Howard had got back to his headquarters before a sound or other indication of the conflict had reached it. "There was no news for me," he says, "except what the scouts brought, and what General Devens had frequently reported, that Lee's columns had been crossing the Plank Road obliquely, between 2 and 3 miles ahead, and apparently aiming toward Orange Court-House. Had I then been familiar with the routes as I am now, I should have distrusted the conclusion. . . . It was already 6 o'clock. Hearing the sound of a skirmish toward Devens' position, I mounted with my staff and rode toward a high ridge."[1]

There on the Taylor height he saw the startled game scampering and scurrying across the fields, and then his disordered and disheartened men with their shooting and yelling pursuers, who, on every side, came swarming out of the thickets which Howard had pronounced to be impenetrable. "It was a terrible gale. The rush, the rattle, the quick lightning from a hundred points at once; the roar redoubled by echoes through the forest; the panic, the dead and dying in sight, and the wounded straggling along; the frantic efforts of the brave and patriotic to stay the angry storm."[2] The hapless commander exerted himself bravely to check these disastrous consequences of his own neglect and disregard of orders. Lieutenant-Colonel Dickinson of Hooker's staff urged him to direct a fire upon the fleeing mass, but he replied: "I will never fire on my own men." Putting away his revolver, he took up a national color and held it against his heart with the stump of his lost arm. Captain Dessauer, another staff officer, fell by his side. His own horse reared and fell with him, but without doing him any serious injury. After a hopeless struggle of ten or fifteen minutes the fragments of his line retreated rapidly and tumultuously toward the Wilderness Church. Devens' four pieces of artillery lately at the Taylor House were taken in flank and rear, and before they could get away, were all captured. They had not fired a shot. Von Steinwehr, as he returned from the Furnace, dropped behind Howard, and at 6:10 p.m. was still on his way to the corps, but he knew from the sound of the firing that the corps was attacked. Schurz had given way before Jackson's left wing, and was falling back on the woods in rear of Hawkins' Farm. The reserve artillery was waiting for its front to be cleared to open fire. In about one hour Jackson had wrecked Devens' division and gained possession of the first point of vantage, the elevation on which stood Taylor's Farm, and of Howard's second line of defence, Hawkins' Farm.

[1] *Autobiography of Gen. O. O. Howard*, I, 368, 370.    [2] *Ib.*

The right center, left center, and left of Jackson's original formation presented a solid front for another advance, but the right was far to the rear. How did this happen? When Jackson's three lines had advanced but a few hundred yards Colquitt, commanding the brigade on Rodes' right $(\frac{4}{2.\ II})$, received a report from his skirmishers that a body of the enemy was on his right flank. His orders and the principles of tactics required him to transmit this report to the second line, and keep right on with the rest of the first line. His own brigade "was least obstructed either by woods or the enemy. It could have moved most rapidly, and might have narrowed the enemy's avenue of escape."[1] He sent word to Ramseur that the enemy was attempting to turn his right, and instead of continuing to advance, and keeping abreast of Doles, moved his brigade by the flank to the right, halted it, and threw his right regiment back into position to meet an attack. Ramseur on receiving Colquitt's message naturally and properly conformed to these movements. He could not pass Colquitt. Paxton with his five regiments of the Stonewall brigade, and Stuart with his two squadrons of cavalry, were condemned to inaction until Colquitt resumed his advance, as the latter had the right of way. Thirteen regiments, about 5000 men, were thus practically eliminated from Jackson's force. After a while Colquitt again sent word to Ramseur that the enemy was threatening his right flank. Ramseur replied in effect that the firing indicated a sharp fight with General Doles, and that his impression was that Colquitt's support was necessary there, and that he would take care of Colquitt's right flank. Regarding the character of the opposition which had caused Colquitt to halt, that officer says in his report: "The enemy's force proved to be a small body of cavalry, which galloped away as soon as the regiment advancing toward them was discovered."[2] Hamlin says in his *Battle of Chancellorsville* (pp. 145, 146): "A few moments after the advance had commenced, Colquitt struck a strong, determined picket reserve, and noticed some cavalry on his right front, and conceived the singular idea that Sickles had moved his forces to the right and was then threatening his flank. Why he should entertain this idea is very strange, as Stuart with his cavalry and the Stonewall brigade of infantry were both on the Plank Road to his right, and guarding it from all attacks from that quarter. Besides this force, the brigades of Archer and Thomas $(\frac{5.\ 6}{1.\ II})$ were still in the rear, guarding the trains, and Colquitt ought to have known that Sickles could not have reached him without first disposing of these forces. . . . The men who made this resistance, which proved of such great importance to the Federal army, belonged to the Fifty-fifth Ohio, but the cavalry Colquitt saw were probably some of Stuart's men,

[1] *Military Memoirs of a Confederate*, by E. P. Alexander, p. 335.
[2] *W. R.*, 39, p. 975.

dressed in the United States uniform, who were halted at the Burton Farm, for no evidence can be found of any cavalry of ours stationed at that point."[1]

About 5:30 the skirmishers from Archer's brigade that were guarding Best's left at the railroad cut were withdrawn. Best received orders from Archer to "move out quickly," but it was too late. Birney's skirmishers had placed themselves across the railroad cut on his left and nearly surrounded him.[2] Best himself and a few of his officers and men escaped, but his regiment as an organization was compelled to lay down its arms and march off into the Federal lines as prisoners.[3] Being commiserated by Pleasonton's cavalry, one of them defiantly spoke up: "You may think you have done a big thing just now, but wait till Jackson gets around on your right." He was laughed at for his supposed bravado. It was not imagined that he would betray Jackson's movement, had he known anything about it.[4]

Soon after 5 p.m. the artillery duel between Turnbull's battery at Welford's Furnace and Brooke's battery at the Welford House was decided by the exhaustion of Turnbull's ammunition. His battery returned to Hazel Grove, and Jastram's was ordered up to replace it. Sims' battery $(\frac{1}{1.\,\text{III}})$ was still in position at Hazel Grove. Sickles, not deeming it "quite time for the effective employment of cavalry in the attack," ordered Devin to report with the 6 N. Y. to Birney, and Pleasonton to send the remainder of the cavalry brigade back to the open space at Hazel Grove to await orders. Accordingly, the 6 N. Y. went to the front, and the brigade to the rear. Pleasonton in person remained with Sickles to receive reports from the front, and Huey remained with Pleasonton to be further posted. Howard and von Steinwehr, on seeing Barlow in position, started back to rejoin their corps.

Posey and Wright had about all that they could do to stand their ground. Any diversion in Jackson's favor could only be made by the forces on their right. McLaws on the Turnpike, and Lee and Mahone on the Plank Road, were impatiently waiting for the sound of Jackson's guns. A shade of anxiety was visible on the faces of both. It was probably nearly 6 o'clock when Mahone exclaimed: "Thank God! There are Jackson's guns," and all along the line, from Anderson's guns on Mahone's left to Perry's brigade on the right, the artillery and infantry coöperated vigorously in "feeling the enemy."[5]    At 6 p.m.

[1] The Federal infantry picket numbered about 40 men (*Papers of Loyal Legion, Commandery of Illinois*, IV, 189). The cavalry may have been a detachment of Pleasonton's.

[2] *W. R.*, 39, p. 980.

[3] Best gives his loss in prisoners as 26 officers and 250 enlisted men (*W. R.*, 39,

p. 980). See also Colquitt's report, *ib.*, 39, p. 977.

[4] *B. and L.*, III, 183; *Berdan's U. S. Sharpshooters*, by C. A. Stevens, p. 251.

[5] *W. R.*, 39, pp. 799, 826, 862, 878; *War Talks of Confederate Veterans*, by G. S. Bernard, pp. 72, 73.

Grandy's battery $(\frac{1}{1.1})$, which had too short a range for use in McLaws' position, was brought over to the Plank Road. From there it was sent off by Lee to the artillery depot at Chesterfield, its horses being unfit for service.[1]

All this time Sickles at the Furnace did not hear a sound of the grand attack on the right, nor did a single fugitive or assailant show himself to him. About 5 p.m. Captain Comstock, Hooker's chief of engineers, and General Warren, his chief of topographical engineers, started out together from army headquarters "to examine the line." They had got to the vicinity of Hazel Grove, when a heavy fire of musketry began on the right, and caused them to hasten in that direction.[2] Meeting fugitives of the XI Corps, Warren sent his aide to inform Pleasonton and Sickles of the rout of the XI Corps and then turned back toward Fairview. Comstock started to report to Hooker.

About 5:30 the head of Reynolds' corps $(\frac{1}{2.1})$, coming up from below Fredericksburg, crossed the Rappahannock at United States Ford, stacked arms near it, and proceeded to rest and refresh itself.[3] The Second and Third Divisions were approaching the ford, followed at a distance of several miles by the First Division.

Lowe, the Federal aëronaut, having observed the depletion of the lines of Fredericksburg, already related, wrote to Butterfield at 5:30 p.m.:

Nearly all the enemy's force have been withdrawn from the opposite side. I can only see a small force in the neighborhood of their earthworks.

I can not at this time get a sufficient elevation to tell what road they take, but should judge, by the appearance of army wagons moving toward Chancellorsville road, that the troops are moving that way also.

### 6:10 to 6:30 p.m. (Map 19)

Jackson's next important objective was Dowdall's Tavern. Between him and this point Schurz's division and the fragments of Devens', together with the brigade and battery of von Steinwehr's division, formed a line of defence extending from Wilderness Church southward and eastward around Dowdall's Tavern and northward along the edge of the wood facing Hawkins' Farm. These forces may be roughly estimated at 5000 men, about 3000 of whom were facing westward. One of the corps batteries, some distance in rear, threw its shot over the heads of the infantry at the masses of the enemy about Hawkins' Farm. Again the Confederate ranks resounded with the command and signal to advance. As they approached Schurz's position and felt its strength, Rodes called upon Colonel Warren, commanding a brigade in his rear, to support him. The troops of the second line had pressed

[1] *W. R.*, 39, p. 884.     [2] *Rep. of Com.*, IV, 45.     [3] *W. R.*, 39, p. 279.

on so ardently that they were already within a few steps of the first and in some places mixed up with them. Warren's and Jones' brigades pushed on with, and through, the first line. After a contest of about twenty minutes, or about 6:30 p.m., Jackson's exultant battalions planted their colors on Schurz's second position (Map 19). Colquitt on receipt of Ramseur's message put his command in march toward the sound of the firing. He was followed by Ramseur, Paxton, and Stuart. These troops were too far behind to overtake those engaged, and could do no more than occupy the conquered positions.

About 6:10 p.m., when Jackson took Schurz's second position, Birney cleared the railroad cut of the enemy. Sickles still knew nothing of the conflict on the Federal right. The moment seemed to him opportune for Pleasonton to pursue. He was about to send a staff officer to bring up his brigade when an aide-de-camp from General Howard rode up, and reported that the XI Corps had yielded the right flank of the army to the enemy, who was advancing rapidly, and indeed was already in Sickles' rear. He did not credit this statement until the aide-de-camp sent by General Warren shortly afterward confirmed it, and asked, in the name of General Howard, for a regiment of cavalry to check the movement. He sent staff officers to recall Birney and Whipple, and directed Pleasonton to comply with Howard's request. Pleasonton ordered Huey to report with his regiment to Howard. At 6:30 p.m. Huey was on his way to his regiment.

While Jackson was rolling up and crushing the Federal right, Hooker with his two aides, Candler and Russell, sat on the veranda of the Chancellor House, enjoying the summer evening. Now and then a shot came from the south and east, where Lee was keeping up a show of force, but nothing occurred to give them anxiety. Not a sound of the fighting at the Taylor Farm or even at the Wilderness Church had reached them. Not an officer from the forces attacked had come to them for aid, or to warn them of the impending danger, and so the hours passed until between 6:15 and 6:30 (about the time when Warren's aide-de-camp reported to Sickles), when the sound of distant cannonading came to their ears, which they attributed to the movements of Birney's force. In Hancock's line it was thought that Stoneman's cavalry or some other Federal force had come up in the rear of a body of the enemy and was driving it toward the Federal lines. The shells, which came sailing through the air toward Chancellorsville from the northwest, were thought to be fired by pursuing Federals. Hooker and his staff were listening attentively and speculating as to the result of Sickles' operations, when Captain Russell stepped out in front, and turned his glass, with some trepidation, it would seem, in the direction of Dowdall's Tavern. A moment later he shouted to General Hooker: "My God, here they come!" meaning Birney's men. Hooker and his aides sprang upon their horses, and rode some distance down the Plank Road before they reached the ambulances and fugitives from Devens' division, and heard from them that the whole rebel army had broken loose upon the flank and rear of the Federal line.[1]   Captain Best, chief of artillery of the XII Corps, began collecting what artillery he could, and massing it on the height of Fairview facing westward, in which he was assisted by Warren on his arrival.[2]   From Chandler's to United States Ford the Federals had two lines of communication: one by the Mineral Spring Road and the road along the river; one by the Ely's Ford Road and the road branching from it to the right, known as the United States Ford Road.   Meade on his own responsibility sent Sykes with his division $(\frac{2}{V})$ to cover these roads.   The exact position taken by Sykes can hardly be determined from the official reports.   General Meade says: "I moved Sykes from the left to the right, and pushed him out on the road to Ely's Ford in front of [beyond] the road to the United States Ford, to cover and hold the same in case the enemy should advance, as I feared, by that [Ely's Ford] road."[3]   General Sykes says: " . . . I took position at double-quick to cover the approach from Ely's Ford to Chancellorsville, my right resting on the road to the United States Ford. . . . "[4]   General Ayres, commanding Sykes' first brigade, says: " . . . moved on the pike, and took a position across the road and facing the ford [Ely's]"[5]   From these statements and those of the other brigade, and the regimental, commanders it appears that the line was a thin or disconnected one; that it crossed the Ely's Ford Road between the Little Hunting Run and the junction of the roads from Ely's Ford and United States Ford, and that it extended on the right to near the United States Ford Road, and on the left to the vicinity of Chandler's (Map 21).   The time when this movement took place is given as about when the XI Corps broke; as "evening," "dusk," "dark," and "night," and by the clock as 5, 6, and 7 p.m.   It was probably about 6:15 p.m.   The position taken was immediately intrenched.   In the meantime the fleeing men of the XI Corps rushed upon it in an uncontrollable torrent.   Little attempt was made by Sykes' men to halt and detain them.   Jackson's bristling battalions might at any moment come dashing at the lines, when a contingent of these spiritless fugitives would prove an element of weakness rather than of strength.[6]   Sykes' place on the Mineral Spring Road was taken by Barnes' brigade on the right of Griffin's division $(\frac{1}{1.\,V})$.   Albright's brigade of French's division $(\frac{3}{3.\,II})$[7] was hurried forward, leaving their

[1] The Battle of Chancellorsville, by A. C. Hamlin, pp. 54, 148; and Memoranda of Colonel Thomas L. Livermore, 5 N. H. Volunteers.

[2] Rep. of Com., IV, 57.

[3] W. R., 39, p. 507.

[4] Ib., 39, p. 526.

[5] Ib., 39, p. 529.

[6] The Fifth Army Corps, by W. H. Powell, p. 450.

[7] 1 Del. and 132 Pa.  The other regiment (4 N. Y.), whose time had expired, but who

knapsacks, overcoats, and blankets behind, and put in position to support Carroll's ($\frac{1}{3.\ \text{II}}$). A portion of it was placed across the road to Chancellorsville to check the retreat of the XI Corps, which it did "by arresting their flight, forming them into companies, and sending them to the rear." [1]

As these changes were taking place and the main body of the I Corps was crossing the river at United States Ford and going into camp, General Reynolds, who preceded the corps, leaving Doubleday in command, reported to Hooker at Chancellorsville about 6:30. Here a military band was playing the national airs as a means of checking the disorder and encouraging the troops. The roads were crowded with panic-stricken men flying in one direction and reserves advancing in another.[2] Had he arrived a little earlier he would have been told to bivouac with his two leading divisions to-night near United States Ford, and proceed in the morning to take position on Howard's right. He was directed instead to place his available troops on the "ground vacated by a portion of the XI Corps." [3] Captain Candler and Captain Paine of Hooker's staff were sent to Doubleday with orders for him to march rapidly to the front. Reynolds proceeded to join his corps.

### 6:30 to 7:10 p.m. (Map 20)

Schurz fell back upon Buschbeck's line. The two reserve batteries not yet engaged came into action—one on the left of Schurz's battery, south of the Plank Road; one in Buschbeck's rifle-pit, north of the Plank Road; and the corps battery previously in action ceased firing on account of the exhaustion of its ammunition. About this time the corps artillery was all ordered to withdraw to Chancellorsville. Schurz's and von Steinwehr's batteries fell back to the Buschbeck line, the former having lost one piece and the latter two pieces, making a total loss for the corps of nine pieces, or 25 per cent. of its artillery. Captain Dilger, commanding Schurz's battery, put one gun in the Plank Road; this being all the artillery that he could use, he sent his four remaining pieces to the rear under charge of a lieutenant, with orders to report to the first artillery officer he should meet. Captain Wiedrich, commanding von Steinwehr's battery, took his four pieces back to near Chandler's and proceeded to refit it.[4] The infantry on Buschbeck's line now consisted of Buschbeck's brigade of four regiments, two regiments and two companies of Schurz's first brigade, three regi-

---

volunteered to remain through the fight, had been on special duty as guard to the corps hospital at Chandler's since the 1st.

[1] *History of the 1st Regiment Delaware Volunteers*, pp. 66, 69.

[2] *The Fifth Army Corps*, by W. H. Powell, p. 450.

[3] Hooker and other officers were under the impression that the position lately held by the XI Corps inclined more than it did toward the Rapidan (*W. R.*, 39, pp. 225, 263, 279, 282, 288, and maps, pp. 673, 683).

[4] *Ib.*, 39, p. 647.

ments of his second, and his unattached regiment, altogether ten regiments and two companies, besides fragments of Devens' division (Map 20). This whole force may be estimated as 4000 men. The work was but a shallow shelter trench, and many of the men were badly shaken; on the other hand, the line was not 1000 yards in length, and among its defenders were entire regiments which were perfectly fresh. If the foregoing estimate is correct, there were more than four men of fairly good *morale* to the running yard; these men were capable of standing off all the infantry that Jackson had in front of them or could possibly put there. But Jackson had reckoned on just such a case as this, and he was prepared to meet it. With his broad mass he assailed the Federal line along its whole front and converged with crushing force upon both its flanks.[1] About 7:10 p.m. he gained possession of this third and last line of Howard's corps. The latter retired in two bodies: one of five regiments, under Schurz, north of the Plank Road; one of four, under Buschbeck, south of it. Dilger with his single piece of artillery, supported by two companies of infantry, and a cavalcade of officers forming a sort of mounted escort for it, took the Plank Road. The first halting-place or line of defence for these troops was one formed by the works covering the right of the XII Corps, and constructed by the men of Williams' division ($\frac{1}{XII}$). These were stout barricades of logs, with abatis on the western side and extending from the south of the Plank Road to a point about 400 yards north of it, with a break of 100 yards at the road. Troops prolonging the line beyond the works, assuming that these were adequately manned, would derive some advantage from resting their left flank on a fortification. The whole line may be designated for convenience as the line of Slocum's Log Works. The only troops in the works were the four companies of the 28 N. Y. which had been left in them to guard the baggage of Williams' division when it moved out to support Sickles' corps. About ¾ of a mile in rear of this line the plateau of Fairview constituted the last point of vantage for the defence. Here Captain Best was engaged in placing his batteries.

About 6:30 p.m. Jastram's battery ($\frac{2}{1.\,III}$) arrived at the Furnace, and about the same time Birney received orders from Captain Moore of Hooker's staff "to advance rapidly."[2] Leaving two of Jastram's pieces at the Furnace, he promptly advanced with his three brigades and the remainder of Jastram's battery. Placing his four pieces in position, he wasted some ammunition on the retreating column, and

[1] "Along this line the contest raged for some time. Hooker states that it was an hour [6:10 to 7:10]; but the actual fighting did not last over twenty minutes, prob-

ably" (*The Battle of Chancellorsville*, by A. C. Hamlin, p. 76).

[2] *History of Battery E, 1 R. I. Light Artillery*, by George Lewis, p. 162; *W. R.*, 39, p. 408.

then, about 7 p.m., without orders from Sickles or from Hooker, prepared to go into bivouac. At this moment he was informed by Lieutenant-Colonel Hart, Sickles' adjutant-general, that the XI Corps had given way in disorder, and that Sickles ordered his immediate return. He withdrew in good order, leaving two regiments $(\frac{63}{1.\,1.\,\mathrm{III}}, \frac{20}{2.\,1.\,\mathrm{III}})$ in position south of the railroad cut as rear-guard, and sent an order to Barlow to follow him. By this time he had caught the sound of the infantry and artillery fire on the Plank Road.[1] Soon afterward he met Devin coming to report to him with the 6 N. Y. Cavalry, and ordered him to return with his regiment, and ascertain whether the Plank Road was open to Chancellorsville.[2] Barlow had lost all touch with the troops on his right and left, and was marching on alone in search of Birney or Jackson in the direction of Orange Court-House. Whipple and Williams received orders to withdraw, the former from Sickles, the latter from Slocum, about the time when Birney received his from Hooker, or about 7 p.m.

Buschbeck, as he fell back, halted in line of battle on the edge of the wood to check pursuit. Not being pressed, he filed his brigade into the road and went on toward Chancellorsville, covered in rear by Dilger with his piece of artillery.[3]

About 6:45 p.m. the 8 Pa. mounted and, headed by Major Huey, started off for the Plank Road in column of twos.[4] The roar of battle, which rolled on past Chancellorsville, through the Federal lines, and out in feeble accent to the enemy on the Turnpike, had not broken the stillness of Hazel Grove, or if it had, had not disturbed the serenity of the few troops assembled there.

No one in the regiment except its commander, Major Huey, knew where it was going. As the column entered the forest which extends about a mile south of the Plank Road, the officers and men saw halted

---

[1] *Four Years in the Army of the Potomac*, by P. R. de Trobriand, p. 441.

[2] *W. R.*, 39, p. 781.

[3] "Dilger's resolute action while retreating with his single gun, supported by the two companies of brave Irishmen of the Sixty-first Ohio, keeping the enemy at bay and the Plank Road free from active pursuit, forms one of the bright and pleasing episodes of this ill-fated campaign, but which has not received even at this late day [1896] the least notice whatever" (*The Battle of Chancellorsville*, by A. C. Hamlin, p. 78).

[4] The time of day is given by C. A. White, late Adjutant of the 8 Pa. Cavalry, as "shortly after six o'clock" (*The Charge at Chancellorsville*, by Pennock Huey, pp. 99, 105). A. B. Wells, late captain in the regiment, says with reference to it: "This was at twenty minutes past six in the evening. I remember it, for I looked at my watch . . ." (*ib.*, p. 71). T. E. Carpenter, late captain in the regiment, gives it as "about half-past six o'clock in the evening" (*ib.*, p. 78). Huey gives the time when Sickles gave the order to Pleasonton as "half-past six o'clock—not later" (*ib.*, pp. 14, 15). This must make the time when Huey put the order into execution later than half-past six. According to Hamlin, Huey received the order "shortly" before seven and put it in execution some time after seven (see his *Battle of Chancellorsville*, pp. 82, 142).

by the roadside, in the opening called the Vista, caissons, guns, carriages, and other material, belonging to the Federal troops who had gone down to the Furnace. None of the soldiers and camp-followers there seemed to be aware that a conflict had taken place in the vicinity or that the least danger was impending. Not a straggler from the line of battle had yet reached this spot to give the alarm. And so Huey and his men marched along with their sabers in their scabbards and their pistols in their holsters. Being, as they thought, well within their own lines, they had no regular advance-guard or flankers. About a third of a mile from the Plank Road a narrow road or path coming from near Dowdall's Tavern joins the road leading directly from Hazel Grove to the Plank Road. As Huey reached this point he saw several men in gray uniforms moving about in the twilight some distance from him, but he took them to be Federal scouts dressed in Confederate gray, and passed on. As he approached the Plank Road he saw, to his astonishment, groups of Confederates in his front between him and the Plank Road, moving in the direction of Chancellorsville, and others on his left approaching his left flank. It flashed upon him that he had marched up against a part of Lee's army, that it was too late to retreat, that the best thing he could do would be to break through the crowd in his front, gain the Plank Road, turn to the right, and fight his way to Chancellorsville. He instantly ordered his men to draw sabers and follow him at a gallop. This was about 7:30 p.m., about the time when Stuart started off for Ely's Ford. When he struck the Plank Road he saw, to his dismay, a crowd of Confederates blocking the way on the right. The XI Corps had all gone by, and he was in the midst of the enemy's advance troops, the main body being to his left, but out of sight. He led the column in the direction which seemed to be that of least resistance, or to the left. After he had gone about 100 yards he was met with a murderous volley from concealed troops in the woods. He turned his staggered column to the right, and passed on eastward.[1]

At 7 p.m. Seeley's battery $\left(\frac{4}{2.\ \text{III}}\right)$ took up the march from United States Ford for Chancellorsville.[2] Berry was still near the Chancellor House with two of his brigades. The noise of the rapid flight and the close pursuit of Jackson's troops was borne to the ears of his men, first in faint, indistinct murmurs, constantly increasing in volume until it seemed as though pandemonium had broken loose. Then came the fugitives, frantic and terror-stricken, blindly pushing their way through his steady ranks. In the midst of the rout and tumult Hooker hurried up.

[1] *The Battle of Chancellorsville*, by A. C. Hamlin, p. 92. See also *Papers of Mil. Hist. Soc. of Mass.*, V, 212.

[2] It appears that in the impending battle this battery had but four pieces engaged. The other two pieces may have been left on the north side of the Rappahannock, but the author assumes that they were left on the south side, in the vicinity of United States Ford.

"General," he shouted, "throw your men into the breach—receive the enemy on your bayonets—don't fire a shot—they can't see you!"

Berry at once advanced at double-time with his 1st and 2d brigades.[1] Hooker, sitting on his white horse, a familiar sight to his old division, watched them go hurrying by—remarking from time to time as he looked down into their upturned faces: "Receive them on your bayonets, boys! Receive 'em on your bayonets!"[2] Hays' brigade $\left(\frac{2}{3.\,\text{II}}\right)$, ordered to support Berry's division, followed at double-time. There can hardly be a severer test of discipline and *esprit de corps* than the one to which these troops were now subjected. Berry's division was the largest and one of the best in the Army of the Potomac, and the II Corps, from which came Hays' brigade, was making a splendid record. Through the surging rout of the XI Corps these sterling organizations forged their way, unchecked and unshaken, toward the mass of yelling and firing assailants. Berry was ordered "to cover the rear of the XI Corps, and if possible to seize and hold at all hazards the high ground which had been abandoned by that corps."[3]

General Reynolds, on reaching United States Ford, was joined by Captains Candler and Paine of Hooker's staff, and about 7 p.m. took up the march with his two divisions, accompanied by these two officers as guides, his 1st brigade, Second Division, in front. Through the dark woods, with here and there a moonlit opening, in and out among wagons, ambulances, and gun-carriages, they pushed slowly but steadily on. A regiment $\left(\frac{94}{1.\,2.\,1}\right)$ was deployed across the road, and as it advanced, drove back hundreds of fugitives of the XI Corps. Reynolds left behind near the ford one regiment of infantry $\left(\frac{135}{1.\,3.\,1}\right)$ and all his artillery.

Williams was getting into position to coöperate with Whipple and Birney in pressing Anderson back upon the Plank Road, when about 7 p.m., as Jackson was carrying Buschbeck's position, he received an order to reoccupy his log works at once. Apprehending that some disaster had happened to the corps on his right, he ordered his brigades to retire in good order, but without loss of time.

---

[1] *Major-General Hiram G. Berry*, by Edward K. Gould, pp. 258, 297. The reports show a great diversity of statement as to the hour of the receipt and execution of this order. Captain Poland, Berry's acting assistant inspector-general and chief of staff, and Captain Tyler, commanding the 74 N. Y., give it as 4 p.m. Both of the brigade commanders and Colonels McLaughlin and Farnum, commanding the 1 Mass. and 70 N. Y., respectively, give it as 5 or about 5 p.m. Lieutenant-Colonel Merriam,

commanding the 16 Mass., gives it as 6:30 p.m. Lieutenant-Colonel Westbrook, commanding the 120 N. Y., gives it as sundown. A. C. Hamlin, in his *Battle of Chancellorsville*, indicates on his maps that it was about 7 p.m.

[2] *Men and Things I Saw in Civil War Days*, by James F. Rusling, p. 303.

[3] Hooker's testimony, *Rep. of Com.*, IV, 126; Hooker's letter to Ross, *B. and L.*, III, 223.

*7:10 to 8 p.m.* (Map 21)

The XI Corps continued its retreat to the position of Fairview without making any stand on the line of Slocum's Log Works. Buschbeck started to do so south of the Plank Road, and was ordered by a staff officer to continue his march.[1] When Schurz reached the line Buschbeck had doubtless abandoned it, as he moved faster than Schurz. From Slocum's Log Works Schurz retreated by the Bullock Road. Rodes' and Colston's men went over the works of Buschbeck's line together, becoming mingled in inextricable confusion. They proceeded with apparently inexhaustible ardor and endurance to the edge of the woods beyond the works. Here about 7:15 p.m. Rodes brought them to a halt (Map 21). In his official report he accounts for this action by the statement: "The right becoming entangled in an abatis near the enemy's first line of fortifications, caused the line to halt, and such was the confusion and darkness that it was not deemed advisable to make a further advance."[2] He sent word to Jackson urging him to push forward the comparatively fresh men of the third line in order that his own line might be reformed. A portion of the Confederate force failed to hear or to heed the command to halt; parts of three brigades pushed on up the Plank Road or in the woods on either side of it, thus forming an advance body of foragers or ground scouts, but there was no line of skirmishers. Paxton had taken position in the rifle-pits of Buschbeck's old line. Colquitt and Ramseur had halted near Dowdall's Tavern.

About 7:30 Barlow, about a mile below the railroad cut, with his brigade, was overtaken by the bearer of Birney's order recalling him. He at once proceeded to return.

On the opposite side of the battle-field the Second and Third Divisions of the I Corps were advancing from United States Ford. At 8 o'clock the First Division, on the north side of the river, was about 4 miles from the ford.

Colonel Munford, with the 2 Va. Cavalry, had got within sight of Ely's Ford, having skirmished with some Federal cavalry, probably the squadron of the 6 N. Y. left in the vicinity of the ford. He sent back reports of his progress to Jackson,[3] who perhaps communicated them to Stuart. At any rate, about 7:30 p.m., Stuart, seeing nothing else for him to do, proposed to Jackson that he "take some cavalry and infantry over and hold the Ely's Ford Road." The proposition was approved and acted upon.[4]

Jackson's artillery having arrived at the front under Crutchfield,

[1] *The Battle of Chancellorsville,* by A. C. Hamlin, pp. 77, 97, 148, 149.

[2] *W. R.,* 39, p. 941.

[3] Private letters of Colonel Munford to the author.

[4] *W. R.,* 39, pp. 799, 887; *Chancellorsville,* by Hotchkiss and Allan, pp. 57, 58; *The Battle of Chancellorsville,* by A. C. Hamlin, pp. 81, 181; *Memoirs of the Confederate War,* by H. von Borcke, II, 227.

Chief of Artillery, the horse artillery, about 8 p.m., withdrew from its advanced position on the Plank Road, leaving there Captain Moorman with 2 pieces which had not been engaged. The men and horses in general were exhausted, not having been fed for forty-eight hours.[1]

Huey, pushing eastward through the woods with a formed remnant of the 8 Pa. Cavalry, outstripped the Confederate troops marching on the road, and striking the Mountain Road, led his men to the Plank Road, where he met Captain Best, Chief of Artillery of the XII Corps, placing his artillery in position. He requested the captain not to fire his guns down the road, as many of his men were still in the woods trying to work their way out. The rear of the column, hearing the attack on the head, turned to the right out of the road on which the column marched from Hazel Grove, and made its way through the woods and over or past the intrenchments of the XII Corps to the Fairview plateau. The regiment, on assembling, took position to support Best's artillery, but from this duty it was soon relieved by the infantry. It then fell back to Chancellorsville, where it was formed in a line of skirmishers for the purpose of intercepting and gathering up stragglers.[2]

Most of the fugitives of the XI Corps preceded the formed or intact bodies under Schurz and Buschbeck. The remainder kept coming in until late in the night. But besides the swarms of XI Corps men which issued from the Plank Road and the roads on each side of it, a current of fleeing soldiery of two other corps reached Chancellorsville from the direction of Hazel Grove. To account for this fact it is necessary to go back a little in the narrative. When the 8 Pa. started to report to Howard it left at Hazel Grove the battery attached to Pleasonton's cavalry, 6 pieces; the three batteries of Whipple's division $(\frac{3}{\text{III}})$, 16 pieces;[3] the 17 Pa. Cavalry, and the 110 Pa. Infantry. Everything was quiet there, when suddenly a sharp fire of musketry broke out from the woods in the direction of the XI Corps. Captain J. F. Huntington, the senior artillery officer present with Whipple's three batteries, assumed command of them, and proceeded to place them in position.[4] Pleason-

---

[1] *W. R.*, 39, p. 1050.

[2] This account of the movements of the 8 Pa. Cavalry is substantially, and in large part verbatim, that given by A. C. Hamlin in his *Battle of Chancellorsville*, pp. 90–92. The author was favored, however, in the preparation of it by the use of a manuscript article by Colonel T. A. Dodge, U. S. Army, retired, entitled "A Romance of Chancellorsville," and of Major Pennock Huey's history of the event. He, moreover, consulted the official reports, *W. R.*, 39, pp. 772–789. It appears from a map in Major

Huey's book (p. 31) that the regiment while in line of skirmishers at Chancellorsville occupied the River Road and Turnpike and the span between them. The road to United States Ford was barred by the head of the I Corps.

[3] These batteries numbered 18 pieces. Two pieces were with Muhlenberg on the Plank Road (*W. R.*, 39, p. 726).

[4] Captain von Puttkammer, the chief of artillery of the division, had left the field to look for orders,—which led to his trial by court-martial, and dismissal from the

ton's battery (Martin's) formed not far from Huntington's, making a total of 22 guns ready to fire. Before the line was formed a mass of fugitives, together with caissons, guns, ambulances, beef-cattle, mules, etc., came surging out of the Vista, and dashed through the incomplete formation, nearly carrying it away.[1] Soon afterward, the line meantime being formed, a regiment of the enemy's infantry $\left(\frac{4}{2.\,2.\,\text{II}}\right)$, about 200 strong, issued from the woods. At once the 22 guns opened fire with canister. The assailants were probably surprised, having reason to believe that everything in this quarter was well started to the rear. They quickly retreated to the woods, taking with them a gun of Turnbull's battery $\left(\frac{3}{1.\,\text{III}}\right)$, three caissons, and the whole mule-train of small-arms ammunition of the III Corps. The forementioned mass of fleeing men, animals, and material was made up of Birney's park of artillery, which was left at Hazel Grove, camp-followers, and fugitives of the XI Corps. As it went through Williams' division $\left(\frac{1}{\text{XII}}\right)$, which was trying to regain its old position in the log works, it was increased by a contribution from that organization.

A few moments after Dilger with his pieces of artillery and escort passed Slocum's Log Works, the Confederate advance troops (foragers or ground scouts) arrived there, surrounded the four companies of the 28 N. Y., and demanded their surrender. Escape seeming impossible, the colonel complied, ordering the men to lay down their arms. Sixty-seven men were thus taken prisoners.[2] The rest, numbering about 40 men who escaped, retired rapidly through the woods,[3] joining in their flight the portion of Huey's cavalry retreating south of the Plank Road. The demoralized crowd carried with it the 13 N. J., also of Williams' division $\left(\frac{13}{3.\,1.\,\text{XII}}\right)$, which had been left in reserve at Hazel Grove.[4] The stampede is thus described by Captain Osborn, Chief of Artillery of Berry's division $\left(\frac{2}{\text{III}}\right)$: "As we passed General Hooker's headquarters, a scene burst upon us which, God grant, may never again be seen in the Federal army of the United States. The Eleventh Corps had been routed, and were fleeing to the river like scared sheep. The men and artillery filled the roads[*sic*], its sides, and the skirts of the field; and it appeared

service (J. F. Huntington, in letter to Major Huey, *The Charge of the 8 Pennsylvania at Chancellorsville*, p. 65).

[1] With reference to this incident, Lieutenant Martin, commanding the battery of horse artillery, says in his report: "Carriages, wagons, horses without riders, and panic-stricken infantry were rushing through and through my battery, overturning guns and limbers, smashing my caissons, and trampling my horse-holders under them.

"While Lieutenant Browne was bringing his section into position, a caisson without drivers came tearing through, upsetting his right piece, and severely injuring one of his drivers, carrying away both detachments of his horses, and breaking the caisson so badly as to necessitate its being left upon the field" (*W. R.*, 39, pp. 787, 788).

[2] *History of the 28 Regiment N. Y. State Volunteers*, by C. W. Boyce, p. 54.

[3] *W. R.*, 39, p. 693.

[4] This regiment was rallied about dark and formed in rear of Ruger's brigade $\left(\frac{3}{1.\,\text{III}}\right)$ (*W. R.*, 39, p. 715).

that no two or one company could be found together. Aghast and terror-stricken, heads bare and panting for breath, they pleaded like infants at the mother's breast that we should let them pass to the rear unhindered."[1]

The hospitals of the XI Corps had been formed in rear of their respective divisions. The retreat of the corps compelled their hasty evacuation; all the wounded who could walk were sent to the rear on foot, the more severe cases were carried in ambulances. Small parties of slightly wounded men, "scattered all through the woods," were collected and sent to hospitals finally established on the north bank of the river, from which they were transported to those at Brooke's Station. A number of medical officers were taken prisoners, among whom was Surgeon George Suckley, Medical Director of the corps.[2] Birney's division ($\frac{1}{III}$) had its hospital in the Old School-House on the Plank Road, about a mile west of Chancellorsville. "The fleeing Dutchmen," says Medical Director Sim, "actually ran over our hospital." The wounded had to be carried on stretchers to the new hospital established at Chandler's, where for a while the enemy's shells came thick and fast. A number of the surgeons ran away, and did not stop until they got about a mile beyond the river.[3] One of the hospitals of the XII Corps was also run over by the XI Corps and ruined.[4]

"Some of the fugitives," says General Francis A. Walker in his life of General Hancock, "were so completely beside themselves with fear that they ran past the Chancellor House, down the Fredericksburg Pike, through Hancock's line, and into the hands of the Confederates without being stopped. One ingenuous German approached Hancock and begged to be directed to the pontoons. The answer he received has been handed down by tradition, but it is best not to put it into cold and unsympathetic type!"[5]

An officer of the III Corps writes: "The officers of other corps made themselves speechless by striving to rally the 'flying Dutchman,' who was no longer an illusion, but a despicable reality; and the cavalry with their sabers, generals and staffs with revolvers, and artillerists with whips and rammers, vainly attempted to stop the disgraceful flight, which was finally checked by the Rappahannock. 'Var ish de pontoons?' 'Der wash too many mens for us.' 'I ish going to mine company,' they continually exclaimed. . . . The Germans sought to escape the censure which the whole army justly bestowed upon them, by tearing the badges from their caps,—for the crescent was recognized as the

---

[1] *W. R.*, 39, p. 483.

[2] *Medical Recollections of the Army of the Potomac*, by Jonathan Letterman, p. 133.

[3] *W. R.*, 39, p. 401.

[4] *Medical Recollections of the Army of the Potomac*, by Jonathan Letterman, p. 134.

[5] *General Hancock*, in Great Commanders Series, p. 83.

insignia of a poltroon,—and giving the number of one of the reliable corps, if they were questioned about the command to which they belonged.''[1]  Many of these men had thrown away their arms.  A number of them, however, with arms, were placed in the trenches of Geary's line.[2]

Rodes galloped up the Plank Road some distance and satisfied himself that there was no line of battle between his troops and Fairview. He apparently did not overtake Buschbeck $(\frac{1}{2. \text{XI}})$.  Schurz $(\frac{3}{\text{XI}})$, who had halted on the Bullock Road, was concealed from him by the woods. Williams $(\frac{1}{\text{XII}})$, Berry $(\frac{2}{\text{III}})$, and Hays had not yet reached their positions (Map 21).

Buschbeck $(\frac{1}{2. \text{XI}})$ reached the field of Fairview about 7:45 p.m., and posted his brigade, together with rallied soldiers of Devens' and Schurz's division $(\frac{1. 3}{\text{XI}})$, in front of the line of guns which Best was still engaged in forming (Sketch 3).  Dilger found his four pieces in position with Best's guns, and united his single piece with them.  Buschbeck's brigade numbered about 1000 men, and the men with Schurz from 1200 to 1500.[3]  On a line with Buschbeck $(\frac{8}{2. \text{XI}})$, in front of Best's guns, were 150 men of McLean's brigade $(\frac{2}{1. \text{XI}})$, and other men of the XI Corps, making, together with the men under Schurz, from 3500 to 4000 men available for action.[4]  On his return Rodes communicated the result of his observation to Crutchfield, Jackson's chief of artillery, who sent three pieces up the Plank Road about half a mile beyond Dowdall's Tavern to fire on Fairview.[5]  These pieces opened fire accordingly about 8 p.m.  Best replied with a fire of four pieces.[6]  At this time the positions of the Federal forces were as follows: Pleasonton with the 6 N. Y., 17 Pa., and Martin's battery at Hazel Grove.  Devin did not go northward beyond this point with the 6 N. Y., but sent a detachment of infantry from here on to ascertain if the Plank Road was open to Chancellorsville.  This detachment, of course, was brought to a halt by the enemy.  Behind Pleasonton, at Hazel Grove, was Whipple's division $(\frac{3}{\text{III}})$, and behind Whipple's, Birney's $(\frac{1}{\text{III}})$, accompanied by Jastram's battery (1. III), forming up.  About a mile south of the unfinished railroad was Barlow's brigade $(\frac{2}{2. \text{XI}})$, marching south, still looking for Birney or the enemy.  Berry with his two brigades $(\frac{1. 2}{2. \text{III}})$ had taken position between the Plank Road and the Bullock Road (Sketch 3), and proceeded to intrench.[7]  Williams' division $(\frac{1}{\text{XII}})$ had

[1] Three Years in the Army of the Potomac, by H. N. Blake, late Captain 11 Mass., p. 180.

[2] W. R., 39, p. 734.

[3] The Battle of Chancellorsville, by A. C. Hamlin, pp. 80, 126.

[4] Ib., pp. 77, 78.

[5] Moorman's pieces were not used, not having sufficient range (W. R., 39, p. 1050).

[6] Two sections of Dimick's battery, Second Division, III Corps (W. R., 39, p. 483).

[7] He formed a line of works which will be referred to as Berry's Log Works.

returned to its corps, but not to its former position. Its 2d brigade was in the old works on Geary's right; the 3d and 1st brigades extended the line northward toward, but not to, the Plank Road. The left regiment of the 3d brigade, the 27 Ind., was formed astride of the old works, the eight right companies inside, the other two outside, of them facing west. Colonel Colgrove of this regiment got Lieutenant Lewis to place two of his 12-pound Napoleon guns (1. 3. III) on a piece of high ground on his left to enfilade a ravine that extended along his front.[1] In rear of these guns, as support, he put about 200 men of the 110 Pa. (3. 3. III), placed at his disposal by an officer of that regiment.[2] On the right of Williams' line were Buschbeck's brigade and other fragments of the XI Corps. When the division had been in this position about fifteen minutes, the 1st brigade, on the right of the line, was sent forward through the darkness to retake its original position, where it had left its knapsacks. It advanced in line of battle with skirmishers in front, and arrived behind the barricades, or log works, south of where they were occupied by the enemy, without knowing that the enemy was in possession of any portion of them.

About dark Perry's brigade of Anderson's division ($\frac{3}{1.1}$) moved, by order of General Lee, from the right of McLaws' to the right of its own division (Map 22).

### 8 p.m. to 9:30 p.m.

Sickles was now undecided as to whether he should conform to the retreat of the Federal right or maintain his position. His last communication from Hooker was the order to attack, which he received about 5 p.m. To open communication with him he sent Lieutenant-Colonel Hart, his assistant adjutant-general, with a small mounted escort, detailed by General Pleasonton, taking the precaution of seeing that no orders, communications, or memoranda, of a nature to be of value to the enemy, should be found upon him in case of his capture. Colonel Hart reported back, probably about 9, with orders for Sickles to hold Hazel Grove. He was then sent to inform Hooker that a portion of Whipple's ammunition (mule) train, some of the caissons of his batteries, and two or three of his cannon were in the woods occupied by the enemy, between Sickles' line of battle and the Plank Road, and that to recover these, as well as the line of the Plank Road, he would, with Hooker's sanction, make a night attack, if supported by the line of Williams' and Berry's divisions $\left(\frac{1}{XII}, \frac{2}{III}\right)$.

In rear of Crutchfield's guns, A. P. Hill's division $\left(\frac{4}{1}\right)$ moved up the Plank Road to deploy, but as it approached the artillery it was raked by the fire from Fairview, and forced to seek shelter on the side of the

[1] These pieces came from Hazel Grove.     [2] W. R., 39, p. 711.

road. Lane stated that he could not deploy unless the artillery firing ceased, and asked General Hill to stop it. Colonel Crutchfield after a delay of about fifteen minutes was ordered to stop firing. The Federal artillery ceased firing; A. P. Hill's division commenced deploying in front of Rodes' and Colston's, and the latter to withdraw and reform.[1] The only part of Hill's division immediately available was Lane's brigade, which had followed the three lines by the road in column. The two brigades which had been deployed in the third line (Heth's and Pender's) had taken to the road. It is not easy to see why they could not have kept in line as well as the other brigades, but as they did not, it would have been better had they marched in column from the start.[2]

By 8:45 p.m. Lane's brigade $(\frac{4}{1.\,\mathrm{II}})$ had deployed on either side of the Plank Road just in advance of Slocum's Log Works, with two or three guns in the road. He did not know of the existence of the log works, or he would have taken position behind them. One of his regiments (33 N. Ca.) was posted in line of skirmishers as a picket from 200 to 300 yards in advance of his main line.

About 8:30 p.m. Schurz with his five regiments retired to the vicinity of Chancellorsville.[3] Hooker learned that the enemy was in possession of the high ground that Berry was to have seized, and that he (Berry) had consequently established his line ''in the valley on the Chancellorsville side of that high ground.'' The ground occupied by Berry was a ridge which in the hands of the enemy would command an open ground, or plain, that extended back to Fairview. As soon as Hooker learned of Berry's position, he directed General Warren and Captain Comstock to lay out a new line of defence to the rear of the one which he then held, and to do it that night, as he would not, he said, be able to hold the line which he then held after the enemy should renew his attack in the morning.[4] The new line, which he pointed out on a map, extended from Chandler's along the Mineral Spring Road, and along the Ely's Ford Road and the Little Hunting Run.

Albright's brigade $(\frac{3}{3.\,\mathrm{II}})$ was withdrawn to its former bivouac between Chandler's and Chancellorsville,[5] leaving Berry's right flank ''in the air.'' Berry dispatched an aide and patrols to the right in search of troops who were supposed to protect that flank or connect with it. These troops could not be found. He reported to Hooker and was informed that the II Corps would connect with his right. At 9 p.m. Hays reported to him with his brigade $(\frac{2}{3.\,\mathrm{II}})$ and was placed obliquely about 300 yards in rear of the second line facing southwest (Plan 2),[6] on

---

[1] *So. Hist. Soc. Papers*, XXX, 112.

[2] It seems that Heth took to the road on his own responsibility, and that Pender was ordered to do so (*W. R.*, 39, pp. 890, 935).

[3] *Ib.*, 39, p. 657.

[4] Hooker's testimony, *Rep. of Com.*, IV, 127.

[5] *History of the 1st Regt. Del. Vols.*, pp. 66, 69.

[6] *W. R.*, 39, p. 389.

account, no doubt, of the threatening appearance of things on the Plank Road. Between his right and the troops on the Ely's Ford Road was a gap of about 600 yards (Map 22). The seven regiments in his front line on the right of the road took up about 700 yards, or about 2 yards to a man. With the regiments in the second and third lines there was less than a man to a yard. On the left of the road Berry connected with Slocum. The 11 Mass. of Berry's 1st brigade was still on the Turnpike in front of Hancock. Neither Jackson nor Hill nor Lane was aware of the line of battle formed by Berry and Hays, to say nothing of Sykes ($\frac{2}{v}$) on the Ely's Ford Road, and the two divisions under Reynolds ($\frac{2.3}{I}$) plodding on by the road from United States Ford in pursuance now of the following order:

Chancellorsville, Va., May 2, 1863, 8:15 p.m.

*Major-General Reynolds:*

The general commanding understands that General Meade has sent General Sykes' division on [to] the Hunting Run. He [Sykes] will establish his line on that [stream], resting on the Rapidan, and extend it in the direction of Chancellorsville, along the line of the Chancellorsville and Ely's Ford Road, as far as he can defend it. The general desires that you connect your right with General Sykes' left along the same line or road.

J. H. VAN ALEN,

Brigadier-General and Aide-de-Camp.

The First, or rear, Division of this corps ($\frac{1}{I}$) halted about 9 p.m. on the north side of the river about 2 miles from United States Ford.[1]

The Confederate commanders were under the impression that the Federal infantry was back of the guns at Fairview except for a line of skirmishers, or pickets, which they knew to be nearer. Where the Federal picket line crossed the Plank Road were two pieces of Lieutenant Dimick's battery ($\frac{3}{2.III}$), thrown out from Fairview and commanded by the lieutenant; at the corresponding point of Lane's line were the three forementioned pieces of Crutchfield's. Lane in placing his regiments had cautioned them to keep a sharp lookout for the enemy, as he was far in advance and alone, and they must be prepared to repel an attack. As soon as his line was formed he went to report for further orders. When he called out in the darkness for General Hill he was answered by Jackson. He found the latter at the junction of the Bullock Road, Hazel Grove Road, and Plank Road, where he had intended to change direction toward the rear of Chancellorsville. But Jackson did not order any change of direction. He had not yet estab-

---

[1] The Itinerary of the I Corps (*W. R.*, 39, p. 257) represents the First Division as crossing the river ahead of the other two divisions. For my authority to the contrary see reports of the inspector-general and of brigade and regimental commanders (*ib.*, pp. 261, 263, 264, 266, 268, *et seq.*).

lished connection with Lee. This he meant to do by pushing Lane's brigade straight on toward Chancellorsville. While Lane and Lee engaged the attention of the enemy in that direction, Jackson with Heth's and Pender's brigades ($\frac{1.\ 2}{1.\ II}$) on the Plank Road, and others at hand ready to follow, would deliver a thrust in Hooker's rear. Colquitt was still in the vicinity of Dowdall's Tavern. Paxton was in rear of his left. Archer's brigade ($\frac{5}{1.\ II}$) went into bivouac about 9 o'clock at the intersection of the Brook Road and Germanna Plank Road.[1] Jackson's front had contracted from about 2 miles to about half a mile. He probably did not know or rightly estimate the force that the Federals put forth in the course of the day beyond the Furnace, and thought that Lane in advancing on Chancellorsville would leave that force at a safe distance behind him or to his right. In answer to Lane's application for orders he raised his arm in the direction of the enemy and exclaimed: "Push right ahead, Lane; right ahead." This was about 9 p.m. Lane at once rode along his line to prepare for the movement; he was on the extreme right, ready to clasp hands with Anderson on Lee's left, and was about to give the signal to advance when one of his bravest officers begged him not to do so until he could ascertain whether the troops and trains heard moving on his right and rear were Lee's or Hooker's. While General Lane was considering what he should do, a Federal officer came up along Slocum's Log Works from the right flank, waving a handkerchief and demanding information as to what troops were in his front. The officer proved to be the colonel of the 128 Pa. of the 1st brigade of Williams' division, looking in the darkness for the former position of his regiment in the log works. He was promptly seized and brought before General Lane. After a moment's conversation with him, Lane had a patrol sent into the woods on the right to ascertain how much of a hostile force was concealed there. About as the patrol disappeared on Lane's right, a Federal officer, probably General Knipe, rode up in the woods in his front, and called out for General Williams, commanding his division. This drew the fire of a part of Lane's skirmish line (33 N. Ca.); the fire was returned by portions of the Federal line confronting it. Part of Lane's line of battle fired a volley at the Federal officer and incidentally into the rear of the line of Confederate skirmishers. This made the latter rush forward for shelter, and this rushing forward gave the Federals the impression that a charge was being made and caused a number of Federal regiments to fire into the woods. Soon after Lane left Jackson, about 9 p.m., the latter was joined by Hill and some of his staff, and Jackson gave Hill his orders in the brief sentence: "Press them; cut them off from the United States Ford, Hill; press them." Hill replied that none of his staff were familiar with the country. Jackson turned to Captain

[1] W. R., 39, p. 929.

Boswell, his chief engineer officer, who was well acquainted with all the roads and paths, and ordered him to report to Hill. Then, about as General Knipe had started toward the Confederate lines, he went with Hill and a number of staff officers out in advance of Lane's line of battle to look and listen, or reconnoiter. The party was preceded by a mounted orderly as a *point*. When this man, having passed through the line of the 33 N. Ca., came into view to the Federal troops across the Plank Road, an attempt was made to capture him. As he turned and galloped away, making his escape, a desultory fire was sent after him.

Jackson with his party had halted in rear of the 33 N. Ca. After listening for a while to the sounds coming from the Federal lines—the ringing of axes in the building of log works and abatis, and the voices of officers giving commands—he turned his horse about and went back toward the Confederate lines. He had halted a second time to listen, when, about 9:15, the sound of the firing caused by General Knipe's call for General Williams and by the appearance of his orderly in front of the Federal lines broke upon his ears. A moment before, the colonel of the 18 N. Ca. of Lane's brigade, with his adjutant, had gone forward on the Plank Road to consult with the colonel of the 33 N. Ca. At the sound of this firing these officers dashed back on the Plank Road to regain their positions in line. Jackson and his party hurriedly left the Plank Road, and pursued their way to the rear through the woods on the right, or north, side of the Plank Road. The Confederate troops were now keenly alert, having been warned against a possible attack by the Federal cavalry.[1] The thumping of hoofs and the clanking of sabers produced by Jackson and the forementioned colonel with their escorts caused an impression in the line that a charge was about to break upon it. The order was given to fire and repeat the firing. The returning party was at this time not more than 20 paces from the line,[2] and could perhaps be vaguely descried through the darkness. The fire of the North Carolina mountaineers, some of which may have been aimed at indistinct, shadowy forms, but most of which was delivered unaimed in the direction of the approaching sounds, was fearfully effective.

[1] *Memoirs of R. E. Lee*, by A. L. Long, p. 257. Randolph Barton, Esq., of Baltimore, at that time on General Paxton's staff, writes to the author: "I have a decided impression, almost a conviction, that when Jackson's assault had carried us to east of Dowdall's Tavern, a rumor ran through our immediate command, of a cavalry attack, and that we must look out for cavalry. This rumor had, no doubt, filtered through from the front, and undoubtedly referred to the remarkable experience of the 8 Pa. Cavalry under Major Huey. . . . This encounter was most unexpected to both sides. An attack from, or an encounter with, cavalry in that dense country seemed to be as unlikely as an attack from a gunboat. But I am sure that the feeling of a possible attack after Huey's affair had impressed the army, and I think our men had become supersensitive on the subject."

[2] *Memoirs of R. E. Lee*, by A. L. Long, p. 257.

Captain Boswell and his horse fell dead. One of the orderlies was killed and one wounded. Jackson received three balls at the same instant. One penetrated the palm of his right hand, a second passed around the wrist of his left hand, and a third passed through the left arm half-way between the shoulder and elbow. It splintered the bone to the elbow-joint, and severed the artery. His horse, frantic with terror, plunged into the wood and rushed toward the Federal lines. An overhanging bough struck him violently in the face, tore off his cap, and nearly unhorsed him; but recovering his seat, he managed to seize the bridle with his bleeding hand, and turn his horse toward the road. In spite of this he would probably have been carried into the Federal lines, had not Lieutenant Wynn of his staff, whose horse had also broken toward the Federal lines, caught Jackson's horse by the bridle and stopped it about 100 yards from a line of Federal skirmishers. The voices of the latter, says Lieutenant Wynn, could be distinctly heard. The lieutenant, with the aid of Captain Wilbourn, took Jackson from his horse, and laid him under a tree. Then giving him some water, he got on his horse, reported to General A. P. Hill, and after taking the latter to Jackson, proceeded to the rear for an ambulance. In the meantime Jackson's broken arm was bandaged with a handkerchief. Soon afterward members of his staff started to bear him to the rear. The party, swollen by the arrival of officers desiring to render him assistance, drew the fire of Dimick's two guns on picket. This was taken by the artillery at Fairview as a signal that the enemy was advancing in force, and immediately, or about 9:30 p.m., it commenced firing by the light of the moon with canister over the heads of the Federal infantry at the Confederate lines of battle.[1] It was in this iron tempest that Stonewall Jackson gave his last order. General Pender, who had not deployed his brigade $\left(\frac{2}{1.\,\mathrm{II}}\right)$, expressed to him a doubt as to his ability to hold his men in their position in the road. Pushing aside the men who supported him, Jackson stretched himself to his full height, and answered feebly, but distinctly enough to be heard above the din: "You must hold your ground, General Pender; you must hold your ground, sir." Still more exhausted by this effort, he asked to be permitted to lie down for a few moments; but the danger from the fire and of capture by the Federal advance was too imminent, and his aides hurried

---

[1] Captain Best gives the number of guns in his line, or mass, as 34 (*W. R.*, 39, p. 675); General Hunt gives it as 38 (*ib.*, p. 249); A. C. Hamlin, in his *Battle of Chancellorsville*, p. 104, gives it as 43. It consisted of the artillery of the XII Corps, except Atwell's and Hampton's batteries and Muhlenberg's section of Crosby's battery (*W. R.*, 39, pp. 675, 721, 249)—14 guns; the artillery of Berry's (2d) division, III Corps (except Seeley's battery and one section of Dimick's, in front on the Plank Road) (*ib.*, pp. 483, 484, 162, 249, 488)—16 guns; one section of Hill's battery and Dilger's battery of the XI Corps (*ib.*, pp. 249, 167, 656, 657)—7 guns; total 37 guns. Dimick's battery was on and to the right of the Plank Road. The other batteries were

him on. A litter having been obtained, he was placed on it, and the bearers passed on as rapidly as the thick woods and rough ground permitted. One of the bearers, shot in the arm, let go the handle, and the general was thrown from the litter upon his wounded arm. For the first time a groan escaped him. His aide, Captain Smith, sprang to his side. As he raised his head, a bright beam of moonlight made its way through the thick foliage and rested upon the pale face of the sufferer. The captain was startled by its great pallor and stillness, and cried out: "Oh, General, are you seriously hurt?" "No," he answered; "don't trouble yourself, my friend, about me," and presently added something about winning the battle first, and attending to the wounded afterward. Again he was placed on the litter; and the party turned from the wood into the road and carried him a few hundred yards to where Dr. McGuire was waiting for them with an ambulance. Having readjusted the bandage so as better to stop the flow of blood, the doctor placed him in the ambulance, which already contained Colonel Crutchfield, Jackson's chief of artillery, who was wounded by Best's artillery, and went with them to the hospital at Wilderness Tavern.[1] Crutchfield was succeeded by Colonel Alexander, commanding a battalion of the I Corps, and senior artillery officer present.

We left Lane awaiting the return of a patrol from his right. In a few moments it returned, bringing with it 150 or more men of the 128 Pa. (1. 1. XII), who had become bewildered in the dark forest, and surrendered to it.[2] While their colonel, previously taken prisoner as already stated, was protesting against the capture of these men as an abuse of the handkerchief of truce, the Federal batteries commenced

on the left of the Plank Road, with Winslow's on the right (*W. R., 39*, p. 487).

[1] *Lee's Last Campaign, with an Accurate History of Stonewall Jackson's Last Wound*, by Captain J. C. Gorman, p. 56; *Chancellorsville*, by Hotchkiss and Allan, p. 56; *Stonewall Jackson and Chancellorsville*, by J. P. Smith, *Papers of Mil. Hist. Soc. of Mass.*, V, 372–374; *Stonewall Jackson and the American Civil War*, by G. F. R. Henderson, II, 553–558; *The Richmond Howitzers in the War, by a Member of the Company*, pp. 73 et seq.; *The Battle of Chancellorsville*, by A. C. Hamlin, pp. 109 et seq.; and manuscript letters of Confederate officers in the possession of Captain I. P. Gragg, U. S. Volunteers.

The horse which Jackson rode was called by the soldiers "Little Sorrel" and by the staff "Fancy." Jackson captured him at Harper's Ferry in 1861, and rode him during the Valley campaign, at the battles around Richmond, and at Cedar Run, Bull Run, Antietam, and Fredericksburg. After the general was lifted from him the horse was turned loose and dashed into the Federal lines. The saddle being an ordinary one, free from the housing and trappings of an officer, he was not recognized as Jackson's horse, and was turned over to the cavalry. In the course of the summer of 1863 General Stuart captured a squad of cavalry, and among its horses one was recognized as Little Sorrel. In 1879 this horse was in the possession of Captain J. G. Morrison, formerly of Jackson's staff, and one of whose sisters Jackson had married (Manuscript letters from Captain Morrison and General D. H. Hill to Captain I. P. Gragg, U. S. Volunteers).

[2] *The Battle of Chancellorsville*, by A. C. Hamlin, p. 112; *So. Hist. Soc. Papers*, XXX, 113.

their firing. At this the Federal prisoners and the Confederate infantry sprang together to the safe side of the log works, where they
remained in a temporary informal truce, waiting for the artillery storm
to blow over. Williams' 1st brigade, attacked on its right and rear,
returned to its position in the division line, and there took ground to the
right so as to connect with Berry's left (Map 22).

About 9 p.m. the corps artillery of Couch's corps, numbering 12
pieces, and 3 pieces of Thomas' battery $\left(\frac{2}{1.\text{ II}}\right)$ under Thomas were placed
in position by Captain Comstock of the engineers "to the right of
the Plank Road and beyond the Chancellor House." [1] Who commanded
these pieces is not known. The group will be considered as Comstock's.
Together with Muhlenberg's 20 pieces and Hancock's 3, it made the
pieces in position about Chancellorsville number 38.

About this time Barlow's brigade commenced arriving at Hazel
Grove. The two divisions of the I Corps were still coming up from
United States Ford. A member of the 13 Mass. (3. 2. I) writes of this
march:

Tramp, tramp, all day until nearly 8 o'clock at night, when we filed down between the hills to the ford, which we crossed on pontoons, and then half a mile
further, when, tired and weary, we gladly received the order to halt for the
night. Our bivouac fires were scarcely lighted and preparations made for sleep
when the drums were sounded, followed by orders to "fall in!" and then
"*f-o-r-w-a-r-d, march!*" and at a good round pace we started for Chancellorsville, wondering what had happened to necessitate this sudden change in our
programme. Something serious, for mounted officers were hurrying about with
orders urging forward the troops. We had not long to wait, however, before
we got some idea of the disaster which had overtaken the army. Very soon we
saw men of the XI Corps hurrying to the rear, many of them panic-stricken
with fear. Orders were received to drive back to the front all men who were
not wounded. . . . "Halt, there! Where in hell are you going?" was frequently
heard, followed by "Turn back, you cowards." [2]

At 9 p.m. Hooker had the following dispatch sent to Butterfield and
to Sedgwick, under the impression that the latter was still on the north
side of the Rappahannock:

The major-general commanding directs that General Sedgwick cross the
Rappahannock at Fredericksburg on the receipt of this order, and at once take
up his line of march on the Chancellorsville road until you [he] connect[s] with
us, and he will attack and destroy any force he may fall in with on the road.
He will leave all his trains behind, except the pack-train of small ammunition,
and march to be in our vicinity at daylight. He will probably fall upon the rear
of the forces commanded by General Lee, and between us we will use him up.
Send word to General Gibbon to take possession of Fredericksburg. Be sure not

---

[1] *W. R.*, 39, pp. 726, 309.
[2] *Three Years in the Army,* by C. E. Davis, Jr., p. 203.

to fail. Deliver this by your swiftest messenger. Send word that it is **delivered** to General Sedgwick.

Testifying before the Committee on the Conduct of the War, Hooker said:

. . . I was of the opinion that if that portion of the army advanced on Lee's rear, sooner than allow his troops to remain between me and Sedgwick, Lee would take the road that Jackson had marched over on the morning of the 2d, and thus open for me a short road to Richmond, while the enemy, severed from his depot, would have to retire by way of Gordonsville. . . .[1]

Every disposition was made of our forces to hold our line as long as practicable, for the purpose of being in readiness to coöperate with the movement which had been ordered to be made on our left.[2]

. . . When I gave the order to General Sedgwick I expected that Lee would be whipped by manœuver. I supposed that he would be compelled to march off on the same line that Jackson had. He would have been thrown on the Culpeper and Gordonsville road, placing me 50 or 60 miles nearer Richmond than himself.[3]

To the question: "Did you expect General Sedgwick to form a junction with you?" he answered:

No, sir; but I expected that while he attacked Lee's rear, I would attack him in front, and compel him to move off toward Gordonsville.[4]

General Warren says:

By our leaving a sufficient force in front of the right wing of the enemy [under Lee] to hold our breastworks, the whole of the rest of our force was to be thrown upon his left at dawn of day, with every prospect of annihilating it.[5]

From all this evidence, it may be concluded:

1. That Hooker meant, if forced from his present line, to take up and hold his new or second one.

2. That if Hooker attacked at all, it was to be against the left flank of Lee's left wing, under Stuart; or against Lee's front; the latter in case Sedgwick should attack Lee.

3. That with Stoneman operating against Lee's communications with Richmond, Hooker was trying to force Lee to retreat upon Gordonsville.

The Federal telegraph line was extended to-day from the Red House near United States Ford to near Hooker's headquarters, but before it could be put in operation, wagons tearing down the road to the ford at a full gallop knocked down many of the poles. Trees in which the wires were placed were cut down to open a way for stalled wagons. The line was thus rendered unserviceable.

---

[1] *Rep. of Com.*, IV, 131.
[2] Testimony, *ib.*, 127. For memoranda of Hooker's see *W. R.*, 40, p. 359.
[3] *Rep. of Com.*, IV, 145.
[4] *Ib.*, 148.
[5] *W. R.*, 39, p. 201.

## 9:30 to 11 p.m. (Map 22)

Best's guns kept up a destructive fire with intermissions until 10 o'clock. Shots fired from some of the rifled pieces of Jackson's corps passed over the heads of the Federals and fell in rear of the Confederates beyond them. Reverberations of the conflict reached the Federal camps on the north side of the Rappahannock. Among the victims of the Federal gunnery was A. P. Hill, who had shortly before succeeded Jackson in command.

When the Federal artillery ceased firing Lane's prisoners were sent to the rear. Soon afterward General Pender informed Lane of the accident to Jackson and the wounding of Hill, and advised Lane not to attack. Hill sent Rodes information that he himself was disabled and that the command of the corps devolved upon Rodes,[1] who was next in rank.

This morning Averell, who was still at Rapidan Station, opposed by a Confederate rear-guard, received Hooker's order of the 1st inst. recalling him, and proceeded to execute it. He sent off the following report:

*En route* to United States Ford, May 2, 1863, 7:20 a.m.

*Captain Candler, A. D. C., etc.:*

Your dispatch of yesterday, stating that the major-general commanding did not understand what I was doing at Rapidan Station, was received at 7:05 a.m. to-day, and I have the honor to state in reply that I have been engaged with the cavalry of the enemy at that point and in destroying communications, and beg to inclose a copy of an order received from headquarters cavalry corps.[2]

Respectfully, your obedient servant,

WILLIAM W. AVERELL,

Brigadier-General.

About 10:30 p.m. he arrived at Ely's Ford with his command of 3400 sabers and 6 guns (Averell's division, Davis' brigade of Pleasonton's division, and Tidball's battery), and went into bivouac on the north side of the river, confronted on the south side by Stuart with his available cavalry and the 16 N. Ca. infantry, numbering together about 1000 men.[3] The squadron of the 6 N. Y. lately on picket at Ely's Ford had fallen back toward United States Ford. Stuart prepared to attack. In the meantime Rodes held a conference with the other division commanders (Colston and Heth) and decided that it would be unadvisable to attempt to carry out a night attack. One of the reasons was that the troops were considerably shaken by the fire of the Federal artillery. The "confusion and disorder" among them, especially on the Plank

[1] *W. R.*, 39, p. 942.

[2] Dated April 30, turning the enemy over to Averell (p. 228 *ante*).

[3] Von Borcke gives the strength of the infantry alone as about 1000 men (*Memoirs of the Confederate War*, II, 228).

Road, were such as to necessitate his placing guards across the road to stop stragglers.[1] Another was the apprehension of danger to his right and rear from the direction of Hazel Grove. But the one to which he doubtless gave the greatest weight was the general uneasiness and perhaps dismay and paralysis likely to result from the loss of Jackson. It was decided to attack in the morning. Jackson's idea of taking Chancellorsville in rear was not known to Rodes or his advisers. Moreover, Captain Boswell, the officer assigned to Hill to guide him to the rear of Chancellorsville, was killed or mortally wounded by the fire which wounded Jackson. Rodes made his disposition with a view to throwing his force directly upon Chancellorsville. His first line was to be formed of Hill's (now Heth's) division. About 9:45 p.m. Pender deployed his brigade $\left(\frac{2}{\text{I. II}}\right)$ on Lane's left, and about 11 p.m. Thomas deployed his $\left(\frac{6}{\text{I. II}}\right)$ on Pender's left. The other brigades were not yet up. But while Rodes was making these preparations, steps were being taken to give the corps another commander. About 10 p.m. Hill, who had remained in a litter near the line of battle, and had, as already stated, turned the command of the corps over to Rodes, sent to Ely's Ford for Stuart to come and take command of it. Rodes says that Stuart was sent for by Major Pendleton, Jackson's assistant adjutant-general.[2] Hill and R. E. Lee say that he was "sent for," but do not specify by whom.[3] Stuart says that the message was borne and delivered to him by Captain Adams of General Hill's staff.[4] A Southern writer says that Jackson upon the wounding of Hill "expressed a desire that General Stuart should direct the subsequent movements of his corps." But he adds that General Rodes had already dispatched a messenger to Stuart.[5] According to another Southern writer, Jackson was not instrumental in transferring the command of his corps to Stuart, but was in a measure responsible for it. He might have prevented it, but permitted it, and acquiesced in it.[6]

The brigadiers of General Jackson's corps, after determining to offer the temporary command to General Stuart, sent Captain Wilbourn [Jackson's signal officer] to General Lee to announce what had been done, and to request that he would himself come to that side and assume the direction of affairs![7]

Captain Wilbourn was accompanied on this errand by Captain Hotchkiss, one of Jackson's topographical engineer officers.

On the side of the Federals, Reynolds' two divisions continued moving up from United States Ford, catching more and more of the din and

[1] Rodes' report, W. R., 39, p. 942.
[2] Ib.
[3] Ib., 39, pp. 885, 799.
[4] Ib., 39, p. 887.

[5] Life of Stonewall Jackson, by A Virginian, p. 255.
[6] Life of Lieutenant-General T. J. Jackson, by Dabney, II, 474, 475.
[7] Ib., p. 478.

roar of the contest in front of Fairview. At last, not far from Chandler's, they halt and load their pieces, but only to unload them, and be off in obedience to another order:

Chancellorsville, Va., May 2, 1863, 9:45 p.m.

*General Reynolds:*

The orders for the position of your corps and Sykes' divisions were communicated to you under the impression that General Sykes was already on Hunting Run. This is not the case; hence the general desires that you will hold the right of the line extending along Hunting Run and resting on the Rapidan, and that General Sykes' right will rest on your left along the Ely's Ford and Chancellorsville road. The general desires that you make yourself particularly strong where this road crosses Hunting Run.

J. H. VAN ALEN,

Brigadier-General and Aide-de-Camp.

As their shuffling footfalls pass on down the moonlit road, the thickets are awakened with cheers and the strains of the grimly humorous Northern song: "John Brown's body lies a-mouldering in the grave."

About 10 p.m. Mott's brigade $\left(\frac{3}{2.\ \mathrm{III}}\right)$, except the 7 N. J., started from the United States Ford for Chancellorsville, and Sickles received through Colonel Hart permission to make his proposed attack. The colonel was sent to communicate with Williams and Berry, and returned at 11 with the report that those officers were ready.[1] This report appears to have been erroneous and unwarranted. General Berry, who was killed next day, left no report of his action or understanding in the matter; the report of Captain Poland, his chief of staff, contains no mention of it, nor is there any reference to it in the report of General Carr, who succeeded Berry, or in that of either brigade commander present.[2] General Williams says:

During the evening a staff officer of General Sickles' corps communicated to me the intention of attacking the enemy on his [the enemy's] right flank in the woods with at least one brigade of that corps [Sickles']. On account of the position of most of my line, at right angles to the position of General Sickles' troops on the left, and from the evident danger of confusion and mishap in the darkness of the night, I asked this officer to have the attack deferred until I could communicate with General Slocum, who was then at the headquarters of the army. The attack, however, began before I could see General Slocum. . . .[3]

General Ruger, commanding Williams' 3d brigade, heard unofficially that a night attack was talked of, but had no official notice regarding it.[4] The other brigade commanders and the corps commander General Slocum appear to have been unprepared for it.[5]

[1] *W. R.*, 39, p. 389.
[2] *Ib.*, 39, pp. 450, 445, 461, 462.
[3] *Ib.*, 39, p. 679.
[4] *Ib.*, 39, p. 709.
[5] *Ib.*, 39, pp. 686, 698, 670.

About 11 p.m. the XI Corps was reorganized in the vicinity of Chancellorsville.[1]  Regarding the artillery of this corps, the battery of the First Division (Dieckmann's) was lost.  The battery of the Second Division (Wiedrich's) lost two pieces; the remaining four were still at Chandler's, refitting and recuperating.  The battery of the Third Division (Dilger's) lost one piece; the remaining five pieces were in the line of artillery at Fairview.  Here, too, was one section of Hill's West Virginia battery of the reserve, or corps, artillery.[2]  The other two batteries and the remainder of Hill's battery were probably at Chandler's.

Regarding the situation about Fredericksburg, Van Alen wrote to Butterfield at 10 p.m.:

General Sedgwick's dispatch [of 8 p.m. to Butterfield] has been received.  It does not alter in any sense the character of the instructions sent General Sedgwick [at 9 p.m.].  They must be fully carried out to the very letter.  This is vitally important.  Gibbon must cross the river to-night.

### 11 p.m. to 12 p.m. (Map 23)

Sickles, having authority for his night attack, and, as he understood, assurance of coöperation from Williams and Berry, ordered Birney to advance.  Pursuant to this order, Birney's 2d and 3d brigades (Ward's and Hayman's) were formed one in rear of the other, or in two echelons.  In the first line of the first echelon were the six regiments of the 2d brigade, except the 20 Ind., which had not yet returned from its position south of the railroad cut.  In this echelon were also the 63 Pa. of the 1st brigade (Graham's) and the 17 Me. of the 3d.  These two regiments followed the 40 N. Y. of the 2d brigade, and the three regiments marched by the road and the open space on each side of it (the Vista) in column of companies at full distance.[3]  On their right the other regiments of the first echelon (2d brigade) formed a line of companies at deploying intervals, each company in column of fours.  The second echelon was about 100 yards in rear of the first, and consisted of the four remaining regiments of the 3d brigade, also in company columns of fours at deploying intervals.  The lines advanced by the light of the moon, with bayonets fixed and pieces uncapped, and with orders not to fire until the Plank Road and Slocum's Log Works were reached.[4]  There were no skirmishers or ground scouts in advance, and the enemy's position had not been located.  The center of the Federal mass rushed into the

[1] Schurz's report, *W. R.*, 39, p. 657.

[2] *Ib.*, 39, p. 249.

Warren says in his report: "To the credit of the artillery of the Eleventh Corps that came off the field, it went into battle on this line [Fairview] with the greatest alacrity" (*W. R.*, 39, p. 200).  It does not seem probable, however, that more than

Dilger's five and Hill's two pieces took position there.

[3] The average company was about 40 strong, or the equivalent of a platoon in the U. S. Army of to-day on a war footing, as contemplated in its present drill regulations.

[4] Birney's report, *W. R.*, 39, p. 409.

interval between the Federal and Confederate lines; the right struck the center of Williams' division $\left(\frac{1}{XII}\right)$; and the left, the right of Lane's brigade $\left(\frac{4}{I.\ II}\right)$. Receiving the cross-fire of friend and foe, the troops, despite the injunction to the contrary, opened fire, and dashed through the darkness at whatever might be in front of them. Those on the right charged a battery of the XII Corps before they discovered that they were attacking friends.[1] The three regiments in column of companies had to change, on reaching the end of the Vista, into a column of fours. The two foremost regiments were thrown into considerable disorder, but were reformed, and this portion of the line produced some consternation in Lane's brigade. But it was repulsed. The troops in the center, practically beating the air, reached the Plank Road, but could not hold it. Slocum says: "As I had not been informed that a night attack was contemplated by our forces, I supposed on hearing the firing that the enemy were advancing on Williams' division, and at once opened upon them with our artillery. General Williams also fired upon all lines that made their appearance in his front. I have no information as to the damage suffered by our troops from our own fire, but fear that our losses must have been severe."[2] But Best, who commanded the artillery, says: "So far as I can learn, and I am happy to record it, not one of our men was killed by our fire or indeed wounded." Ruger, whose brigade $\left(\frac{3}{I.\ XII}\right)$ was nearest Sickles' corps, reports that when the attack occurred he gave orders to his regimental commanders to keep their men steady, and not to fire unless fired into, as he "believed the attack was by Federal troops."[3] These orders were obeyed as well as could have been expected. A volley of bullets whistling over the heads of the 3 Wisc. of Ruger's brigade started that regiment partly to firing and partly to running, and the fleeing portion caused the 13 N. J., in its rear, to fire into it. The firing of the 3 Wisc. was kept up briskly for about half an hour.[4] Knipe's brigade, on Ruger's right, repulsed two advances of the enemy,[5] and Berry's line, one.[6] General Williams, describing the operation in a private letter, says:

A tremendous roll of infantry fire, mingled with yellings and shoutings, almost diabolical and infernal, opened the conflict on the side of Sickles' division. For some time my infantry and artillery kept silent, and in the intervals of the musketry I could distinctly hear the oaths and imprecations of the rebel officers, evidently having hard work to keep their men from stampeding. In the meantime Sickles' artillery opened fire over the heads of the infantry, and the din of arms and inhuman yellings and cursings redoubled. All at once Berry's division, across the road on our right, opened in heavy volleys, and Knipe, commanding my right brigade next to the road on the south, followed suit.

Best began to thunder with his thirty-odd pieces. In front, and on the flank,

[1] *W. R.*, 39, pp. 430, 437.    [3] *Ib.*, 39, p. 708.    [5] *Ib.*, 39, p. 687.
[2] *Ib.*, 39, p. 670.    [4] *Ib.*, 39, pp. 715, 720.    [6] *Ib.*, 39, p. 449.

shell and shot and bullets were poured into these woods, which were evidently crowded with rebel masses preparing for the morning attack. . . .

Human language can give no idea of such a scene—such an infernal and yet sublime combination of sound and flame and smoke, and dreadful yells of rage, of pain, of triumph, or of defiance.

As Sickles' two brigades fell back from the Plank Road, portions of them were thrown into confusion, and ran to the rear, apparently as much panic-stricken as any of Howard's men had been, having to be rallied at the point of the bayonet.[1]

The start and the return of these troops were witnessed by Barlow's brigade $\left(\frac{2}{2.\ XI}\right)$, which had formed up at Hazel Grove (Map 23). The brigade had lost all its knapsacks by leaving them in its camp near Dowdall's Tavern.

What sort of support Sickles expected from Berry's and Williams' lines can only be conjectured, but it is safe to say that it was something aggressive, and was not furnished. For this, Berry does not seem to have been at all responsible. Williams, in the absence of his corps commander, should have made all necessary arrangements for action by his division. But in spite of faults and mishaps, Sickles' night attack justified itself. The gun and three caissons which had been lost in the Vista were retaken and brought in. Sickles took up and held a more advanced position. He did not gain the Plank Road, and so could not establish the desired connection with the main force under Hooker. But he got where he could cut a road that would answer his purpose. His pickets formed connection on their right with those of the XII Corps.

We left Stuart preparing to attack Averell. Before his preparations were completed he received Hill's message to the effect that both Jackson and Hill had been wounded, and that the command of Jackson's corps devolved upon him. His infantry, the 16 N. Ca., having already deployed, he ordered it to fire three rounds into the enemy's camp, and then retire and join its brigade. Without awaiting the result of this fire, and leaving Fitzhugh Lee and his cavalry to guard the road from Ely's Ford, he hastened to assume the responsibility so unexpectedly devolved upon him.[2]

Across the Rapidan Averell's men had lighted fires, made coffee, and were enjoying their pipes, some had already lain down to sleep, when they were startled by a rattle of musketry and a rain of bullets. The horses stampeded, creating confusion among the men. The men rushed

[1] *The Three Years' Service of the 33d Mass. Infantry Regiment*, by A. B. Underwood, pp. 68, 69; *W. R.*, 39, p. 418.

[2] *Campaigns of Stuart's Cavalry*, by McClellan, p. 235. The cavalry remained in observation between the left of Stuart's infantry and Ely's Ford. The 16 N. Ca. rejoined its brigade $\left(\frac{2}{1.\ II}\right)$ at 3 a.m. (*W. R.*, 39, p. 937).

for their arms and returned the fire until it stopped.[1] It was necessary to wait for morning to try to recover the scattered horses.

Averell received the following communication from Butterfield, sent probably before Jackson's attack:

The major-general commanding has directed that you report to him in person with your entire command, save one regiment. This regiment you will direct, in accordance with the commanding general's instructions, to be employed in patrolling the country between the Aquia Railroad and Orange and Alexandria Railroad. This regiment must be kept well thrown out, for the purpose of giving timely notice of any raids, and destroying any guerilla parties that may invade that district. . . .

Similar instructions to the above were sent you when your command was at Rapidan Station. Up to this time they have not been complied with. The major-general commanding directs it to be done immediately.

Best's artillery and Berry's infantry covered themselves with hasty intrenchments. About midnight the 7 N. J. started from Humphreys' left and the 11 Mass. from Hancock's front to rejoin their respective brigades $\left(\frac{3.\ 1}{2.\ \text{III}}\right)$.[2]

Reynolds, with his two divisions $\left(\frac{2.\ 3}{1}\right)$, was toiling on, harking to the diapason of musketry and artillery on the Plank Road, and pondering on a sound as of infantry volleys coming for a short time from the direction of Ely's Ford. The noise finally subsided, and the tired soldiers of both armies lay down, looking up through the dark foliage at the moon and stars, and lulled by "the weird, plaintive notes of the whippoorwills, which were never known to sing so long and loud as they did that Saturday night at Chancellorsville."[3]

As it appeared that the Chancellor House would be under fire, all the wounded, except five or six severe cases which were likely to be injured by being moved, were sent to-day to the corps hospitals in the vicinity of Potomac Bridge.

In the course of the day the Federal right wing gained by reënforcement about 9000 men and 45 pieces of artillery. Estimating the losses at about 3000 men and 8 pieces of artillery, Hooker had at midnight under his immediate command about 76,000 men with 244 pieces of artillery. The Confederates received no reënforcements. They lost one battery of 4 pieces, sent away by General Lee, one regiment of infantry detached from McGowan's brigade, and about 1250 men killed, wounded, or missing. This left them at midnight, under Lee and Stuart, facing Hooker, about 43,000 men with 132 pieces of artillery.[4]

[1] *History of the 3 Pa. Cav.*, by Committee, pp. 232, 233.
[2] *W. R.*, 39, pp. 478, 452.    [3] *Slocum and his Men*, by Committee, p. 164.

| [4] | INFANTRY | CAVALRY | ARTILLERY | AGGREGATE |
|---|---|---|---|---|
| Federal . . . . . . | 70,207 | 1,175 | 4,841 | 76,223 |
| Confederate . . . . . | 38,470 | 1,933 | 2,640 | 43,043 |

Captured pieces are not counted.

# CHAPTER XXI

A T 5:05 a.m. Butterfield telegraphed to Hooker:

Dispatch dated 1:55 o'clock [a.m.] for removement of Reynolds and bridges just received 4:55 o'clock [a.m.]. . . . Copy has been delivered to Sedgwick.[1] It cannot be complied with as regards before daylight.

The bridges could hardly be taken up without attracting the attention of the enemy and indicating to him that he was free to move upon Chancellorsville, for taking up the bridges meant withdrawing all the Federal troops from the south side of the river. But the troops were needed at Chancellorsville. An attempt had, therefore, to be made to get them there, and at the same time to keep the enemy from going in that direction. Reynolds' Second and Third Divisions, on the north bank, were put in motion up the river, and his First Division, on the south bank, was ordered to recross and follow them. Newton's division $\left(\frac{3}{VI}\right)$ came down from Franklin's Crossing to cover these operations and make a show of force, but could not prevent the enemy's artillery from firing with effect at the division recrossing the river. Sedgwick at 8:55 a.m. sent the following report to Butterfield:

General Reynolds' movement will be a little delayed in consequence of the heavy shelling they have given him. His infantry have been in motion for some time, and the whole movement will be pushed.[2]

He received the following dispatch from Reynolds, sent at 11:05 a.m.:

The troops are all [back] across [the river] and moving up the road. The bridge is on this side and being taken apart. The enemy interfered in no way except with his artillery, one shot striking the bridge while the troops were crossing, delaying us until a new boat could be put in. I report that pontoon bridge will be piled on this side and left. There are no trains to haul them off.[3]

The bridge material was guarded by Wheaton's brigade $\left(\frac{3}{3. VI}\right)$ from Franklin's Crossing.[4]

Reynolds remained at the crossing below to superintend the with-

---

[1] Butterfield's dispatch transmitting the order was marked 5 a.m. (*W. R.*, 40, p. 361). Sedgwick received it at 5:25 a.m. (*ib.*, 39, p. 558), and Reynolds at 7 a.m. (*ib.*, 39, p. 254).

[2] *Ib.*, 107, p. 1034.     [3] *Ib.*

[4] For the story of a curiously erroneous description of this operation, the reader is referred to *Campaigns of the Army of the Potomac*, by William Swinton, p. 274, foot-note.

drawal of his First Division, and having done so, proceeded to overtake the head of his column. He was in doubt, it seems, as to whether he should direct his march with regard primarily to rapidity or to concealment. On this point he was advised by Butterfield as follows:

In regard to your line of march, the general indicated no route. Under present circumstances the shortest line would seem to be the one [for you to take], but you must consider whether the fire your troops would receive from the enemy's artillery while passing along the River road, the guns of the enemy in position, etc., would make it proper for you to diverge for a short time to avoid it; time is everything. . . .

The head of his column was already directed upon Hartwood Church to proceed thence to United States Ford. There was no attempt made to conceal the march, and it was observed, at least in part, by the enemy. Pendleton says that he and Barksdale united in a note to Early stating that the Federals "appeared massing troops toward Falmouth."[1] Barksdale says: "appearances indicated that the enemy were leaving their encampments on this side the river, and were marching to reënforce Hooker."[2] Early makes no reference to the movement or to the note mentioned by Pendleton. Reynolds was probably in the vicinity of Falmouth when he received from Butterfield the following dispatch:

The telegraph operator just reports that the rebels are evacuating Banks' Ford and moving toward the firing [Chancellorsville].[3] It may be that this ford will be opened at any time and the bridge[s] thrown over. Keep yourself in communication with me as far as possible, to be advised of this. It would seem to be proper, if an opportunity occurs, that you should cross there, and reënforce General Hooker, and so shorten the line. You had better send a staff officer ahead to Banks' Ford, if communication is opened there, and communicate with General Hooker.

Reynolds went to the ford himself, but finding that no bridge had been thrown, made no change in his line of march.

On the withdrawal of Reynolds' corps (I) the only Federal troops left on the Confederate side of the Rappahannock below Fredericksburg were Brooks' division $\left(\frac{4}{\text{I. VI}}\right)$ and Burnham's light division $\left(\frac{4}{\text{VI}}\right)$ with Williston's battery $\left(\frac{4}{\text{I. VI}}\right)$.

At Franklin's Crossing the enemy was much more threatening than he was at Reynolds'. The danger of recrossing the river and taking up the bridges in the presence of the enemy, together with the significance of such action to the enemy, determined Sedgwick to leave things as they were, until he could hear from headquarters. He wrote to Butterfield:

I have not dared to take up the bridge at Franklin's Crossing. Reynolds' bridge ought not to be taken away until after dark; it may cost the loss of many

---

[1] *W. R.*, 39, p. 811.      [2] *Ib.*, 39, p. 839.      [3] This report was without foundation.

boats. Will pontoon wagons be sent to take them at dusk? Shall the bridges at Franklin's Crossing be taken up at dark without further instructions? Please communicate [answer].

This message was delivered to Butterfield and repeated by him to Hooker at 10 a.m. In a dispatch of 2:30 p.m. Van Alen said to Butterfield: "The bridge[s] can be taken up at such time as General Sedgwick thinks best." Under this authority the three bridges were left, one piled on the bank of the river at Fitzhugh's Crossing, the other two spanning the river at Franklin's Crossing.

The telegraph line was extended this morning by a spur from England to the vicinity of Scott's Ford. The regiment and brigade ordered to Banks' Ford $\left(\frac{19}{1.\ 2.\ II}, \frac{2}{2.\ II}\right)$ arrived there at an early hour, also a signal party which established a flag and torch station to open communication with the troops on the south bank as they approached the ford. But only Confederate troops showed themselves. Wilcox with his brigade $\left(\frac{4}{1.\ I}\right)$ and two batteries $\left(\frac{2\ 4}{1.\ I}\right)$ arrived on the south bank about the same time as the Federals on the north bank. The Federal regiment left at Falmouth $\left(\frac{20}{3.\ 1.\ V}\right)$ took post probably between Banks' Ford and United States Ford to guard the telegraph line.[1]

Wilcox received an order from Lee to leave a small force to watch the ford, if in his judgment the enemy did not intend to cross there, and move up the Plank Road, reporting the fact to Lee. But the movements of Federal troops on the opposite side of the river determined him to remain at the ford.[2]

At 10:13 a.m. Butterfield wrote to Hooker inquiring whether General Gibbon was to move to-day with his division to Banks' Ford or to wait until the ford was uncovered. At 2:30 p.m. he received the reply:

. . . no orders have been sent for General Gibbon's division to move to Banks' Ford. The order was only for one brigade of his division.

Butterfield wrote further:

*To Gibbon, 10:20 a.m.*

Two bridges ready to be thrown across [at Banks' Ford] whenever the ford is uncovered. Stoneman's cavalry is supposed to be in the enemy's rear, on the line of his railroad.[3] . . .

*To Hooker, 2:10 p.m.*

. . . Supplies of Howard's, Slocum's, and Meade's infantry expire a.m. of Monday [May 4], unless replenished from the trains. All quiet here.

[1] *W. R.*, 39, p. 519; *Maine in the War for the Union*, by W. E. S. Whitman and C. H. True, p. 492.

[2] *W. R.*, 39, p. 855.

[3] For approximate position of Stoneman's cavalry see Map 22, sketch in upper right-hand corner.

The trains were still on the north side of the river, waiting for the opening of Banks' Ford and the crossings below. Reynolds' trains moved to the vicinity of Hamet, about 2½ miles from Hartwood Church.

When Lee decided upon Jackson's flank march it may have occurred to him that he might favor it by making a feint of withdrawing his whole army toward Richmond or Gordonsville or both. At any rate, there were movements among his troops to-day that had more or less the effect of such a stratagem. Back of Fredericksburg, as Early and Pendleton were standing about 11 a.m. on Lee's Hill, watching the movement of Reynolds' corps, the rear of which had recrossed the Rappahannock and marched about half an hour on the way to United States Ford, Colonel Chilton, Lee's chief of staff, came up and delivered verbal orders for one brigade and 8 or 10 pieces of artillery to be left at Fredericksburg as a guard,—the remainder of the infantry to march to join Lee, and the remainder of the artillery to be returned to the depot at Chesterfield. Early had for some time been deliberating as to whether, under his instructions of yesterday, he should withdraw two of his brigades and send them to reënforce Lee. He now had no discretion in the matter. His orders were peremptory. The defence of Fredericksburg and the heights back of it was committed to Hays' brigade $\left(\frac{4}{3.\,\mathrm{II}}\right)$ and a regiment of Barksdale's, and 15 pieces of artillery, numbering about 2500 men. The remainder of the infantry moved to the Plank Road and started for Chancellorsville; 22 pieces of artillery were put on the march for Chesterfield depot, and 11 others were withdrawn from position and held in readiness to follow. While the pieces were being withdrawn, a display of artillery horses and carriages was made as if bringing up instead of taking away guns. The withdrawal of the infantry in full view of the enemy could not be disguised. It may have been ascribed by the Federals to Stoneman's cavalry, which was thought to be capable by itself of determining Lee to retreat. Regarding this cavalry, there were plenty of rumors and conjectures, but no authoritative reports. In the hope of obtaining one, Butterfield telegraphed at 11:30 a.m. to Keyes at Yorktown:

Our cavalry ought yesterday to have been in rear of the enemy on the Richmond and Fredericksburg road, at its crossing of the Pamunkey, or in that vicinity, and have destroyed it. Use every possible means to get any information, and telegraph it to us, and oblige.

Things are very lively here now.

After the Confederate infantry, withdrawing from their line, had assembled on the Plank Road and advanced about a mile toward Fredericksburg, Early received a letter from Lee expressing apprehension that his wishes had been misunderstood, and stating that he had not intended to require a withdrawal, but to leave the question of such a movement, as he did in his order of yesterday, to Early's discretion,— to be decided "according to the force and movements of the enemy near Fredericksburg." By this time it was late in the afternoon. The column was immediately faced about and marched back toward the heights.

On the north side of the Rappahannock numerous dispatches were sent to report movements in rear of Fredericksburg:

*Gibbon to Butterfield, 3 p.m.*

Reports from my picket line on the right state that the rebels are withdrawing their pickets all along the river above the dam.

*Lowe to Butterfield, 4:12 p.m.*

The enemy have entirely withdrawn their advance lines with the exception of a small picket force.[1]

About 3 p.m. the flag and torch station at Seddon's was broken up, and the telegraph line drawn in from Reynolds' to Sedgwick's headquarters.

Hooker's dispatch of 4:10 p.m. ordering Sedgwick to cross the river, and reporting Sickles among the enemy's trains, reached Sedgwick at 6 p.m. Sedgwick supposed that Hooker when he sent this dispatch had a substantially correct idea of Sedgwick's position on the south side of the Rappahannock between Franklin's Crossing and Fitzhugh's Crossing. He was puzzled, therefore, at being directed to combine a movement on Richmond with the capture of Fredericksburg. He thought that possibly the pursuit which he was to make was not to be directed by the Bowling Green Road, as previous dispatches had indicated, but by the road to Gordonsville. He accordingly sent a request for information.

In reply he received the following dispatch, sent by Butterfield at 7:05 p.m.:

The major-general commanding directs you to pursue the enemy on the Bowling Green road.

He now knew that the capture of Fredericksburg, if expected of him at all, was subordinated to the pursuit of the enemy, and he believed that a march on Richmond would cause the evacuation of the heights and town of Fredericksburg. He therefore ordered his Second and Third Divisions to cross at his lower bridge, or near Mansfield, and had his First Division, Brooks', and one regiment of the light division $\left(\frac{31}{\text{O. 4. VI}}\right)$ push across the River Road, driving the enemy back behind the

[1] *W. R.*, 107, p. 1035.

railroad, and so open the way to the Bowling Green Road. At 8 p.m. he reported to Butterfield:

General Brooks $\left(\frac{1}{VI}\right)$ has taken the Bowling Green road in front of him; is still skirmishing, and will advance as long as he can see, and will then take position for the night.

Newton $\left(\frac{3}{VI}\right)$ is moving in the direction of Hamilton's crossing, and at daylight the entire corps will be in motion.

Sedgwick thought that the Bowling Green Road went through Hamilton's Crossing. By *Bowling Green road* he meant *River* road. When he wrote this dispatch Newton's division was in the act of crossing, about half of it having crossed. Howe's division was in rear of Newton's, waiting for a chance to cross. Sedgwick doubtless intended that, under cover of Brooks' division, the remainder of the corps should file off by the Bowling Green Road toward Richmond, and Brooks bring up the rear. Butterfield believed that an attack upon almost any point of Early's line ought to succeed, and that an attack upon some point of it was about to be made.[1]

According to the instructions sent by Van Alen at 10 p.m., Butterfield transmitted to Sedgwick at 10:10 p.m. the instructions contained in the dispatch of 9 p.m. to march through Fredericksburg on Chancellorsville. These reached Sedgwick at 11 p.m.; those of 9 p.m. sent directly to him had not come. If there had been a bridge at Fredericksburg in the possession of the Federals, he would not have hesitated to recross the river where he was and cross it again at Fredericksburg. But there being none, recrossing and crossing again would have been an all-night operation. It was light enough for the enemy to fire with effect upon a party attempting to lay a bridge. It would therefore be necessary, before a bridge could be laid, to drive the enemy away from the opposite bank. To do this from the south bank meant stealing a passage above or below the enemy, as was done at the first battle of Fredericksburg. Sedgwick decided not to recross, but to march by the south bank to Fredericksburg. His four divisions were to march in the following order: Newton$\left(\frac{3}{VI}\right)$, Burnham $\left(\frac{4}{VI}\right)$, Howe $\left(\frac{2}{VI}\right)$, Brooks $\left(\frac{1}{VI}\right)$; Burnham's division had been attached to Newton's.[2] At midnight, or

---

[1] He wrote:

*To Sedgwick, 8 p.m.:* "Their horses are poor. They cannot but be panic-stricken if you give them a sharp blow in the night. Your opportunities are grand beyond question. I know you will improve them." *Ib.*, *8:25 p.m.:* "Can't you take Fredericksburg to-night, so we can commence railroad and telegraph, and pontoon bridge, by daylight?"

*To Gibbon, 8:25 p.m.:* "Everything working well. Sickles is in the enemy's trains. Sedgwick is pursuing here. Be ready to spring with your full supplies whenever you receive the order. Expect it at any moment."

*To Haupt:* "Have all your material, men, and everything ready to move to-night with [construction] train to commence work in the morning, if required. I may telegraph you at any moment."

[2] W. R., 39, p. 563.

an hour after Sedgwick received his orders, the 1st brigade of Newton's division (Shaler's), which was to form the advance, having thrown out a line of skirmishers, drew out into column of march, and pushed on in the direction of Fredericksburg. Considering that his troops had to be roused and formed, and his orders issued and transmitted, the time spent in initiating the movement was perhaps not excessive. The 1st brigade was followed by the 3d (Wheaton's), and this by the 2d (Browne's). Butterfield, about when he received and transmitted the 9 p.m. dispatch from Hooker directing Sedgwick's movement, sent to Sedgwick a negro who knew the Plank Road to Chancellorsville, and wrote or telegraphed:

*To engineer officer:* To be ready to lay the pontoon bridge brought up from Fitzhugh's Crossing by midnight, place to be indicated.[1]

*To Gibbon* (received 11 p.m.): To get under way soon and cross the river to Fredericksburg to-night, taking care not to come into contact with Sedgwick.

*To Sedgwick:* To push on without delay, taking care not to come into contact with Gibbon; to seize citizens and put them to death if they failed to put him on the right road.

Captain Razderichin of Hooker's staff[2] was sent from Chancellorsville to deliver verbally and explain the instructions forwarded by telegraph. He instructed Sedgwick that he was to fall upon Lee's rear at daylight. At midnight Butterfield wrote to Sedgwick: "It seems to be of vital importance that you should fall upon Lee's rear with crushing force. . . . Give your advance to one who will do all that the urgency of the case requires." General Warren, Hooker's chief of topographical engineers, who knew much of the road which Sedgwick was to march over, left Hooker's headquarters about 10:30 p.m. to join Sedgwick and guide his column from Fredericksburg to Chancellorsville. He was charged, no doubt, too, with keeping Hooker posted as to the progress of Sedgwick's movement.

At 11 p.m. General Gibbon broke up his headquarters, and moved in person down to the river near the Lacy House, where the engineers were at work laying a pontoon bridge, but these were fired on by the enemy in Fredericksburg, and forced to suspend work.

It was night before the Confederates, withdrawn this forenoon from the heights of Fredericksburg, reached them on their return; at

---

[1] This bridge had been moved by teams to the Lacy House. Benham says in his report that it was moved on the 3d (*W. R.*, 39, pp. 214, 215), but this dispatch and the following one (*ib.*, 40, pp. 360, 368) seem to show that it was moved on the 2d, though not laid until the 3d. The two bridges at Franklin's Crossing were not moved until the 3d.

Butterfield thought that by midnight Sedgwick might be in possession of Fredericksburg.

[2] A volunteer aide-de-camp not appointed in orders (*The Campaign of Chancellorsville*, by T. A. Dodge, p. 169).

11 o'clock Early was still engaged in reëstablishing and adjusting his lines. Much of his artillery, it seems, went too far to be recalled; at any rate, only a portion of it was brought back.

The participation of the Federal War Department in the direction of operations led to the following correspondence:

### Halleck to Dix, 10 a.m.

. . . If, as is supposed, the mass of Longstreet's troops has joined Lee, the demonstration agreed upon [against West Point] should be immediately made.[1]

### Dix to Halleck

. . . deserters from Pickett's division state that they saw Pickett yesterday, and that no brigades have gone from Longstreet's command. . . . One of the deserters—a Texan—says that Hood was there [before Suffolk] yesterday. Jenkins' division is before Suffolk.[2]

The substance of the latter dispatch was communicated by Peck directly to Hooker.

Schenck telegraphed to Stanton:

. . . it is desirable I should know whether [whatever?] you can tell me of General Hooker. The night is full of rumors.

Stanton replied:

You may rest assured that General Hooker's operations are progressing successfully and in all respects as desired unless you are otherwise advised by this department.

Any mishap you will be promptly notified of, but, for obvious reasons, details of his movements and position cannot be given while in successful progress.

That the Confederate public was better posted than it should have been on the general situation of the Army of the Potomac may be inferred from the following communication:

Washington, D. C., May 2, 1863, 11 a.m.
*Major-General Hooker:*

We can not control intelligence in relation to your movements while your generals write letters giving details. A letter from General Van Alen [aide-decamp] to a person not connected with the War Department describes your position as intrenched at Chancellorsville—can't you give his sword something to do, so that he will have less time for the pen?

EDWIN M. STANTON.

### COMMENTS

Jackson's flank march was as brilliant an operation as Hooker's grand turn. His manœuver, like Hooker's, was little favored by secrecy

---

[1] *W. R.*, 26, p. 682.

[2] Jenkins commanded a brigade of French's division on the Blackwater.

or concealment, and owed its success particularly to being mistaken for a retreat.  The principal circumstances which led to this mistake were:

1. Statements of deserters the day before.

2. The direction of Jackson's march after he turned off the Furnace Road.

3. The expectation that Lee would retreat in consequence of the operation of Stoneman's cavalry.

4. The indications about Fredericksburg that the Confederates were retreating from there,—due to the misinterpretation of the verbal order sent by Lee to Early.

While the Confederate cavalry under Stuart was feeling the Federal lines and driving back their patrols and scouting parties, the Federal cavalry was for the greater part lying idle in camp.[1]  Just before Jackson rushed upon Howard's right a reconnoitering party of Howard's cavalry went into the woods in front of the 26 Wisc.  On returning about ten minutes later, it informed the officers of this regiment that "it was all right," and then went quietly to rest behind Hawkins' Farm.[2]

Jackson's attack, which was to give effect to his manœuver, terminated without having attained its object.  Lee's separate fractions, by their skilful and vigorous coöperation, had dealt Hooker a staggering blow, but not a finishing one.  They were now themselves in a most critical position.  The force which held them at bay might turn against either one and overpower it.  It was particularly to prevent such a situation that Jackson had issued his explicit orders that there should be no pause in the advance.  He had no doubt expected that before dark he would join hands with Lee and be thanking God with him for the complete rout of the Federal army.  He meant that the Federals should be given no time in which to recover from their first surprise and confusion.  In this he was disappointed by the halting of his lines as stated about 7:15 by General Rodes.

It is harder to find a commander who will require of troops all that they are capable of than to find one who will not call upon them for more than they are capable of; how rarely and imperfectly, too, are troops prepared by drill or field exercise for doing anything in a state of disorder!  Neither Rodes nor Colston asserts or implies that the troops were exhausted or incapable of another effort.  They account for their halting by the two conditions of *confusion* and *darkness*.[3]  If Jackson had been at the front, the advance would have continued.  What the effect would have been is a question on which historians differ.  With Map 21 and the foregoing account before him, the reader may be able to answer it to his satisfaction.

Had Jackson not been wounded and disabled, he might have carried

[1] The 8 Pa. took this occasion to change its organization from a three-battalion to a two-battalion regiment.

[2] *W. R.*, 39, p. 654.

[3] *Ib.*, 39, pp. 941, 1004.  See also Colston in *B. and L.*, III, 233.

out his purpose of resuming the advance, coupling with it a movement against Hooker's line of retreat. But he would not have gone far. A good part of his force would have been checked or paralyzed by the artillery at Fairview or the infantry in front of it and at Hazel Grove (Map 22). The remainder would have brought up, more or less of it in column, against the lines of Berry and Williams, and been at least repulsed. What was perhaps possible at 7:15, when Rodes brought the lines to a halt, was no longer feasible at 9, when Jackson was ready to resume the advance.

Had Sickles been supported as he should have been in his movement beyond the Furnace, he would have sent Jackson's column flying toward Richmond. He has been criticized for causing a gap in Hooker's line, which left the XI Corps without support. The officer responsible for this gap was the one who remained behind, and not the one who advanced; that was Howard and not Sickles.[1] That Sickles was not cut off from Hazel Grove was due to Colquitt's blunder.

It may be asked whether Sedgwick would not have done well to have departed further from his instructions than he did, to have attacked Early's right, and made a bee-line for Chancellorsville? He did not know the roads to Chancellorsville, and had no guide. He may have thought that he would find his way more easily, and would more readily procure a guide, going through Fredericksburg than going straight across country. He may have felt bound to go to Fredericksburg to open a crossing there for Gibbon. Would it not then have been better to roll up the enemy's line toward Fredericksburg than to risk a march by the flank along the front of his line to that point? Sedgwick probably asked himself such questions, but under the representations of the enemy's weakness and the urgings to make haste which came to him from Hooker and Butterfield, he thought himself bound to disregard any danger or difficulty there might be in an immediate and direct march upon Fredericksburg. The result was the singular spectacle of a body of troops practically on its enemy's flank moving to the enemy's front in order to attack him. But this apparent blunder was perhaps good luck. The center of the enemy's line was the most weakly manned, and probably, all things considered, the most vulnerable. The enemy expected, both from recent indications and from the course of the first battle of Fredericksburg, that the Federal attack would be made against his right. But there is no evidence that this expectation was known to the Federals.

[1] "General Hooker's plan of operations for the day, as I understood it, was to allow this movement of the enemy [Jackson] to develop itself until he [Lee] had divided his army, then to put my corps, well supported, on Lee's line of communication so as to prevent the junction of their forces, and then gather his army in hand, and fall upon the two wings of the enemy in detail and destroy them both" (Sickles, *Rep. of Com.*, IV, 6).

# CHAPTER XXII

## *Preparation* (Map 23, Plan 3)

STUART arrived from Ely's Ford about midnight.[1] The command of Jackson's troops was formally turned over to him by General Hill, though he himself had previously yielded it to General Rodes.[2] How this treatment of General Rodes was taken by that officer is best told in his own words:

> I yielded the command to General Stuart, not because I thought him entitled to it, belonging as he does to a different arm of the service, nor because I was unwilling to assume the responsibility of carrying on the attack, as I had already made the necessary arrangements and they remained unchanged, but because, from the manner in which I had been informed that he had been sent for, I inferred that General Jackson or General Hill had instructed Major Pendleton to place him in command, and for the still stronger reason that I feared that the information that the command had devolved on me, unknown except to my own immediate troops, would, in their shaken condition, be likely to increase the demoralization of the corps. General Stuart's name was well and very favorably known to the army, and would tend, I hoped, to reëstablish confidence. I yielded because I was satisfied the good of the service demanded it.[3]

Stuart heard of Sickles' "midnight" attack, and was informed that there was much confusion on the Confederate right owing to the fact that certain troops there had mistaken friends for the enemy and fired into them. Apprehending that the Federals would repeat their attack, and the Confederates their mistake, he decided to suspend operations until daylight.[4] He had no intimation from Jackson that the latter was aiming at the White House (Chandler's). No one under Jackson knew of his intention of gaining Hooker's rear except A. P. Hill, his second in command.[5] The Confederates, it seems, did not know by what troops they had been attacked on their right, or that Sickles had returned from the Furnace. They apprehended a hostile force being somewhere in that direction, but seemed not to suspect the proximity

---

[1] Stuart erroneously says 10 p.m. (*W. R.*, 39, p. 88). See McClellan's *Campaigns of Stuart's Cavalry*, pp. 235, 247, 248.

[2] *W. R.*, 39, pp. 887, 942.

[3] *Ib.*, 39, pp. 942, 943.

[4] *Ib.*, 39, p. 887.

[5] *Stonewall Jackson and the American Civil War*, by Lieutenant-Colonel Henderson, II, 560.

of so large a force as Sickles'. T. J. Leigh, aide-de-camp to General Ward, was taken prisoner between 12 and 1 a.m. Some of the enemy said to him in a very confident tone: "We got Dan Sickles' corps cut off, and we 'll capture the whole of them." [1]

All through the night Confederate troops came up from the rear and took their places in the new lines. About 12 p.m. McGowan $\left(\frac{3}{\text{I. II}}\right)$ formed on Lane's right, obliquely to Lane, so as to face Sickles. Brockenbrough, commanding Heth's brigade $\left(\frac{1}{\text{I. II}}\right)$, formed it in rear of Pender's and Lane's, in immediate support of the center. Archer's brigade $\left(\frac{5}{\text{I. II}}\right)$ broke up its bivouac about midnight, and took up the march for the front. In rear of A. P. Hill's (now Heth's) (1st) division, Colston's (4th) division formed an irregular second line.[2] Rodes' (2d) division was at Dowdall's Tavern, reformed or reforming.[3] At 3 a.m. the 16 N. Ca. rejoined its brigade $\left(\text{Pender's} \frac{2}{\text{I. I}}\right)$ from Ely's Ford. The cavalry, under Fitzhugh Lee, was in observation between Ely's Ford and the left of Stuart's infantry.

Stuart dispatched Major Pendleton, Jackson's assistant adjutant-general, to inform Jackson of the situation, obtain his views upon it, and learn his wishes. Jackson had been conveyed to the corps hospital at Wilderness Tavern. Chloroform having been administered to him, a round ball, used with the Springfield musket, was removed from his right hand, and his left arm amputated two inches below the shoulder. He was recovering from the effects of these operations when, about 3:30 a.m., Major Pendleton arrived at the hospital, and asked to see him. At first the surgeon declined to permit an interview, but the major urged that the safety of the army and the success of the cause might depend upon his seeing him, and he was permitted to do so. Pendleton briefly explained the condition of affairs, and asked what should be done. Jackson was at once interested, and asked, in his quick, rapid way, a number of questions. When they were answered he remained silent for a moment, evidently trying to concentrate his thoughts. He seemed to have succeeded, but it was only for a moment. Presently he answered very feebly and sadly: "I don't know, I can't tell; say to General Stuart he must do what he thinks best."

Stuart doubtless heard from Hill of Jackson's purpose of turning the position of Chancellorsville;[4] but, as previously stated, the officer who

---

[1] W. R., 118, pp. 624, 625.

[2] A. P. Hill in his report places his division in the second line (W. R., 39, p. 886). But see Heth's report (ib., p. 891), and Colston's (ib., pp. 1005, 1008).

[3] The 12 S. Ca. of McGowan's brigade and 23 Ga. of Colquitt's were absent,—the former guarding prisoners, the latter captured.

[4] Hunter McGuire, late medical director of Jackson's corps, says: ". . . after the battle, when still well enough to talk, he [Jackson] told me that he had intended, after breaking into Hooker's rear, to take and fortify a suitable position, cutting him off from the river and so hold him until, between himself and General Lee, the great Federal host should be broken to pieces.

was to have guided the column in this movement was killed or mortally wounded. Besides, he must have doubted the feasibility of this operation. Having decided not to act until morning, he could not expect to find the direct way to Hooker's rear unguarded. Moreover, a movement by his left would take him further away from Lee. He decided to consult Lee. In the meantime he ordered Colonel Alexander, his senior artillery officer, to occupy with artillery all points along the line bearing upon the Federal position. In this duty Alexander was engaged most of the night. He placed Marye's and Brunson's batteries of Walker's battalion (1. II), numbering 8 pieces, in two lines about 300 yards apart, on and near the Plank Road, the second line to fire over the first and the adjoining infantry. The other three batteries of Walker's battalion and Page's battery of Carter's battalion (2. II)—18 pieces—were posted or massed on or near roads leading to Hazel Grove, to support or accompany infantry advancing upon that point.[1] This left him a reserve of 96 pieces, without counting the 10 pieces of horse artillery which were sent to the left to coöperate with the cavalry under Fitzhugh Lee in guarding against an attack from Ely's Ford. The corps artillery was parked near Dowdall's Tavern.

The messengers from Jackson's corps, Captain Wilbourn and Captain Hotchkiss, making a wide detour to avoid Sickles' scouts and pickets, reached General Lee's headquarters between midnight and three o'clock this morning, and found the commander-in-chief resting upon a bed of straw. When he heard of General Jackson's misfortune, he exclaimed with emotion: "Thank God it is no worse! God be praised he is still alive!" Then he added: "Any victory is a dear one that deprives us of the services of Jackson, even for a short time." When reminded that General Rodes was now the senior officer in the corps, he said he was a gallant, efficient, and energetic officer. But he acquiesced in the selection of General Stuart to lead the troops on that day.[2] One of the officers remarked that he believed it was General Jackson's intention to have pressed the enemy on Sunday, had he been spared. General Lee said quietly: "These people shall be pressed to-day." He wrote to Stuart:

*3 a.m.* It is necessary that the glorious victory thus far achieved be prosecuted with the utmost vigor, and the enemy given no time to rally. As soon, therefore, as it is possible, they must be pressed so that we can unite the two wings of the army.

He had no fear. It was then that I heard him say: 'We sometimes fail to drive them from position, they always fail to drive us'" (*So. Hist. Soc. Papers*, XXV, 110). It would seem that Jackson never knew of Colquitt's blunder and the danger of an attack from the direction of Hazel Grove. Had he known the situation as it was, he would hardly have thought of directing his main force toward Hooker's communications. J. B. Jr.

[1] Alexander and Pegram differ in their reports as to the strength and disposition of this artillery (*W. R.*, 39, pp. 823, 938).

[2] *Life of Lieutenant-General T. J. Jackson*, by R. L. Dabney, II, 479.

Endeavor, therefore, to dispossess them of Chancellorsville, which will permit the union of the whole army.

I shall myself proceed to join you as soon as I can make arrangements on this side, but let nothing delay the completion of the plan of driving the enemy from his rear and from his position.

I shall give orders that every effort be made on this side at daylight to aid in the junction.

This dispatch of Lee's suggested, if it did not require, a movement to Hooker's rear. Stuart probably requested to be enlightened on this point. At any rate, at 3: 30 a.m. Lee wrote him again:

I repeat what I have said half an hour since. It is all-important that you still continue pressing to the right [toward me], turning, if possible, all the fortified points, in order that we can unite both wings of the army. Keep the troops well together, and press on, on the general plan, which is to work by the right wing, turning the positions of the enemy so as to drive him from Chancellorsville, which will again unite us. Everything will be done on this side to accomplish the same object. Try and keep the troops provisioned and together, and proceed vigorously.

When Lee wrote this dispatch he perhaps did not fully realize the difference of the present situation from that in which Jackson had been able to "press on," "turning the positions of the enemy." Instead of overlapping the enemy, the lines under Stuart were now overlapped themselves. At Hazel Grove, on Stuart's right, Sickles had Birney's and Whipple's divisions $\left(\frac{1.3}{\text{III}}\right)$, Barlow's brigade $\left(\frac{2}{2.\,\text{XI}}\right)$, 20 of the 22 guns with which Huntington and Martin opposed Jackson the evening before, and the 18 guns of Birney's division $\left(\frac{1}{\text{III}}\right)$—38 guns. On Stuart's left and front the Federal lines had been materially strengthened and extended. About 1 a.m. Reynolds arrived with his infantry $\left(\frac{2.3}{\text{I}}\right)$ on the ground which he was to occupy, and proceeded, with the guidance of Captain Candler and Captain Paine of Hooker's staff, to put it in line. This was accomplished between 3 and 4 a.m. His men had marched through heat and dust since the previous morning, carrying eight days' rations, about 23 miles, without a halt of more than twenty minutes. Some of them were too tired to eat. But numbers of them had to go on picket, and most of the remainder were put to work intrenching. One 4-gun battery $\left(\frac{3}{2.\,\text{I}}\right)$ arrived at the front about 2 a.m., but at 5 a.m. had not been put in position,[1] and no other battery of the corps had come up. To supply this deficiency, Atwell's battery of 6 guns $\left(\frac{1}{2.\,\text{XII}}\right)$ was taken from Muhlenberg and sent to report to General Reynolds; and the available artillery of the XI Corps, consisting of its three batteries of corps artillery and Wiedrich's battery (numbering some 20 pieces), reported also to Reynolds and was posted on his line.

[1] W. R., 39, p. 286.

Sykes' infantry (2. V), contracting its line, took position along the Ely's Ford Road, on the left of the I Corps, covering the road to United States Ford, its left near the junction of this road and the Ely's Ford Road. The infantry of Griffin's division $\left(\frac{1}{V}\right)$ formed on Sykes' left, connecting him with Chandler's (Map 23). At 5 a.m. Humphreys' infantry (3. V) was moving up toward Chandler's. Wadsworth's division $\left(\frac{1}{I}\right)$ reached United States Ford and commenced crossing about 3 a.m. At 5 a.m. its four brigades were taking up positions, the 2d and 4th in support of Sykes $\left(\frac{2}{V}\right)$, and the 1st and 3d in support of Robinson $\left(\frac{2}{I}\right)$. The battery which crossed the river with it $\left(\frac{3}{1.\,I}\right)$ joined the artillery park, it seems, at the Red House.

The infantry of the XI Corps formed on the ground vacated by that of the V. Schurz (3. XI) took the left, von Steinwehr (2. XI), with only Buschbeck's brigade, the center, and Devens (3. XI) the right.

Seeley with 4 guns of his battery $\left(\frac{4}{2.\,III}\right)$, together with Mott's brigade $\left(\frac{3}{2.\,III}\right)$, including the 7 N. J., arrived at the front about 2 a.m. Mott's brigade took position in rear of Williams' line on the left of the Plank Road. The battery was held in reserve near Chancellorsville. The 5 pieces of Dilger's battery (1. XI) and the 2 pieces of Hill's went from Best's line at Fairview to United States Ford. Of the 34 pieces of the II Corps at the front, 27 (including the 15 of Comstock's line) were sent by the corps commander, General Couch, pursuant to an order from Hooker, to the Red House near United States Ford.[1] The 4 N. Y., a 6-gun battery of Berry's division, was sent from Best's line by order of General Hooker to the ford, to be unhorsed and dismantled to refit other batteries of the division.[2] So, through the gray of the morning, 40 guns and caissons went rumbling past the sleeping camps, rocking and reeling, further and further away from the impending battle. Bailey's battery $\left(\frac{1}{1.\,XII}\right)$ of 4 guns, in Best's line, was broken up. Two pieces were sent to General Meade, and 2 to Muhlenberg. Hampton's battery $\left(\frac{2}{2.\,XII}\right)$ of 6 guns was sent from Muhlenberg to Best. This left Muhlenberg with 10 pieces and Best with 26, without counting the 2 pieces of Dimick's in line with the infantry.[3]

Chancellorsville was covered on the east, or the side of Fredericksburg, by Hancock's division $\left(\frac{1}{II}\right)$ and Carroll's (1st) brigade of French's

---

[1] W. R., 39, pp. 309, 360, 380; ib., 40, Memoranda, p. 359; B. and L., III, 167. The pieces of the II Corps left at the front were the 4 of Pettit's (1. 1. II) with Muhlenberg, and the 3 of Thomas' (2. 1. II) with Hancock.

[2] W. R., 39, pp. 406, 484, 485.

[3] Muhlenberg....Pettit $\left(\frac{1}{1.\,II}\right)$ 4 pieces, Lewis $\left(\frac{1}{3.\,III}\right)$ 2 pieces,
Bailey $\left(\frac{1}{1.\,XII}\right)$ 2 pieces, Crosby $\left(\frac{3}{1.\,XII}\right)$ 2 pieces.

Best.......... Winslow $\left(\frac{1}{2.\,III}\right)$ 6 pieces, McLean $\left(\frac{2}{2.\,III}\right)$ 6 pieces,
Dimick $\left(\frac{3}{2.\,III}\right)$ 4 pieces, Winegar $\left(\frac{2}{1.\,XII}\right)$ 6 pieces,
Crosby $\left(\frac{3}{1.\,XII}\right)$ 4 pieces.

division $\left(\frac{3}{\text{II}}\right)$, on the south by Geary's and part of Williams' divisions $\left(\frac{2.1}{\text{XII}}\right)$, and on the west by the remainder of Williams' division (except the 10th Maine battalion), Berry's division $\left(\frac{2}{\text{III}}\right)$, Hays' brigade $\left(\frac{2}{3.\text{II}}\right)$, and Mott's brigade $\left(\frac{3}{2.\text{III}}\right)$. The 10th Maine battalion (three companies) was placed on guard at the rear to prevent the escape of stragglers.[1]

Before dawn the 11 N. J., on the left of Berry's second line, was moved to the left, where it rested on the Plank Road. The 11 Mass., on arriving from in front of Hancock, was placed on the right of this regiment. The 16 Mass. was moved to the right in support of the 26 Pa. The 73 N. Y. was relieved by the 3 Md. of Slocum's corps, and placed in the second line. It was ordered to take position on the right of the division, and its commander says in his report that it did so. But the reports of other commanders indicate that it did not, and that it was practically lost.[2] It must, however, be reckoned as a part of Berry's available force. The 7 N. J. of Mott's brigade $\left(\frac{3}{2.\text{III}}\right)$ was detached to the left to complete the connection between Sickles and Slocum. The formation of the opposing forces on either side of the Plank Road about 5 a.m. is shown in Plan 3. The infantry, including Birney's and Whipple's at Hazel Grove, numbered in effective officers and men about 21,500. Stuart's infantry numbered about 26,500.[3] The new lines formed during the night and morning, extending from near Hazel Grove generally northward to the right of Reynolds' corps, had been or were being strengthened with rifle-pits or log works, except, it would seem, a portion of Williams' line.[4] These works were about 3 feet high, made for men to fire over kneeling, and were covered with abatis.

The chief obstacle in the way of Lee's junction with Stuart was the presence of Sickles with his command on the height of Hazel Grove. There were other considerations which made Hazel Grove an important objective to the Confederates and a valuable possession to the Federals. It was but little inferior to Fairview in elevation, and was an exceptional position from which to prepare an attack upon that point. It was in prolongation of the line formed by Geary's and a portion of Williams' divisions $\left(\frac{2.1}{\text{XII}}\right)$ south of Chancellorsville. In the hands of the enemy, it would command this front with an enfilade and reverse fire. The eastern face of the Federal front under Hancock and the western one under Berry and Williams may be regarded as refused flanks of the

---

[1] *History of the First- Tenth- Twenty-ninth Maine Regiment,* by Major J. M. Gould, pp. 345, 346.        [2] W. R., 39, pp. 468, 469.

[3]

| Federals | | Confederates | |
|---|---|---|---|
| Hays | 1,400 | Heth | 10,382 |
| Williams | 2,928 | Rodes | 8,460 |
| Sickles | 17,338 | Colston | 7,690 |
| Aggregate | 21,666 | Aggregate | 26,532 |

[4] *The 27 Indiana Vol. Infantry,* by a Member of Company C, p. 343.

southern face. Should either of these refused flanks be forced, or the artillery fire from Hazel Grove prove too much for the southern face, or an attack from the south succeed in breaking it, the defences of Chancellorsville would crumble away. To the Federals Hazel Grove afforded an opening by which to sally and roll up the separate wings of the enemy, cutting them both off from their lines of retreat.

In the dead of night an aide was posted to Hooker's headquarters to report the situation at Hazel Grove and request instructions, suggesting that the lines of the army be changed so as to take in this important position.[1] When the aide arrived General Hooker was asleep. General Van Alen, whom he found on duty and in charge of headquarters, would not wake him.[2] He directed the aide to wait. Toward morning Van Alen was prevailed upon to deliver the message, when Sickles was sent for at full speed.[3] Perhaps Hooker went out toward Hazel Grove to meet Sickles. At any rate, it seems that he went to Hazel Grove, and there in person at daylight ordered Sickles to evacuate Hazel Grove, and march his command by the most practicable route to Fairview, and occupy the new line of intrenchments along the skirt of the woods perpendicular to, and on either side of, the Plank Road, his artillery to occupy the field works on the crest of the hill in rear of the line of battle;[4] in other words, to reënforce the face occupied by part of the XII Corps, Berry's division $\left(\frac{2}{\mathrm{III}}\right)$, and Hays' brigade $\left(\frac{2}{3.\ \mathrm{III}}\right)$. Hooker then with his few attendants walked down from the hill and opening of Hazel Grove through a little gully into the field beyond and on toward Chancellorsville. He was silent and seemed very thoughtful.[5] No doubt he was thinking of Sedgwick, who was to be in Lee's rear by daylight. It was then daylight, and no sign or rumor of Sedgwick's approach.

### 5 to 7 a.m. (Maps 24, 25)

Sickles, on receiving his orders, sent out a regiment $\left(\frac{105}{1.\ 1.\ \mathrm{III}}\right)$ to make a road leading over a swamp on his right through Slocum's line to Fairview, and proceeded to withdraw his troops. At the head of his column went the artillery, except Huntington's battery of Whipple's division, which, with Graham's brigade, was to cover the movement. Next went Whipple's division, moving off by the left flank and rear; lastly, Bir-

[1] *The 27 Indiana*, by a Member of Company C, p. 343.

[2] *The Battles of Chancellorsville and Gettysburg*, by A. H. Nelson, p. 62; *Two Days of War*, by H. E. Tremain, p. 365.

[3] General Van Alen, without experience or qualification, had been allowed to assume the duties of acting chief of staff in the field, displacing a brilliant and capable officer—though much junior in rank—who had been Hooker's confidential aide-decamp in all his campaigns, Captain William L. Candler of Boston, Mass. *Two Days of War*, by H. E. Tremain, p. 365; *W. R.*, 40, p. 249.

[4] *W. R.*, 39, p. 390.

[5] *The Three Years' Service of the 33 Mass. Infantry Regiment*, by A. B. Underwood, p. 70.

ney's division followed Whipple's. Barlow with his brigade $\left(\frac{2}{2.\,XI}\right)$ left Sickles to join his corps.

Before daylight Perry's brigade $\left(\frac{3}{1.\,I}\right)$ on Anderson's right was put in motion toward the left and rear to clear the country, if necessary, of the enemy, and feel for Jackson's corps (Map 24). About daylight three rifled pieces of Jordan's battery (Alexander's battalion, I), and Posey's brigade $\left(\frac{2}{1.\,I}\right)$, marched by the west side of Scott's Run to the Furnace. Finding the country clear of the enemy, this force went on past the Furnace in advance of Perry's brigade toward Hazel Grove. At the same time Mahone's brigade $\left(\frac{1}{1.\,I}\right)$ on the right, its right resting on the Plank Road, gained ground to the front; and Wright's $\left(\frac{5}{1.\,I}\right)$, between Posey's and Mahone's, conformed roughly to the movement of Posey's, the whole line pivoting on Mahone's. These movements were through a dense wood and shrubbery, making regular alignments impossible, and progress in any formation slow and fatiguing. No two of these four brigades were in sight or hailing distance of each other. McLaws on the Turnpike felt Hancock's skirmish line with skirmishers.

At early dawn Stuart's men were under arms, but not ready to advance. Rodes was to issue rations, and in the meantime the lines on the right of the Plank Road were to be straightened out perpendicularly thereto.[1] About 5:30 Lane started to execute a partial wheel to the left that should bring his brigade into line with the troops on its left. McGowan and Archer moved out straight to their front. These movements were hardly started when Stuart ordered his whole first line to advance, and the second and third lines to follow. Accounting for this action, he says in his report: " . . . when, as a preliminary to an attack, I ordered the right of the first line to swing around and come perpendicular to the road, the order was misunderstood for an order to attack, and that part of the line became engaged."[2] Colonel Perrin, commanding McGowan's brigade, says: "I received orders to advance, which was done, . . . the plan of the advance not having been communicated to me."[3] Archer makes no mention of orders, but says: "about sunrise we moved forward to the attack."[4] It can hardly be doubted that McGowan and Archer understood the orders which they received, and carried them out, but that they were not the orders which Stuart meant them to receive, and which Lane did receive. It is probable that Stuart gave his orders to Lane in person, and sent them to McGowan and Archer verbally, by a courier or staff officer, who delivered them incorrectly. But if they had been delivered correctly, the result would have been the same. The lines could not be straightened out without a fight. Had the movement been delayed a little longer the Confederates might have occupied Hazel Grove without firing a

[1] W. R., 39, p. 887.  [3] Ib., 39, p. 907.   [4] Ib., 39, p. 925. The sun rose red and
[2] Ib.                                         clear; not a cloud was to be seen.

shot. About 6 a.m. the skirmishers along Stuart's whole front started forward, followed by the first line of battle (Heth's division, including Brockenbrough's brigade). None of the second line (Colston's) started forward at this time. While five of Heth's brigades were still working their way through damp thickets of black-jack and entanglements of swamp trees and vine, Archer's brigade on the right came upon and pressed Sickles' rear-guard at Hazel Grove. Graham's brigade, after firing a few volleys, which checked their advance to some extent, retired rapidly,—closely pursued, and subjected to a hot fire. Huntington's battery, with a regiment on each flank, covered this movement to the last moment, and brought up the rear, losing 3 pieces.

Sims' battery, 4 pieces of Jastram's,[1] and 4 of Seeley's took position in the line of guns at Fairview. These three batteries numbered 14 pieces, making the number of guns at Fairview 40.[2] One section of Lewis' battery was held in reserve at Chancellorsville, and Turnbull's and von Puttkammer's batteries (1. III, 3. III) at Chandler's; Huntington's 3 pieces (3. III) and a section of Jastram's were sent back to United States Ford. Pursuant to an order from Hooker, the two regiments of cavalry reported to him, and were formed as skirmishers "in rear of the line of battle to prevent any stragglers passing through."[3] They had plenty to do. Officers forgot their dignity and ran away as well as privates. Most of them were stopped unless wounded.[4] By Pleasonton's order Martin's battery of horse artillery took position behind Hooker's headquarters at Chancellorsville, and moved thence to United States Ford.

In the V Corps, Humphreys' infantry (3. V) formed in rear of Griffin's (1. V), with instructions to support Griffin, Sykes, or French. Wadsworth's division $\left(\frac{1}{I}\right)$ completed its deployment as support of Robinson's, Doubleday's, and Sykes' divisions $\left(\frac{2.3}{I}, \frac{2}{V}\right)$. At 6 a.m. Thompson's 4-gun battery $\left(\frac{3}{2.I}\right)$ was posted near the right of the line covering the road to Ely's Ford. At 7 a.m. it was joined by Hall's 6-gun battery $\left(\frac{1}{2.I}\right)$. About this time two of the batteries of the XI Corps (probably Jahn's, 2 N. Y., and de Beck's, K, 1 O.), hearing the sound of battle on their left, shamefully abandoned their positions and ran toward United States Ford.[5]

In front of Berry's and Williams' Log Works the woods had been cleared for a space varying in width from 50 to 100 yards. Up to that clearing an advancing enemy would be more or less concealed from

[1] *History of Battery E, 1 R. I. Light Artillery,* by George Lewis, p. 171.

[2] I have been unable to determine the exact location of all the batteries. They were not in one line, nor were they all on the height of Fairview. But for convenience, as they coöperated with the artillery posted there, I refer to the artillery at or near that position as one mass or line.

[3] *W. R.,* 39, p. 782.

[4] *History of Battery B, 1 N. J. Artillery,* by Michael Hanifen, p. 55.

[5] *W. R.,* 39, pp. 255, 276, 277, 279.

view, and the crossing of it was a matter of a few seconds, but this would bring him to the abatis, where he would be delayed. On this delay the defence relied for overwhelming the assailants with fire, pending which the proximity of the lines to each other would make the fire of the guns at Fairview dangerous to friend as well as to foe. The preponderance of the Federals in artillery could hardly be turned to account over its own infantry except by firing upon the enemy's supports and reserves. This was in a measure prevented and in a measure favored by the woods. It was prevented by the concealment which the woods afforded, and favored by the obstruction which these presented to the movement of troops. It was further favored by the large distances between the Confederate lines. While the Federal infantry was about 300 yards deep, the Confederate infantry had a depth of about 1300 yards.

When Archer's brigade, following up Sickles' rear-guard, arrived at the Farm-House at Hazel Grove, it halted a few minutes to reform its broken line, and before its formation was thoroughly restored, turned to the left, and proceeded to attack the section of Slocum's line under command of Colonel Ross (Plan 3). It was sharply repulsed. After a feeble attempt at another advance, it returned about 6:45 a.m. to Hazel Grove to await reënforcements.

The Confederates crowned the height of Hazel Grove with 31 pieces of artillery,[1] which enfiladed the southern front of the XII Corps, and made itself felt in Ruger's lines on the west front; at the same time it poured a heavy fire upon Fairview. On the Plank Road were about 30 pieces—of which say 20 were in action between Dowdall's Tavern and Slocum's old works, directing their fire upon Fairview. The Confederates thus had about 51 pieces in action to the 40 under Best, with the advantage of a converging fire opposed to a diverging one. On the other hand, the Federals had the advantage of command, or height, and their pieces were generally intrenched, while those of the Confederates had no cover but that afforded by the ground. For an artillery duel the advantage of position was with the Federals; for firing upon the enemy's infantry the advantage was, on the whole, with the Confederates.

By the time that Lane had completed his change of front he had orders to attack. Accordingly, without halting, he went on with the troops on his left toward the Federal line in his new front. This separated him from McGowan. The latter inclined to the left, separating himself from Archer, and overlapping Lane. But as he proceeded he again became separated from Lane. McGowan, Archer, and Lane were

---

[1] Crenshaw's, Davidson's, and McGraw's batteries ($\frac{11}{1}$), 12 pieces; Page's battery ($\frac{2}{1}$), 6 pieces; and Alexander's battalion (II) (except Eubank's and Rhett's batteries, 1 piece of Jordan's battery, and 2 pieces of Parker's), 13 pieces.

then advancing each without support on his right or left.[1] McGowan's brigade $\left(\frac{3}{\text{I. II}}\right)$ came upon the rear regiment (37 N. Y.) of Hayman's brigade $\left(\frac{3}{\text{I. III}}\right)$ as it was about to take up the march, attacked it in front and on the left flank before a proper fighting formation could be effected, and threw it into disorder, disabling many of its officers. Further on it encountered the 7 N. J. of Mott's brigade and Ruger's brigade $\left(\frac{3}{\text{I. XII}}\right)$, which had advanced. After a musketry duel of about half an hour's duration and an attack upon its right flank, McGowan's brigade was thrown back in disorder to Slocum's Log Works, closely followed by Ruger's brigade, and on the left of the latter by the 7 N. J. (Map 25).

Lane's brigade was supported by the right wing of Brockenbrough's (40 and 47 Va.), and Pender's by the left wing (22 and 55 Va.). Lane and Pender threw themselves upon the center of the Federal line on and near the Plank Road. Here, with its right resting on the road and forming the right of Slocum's line, was the 3d regiment of Maryland Volunteers, composed largely of new men. These green Marylanders could not stand the yell and rush of Lane's veteran North Carolinians, and gave way in unseemly haste. The foremost Confederates cleared the works and took a number of prisoners.[2] Others turned upon Dimick's section of artillery, which had fired volley after volley of canister into the enemy's ranks, and silenced it. The guns now try to save themselves. One is sent off before the enemy can seize it. The other falls temporarily into his hands. Dimick, struck in the foot, conceals his wound, but in a moment is disabled by a shot in the spine, from which he is to die in a couple of days.

Captain Poland, Berry's chief of staff, tries in vain to move forward the 115 Pa. of Mott's brigade $\left(\frac{3}{\text{2. III}}\right)$.[3] The fight abandoned by the 3 Md. and refused by the 115 Pa. is taken up by the 5 and 8 N. J.[4] Lane's brigade is checked, but stands its ground, firing defiantly and threateningly at its new opponents. The right wing of Brockenbrough's brigade, instead of reënforcing it, halted and remained well in rear of it. Lieutenant Sanderson of Dimick's battery (H, 1 U. S. Artillery) galloped up with a limber, and gallantly withdrew the remaining gun

---

[1] W. R., 39, pp. 902, 904, 907, 921.

[2] Lieutenant-Colonel G. P. Robinson, commanding the 3 Md., says in his report: "I was forced from my position by superior numbers, but retired in good order to the rear. . . . my regiment, being composed of a good many new men, stood the fire well" (W. R., 39, p. 703). Captain J. S. Poland, chief of staff of Berry's division, characterizes this movement in his report as a "premature and precipitate withdrawal"

(ib., p. 450). General Carr calls it "an injudicious retreat" (ib., p. 445); and General Sickles "a premature and hasty retirement" (ib., p. 392). Captain J. G. Langston, commanding the 8 N. J. Volunteers, says of the 3 Md.: ". . . at the first volley from the enemy [it] gave way in confusion and fell back" (ib., p. 480).

[3] Ib., 39, p. 450.

[4] Ib., 39, pp. 473, 475, 478, 445.

of Dimick's section amid a storm of musketry.[1]  Pender's right now moved upon the exposed flank of Berry's division, the extreme left of which was held by the 1 Mass., resting on the Plank Road, supported in rear by the 11 N. J.  Captain Poland, discovering the enemy crossing the Plank Road, ordered Colonel McAllister, commanding the latter regiment, to advance and force him back, "but unfortunately," says Poland, "my authority was questioned at an untimely moment."[2] Colonel McAllister sent his adjutant to his brigade commander, General Carr, to find out whether he should advance or remain in his position.[3]

Sickles' infantry brought in from Hazel Grove was placed generally in support of the artillery at Fairview.  Berdan, on the right of the Plank Road, a little in rear of the guns, detached four companies to the right of Berry's line and by 7 a.m. went with the remainder of his force to their support (Map 25).

Hayman's brigade $\left(\frac{3}{1.\,\text{III}}\right)$ had lost the greater part of the 37 N. Y. This regiment was thrown, as previously stated, into confusion by McGowan's brigade.  It was rallied about 100 strong in rear of Chancellorsville, and was marched thence without authority to the vicinity of United States Ford by its lieutenant-colonel, and did not rejoin the brigade until after the battle.[4]

Averell at Ely's Ford sent an officer with a party of 20 men to examine the enemy's position in his front.  He meant to throw his division upon the enemy's flank or rear, "if there was any chance of striking it."[5]  A considerable portion of his command had been out since daybreak, gathering up the horses that were scattered over adjoining fields by the fire of the 16 N. Ca. the night before.[6]

### 7 to 7:30 a.m. (Map 26)

Berry directed Captain J. B. Greenhalgh, his senior aide, to ride to General Hooker's headquarters, and inquire whether he was to continue to hold his position.  Greenhalgh galloped away.  What answer he got was never known to his chief in this world.  General Berry had a custom that is rare among division commanders, of giving his orders in person when it was possible to do so.  He told his staff to remain where they were, while he crossed the Plank Road to communicate with General Mott.  His officers remonstrated and offered to go in his stead, pointing out that the enemy's sharpshooters were posted in the trees

---

[1] W. R., 39, p. 450.  The two pieces were sent to the rear.

[2] Ib., 39, p. 450.    [3] Ib., 39, p. 457.

[4] Ib., 39, pp. 433, 442.

[5] Ib., 39, p. 1079.

[6] History of the 3 Pa. Cav., by Committee, pp. 232–234.  The horses were not marked for identification.  After the campaign each regiment was furnished with a branding-iron, with a number and letter upon it, and the horses were branded on the hoof of the right fore foot, 3 P. or 16 P., as the case might be (ib.).  This may be the origin of the present practice in our army, of branding cavalry horses on one hoof.

and sweeping the Plank Road with their unerring rifles. The general replied that he preferred to give the order in person, and started on his way. He crossed the Plank Road in safety. On reaching General Mott, he conversed with him a short time, and started to return. He had gained the Plank Road, and was recrossing it, having nearly reached the place where his staff officers were standing, when, from the trees in which the North Carolina sharpshooters were posted, came a wreath of smoke, followed by the sharp crack of a rifle. Major-General Hiram G. Berry had fought his last battle. The minie-ball struck him in the arm close to the shoulder, passed downward through his vitals, and lodged in his hip.[1] He fell in the center of the road. At 7:26 o'clock, with a group of sympathetic staff officers and comrades by his side, and the embattled lines of his division about him, he breathed his last at the age of thirty-eight, one of the most promising young generals that the Civil War had produced.

Captain Poland, on seeing Berry fall, sent an officer to General Carr, lately commanding the 1st brigade, with notice that he commanded the division. Carr at once ordered the 11 N. J., on the left of his second line, to support Dimick's section of artillery. The 1 Mass. fell back, carrying with it or closely followed by the 11 Mass., both more or less shaken and broken. These regiments reformed about half a mile from the front line, probably in rear of Hays' brigade and the artillery at Fairview. The 11 N. J. remained covering the right flank of Mott's brigade. The hostile irruption was stayed on the left of the Mountain Road, but not on the right. The remainder of Carr's line, consisting of the 2d brigade and the 26 Pa. and 16 Mass. of the 1st brigade, broke off regiment by regiment from the left as Pender and Thomas in succession threatened to crush its flank, and fell back in a northerly direction. In the meantime Knipe's brigade $\left(\frac{1}{1.\,XII}\right)$ was crippled by the departure of the 46 Pa. and portions of the 5 Conn. and 128 Pa.[2] Ward was sent with his brigade $\left(\frac{2}{1.\,III}\right)$ to form on the right of General Carr and act as his support. Not finding Carr, he reported to French, who placed him near Chandler's. Carr had gone to the left of the Plank Road, where he found Mott's brigade advancing upon the enemy in two lines. Lane's

---

[1] *Major-General Hiram G. Berry,* by Edward K. Gould, pp. 266, 267; and Captain Poland's report, *W. R.,* 39, p. 450.

[2] These troops were marched without orders or authority, by Lieutenant-Colonel Betts of the 5 Conn., to United States Ford, where they were taken charge of by General Patrick, Provost-Marshal-General, moved across the river, and placed on guard over prisoners (*W. R.,* 39, pp. 689, 696). The brigade was thus reduced to two weak regiments, the 5 Conn. and 128 Pa.

(*ib.,* 39, pp. 688, 690, 692, 695, 696). General Williams, the division commander, says that three regiments of this brigade, "soon after the fight began, moved to the breastworks." It would appear, however, from the reports of the brigade and regimental commanders, that the regiments that remained on the field, with the possible exception of the 5 Conn., were in reserve from beginning to end of the fight (*ib.,* 39, pp. 680, 681, 696). Every regiment of the brigade lost its commanding officer yesterday.

brigade had suffered from the artillery at Fairview: Struck now by Mott's brigade in front and threatened by the 123 N. Y. and Ruger's brigade in flank and rear, it wavers, breaks, and dissolves (Map 26). One regiment, the 28th, rallies and reforms in rear of Slocum's Log Works. The other four regiments go on to a safer distance. Brockenbrough's right wing goes back to Slocum's Log Works.

Ruger's brigade, which had followed the retreating remnants of McGowan's, Lane's, and Brockenbrough's brigades $\left(\frac{3. 4. 1}{1. II}\right)$, stood up in the open within a stone's throw of these troops, now on the safe side of Slocum's Log Works, and went to loading and firing as fast as they could. Colonel Colgrove of the 27 Ind. says: "I can safely say that I never witnessed on any other occasion so perfect a slaughter. Many of them made no attempt to get away, but threw down their arms and came into our lines. I think I am safe to say that we took from 150 to 200 prisoners, and sent them to the rear."[1]

A Confederate writer says: "The onslaught of the enemy was daring and obstinate. They pushed upon the very works, and one color-bearer even planted his flag upon them."[2] General McGowan was wounded standing upon the works. Colonel O. E. Edwards, who succeeded him, was soon wounded also, when Colonel D. H. Hamilton took command of the brigade.

### 7:30 to 8 a.m. (Map 27)

Pender's brigade $\left(\frac{2}{1. II}\right)$, followed by the left wing of Brockenbrough's $\left(\frac{1}{1. II}\right)$, penetrated to the line of Hays' brigade $\left(\frac{2}{1. III}\right)$, but there, with the exception of its left regiment, the 13 N. Ca., was brought to a halt by a combined fire of infantry and artillery. The 13 N. Ca. and Thomas' brigade $\left(\frac{6}{2. II}\right)$, less exposed, went on, struck the right of Hays' line, partially broke it, and threw the line back on its left (Map 27). General Hays was taken prisoner with all his staff except one officer. A fleeing color-bearer barely saves his color by tearing it from its staff.

Stuart's first line, numbering about 10,000 men, practically unsupported by artillery, had forced the Federal first line, manned by about 9000 infantry, intrenched, and materially supported by artillery. The five regiments to which the assailants were now reduced seemed about to sweep away the last infantry protection on the right of the Federal artillery, and break in a surging mass on the flank and rear of the guns at Fairview, when their victorious progress was arrested by opposition from two directions. In their front Franklin's brigade had come into line, with orders to repulse any attack and cover the artillery at all hazards. On their left and rear went up the savage roar of a Federal charge. About 7 o'clock this morning, General French, by authority of

---

[1] *W. R.*, 39, p. 712; *The 27 Indiana*, by a Member of Company C, pp. 334, 335.

[2] Caldwell, *History of McGowan's Brigade*, p. 81.

his corps commander, withdrew the 7 W. Va., 4 and 8 O., and 14 Ind. of Carroll's brigade $\left(\frac{1}{3.\ \text{II}}\right)$ from the rifle-pits on Hancock's left, leaving to hold this portion of the line the 24 and 28 N. J. of the same brigade. The four forementioned regiments he drew up in a single line of battle in a plain in rear of their former position, facing obliquely toward the Plank Road, which was concealed from him by the woods. On his right he formed Albright's brigade $\left(\frac{3}{3.\ \text{II}}\right)$ to support the left of a line of guns of the V Corps. Hooker came up and noticed these dispositions. Masses of troops were arriving from the front and forming in rear of French's lines. The situation seemed to have aroused Hooker's combativeness. At any rate, he dispatched a staff officer to French with an order for him to move forward with his division, "attack the enemy, and drive him through the woods."[1] It was about 7:30 when French received this message. In a moment his eager men were stripped to light fighting order, and striding in line of battle across the plain. At the verge of the surrounding woods, receiving some of the enemy's fire, they fired once, and dashed forward with a cheer. Thomas' men, threatened in flank and rear, turned and ran, receiving volley after volley, well put in by Carroll's Western regiments, the 14 Ind., 4 O., and 7 W. Va. Through some mistake the 8 O. remained behind supporting the artillery. French brought up on Carroll's right the 132 Pa. and 1 Del. of Albright's brigade $\left(\frac{3}{3.\ \text{II}}\right)$[2] and the last regiments of Carroll's (24 and 28 N. J.),[3] and drove Thomas' and Pender's brigades over Berry's Log Works back upon Slocum's Log Works and Jones' artillery (Map 28), making several hundred prisoners and releasing a battalion of the III Corps captured by the enemy. Brockenbrough's left wing, after a sturdy effort to breast the tide of Federal success, its left flank being turned, joined the retreat.

South of the Plank Road, Lane's and McGowan's brigades were still hugging the log works for protection against Ruger's line. In rear of them Williams' and Garnett's brigades of the second line halted within supporting distance, but rendered no active support.[4] By Ruger's advance south of the Plank Road and French's advance north of it, Stuart's first line was completely shattered. It devolved on the second line to hold the present position until the third line, which was coming up under Rodes, should warrant another general advance. The second

---

[1] W. R., 39, p. 363.

[2] The other regiment was, as previously stated, on guard duty at the corps hospital.

[3] The places of these regiments on Hancock's left were filled by troops falling back from other commands (W. R., 39, p. 363).

[4] The colonel of the 1 S. Ca., McGowan's brigade, says: ". . . we were reënforced,

or rather encumbered, by a portion of General Colston's command, for instead of pushing rapidly to the right and occupying the position, they took refuge (many of them) in rear of my line and annoyed my regiment very much by firing over their heads, in some instances wounding my men, and in one instance killing one of my best subalterns" (ib., 39, pp. 902, 903).

line was hard pressed on the right by Ruger's left; to meet this danger Paxton's brigade was ordered to the right of the Plank Road and directed upon Slocum's Log Works. At the same time Garnett's brigade was ordered to advance.[1] Rodes had directed his brigade commanders to push forward until the enemy was encountered, and "engage him vigorously, moving over friend and foe alike, if in the way."

On the extreme right of the third line Colquitt's brigade $\left(\frac{4}{2.\,\text{II}}\right)$ had been ordered to support Archer $\left(\frac{5}{1.\,\text{II}}\right)$. Being too late for that, it was ordered toward the left to relieve the pressure there. Doles' brigade $\left(\frac{2}{2.\,\text{II}}\right)$ broke into halves. One half, under Colonel Mercer, drifted to the right and was ordered by Stuart to support the artillery at Hazel Grove in conjunction with Archer's brigade. The other half moved on in touch with Ramseur, who, with the rest of Colston's line, reached the front about 8 a.m.

Paxton, with the Stonewall brigade $\left(\frac{1}{4.\,\text{II}}\right)$, came upon the lines cowering six and eight deep behind Slocum's Log Works.[2] "At this point," says Colonel Funk of the 5 Va., "we found a large number of men of whom fear had taken the most absolute possession. We endeavored to persuade them to go forward, but all we could say was of but little avail." The brigade prepared to proceed, if necessary, alone. As soon as the lines were formed, it crossed the works, passing in part over McGowan's men, and advanced, accompanied on its right by Garnett's brigade. "We will show you," said Colston's men to McGowan's, "how to clear away a Yankee line." Before they crossed the works, General Paxton and Colonel Garnett fell, mortally wounded. Gallantly do surviving officers cheer and lead on, and bravely are they followed. Major McKim of the division staff is killed, two other members are wounded. The line pushes on through a terrific fire to within 70 yards of Ruger's line, but only to break and rush back in disorder to where it started from. General Paxton is succeeded by Colonel Funk, and Colonel Garnett by Colonel Vandeventer.

Ruger, having been in action nearly three hours and having repulsed three separate assaults by fresh troops (Archer's, McGowan's, and Paxton's), had reported that his ammunition was nearly exhausted.

As no ammunition could be furnished him, Graham was sent with his brigade to relieve him.[3] By this time the two pieces of Lewis' battery had probably retired from Slocum's western front and taken position near Chancellorsville. About as Paxton advanced to the support of Lane and McGowan, J. M. Williams advanced to the support of Thomas and Pender.

Upon the death of Berry, the command of his division $\left(\frac{2}{\text{III}}\right)$ devolved, as already stated, upon General Carr, who assumed it at 7:30. But

---

[1] *W. R.*, 39, pp. 1005, 1006.        [2] *Ib.*, 39, p. 1006.        [3] *Ib.*, 39, pp. 409, 709.

General Revere, commanding the 2d brigade, thought that he succeeded to the command of the division, and before 8 o'clock he marched his own command, which went by the inspiring name of the "Excelsior Brigade," and part of the 1st brigade, the larger part of nine regiments, off the field, and proceeded with this force to the vicinity of United States Ford, on the ground that the division needed to be reorganized and supplied with ammunition and rations, and that it was necessary that it intercept stragglers.[1] The remainder of Carr's division reformed about 8 a.m. in rear of Franklin's brigade, and was there joined by Ward's brigade. Reynolds had still two batteries of his corps $\left(\frac{1.\ 3}{2.\ 1}\right)$ and two of the XI Corps, about 20 pieces, on his line. At 8 a.m. these pieces and the 6 of Atwell's battery $\left(\frac{1}{2.\ \text{XII}}\right)$ sent him from the XII Corps were in position; Stewart's, Leppien's, and Ransom's batteries $\left(\frac{3}{1.\ 1}, \frac{2.\ 4}{2.\ 1}\right)$, numbering 17 pieces, were moving up to report to him.

## 8 to 8: 15 a.m. (Map 28)

The artillery at Fairview could hold its own against any front attack of infantry. Its immediate danger was that the artillery at Hazel Grove would break down the bulwark of the XII Corps on its left or that a body of infantry would gain a lodgment on its right. Another danger, no less serious, was beginning to threaten it. The ammunition, both in the infantry and in the artillery, was running short. Repeated and urgent requests for a fresh supply sent to army headquarters met with no response, or with the impatient reply: "I can't make ammunition."[2] The artillery was being reduced to canister, which could not generally be fired over its own infantry, and would not reach the enemy's artillery. About 8 a.m. a limber and caisson exploded, mortally wounding the battery commander, Captain Hampton.

On the offensive, artillery is essentially an arm of preparation. It enables a commander to shake the enemy's infantry without exposing his own. Its principal function is the facilitation of the infantry attack. This requires that its fire be concentrated on the point determined upon for that attack. For the artillery to fire upon one point while the infantry attacks at another is a squandering of tactical power. That is

[1] W. R., 39, pp. 446, 452, 460, 462. General Revere was tried by a court-martial, of which General Hancock was president, on charges of misbehavior before the enemy and neglect of duty, preferred by General Sickles. He was found *not guilty* of both charges, but guilty of "conduct to the prejudice of good order and military discipline," and sentenced to dismissal. President Lincoln approved the sentence, but afterward revoked it, and accepted General Revere's resignation. He could not in justice have let it stand without ordering the trial of the other officers who had taken their commands to the rear without authority; and this he doubtless deemed on political grounds to be inexpedient. The proceedings in the case of General Revere, together with that officer's comments thereon, were published in the form of a pamphlet entitled "A Statement of the Case of Brigadier-General Joseph W. Revere."

[2] *History of the II Army Corps*, by F. A. Walker, p. 242.

about what is taking place between Hazel Grove and Chancellorsville. Stuart's artillery is for the greater part pounding away at the south face of the Federal salient, while his infantry is straining every nerve to break through the west face. Anderson's disjointed line of from one to two men to the running yard has driven in the Federal skirmishers. Its left, without connecting with Archer, has passed by the position of Hazel Grove and gone on toward the Federal salient. Its right is bracing itself for a general assault.

When Pender and Thomas were driven back, Hays withdrew to Chandler's, leaving Franklin and Berdan, supported by Ward and Carr, covering Best's right. Allabach's brigade of Meade's corps $\left(\frac{2}{3.\,V}\right)$ formed line of battle along the Ely's Ford Road, with some artillery between its two wings (Map 28).[1] Meagher's brigade $\left(\frac{2}{1.\,II}\right)$ arrived from the rear, and took position between Chandler's and Chancellorsville, facing west. Ward's brigade formed on its left.

About 8 a.m. Geary, pressed by Lee's infantry on his left and raked from right to left by Stuart's artillery at Hazel Grove, received an order to retire and form at right angle to his former line.[2] By 8:15 his 1st brigade (Candy's) had been withdrawn and ordered to take position as support in rear of Muhlenberg's line of guns.[3]

### 8:15 to 8:45 a.m. (Map 29)

Jones, with his artillery on the Plank Road, was startled by the swarms of men in butternut that came tearing out of the woods across the road a short distance in front of his guns. Judging from appearances that their pursuers were not far behind them, he ordered the pieces that were in the road to load with canister, and to fire "at the word." As soon as French's men appeared he gave the word. A peal hushing the din of musketry, a harsh fluttering and ripping in the thickets, and the hurrahing, onrushing men in blue were scurrying back. But having gained their distance, they halted and settled down to a lively musketry duel. Jones' batteries went forward on or near the Plank Road to occupy the log works, but found them occupied by Federals, and were compelled to retire to their former position. North of the Plank Road Stuart's third line passed through the second line, most of which refused to advance.[4] About this time Colonel O'Neal, commanding Rodes' 1st brigade, was wounded and succeeded by Colonel Hall. This brigade broke into two parts. One part, under Hall, followed by many men of Brockenbrough's, drifted to the right and encountered the fire of Mott's men and the 11 N. J. on their right. The other part, under

[1] *W. R.*, 39, pp. 508, 547, 555, 513, 1123, 1007.

[2] *Ib.*, 39, p. 731. The records do not show from whom this order was received.

[3] *Ib.*, 39, pp. 734, 735. Colonel Ross, commanding Williams' 2d brigade, was disabled about 8 a.m., when General Knipe assumed the command of this brigade in addition to that of his own.

[4] *Ib.*, 39, pp. 952, 956.

Colonel Pickens, halted at Berry's Log Works. Colquitt's brigade, on its way to the left, was ordered back to the right.

Ruger, being relieved by Graham, withdrew to Chancellorsville and thence to United States Ford. He probably carried with him the men of the 110 Pa., leaving on his left the 7 N. J. of Mott's brigade, and on his right the 123 N. Y. of Ross' brigade.

Ramseur $\left(\frac{5}{2.\text{II}}\right)$, after vainly urging the troops in Slocum's Log Works to advance, went with his brigade (except the 30 N. Ca., detached to support a battery at Hazel Grove) against the Federal infantry in his immediate front. This brought him against the right flank of Graham's brigade (Map 29).

Meanwhile Doles with half of his brigade should have supported Ramseur's right, but in marching through the dense wood he had lost connection with Ramseur. Passing by Graham's left, he went toward the line lately commanded by Colonel Ross and now commanded by General Knipe. The heavy fire of the enemy made it impossible for Williams to get pack-mules to the front. So the only way of supplying ammunition to his infantry was to bring up fresh troops. He sent to Slocum for reënforcements, but none came. Soon afterward he was assured by Sickles that troops of the III Corps had already been sent to replace his line.[1] Bowman had sent a couple of regiments to occupy the works on the right of Ross' line. Doles took the combined line in flank and rear, making many prisoners. The regiments lately under Ross, literally without ammunition,[2] broke away in some disorder from the right and joined Ruger's brigade. Doles went on past the left of Best's artillery toward Chancellorsville.

About 8:30 Colonel Sewell, commanding the 5 N. J. of Mott's brigade $\left(\frac{3}{2.\text{III}}\right)$, was informed that General Mott was wounded, which left him in command of the brigade. He rode to the right of the Plank Road in search of General Berry. General Knipe tried to bring a couple of regiments of Sewell's brigade up to the breastworks from which the 5 and 8 N. J. were firing upon Hall and Ramseur, but could not do so. He says: "Just at this moment a regiment of red-legged Zouaves [the 114 Pa. of Graham's brigade] came pell-mell from our left, with less than half their number of the enemy close at their heels. I endeavored to arrest the fugitives and induce them to defend themselves from behind the rifle-pits over which they had just retreated. This, however, I could not accomplish."[3]

[1] W. R., 39, p. 680.

[2] Ib.

[3] Ib., 39, pp. 687, 688. The commander of this regiment was tried by court-martial on the charge of misbehavior before the enemy, and honorably acquitted (ib., 39, p. 410). It seems that his regiment did its full duty. It was probably to this regiment that the Confederate writer Caldwell referred in describing the fight at Slocum's old works: "A regiment of Zouaves was particularly impetuous, but even they were forced to give way after frightful losses, and leave their disabled comrades behind them."

*8:45 to 9 a.m.* (Map 30)

The withdrawal of Ross' line uncovered the right of Geary's. Geary's right brigade (Greene's) gained ground to the right and threw back two regiments (60 and 102 N. Y.) for its protection on that side. Doles' half brigade, repulsed by these two regiments, veered to its left and went on, protected by the crest of the hill, past the left of the artillery at Fairview, in rear of Geary, to the rear of Sickles (Map 30). Coming under the fire at close range of some of the artillery about Chancellorsville and observing a large force of infantry moving toward its right, it faced about and hastened back to Slocum's Log Works.

Graham's right flank and then the rest of his brigade gave way. On reaching Williams' old line it made a stand, which compelled Ramseur to hold back nearly half of his brigade. The other half, however, drove before it the 5 and 8 N. J. and 123 N. Y., and occupied the intrenchments vacated by these troops on Graham's right (Map 30).

Sewell, on learning of Berry's death, returned to the left of the Plank Road. With the support on his right of the 11 N. J., he stood his ground in rear of the lost intrenchment until nearly 9 o'clock, when the pressure from Hall, reënforced or supported by Pender, Thomas, and others, together with a scarcity of ammunition, compelled him to retire to the rear of the artillery.

Knipe fell back to Chancellorsville, and thence to United States Ford, with what was left of his brigade and Ross'.

The artillery at Fairview had been gradually reduced by the withdrawal of batteries out of ammunition to 20 or 30 pieces. It was now generally free to use its canister, and so to take care of itself, in front, but was imperfectly protected by infantry on its flanks. Hall's men, accompanied on their left by five companies of Iverson's brigade under Colonel Christie, surge around the Federal right, and compel Dimick's guns north of the Plank Road to retire. Skirmishers and sharpshooters get within 100 yards of Winslow's battery on the new flank. They plant their colors by the side of the road, and commence picking off his horses. He loads with canister and blows them back. Again and again they return, to be as often repulsed. The artillery sustains a notable loss in the death of Lieutenant F. B. Crosby. This young officer was a type of the best American volunteer. After the battle of Bull Run he gave up the practice of law to accept a second lieutenancy in the 4 U. S. Artillery. He was assigned to Battery F, and was soon promoted for good conduct and ability to be first lieutenant. On the appointment of Captain Best, his commander, as chief of artillery of the XII Corps, Crosby became commander of the battery. He was pitting his guns against masses of infantry coming on with high, shrill rebel yells—red, blue-crossed battle-flags tossing here and there above them—when a bullet from the right of the battery, probably a sharpshooter's, found its billet in his breast. Five minutes later, at half-past 8 o'clock, his brief, honorable career was ended. His last words were: "Tell my parents that I die happy. Lord, forgive my sins."[1]

Colonel Morgan, Hancock's chief of artillery, received orders from Hooker to bring up all the batteries of the corps that had not been engaged. He had to go to United States Ford for them, as they had all been sent there pursuant to Hooker's order. Captain Randolph, chief of artillery of the III Corps, sent to Chandler's for von Puttkammer's 11 N. Y. Battery (3. III), but it could not be got to the front.[2] The 5 Me. battery (2. I), on its way to the I Corps, was diverted by General Hooker toward Chancellorsville. The following description of the situation was received at 8:45 a.m.:

United States Ford, May 3, 1863.

*General Butterfield,* Headquarters Camp Falmouth:

A most terrible bloody conflict has raged since daylight. Enemy in great force in our front and on the right, but at this moment we are repulsing him on all sides. Carnage is fearful. General Hooker is safe so far. Berry is killed. I return to the front, but will keep you advised when in my power. Our trains are all safe, and we shall be victorious. Our cavalry has not come up.

RUFUS INGALLS,
Chief Quartermaster.

This message was sent by telegraph. The line to United States Ford was put in working order during the night, and a station opened about a mile in rear of Chandler's at 8:30 a.m. The last sentence of the message probably refers to Stoneman, but may refer only to Averell, who, it will be remembered, had been under orders, since the evening of the 1st, to return immediately to United States Ford, and report in person at Hooker's headquarters. He was still at Ely's Ford and had not reported.

General French, having been hotly engaged for about an hour, discovered that the enemy was taking a position on his right to flank him. His corps commander, General Couch, being far away, and Hooker, as he thought, comparatively near, he sent a report of the fact to be delivered to Hooker. For some reason it was delivered to Meade, who directed Humphreys to order a brigade of his division to French's support. Humphreys designated Tyler's $(\frac{1}{3.\text{ V}})$.[3] About 9 a.m. this brigade went into action on French's right, causing Williams to extend his line and change front to the left (Map 30).

---

[1] *Memorial of Lieutenant Franklin Butler Crosby, 4 U. S. Artillery.*

[2] Captain Randolph says: "I regret to report the disgraceful conduct of Captain von Puttkammer. As the matter has come to the eye of the general commanding in another way, I will not enlarge upon it here" (*W. R.,* 39, pp. 406, 485).

[3] *Ib.,* 39, pp. 363, 508, 547, 550, 552, 553.

The 5 Me. Battery $\left(\frac{2}{2.\,1}\right)$ arrived at the front and went into action, dividing its fire between the enemy's advancing infantry and Jones' artillery. It suffered heavily from both. About 9 a.m., all its officers being killed or wounded, the command of the battery was given by Couch to Lieutenant Kirby, whose battery of corps artillery was in reserve.

Colquitt, on his way to Stuart's right, was again ordered to the left.

# CHAPTER XXIII

### *9 to 9:30 a.m.*  (Map 31)

WHILE Ramseur threatened Graham's right, Graham advanced his left against Ramseur's right. This movement was checked for a time by a charge made by the 30 N. Ca., as it came over to join Ramseur from Hazel Grove, but was favored later by a charge against Ramseur's right made by the 7 N. J. falling back on Graham's left. The latter regiment captured the colors and a large part of the *personnel,* including the colonel, of the 2 N. Ca. Colonel Francine, commanding the 7 N. J., now went to the rear, taking with him 400 men of the brigade and leaving 300 with Sewell. Francine had fought his regiment gallantly, and was under the impression that Sewell was wounded, and he in command of the brigade. He had been advised by his surgeon to retire from the field, having lost his voice, but had no excuse, it seems, for taking over half of the brigade with him.[1]

Vandeventer's brigade had not advanced. Ramseur went back and personally exhorted and ordered its officers and men to take position on his right, but in vain. He then reported to General Rodes that unless the enemy was driven from his right he would have to fall back. Rodes made repeated efforts to bring up troops from the rear, but none would move forward. About this time Stuart rode up to Funk's brigade and in his usual happy manner ordered a charge. The order was obeyed with the characteristic enthusiasm of the Stonewall brigade. This attack in front, with Ramseur's pressure on the right, started Graham's brigade, about 9:15, on a disorderly retreat to Chancellorsville. Hayman's brigade ($\frac{3}{1.\text{III}}$), led by Birney himself, covered Graham's movement with a charge, which broke the formation of Hayman's brigade, and caused its withdrawal to Chandler's. From there a portion of the 17 Me. under the regimental commander, Lieutenant-Colonel Merrill, marched without authority to the river to reform.[2] Carr's brigade withdrew to Chandler's.

The Stonewall brigade took position on Ramseur's right (Map 31),

---

[1] *W. R.,* 39, pp. 445, 474, 478.  [2] *Ib.,* 39, pp. 433, 436.

and Ramseur's brigade, with depleted ranks and empty cartridge-boxes, withdrew to the rear of Slocum's Log Works, leaving behind it the 30 N. Ca., which took position on Funk's right.

Geary was engaged in establishing his new line, perpendicular to his old one, when about 9 a.m. Hooker rode up to him and directed him to resume his original position and hold it at all hazards, promising to support him by an attack in force on Stuart's left flank. Candy's men put their caps on their bayonets, swung them over their heads, and rushed with wild cheers back to their old lines. Geary's other two brigades (Kane's and Greene's) had received orders to retire. While the 1st brigade returned to the left of the original line, the 3d brigade, on the right of the latter, left its intrenchments and went to the rear, covered by two of its regiments, the 60 and 102 N. Y. On the opposite side of the field Tyler was pushing back the Confederate left, and Colquitt moving to its support.

About 9 a.m. the remnant of Best's artillery was compelled, by the fire it was receiving from the enemy's infantry on its right, the imminent danger of similar treatment on its left, and a shortage of ammunition, to abandon the position of Fairview.[1] At the same time Pettit's battery was withdrawn from Muhlenberg's line to Chandler's,[2] and O'Donohue's 3 pieces from Hancock's line to Muhlenberg's, which left Muhlenberg 9 pieces. A number of Best's pieces went into action between Fairview and Chancellorsville, forming with other artillery a cordon of 24 pieces about Chancellorsville.[3]

Sickles sent to Hooker his senior aide, Major Tremain, with a most urgent appeal for support. Hooker, on the porch of the Chancellor House, saw him coming, and bent over the rail in his eagerness to hear Tremain's report, when a solid shot struck the pillar against which he had been leaning, splitting it from end to end, and throwing one half of it violently against his body and head. He fell senseless, and for a few moments was thought to be dying, but under the care of his medical director he soon revived sufficiently to show himself to his troops. By great force of will, and with the assistance of his staff, he mounted his horse and started to the rear. In the meantime a rumor that he was killed had spread through the ranks. Couch, the senior corps commander, had heard it, and hastened to the Chancellor House, thinking to himself: "If he is killed, what shall I do with this disjointed army?" He was overjoyed at coming upon Hooker mounted and with his staff also in their saddles. Briefly congratulating him, he went on with his duties at the front. Hooker was not again fit to exercise command dur-

---

[1] *W. R.*, 39, pp. 405, 675.

[2] *Ib.*, 39, p. 349. Pettit's battery was joined at Chandler's by the section detached yesterday to serve with the Irish brigade.

[3] Muhlenberg 9 pieces, Lewis 4 pieces, Jastram 2 pieces, Seeley 4 pieces, Kirby 5 pieces.

ing the campaign. Nearly all the rest of the day he suffered pains which deprived him of the use of his faculties. His right side was partially paralyzed, and was livid for weeks afterward.[1] But as he rode away from Chancellorsville he said nothing to Couch about relinquishing command, nor did he give him any orders. "This," says Couch, "was the last I saw of my commanding general in front."[2] It was the last time that Hooker was to be at the front in command of an army. On riding to the vicinity of Chandler's he had a violent return of pain. He became faint, and would have fallen from his horse had not his staff rushed to his side and helped him to the ground. A blanket was spread, and he was laid upon it. Some remedy was administered to him, and he again revived. Proceeding to mount, he was scarcely on his feet when a solid shot from Hazel Grove struck the blanket in the spot where he had been lying. Being assisted into the saddle, he rode in paroxysms of pain to a less exposed position near Chandler's. Probably about this time he received the following dispatches from Butterfield:

*6:45 a.m.*

Sedgwick's prospects here look unfavorable from reports. He is not out of Fredericksburg.

*7:05 a.m.*

Sedgwick still in front of Fredericksburg, as far as I can judge. Trains were running up all night to vicinity of Hamilton's Crossing. It may be that the enemy were reënforced.

Hooker telegraphed:

*To Sedgwick, 9:15 a.m.*

You will hurry up your column. The enemy's right flank now rests near the Plank road at Chancellorsville, all exposed. You will attack at once.

*To Butterfield*

Communicate with Sedgwick. We are driving the enemy and only need him to complete the job.

Would the forces at Chancellorsville preserve this opportunity for Sedgwick? Their defence could not last much longer. The ever-

---

[1] The paralysis with which during his later years his entire right side was affected was the result of this blow (*The Battle of Chancellorsville*, by S. P. Bates, pp. 126, 127; *Medical Recollections of the Army of the Potomac*, by Jonathan Letterman, p. 137).

Captain Candler, Hooker's aide-de-camp, wrote home on the 7th: "The blow which the General received seems to have knocked all the sense out of him. For the remainder of the day he was wandering, and was unable to get any ideas into his head excepting to remain in the extreme front and under as much fire as could be possibly found. In fact, at no time of trip after Sunday did he seem to be *compos mentis*" (Manuscript).

[2] *B. and L.*, III, 167.

aggressive Sickles wanted to make a counter-attack, but Couch refused to permit it. "It would not have been difficult," says Sickles, "to regain the lost ground with the bayonet, as I proposed to do, but the attempt was not deemed expedient (for the want of supports to hold it) by the senior officer present upon that part of the field, upon whom the direction of operations in front had devolved in the temporary absence of the general-in-chief."[1]

Meade had been hoping for orders or permission to strike a blow at Stuart's left. By his own order, Colonel Webb of his staff had ridden to the left of Stuart's line, and seen it moving forward across his front. He went with Webb to Hooker's tent, and urged that he and Reynolds be allowed to attack the enemy's left, and sweep him from the front of Couch, stating what Webb had seen. Reynolds also besought Hooker for permission to attack, but Hooker, renouncing what offensive designs he may have entertained, positively refused to allow it. He disapproved of Meade's action in sending Tyler's brigade $\left(\frac{1}{3. \text{ V}}\right)$ to the relief of French, and ordered him not to send any more troops forward.[2]

Pursuant to an order received soon after 9, Caldwell, commanding Hancock's 1st brigade, reported to Hooker northwest of Chandler's with the available troops of his brigade and Zook's brigade $\left(\frac{1. \text{ 3}}{1. \text{ II}}\right)$, from 500 to 600 men.[3] He deployed a company facing Chancellorsville to arrest the crowd of fugitives and stragglers going down the road. About 9:30, Hooker, who, in great physical pain, was on his horse, visiting his new lines, ordered him to advance across the open field and through the woods beyond.

### 9:30 to 10 a.m. (Maps 32, 33)

Hall's and Christie's men swarmed over the works of Fairview, but the troops on their left and rear gave way. French's infantry, with the support of Tyler's on its right, and of other infantry and the 5 Me. Battery on its left, forced the Confederates north of the Plank Road back in confusion upon such supports as they could find. In vain does Hall call upon the fugitives to come to his support. One of their officers tells him that "the d——d scoundrels" will not fight. All efforts to

[1] W. R., 39, p. 393.

[2] Ib., 39, p. 508; Life of General G. G. Meade, by R. M. Bache, pp. 272, 273; General Meade, by I. R. Pennypacker, pp. 122, 123; Papers of Mil. Hist. Soc. of Mass., III, 219 et seq. Warren says: "We expected that Jackson's force would assault us in the morning at Chancellorsville, and the intention was that General Sickles, with all his force, was to meet him at once, and the I Corps was also to attack him and envelop him, and if necessary more forces were to be drawn from the left of our line, leaving only force enough to hold Lee's forces in check" (Rep. of Com., IV, 46).

[3] This left in Hancock's main line about eight companies of the 140 Pa. of Caldwell's brigade and none of Zook's brigade.

rally them fail.[1]  The Federals crowd in on his flank and rear.  Franklin's brigade, lately forced back and thrown into some confusion by the enemy's impetuous advance, rallies, and, accompanied by a remnant of Sewell's brigade on its left, dashes back at the artillery position, recovers a number of cannon that the enemy had seized, and hurls him out of the works, taking the flags of Hall's 5 Ala. and 26 Ala. and many prisoners.  The Confederates reform along Berry's Log Works, with their left thrown back to confront Tyler (Map 32).

Caldwell went forward, accompanied on his left by Meagher with his Irish brigade.  As he did so, he met French falling back with Carroll's brigade.  Meagher had not gone far before he came under the fire of Jones' guns, which broke up his column.  He returned to his position as support of the 5 Me. Battery.[2]

Diagonally across the field the Stonewall brigade advanced, broke the Federal line, and captured a Federal flag.  While exulting in the possession  of this trophy and the commanding position of Fairview, from which the Federals could be seen fleeing toward Chancellorsville, Colonel Funk, commanding the brigade, observed a Federal column moving to gain his flank.  He sent an officer to urge forward all supports within reach.  The 26 Ala. of Hall's brigade made a charge, recovering its lost color.  Other regiments came up on his left, but retired before they had fired a volley.  Being thus unsupported and threatened on every side, his force reduced about 30 per cent. and without ammunition, he fell back to Williams' old works, *hors de combat* (Map 33).

The Federals, though they had lost some ground, had beaten back all the men that Stuart had sent against them.  But this they had only been able to do by throwing in fresh troops.  Against Stuart's 26,500 infantry they had had in action from first to last the following forces of the same arm:

| | |
|---|---:|
| Sickles, Williams, and Hays . . . . . . | 22,894 |
| Carroll and Albright . . . . . . . . | 2,276 |
| Tyler  . . . . . . . . . . . . . | 1,711 |
| Meagher  . . . . . . . . . . . . | 1,150 |
| Caldwell . . . . . . . . . . . . | 550 [3] |
| Total . . . . . . . . . | 28,581 |

About 9:45 a.m. Geary's 2d brigade followed the 3d toward Chancellorsville, leaving the 1st and two regiments of the 3d (60 and 102 N. Y.) at the front.  On the left of Geary, the Federals had not yielded an inch.  Hancock's advance line of skirmishers, or picket line, facing toward Fredericksburg, was still under the command of Colonel Nelson A.

---

[1] *W. R.*, 39, p. 954.          [2] *Ib.*, 39, pp. 1044, 410, 328, 327.
[3] *Ib.*, 39, pp. 313, 319.

Miles of the 61 N. Y. Volunteers. It consisted this morning of the following troops:

6 companies of the 148 Pa. of Caldwell's brigade $(\frac{1}{\text{I. II}})$. This was a new regiment, in its first fight. It was commanded by Colonel James A. Beaver, who was to become in after years the Governor of Pennsylvania.

66 N. Y. of Zook's brigade $(\frac{3}{\text{I. II}})$.

64 N. Y. of Brooke's brigade $(\frac{4}{\text{I. II}})$. This was John R. Brooke, later Governor-General of Cuba.

About 8:45 a.m. this force was increased by 250 men of the 145 Pa., also of Brooke's brigade. It was vigorously attacked on its left and pressed along its whole front by the troops under McLaws. Every effort to break it with infantry failed. The enemy then opened on it with artillery, but with no better result.[1] About 9:15 a.m. Colonel Miles was shot through the abdomen and taken, more dead than alive, from the field. As he was carried on a blanket into the Chancellor House he saw General Hooker, covered with dust, going out on the other side of the building.[2]

Hooker had been momentarily expecting to learn that Sedgwick had come up in Lee's rear.[3] Having no thought of attacking if Sedgwick did not attack, or of reënforcing the troops that he had in action, and unwilling to suffer further loss on an uncertainty as to Sedgwick's coöperation, he decided to abandon the field. About 9:30 a.m. one of his staff officers rode up to Couch and requested his presence with Hooker. Couch turned to Hancock, near by, told him to "take care of things," and rode to the rear. Near Chandler's he came upon three or four tents, around which, mostly dismounted, were a large number of staff officers. Meade was present, and perhaps other general officers. Hooker was lying in a tent by himself. Raising himself a little as Couch entered, he said: "Couch, I turn the command of the army over to you. You

---

[1] *W. R.*, 39, pp. 331, 332, 826, 830, 834.

[2] In his report after the battle the brigade commander paid this handsome tribute to the youthful colonel of the 61 N. Y. (Miles was then only twenty-four years old):

"I greatly regret to report that Colonel Miles was severely, if not mortally, wounded on Sunday morning (May 3) while handling the picket line with masterly ability. I have had occasion heretofore to mention the distinguished conduct of Colonel Miles in every battle in which the brigade has been engaged. His merits as a military man seem to me of the highest order. I know of no terms of praise too exaggerated to characterize his masterly ability. If ever a soldier earned promotion, Colonel Miles has done so. Providence should spare his life; and I earnestly recommend that he be promoted, and intrusted with a command commensurate with his abilities" (*W. R.*, 39, p. 321).

Colonel Miles was spared to distinguish himself in many another battle, and destined to attain, and for many years to fill, the highest and most honorable position in the army of the United States.

[3] *Rep. of Com.*, IV, 148. It is not clear how he expected to be informed of this event. With Lee between him and Sedgwick, he could hardly be reached by messenger, and with such a noise as there was about Chancellorsville, a firing by Sedgwick in Lee's rear might not have been heard and recognized in Hooker's line.

will withdraw it, and place it in the position designated on this map,"
as he pointed to a line traced on a field-sketch.[1] In his official report
(*W. R.*, 39, p. 307) Couch says:

I was called to the Chandler House briefly to take command of the army,
simply acting as executive officer to General Hooker in fulfilling his instructions,
which were to draw in the front, and make some new dispositions.[2]

As Couch came out of the tent he met Meade, who looked at him in-
quiringly as if at last to receive the long-wished-for order to "go in."
Colonel Davis, Hooker's assistant inspector-general, broke out: "We
shall have some fighting now." But alas! the words were hardly out of
his mouth when a messenger dashed off with orders for Sickles to retire
to the new line. Hancock received word that, after Sickles had retired,
he and Geary would be ordered to follow him.

Hancock faced his main line about, forming two sides of a square,
one fronting west toward Gordonsville, and one east toward Fredericksburg, about ¾ of a mile apart. Geary with a brigade and a half held
the approach from the south.

The two regiments of cavalry near Chancellorsville withdrew again
and formed a line of skirmishers in rear of Chandler's to intercept
stragglers.[3] The other regiment of cavalry, the 8 N. Y., had probably
by this time started, by Pleasonton's order, to cross the river at
United States Ford and do picket duty, as we shall see, on the north
side.

Colquitt came up on the Confederate left and pressed Tyler's right.
Tyler sent twice for ammunition, but got none. Reporting his situation to French, and asking him for orders, he was told to retire when
his ammunition was exhausted. This soon occurred, when he yielded
to Colquitt's increasing pressure, and fell back to Meade's line.

On the south Anderson's disjointed line had worked its way through
thickets and gullies and over slopes and ridges to the southern front of
the Federal position. As his men crowd over Geary's breastworks,
Lee rides up to Archer at Hazel Grove, and orders him to advance with
the fraction of Doles' brigade attached to his own, which he promptly
does. At the same time the troops under Stuart push forward on the
right and left of the Plank Road. Sickles' line is forced out of the
works of Fairview.[4] Anderson's men arrive on the height comparatively fresh and secure its possession. The Confederate infantry that
reached Fairview was soon followed by artillery from Hazel Grove,
which coöperated with Jones' artillery on the Plank Road and artillery
south of Chancellorsville under Hardaway. The Federal artillery at

---

[1] Couch, *B. and L.*, III, 169, 170.      [4] It does not appear that Sickles had
[2] *W. R.*. 39, p. 307.   [3] *Ib.*, 39, p. 782.   received Hooker's order to withdraw.

Chancellorsville was reduced by the withdrawal of Lewis' battery to 18 pieces, but these were full of fight. The 4 pieces of Seeley's and 2 of Jastram's were astride of the Plank Road, and near them was the section of Bailey's, withdrawn from Muhlenberg's line. Lieutenant Seeley loaded his guns with canister, and reserved his fire until the enemy was within 350 yards of his position, when he opened on them with terrible effect, making them break and take to the cover of the woods. He followed them with solid shot until the ammunition in his limbers was exhausted. The debris of his battery was then drawn from the field to the cheering of his men, and under the fire of three of the enemy's batteries. His loss in *personnel* was 1 officer and 45 men out of a total of 3 or 4 officers and 120 men.[1] The two pieces of Jastram's had lost so many horses that one piece had to be removed by hand and the other abandoned.

Projectiles from the edge of the Fairview plateau on the west, and McLaws' lines on the east, passed over both of Hancock's lines; others from the Plank Road, on the south, enfiladed them. At 10 a.m. Pettit's battery (II), brought back from Chandler's, was placed in position at Chancellorsville. Its fire was combined with that of Leppien's 5 pieces (2. I) and the 3 pieces of Thomas' battery $\left(\frac{1}{\text{II}}\right)$, making a fire of 14 pieces, which was directed upon the artillery enfilading Hancock's lines. Four additional pieces probably fired on the enemy's infantry. It was not long before one of Pettit's caissons exploded. But this did not divert the gunners from their furious work. Stripped of all superfluous clothing, like imps of darkness, jumping back and forth, and in and out, among their devilish implements, as these recoiled with dripping muzzles from their deadly blasts—swabbing and ramming, priming and sighting, bracing themselves with eager ears for the sharp signal *Fire*—they had no thought but for the fierce task of sending as much death and destruction as possible into the enemy's ranks. The wounded lying and reclining about the Chancellor House gloated over their execution.

After the loss of Huntington's 3 guns Hooker still had between United States Ford and Fairview 246 pieces of artillery. Lee had to oppose to them only 132. Yet the line of guns at Chancellorsville was greatly outnumbered by the artillery combating it,[2] and this was not its only disadvantage.

---

[1] In his report Lieutenant Seeley says that his loss in men was probably greater than that of any other battery in the war (*W. R.*, 39, p. 490).

[2] Colonel Carter gives the number of Confederate pieces in action at Fairview alone as "some twenty-five" (*ib.*, 39, p. 1000). According to Major Pegram, they consisted of McGraw's battery (4 pieces), Carter's battalion (20 pieces), and McIntosh's battalion (20 pieces), altogether 44 pieces (*ib.*, p. 938), to which should be added 3 pieces of Jordan's battery, making 47 pieces (*ib.*, pp. 821, 878). Hancock gives the distance of these pieces from his lines as about 900 yards (*ib.*, p. 313).

Colonel Morgan, chief of artillery of the II Corps, says with reference to the position of the Federal artillery:

I do not think it could have been held by any number of guns I could have placed in the contracted ground near the Chancellor House. The enemy's position was greatly superior, and our batteries were subjected to a direct, enfilading, and reverse fire.

Regarding the direction of the artillery fire he says:

I understand that some dissatisfaction has been expressed that the batteries near the Chancellor House did not disregard the artillery fire against them, and turn their attention to the rebel infantry in the woods near by, but from whose fire they [the batteries] were suffering little or nothing. My own judgment is that the only thing that could have enabled us to hold the ground was to have silenced the enemy's batteries.[1]

After Sickles, Geary was ordered to withdraw, and passed in an orderly column to the rear. This left Hancock holding the field alone, except for the remaining artillery. Despite the fact that the southern flanks of his lines, which had been covered by Geary, were entirely exposed and the enemy's infantry only a few hundred yards from them, the 18 pieces of artillery kept the enemy from advancing. It was still of great importance to gain time; to hold the enemy at bay until the roads leading to the rear should be cleared of troops, and the broken and disordered brigades should be reformed. This necessity pressed strongly upon General Couch, and nobly did he set himself to discharge the duty. His example was superb. Of slight stature, and usually of a simple and retiring demeanor, he became sublime as the passion of battle and the high-mounting sense of duty took complete possession of every power and faculty, every thought and feeling, every limb and nerve. His horse was killed; he was himself twice hit. Nobly, too, was he seconded by the chief of his First Division, General Hancock, whose horse was killed, and who was only able to secure a remount on an animal hardly large enough to allow the general's feet to clear the ground.[2]

Meade directed or authorized Captain Weed, his chief of artillery, to collect "all the available batteries," and place them "in position around Chandler's to cover the withdrawal of our troops and check the advance of the enemy." While this was being done, Hooker directed Colonel Wainwright, chief of artillery of the I Corps, in the absence of General Hunt, chief of artillery of the army, to take command of all the artillery.[3] It should be remembered that, under Hooker, Hunt had

[1] W. R., 39, p. 310.

[2] History of the II Army Corps, by F. A. Walker, p. 246.

[3] W. R., 39, pp. 253, 255, 381. Hunt is in error in stating (p. 250) that Wain-wright was placed in general command on the 2d. According to his own statements (pp. 252, 253) this action was not taken until the 3d.

been allowed only administrative control of the artillery. This appointment of an officer to command the artillery was a radical change of organization in the presence of the enemy. Wainwright could exercise but a nominal command over the greater part of it, scattered and intermixed as it was. Weed's line, when formed, extended about 500 yards on each side of a salient in front of Chandler's. It comprised 56 guns, 28 on the right, 24 on the left, and 4 in the angle.[1]

Hooker had probably received the following dispatch from Butterfield:

*8:45 a.m.* Sedgwick at 7:40 o'clock reports about making combined assault on their works: Gibbon on right; Newton center; Howe on left. If he fails, will try again.

This dispatch and no sound of firing in Lee's rear may have given Hooker to believe that Sedgwick was checked or advancing with unnecessary caution. At any rate, at 10 a.m. he repeated his order of 9:15 for Sedgwick to hurry up his column and attack at once.

### 10 a.m. to 1 p.m.

A little after 10 a.m. Hancock received an order from Couch to withdraw. He transmitted it to his artillery, and sent Colonel Morris, who had succeeded Miles in command of the pickets, the following order:

We will soon withdraw our lines. You will have your command ready to follow the movement without delay, and without further instructions, when you see our line falling back. In doing so, use the utmost care not to anticipate our movement, and the greatest judgment and coolness in withdrawing your line. Do not let it be done hurriedly or with confusion.[2]

Pettit's battery was finally silenced, having drawn upon itself the fire of about 18 of the enemy's pieces. It was about to be manned by infantry when orders came for the latter to retire. The battery was brought away by hand. Bailey's section soon followed it.

Under the destructive fire to which it was subjected the 5 Me. Battery was abandoned by its men with the single exception of Corporal James H. Lebroke. The horses had all been killed or wounded, and it looked as if the pieces were about as good as lost. But under the orders of their officers, men of the 116 Pa. of Meagher's brigade, and of the 140 and 53 Pa. of Zook's and Brooke's brigades, rushed at the guns, and, under a galling fire, pulled them by prolonges out of the stiff yellow clay in which they were stuck, and went with them back into the Federal lines. Kirby lay on the ground with a fractured thigh watching the operation. Men came to him to move him from the field. "No," he said; "take off that gun first." And the last of his five pieces was car-

---

[1] *W. R.*, 39, pp. 508, 512.          [2] *Ib.*, 39, p. 318.

ried to a place of safety.[1]  About 10:30 a.m. the artillery had retired, leaving Lieutenant O'Donohue of Thomas' battery in the hands of the enemy, mortally wounded.[2]

About 11 o'clock Allabach, by order of General Humphreys, threw back the two left regiments of his brigade $\left(\frac{2}{3.\,\mathrm{V}}\right)$ perpendicularly to the road to Chancellorsville, and advanced in line of battle with these regiments, under a severe fire of shell and canister, as far as the edge of the wood near Chancellorsville, to cover the final withdrawal.  During this movement, which was effected between 11 and 12—and for some time before—the Chancellor House was subjected to more or less of the enemy's artillery fire.  Missiles pierced the walls or stuck in the brickwork; shells exploded in the upper rooms, setting the building on fire; the chimneys were demolished, and their fragments rained down upon the wounded about the building.  All this time the women and children (including some slaves) of the Chancellor family, nineteen persons in all, were in the cellar.  The wounded were removed from in and around the building, men of both armies nobly assisting one another in this work.  The people in the cellar were rescued and cared for by Colonel Dickinson of Hooker's staff.  The only avenue of escape from the house was the road leading to United States Ford, which for some distance extended through an open field.  One by one those who had been at the house, and who were able to do so, including the women and children, ran the gauntlet of the fire by which this field was swept.  At the edge of the woods they crossed the line of Allabach's men, lying on the ground awaiting orders to advance.[3]  The dry leaves, abatis, and dead wood of the surrounding forest caught fire, and many of the poor cripples whom it was intended to save were forgotten or overlooked, and perished miserably in the flames.  Their cries and groans succeeded, as the fighting subsided, to the fiendish yells and savage shouts, the frightful fusillades and awful detonations, that during the last five hours had rent the air of this beautiful Sabbath morning.  "It was pitiful," says Caldwell, "to see the charred bodies hugging the trees, or with hands outstretched, as if to ward off the flames.  We saw around some of them little cleared circles where they had evidently raked away the dead leaves and sticks to stay the progress of the fire.

---

[1] *W. R.*, 39, pp. 310, 327, 328, 329, 314, 337, 347.  The last shot from this battery was fired by Corporal Lebroke alone.  Captain Leppien died on the 24th of May, on the amputation of his wounded leg, receiving his promotion to a lieutenant-colonelcy of volunteers on his death-bed (*Maine in the War for the Union,* by W. E. S. Whitman and C. H. True, p. 412).

Lieutenant Kirby died on the 28th.  On the 23d President Lincoln had sent him a general officer's commission in recognition of his brilliant abilities, undaunted courage, and faithful service (*History of the II Army Corps,* by F. A. Walker, pp. 245, 246).

[2] *W. R.*, 39, pp. 307, 309.

[3] *History of the First- Tenth- Twenty-ninth Maine Regiment,* by Major J. M. Gould, p. 347.

And there were ghastly wounds there—heads shot off or crushed, bodies and limbs torn and mangled, the work of shells. The smoke and stench were stifling.''[1]

The withdrawal was accomplished between 11 and noon. The two divisions of the II Corps, Hancock's on the right and French's on the left, connected on the right with the V Corps, to which Tyler's brigade $\left(\frac{1}{3.\ \text{V}}\right)$ had returned, and on the left with the XI Corps. Allabach's two regiments remained in their forward position. By an error in the direction given one of the retiring regiments (27 Conn.), the entire body present, consisting of eight companies and most if not all of the field officers, was marched into the enemy's lines and taken prisoner. The capture of this regiment is claimed by General Wright for his brigade $\left(\frac{5}{1.\ \text{I}}\right)$, and by Lieutenant-Colonel Holt, commanding the 10 Ga. of Semmes' brigade $\left(\frac{2}{2.\ \text{I}}\right)$, for his regiment. Wright gives the number of men captured, without counting officers, as from 600 to 700. Holt gives the aggregate (officers and men), including a fraction of another regiment, as 340. According to the Federal official returns, the killed, wounded, and missing in the regiment from the 1st to the 3d of May aggregated 291.[2] On the whole, the Federal withdrawal was as well executed as could have been reasonably expected.[3]

At 10 a.m., about as Hancock received the order to fall back, his chief of artillery started out from United States Ford with three batteries: Arnold's $\left(\frac{1}{2.\ \text{II}}\right)$, Kirby's $\left(\frac{1}{\text{II}}\right)$, and Cushing's $\left(\frac{2}{\text{II}}\right)$, numbering 18 pieces, intending to ''put in'' every gun that could be worked, but as the head of the column arrived at the Chandler House he met the corps falling back.

General Lee rode to the front of his pursuing lines.

His presence was the signal for one of those uncontrollable outbursts of enthusiasm which none can appreciate who have not witnessed them.

The fierce soldiers, with their faces blackened with the smoke of battle, the wounded, crawling with feeble limbs from the fury of the devouring flames, all seemed possessed of a common impulse. One long, unbroken cheer, in which the feeble cry of those who lay helpless on the earth blended with the strong voices of those who still fought, hailed the presence of the victorious chief.

His first care was for the wounded of both armies, and he was among the foremost at the burning mansion, where some of them lay. But at that moment, when the transports of his troops were drowning the roar of battle with acclamations, a note was brought to him from General Jackson.[4]

[1] Colonel Hamilton of the 1 S. Ca. refers to his bivouacking on the night of the 3d "in a swamp, with dead, dying, and roasted Yankees" (*W. R.*, 39, p. 905). See also *History of McGowan's Brigade*, by J. F. J. Caldwell, p. 84.

[2] *W. R.*, 39, pp. 869, 838, 176.

[3] *History of the II Army Corps*, by F. A. Walker, p. 247; Couch, *B. and L.*, III, 170; *Military Memoirs of a Confederate*, by E. F. Alexander, p. 349.

[4] Address by Colonel Charles Marshall, Soldiers' Memorial Meeting, Baltimore.

In the most unpretending words Jackson stated that he had been disabled by his wounds, and had accordingly transmitted his command to the general next in rank, A. P. Hill. He congratulated Lee upon the great victory which God had that day vouchsafed to his arms.[1] Lee at once dictated the following reply:

Headquarters, May 3, 1863.

GENERAL THOMAS J. JACKSON, Commanding Corps.

*General:* I have just received your note informing me that you were wounded. I can not express my regret at the occurrence. Could I have directed events, I should have chosen, for the good of the country, to be disabled in your stead. I congratulate you upon the victory, which is due to your skill and energy.

Very respectfully, your obedient servant,

R. E. LEE,

General.

The rattle and rumble of the conflict was distinctly heard at the hospital. Jackson made frequent inquiries about the fighting, and listened with interest to the accounts that he was able to obtain of the performances of particular officers or organizations. When Lee's message was read to him, he remarked: "General Lee is very kind, but he should give the praise to God." In the early part of the day he suffered in his right side, but in the evening the pain had left him, and he was thought to be doing well.

The falling back of the Federal lines brought the hospitals of the II and III Corps at Chandler's within reach of the enemy's shells, by which several men were killed or wounded. The hospitals were moved further to the rear, in part to near Compback's Mill and in part to the brick house near United States Ford. Great difficulty was experienced in removing the wounded for want of ambulances, plenty of which were parked on the north side of the river. While the surgeons were actively engaged in dressing wounds, extracting bullets, etc., the enemy's shells again found them out, causing a stampede among the wounded who were able to get away, and a considerable perturbation among the poor fellows who could not. The hospital at the brick house became the principal one of the army. A medical depot was established on the north side of the river, near where the ambulance corps was parked. Men able to walk were sent there afoot. As many as possible of these went on by ambulance to the hospitals on Potomac Creek.[2]

## COMMENTS

The chief advantage that the defensive has over the offensive is its superiority of fire. As an offset thereto the offensive has the privilege

---

[1] *Life of Lieutenant-General T. J. Jackson,* by R. L. Dabney, II, 488.

[2] Recollections of Medical Director Letterman, and Report of Medical Director Sim, III Corps.

of determining the time and the point of attack.  The defensive has to
be strong at every point, the offensive has to be strong at but one point.
A commander who attacks when and where his opponent expects him to
suffers all the disadvantages of the offensive without realizing its characteristic advantage.  Hooker expected an attack from the direction of
Jackson's advance on the 2d.  Stuart's attack was made in that direction and in what tacticians call the *parallel order*—in lines parallel to
those of the enemy—against the straight line formed by the western
face of the Federal angle.  His infantry was formed, as under Jackson,
in division lines, one in rear of another.

The Comte de Paris, commenting on the Confederate formation for
attack, or order of battle, on the 2d and 3d of May, says: "In giving
their whole front to a single division and forming the other divisions in
rear of it in successive lines, Jackson and then Stuart, as has been seen,
introduced at the first serious encounter a great complication into their
order of combat.  The brigades, the regiments of the different lines,
were soon mixed up, and each part of the front found itself under the
direction of chiefs whom chance brought to it, whilst the division commanders could not embrace all the movements of their commands.  This
inconvenience, so serious in marching in battle formation through a
thick wood, would have been avoided if each division had been formed
three lines deep, thus presenting but a small front to the enemy."[1]

A corps marching on a single road, as Jackson's was, can by the use
of division lines cover its front with a line of battle in less time than it
can by the formation of divisions with brigade front.  But there was not
the same justification for this formation to-day that there was yesterday, and there was more to be gained to-day by having the divisions
in compacter form.  Perhaps, however, the retention of the original
formation may be justified by the general weariness of the troops and
the importance of their resting before daylight.

As compared with brigade lines, the division lines, in rear of one
another, are less handy or mobile, but may compensate for the lack of
mobility by greater unity and strength.  This possible advantage was
forfeited by the distances between the lines.  Had the three lines attacked together, or supported each other closely, they would probably
have won the field with the first rush.  But about an hour elapsed after
the first line went into action before the second became generally engaged; and there was as long a period after this before the third line
came up to the first and second lines.  This was not "Stonewall Jackson's way."

The preparation by the artillery had, on account of the topography of
the battle-field, to be directed against the south face of the Federal
angle, held by Slocum.  This circumstance, the danger of a counter-

---

[1] *History of the Civil War in America*, by the Comte de Paris, V, 159, 160.

attack from the Federal right, Lee's injunction to Stuart to "work by the right wing," and the presentation of a salient in the Federal line opposite Hazel Grove, combined to demand a massing of Confederate infantry against Hazel Grove and Slocum's right or front, leaving, say, a division astride of the Plank Road as a feint. The first thing to do was to take Hazel Grove as a position for the artillery. After the artillery had fired a sufficient length of time to produce the desired effect, and not before, the mass of the infantry should have been thrown upon the point thus prepared for attack, and the rest launched as a diversion or demonstration against other points of the enemy's lines. Had this mode of operation or some approximation to it been adopted and carried out, the battle would have been decided in about half the time which it actually consumed; and hundreds of the devoted victims of its carnage and conflagration would have survived it.

It was not left to the writer of this history to be the first to criticize the operations of the II Corps under Stuart. The contemporary criticisms that they evoked stirred him to write to Lee on the 9th of May, soliciting a vindication of his generalship. Lee replied, with his characteristic tact:

. . . In the management of the difficult operations at Chancellorsville, which you so promptly undertook and creditably performed, I saw no errors to correct, nor has there been a fitting opportunity to commend your conduct. I prefer your acts to speak for themselves, nor does your character or reputation require bolstering up by out-of-place expression of my opinions.

A general who should think of adopting the tactics that Lee and Stuart employed at the battle of Chancellorsville should be sure, before doing so, that he realizes the conditions under which these tactics succeeded— the mental collapse of the enemy's commanding general, and a lack of ammunition. To try them on a commander in his senses, whose troops are supplied with ammunition, would be to court defeat and invite disaster, as was to be shown a couple of months later at the battle of Gettysburg. Lee and Stuart won the battle because:

1. Their bad tactics were opposed by worse tactics on the part of Hooker;

2. Hooker's careful provisions for the supply of ammunition[1] proved ineffective.

Referring to the ammunition supply, General Abner Doubleday says: "There should have been some staff officer specially charged with this

[1] "G. O. No. 30, March 25, 1863:

". . . Division ordnance officers will be held responsible that the following supply of ammunition is kept constantly on hand: For infantry, 140 rounds, with that in the cartridge-boxes; for cavalry, 100 rounds of carbine and 40 rounds pistol, with that in the cartridge-boxes; for artillery, 250 rounds, with that in the ammunition-chest. . . .

"The wagons containing the reserve ammunition will be under the control of the division ordnance officers. Ammunition-wagons will be distinguished by a horizon-

subject, but there seemed to be no one who could give orders in relation to it.'' [1]

This is a singular statement to be made by a historian who participated in the campaign as a division commander. Lieutenant Flagler, the chief ordnance officer of the army, was on the field, so were the ordnance officers of the several corps and divisions. These officers were specially charged with seeing in their respective spheres to the supplying of ammunition, and were competent to give orders regarding it. There was an abundance of ammunition between United States Ford and Chancellorsville. Why was it not forwarded and distributed to the troops? General Williams, as already stated, considered it impossible to get ammunition across the fire-swept zone in rear of the lines. But General Geary, commanding the other division of Slocum's corps, says, referring to his ordnance officer, Captain G. M. Elliott:

By dint of great exertion he had succeeded in bringing forward a large supply-train of ammunition, the arrival of which was most opportune. Many divisions besides our own had expended their entire stock, and could not have continued the action had it not been for the timely supply afforded by the foresight and energy of Captain Elliott, who prosecuted his duties under the hottest fire.[2]

### And Birney, commanding Sickles' First Division, says:

Lieut. C. H. Graves, Fortieth N. Y., the division ordnance officer, kept us well supplied with ammunition.[3]

In Hancock's division ammunition was brought to the firing-line by Captain H. H. Bingham, division judge-advocate, and by the pioneers of the 64 N. Y.[4] Hancock says nothing about lacking ammunition, nor does any of his brigade commanders, nor his corps commander. French says:

Lieut. W. E. Potter, ordnance officer, was indefatigable, brave, and zealous. His department was never better served.[5]

tal stripe, 6 inches wide, painted on each side of the cover; for artillery ammunition, red; for cavalry, yellow; for infantry, light blue. The wagons will also be distinctly marked with the number of the corps and division to which they belong and the kind and caliber of ammunition contained. The main depot for the army will be designated by a crimson flag marked 'Ordnance Depot, U. S. A.' Upon the march, or when the brigades are widely separated from each other, the wagons containing the reserve ammunition for each brigade may, at the discretion of the division commander, be turned over to the brigade quartermaster, who will draw his supplies from the division ordnance officer.

"In time of action, division ordnance officers will be careful to get explicit instructions from their division commanders in regard to the disposition to be made of their trains, and they will themselves remain with their trains to attend to the issue of ammunition. If it should be necessary during a prolonged action to replenish the trains, the division ordnance officers will be informed where the ammunition can be obtained. . . ." (*W. R.*, 40, pp. 156, 157).

[1] *Chancellorsville and Gettysburg*, p. 49.
[2] *W. R.*, 39, p. 732. See also Knap's report, *ib.*, p. 772.
[3] *Ib.*, 39, pp. 410, 411.
[4] *Ib.*, 39, pp. 317, 344, 349.
[5] *Ib.*, 39, p. 364.

In the V Corps, Tyler's brigade ran out of ammunition, but there was apparently a supply for it with the division. Referring to the ammunition for which Tyler had asked, Humphreys says: "This it would have been impracticable to distribute had it been with the brigade, and it would probably have fallen into the hands of the enemy, had it been sent, so close was the brigade pressed by them. General Tyler was therefore directed to withdraw when his ammunition was expended."[1]

The lack of ammunition was a serious factor in Tyler's brigade, in Berry's and possibly Whipple's divisions, in Williams' division, and in Best's line of guns. But it can hardly be considered as general.

Its two fundamental causes were:

1. Inefficiency on the part of certain ordnance officers.

2. Division of responsibility between the quartermaster's and ordnance departments in the handling of ammunition-trains.[2]

Stuart's attack made up in spirit for what it lacked in skill. His first line, without any material support from the second or third, forced Williams' intrenchments, and penetrated in part to his and Berry's last infantry reserves. This feat may be accepted as a signal proof of the valor of our Southern countrymen. But the battle was not decided by native valor. That quality did not count for as much as the artificial valor, the combination of steadiness and obedience, which come of military training and experience. On the part of the Confederates there was no such wholesale marching to the rear as there was on the part of the Federals. The Federal organizations that were taken off the field by their officers without authority must have numbered over 5000 men. The individual skulking probably came up to an equal number. This discreditable showing should be ascribed to inefficiency on the part of officers rather than to poltroonery among the men. Say what one will about the man behind the gun, he is about what his officers make him. Good officers will make good soldiers of almost any kind of men; the best men under poor officers will make but indifferent soldiers. On the *morale* of the opposing armies Hooker expressed himself as follows: "Our artillery had always been superior to that of the rebels, as was also our infantry, except in discipline, and that, for reasons not necessary to mention, never did equal Lee's army. With a rank and file vastly inferior to our own, intellectually and physically, that army has by discipline alone acquired a character for steadiness and efficiency unsurpassed, in my judgment, in ancient or modern times. We have not been able to rival it, nor has there been any near approximation to it in the other rebel armies."[3]

The fire of Pegram's artillery from Hazel Grove on Slocum's flank

[1] *W. R.*, 39, p. 547.

[2] This defect of administration was remedied by a reorganization of the artillery after the campaign (*Journal of the Mil. Service Inst. of the U. S.*, XIII, 302).

[3] *Rep. of Com.*, IV, 113.

and along his line was annoying and effective, but could not prove decisive. It was the giving way of Williams' division and Graham's brigade
on his right, under the pressure of Stuart's infantry, accompanied or
followed by the assaults of Anderson's infantry in his front, and not
the flanking and raking fire of Pegram's guns, trying as that was, that
forced Geary out of his intrenchments; and so with the Federal artillery, it was the loss of their infantry supports and the approach of the
enemy's infantry on their flanks, rather than the lack of ammunition or
the execution of the enemy's artillery, that made Best's guns retire
when they did. With the canister left in their chests they might have
held out some time longer against front attacks.

The position to which Hooker retreated, like the one he abandoned,
had the general form of an angle. The left side was occupied by the II
and XI Corps, the right by the I and V. The III Corps was formed at
the salient, or between the II and V Corps, except the portion under
General Revere, which did not return from United States Ford until
about 3 p.m. The XII Corps was assembled in a central position as a
general reserve. The artillery by 12 m. formed four groups or masses,
one of 26 pieces on the left under Captain Randol, chief of artillery of
Humphreys' division $\left(\frac{3}{V}\right)$; one of 48 pieces in the center under Weed,
chief of artillery of the V Corps; and two groups, one of 10 and one of
18 pieces, on the right, under Wainwright, chief of artillery of the I
Corps. Four pieces of Waterman's battery stood between Weed's and
Randol's masses, and 140 lay in reserve between Chandler's and United
States Ford (*Appendix 16*).

In the course of the day the Federal right wing was reënforced by
about 7700 men with 6 pieces of artillery and lost about 8400 men and 4
pieces of artillery, which left it numbering about 75,500 men with 246
pieces.

The Confederates lost about 8800 men, which reduced them to about
34,000 with 132 pieces of artillery.[1]

The Confederate forces formed on Chancellorsville as a center and
extending therefrom to the right and left in the general direction of the
Plank Road and Turnpike. Colston was in the center with two brigades
on each side of Chancellorsville; Rodes some distance to the left of
Colston. On Colston's right were Anderson's and McLaws' divisions,
and Heth's division was on the left of Rodes.

Lee had no idea that the Federals were in position to give battle. He
had mistaken Hooker's withdrawal to his new lines for a retreat. He
was about as badly deceived to-day by Hooker's retrograde movement

---

[1]

| | INFANTRY | CAVALRY | ARTILLERY | AGGREGATE |
|---|---|---|---|---|
| Federal . . . . | 69,618 | 1,175 | 4,714 | 75,507 |
| Confederate . . | 30,013 | 1,933 | 2,300 | 34,246 |

The losses were insignificant after 12 m.

as Hooker was yesterday by Jackson's manœuver. Regarding the campaign as decided, he announced its successful termination in the following bulletin:

Milford, May 3, 1863.

*President Davis:*

Yesterday General Jackson, with three of his divisions, penetrated to the rear of the enemy, and drove him from all his positions from the Wilderness to within 1 mile of Chancellorsville. He [the enemy] was engaged at the same time in front by two of Longstreet's divisions. This morning the battle was renewed. He was dislodged from all his positions around Chancellorsville, and driven back toward the Rappahannock, over which he is now retreating. Many prisoners were taken, and the enemy's loss in killed and wounded large.

We have again to thank Almighty God for a great victory. I regret to state that General Paxton was killed, General Jackson severely, and Generals Heth and A. P. Hill slightly wounded.

R. E. LEE,

General Commanding.

He was on the point, about 12:30 p.m., of throwing his 34,000 men against Hooker's 75,000, when his hand was stayed by the ominous tidings that the Federals had carried the heights of Fredericksburg and were advancing in his rear by the Plank Road. He rode up to McLaws, and directed him to march with Kershaw's brigade, and Manly's battery of his division, and Mahone's brigade of Anderson's, to meet the enemy. Learning afterward that an aide-de-camp of General Sedgwick's, captured near Banks' Ford, reported two corps under Sedgwick,[1] he directed McLaws to take the remainder of his division, which he did. Later Alexander with his battalion of artillery was ordered to McLaws' support.

Averell with his division crossed the Rapidan at Ely's Ford at 1 p.m., proceeded to United States Ford, and reported to Hooker, who placed him in support of Howard, on the left near the river. The following order was issued probably not long afterward, but was not received to-day:

Camp near ——, May 3, 1863.

Brigadier-General Pleasonton will assume command of the division of cavalry now held by Brigadier-General Averell. The latter will, on being relieved, report for orders to the Adjutant-General of the Army.

By command of Major-General HOOKER:

J. H. VAN ALEN,

Brigadier-General and Aide-de-Camp.

[P.S.] General Pleasonton will please deliver the above to General Averell.[2]

While Lee's detachments were marching toward Fredericksburg, and Averell with his cavalry toward United States Ford, was perhaps the

---

[1] *W. R.*, 39, pp. 801, 826, 844, 888.      [2] *Ib.*, 39, p. 1080.

most critical time for Lee during the campaign. It was a grand chance for Hooker to make a decisive counter-attack. Hooker had apparently forgotten President Lincoln's parting injunction: "In your next fight, put in all your men." The I Corps, except a small part of its artillery, and three fourths of the V Corps, had not been engaged at all. These forces with 8000 reliable men of the XI Corps, and the 3400 men under Averell, formed a fresh army about 35,000 strong, which if thrown, with the support that was available, against Stuart's tired men, should have wiped them off the field. But there was not the necessary leadership. Couch did not for a moment exercise supreme command. To do so he would have had to supersede Hooker against the latter's wishes, and without the sanction of the chief of staff or the chief medical officer. It does not appear that he had any information from either of these officers to the effect that Hooker was disabled. Hooker was not officially reported among the wounded. It looks as if the medical director failed to do his full duty toward freeing the army of its disqualified and incompetent commander.

On a rumor that Fitzhugh Lee had crossed the Upper Rappahannock, the 8 Pa. Cavalry was sent across the river, and for a number of hours picketed the road from Hartwood Church to Kelley's Ford. Not finding any enemy, it returned to United States Ford, where it bivouacked for the night.[1]

About nightfall the 17 Pa. Cavalry was sent by Pleasonton's order to the north side of the Rappahannock at United States Ford to supply itself with rations and forage. It did not return during the campaign. The 6 N. Y. was kept in rear of the line of battle. The squadron which had been picketing Ely's Ford, having been completely cut off from the army, fought its way through the enemy's skirmishers, and rejoined the regiment.

Before we go back to the VI Corps, which we left at midnight just taking up the march for Fredericksburg, let us run our eyes over the following reports of Hooker's recent operations and present prospects:

May 3, 1863.

*General Humphreys,*
    Commanding 3d Division [V Corps]:
    . . . Everything goes well. Sedgwick has Fredericksburg. Sickles is in Jackson's rear.

Very respectfully,
Your obedient servant,
FRED T. LOCKE,
Assistant Adjutant-General [V Corps].[2]

---

[1] *History of Pennsylvania Volunteers, 1861–1865,* by S. P. Bates, III, 165; *The Charge at Chancellorsville,* by P. Huey, p. 73.
[2] *W. R.,* 107, p. 1036.

Headquarters Army of the Potomac, May 3, 1863, 12:45 p.m.

*General Butterfield:*

I think we have had the most terrible battle ever witnessed on earth. I think our victory will be certain, but the general told me he would say nothing just yet to Washington, except that he is doing well. In an hour or two the matter will be a fixed fact. I believe the enemy is in flight now, but we are not sure.

RUFUS INGALLS,
Chief Quartermaster.

Headquarters Army of the Potomac, near Chancellorsville,
1:25 p.m., May 3, 1863; by orderly to U. S. Ford, thence
by telegraph 3:30 p.m.   Received at 4 p.m.[1]

*His Excellency A. Lincoln*, President United States:

We have had a desperate fight yesterday and to-day which has resulted in no success to us, having lost a position of two lines, which had been selected for our defence. It is now 1:30 o'clock, and there is still some firing of artillery. We may have another turn at it this p.m. I do not despair of success. If Sedgwick could have gotten up, there could have been but one result. As it is impossible for me to know the exact position of Sedgwick as regards his ability to advance and take part in the engagement, I can not tell when it will end. We will endeavor to do our best. My troops are in good spirits. We have fought desperately to-day. No general ever commanded a more devoted army.

JOSEPH HOOKER,
Major-General.

[1] *Rep. of Com.*, IV, 225.

# CHAPTER XXIV

MAY 3 . . . SECOND BATTLE OF FREDERICKSBURG.  ENGAGEMENT AT
SALEM CHURCH

## *Battle of Fredericksburg* (Map 34, Plans 4 and 5)

SEDGWICK'S orders required him to be in the vicinity of Chancellorsville at daylight.  The night was bright moonlight, but the fog which hung heavily over the river and the adjacent country made an atmosphere peculiarly difficult to see through.  Under the most favorable sky, and assuming that he met with no resistance, and that his corps already possessed the marching power for which it was later to be distinguished, Sedgwick would have done well to cover the 10 miles between the head of his column and "the vicinity of Chancellorsville" by a night march of about five hours' duration.  For daylight comes at this time of the year in Virginia at about 5 o'clock.

As soon as the head of his column moved away from the vicinity of the bridge it found itself opposed by hostile skirmishers.  At the same time Brooks, facing the heights, was sharply pressed as if to find out whether the force behind him was withdrawing.  Under these circumstances the progress of Sedgwick's column was necessarily slow and cautious.  It was about 2 a.m. when the advance reached the outskirts of Fredericksburg and commenced driving the enemy through the town.  A negro came into the lines and reported that the heights were occupied and the enemy was cutting the canal to flood the roads.  The investigation which followed caused a considerable delay.  In the meantime the troops, as they arrived, were halted in the streets.  It was about 3 o'clock when the Second and Third Divisions took up the march.  About this time General Warren, coming from Hooker's headquarters, crossed the river and joined Sedgwick near Franklin's Crossing, where Sedgwick's bridges were still down, and proceeded with him toward Fredericksburg.  He gave Sedgwick another copy of Hooker's last order, and explained to him "somewhat confidentially" the exact position of things at Chancellorsville, that he might know the importance of the order.[1]  About 4 o'clock the head of the Second Division reached Hazel Run, and that of the Third Division, Deep Creek.

[1] *Rep. of Com.*, IV, 46.

Butterfield used all his influence and authority to secure vigorous coöperation on the part of Gibbon and Sedgwick, and kept Hooker posted as to the progress made. He wrote:

*To Gibbon, 12:20 a.m.*

Push everything to get that bridge over. If you are likely to fail with the bridge, keep your ammunition dry, and push over the ford, if practicable. You must cross to-night.

*1:45 a.m.*

If it is found to be entirely impracticable to lay a bridge or cross at the fords near Falmouth, you can go *via* Sedgwick's [Franklin's] crossing, where the two bridges remain. . . .

*To Sedgwick, 1:45 a.m.*

Captain Razderichin's (aide-de-camp of General Hooker's staff) explanations will tell you how necessary it is that you should push through every obstacle in your path. The enemy will no doubt make every effort to delay and stop your force by a smaller one, that their main force may be used upon the right wing of our forces [at Chancellorsville].

At 2 o'clock Gibbon's division moved to the banks of the river directly opposite Fredericksburg. Twenty-five men of the 19 Mass., and an equal number from the 20 Mass., having volunteered therefor, were designated to cross over in boats, drive the enemy from rifle-pits near the city, and cover the laying of the bridges.[1] At the same point of crossing as before, with pontoons ready to be slid into the water, the detachments lay waiting for daylight to enter upon their perilous duty. Opposite these Massachusetts men, on the right bank of the river, were the same riflemen from Mississippi who opposed them in December. Everything indicated a repetition of the contest at this point.[2] Dispatches were sent as follows:

*Butterfield to Hooker, 2:25 a.m.*

General Sedgwick just reports three regiments threatened his left flank and have engaged his pickets; [that] there is still a force in Fredericksburg; that he is marching as rapidly as possible, but can not reach you by daylight.

*Butterfield to Sedgwick, 2:35 a.m.*

. . . Everything in the world depends upon the rapidity and promptness of your movement. Push everything. . . .

*Barstow, Assistant Adjutant-General, Falmouth, to Sedgwick, 3:15 a.m.*

Gibbon telegraphed at 2:40 o'clock that he is putting his pontoons [brought up from Reynolds' Crossing] in the water just above the Lacy House without opposition. The two guns were Gibbon's answer with canister to a volley of musketry from the opposite shore. No firing since.

[1] *W. R.*, 39, p. 358.
[2] *The 20th Regiment Mass. Vol. Inf.*, by G. A. Bruce, p. 250.

Gibbon was permitted to put his pontoons in the water, but was still prevented by the enemy's fire from laying a bridge.

*Van Alen to Butterfield, 4:10 a.m.*

The general commanding directs me to say that any force in front of General Sedgwick must be a small one, and must not check his advance.

In spite of Butterfield's and Hooker's assurances, Sedgwick was not convinced that the force in front of him was "a small one." Having halted and faced it from column of route, he had Newton on his right, Burnham as right center, Howe as left center, and Brooks on the left. The Confederate position may be considered as divided, like the Federal line, into four sections: right, right center, left center, and left (Map 34); the right extending from Hamilton's Crossing to a point known as the Brick Cabin (5600 yards); the right center, from the Brick Cabin to Hazel Run (1650 yards); the left center, from Hazel Run to the Plank Road (900 yards); the left, from the Plank Road to the Rappahannock (3200 yards). The position was fortified from one end to the other.[1]

Perhaps the strongest section topographically was the left center, Marye's Hill (Plan 4). The artificial defence at the base of it consisted mainly of a stone fence partially covered in front with earth thrown up from behind. This intrenchment was already famous as the position against which Burnside's columns were shattered in the battle of December, 1862. From the Pike to the Plank Road and beyond it a shelter trench was constructed in prolongation of the stone wall. The low ground in front of this trench beyond the Plank Road had been flooded and thus rendered difficult, if not impracticable; the low ground to the left or east of the Plank Road was naturally boggy and difficult. In general the land behind the town formed an open plain extending back a quarter of a mile to the base of the ridge.[2]

---

[1] In a letter of April 26, Major A. S. Pendleton of Jackson's staff described the fortifications as follows:

"The greatest destruction, and change in the appearance of the country, is from the long lines of trenches and the redoubts which crown every hillside from ten miles above Fredericksburg to twenty miles below. The world has never seen such a fortified position. The famous lines at Torres Vedras could not compare with them. As I go to Moss Neck I follow the lines, and have a ride in the trenches. These are five feet wide and two and a half deep, having the earth thrown toward the enemy, making a bank still higher. They follow the contour of the ground and hug the bases of the hills as they wind to and from the river,

thus giving natural flanking arrangements; and from the tops of the hills frown the redoubts for sunken batteries and barbette batteries *ad libitum*,—far exceeding the number of our guns; while occasionally, where the trenches take straight across the flats, a redoubt stands out defiantly in the open plain to receive our howitzers, and deal destruction broadcast to the Yankees, should their curiosity tempt them to an investigation" (*Memoirs of William Nelson Pendleton, D.D.*, by his daughter Susan P. Lee).

[2] I visited this position in September, 1897, and, from what I saw and heard, am satisfied that the stone wall was at both battles substantially as it was before the war. I saw other walls in the country

General Sedgwick directed Newton to feel the enemy's position, and learn what he could regarding the nature of the defences, and number of men and guns, etc., behind them. Newton's leading brigade was not available, being engaged in clearing the town of the enemy. So the next brigade in the column, the 3d, was designated for the reconnaissance. Its commander, General Wheaton, selected the 62 N. Y. and 102 Pa. for his first line, deployed them in the gray of the morning just below a crest about 450 yards from the stone wall, and about 4 o'clock, supported by one or two batteries, the first in position, marched upon the enemy. He intended that his other three regiments, which were a short distance in rear, should follow when these two had got the distance usual between lines of battle, or about 200 yards. Before they had done this they were fired on by infantry and artillery with terrible effect, and compelled to fall back. They halted and lay down. The remaining three regiments and McCarthy's battery $\left(\frac{3}{VI}\right)$ now came up on a line with them. The brigade thus reënforced maintained its position, but was *hors de combat* so far as assaulting the stone wall was concerned. Sedgwick rode out near the left of the line and witnessed the repulse of his men. The enemy, perceiving a commanding officer whose presence indicated authority, directed their fire upon him. After a few seconds of delay Colonel McMahon, his adjutant-general, ventured to suggest to him to retire from his exposed position. Sedgwick replied, "By Heaven, sir, this must not delay us," and slowly turned his horse and rode back into the town.

During the few moments that he stood gazing at the enemy's works his plans for carrying Marye's Heights were completed. Gibbon was to attack on the right, Howe on the left, and Newton to demonstrate against the front. Beyond Newton, on the extreme left, Brooks was to hold the enemy in check. Apprehending a general counter-attack, which might endanger his communications, he wrote to Butterfield at 5:30 a.m.:

My command is all in Fredericksburg, and I have no men [at work] on the bridges. These bridges should be taken up as soon as possible. We are warmly engaged on Sumner's old ground [1] and on the right.

On this report officers of Hooker's staff at Falmouth issued orders in his name:

*Williams to Engineer Officer at Franklin's Crossing:*

. . . proceed immediately to take up the two bridges at Franklin's Crossing, and relay them in the vicinity of the Lacy House. The transfer must be made

about Fredericksburg covered, as this one undoubtedly had been, by the earth excavated in digging draining-ditches along the road. Plan 4 represents the wall and the road as I conceive them to have been. The dimensions given are my own measurements or estimates. J. B. Jr.

[1] Referring to Brooks' position and the battle of Fredericksburg, December, 1862. This sentence, it will be observed, contra-

in the most expeditious manner possible, and it is suggested whether time might not be saved by floating the boats up to the point indicated. The bridges will be removed one at a time.

*Butterfield to Sedgwick, 6:20 a.m.*

Have telegraphed your dispatch [of 5:30] to General Hooker. You know how much depends on your pushing, and of course will do everything in your power. . . .

It was probably left to Sedgwick to designate the exact places where the bridges were to be laid as well as to furnish troops of the line to assist in laying them and to guard them. They were promptly towed upstream, accompanied on the right bank by the artillery that had covered them below, and by Sedgwick's main train. The latter on arrival was parked near the Lacy House. In the meantime the leading detachments had proceeded to cross. Two boats were taken from their carriages, pushed into the stream, and manned. The orders were to wait until the guns of Sedgwick's skirmishers were heard. The oarsmen were ready, and at the first sound of fire the boats pulled out into the stream. The firing increased and was now heard well into the city. The men of Sedgwick's corps were occasionally seen as they moved in and out among the buildings in their work of driving out the enemy. Just as the sun cast its first rays over the waters, the men landed on the Fredericksburg shore at the same place where two regiments landed on December 11, 1862.[1]

About 5 o'clock Colonel Johns with the 7 Mass. took a defensive position in a cemetery, and the Federals came into complete and secure possession of the town. The special service of the 19 and 20 Mass. regiments thus became unnecessary. General Sedgwick crossed in a boat to the Stafford shore, and held a conference with General Gibbon. As a consequence, the bridge which was brought up yesterday from Fitzhugh's Crossing was laid just above the Lacy House between the hours of 5:15 and 6:30. The two bridges from Franklin's Crossing were laid somewhat later—one near the Lacy House, the other below the ruined railroad bridge.[2] As soon as the first bridge was laid at the Lacy House, Gibbon crossed on it, with his two brigades (1st and 3d), numbering about 3400 men, and two batteries $\left(\frac{1}{2.\ II},\ \frac{2}{3.\ II}\right)$, numbering 12 guns, which gave Sedgwick about 24,400 infantry and 11 batteries, or about

dicts the opening one and so prohibits the suspicion that Sedgwick meant to deceive Butterfield into believing that the whole of the VI Corps was in Fredericksburg.

[1] *History of the 19th Regt. Mass. Vol. Inf.*, by Committee, p. 203; *History of the 20 Mass.*, by G. A. Bruce, p. 251.

[2] According to Benham's *Tabular Statement of Bridges Laid*, etc. (W. R., 39, p.

215), these two bridges and the bridges from Fitzhugh's Crossing were laid at the same time. But it would seem from the text of his report (*ib.*, p. 214), the foregoing dispatches, and other evidence, that they were laid as stated, the single bridge first, and the couple of bridges some time afterward. J. B. Jr.

25,600 men and 66 guns. Of Gibbon's 1st brigade the 19 Me., lately detached to Banks' Ford, returned to-day to Falmouth, where it remained as a camp guard. The 2d brigade remained at Banks' Ford. There were no bridges now below Fredericksburg.

In compliance with Lee's order of yesterday, Wilcox prepared this morning to march toward Chancellorsville, leaving about 50 men and 2 pieces of artillery at Banks' Ford and taking with him about 1700 infantry, the remaining pieces of his two batteries,[1] and 50 cavalrymen (15 Va.); but learning of Gibbon's movements between the river and the canal, he directed his march toward the canal, taking with him all his artillery (8 pieces). Arriving behind Taylor's Hill, he left his force there, and went on to Marye's Hill, where he conferred with General Barksdale.

The Confederate infantry was disposed as follows (Map 34, Plan 5): on the right, between Hamilton's Crossing and Brick Cabin, Gordon's, Hoke's, and Smith's brigades of Early's division (about 6100 men); in the right center, between Brick Cabin and Hazel Run, one regiment of Hays' brigade, same division, and two regiments of Barksdale's brigade of Anderson's division (about 1300 men); in the left center, between Hazel Run and the Plank Road, two regiments of Barksdale's brigade (about 900 men); on the left, between the Plank Road and the Rappahannock River, part of Wilcox's brigade and four regiments of Hays' brigade (about 3300 men). These forces, aggregating about 11,600 men, gave the Confederates a little more than 1 infantryman per yard. The Federals had more than 2 infantrymen per yard.

The Confederate artillery on the field numbered 48 pieces, of which 42 were in position as follows: 16 in two batteries on the right (Andrews'); 12 in the right center (Fraser 4, Patterson 4, Carlton 4); 7 in the left center, including the piece on the Plank Road (Parker 2, Washington Artillery 5); and 7 on the left (Washington Artillery 1, Penick 4, Moore 2).[2] The Federals had 66 pieces on the south side of the river; these could be more or less supported by the 40 pieces on the north side, among which were 12 guns of position (20-pounder Parrotts and 4½-inch siege-guns).

At 7:40 a.m. Sedgwick reported to Butterfield that he intended to make a general assault. But at 9:30 Gibbon's troops were still marching through Fredericksburg, and the operation was not to commence until all the troops were in position. In Gibbon's front was a canal which he would have to cross twice in order to get at the enemy. He crossed it once, but before he could do so the second time the enemy broke up the

[1] Penick's and Moore's $\left(\frac{2.4}{1.1}\right)$.

[2] The six pieces not in position were four of the Washington Artillery, under Richardson, moving from the right to report to Pendleton, and two of Moore's battery. The places given on Map 34 to the pieces in position are partly conjectural.

only bridge by which it was spanned, and opened on him from the heights with artillery. This canal was about thirty feet wide, about six feet deep, and under the full fire of the enemy's batteries. He could not cross it in line of battle; to construct a bridge and pass over it under the fire which would be concentrated on him, would be suicidal. He halted his infantry, and bringing up his artillery, replied with it to the artillery of the enemy.[1]

Howe, on the left, found that to turn the line of works on Marye's Heights would involve his crossing the stream and gully of Hazel Run, and, what was more serious a matter, exposing his flank to a line in rear of the former and in echelon thereto. In short, the combined turning movement proved impracticable, and there was nothing left but to make a direct or front attack, supported by demonstrations on the right and left. The main attack was to be made by Newton, who proceeded to prepare for it between 9:45 and 10 a.m. A cannonading had been kept up since about 6. It now ceased altogether. The enemy plainly saw the preparations for the assault, and evidently did not wish to interfere with them. He seemed perfectly confident of his ability to repel it.

While Sedgwick's troops were forming for the attack and the demonstrations, and the enemy was being "prepared" by the fire of artillery, the following dispatches were sent off:

*Butterfield to Sedgwick, 9:05 a.m.*

. . . General Hooker seems from the sound to be pushing this way.

*9:40 a.m.*

General Hunt reports from Banks' Ford that, from the sound, he judges that General Hooker is pushing the enemy toward the river [in the direction of Fred-

---

[1] "Gibbon's command came under fire and lost some men; but the impossibility of getting across the canal which carried water from the river above the town to the mills of Fredericksburg prevented its being generally engaged. The misadventure was in no sense Gibbon's fault, but was wholly due to the astounding ignorance of the Fredericksburg plain and Marye's Heights, which characterized all the operations from the 17th of November, 1862, down to the day of which we now speak. I well remember on the 12th of December, 1862, carrying a message to Burnside from Couch, saying that so far as the latter could judge from the reports of citizens, contrabands, and deserters, a deep trench or canal ran around the town, between it and the hills, which would prove a serious obstacle to the passage of troops; and I never shall forget how indignantly and even angrily Burnside rejected the suggestion. What came of this ignorance, on the 13th of December, is a part of the history of the war, and one of the most painful and distressing parts of that history. And here, again, after the occupation of Fredericksburg plain for four or five days in December of 1862, we find the staff of the Army of the Potomac so ignorant of the features of that field as to allow Gibbon to be sent into a position which was an impossible one—ordered to attack the enemy's extreme left, he simply could not get his troops into action, because of the intervening watercourse" (*General Gibbon in the II Army Corps*, by General Francis A. Walker, N. Y. Commandery, Loyal Legion, II, 304, 305).

ericksburg], and that the enemy appear to be evacuating their intrenchments at Banks' Ford.

### About 9:50 a.m.?

. . . I wish to facilitate your operations in every way. Command me in any way, and I am at your disposal. Telegraphic communication with the general *via* United States Ford is broken. Will advise you when restored. I am of no service here while the line is down. If I can aid you on the field, command me. . . .

P.S. My orders were to remain here, from General Hooker, but I feel like disobedience now. Please consider this confidential.

### 10:05 a.m.

What can I say to General Hooker of your position [and] prospects, and what he can expect? Telegraph is open to him partially.

The answer to this inquiry, if there was one, is not known. About this time, however, Sedgwick informed Howe that an attack was about to be made between Hazel Run and Fredericksburg, stating that he wished Howe to assist. Howe at once [1] placed his divisional artillery where it could fire effectively upon the enemy's works without interfering with the advance of his infantry, and formed the mass of the latter in three lines as follows:

*First line*—33 N. Y., 7 Me., ½ of 21 N. J., and 77 N. Y. of General Neill's brigade (3. 2. VI), the 77 N. Y. deployed as skirmishers.

*Second line*—2 Vt., 6 Vt., and 26 N. J. of Colonel Grant's brigade (2. 2. VI).

*Third line*—3 Vt. and 4 Vt. of Grant's brigade, and ½ of 21 N. J. of Neill's brigade, under Colonel Seaver.[2]

The 5 N. J. was placed in support of a battery.[3] The two remaining regiments (20 and 49 N. Y.) were, it seems, similarly employed or held in reserve.

Newton's men had long been standing in the streets of Fredericksburg listening to the rumble of the cannon at Chancellorsville, and were impatient to advance. At last everything was ready. The necessary commands were given and transmitted. At 10: 35 a.m. Butterfield reported to Hooker:

Sedgwick at this moment commences his assault. He is on our old ground of December [1862]. The force in his front is small but active. Will post you speedily as to result.

Two regiments in column of fours took the Telegraph Road; and four regiments in like formation, the Plank Road. On the left of these col-

---

[1] He gives the time erroneously as *about 11 a.m.* (*W. R.*, 39, p. 599). Neill gives it as *about 10 a.m.* (*ib.*, p. 608).

[2] Howe's division comprised a 2d and 3d brigade, but no 1st.

[3] *W. R.*, 39, p. 603.

umns four regiments marched in line of battle, under Colonel Burnham. Three of them formed the main or middle line; the other regiments formed a line of skirmishers and a third line. These ten regiments were taken from Newton's and Burnham's divisions, and numbered about 4700 men. The ten other regiments of these two divisions did not take part in the attack. One of them $\left(\frac{2}{2.\ 3.\ \text{VI}}\right)$ was supporting a battery of Gibbon's.[1] The other nine (about 4230 men) were available as a reserve.

The stone wall was manned by the 18 Miss. and three companies of the 21, altogether about 600 men. Seven companies of the 21 Miss. were on Marye's Hill. At the base of the hill, on a line with the stone wall, were two howitzers. On the hill itself were five guns, one of which was north of the Pike, on the Plank Road, to command that road. The Federal troops, in light marching order, advanced in double time at *trail arms*. The men had been cautioned not to fire a shot, whatever the provocation, but to trust to cold steel. The artillery on Marye's Hill opened on them with shot and shell, but without effect, as the pieces could not be sufficiently depressed. When the assailants were about 300 yards from the stone wall, the two howitzers on a line with it, and the gun on the Plank Road, opened on them with canister. The right column, commanded by Colonel Spear of the 61 Pa., advancing on the Plank Road, was almost literally swept away. Spear himself was killed. The other column, commanded by Colonel Johns of the 7 Mass., moved unflinchingly on. It comes in sight of the stone wall with its fringe of gleaming muskets. An ominous silence prevails along that line. Its defenders are biding their time. The assailants hear only officers cautioning their men: "Steady, you 'uns! Hold your fire! Let 'em come on." On they come. They are perhaps 50 yards from the wall, when "crack" goes a gun, a single shot, the twitch of some shaky hand.[2] Then "Fire" rings out, and every muzzle and cannon mouth leaps flame. From the rifle-pits at the base of the hill the smoke curls up the grassy slope and softens its dark green with shades of blue and gray, covering it as with a beautiful carpet. Ping, ping, zip, zip; bullet and canister cut up the ground about the slender column. At first there was a wavering, with cries of "Retreat!" But others yelled: "Forward! don't go back! We sha'n't get so close again." The head of the column was broken; Colonel Johns promptly rallied it. Again it was broken, and again the gallant colonel succeeded in reforming it. But he was now badly wounded, and the command had to be taken over by Lieutenant-Colonel Harlow. Colonel Burnham, commanding the line of bat-

---

[1] This regiment rejoined its brigade about 1 p.m.

[2] In the *History of Battery B, First R. I. Artillery*, the distance is given as 30 or 40 yards. A private of Company F, 7 Mass., the leading company, gives it as within 25 yards. J. B. Jr.

tle on the left, fell wounded from his horse. The line and column recoiled some distance, and took shelter.

In front of the stone wall, facing down the road, was a house inclosed by a high board fence. While the 7 Mass. was enjoying a breathing-spell behind the latter, some of the men, looking between the boards, caught sight of the enemy's unprotected flank. A flag of truce was sent forward, probably by a brigade commander. The officer bearing it asked to be allowed to remove the dead and wounded in front of the 18 Miss. Colonel Griffin, the regimental commander, without referring to his brigade commander, granted the request, and allowed his own men to show themselves while the wounded were being delivered. The feebleness and vulnerability of the defence was soon reported and passed along the line of the assailants.[1] On the right the thrilling cry rang out: "Massachusetts colors to the front!" With a rallying shout from the color-guard the colors of the 7 Mass. were thrust forward; in a moment a mass of men rushed to the board fence, and went through it pell-mell, directly upon the enemy's flank, giving them the contents of their muskets point-blank.[2] On the left Colonel Allen of the 5 Wisc. took the place of Colonel Burnham, and electrified his men with the words: "When the signal *forward* is given, you will start at double-quick, you will not fire a gun, and you will not stop until you get the order to halt. You will never get that order."[3]

The charge was sounded. The first line sprang forward with a cheer, followed at 30 steps by the second, which was followed by the third, all accompanying the columns on the right. The stone wall, which had cost the Federal army so many brave lives, was gained and cleared. A short rest, a final rush, and the works on Marye's Hill shared the fate of the stone wall.

Newton's reserves followed the assaulting columns up the heights, and secured the conquered positions. The gallant feat cost little more time than it takes to describe it. At 10:50 a.m., as Lee was sweeping Hooker's rear-guard out of Chancellorsville, Butterfield telegraphed to Hooker:

Am signaled that Sedgwick has carried Marye's Heights, and, officer thinks, captured the guns.

Howe, as soon as he heard the firing in front of Marye's Hill, proceeded to attack. Five of his regiments obliqued to the right, and crossing the Run, united or coöperated with Burnham's division. One of them (6 Vt.) was the second regiment to gain Marye's Heights.[4] In-

---

[1] *W. R.*, 39, p. 840; *Military Memoirs of a Confederate*, by E. P. Alexander, p. 351.

[2] *Stories of our Soldiers*, collected from the Boston *Journal*, p. 192; *History of Battery B, 1 R. I. L. A.*, by J. H. Rhodes, pp. 172, 173.

[3] *History of the Army of the Potomac*, by J. H. Stine, p. 373.

[4] *Chancellorsville*, Hotchkiss and Allan, p. 82; *History of the Army of the Potomac*, by J. H. Stine, p. 373.

Since the battle Marye's Heights has

cluding these five, there were 15 regiments (about 7500 men) that participated in the assault, and they were none too many. Their preponderance of 7½ to 1 was none too great.[1]

As Newton's regiments advanced to the assault, his batteries concentrated their fire upon the stone wall, and continued to do so until the advancing infantry had neared the wall, when they directed it upon the crest beyond. Howe's batteries coöperated in like manner with his infantry. Gibbon's two batteries on the right and three of Brooks' on the left directed their fire also upon the enemy in their front. There were thus 10 batteries, or 60 guns, in action, without counting the guns on the north side of the Rappahannock. But it does not appear that a sufficient fire of artillery was brought to bear upon any one point to shake the enemy's infantry.

Brooks on the left had preserved on the whole a defensive attitude. Bartlett's brigade in the valley of Deep Run supported two batteries which engaged the batteries in their front. His two other brigades, with a battery, prolonged the line to the river. This battery was not engaged. Another battery on the plateau between the Bowling Green Road and the river fired occasionally at the batteries of the enemy.

The loss of the VI Corps in killed, wounded, and missing may be estimated at 1500 men, or about 7 per cent. of its strength.[2] That of Gibbon's command was unappreciable.[3] Hospitals were at once established in the town, and by 2 o'clock all the wounded were collected within them.

When Barksdale saw the Federals debouch in force and advance upon the stone wall, he called on Hays and Wilcox for assistance. One regiment of Wilcox's brigade and the four regiments of Hays' brigade were marching toward him in compliance with that request. But before they reached him Sedgwick's victorious columns broke over his position.

"Upon reaching the summit of the sharp hill after passing through the extensive and well-wooded grounds of the Marye House, an exciting scene met the eye. A single glance exhibited to view the broad plateau

been commonly understood to include the two positions of Willis's and Marye's Hills.

[1] Newton says: "If there had been a hundred more men on Marye's Hill we could not have taken it" (*Chancellorsville and Gettysburg*, by Abner Doubleday, p. 59). It may safely be asserted that without Howe's vigorous assistance Newton would have failed to carry it.

About 100 men of the 20 N. Y. Volunteers (Neill's brigade) refused to cross the Rappahannock on the plea that their term of enlistment had expired. They were court-martialed, and sentenced to hard labor during the war, with forfeiture of all pay and allowances due them.

[2] The *War Records* (39, p. 191) give the loss of the VI Corps for the 3d and 4th of May as 4950, but do not give the loss for this particular action. General Barksdale says in his official report that the Federal papers gave the loss of the Federals in *killed* and *wounded* as 1000, but that according to statements from intelligent citizens it reached 2000 (*W. R.*, 39, p. 840). Colonel Cabell says substantially the same thing. Medical Director Letterman gives the wounded alone in this engagement as over 1000 (*Medical Recollections*, p. 134).

[3] The *War Records* (39, p. 191) give the loss of Gibbon's division during the 3d and 4th in killed, wounded, and missing as 110.

alive with fleeing soldiers, riderless horses, and artillery and wagon-trains on a gallop. The writer hurried back to Sedgwick, who was giving directions for Brooks and Howe to come up, and suggested that it was a rare opportunity for the use of cavalry. With evident regret Sedgwick replied that he did not have a cavalryman. The carrying of the heights had completely divided the enemy's forces, throwing either flank with much confusion on opposite roads, and it seemed as though a regiment of cavalry might not only have captured many prisoners, guns, ammunition, and wagons, but also have cleared the way for the corps almost as far as the immediate rear of Lee's army at Chancellorsville."[1]

Gibbon's men, after cheering the victors, marched through the city and out by the Pike to the rear of the Confederate defences.

Butterfield received the following dispatch, and transmitted it as indicated to Sedgwick:

United States Ford, May 3, 1863, 12 m.

*General Butterfield:*

. . . We have plenty of fresh troops still left, but have gained no ground to-day, yet our lines are strong; but no doubt another desperate effort will be made to force our position. We feel confident that Sedgwick must press them fast. Answer me here. I will take it to General Hooker. He wants Sedgwick to press them.

RUFUS INGALLS,
Chief Quartermaster.

[Indorsement]

May 3, 1863, 12 m.

*General Sedgwick:*

What answer can I send General Hooker?

BUTTERFIELD.

Evidently without waiting to hear from Sedgwick, Butterfield replied:

May 3, 1863, 12 m.

*R. Ingalls,*

Chief Quartermaster:

Sedgwick is by this time (12 m.) probably free from all obstacles of earth-works. He has carried the heights on right of Telegraph road [Marye's]. Two lines of his troops have disappeared in the wood on the hills, and all seems going well. Will advise you further as soon as I can get word from Sedgwick.

BUTTERFIELD.

Lieutenant Pitzer of Early's staff, who was on Lee's Hill when it was captured, galloped at once to General Lee, and informed him of the loss of that position.[2] Early with his main force retreated by the Telegraph Road to Smith's on the Ny River (Map 2), leaving Gordon's brigade to cover the movement at Cox's (Map 34). Barksdale rallied and reformed his fleeing regiments on Lee's Hill, under cover of Carlton's and Fra-

---

[1] Brevet Lieutenant-Colonel H. W. Jackson, U. S. Volunteers, *B. and L.,* III, 229, 230.

[2] Fitzhugh Lee's *Chancellorsville Address.*

ser's batteries. From this point his brigade and these batteries fell back to Leach's, where they formed line of battle and succeeded in checking the pursuit in that direction (Second Position, Map 34). The whole force then proceeded down the Telegraph Road to Cox's (Third Position, Map 34). Wilcox retired in the direction of Chancellorsville, with the object of opposing the Federal advance. He tried to induce Hays to do likewise, but the latter, intent upon rejoining his commanding general, went on to Cox's.

It would now be easy for Sedgwick to turn upon Early's force, disperse it, and destroy the depot at Hamilton's Crossing. But his orders required him to march with the least possible delay toward Chancellorsville. The chief advantage of breaking through an enemy's center is gaining access to his line of communication. But herein lies the chief danger of the operation. The attraction of the enemy's trains and depots, and the eagerness to cut off his retreat, may carry the attackers through and beyond the enemy's line of battle, leaving the separate fragments of the latter in a position to take their late assailants in rear. Instances are not wanting in which an attacking force, having carried everything before it, and gone to pillaging the enemy's camp, was itself attacked and put to rout. Having broken a portion of the enemy's line, the assailant must turn on the separate fractions and disperse them before he can safely proceed to the enemy's rear. This principle Sedgwick was required, it seems, to ignore. At any rate, he pushed on from Marye's Heights with Newton's division directly toward Chancellorsville. Howe was prevented by Barksdale from following him. Brooks had broken away from the enemy with the greater part of his division, and was marching with it toward Fredericksburg. Gibbon remained with his division (less one brigade) on the heights of Fredericksburg. Sedgwick did not consider himself authorized to order him forward, nor Gibbon to advance without orders. Sometime between 11 and 1, probably about noon, Sedgwick found himself as far from support as he dared go with his single division, and halted to await the arrival of another division. At 1 p.m. Warren reported the situation to Butterfield as follows:

We have advanced with Newton's division on the Plank road as far as Guest's House. The heights were carried splendidly at 11 a.m. by Newton. Howe immediately afterward carried the heights to the south of Hazel Run. We have been waiting to get his [Howe's] division behind us before advancing, to get up batteries and stragglers, and get the brigades straightened out, which were a little disorganized by a successful charge and pursuit. Our loss, though honorable proof of a severe contest, is not very severe. The Sixth Corps is in splendid spirits. We captured several guns. General Howe reports a force yet in his front.

P.S. Brooks' division were kept by the enemy's fire in position on our left, and after the heights were carried he had 3 miles to march to join us. He is not yet up.

This dispatch was received and transmitted to Hooker at 2:30 p.m. About the time when it left Warren's hands the following one came into Butterfield's:

U. S. Ford, May 3, 1863.

*General Butterfield:*

Do not expect dispatches much from General Hooker at present. He wishes to hear constantly from you, but he is too engaged. He has been slightly hurt, but not at all severely. No firing for an hour. Am just back from Hooker's headquarters. The slaughter has been fearful on both sides. The enemy must have suffered most, as he has been forced to attack every time. Your last dispatch [12 m.?] is received and forwarded.

RUFUS INGALLS,
Chief Quartermaster.[1]

This elicited the following message:

Headquarters Army of the Potomac, May 3, 1863, 1:15 p.m.

GENERAL HOOKER.

*Dear General:*

I deeply regret to hear that you are even slightly wounded. I have put every officer and man here in use during the operations, even to the Twentieth Maine.[2] As I can not now by any possibility be able to join you if permitted,[3] can I join General Sedgwick? The enemy will undoubtedly make a desperate effort, as his custom is, toward dusk, if he lasts that long. Our troops are still advancing, cheering lustily. A portion of Sedgwick's force is moving to the right, on Bowling Green road.[4] Haupt is at Falmouth with his force, ready to spring with the railroad bridge when ordered. Affairs seem to justify it now here. Am sending 200 prisoners to the rear; [including] 1 colonel. While I do not know who could replace me here, I am heartsick at not being permitted to be on the actual field, to share the fate and fortune of this army and my general.

BUTTERFIELD.

Under the impression that Gibbon advanced with Sedgwick, Butterfield wrote at 2 p.m. to Hunt:

General Gibbon, right of Sedgwick's advance, should be about 2 or 3 miles from Fredericksburg, moving toward Chancellorsville. We can not now tell where he is. Send scouts to swim the river, and report to you. Act according to orders from General Hooker. Keep him advised of Sedgwick's advance, with time. . . . Better lose a few men as scouts than not have news and report of our advance on Chancellorsville Plank road.

Sedgwick was anxious to communicate with Benham at Banks' Ford, as he wanted a bridge laid there. For some time his attempts to get a

---

[1] *W. R.*, 107, p. 1035.

[2] This regiment of infantry $\left(\frac{20}{2.\ 1.\ \text{v}}\right)$, left in camp near Falmouth on account of smallpox, was employed guarding the telegraph line to U. S. Ford (Report of brigade commander, *ib.*, 39, p. 519).

[3] This assertion would seem to be based on the delusion that Hooker was pursuing Lee.

[4] No portion of Sedgwick's force was moving on or toward the Bowling Green Road. J. B. Jr.

message to the ford were frustrated by roving bands of Confederate cavalry to which he had nothing to oppose. But he was finally successful.[1]

Brooks' and Howe's divisions joined Newton's at the Guest House about 2 p.m. Brooks' seemed to be in better fighting and marching trim than either of the other two, and was deemed the best qualified "to do everything that the urgency of the case required." It was therefore ordered to take the advance. Shortly afterward the following report was made to Butterfield by an aide-de-camp, whom he sent to Sedgwick to keep him posted as to the latter's movements.

*2:20 p.m.* Brooks' division has just moved ahead again, and other two divisions will follow shortly. Sedgwick says loss heavier than he expected, having lost several colonels and many field officers. Warren thinks 1½ miles beyond this [beyond Guest's House, or at the Toll-House] the enemy have halted and will make a stand. The men show much fatigue, but Sedgwick intends to push vigorously. . . .

This dispatch was transmitted to Hooker at 3:25.

Brooks had with him Brown's and Bartlett's brigades $\left(\frac{1.\ 2}{1.\ VI}\right)$ and his four batteries of artillery, having left Russell's brigade behind to cover his withdrawal. The country being open, the division was formed on a broad front, one brigade on each side of the Plank Road, each brigade in two lines, the front and flanks covered by a line of skirmishers. The artillery formed in column on the road between the brigades. The bridge that was being thrown was a portion of the one of the two bridges brought up from Franklin's Crossing. Its location was Scott's Ford, about a mile below Banks' Ford, but was commonly called Banks' Ford in subsequent dispatches and reports. Hooker, it seems, was opposed to the laying of a bridge at this point as tending to weaken Sedgwick's resolution to push on. With a view to improving his own communications, he issued an order at 2:30 p.m. for another bridge to be laid at United States Ford, authorizing the use of Comstock's canvas pontoons "as far as they would go."

Wilcox had posted a small force of dismounted cavalry and 4 pieces of artillery on the Plank Road about three fourths of a mile west of the Guest House, and about a mile from Salem Church. With his main force he took position at the Toll-House. McLaws with his three brigades, Mahone's brigade of Anderson's division, Manly's and McCarthy's batteries (8 pieces), and Alexander with his battalion (14 pieces), were marching in the direction of Fredericksburg; McLaws by

[1] T. W. Hyde, Provost-Marshal and Acting Aide-de-Camp on General Sedgwick's staff, says: "Colonel Tompkins was sent there with a message. He did not return. Captain Farrar was sent. He came back to us some months after by way of Richmond exchange. Then General Sedgwick in impatience sent me. I did not take the road, but took a bee-line across country, most fortunately, for I was back in an hour, having seen no wandering rebels" (*Following the Greek Cross*, p. 129).

the Turnpike, and Alexander by the Plank Road. Lee seemed to be thinking more of Stoneman than of Sedgwick. He wrote to Seddon:

I request that Ransom's and Pettigrew's brigades [coming up from D. H. Hill's command] be stopped at Hanover Junction, with orders to protect the railroads from the enemy's cavalry.

It is reported that the enemy has crossed at Fredericksburg, and driven back our force that was left there. I have sent back reënforcements.

### Battle of Salem Church (Map 35)

About 2 p.m. McLaws arrived at Salem Church, and formed line of battle on the edge of a strip of wood, about 250 yards wide, pushing his skirmishers out to the far edge (Map 35). The ground fell away from his line to the Toll-Gate, where a slight rise gave command of it back to the wood. The intervening ground, though generally clear and open, was intersected by a number of ravines parallel to McLaws' position, which would throw disorder into lines advancing upon it and break the *élan* of a charge. From the Toll-Gate to McLaws' line was about 1000 yards. Leaving an interval in the center for Wilcox, McLaws threw Kershaw's and Wofford's brigades $\left(\frac{1.3}{2.1}\right)$ out to the right, and Semmes' and Mahone's $\left(\frac{2}{2.1}, \frac{1}{1.1}\right)$ to the left. His artillery had not yet come up. Hays had by this time joined Early. It was about 3:15 p.m., more than four hours after the capture of Marye's Heights; more than an hour after the assembly of the VI Corps at the Guest House, and the arrival of McLaws in the intrenched position of Salem Church; and about an hour after the departure of Brooks' division for Chancellorsville, when Newton's and Howe's divisions took up the march, the former to follow Brooks', and the latter to follow Newton's. These divisions marched in column of route. Sedgwick's corps might have made an earlier start from Fredericksburg, had Newton's division, when it gained the heights, been thrown against the inner flank of the line confronting Howe and Brooks, instead of being marched on to the Guest House, where it was kept inactively waiting for the other divisions to break away from their plucky, tenacious opponents. Nothing was gained and precious time was lost by moving toward Chancellorsville with a single division. Butterfield, dissatisfied with the rate of Sedgwick's progress, started three times to relieve him from command.

Hunt at Banks' Ford wired to Butterfield at 3 p.m.:

Parties [of skirmishers] across from this command. Colonel Doull[1] sent over with directions to ascertain and report the distance of Sedgwick's and Gibbon's advance on the Plank road. The bridge is being thrown.

The [telegraph] wires are across; taken by swimmers of the signal corps.[2]

---

[1] Major Alexander Doull, Inspector of Artillery on General Hunt's staff, probably brevet colonel, crossed the river by swimming his horse.

[2] "This movement, though bold and dar-ing, was of no immediate importance, and the instruments and wires were brought back in the evening" (*The Signal Corps in the War of the Rebellion,* by J. W. Brown).

This dispatch was repeated to Hooker.

Two signal stations were established to connect Sedgwick with Butterfield, one in a church tower in Fredericksburg, and one on the heights beyond, but no signal communication was opened. There was no signal officer with Sedgwick, his two signal officers having remained behind to form the station in the church tower.[1] Moreover, Sedgwick understood that signaling was prohibited.[2]

About 3:25 Sedgwick's advance came upon the dismounted cavalry covering Wilcox, and engaged it. Wilcox supported it with the fire of two pieces of artillery at the Toll-House. Brooks' division had been compelled, it seems, to change its formation to two parallel columns, preceded by a line of skirmishers, each column consisting of the main body of a brigade. One of his brigades had to come up and deploy, and a battery of artillery to open fire, before Wilcox's outpost fell back upon the brigade, and the Federal advance could be resumed. About 4 p.m. Wilcox, with his whole command, fell back upon McLaws' line, and took position at Salem Church. His five regiments of Alabama infantry were disposed for defence—the 11th and 14th on the left of the road, the 10th and 8th on the right, the 10th and 11th being next to the road. In the rear of the 10th was the 9th, of which one company was stationed in the school-house, a one-story building about 60 yards in front of the line, and one in the church. The company in the church was ordered to fire from the window of the ground floor and from those of the gallery. Between the 10th and 11th regiments was an interval of from 75 to 80 yards, which was occupied by Penick's battery of four guns. Hardly were these dispositions completed when the Federals were seen advanc-

---

[1] *W. R.*, 39, p. 240.

[2] Butterfield had written to Sedgwick: "*2:05 a.m.* I don't want any signal. It will betray the movement for miles. The enemy read our signals." As a consequence, Captain Cushing, the acting chief signal officer of the Army of the Potomac, who knew nothing about the order, found it impossible to "call" Sedgwick's signal station, and thought that the officers stationed with Sedgwick were neglecting their duty. He was about to order their arrest, when their conduct was satisfactorily explained to him by the following dispatch borne by an orderly:

"On the march, May 3, 1863, 4 a.m.
"*Captain Cushing:*
"General S. has received an order from General Butterfield not to use signals, as the enemy can read them. What will we do? Let us know by the next orderly that

comes to General Sedgwick from headquarters.
"CAPTAIN PIERCE,
"Signal Officer VI Corps"
(*W. R.*, 39, p. 220).

He wrote in answer:

"May 3, 1863, 7:15 a.m.
"*Captain Pierce:*
"Use your cipher to send important messages. Tell General Sedgwick that messages may be sent to him giving him information regarding position of the enemy, which will not aid the enemy much, and may aid him. . . .
"SAMUEL T. CUSHING"
(*W. R.*, 39, p. 220).

At 9:05 a.m. Butterfield wrote to Sedgwick: "My dispatch last night [2:05 a.m.] in regard to not using signals was intended for night signaling only, as a signal last

ing up the Plank Road in line of battle. A 6-gun battery, accompanying their advance, halted at the Toll-Gate, and opened fire.[1] Penick's battery at the church fired one shot in reply, and retired by order of General McLaws to a point several hundred yards from the church.[2] Moore's battery could not find an eligible position and so was sent to the rear. Manly's and McCarthy's batteries were just coming on the field; Alexander's battalion was still far off. The Confederates at Salem Church and the Toll-Gate now numbered about 10,000 men and, except in front of Wofford on the extreme right, were covered with intrenchments. The battery with the Federal advance (reënforced probably by one or two others) shelled the woods to the right and left of the road for a short time. When the artillery ceased firing, Brooks' division advanced to the attack.

The Confederate skirmishers are pushed back to the wood and then upon their line of battle. The Federals follow quickly. Reaching the edge of the wood, they give a cheer and rush forward to the charge. Within 80 yards of the enemy's line they receive his fire. They waver, but only for a moment. Bartlett with the 2d brigade dashes forward, surrounds the school-house, and captures the garrison. Pushing on, he delivers all the impetus of his attack on the 10 Ala., and shatters it. A little further on, and the victory will be won. Wilcox still has the 9 Ala. in reserve just behind this part of the line. In a moment he hurls it upon the advancing Federals. The Alabamians deliver a deadly fire at close quarters, and rush forward to gain what has been lost. Gallantly does Bartlett strive to hold the advantage he has won. A fierce struggle, and in turn the Federal line gives way. No time is allowed it to rally. Wilcox follows closely, increasing at each step the confusion and carnage in the Federal ranks. The school-house is reached, the captured garrison is set free, and their captors are in turn captives. It is now 6:30 p.m. In vain do the Federals try again to turn the tide of battle. Once more their line is broken, and rushes in confusion to the rear. The field is cleared of Federal troops to the Toll-Gate.[3] A fresh regiment of Bartlett's brigade, just arrived from Fredericksburg, is drawn up across the road to stop stragglers. As the broken lines come back they are reformed in front of it.[4] Newton's division comes up on the right, too late to turn the tide of battle, but reënforcing and restor-

---

night might have informed the enemy of your movements, which it was desirable to avoid. . . ." But this message had not reached Sedgwick, and Cushing's instructions of 7:15 Sedgwick did not consider as authoritative.

[1] *W. R.*, 39, p. 858.

[2] Report of Lieutenant Penick, *ib.*, 39,

p. 884, but Wilcox says in his official report: "The two batteries fired some 15 or 20 minutes, when ours was withdrawn for the want of ammunition" (*ib.*, 39, p. 858).

[3] *Chancellorsville*, by Hotchkiss and Allan, pp. 86, 87.

[4] *History of the 27th Regiment N. Y. Volunteers*, by C. B. Fairchild, p. 169.

ing Brooks' line. Howe's halts in column of march, and wheels into line facing to the left.[1]

Under the protection of skirmishers who had forded or swum the river, and of the artillery on the north bank, the bridge at Scott's Ford was completed about 4:30 p.m.[2] Owen's brigade $\left(\frac{2}{2.\text{ II}}\right)$ immediately crossed it and took position to cover it, throwing out a regiment as skirmishers about ¾ of a mile beyond it. He also sent his adjutant-general to report to General Sedgwick, requesting that he "be assigned a position and be allowed to take part in the fight." In reply he was informed that Sedgwick was strong enough for the enemy, and was advised to prevent the [detachments of the] enemy from either crossing or destroying the bridge.[3]

A soldier writes: "We slept in line that night with the dead of the day's battle lying near us. The stretcher bearers with their lamps wandered here and there over the field, picking up the wounded, and the loaded ambulances rattled dismally over the broken plank road. The pickets were unusually still, for the men of both armies were tired, and went willingly to rest. . . . Sedgwick scarcely slept that night. From time to time he dictated a dispatch to General Hooker. He would walk for a few paces apart and listen; then returning would lie down again in the damp grass, with his saddle for a pillow, and try to sleep. The night was inexpressibly gloomy. Fires were not allowed to be lighted, and there was not even the excitement of a picket alarm to relieve the singular stillness."[4]

When Sedgwick advanced from Fredericksburg he had with him ten regiments and six companies of the First Division, and his nine batteries of artillery; when he made his attack he had been joined by troops from the rear, who brought his infantry up to eleven regiments, or about 5000 men. Allowing for the loss at Fredericksburg, he had in the VI Corps about 19,500 infantry, or about 20,500 men, and yet with 5000 men he assailed an intrenched position manned by about 10,000 practically untouched by artillery. For there was hardly any preparatory artillery fire. While the attack was in progress the number of batteries at the

---

[1] Doubleday says: "It was now decided that a second attempt should be made by Newton's division, but Newton states that the design was abandoned, because Howe's division, which was to support him, had gone into camp without orders, and was not immediately available. Before new arrangements could be made darkness came on, and both armies bivouacked on the ground they occupied" (*Chancellorsville and Gettysburg*, p. 61). Howe says: "I soon received orders to throw my division to the left to check a flank attack. I did so. No

flank attack being made, and night coming on, I encamped my division in the road" (*W. R.*, 39, p. 600).

[2] Benham says in his report that this bridge was laid between 3 and 4:30. In his statement of *Bridges laid*, etc., he gives the time of laying as 3 to 4 p.m. (*W. R.*, 39, pp. 213, 215).

[3] *Ib.*, 107, p. 178. See also *History of the Philadelphia Brigade*, by C. H. Banes, pp. 161, 162.

[4] *United States Service Magazine*, V, 211.

Toll-Gate was increased to three, but this new line of guns did not open fire until the infantry came running back with the enemy after them; the artillery then fired over the heads of the infantry, and by their excellent practice checked the pursuit. These batteries were afterward replaced by three others kept in reserve. Of the nine batteries of the VI Corps, not more than three were in action at any one time; and two (Martin's and McCartney's) were not engaged at all. The corps seems to have lost in this engagement about 1500 officers and men.[1] With reference to the Confederates, Penick's four guns probably went into action a second time as the Federal infantry advanced, and expended the remainder of their ammunition; at any rate, they had no ammunition with which to fire on the Federal infantry as they retreated. Manly's and Mc-Carthy's batteries did not get into position until after the main attack was repulsed. Alexander with his battalion of 14 pieces did not reach the field until the fighting was all over. Like the "Battle of Chancellorsville," the engagement at Salem Church was essentially an infantry fight.

The following correspondence explains itself:

*Butterfield to Hooker, 4:05 p.m.*

Gibbon's division still in and around Fredericksburg. Shall it be pushed after Sedgwick or remain here?

*5:30 p.m.*

[A] Captain of the Washington Artillery captured reports Hood's and Pickett's divisions as expected to-night. . . . The general impression of the prisoners seems to be that we shall hear from Hood before long.[2]

*To Gibbon, 6:20 p.m.*

General Hooker wishes you kept at Fredericksburg.

It was not expected that Gibbon would be able to hold the heights of Fredericksburg in case of an attempt to retake them, and they were only guarded by a picket line. The duty assigned him was to keep the town, and preserve the bridges in the event of the VI Corps finding it necessary to return by that route. His force was stretched out from Hazel Run across the plain to the river above Fredericksburg, to meet an attack—should one be made—along the Bowling Green Road on the left, or the River Road on the right, or over the heights in front.[3]

---

[1] Bartlett reports a loss of 580 out of his four regiments numbering less than 1500 (*W. R.,* 39, p. 582). The 121 N. Y., commanded by Colonel Emory Upton, having never been in action before, lost 276 out of an aggregate of 453 (*ib.,* pp. 189, 589).

[2] Hood and Pickett had orders from Longstreet to "move back from front of Suffolk to the right bank of the Blackwater immediately after dark." It is safe to say that Lee did not expect either of these commands or any other reënforcement to-day.

[3] *History of the 20 Mass. Volunteers,* by Colonel Bruce, p. 257.

Early reported to Lee that the Federals had possession of the town of Fredericksburg, and described his situation. Lee wrote at 7 p.m.:

### To Early

I very much regret the possession of Fredericksburg by the enemy. I heard to-day of their taking the hills in rear of the city, and sent down General McLaws with two brigades of Anderson's division and three of his own, to unite with the forces under you, and endeavor to drive them back. I heard this afternoon that he had halted at Tabernacle Church. . . . If they are attacking him there, and you could come upon their left flank, and communicate with General McLaws, I think you would demolish them. See if you cannot unite with him, and together destroy him. . . .

P.S. I understand that Wilcox is with him also.

### To McLaws

I presume from the firing which I hear in your direction that you are engaged with the enemy. . . . I have just written to Early . . . to unite with you to attack the enemy on their left flank. Communicate with him, and arrange the junction, if necessary and practicable. It is necessary that you beat the enemy, and I hope you will do it.

By the time this dispatch reached McLaws, Early had moved his main force back to Cox's, concentrating his command at that point. Lee's instructions contemplated an attack on Sedgwick's left flank. They were evidently issued under the impression that Sedgwick's whole force was in line of battle facing Salem Church. Such would have been the case had Sedgwick marched, as perhaps he should have done, in some approximation to a line of battle, say with his four divisions abreast or two abreast followed by the other two, also abreast, each division forming a line of short columns. It should be said in justice to Sedgwick that he might have adopted such a formation had he not been continually urged to make speed and to abandon all thought of serious opposition.

Under Hooker's order of 2:30 a portion of the unutilized bridge at Banks' Ford, sufficient to span the river, was forwarded to United States Ford, where it arrived about 10:30. The remnants of this bridge, and of the one already laid at Scott's Ford, were held ready to be laid, if necessary, as a second bridge at Scott's Ford. The bridge that was moved to United States Ford was not laid to-day.

The line of signal stations in Sedgwick's rear broke up about 5 p.m. for lack of protection.[1] A telegraph line was pushed across the river from the Lacy House to the outskirts of Fredericksburg, but as Sedgwick was constantly moving, it was not of much use.[2] Supplies of ammunition and forage were forwarded to him to-night from his main train at the Lacy House.

---

[1] *W. R.*, 39, pp. 221, 245.        [2] *Ib.*, 39, pp. 220, 221.

At 10 p.m. General Hunt, chief of artillery, reported in person to Hooker in obedience to an order from Butterfield. The service rendered by the Federal artillery would have been greater and more effective if Hooker had kept his chief of artillery with him, and allowed him to discharge his proper functions. ''There was no one upon the field whose special business it was to look for eligible positions for batteries, and having found them, with authority to post them there, and to command them when so posted; to select rifle batteries for positions requiring such pieces, and smooth-bores for service adapted to their kind. It was not until after disaster had befallen his army, and everything was in confusion, that Hooker recalled his chief of artillery, and invested him with authority to restore order.'' [1] During the battle Hooker's Chief of Staff, Chief of Artillery, Chief Engineer Officer, and Chief Signal Officer were all on the north side of the Rappahannock, to observe, direct, and assist Sedgwick, on whose fighting the success or failure of the campaign was so largely to depend. Warren returned this evening to Hooker's headquarters, arriving there at 11 p.m. He found Hooker in a deep sleep and still suffering from the concussion of the morning. He asked him if he had instructions to send to Sedgwick, and was answered, ''None.'' Rather than leave Sedgwick in the dark as to how matters stood, he wrote to him at midnight on his own responsibility:

I find everything snug here. We contracted the line a little, and repulsed the assault with ease. General Hooker wishes them to attack him to-morrow. If they will, he does not desire you to attack them again in force unless he [Hooker] attacks him [them] at the same time. He says you are too far away for him to direct. Look well to the safety of your corps, and keep up communication with General Benham at Banks' Ford and Fredericksburg. You can go to either place, if you think it best. To cross at Banks' Ford would bring you in supporting distance of the main body, and would be better than falling back to Fredericksburg. [2]

Several messages passed to-day between Hooker's chief of staff and the President:

*Lincoln to Butterfield, 4:35 p.m.*

Where is General Hooker? Where is Sedgwick? Where is Stoneman?

*Butterfield to Lincoln, 4:40 p.m.*

General Hooker is at Chancellorsville. General Sedgwick, with 15,000 to 20,000 men, at a point 3 or 4 miles out from Fredericksburg, on the road to Chancellors-

---

[1] *Artillery Service in the Rebellion,* by Tidball.

[2] The abandonment of Chancellorsville, and taking up a position of which the nearest point is ¾ of a mile and the center 1½ miles from Chancellorsville, Warren calls *contracting the line a little.* Referring especially to this incident, A. C. Hamlin says in his *Battle of Chancellorsville* (p. 164): "This deceptive and dangerous dispatch to Sedgwick may be excused perhaps in war, but it was false, and Warren was aware of it." Warren says in his official report: "This dispatch was written at a time when I was exceedingly exhausted."

ville. Lee is between. Stoneman has not been heard from. This is the situation at the hour from latest reports, 4:30 p.m.

The state of the supplies occasioned the following correspondence:

### Butterfield to Ingalls, 8 p.m.

How about the question of forage for animals? How can they fare and get on? The rations of the Eleventh, Twelfth, and Fifth expire to-night unless replenished from trains [on north side of Rappahannock]. I telegraphed the general yesterday, and reply came that orders would issue to-day. Have heard nothing. How stands it? Advise me.

### Ingalls to Butterfield, 8:15 p.m.

We can do nothing at present about forage and subsistence. If we succeed, we shall march at once to Fredericksburg. If we fail, we must try soon to reach our depots [by retreating]. The question must soon resolve itself. I propose to order all empty teams down to Falmouth.

Major Rusling wrote home:

. . . It has been a sad day here. General Berry was killed this morning at the head of our division. General Mott was again wounded; and every colonel in his brigade, except one, either killed or wounded. The carnage on both sides has been awful. Oh, what a Sunday!

. . . We hope and believe that to-morrow will wind up a week's fighting with a great and overwhelming victory.

At 3 p.m., as Howe and Newton started to follow Brooks toward Chancellorsville, Lee initiated a movement toward Hooker. In a low, quiet tone he gave his orders to Colston (Map 36):

General, I wish you to advance with your division on the United States Ford road. I expect you will meet with resistance before you come to the bend of the road. I do not want you to attack the enemy's positions, but only to feel them. Send your engineer officer with skirmishers to the front to reconnoiter and report. Don't engage seriously, but keep the enemy in check, and prevent him from advancing. Move at once.[1]

Pursuant to this order Colston advanced with two of his brigades on each side of the road and two Napoleon guns in the road between them. He had hardly started when he received a terrific fire of shell and canister from Weed's artillery. In less than two minutes 50 officers and men fell, killed and wounded, by his side. By this time he was aware that the Federals occupied a formidable position. To advance against it with a division so much reduced as his was, would have been only to insure its destruction, and would have been contrary to the

---

[1] General Colston, *B. and L.*, III, 233; and *W. R.*, 39, pp. 1006, 1007.

instructions that he had received.  He accordingly reported to Stuart that he was not able to attack with any prospect of success,[1] and about 3:45 was ordered to return with his division to his place in line.

At 4 p.m. Anderson proceeded, by order of General Lee, with the three brigades then present (Wright's, Perry's, and Posey's), to the River Road, opposite the Federal left (Map 36), "to watch that road, and to threaten the enemy's communications, and his line of retreat from Chancellorsville."  Major Hardaway with a battery of 13 rifled pieces was attached to this command.  He selected a position near Hayden's, from which to fire at the Federal camps across the river in the vicinity of United States Ford.[2]  These dispositions were completed about nightfall.

It may have been in consequence thereof that about 10 p.m. the Federal XII Corps (excepting Knipe's regiments guarding prisoners) was moved from its position as a general reserve to the left of the XI Corps, between that corps and the Rappahannock—Geary $\left(\frac{2}{XII}\right)$ on the right. To make room for it, Schurz's division $\left(\frac{3}{XI}\right)$ was withdrawn from the left of the XI Corps, and placed in rear of Devens' division $\left(\frac{1}{XI}\right)$.

Anderson remained quiet, watching Slocum; and McLaws slept on his arms in front of Sedgwick.  Early wrote to McLaws that he purposed attacking Marye's Hill and Sedgwick's rear at daylight, and McLaws transmitted this message to Lee.

---

[1] *W. R.*, 39, p. 1007.  See also the report of Colonel Hinrichs, chief engineer, *ib.*, pp. 1011, 1012.

[2] *Ib.*, 39, pp. 857, 879, 880.  The pieces were 3 of Hurt's, 4 of Jordan's, 2 of Carter's $\left(\frac{2}{n}\right)$, 2 of Fry's $\left(\frac{2}{n}\right)$, and 2 of Marye's $\left(\frac{1}{n}\right)$.

# CHAPTER XXV

MAY 4 . . . SEDGWICK FALLS BACK TO SCOTT'S FORD.   AVERELL RELIEVED

ANDERSON had prepared during the night for a demonstration against the extreme left of Hooker's line.  A large park of wagons was discovered on the north side of the river within range of the rifled artillery, and before daybreak Major Hardaway opened fire upon it with 10 rifled pieces.  "At 3:30 o'clock," says Lieutenant-Colonel Woods, chief commissary of subsistence of Sickles' corps, "[I] was awakened by the rapid explosion of shells near where I was, some of them falling in the same field where the beef-cattle were, but the most of them falling in a cavalry camp, about ⅓ of a mile away, among some rebel prisoners, and amid the ammunition-trains of one of the other corps.  This shelling lasted for the space of about seven minutes.[1]

"During this time the entire park had become the scene of the greatest confusion; teamsters and drivers of ambulances were fleeing to the rear in great haste upon their horses, in many instances without saddles, boots, or hats, and every path appeared to be filled with those wearing the crescent.  We attempted in vain to stop the incipient panic, and the fortunate cessation of the shells soon restored order."[2]  Meanwhile Anderson pushed forward his skirmishers and found the Federals holding and fortifying the high ridge along the Mineral Spring Road.  It appearing therefrom that Hooker would not advance down the river, Lee decided that Anderson should proceed to Salem Church and unite with McLaws and Early.  The three divisions and the corps artillery of Jackson's old corps, and Stuart's cavalry, about 25,000 men, were to remain under Stuart in front of Hooker's 75,500 men, and the divisions of Anderson, Early, and McLaws, with the corps artillery of the I Corps and a portion of the General Artillery Reserve (about 23,000 men), were to be thrown against Sedgwick, whose corps now numbered about 19,000 men.  Lee was not aware that Reynolds' corps had been transferred from Sedgwick's command to Hooker's, and was under the impression that Sedgwick had two corps with him.  Sedgwick believed that Early had been reënforced by a column 15,000 strong from Richmond and that it was this force or a part of it that had occupied the heights of

---

[1] Hardaway himself heard the crashing of the wagon bodies (*W. R.*, 39, p. 880).
[2] *Ib.*, 39, p. 398.

Fredericksburg, cutting him off from the town.[1]  Thus Lee and Sedgwick each estimated the other's strength in this quarter as about twice as great as it was.

Sedgwick continued anxious and perplexed.  At 1: 30 a.m. he wrote to Hooker:

We were checked here [near Salem Church] last night and held until dark.  I believe the enemy have been reënforcing all night, and will attack me in the morning.  How do matters stand with you?  Send me instructions.

At 6: 20 a.m. he wrote to Butterfield:

I am anxious to hear from General Hooker.  There is a strong force in front of me, strongly posted.[2]  I can not attack with any hope of dislodging them until I know something definite as to the position of their main body and ours.  I have sent two or three messengers to Banks' Ford, but none have returned, nor have I heard from the general since yesterday.

Ten minutes later he received Warren's dispatch of midnight.  He naturally concluded that he was not expected to do more than take care of himself unless Hooker attacked, but in that case he was to attack also.  As with Hooker yesterday at Chancellorsville, he was deterred from falling back to a stronger position by the prospect of assistance coming to him from the enemy's rear.

McLaws received the following dispatch sent at midnight by Lee's adjutant-general:

I am directed by General Lee to say that he thinks well of what General Early proposes, if it is practicable.  Such a movement would be a virtual relief to you, and might cause the enemy to pause or retire, and should this occur, he [General Lee] would desire that you press them so as to prevent their concentration on General Early.

The general says General Anderson is on your left [facing westward], watching for any movement down the river; has not yet heard from him; thinks his presence there will render your left flank secure.

This dispatch was forwarded by McLaws to Early.

About 7 a.m. Anderson was relieved on the River Road by Heth with three brigades of his division, and started for Salem Church.  By 8 a.m. Early had taken the heights of Fredericksburg, leaving Gibbon in possession of the town, but severing all tactical connection between him and Sedgwick, and capturing six empty wagons and a number of packmules of Stoneman's that were returning to the main train at the Lacy

---

[1] *W. R.*, 39, p. 560; Butterfield to Hooker, 11:30 a.m., *ib.*, 40, pp. 399, 340.

Pickett's and Hood's divisions were ordered to-day to march from in front of Suffolk *via* Ivor to Richmond (*ib.*, 26, p. 1045).

[2] McLaws, now numbering about 9000 men.

House.  He left Barksdale's brigade (about 1300 strong) and Andrews' battalion (4 batteries), altogether about 1600 men with 16 pieces, to hold Gibbon in check, and with the remainder of his force (about 10,400 men) formed line facing a little west of north.  He sent information of the state of affairs to McLaws, and waited to hear from him.

While Early retook the heights two Federal signal officers escaped to General Sedgwick, and established a station within his lines.  The messages went therefrom by signal either to Scott's Ford or to the vicinity of Falmouth, and *via* United States Ford, by telegraph, to within a mile of Hooker's headquarters.

Sedgwick received the following dispatch from Van Alen, sent at 6 a.m.:

The general commanding desires that you telegraph to him your exact position. What information have you respecting the force of the enemy in front and rear? What is your own strength?  Is there any danger of a force coming up in your rear and cutting your communications?  Can you sustain yourself acting separately or in coöperation with us?

Sedgwick wrote in reply:

*8:30 a.m.*

I am occupying the same position as last night.

*9 a.m.*

. . . I have secured my communication with Banks' Ford.  The enemy are in possession of the heights of Fredericksburg in force.  They appear strongly in our front, and are making efforts to drive us back. . . . It depends upon the condition and position of your force whether I can sustain myself here.  Howe reports the enemy advancing upon Fredericksburg [from the heights].

*9:45 a.m.*

The enemy are pressing me.  I am taking position to cross the river whenever necessary.

He formed his corps on three sides of a rectangle covering Scott's Ford,—with Howe on the left, Brooks in the center, and Newton on the right.  Batteries were posted along the line at the weaker points (Map 37).  This line, about 6500 yards in length, numbered about 3 men per running yard.

The 8 Pa. Cavalry, except one squadron, which was ordered to report to General Schurz, crossed the Rappahannock this morning at Scott's Ford, and reported to General Sedgwick, who ordered it to report to General Howe, by whom it was sent to the rear to cover the communications with Scott's Ford.[1]

---

[1] *The Charge at Chancellorsville*, by Pennock Huey, p. 73; *History of Pennsylvania Volunteers, 1861–1865*, by S. P. Bates, III, 115.

Gibbon had one of his two brigades in the town of Fredericksburg, and the other one and his two batteries on the north side of the Rappahannock at the bridges. He wrote to Butterfield that if Sedgwick had gone forward and he (Gibbon) was forced out of Fredericksburg, he would take up the bridges; and that if Sedgwick had "gone away" [by Scott's Ford], he "had better withdraw at once and take up the bridges."

Butterfield replied:

"Hold on to the last extremity, until further orders. Sedgwick holds the same position as he did."

He wrote also:

### To Hooker, 9:40 a.m.

. . . No information yet received shows more than a [Confederate] division in front of Fredericksburg. Should Sedgwick throw himself rapidly and boldly on their flank, he would capture or destroy them, if circumstances of your movements and position, and presence of enemy on his front and left, permit.[1]

### To Gibbon, 10:27 a.m.

Make your disposition so that no confusion or panic ensues. . . . Short of the loss of every man of your command, do not permit the enemy to cross. In case you retire from the town, be vigilant. I am just ordered to General Hooker and leaving here. Keep the fords well guarded by batteries and your picket line strong. Keep an eye out for the pontoon train that was reported at Hamilton's Crossing.[2] Much may depend on you. . . . You perhaps had better take up your lower bridge, and get boats out of water, and hold engineer force ready to work on others. Use your discretion.

At 10:35 a.m. Van Alen wrote to Butterfield:

. . . Gibbon's command is to remain where it is. The bridges, of course, are to remain. It would seem from your dispatch that Gibbon and the enemy are retreating from each other.

General Early, not receiving any message from McLaws nor hearing any sound of firing in his direction, sent out Smith's brigade to feel the Federal lines. It went up against Neill's brigade of Howe's division, which, with the assistance of two pieces of Martin's battery $\left(\frac{2}{2.\,VI}\right)$, drove it back, capturing the flag of the 58 Va. Concluding that the Federals were too strong for him to attack alone, Early reported the situation to McLaws, "requesting him to move."[3] He stated that if McLaws would attack in front, he would advance two brigades, and strike the enemy in flank and rear. McLaws did not consider himself

---

[1] A copy of this dispatch was sent to Sedgwick.
[2] There was no pontoon train at Hamilton's Crossing.
[3] W. R., 39, p. 1002.

strong enough to attack in front, but he thought that if Early would attack in flank and rear the Federals would be obliged at least to move, and would probably expose a flank or other weak point. So he agreed to advance provided Early would attack first. He informed General Lee of the plan proposed and asked for reënforcement.[1] Lee in reply sent him word of Anderson's movement toward him, and McLaws, on receiving it, gave orders that no attack should be made until General Anderson arrived. In the meantime Early was also informed that Anderson was coming, and was not to attack until he was in position on McLaws' right, connecting with Early's left. Anderson arrived at Salem Church at 11 and reported as directed to McLaws. Lee arrived soon afterward, and took charge of affairs. He directed Anderson to form his three brigades (Posey, Perry, and Wright) on Early's left, and sending for Early, gave him his instructions. A general attack was to be made at a signal of three guns to be fired in rapid succession. Three of Early's brigades—Hoke's, Hays', and Gordon's—were to join in the assault. The other brigade, Smith's, was to be held in reserve to reënforce Barksdale, if necessary, or portions of the attacking line. Anderson's three brigades on Early's left and the two brigades on McLaws' right (Kershaw's and Wofford's) were also to advance at the signal or when firing was heard on the right. The remainder of McLaws' force was to maintain a defensive attitude at least until the enemy in its front was in retreat.[2] Hardaway with his rifle battalion of 13 pieces, 2 pieces of Parker's battery of Alexander's battalion (I), Penick's battery $(\frac{1}{1})$, and 2 pieces of McCarthy's battery, altogether 21 pieces, took position on Smith's Hill (Map 36).

Sedgwick had decided to hold his present position until dark and then fall back upon his bridges.[3] He wrote:

*To Butterfield and Hooker, 11 a.m.*

. . . If I can hold until night, I shall cross at Banks' Ford, under instructions from General Hooker, given by Brigadier-General Warren.[4]

*To Hooker, 11:15 a.m.*

. . . It is not improbable that bridges [5] at Banks' Ford may be sacrificed. Can you help me strongly if I am attacked? . . . My bridges [5] are two miles from me. I am compelled to cover them above and below from attack, with the additional assistance of General Benham's brigade alone.[6]

---

[1] W. R., 39, p. 827.

[2] Ib., 39, pp. 802, 828, 831.

[3] Ib., 39, p. 560.

[4] Warren's dispatch of midnight, p. 403 ante.

[5] Only one bridge was laid at Scott's Ford, but Benham had the material for laying another.

[6] Owen's brigade of Gibbon's division $(\frac{2}{2. \text{II}})$.

*To Hooker, 1:40 p.m.*

. . . I have no means of judging of the enemy's force about me; deserters say 40,000. I shall take position near Banks' Ford and the Taylor house, at the suggestion of General Warren. Officers have already gone to select a position.

It is believed that the heights of Fredericksburg are occupied by two divisions of the enemy.

Messages now arrived from Hooker's headquarters:

*1, 10:30 a.m.*

The commanding general directs that in the event you fall back, you reserve, if practicable, a position on the Fredericksburg side of the Rappahannock, which you can hold securely until to-morrow p.m.

*2*

. . . I inclose substance of a communication sent last night [Warren's midnight dispatch]. Its suggestions are highly important, and meet my full approval. There are positions on your side, commanded by our batteries on the other side, I think you could take and hold. The general would recommend as one such position the ground on which Dr. Taylor's is situated.

HOOKER.

These dispatches would seem to sanction the withdrawal of Sedgwick's corps, provided a portion of it was left in a commanding position south of the Rappahannock. But it is safe to say that none of them was written or dictated by Hooker, notwithstanding that the last one was signed with his name. They were doubtless all written by staff officers, and sent off without being shown to Hooker, who since he was injured at Chancellorsville had been almost continuously alternating between sleep and stupor. It seems that on coming to himself and realizing their tenor he apprehended that Sedgwick would recross the river, and to prevent it, wrote or dictated the following dispatches:

*To Sedgwick, 11 a.m.*

The major-general commanding . . . does not wish you to cross the river at Banks' Ford unless you are compelled to do so. The batteries at Banks' Ford command the position. If it is practicable for you to maintain a position [on the] south side [of the] Rappahannock, near Banks' Ford, you will do so. . . .

*11:50 a.m.*

If the necessary information shall be obtained to-day, and if it shall be of the character he anticipates, it is the intention of the general to advance to-morrow. In this event the position of your corps on the south bank of the Rappahannock will be as favorable as the general could desire.

*1:20 p.m.*

I expect to advance to-morrow, which will be likely to relieve you.

You must not count on much assistance without I hear heavy firing. Tell General Benham to put down the other bridge, if you desire it.

Sedgwick replied at 2 : 15 p.m. :

I shall do my utmost to hold a position on the right bank of the Rappahannock until to-morrow.

Hooker's intentions at this time were later expressed by himself as follows :

I proposed to leave troops enough where I was to occupy the enemy there, and throw the rest of my force down the river and reënforce Sedgwick; then the whole of Lee's army except that which had been left in front of Sedgwick would be thrown off the road to Richmond, and my army would be on it.[1]

As previously stated, Sedgwick informed Benham yesterday that he wanted another bridge put down. He signaled to him to-day: "I wish the second bridge laid close by the first one."[2] At 1 p.m. Benham commenced laying this bridge, using the material left over from the bridges already laid at Banks' Ford and at United States Ford. He reported to Sedgwick at 3 p.m. :

I will have the [second] bridge done by 3 :30 o'clock.[3]

But he was reckoning without Hardaway's battery of 21 guns, which, whether intentionally or not, dropped an occasional shell annoyingly near the crossing, which delayed the construction of the bridge. Points of direction were established for night firing from Smith's Hill upon Scott's Ford.[4]

The reoccupation of Marye's Heights gave the Confederates control of the country between the Federal hospitals and the VI Corps. This necessitated the removal of the wounded across the river and the reëstablishment of communication with the corps by way of Scott's Ford. By 10 a.m. the hospitals were established in tents on the north side of the river; and by 11 all the wounded were removed to them. The ambulances were then dispatched to Scott's Ford, but as the pontoon bridge, on their arrival there, was found to be under fire, they could not cross the river.

About the middle of the afternoon, Hooker was waked out of one of his slumbers by Pleasonton handing him a paper with the remark: "General, this is a dispatch from the President." He took the paper, and read :

Washington, D. C., May 4, 1863, 3 :10 p.m.

*Major-General Hooker:*

We have news here that the enemy has reoccupied heights above Fredericksburg? Is that so?

A. LINCOLN.

---

[1] *Rep. of Com.*, IV, 148.      [3] *Ib.*
[2] *W. R.*, 39, p. 236.      [4] *Ib.*, 39, p. 821.

Having waited for some time in silence, Hooker at 4:20 p.m. had Pleasonton answer the message as follows:[1]

I am informed that it is so, but attach no importance to it.

JOSEPH HOOKER,

Major-General.

The bridge brought up yesterday from Banks' Ford to United States Ford was laid at the latter place this morning between 10 and 11:30, making three bridges at United States Ford.

Anderson got into the position assigned him about 12 m.[2] McLaws swung his two right brigades to the left, bringing his right within about ¾ of a mile of Anderson's left. This gap was to be closed as the troops advanced. The afternoon, however, wore away in skirmishing for information and getting into position.[3] Excluding Barksdale's brigade and Andrews' battalion (about 2000 men), neutralized by Gibbon, Lee had 21,000 men confronting the 19,000 under Sedgwick.[4] Had he become aware of the thinness of Hooker's line, he might have planned to break through it. According to Doubleday, Lee, after personally examining Sedgwick's position, ''gave orders to break in the center of the Sixth Corps so as to defeat the two wings, throw them off in eccentric directions, and scatter the whole force.''[5] But he gives no authority for this statement, and his own description of the action seems inconsistent with such a plan. Lee's general idea seems to have been to crush the Federal left under Howe and drive the corps in the general direction of the Plank Road toward McLaws, who, together with Heth on the River Road, was to prevent a junction of Sedgwick with Hooker. Anderson and McLaws' right were to press the retreating Federals toward the Rappahannock. To prevent their crossing it, Hardaway's artillery was to riddle their bridges, and Early's right brigade, Gordon's, to push toward the crossing and intercept or harass their retreat.

About 1 p.m. Howe received reliable information that the enemy was assembling a force largely outnumbering his division immediately in rear of Fredericksburg for another attack. In view of his repulse of Smith's brigade in the morning, he expected that if the enemy made a second attempt it would be against his left. He therefore carefully examined the ground, and made arrangements, in case his left was unable to hold its position, to withdraw it to a position of safety. His formation was in two lines (advanced line and main line) besides his line of skirmishers. His advanced line and skirmish line were formed of

[1] Pleasonton in *Rep. of Com.*, IV, 31.

[2] *W. R.*, 39, pp. 802, 852.

[3] This delay is not satisfactorily accounted for in the records. The only reference to it that the author finds is in Lee's report (*W. R.*, 39, p. 802).

[4] Without counting Owen's brigade at Scott's Ford.

[5] *Chancellorsville and Gettysburg*, p. 65.

Neill's brigade and two regiments (4 Vt. and 5 Vt.) of Grant's brigade; his main line, of Grant's brigade and 12 pieces of artillery.

It was about 5:30 p.m. when Lee's three signal shots were at last fired,[1] and his troops advanced to the attack. Hays' brigade moved to the right across the front of the 5 Vt. and the 2 pieces of artillery which it supported. The latter had exhausted their ammunition, but the 5 Vt. poured a heavy enfilading fire into the enemy's ranks, and kept this up until Hoke's brigade, coming up on its right and rear, threatened to cut it off, when it withdrew to the right of the 3 Vt. Hays struck the 20 N. Y. in flank, front, and rear, and flung it back on Rigby's battery $\left(\frac{3}{1.\ VI}\right)$, which threw this organization into such confusion that "it could do nothing."[2] It withdrew without firing again. The 20 N. Y. went on to the rear and could not be rallied.[3] Hoke coming up in the dusk on Hays' left, the two brigades fired into each other and were thrown into such confusion that they had to fall back to reform. A portion of Smith's brigade came up to their assistance, and presumably covered their withdrawal.[4] Howe now extended his left and sent to Sedgwick for reënforcement. Gordon, meanwhile, had moved northward, compelling the withdrawal of Howe's skirmishers and advanced line. Howe was compelled to yield some ground, but at the end of the contest his main line was practically where it was at the beginning. Thanks to his preparations on his left, and to his being reënforced with a battery and seven regiments of infantry, he presented in his new position an effective barrier to the enemy's progress[5] (Map 38). The attack on Brooks was easily repulsed, principally by his skirmishers and artillery. The only force that he had to oppose was Wright's brigade, as it masked the movements of Posey's and Perry's brigades. McLaws' two right brigades worked their way slowly and laboriously through the wood and underbrush in the direction of Brooks' right, but did not reach it. Newton and Burnham were not molested. Hardaway, on Smith's Hill, opened fire with 18 pieces on 12 Federal pieces near Banks' Ford, which were in position to enfilade McLaws' line of battle.[6] He states in his report that he disabled 6 pieces and drove 2 off the field, but, according to one of his battery commanders, 16 of Hardaway's pieces were silenced by the Federal fire.[7] Such was the situation when, about 6:45 p.m., Sedgwick, in accordance with his decision of this morning, issued orders for a general withdrawal. General Newton, a trained engineer

---

[1] The Federal authorities generally say 5, the Confederates 6 p.m.

[2] W. R., 39, p. 597.

[3] Ib., 39, p. 610.

[4] Chancellorsville, by Hotchkiss and Allan, pp. 93, 94.

[5] His reënforcements consisted of Butler's regular battery $\left(\frac{2}{3.\ VI}\right)$, Wheaton's brigade,

and two regiments of Burnham's brigade (W. R., 39, p. 561).

[6] Ib., 39, p. 881. The Confederate pieces in action were 5 of Parker's and Penick's (1. I), 2 of McCarthy's (2. I), and the 13 of Hardaway's mixed battalion brought up from the River Road, except 2 of Hurt's.

[7] Captain McCarthy (W. R., 39, p. 848).

officer, was sent back to select and prepare the new line of defence. The movement was successfully executed. Pursuit was checked on the Federal left by Howe, and was not promptly undertaken anywhere else. A dense fog settled over the field, increasing the obscurity, and necessitating caution to avoid collision with one's own troops.[1] About 9:30 Wilcox with the 8 and 9 Ala. of his brigade, Kershaw's brigade, and Manly's battery, began following the retreat. He was too late to interfere with it, but reached the river near Banks' Ford, and there succeeded in capturing a few prisoners.[2]

The Federals now found themselves on high ground with shelter trenches in front of them and 34 pieces of artillery on the still higher ground behind them. Their second bridge, on which they had been working, was completed at 10 p.m.

About this time Colonel Alexander of the Confederate artillery received orders "to fire upon the ford over which the enemy was retreating." The guns of Hardaway's rifle battalion (probably 11 pieces) opened fire, and continued firing one gun at intervals of twenty minutes until half an hour after sunrise on the 5th;[3] and Manly's battery shelled the woods along the river and the ford for about half an hour from the advanced position occupied by Wilcox.[4]

The two following dispatches show how matters were viewed by Lee and Sedgwick:

Downman's House, May 4, 10 p.m.

MAJOR-GENERAL McLAWS.

*General:*

. . . We cannot find any of the enemy south of the Plank road. But if we let them alone until morning we will find them again intrenched, so I wish to push them over the river to-night. . . .

Direct Colonel Alexander to endeavor to arrest all movements [of the enemy] across Banks' Ford, or up the river road [toward Hooker]. Anderson and Early are north of the Plank road.

I am, very respectfully yours,

R. E. LEE,

General.[5]

Banks' Ford, Va., May 4, 1863, 11:50 p.m.

*General Hooker*, United States Ford:

My army is hemmed in upon the slope, covered by the guns from the north side of Banks' Ford. If I had only this army to care for, I would withdraw it to-night. Do your operations require that I should jeopard it by retaining it here? An immediate reply is indispensable, or I may feel obliged to withdraw.

JOHN SEDGWICK,

Major-General.

[1] *W. R.*, 39, p. 802.
[2] Thirteen officers and 150 men (*W. R.*, 39, p. 860).
[3] *Ib.*, 39, pp. 821, 882.
[4] *Ib.*, 39, p. 831.
[5] *Ib.*, 40, pp. 860, 861.

All this time Hooker with his 75,500 men, and the sound of Sedgwick's guns ringing in his ears, was held in check by Stuart with his 25,000. He allowed the day to pass without discovering the feebleness of his opponent and appreciating the opportunity presented to him for crushing this fraction of Lee's army. Behind his intrenchments bristling with cannon and swarming with men, he waited supinely for Stuart to attack him or Sedgwick to attack Stuart. Reynolds begged to be allowed to attack the enemy's left flank, and failing to receive permission, sent Stone's brigade on a reconnaissance, hoping that it would bring on a general engagement. Stone got near enough to hear the voices of Stuart's men, but prudently withdrew, not dreaming of the real purpose of the movement, of which Reynolds informed him afterward.[1] The 12 and 13 Mass. with Hall's battery, and accompanied by General Robinson, made a reconnaissance to near Ely's Ford. They found the enemy in force, but then, having orders not to bring on an engagement, simply retraced their steps.[2] Among the notable casualties of this day's desultory fighting was the death of Major-General Whipple. While standing near Ricketts' battery, directing the construction of some earthworks, he was mortally wounded by a sharpshooter sitting in a tree, who had been annoying the Federal officers with his fire directed especially upon them. General Sickles had sent instructions to Whipple to have Berdan detach a portion of his command to dislodge him. Whipple was on his horse writing an order to this effect when he was hit. The bullet passed through his belt and stomach, and came out at the small of his back close to the spinal column. The sharpshooter proceeded to load, but he never fired again. A lieutenant of Berdan's, carrying a loaded rifle, stalked across the Federal line of battle, crept through the line of skirmishers, and felt his way into the woods beyond till he caught sight of the Confederate marksman. Before the latter could finish reloading the lieutenant drew a bead on him and fired, bringing him down a corpse. On his return he exhibited as trophies an extra rifle, a foxskin cap, $1600 in Confederate money, and $100 in greenbacks.[3]

One of Knipe's regiments $\left(\frac{128}{\text{1. 1. XII}}\right)$, guarding prisoners under Patrick, returned to its brigade. Another, the 4 Pa., recrossed the river *en route* to the front.

The two-year men of the 5 N. Y. Volunteers, Duryee Zouaves

---

[1] Address, July 1, 1899, by H. S. Huidekooper; *History of the 150th Regiment Pa. Volunteers*, by Lieutenant-Colonel Thomas Chamberlin, p. 95.

[2] *History of the 12 Mass. Vol.*, by Lieutenant-Colonel B. F. Cook, p. 93.

"Between the 3d and 4th, reconnaissances were made on the right [in the right wing] from one end of the line to the other, to feel the enemy's strength, and find a place and way to attack him successfully; but it was ascertained that it could only be made on him behind his defences, and with slender columns, which I believed he could destroy as fast as they were thrown on to his works" (Hooker's testimony, *Rep. of Com.*, IV, 133).

[3] New York *Herald*, May 7, 8; *Historical Sketch of the 118th Regiment Pa. Volunteers*, by H. T. Peck, p. 202.

(3. 2. V), were relieved to-day from duty with the army in order that they might return to the place where they had been mustered in, and arrive there in time to be mustered out on the expiration of their period of enlistment. They were honored with a complimentary order.[1]

To the music of the enemy's bullets, amid the rattling of their comrades' rifles and the thundering of their cannon, officers and soldiers turned their backs on the field of battle, and marched to the rear. After crossing the pontoon bridge at United States Ford, they took up the other two-year men of the regiment, who were guarding the wagons, and proceeded briskly, about 200 strong, toward Stoneman's Switch. As they passed Banks' Ford they saw firing between Sedgwick's men and Lee's, and were harassed with fears that they would be again ordered to the front. But they reached the railroad without any such *contretemps*, and were safely conveyed North, receiving on the way and at their destination the ovations with which our people are wont to honor their military heroes.

In contrast with this incident it is pleasant to consider that the 123 Pa. of Allabach's brigade (Colonel J. B. Clark) should, under existing orders, have been on its homeward march to-day. But it remained on the field of battle, and did not leave the army until the 8th, the day on which its term of enlistment expired.[2] The 4 N. Y. (Colonel J. D. McGregor) was enlisted, for the greater part, to be mustered out on the 1st of May. The whole regiment remained with the army through the campaign, and was not mustered out till the 25th.[3]

This morning the New York *Herald* said in an editorial:

The city yesterday was full of absurd rumors of defeat and disaster, which we hope will be completely dispelled by official intelligence to-day of the greatest achievement of the war; . . . considering the numbers of the rebel forces en-

---

[1] "Headquarters 2d Division, V Corps,
"Camp near Chancellorsville, Va.,
                    "May 4, 1863.
"General Order No. 99.

"I. The term of service of a portion of the 5th Regiment being about to expire, the Major-General commanding desires the officers and men to know that he parts from them with very great regret, a regret which he is confident is shared with the whole division. The regiment has been distinguished in all the operations of his command, especially at Gaines' Mill and the battle of Manassas Plains. Its ranks, thinned and scarred by battle, are the best and proudest witness of the fact. The General hopes to see again the brave men who have served under him. Many of their comrades still have to hold in trust the respect of the old

regiment, and the General has no fears but that it will be sacredly guarded and preserved. The officers and men who are to leave this army will proceed to New York on the 5th. Colonel Winslow will turn in to the proper department at Aquia Creek all ordnance stores and all supplies of property not needed for the men who remain.

.    .    .    .    .    .    .

"By command of General SYKES:
"G. RYAN, Captain, A. A. General."

*Camp and Field Life of the 5 N. Y. Volunteer Infantry, Duryee Zouaves,* by A. Davenport, pp. 387, 388.

[2] *W. R.,* 39, p. 549.

[3] *New York in the War of the Rebellion,* by F. Phisterer, p. 377.

gaged elsewhere, east and west, we believe it simply impossible that General Lee could muster an army capable of standing five hours outside of his works before the powerful army of General Hooker.

A few hours later Horace Greeley, editor of the New York *Tribune*, entered a room at the *Tribune* office, holding in his hand the latest telegram from the front. His face was pallid, his step almost tottering, and his lips trembled. "My God!" he exclaimed, "it is horrible—horrible; and to think of it, 130,000 magnificent soldiers so cut to pieces by less than 60,000 half-starved ragamuffins!"[1]

At daylight to-day Averell received Hooker's order relieving him from command. About 10 a.m. his division, now under Pleasonton, broke camp. It crossed the Rappahannock at United States Ford, and camped 5 miles therefrom in the direction of Falmouth.

The main train of the II Corps moved to-day to United States Ford.[2] Instructions were issued by the chief quartermaster of the army looking to the safety of the depots and trains in case of a general failure or reverse.[3] At Aquia Landing everything movable was put on boats.[4]

Rear-Admiral Lee wrote to Dix:

. . . I respectfully and earnestly propose to you a joint expedition to take Fort Powhatan, Petersburg, and perhaps Richmond. I am ready to move at a moment's notice, and will coöperate with you in any and every way possible. My gunboats and a few companies will hold your posts at Suffolk and Yorktown.

The opportunity for striking a great blow is such as rarely presents itself in the history of nations. I am confident you will improve it.[5]

This suggestion was not favorably considered by General Dix, and the operation was not undertaken.

[1] *Personal Recollections of Abraham Lincoln and the Civil War*, by J. R. Gilmore, p. 103.

[2] *W. R.*, 39, p. 549.

[3] *Ingalls to Haupt, 1, 12 m.*

"The [railroad] bridge need not be built of course at present. You doubtless will see that your road stock is not molested by any raid of the rebels."

2

"I do not wish any more supplies taken up [from Aquia to Falmouth] until further notice. I hope you will ask for protection at Aquia in case of necessity, though we trust to fight it out in excellent style yet."

*To Thompson, Quartermaster, Aquia, 12 m.*

"Keep as much of the public property afloat as you can until further orders. Be prepared to act at short notice. See that your depot is kept constantly prepared [to move]."

*To Rankin, Quartermaster, Falmouth, 12 m.*

"Do not come up here yourself. Perhaps no one had better come just yet. Keep quiet; do not make any excitement. We are in great trouble, but we shall fight [it] out. Do not communicate with Washington on the subject."

[4] *History of the 9 N. Y. Cavalry*, by N. Cheney, p. 89.

[5] *W. R.*, 26, pp. 693, 694.

# CHAPTER XXVI

AT midnight (4th–5th) all the corps commanders of the Army of the Potomac, except Sedgwick and Slocum, assembled in a large tent at Hooker's headquarters in consultation. Hooker, Warren, and Butterfield were also present. Slocum was called, but, on account of the long distance from his post, did not arrive until after the meeting broke up. Hooker set forth the condition of affairs in the right wing, expressing apprehension of a want of steadiness on the part of some of the troops, exhibited, it seemed to him, by uncalled-for firing along parts of the line, and gave his hearers to understand that he was in favor of withdrawing the army to the north bank of the Rappahannock. He presented for consideration the question whether the army should advance or withdraw. Hooker and Butterfield then retired. Warren, thinking that some information might be wanted of him, remained. Meade and Howard spoke in favor of advancing.[1] Reynolds said that, as his corps was the only one that had not been engaged, he would not urge his opinion, but that he agreed with Meade. He asked Meade to vote for him, and then went to sleep. Couch expressed himself as incompetent from lack of knowledge to give an opinion. The knowledge which he felt himself lacking was whether in case of an advance Hooker would be in active command, and how he purposed to operate. Couch said that he favored an attack, provided he could choose the point of attack. Sickles modestly remarked that his profession had not been that of a soldier, and that therefore his opinion was perhaps entitled to but little consideration. He then presented reasons for retiring. He created a little stir as he went on to remark that he was astonished at the manner in which the commanding general had presented the subject, that he had not expected that "the responsibilities" would be thrown on the corps commanders. At this point the loyal Warren, perceiving that his chief was coming in for some criticism, withdrew.

The question was raised and discussed whether a withdrawal could be safely effected. Before the assemblage dissolved, Hooker returned to

---

[1] "Howard voted to remain, without reference to the situation of the army, because, in his opinion, his corps had behaved badly, and he wished to retrieve his reputation" (*Chancellorsville and Gettysburg*, by A. Doubleday, p. 68).

the tent and stated as his decided opinion that he could withdraw the army without loss of men or material. This statement and perhaps other circumstances satisfied Couch that Hooker would be in command, whichever way the army moved. So when the vote was taken Meade, Reynolds, and Howard voted for an advance, and Sickles and Couch for a withdrawal.[1] Hooker thereupon announced that he would take upon himself the responsibility of withdrawing. As the officers stepped out of the tent, Reynolds broke out: "What was the use of calling us together at this time of night when he intended to retreat anyhow?"[2] Thus Hooker, after stating to Sedgwick that he would advance in the morning, decided, against the advice of his corps commanders, to leave his lieutenant in the lurch. He directed General Warren to prepare a new and shorter line of defence in his rear to secure the army against any attempt of the enemy to interrupt its passage of the river, and ordered the corps commanders to cut roads where necessary, leading from their positions to United States Ford. He ordered Pleasonton "to cover all the fords, and prevent the enemy crossing until the army had got over."[3] General Hunt, chief of artillery, was instructed at daybreak to cross all the batteries not in line of battle to the north bank of the Rappahannock, under cover of the fog, and send them by way of Hartwood Church to their old camps. This duty Hunt delegated to Captain Best, chief of artillery of the XII Corps, directing him to select positions to protect the recrossing of the army. The V Corps was designated as rear-guard. This corps was the best posted to cover the main roads to United States Ford; its advanced position naturally suggested it as the one to retire last. It had, moreover, been the least engaged of all the corps, except the I, whose position on the extreme right was not suitable for the rear-guard. It had been the last to cross the Rappahannock at Kelley's Ford, and its commander had discharged the duty of bringing up the rear of the army on that occasion in a satisfactory manner. Finally, it comprised the regular division. These considerations may all have had weight in determining its selection as rear-guard.

Hooker was still unwilling that the VI Corps should recross the Rappahannock. "My desire," he says, "was to have General Sedgwick retain a position on the south side of the river in order that I might leave a sufficient force to hold the position I was in, and with the balance of

---

[1] "Whenever afterward Couch's action was challenged he replied: 'And I would do it again under such a commander'." (*History of the II Army Corps*, by F. A. Walker, pp. 250, 251).

[2] Testifying before the Committee on the Conduct of the War, Hooker said: "Being resolved on recrossing the river, . . . I called the corps commanders together, not as a council of war, but to ascertain how they felt in regard to making what I considered a desperate move against the enemy in our front" (*Rep. of Com.*, IV, 134).

[3] *Ib.*, 32. Pleasonton stated that he started at midnight to execute this order. The hour was probably later.

my force recross the river, march down to Banks' Ford, and turn the enemy's position in my front [at United States Ford] in so doing."[1]

Benham and Sedgwick had been classmates and friends at West Point. As they walked up and down upon the slope on which the men were lying at Scott's Ford, Benham cautioned Sedgwick not to recross the Rappahannock under any circumstances without his entire command, nor without Hooker's express sanction.[2]  Acting upon this suggestion, Sedgwick wrote to Hooker:

### Second Dispatch

I shall hold my position, as ordered, on south [side] of Rappahannock.

The messenger with his first dispatch (11:50 p.m., May 4)[3] had to ride perhaps 3 miles to reach the place of telegraphing, and Sedgwick thought that the messenger with the second one would overtake him, but he did not.  To Sedgwick's first dispatch Butterfield replied:

*1 a.m.*  Dispatch this moment received.  Withdraw.  Cover the river, and prevent any force crossing.  Acknowledge this.

About ten minutes later he received Sedgwick's second dispatch.  In reply thereto Hooker wrote:

*1:20 a.m.*  Yours received, saying you should hold position.  Order to withdraw countermanded.  Acknowledge both.

Having received the dispatch of 1 a.m., Sedgwick wrote to Butterfield:

*2 a.m.*  General Hooker's order received.  Will withdraw my forces immediately.

He acted accordingly.  Hooker's messenger with the dispatch countermanding the order to withdraw was delayed *en route*.  To this dispatch Sedgwick replied:

*2:30 a.m.*  Yours just received, countermanding order to withdraw.  Almost my entire command has crossed over.

The crossing being completed, this message was supplemented with the two following ones to Butterfield:

*5 a.m.*  The bridges at Banks' Ford are swung, and in process of being taken up.  The troops are much exhausted.  The dispatch countermanding my movement over the river was received after the troops had crossed.

*7 a.m.*  I recrossed to the north bank of the Rappahannock last night, and am in camp about a mile back from the ford.  The bridges have been taken up.

---

[1] *Rep. of Com.*, IV, 133.
[2] *Chancellorsville and Gettysburg*, by A. Doubleday, p. 66.
[3] P. 415 *ante*.

The retreat was covered by the 8 Pa. Cavalry, two companies of which swam the river after the pontoons were removed.[1]

Early this morning Hall's brigade withdrew from Fredericksburg to the north side of the Rappahannock. The 19 Mass. acted as rear-guard. Its left wing moved noiselessly to the river-bank and held the head of the pontoon bridge, while the right wing as silently fell back upon it. The enemy, discovering the movement, followed it up, but as he neared the defensive line, received a volley which turned him back. The Massachusetts regiment made a rush for the river, and gained the pontoon bridge. Two officers and half a dozen men with axes severed the shore lines which held it on the south side, then leaped into the boats and poled across. The bridge slowly drifted down with the current to the north shore, and the enemy did not attempt to follow it.[2] The three bridges were dismantled and taken up between 3 and 7 p.m.

In preparation for Hooker's withdrawal, Warren and Comstock prepared an inner line of intrenchment covering the bridges at United States Ford. Continuous "cover and abatis" were constructed from the Rappahannock at Scott's Dam around to the mouth of Hunting Run on the Rapidan, a distance of 3 miles. This was the third line of defence that Hooker had caused to be prepared. It was not occupied to-day. The line which the army had been occupying since the 3d will be referred to hereafter as the Chandler line.

Captain Best, pursuant to Hunt's directions of this morning, put 44 guns in position on the north bank of the Rappahannock:[3] 10 in the bend below United States Ford, to sweep the front of the left of Hooker's line, and command all the open ground upon which the enemy could place guns to shell the bridges,[4] and 34 to command the ford so as to hold the enemy in check, should he attempt to follow the army on its withdrawal.[5] The following instructions were issued:

Circular:

The Major-General commanding directs that every vehicle in your command on this side (south) of the river be sent to the north bank without unnecessary delay, under cover of the present fog; all extra animals of every kind to be sent over also. This, of course, does not include your necessary artillery and a very few ambulances.

*To Reynolds, 8:45 a.m.*

. . . send a most reliable [infantry] regiment (good shots), with a battery, to Richards' Ford, axemen with them, to fell trees, and make every possible obstacle to the passage of troops on our flank; to move quickly. The regiment and battery

---

[1] *The Charge at Chancellorsville*, by Pennock Huey, pp. 73, 74.

[2] *History of the 19th Regiment Mass. Vol. Infantry*, by Committee, p. 208.

[3] 8 of the I Corps, 18 of the II Corps, and 18 of the XII Corps (*W. R.*, 39, pp. 676, 206, 303, 310, 350, 361, 674).

[4] $\frac{1}{2.\,\text{XII}}$, $\frac{3}{2.\,\text{I}}$.

[5] $\frac{2}{1.\,\text{XII}}$, $\frac{1}{1.\,\text{II}}$, and others.

must intrench themselves, and be instructed (confidentially) to fight to the death in case the enemy approach there. Let them have good supply of rations and ammunition by pack-train. I inclose a copy of dispatch to General Pleasonton, who will move to the right of Richards' Ford, as soon as he can, from Falmouth.

[Inclosure]

*To Pleasonton, 8:45 a.m.*

. . . send a brigade of cavalry and a horse battery to guard our right, above Richards' Ford. Take intrenching tools with them. General Reynolds will be directed to send a regiment of infantry and a battery to Richards' Ford. Obstruct all fords or possible crossings up to Rappahannock Station. Officers and men must be instructed to fight to the death to guard our right. Put most reliable and true men on this duty. Will send copy of Reynolds' instructions.

*To Sedgwick, 2:30 p.m.*

. . . you are charged with the duty of guarding the river. General Gibbon's command is temporarily placed at your disposal for this purpose. The probabilities now are that [all] the forces on the south bank will retire [across the river] to-night. You will make dispositions accordingly. . . .

Pleasonton wrote to Butterfield at 10:10 a.m.:

. . . Have sent [ordered] a brigade of five regiments under Colonel Davis, and Martin's battery, above Richards' Ford. . . .

A. PLEASONTON.

The situation of the army was reported to President Lincoln by the following dispatch of 11 a.m. to-day, which was not received until 10:45 a.m. on the 6th:[1]

. . . The Cavalry [Corps], as yet learned about, have failed in executing their orders. Averell's division returned; nothing done; loss of 2 or 3 men. Buford's Regulars not heard from. General Sedgwick failed in the execution of his orders, and was compelled to retire, and crossed the river at Banks' Ford last night; his losses not known.

The I, III, V, XI, XII [Corps], and two divisions of II Corps are now on south bank of Rappahannock, intrenched between Hunting Run and Scott's Dam. Trains and Artillery Reserve on north bank of Rappahannock. Position is strong, but circumstances, which in time will be fully explained, make it expedient, in the general's judgment, that he should retire from this position to the north bank of the Rappahannock for his defensible position. Among these is danger to his communication by possibility of enemy crossing river on our right flank and imperiling this army, with present departure of two years' [troops] and three months' [nine months'] troops constantly weakening him. The nature of the country in which we are prevents moving in such a way as to find or judge of

[1] *Rep. of Com.*, IV, 226.

position or movements of enemy.  He [Hooker] may cross to-night, but hopes to be attacked in this position.

> DANIEL BUTTERFIELD,
> Major-General, Chief of Staff.

Owing to the censorship of the telegraph by the War Department, the news that reached the general public was meager, and the newspapers complained bitterly.  One of them which supported the administration expressed itself thus:

> What does the government mean by this persistent suppression of telegraphic war dispatches from Washington?  The whole country is in an agony of expectation to know the progress of the tremendous combat which is going on in Virginia.  Why should it not be allowed to know?  We have too much respect for the members of the cabinet to suppose for a moment that it is done for the benefit of stock-jobbers, and yet the whole effect of it is to give them the opportunities they so much desire.[1]

As a contemporary record indicative of the state of the public mind at this time, the following extract from the diary of a son of General Dix is worthy of perusal:

> . . . It would seem that Hooker has beaten Lee, and that Lee has beaten Hooker; that we have taken Fredericksburg, and that the rebels have taken it also; that we have 4500 prisoners, and the rebels 5400; that Hooker has cut off Lee's retreat, and Lee has cut off Sedgwick's retreat, and Sedgwick has cut off everybody's retreat generally, but has retreated himself although his retreat was cut off; that Longstreet has not left Suffolk at all, and again that he has never been there.  In short, all is utter confusion.  Everything seems to be everywhere, and everybody all over, and there is no getting at any truth.[2]

Pleasonton's orders brought him into conflict with Gibbon, to whom Sedgwick had practically delegated his authority for the defence of the river (*Appendix 17*).  Pleasonton refused to receive orders from Gibbon.  Regarding his own dispositions he wrote to Butterfield at 2: 30 p.m.:

> [I] Have two regiments of cavalry below Fredericksburg, watching river and Neck over ten miles down.  Hear the rebels did have one pontoon train at Hamilton's Crossing.[3]  Have sent for another horse battery to be placed [below]; one [is now] at Richards' Ford.  Will pounce on them if they try to cross in that way [by pontoon] to-night below.  Would it not be well for the gunboats to push

---

[1] New York *Evening Post*, May 5, 1863; quoted from Rhodes, *History of the U. S.*, which see, Vol. IV, pp. 267 and 268 (footnotes), for details of the telegraph censorship.

[2] Quoted in *Memoirs of John Adams Dix*, compiled by his son Morgan Dix, II, 57.

[3] There had been no pontoon train at Hamilton's Crossing.

up the Rappahannock as far as they can? They can help a great deal. All quiet up to 12 m., at last accounts, up the river and to the rear toward Dumfries.

A. PLEASONTON,

Brigadier-General Commanding.

Butterfield inquired of Magaw whether it would be possible for him to send any gunboats up the Rappahannock and received an unfavorable reply, ending, however, with the statement: "If you will assume the responsibility, I will send everything under my command up the Rappahannock."[1] This offer, it seems, was not accepted.

Lee learned this morning that Sedgwick and Gibbon had withdrawn across the river; and regarding Hooker, received the following communication:

Stuart to Taylor, 8:45 a.m.

. . . the forced reconnaissance in our front, which I have ordered, discovered the enemy in force in earthworks, artillery and infantry. About thirteen pieces of artillery are said to bear on our center. About 200 spades and picks would be very acceptable toward burying the dead of the enemy and horses dead near the hospital [Chancellorsville?] and lines. Can they be had from Early's line? Our own dead are nearly all buried.[2]

Hooker to Lee

I would most respectfully request the privilege of sending a burial party on the field of Chancellorsville, to bury the dead and care for the wounded officers and soldiers of my command.

No answer was made to this dispatch to-day. Medical Director Letterman was ordered this morning to remove all the wounded without delay, but to use only ambulances already on the south side of the river; the provost marshal at the river had orders to allow no ambulances to return when they had once passed to the north bank. Numbers of the wounded would have been left behind, had not the medical director, after much solicitation, obtained permission late in the day to take ambulances from the north side of the river. With the transportation thus secured, all the wounded were got across before the troops commenced crossing.[3]

The telegraph station was moved half a mile back toward the river to be reëstablished, but the line was broken by the retreating troops.

By General Lee's order, Jackson was moved to-day from the hospital at Wilderness Tavern to a house near Guiney's Station. Being asked what he thought of Hooker's plan of campaign, he replied:

It was in the main a good conception, an excellent plan. But he should not have sent away his cavalry; that was his great blunder. It was that which enabled

---

[1] *Naval W. R.*, Series I, Vol. V, p. 264.  [3] *Medical Recollections of the Army of*
[2] *W. R.*, 108, p. 702.                      *the Potomac*, by Jonathan Letterman, pp. 137, 138.

me to turn him without his being aware of it, and to take him in the rear. Had he kept his cavalry with him, his plan would have been a very good one.[1]

Lee wrote to President Davis from Guiney's Station:

At the close of the battle of Chancellorsville on Sunday [3d] the enemy was reported advancing from Fredericksburg in our rear. General McLaws was sent back to arrest his progress, and repulsed him handsomely that afternoon at Tabernacle Church. Learning that his force consisted of two corps under General Sedgwick, I determined to attack it. Leaving a sufficient force to hold General Hooker in check, who had not recrossed the Rappahannock, as was reported, but occupied a strong position in front of the U. S. Ford, I marched back yesterday with General Anderson, and uniting with McLaws and Early in the afternoon, succeeded, by the blessing of Heaven, in driving General Sedgwick over the river. We have reoccupied Fredericksburg, and no enemy remains south of the Rappahannock in its vicinity.[2]

Leaving Early's division and Barksdale's brigade to hold the lines of Fredericksburg as before, and disregarding for the present the position of Banks' Ford, Lee ordered McLaws' and Anderson's divisions (including Wilcox's brigade) to march to the vicinity of Chancellorsville. The marching and fighting of the last four days had reduced the numbers and sapped the strength of the troops, but did not prevent their responding with alacrity to this new call upon their martial spirit. "As I sheltered myself," says the correspondent of the London *Times*, "in a little farm-house on the Plank Road, the brigades of Anderson's division came splashing through the mud in wild tumultuous spirits, singing, shouting, jesting, heedless of soaking rags, drenched to the skin, and burning again to mingle in the mad revelry of battle."[3] Lee had resolved to attack Hooker on both flanks, directing Anderson and McLaws against his left on the Mineral Spring Road, and Stuart against his right on the Hunting Run. Before the lines could be formed for attack Stuart's troops had to be relieved by Anderson and McLaws opposite the Federal left. It was late and dark when the preparations for the assault were completed, and Lee was obliged to put off the formidable task till the morrow.[4] He directed Colonel Alexander of the artillery to accompany Captain Johnston of the engineers to reconnoiter a position whence the Federal line of battle on the Mineral Spring Road "could be reached." Alexander moved his whole battalion by the River Road to such a position, and in the course of the night had six gun-pits partially constructed. The Federal artillery

---

[1] *Stonewall Jackson and the American Civil War,* by Lieutenant-Colonel F. G. R. Henderson, II, 572.
[2] *W. R.,* 39, pp. 794, 795.

[3] *Stonewall Jackson,* by Lieutenant-Colonel Henderson, II, 571.
[4] *The Crisis of the Confederacy,* by Cecil Battine, p. 91.

across the river, without having observed the work of the Confederates, intrenched itself also during the night.

Under cover of darkness and a drenching rain, the retreat of the Federals commenced about 7:15 p.m., the artillery leading. The bridges were covered with pine boughs to deaden the sound. About 10 o'clock, hardly half of the artillery having crossed, the movement was interrupted by a sudden rise in the river so great as to submerge the ends of the bridges on the north side, and the velocity of the current threatened to sweep them away.[1] Some of the batteries that had moved toward the river were sent back to their positions. The infantry was still in the Chandler line, with pickets out (Map 39).

[1] Captain Candler says that the river rose 6 feet 8 inches in two hours (manuscript).

# CHAPTER XXVII

### RETURN TO STAFFORD HEIGHTS.  DEATH OF JACKSON

MAY 6.  When the order was given for the army to recross the river, General Hooker was almost the first man to cross, "leaving everything to his corps commanders."[1]  At midnight (5th–6th) Meade sent word to Couch that the river was over the bridges, that Hooker was on the other side, and that communication with him was cut off.  Couch immediately rode over to Hooker's late headquarters, and satisfied himself that he was in command of the army.  He proceeded with Sickles and Reynolds to Meade's headquarters to confer as to what should be done, and told Meade that the crossing was suspended.  "We will stay where we are," he said, "and fight it out." He then went to his tent, and turned in, as he thought, for the night.

Meade, it seems, was not satisfied with the situation in which Couch had thus placed him.  At any rate, he directed Major Biddle of his staff to cross the river by way of United States Ford, find General Hooker, and ask for orders.  The aide found the army commander fast asleep on the floor of a house.  He awakened Butterfield, and reporting the situation, was told that the order for a retreat was imperative.  On communicating this reply to Meade, Biddle was directed to transmit it to Reynolds.  "Tell General Meade," said Reynolds, "that some one should be waked up to take command of this army."  Who, if any one, was consequently waked up, history does not tell.  At 2 a.m., however, Couch was roused to receive a sharp message from Hooker about recrossing the army as he had directed.

One of the bridges had been taken up, and used to piece out the other two, making the passage feasible.  It was now resumed, and was continued through the dark, rainy night.  The batteries which were waiting at the river commenced again to recross.  General Hunt sought General Hooker on the north side of the river, and proposed to him to postpone the movement for one day, as it was certain that the army could not all cross in a night.  He expressed himself as doubtful whether the artillery could all go over before daylight.[2]  But Hooker refused to suspend the movement, and it proceeded, disturbed only by the rain, which

---

[1] Private letter of Captain Candler, aide-de-camp, May 7, 1863. "It was so different," says Candler, "from his former acts."

[2] *The Campaign of Chancellorsville*, by T. A. Dodge, p. 230.

flooded the trenches so that they had to be cut through to let the water out. The infantry commenced withdrawing from the intrenchments, leaving its pickets out. These were to veil the retreat of the army at all hazards. Under their protection the columns marched back by their several roads to the vicinity of the ford, except the infantry of the V Corps, which took position on the third line of defence, the Second and Third Divisions in the trenches, the First Division in rear of them as support. The bulk of the infantry, near the ford, was ployed into masses to wait for their turns to cross (Map 39). Every effort was made to keep the ammunition dry, but it is doubtful whether at this time half of the muskets in the army could have been discharged. Sleep was out of the question. It has been remarked by writers on this campaign that a sudden onset by the enemy or a few shells dropped among the masses of troops assembled near the bridges would have precipitated a panic that would have resulted in the destruction of the army.[1] It may be answered that the V Corps, reënforced perhaps by other troops, would have taken care of the onset, and that the Army of the Potomac had been so inured to shell-fire that its only effect in this case would have been to cause a deployment of the masses into lines of battle. The army might, however, have been placed in a serious predicament, had the enemy been able to train a gun upon its bridges. As already stated, this danger had been anticipated and provided against by General Hunt. As Hunt had apprehended, it was daylight before the artillery had all crossed. About this time the infantry pickets commenced falling back, unobserved by the enemy. The artillery being all over, the masses of infantry, soon after daylight, commenced recrossing. Parties of Confederate skirmishers moved out to feel the Federal pickets, and finding them gone, pushed on after them. The Federal pickets halted occasionally to fire at them. In the meantime the masses of infantry had finished crossing; they were followed by the Third and Second Divisions, and these by the First Division of the V Corps. The First Division (Griffin's) was selected to cross last because it was strong in numbers, composed of veterans who had fought on the Peninsula, while Sykes' division was numerically weak, and Humphreys' was made up almost wholly of new regiments. The last brigade to cross was Barnes', Griffin's 1st brigade. It waited on the south bank the arrival of the pickets coming from the front under General Ayres, the field officer of the day. As the main column toiled up the north bank of the Rappahannock, many a backward look was taken at these last troops in contact with the enemy. Before they reached the bridges or the protection of Barnes' brigade they came under cover of the Federal artillery on the north side of the river. The pickets having crossed, Barnes' brigade

---

[1] *Reminiscences of Carl Schurz*, II, 432; *The Campaign of Chancellorsville*, by T. A. Dodge, pp. 231, 232.

proceeded to follow them, with a rear-guard formed of detachments from the 18 Mass. and 118 Pa.

A portion of the army supposed that it was making a flank march of great importance, but the general belief among officers and men was that they were retreating beaten. "The wonder of the private soldiers was great. How could they have been beaten with so little fighting? How had one half of the army been defeated while the other half had not fought? The muttered curses were prolonged and deep as they plodded back in the mud to their old camps."[1] Somewhere among the disgruntled soldiery, having recrossed the river with the army, was the party of ladies that had experienced the bombardment of the Chancellor House.[2] On account of the information which they possessed they could not be sent into the Confederate lines until after the campaign.

Lee, having passed the night in complete ignorance of Hooker's movement, sent off this morning a report in which, after correcting a former misrepresentation, he makes another as serious as the one that he corrected.

Near Chancellorsville, *via* Fredericksburg, May 6, 1863.

HON. SECRETARY OF WAR.

*Sir:*

General Hooker did not recross the Rappahannock after his defeat on Sunday (May 3), but retreated to a strong position in front of the United States Ford, where he is now fortifying himself, with a view, I presume, of holding a position this side of the Rappahannock. I understand from prisoners that he is awaiting reënforcements, and that, among others, General Heintzelman [commanding Department of Washington] is expected. I have received none of the troops ordered from south of the James River. . . . I had hoped that Longstreet would have been here before this time. . . . I hope every effort will be made to restore the railroads, else we shall have to abandon this country.

Very respectfully,

R. E. LEE,

General.

Lee says in his report of the campaign:

Preparations were made to assail the enemy's works at daylight on the 6th, but on advancing our skirmishers, it was found that under cover of the storm and darkness of the night he had retreated over the river.[3]

This statement is incorrect. The Federals had not completed their crossing at daylight. Their retreat was not performed under cover only of "the storm and darkness of the night." That some of them were not driven into the river was due mainly to the protection afforded

---

[1] *Recollections of a Private,* by Goss, p. 163.
[2] Manuscript letter of Captain Murray F. Taylor, C. S. A.
[3] *W. R.,* 39, p. 802.

by the Federal artillery on the north bank, as Lee himself testified, writing to Davis on the 7th:

. . . The line of skirmishers was pressed forward until they came within range of the enemy's batteries, planted north of the Rappahannock, which, from the configuration of the ground, completely commanded this side.  His army, therefore, escaped with the loss of a few additional prisoners.[1]

It would seem from the statements of a prominent Southern writer that Lee was dissatisfied with some of his own officers for having failed to discover Hooker's retreat and to intercept or harass it.  Jed. Hotchkiss says:

Just at dawn, on the morning of the 6th, as Lee was about to order an advance, General Pender came galloping to his field headquarters under a tent-fly at Fairview cemetery, and informed him that his skirmishers had advanced and found Hooker gone.  In surprise he exclaimed: "Why, General Pender!  That is what you young men always do.  You allow these people to get away.  I tell you what to do, but you don't do it."[2]

This interview must have taken place after "dawn."  It was some time after daylight before the Confederate skirmishers discovered that the Federal army had withdrawn.

Before the Committee on the Conduct of the War Hooker represented that his recrossing of the river was consequent upon Sedgwick's withdrawal, and with a view to resuming offensive operations below Fredericksburg.  "As soon," he said, "as I heard that General Sedgwick had recrossed the river, seeing no object in maintaining my position where I was, and believing that it would be much more to my advantage to hazard an engagement with the enemy at Franklin's Crossing, where I had elbow-room, than where I was, the army on the right was directed to recross the river."[3]  Almost in the same breath he gave the testimony already cited to the effect that he had decided on withdrawing before he called his corps commanders together, or before Sedgwick commenced to withdraw.

Sedgwick's withdrawal deprived him of all hope of flanking Lee and driving him off the direct line of communication with Richmond.  Butterfield said:

He [Hooker] felt that he could remain perfectly well on the south side of the river, and possibly force the enemy to fall back; but as the enemy would fall back toward Richmond, they would constantly become stronger and go into their fortifications there, while we should grow weaker.[4]

At dawn this morning Colonel Alexander put Eubank's 4 Napoleons and 2 of Jordan's rifles in his unfinished gun-pits under Jordan, and

[1] Richmond *Whig*, May 8, 1863.          [3] *Rep. of Com.*, IV, 133, 134.
[2] *Confederate Military History*, III, 392.     [4] *Ib.*, 77.

proceeded with the construction of his works. The Federal artillery across the river was on the lookout for him. Winegar's and Pettit's batteries $\left(\frac{2}{1.\,\mathrm{XII}}, \frac{1}{1.\,\mathrm{II}}\right)$ in the main line of guns and Atwell's $\left(\frac{1}{2.\,\mathrm{XII}}\right)$ in the flank position opened an annoying fire on the men working on the pits. One of their first shells went through the roof of the Hayden House, and some of the inmates left it with agonizing screams. About 9 a.m. Alexander undertook to drive off the Federal pieces with Moody's and Parker's batteries and a 24-pounder howitzer of Woolfolk's—7 guns in all. They took position in front of Winegar's and Pettit's batteries, and opened fire, assisted by the six guns in the pits. The Federal batteries continued their fire, and Thompson's $\left(\frac{3}{2.\,\mathrm{I}}\right)$ joined Atwell's $\left(\frac{1}{2.\,\mathrm{XII}}\right)$ in firing from a position on which Alexander's guns could not be brought to bear. After a duel of about three quarters of an hour between the 22 Federal and 13 Confederate pieces, the latter were silenced. In the meantime Alexander had perceived that the Federals had all withdrawn across the river, and his works were therefore useless.

At 6:30 a.m. the following instructions were issued, looking to the reunion of the wings of Hooker's army:

General headquarters to-night will be at the old camp near Falmouth. Corps commanders will send a staff officer for orders at 6 p.m., to report their locations for the night, as fixed on the old map of the camp of occupation. . . .

Barnes' brigade was left at United States Ford to assist in taking up the bridges. About 9 a.m., the troops having crossed, the bridges were *swung*. So nervous were the engineers lest the enemy should come upon them at their work, that they did not even wait to pull up anchors, but cut every cable, and cast loose,—glad enough to see their flotilla on the retreat after the army, and more gratified still at not being attacked during the operation.[1] The engineers and the men of Barnes' brigade assisting them were the last troops to cross the river. It was half-past four in the afternoon when the bridges were dismantled and loaded on the trucks, and the train started for Falmouth, escorted by Barnes' brigade. The storm was still raging.

Captain Candler wrote home:

. . . I hear the army moves at 12 m. [to-morrow]. If so, thank God. If not, Heaven only knows what will be the end. The army is in as good spirits as when we went out. It is perfectly marvelous. . . . I have not had twelve hours' sleep in five days.

Regarding the danger of a passage of the Rappahannock by the enemy above Hooker's right, Pleasonton wrote to Butterfield at 7 a.m.:

[1] *Hard Tack and Coffee*, by J. D. Billings, p. 388.

Just heard from brigade on the right $\left(\frac{2}{2.6}\right)$ up to 6 p.m. last night. Were at Deep Run, and found that stream impassable. The Sixteenth Pennsylvania Cavalry have pickets at Morrisville, Kelley's and Ellis' Fords. Scouts from the other side of the river report no enemy this side of the Rapidan. The brigade is 1700 strong, without the battery.

Lee could not venture across the Rappahannock. Assuming that he could have gathered together the necessary bridge material, and that the Army of the Potomac was as inferior in prowess to the Army of Northern Virginia, or as demoralized by its recent reverse, as he now naturally believed it to be, he could not, for lack of supplies, have kept his army north of the Rappahannock long enough to strike or attempt to strike an effective blow. He must have appreciated, too, the risks that he would run of losing, or being severed from, his bridges over the high and turbulent river in his rear. "At Chancellorsville," he is reported to have said, "we gained another victory; our people were wild with delight. I, on the contrary, was more depressed than after Fredericksburg; our loss was severe, and again we had gained not an inch of ground, and the enemy could not be pursued." [1]

A detachment was left at Chancellorsville to guard the battle-field, while the wounded were removed, and the captured property collected. The rest of the army returned to the lines of Fredericksburg.

Lincoln telegraphed to Hooker, 12:25 p.m.:

We have through General Dix the contents of Richmond papers of the 5th. . . . The substance is, General Lee's dispatch of the 3d (Sunday) claiming that he had beaten you, and that you were then retreating across the Rappahannock, distinctly stating that two of Longstreet's divisions [2] fought you on Saturday, and that General Paxton was killed, Stonewall Jackson severely wounded, and Generals Heth and A. P. Hill slightly wounded. The Richmond papers also stated, upon what authority not mentioned, that our cavalry have been at Ashland, Hanover Court-House, and other points, destroying several locomotives, and a good deal of other property, and all the railroad bridges to within 5 miles of Richmond.

*12:30 p.m.*

Just as I had telegraphed you contents of Richmond papers, showing that our cavalry has not failed, I received General Butterfield's, of 11 a.m. yesterday. This, with the great rain of yesterday and last night, securing your right flank, I think, puts a new face upon your case, but you must be the judge.

Lincoln wrote this dispatch under the impression that Hooker was still on the south side of the Rappahannock. By referring to Butterfield's dispatch, it will be seen that it was Hooker's line of communication, not his right flank, that was thought to be imperiled.

[1] *Address of Colonel Chapman Biddle,* Hist. Soc. of Pa., March 8, 1880.
[2] Anderson's and McLaws'.

Hooker, probably on receipt of this message, issued the following circular:

*Corps Commanders:*

The major-general commanding directs that you have your command well in hand, arms inspected, ammunition dry, and everything in readiness for action by to-morrow p.m.

To Noah Brooks, who was at the White House, Lincoln stated that, while still without any positive information as to the result of the fighting at Chancellorsville, he was certain in his own mind that "Hooker had been licked." He was only then wondering whether Hooker would be able to recover himself and renew the fight. Later in the day he got positive information. "I shall never," says Noah Brooks, "forget that picture of despair. He held a telegram in his hand, and as he closed the door and came toward us, I mechanically noticed that his face, usually sallow, was ashen in hue. The paper on the wall behind him was of the tint known as 'French gray,' and even in that moment of sorrow and dread expectation I vaguely took in the thought that the complexion of the anguished President's visage was almost exactly like that of the wall. He gave me the telegram, and, in a voice trembling with emotion, said, 'Read it—news from the army.' "[1]

It read as follows:

Headquarters Army of the Potomac, May 6, 1863, 1 p.m.[2]

*His Excellency Abraham Lincoln,* President of the United States:

I have just returned from above, and find your two dispatches to General Hooker, and one from him to me, directing me to telegraph you that the army has recrossed the river; that the bridges are up, and that all are under orders to return to camp. Your dispatches were sent to him, and by this time he has probably received them.

DANL. BUTTERFIELD,
Major-General, Chief of Staff.

"The appearance of the President," says Noah Brooks, "as I read aloud these fateful words, was piteous. Never, as long as I knew him, did he seem to be so broken up, so dispirited, and so ghostlike. Clasping his hands behind his back, he walked up and down the room, saying, 'My God, my God, what will the country say! What will the country say!' He seemed incapable of uttering any other words than these, and after a little time he hurriedly left the room. . . . "

The New York *Herald* said in an editorial:

Terrible will be the responsibility of President Lincoln and his cabinet and his chiefs of the war office should their ruinous policy of underrating the enemy

---

[1] *Washington in Lincoln's Time,* by Noah Brooks, p. 57.

[2] The *Report of the Committee on the* *Conduct of the War* gives the hour of sending as 1:15 and the hour of receipt as 1:35 (IV, 227).

and trusting to luck result in another disastrous campaign of the Army of the Potomac. We shrink from the contemplation of the fearful consequences which in this event may befall the administration and the country.

Before the day was out a correspondent wrote to the New York *Times*:

The news that Hooker and his army had recrossed the Rappahannock flashed through Washington about 5 o'clock this afternoon. The impression produced by it was profound. Men's minds were cast down from the congratulatory cheerfulness with which all had for three days discussed the events which succeeded the brilliant passages of the Rappahannock and the Rapidan. . . . It made men silent and thoughtful beyond anything I have ever seen in Washington.

The wildest rumors were set on foot; but it was known that the President and General Halleck had gone to the front, taking a special steamer at the navy yard at four o'clock that afternoon. It was commonly believed that Hooker was or would be put under arrest; that Halleck would be placed in command of the Army of the Potomac; that Stanton had resigned; that Lee had cut Hooker to pieces, and was approaching Washington by way of Dumfries; that McClellan was coming on a special train from New York, and that Sigel, Butler, Fremont, and several other shelved generals had been sent for.[1] Many men who were earnest in support of the war gave up all idea that the South could be conquered. But the general feeling of the country, as well as of the army, was one of disappointment and mortification rather than of discouragement or despair. The general gloom and sickness at heart that followed the first and second Bull Run, the defeat of McClellan before Richmond, and the battle of Fredericksburg, did not manifest themselves in anything like the same degree.[2]

The following messages went over the wires:

*Governor Morgan, New York, to President Lincoln, 3 p.m.*

Nothing will so cheer the hearts of all good men as the immediate reënforcement of General Hooker by troops from around Washington, Fort Monroe, and Suffolk.

*Hooker to Lincoln, 4:30 p.m.*

Have this moment returned to camp. On my way received your telegrams of 11 a.m.[3] and 12:30. The army had previously recrossed the river, and was on its return to camp. As it had none of its trains of supplies with it, I deemed this advisable. Above, I saw no way of giving the enemy a general battle with the prospect of success which I desire. Not to exceed three corps, all told, of my troops have been engaged. For the whole to go in, there is a better place nearer at hand. Will write you at length to-night. Am glad to hear that a portion of the cavalry have at length turned up. One portion did nothing.

---

[1] *Washington in Lincoln's Time*, by Noah Brooks, pp. 58, 59.
[2] Rhodes' *History of the U. S.*, IV, 266.        [3] Not found.

### Seward, Secretary of State, to Morgan, Governor of New York

General Hooker has had, has now, and will have, everything he asks for by telegraph, which is always in full connection with the War Department. He knows best what he wants, and when and where, and directs everything according to his own plans. He reports confidentially that only three corps of his army, all told, have been engaged. You need not be told that this is less than half of the army in his command and actually with him. Further accumulation of troops, not called for by him, would exhaust his supplies and endanger his plans. Be patient.

### Lee to Hooker

I have had the honor to receive your letter of yesterday, requesting permission to send a burial party to attend to your dead and wounded on the battle-field of Chancellorsville. I regret that their position is such, being immediately within our lines, that the necessities of war forbid my compliance with your request, which under other circumstances it would give me pleasure to grant. I will accord to your dead and wounded the same attention which I bestow upon my own; but if there is anything which your medical director here requires which we cannot provide, he shall have my permission to receive from you such medical supplies as you may think proper to furnish. Consideration for your wounded prompts me to add that, from what I learn, their comfort would be greatly promoted by additional medical attendance and medical supplies.

### Stanton to Hooker, 8:30 p.m.[1]

The President and General-in-Chief left here this afternoon at 4 o'clock to see you. They are probably at Aquia by this time.

*May 7.* About 10 o'clock this morning a special train consisting of a locomotive and a single box car arrived at Falmouth, bringing from Aquia Creek the President and Major-General Halleck. They were immediately conducted to a carriage, and, with a solitary cavalryman on either side, escorted to the headquarters of General Hooker. The President, after he had conferred with Hooker, returned to Washington, writing him the following letter probably *en route:*

The recent movement of your army is ended without effecting its object, except, perhaps, some important breakings of the enemy's communications. What next? If possible, I would be very glad of another movement early enough to give us some benefit from the fact of the enemy's communication being broken; but neither for this reason or [sic] any other do I wish anything done in desperation or rashness. An early movement would also help to supersede the bad moral effects of the recent one, which is said to be considerably injurious. Have you already in your mind a plan wholly or partially formed? If you have, prosecute it without interference from me. If you have not, please inform me, so that I, incompetent as I may be, can try and assist in the formation of some plan for the army.

[1] *Rep. of Com.,* IV, 228.

The President left Halleck with the army, to remain until he knew "everything." The President's letter elicited the following reply:

. . . I do not deem it expedient to suspend operations on this line, from the reverse we have experienced in endeavoring to extricate the army from its present position. If in the first effort we failed, it was not for want of strength or conduct of the small number of troops actually engaged, but from a cause which could not be foreseen, and could not be provided against.[1] After its occurrence, the chances of success were so much lessened that I felt another plan might be adopted in place of that we were engaged in, which would be more certain in its results. At all events, a failure would not involve a disaster, while in the other case it was certain to follow the absence of success. I may add that this consideration almost wholly determined me in ordering the army to return to its old camp. As to the best time for renewing our advance upon the enemy, I can only decide after an opportunity has been afforded to learn the feeling of the troops. They should not be discouraged or depressed, for it is no fault of theirs (if I may except one corps) that our last efforts were not crowned with glorious victory. I suppose details are not wanted of me at this time. I have decided in my own mind the plan to be adopted in our next effort, if it should be your wish to have one made. It has this to recommend it: It will be one in which the operations of all the corps, unless it be a part of the cavalry, will be within my personal supervision.

The following circular was issued at 12:15 p.m.:

Corps commanders will have three days' rations issued and ready to cook at short notice; lost knapsacks replaced, and supplies on hand to fill them; arms and equipments in order; a full supply of ammunition; everything prepared for at once resuming active operations.

Captain Candler wrote home:

I am of the opinion that we will move within twenty-four hours. The report now is that Johnny Reb retreated at the same time we came back, and that the pontoons are to be thrown across at Fredericksburg to-morrow morning. . . . it will be found out that the enemy was retiring at the same time we were. . . . It is my opinion that already they have commenced their retrograde march on Gordonsville, and that the troops seen in our front are only a rear-guard. We shall undoubtedly attack again in twenty-four hours.

Lee wrote:

### To Critcher

. . . take position on the right of the infantry, beginning at Moss Neck Mill, and picketing as before down the Rappahannock. Keep a good lookout and report any movement of the enemy that may be discovered.[2]

---

[1] The rout of the XI Corps.      [2] *W. R.*, 108, p. 705.

*To Longstreet*

. . . My letter of the 1st instant [1] to which you refer was intended to apprise you of my intended movement [Jackson's flank march] and to express the wish rather than the expectation that one of your divisions could coöperate in it. I did not intend to express the opinion that you could reach me in time, as I did not think it practicable. The emergency that made your presence so desirable has passed for the present. . . . The only immediate service that your troops could render would be to protect our communications from the enemy's cavalry, and assist in punishing them for the damage they have done.

Longstreet wrote to the Secretary of War:

His Excellency the President expressed the desire last night [May 6] that I should join General Lee at Fredericksburg at once.

I regard the opening and securing the communication of General Lee's army with this city [as] of the first importance, and fear that this may not be accomplished if I leave it unfinished. There are some indications, too, that the enemy may bring one or two other columns against this city with the hope of getting possession by a sudden dash. I think it more important that these things should be considered, and that we should have our forces so in hand as to meet any such contingency. I propose, therefore, to remain here until I can so arrange and dispose of my forces as to free General Lee's army of the force which now threatens his communications. [2]

For the reassurance of the Federal armies and the Northern public the following bulletin was sent from the War Department to Generals Grant, Rosecrans, Dix, Pope, Burnside, and Curtis, and to the governors of all the Northern states:

. . . . . . . . .

The President and General-in-Chief have just returned from the Army of the Potomac. The principal operation of General Hooker failed, but there has been no serious disaster to the organization and efficiency of the army. It is now occupying its former position on the Rappahannock, having recrossed the river without any loss in the movement. Not more than one third of General Hooker's force was engaged. General Stoneman's operations have been a brilliant success. A part of his force advanced to within 2 miles of Richmond, and the enemy's communications have been cut in every direction. The Army of the Potomac will speedily resume offensive operations.

The melancholy correspondence relating to the Federal dead and wounded proceeded as follows:

*Hooker to Lee, 8 p.m.*

. . . If agreeable to you, I would like to send medical supplies and attendance to my wounded, and, at such times as the state of the stream will permit, send ambulances for them *via* the fords designated in your communications, viz.,

---

[1] Not found. J. B. Jr.          [2] *W. R.*, 26, p. 1050.

United States and Banks' Fords. . . . Upon an intimation from you as to any deficiency in your immediate necessities of medical supplies of your own, by reason of their use for my wounded or other causes, I shall with pleasure replace them.

### Lee to Hooker

The reasons that prevented me from complying with your request with reference to your wounded no longer existing, I have the honor to inform you that you can extend to them such attention as they may require. All persons whom it may be necessary to send within my lines for this purpose will remain until the wounded are finally disposed of. The burial of your dead has already been provided for.

At daylight this morning Dr. McGuire, Jackson's medical director, was aroused and informed that the general was suffering great pain. An examination disclosed pneumonia of the right lung. This complication was due to Jackson's persisting, in opposition to Dr. McGuire's urgent dissuasion, in treating a cold which he had by the application of wet blankets.[1]

Toward evening he became better, and hopes were again entertained of his recovery. Mrs. Jackson arrived with her infant child, and contributed her tender and faithful nursing to the skilful and no less faithful attendance that he was receiving from the doctor.

*May 8.* The hopes that Jackson would recover were of short duration. On the 8th his wounds were found to be doing well, and the pain in his side had disappeared, but he breathed with difficulty, and complained of a feeling of exhaustion. On the 9th his breathing was less difficult, but he grew steadily weaker. About daylight on the 10th Mrs. Jackson informed him that his recovery was very doubtful. He continued to lose strength with increasing rapidity. About half-past one he was told that he had but two hours to live. "Very good, it is all right," he answered feebly, but firmly. After lying for some time unconscious, he came to himself, crying out: "Order A. P. Hill to prepare for action! Pass the infantry to the front! Tell Major Hawks—" leaving the sentence unfinished. Once more he was silent; but soon afterward said very quietly and clearly, with an expression as if of relief: "Let us cross over the river, and rest under the shade of the trees." It was his last utterance. General Stonewall Jackson was dead.

[1] *Memoirs of the Confederate War,* by H. von Borcke, II, 259; General Pendleton, in *Memoirs of William Nelson Pendleton, D.D.,* by his daughter, p. 269.

# CHAPTER XXVIII

## OPERATIONS OF INDEPENDENT CAVALRY

### Mosby

THE movement which Stuart suggested to Mosby on the 26th of April, with a view to interrupting the railroad communication in rear of Stoneman's camp, culminated on the 3d of May in a dash at a brigade of Major-General Stahel's cavalry division at Warrenton Junction. About daylight Mosby started with a following of from 75 to 100 men from the vicinity of Warrenton, intending to strike at Hooker's trains and depots, between Aquia and United States Ford. But arriving within a couple of miles of the Orange and Alexandria Railroad, and learning that a force of Federal cavalry was encamped on it, he changed his plan and adopted this force as his objective. He succeeded in surprising the outpost of the 1 W. Va. Cavalry. A large part of the regiment was caught in a building and compelled to surrender. The attackers were then in turn attacked by the 5 N. Y. Cavalry. The Northern sabers soon drove the Southern pistols from the field, and compelled the release of most of the prisoners.[1] Another Federal regiment (1 Vt.) was at hand, but not engaged. It was this affair that gave rise to-day in Hooker's army to the rumor that Fitzhugh Lee had crossed the Upper Rappahannock.[2]

Mosby himself comments on it as follows:

"These [Federal] troops had just been sent up [from Fairfax Court-House] to replace Stoneman's. I committed a great blunder in allowing myself to be diverted by their presence from the purpose of my expedition. They were perfectly harmless where they were, and could not help Hooker in the battle then raging. I should at least have endeavored to avoid a fight by marching around them. If I had succeeded in destroying them all, it would hardly have been the equivalent of the

[1] One of the Federal commanders says all but 2 (*W. R.*, 39, p. 1106). Mosby says he kept 8 (*ib.*, 40, p. 861). He gives the strength of his command as "not over 100 men." The Federal General Stahel says it consisted of Mosby's "band of guerillas, together with a portion of the Black Horse cavalry and a portion of a North Carolina regiment [2d]" (*ib.*, 39, p. 1104).

Brigadier-General Abercrombie (Federal) puts the attacking force at "about 125 men" (*ib.*, pp. 1105, 1106). Major Chamberlain, commanding the 1 W. Va., says his men were attacked "by about 1000 rebel cavalry" (*ib.*, p. 1106). See also *ib.*, pp. 1104 and 1105, and *Historic Records of the 5 N. Y.*, by L. N. Boudrye, pp. 55, 56.

[2] P. 380 *ante*.

damage I might have done to Hooker by appearing at United States Ford during the agony of the fight. There all of his wagons were parked. It would be difficult to calculate the demoralizing effect of the news on his army that the enemy was in the rear, and their trains and rations were burning up.''[1]

### Stoneman

On the 29th of April, having followed the army across the Rappahannock, Stoneman camped, as already stated, at Madden (Map 10).

*April 30.* At daylight this morning he prepared to resume his march with as few encumbrances as possible. All the pack-mules and led horses were started toward Germanna Ford to follow in rear of the army. No supplies were retained except three days' subsistence and three days' short forage (ten pounds to the ration), and forty carbine and twenty pistol cartridges per man, all of which were to be carried on the horses of the men and officers. Not a wheel of any description accompanied the expedition, outside of the artillery.[2] Stoneman wanted to reach Verdiersville by the interval between Mountain Run and Clark's Mountain, and selected Raccoon Ford as his point of crossing. But satisfied that he would find this point guarded, he ordered Buford to cross at Mitchell's Ford, about 6 miles below, and open up Raccoon Ford. At 9 a.m. he received Averell's note of the 29th informing him that Stuart was ignorant of his (Stoneman's) whereabouts.[3]

Buford reached Mitchell's Ford about 11 a.m. and found it impracticable. His leading squadron under Lieutenant Mason swam across, and marched up the right bank. About 12 m. the remainder of the brigade crossed at Morton's Ford, and detached a squadron to accompany Mason's as advance-guard.

The two squadrons under Mason scoured the country to Somerville Ford. The remainder of the brigade marched to Raccoon Ford, and finding it practicable, was joined by the main body under Stoneman. The rear of the column got over about 10 p.m., when the whole command went into bivouac. Stoneman heard that Stuart with Fitzhugh Lee's brigade crossed this morning at Somerville Ford, and that he proceeded toward Fredericksburg.[4] He had allowed no fires to be made, as his camp was in plain view of the Confederate signal station on Clark's Mountain, and issued orders for the command to be in the saddle at 2 o'clock in the morning, and in the meantime to stand to horse without unsaddling. A dense fog settled down in the valley; it became very

---

[1] *Mosby's War Reminiscences*, pp. 130–132.

[2] For further details of the logistics of "Stoneman's Raid" the reader is referred to the report of Stoneman's chief quartermaster, Lieutenant-Colonel C. G. Sawtelle, U. S. Army (*W. R.*, 39, pp. 1067 *et seq.*).

[3] P. 202 *ante.*

[4] Stuart crossed, as previously stated, about midnight (29th–30th) at Raccoon Ford (R. E. Lee's report, *W. R.*, 39, p. 797; Stuart's report, *ib.*, p. 1046; *Campaigns of Stuart's Cavalry*, by H. B. McClellan, p. 227).

cold.  The mud was deep, and froze so that it bore a horse.  All clothing being wet, the men suffered greatly.  Many sank exhausted at their horses' heads, and, with reins fastened to wrist, slept for hours despite their discomfort.[1]

*May 1.*  Stoneman intended to take up the march at 2 o'clock this morning.  But at that hour the country was covered with the usual morning fog, and as he had no guide he delayed his start until daylight,[2] when he marched to Verdiersville.  He did not find Stuart there, but struck his trail on the Turnpike, and saw therefrom that he had gone toward Fredericksburg.  He sent Gregg's division ahead toward Louisa Court-House, on the Virginia Central Railroad (Map 1, sheet A).  In the course of the day Major Falls of General Gregg's staff, who had been out foraging for a guide, came galloping along the column with an "intelligent contraband" astride his horse behind him.  At midnight Gregg was still on the march, probably in the vicinity of the North Anna.  The remainder of Stoneman's command, consisting of Buford's brigade and corps headquarters, followed in the same general direction, and camped on the south side of the North Fork of the North Anna.  For the first time in three days and nights the horses of this portion of the command were unsaddled and the men allowed to make fires.  For Gregg's division there was to be no unsaddling, and no sleep, except what the men might succeed in getting in their saddles.

W. H. F. Lee, who had been opposing Averell at Rapidan Station, received an order from R. E. Lee to burn the bridge and fall back on Gordonsville.  The Federals had started to burn the bridge, but desisted on seeing that the enemy had anticipated them.  Averell withdrew under the erroneous impression that the bridge was destroyed;[3] saturated by the recent rains, it had proved refractory to all the fire that was brought to bear upon it.  Though the effort to burn it was not abandoned till retreat made it necessary, the structure was then left standing and serviceable.[4]

*May 2.*  Gregg's division, detached yesterday from Stoneman's command, arrived within three fourths of a mile of Louisa Court-House at 3 a.m.  Its four pieces of artillery were placed in a commanding position and the 2d brigade detailed as support.  The 1st brigade was then ordered forward in three columns of attack, the central column to take the town, the other two to strike the railroad one mile to right and left of it.  No enemy being found, the pioneer corps went to work destroying the railroad, which it effectually did for a stretch of 5 miles.  The

[1] *Annals of the 6 Pa. Cavalry*, Gracey, pp. 138, 139; *The Battles of Chancellorsville and Gettysburg*, by Captain A. H. Nelson, p. 23.

[2] Stoneman's and Buford's reports, *W. R.*, 39, pp. 1060, 1089.  According to the report of Captain Harrison, 5 U. S. Cavalry, the march was resumed at 4 a.m. (*ib.*, 39, p. 1092).

[3] *Ib.*, 39, p. 1079.

[4] *History of the 9 Va. Cav.*, by R. and T. Beale, p. 63.

water-tank was also destroyed, and some commissary stores were seized at the depot. About 10 a.m. Stoneman arrived at Louisa Court-House with the remainder of his corps, and pushed out a squadron of the 1 Me. under Captain Tucker toward Gordonsville, to ascertain the whereabouts of the enemy. When W. H. F. Lee about 11 a.m. reached Gordonsville, he heard it rumored that "a large body of the enemy was at Trevilian's Station and Louisa Court-House." He at once detached the 9 Va. Cavalry in the direction of those places. It had hardly started when its pickets were driven in by the squadron of the 1 Me. The latter was then in turn forced back by the 9 Va. Both sides were subsequently reënforced and the contest resumed, with the net result that each of the opposing commanders gained the information which he desired. W. H. F. Lee learned that there was "no large body of the enemy" at Trevilian's Station, but that Stoneman, with his whole corps, was at Louisa Court-House; and Stoneman learned that W. H. F. Lee was at Gordonsville with infantry, cavalry, and artillery. A train which started from Gordonsville for Charlottesville had to turn back on account of the presence of a force of Federal cavalry at Cobham Station. At 4 o'clock this afternoon there were three trains at Gordonsville that could not leave by any of the railroads.[1]

Stoneman put an operator in the telegraph office at Louisa Court-House, who received messages from Richmond giving information of the success of Hooker's operations up to that time. For nearly an hour Confederate messages continued to arrive. When the discovery was made in Richmond that the "Yankees" held the line, a few forcible remarks came over the wires, and communication ceased.[2]

Stoneman's present duty, under his orders from Hooker, was to make all haste for Hanover Junction. But no such thought, it seems, entered his mind. He detached Captain Lord with 265 officers and men of the 1 U. S. Cavalry to destroy the track and buildings of the Virginia Central Railroad as far as Frederickshall, a distance of 12 miles, and, if possible, Carr's bridge over the North Anna, about 6 miles north of Frederickshall, on the main road from Spottsylvania to Goochland on the James. From Louisa Court-House the main column proceeded to Yanceyville, where the South Anna was crossed on a bridge. From this point Captain Merritt was detached with a squadron of the 1 Md., about 50 strong, including pioneers, to destroy the bridges and the fords as far as possible down the South Anna. Stoneman went on to Thompson's Cross-Roads, where he arrived at 10 p.m.; his rear-guard, consisting of the 1 Me., came up with him here about midnight. This regiment of Gregg's was again to pass the night without unsaddling and without sleep except what it might get in the saddle. At mid-

[1] Stahel to Heintzelman, *W. R.*, 40, p. 433.
[2] *Annals of the 6 Pa. Cavalry,* by S. L. Gracey, pp. 140, 142.

night Lord's and Merritt's detachments were still out. W. H. F. Lee, being joined by Rhett with 1400 men from Richmond, settled down to the defence of Gordonsville. His force now numbered about 2400 men and 6 guns.

*May 3.* At Thompson's Cross-Roads Stoneman captured the baggage-wagon of a surveying party under a Captain Blackford, in which he found a set of section maps of this part of Virginia, which were to prove very useful to him. The maps that he had brought with him had been prepared by the U. S. Topographical Engineer Corps, and were based upon surveys made years before the war.

In the course of the forenoon he caught sounds of the artillery firing at Chancellorsville, 35 miles off as the crow flies, and was more or less disquieted by it.[1]   Respecting his intentions he says in his official report:

At this point the James and South Anna Rivers are less than 12 miles apart, and here I determined to make the most of my 3500 men in carrying out my previously conceived plan of operations. I called together all my regimental commanders, showed and explained to them the maps, and gave them an idea of what I wished done. I gave them to understand that we had dropped in that region of country like a shell, and that I intended to burst it in every direction, expecting each piece or fragment would do as much harm and create nearly as much terror as would result from sending the whole shell, and thus magnify our small force into overwhelming numbers, and the results of this plan satisfied my most sanguine expectations. . . .

According to instructions thus issued, parties went out as follows:

1. COLONEL WYNDHAM, with the 1 N. J. and 1 Md., about 400 men, to strike the James River at Columbia (the junction of the James and Rivanna Rivers), destroy, if possible, the canal-aqueduct over the Rivanna, and proceed along the canal in the direction of Richmond, doing all the damage possible. If thought expedient, a detachment was to be sent across the James River to make a dash on the railroad bridge over the Appomattox.

2. COLONEL KILPATRICK, with the 2 N. Y., about 400 men, to push on to the railroad bridges over the Chickahominy, destroy them and the telegraph, and operate in the direction of Richmond, about 4 miles from the Chickahominy bridges, doing as much damage as possible.

3. LIEUTENANT-COLONEL DAVIS, with the 12 Ill. Cavalry, about 300 men, to penetrate to the Richmond and Potomac Railroad, and, if possible, to the Virginia Central, and destroy communications.

4. BRIGADIER-GENERAL GREGG, with the 1 Me. and 10 N. Y. and 2 pieces of artillery, to destroy the bridges, including, if possible, the two railroad bridges, on the South Anna.

---

[1] My authority for this statement is Lieutenant-Colonel A. S. Austin, Stoneman's commissary officer.   J. B. Jr.

The bulk of Buford's regular brigade and the 6th Lancers remained in camp as a reserve and provost guard.

The raiding parties were all off by 3 a.m. They were instructed to endeavor to strike the railroad and telegraph at 3 p.m. of this day, in order that, all striking at the same time, they should find some at least of their objectives unguarded.

The first three commanders, Wyndham, Kilpatrick, and Davis, were directed, if they crossed the Virginia Central Railroad, to push on to Williamsburg on the Peninsula as a place of refuge. Gregg was ordered to return to the reserve. It will be observed that none of these parties (6, including Lord and Merritt) was directed upon Hanover Junction, "somewhere in the vicinity" of which Hooker expected the main blow to be struck.[1] Gregg's column was directed to the railroad crossing of the South Anna about 5 miles south of the Junction, and the other three columns upon or toward Richmond. Stoneman was apparently less intent upon checking a retreat of Lee's army than he was upon entering Richmond, which Hooker did not expect him to do.[2]

Elzey wrote to Lee:

One regiment has been sent to [railroad] bridge on North Anna, one to Hanover Junction, and a force to [railroad] bridge over South Anna. General Pettigrew's brigade arrived to-day from Petersburg. General Lee from Gordonsville reports enemy moving toward Columbia on James River. They have left the [Virginia Central] railroad. General Lee is moving after them. I shall detail Pettigrew's force here to-day.

Captain Lord, sent out by Stoneman yesterday, and Colonel Wyndham, sent out this morning, returned to-day. Lord destroyed Carr's bridge over the North Anna, and disabled the Virginia Central Railroad for a distance of 15 miles. Wyndham cut the James River Canal at Columbia, burned five bridges, and destroyed a large quantity of supplies. For want of proper implements, he did not succeed in materially injuring the stone aqueduct across the Rivanna. Hearing that W. H. F. Lee was after him with cavalry and artillery, he did not attempt to reach the Appomattox or to proceed as ordered in the direction of Richmond, but took up the march to return to Thompson's Cross-Roads. W. H. F. Lee marched all night in pursuit of him.

Kilpatrick, making a forced march for Hungary Station, went into camp at daylight about 15 miles from his objective, and remained in camp, concealed, all day and about half of the night. At midnight he was again on the march, but not far from his late camp. Davis destroyed one bridge on the South Anna. He struck the Richmond and Potomac Railroad at Ashland, catching an ambulance-train from Fredericksburg that contained 250 sick and wounded. He received their

---

[1] Williams to Stoneman, April 12.     [2] *W. R.*, 39, p. 1065.

version of the fight at Chancellorsville, paroled them, and let them go. He destroyed a railroad trestle bridge, and went on to the Virginia Central Railroad at Hanover Station, arriving about 8 p.m. Here also he destroyed a trestle bridge. Proceeding to Hanover Court-House and thence to within 7 miles of Richmond, he halted and camped for the night.

Merritt, sent out yesterday, left intact the bridge at Yanceyville and one a few miles below it. The latter, it seems, was afterward destroyed by some one else. The second bridge below Yanceyville he destroyed. Overtaken by Gregg, he proceeded with him down the river, destroying a ford at Paine's Mill, then a bridge known as the Factory Bridge, and, a few miles further down, the Ground Squirrel Bridge. Late in the afternoon Gregg halted his column at Rocky Mills, 15 miles from Richmond. Here his horses were fed and groomed, and the more fortunate of his men got something to eat. On a report that the railroad bridge across the South Anna was guarded only by a small cavalry picket, a detachment of 200 men, under command of Lieutenant-Colonel Smith of the 1 Me., was sent about an hour before sunset, with a negro guide, to destroy it. Captain Merritt joined this party with his squadron. An erratic ride through the woods with no roads, seemingly in no particular direction (the guide knowing little about the country), and for the greater part at a trot, brought the column to the bridge. There it was discovered that the enemy had sent a force of infantry and artillery for its protection. The bridge was not destroyed, but a portion of the railroad track was torn up and some storehouses were burned. At midnight the column was on its return march to Rocky Mills. Another night for the 1 Me. without unsaddling. Two thirds or more of the men allowed themselves to go to sleep and their horses to wander at will. The column was immensely strung out. The utmost efforts of the officers and of the men who were not asleep no more than sufficed to keep the rest of the men in the straggling column of files. Twenty wide-awake determined Confederate soldiers could have captured the whole 200.[1]

The people of Richmond were seized with apprehension. A "Rebel War Clerk" wrote in his diary:

There has been some commotion in the city this afternoon and evening, but no painful alarm,—caused by intelligence that the enemy's cavalry had cut the road at Trevilian's Depot, had reached Ashland, and destroyed the depot. Subsequent rumors brought them within 8 miles of the city, and we have no force of any consequence here. . . . I think they will disappear down the Pamunkey, and of course will cut the Central and York roads and the wires. Thus communication with Lee is interrupted. The Fredericksburg train of course failed to come in to-day at 6 p.m., and it is rumored there were 700 of our wounded in it.

[1] *History of the First Maine Cavalry*, by E. P. Tobie, p. 139.

The Philadelphia correspondent of the New York *Times* wrote:

The latest news from Chancellorsville is that Stoneman has cut the railroad.

That Stoneman had cut Lee from Richmond, at least for a time, must have been known this evening both to Lee and to Hooker.[1]

There were anxious moments now for Stoneman, waiting for the scattered fragments of his "bursting shell" to do their work and come together again. Apprehending an attack upon his feeble reserve at Thompson's Cross-Roads, he sent Lieutenant Mason with a squadron of the 5 U. S. to guard the bridge at Yanceyville, and prepare to destroy it, should that become necessary. With a view, in this case, to passing the river by a ford, he detached Captain Drummond with 200 picked men and 4 officers of the 5 U. S. to examine all the fords of the South Anna as far down as Allen Creek. The captain was directed to proceed, if possible, from the mouth of that stream to Goochland Court-House on the James River, and clear the place of any hostile force that might be found in it. He found the upper ford practicable and the others impracticable. An hour or two after midnight he went into camp below Allen Creek. Captain Harrison with the remainder of the 5 U. S., numbering 119 officers and men, was sent to Shannon's Cross-Roads with orders to scout the country in the directions of Gordonsville, Fluvanna,[2] and Columbia.

Uneasy as Stoneman may have been as to the result of the pending operations, he was not influenced, it seems, by a single thought of what he should have been doing. Breaking up his command and sending it off on separate expeditions would have been very well if his sole duty had been to make raids. But his principal duty was to check the enemy's retreat, and if this failed, to fall upon his flanks and harass or delay him.[3] The operation that has gone into history as Stoneman's Raid was to have been a part of a grand tactical and strategic manœuver. Without Averell, Stoneman's force numbered only about 4000 sabers, but outnumbered the cavalry opposed to it about 2 to 1. The latter advantage was thrown away in order to spread alarm through the enemy's country.

The measures taken for the protection of Lee's communications appear in the following dispatches:

Richmond, May 3, 1863.

GENERAL R. E. LEE.

*General:*

One regiment has been sent to bridge on North Anna, one to Hanover Junction, and a force to bridge over South Anna. General Pettigrew's brigade arrived to-day from Petersburg. . . .

ARNOLD ELZEY,

Major-General.

---

[1] For Butterfield's erroneous or misleading testimony on this point, see *Rep. of Com.*, IV, 77.
[2] About 13 miles northwest of Columbia. Not shown on map.
[3] Williams to Stoneman, April 12, pp. 142–144, *ante*.

War Department, C. S. A., Richmond, May 3, 1863, 12 midnight.

*General Hampton,* Lynchburg, Va.:

I do not think Farmville or Lynchburg threatened. The enemy have, I learn, turned down the river on the north side, either for a daring dash on this city, or, more probably, to escape by the Peninsula to Yorktown or around Port Royal. Move with your forces, as you concentrate, toward Gordonsville.

J. A. SEDDON,
Secretary of War.

*May 4.* Apprehending the approach of hostile cavalry, Stoneman moved back to Shannon's Cross-Roads, about 6 miles in his rear. There he had an encounter with the brigade of W. H. F. Lee, set free by the recall of Averell's command. The raiding column under Davis $\left(\frac{12}{2.\ 3.\ C}\right)$ started at 8 o'clock this morning from its camp, about 7 miles from Richmond, for Williamsburg. At Tunstall Station it was met by a train of cars filled with infantry and a battery of 3 guns run out from White House. The Confederates took position in a line of intrenchments and repelled the Federal assault. Davis withdrew, and determined to cross the Pamunkey and Mattapony Rivers and make for Gloucester Point.[1]

Kilpatrick with his regiment $\left(\frac{12}{2.\ 3.\ C}\right)$ reached Hungary, on the Richmond and Potomac Railroad, at daylight, and destroyed the depot, telegraph wires, and railroad, for several miles, charged a battery, and drove it to within 2 or 3 miles of Richmond. He was now with his single regiment within the line of fortifications of the enemy's capital. A Confederate officer rode up to him with the question, "What regiment?" and was answered, "The Second New York, and you, sir, are my prisoner." This officer proved to be an aide to General John H. Winder. "You're a mighty daring sort of fellows," he remarked, "but you will certainly be captured before sundown." "That may be," said Kilpatrick, "but we intend to do a deal of mischief first."

Kilpatrick appropriated the specially fine horse which the prisoner was riding, secured the 11 men by whom he was escorted, and made off with his booty and captives. He forded the Chickahominy above Meadow Bridge, burned that bridge, by which the Virginia Central Railroad crossed the Chickahominy, and ran a train of cars into the river. Having now crossed the railroad, he was debarred by Stoneman's orders as well as by circumstances from returning to the cavalry corps. Instead, however, of proceeding toward Williamsburg, he decided, as Davis had done, to cross the Pamunkey and Mattapony Rivers, and make for Gloucester Point. Picking up an intelligent negro who knew the roads, he made him act as guide, and in less than two hours reached Hanovertown. There he performed the tedious operation of crossing the Pamunkey on a ferry-boat that would not carry

[1] *W. R.,* 39, p. 1087.

more than 20 horses with their riders. The last load being safely landed, he destroyed the ferry just in time to check a force of pursuing cavalry, burned a train of 30 wagons loaded with bacon, took 13 prisoners, and camped for the night about 5 miles beyond the Pamunkey. The two railroads connecting Hanover Junction with Richmond were now both cut, each in two places.

Captain Harrison, with his 119 officers and men of the 5 U. S., arrived at Shannon's Cross-Roads about half-past 2 o'clock a.m. and established pickets. He had hardly done so when he was attacked by a regiment of Virginia Cavalry, about 800 strong, under W. H. F. Lee, and driven back upon Lieutenant Mason at Yanceyville, where he made arrangements to hold the bridge. Word was sent to Stoneman of the proximity of the enemy, and Buford's command and the lancers (6 Pa.) came up at a trot, accompanied by Stoneman, but not in time to strike the enemy. Captain Harrison, in this affair, lost 2 officers and 30 men captured, and 4 men wounded, one having seven saber-cuts. W. H. F. Lee returned to Gordonsville. Captain Drummond with his 200 men, also of the 5 U. S., took up the march about daylight for Goochland Court-House. Halting in the vicinity of that place, he had it examined, and found it unoccupied and almost deserted. He then returned to Thompson's Cross-Roads, but not to his regiment, which was now with the reserve at Yanceyville.[1]

About 2 a.m. Lieutenant-Colonel Smith with his 200 men, returning from his attempt to destroy a bridge, arrived at Rockville, and found that the remainder of Gregg's command had gone. Without stopping to rest, he pushed on in search of it. Men who had thus far kept awake gave up in despair. Arguments, orders, curses, and even blows, could not keep them awake. About 3:30 a.m. the detachment found the command about 3 miles from Rockville, standing "to horse," and expecting every moment to receive orders to move. Oblivious to this circumstance, the exhausted troopers threw themselves upon the ground to rest, and got about an hour's sleep.[2] Half a dozen of them did not get this much, for as soon as they arrived they were sent off by General Gregg to carry dispatches to General Stoneman at Thompson's Cross-Roads. They reached Stoneman, and delivered the dispatches, just as he was starting out from the Cross-Roads for Yanceyville. W. H. F. Lee wrote to Elzey, magnifying Stoneman's 11 regiments of cavalry to 28.[3]

This was the sixth day since the cavalry corps crossed the Rappahannock, the last, according to Stoneman's understanding, that he had to wait to hear from Hooker. He had not received any communication

---

[1] This detachment did not rejoin the regiment until noon of the 6th.
[2] *History of the First Maine Cavalry,* by E. P. Tobie, p. 140.
[3] *W. R.,* 39, p. 1097.

from him, and since the 2d had heard nothing as to the situation of the army, except vague rumors of its defeat and capture; the rations for man and beast which he had carried with him were exhausted, and foraging was becoming more and more difficult. So in a council of war which he called this evening it was decided that the portion of his corps that he now had with him should return to the army by the route that it had come by.

*May 5.* To deceive the enemy, a detachment of 646 men of the regular brigade on picked horses was sent under Buford to threaten any force that might be in the vicinity of Gordonsville, and induce W. H. F. Lee and Hampton to believe that Stoneman was to march that way. The outlying detachments were left to find their way to the main body as best they could. Buford was to rejoin it at Orange Springs on the following day. The main body started this evening in a thunder-shower, with the 1st Maine regiment as advance-guard. It had as guide a negro, who, to gain his freedom, engaged to pilot the column by a route out of reach and observation of the enemy, who occupied the main roads.[1]

The shower settled into a steady rain; the night was very cold. The men, who during the day had been inclined to complain of the heat, now shivered in their saddles. After crossing the South Anna at Yanceyville the bridge at that point was destroyed. Proceeding northward, the column crossed the railroad at Tolersville. It was so dark that a trooper could hardly see his file-leader unless he rode a white horse; the way lay through swamps, thickets, woods, cow-paths, by-paths— every sort of communication except a highway. The dismal ride was made more dismal by an occasional shot from a guerilla, and the doleful note of a whippoorwill that followed the column all night.[2]

Captain Drummond, with his 200 men of the 5 Cavalry, and another outlying detachment of about 100 men, under Captain Rodenbough, started separately from Thompson's Cross-Roads to find and rejoin the main body. Rodenbough took up the march at 8 p.m., crossed the South Anna by the bridge at the Cross-Roads, and then set fire to it. Where Drummond crossed the river is not known.[3]

Davis $\left(\frac{12}{2.\ 3.\ C}\right)$ crossed the Pamunkey at Putney's Ferry and the Mattapony at Walkerton without meeting with serious opposition. Between the two ferries a portion of his command under Major Bronson became separated from the rest.

Kilpatrick $\left(\frac{2}{1.\ 3.\ C}\right)$ was on the march at 1 a.m. At Aylett's on the Mattapony he captured 2 officers and 33 men, burned 45 wagons and a depot containing more than 60,000 barrels of corn and wheat, and quan-

[1] Manuscript narrative by Brigadier-General E. V. Sumner, U. S. Army, retired— lieutenant and aide-de-camp on General Stoneman's staff.

[2] *History of the First Maine Cavalry*, by E. P. Tobie, p. 141.

[3] The author has been unable to learn the route followed by this column.

tities of clothing and commissary stores. Crossing the Mattapony, he destroyed the ferry just in time again to check the enemy's cavalry. Late in the evening he destroyed a third wagon-train and a depot a few miles above and west of Tappahannock on the Rappahannock. Through the night he continued his march southward, aiming at King and Queen Court-House, and pursued by cavalry which he supposed to be a portion of Stuart's.

At Aylett's Lieutenant Estes of the 1 Me., serving on Kilpatrick's staff, was detached with 10 men to dash across country northward, and communicate, if possible, with Hooker. He struck the Rappahannock at Tappahannock, and found the river too much swollen to cross, but surprised, captured, and paroled a lieutenant and 15 men. The county militia, about 400 strong, assembled under a General Mule, and took the field against him. Summoned to surrender, he refused, mounted, and spurred rapidly with his escort down the river. *En route* he caught a Confederate major, 2 captains, and 3 privates, going to join their regiments, and paroled them. General Mule with about 300 of his men followed closely, and soon had the little party in a *cul-de-sac* between the swollen river and the Dragon Swamp. They again refused to surrender, abandoned their horses, destroyed their arms, and took to the swamp. Here the militia gave up the pursuit, but the planters turned out, and went after them with bloodhounds. At midnight they were probably in full cry on a hot trail.

The perplexity of President Davis and others at having to reconcile Lee's report of a "great victory" with rumors created by Stoneman's cavalry occasioned to-day the following communications:

### Seddon to Lee

. . . The enemy's cavalry in detachments, varying in numbers from 500 to 2000, reported by General W. H. F. Lee to be twenty-seven regiments [say 8100 men], have been making raids from Louisa Court-House to Columbia; in Goochland [County], to Ashland, Hungary Station, Hanover Court-House; [and] the line of the [Virginia] Central Railroad to the Chickahominy. They have been hovering around the city with two or three regiments, apparently menacing attack, probably covering escape of all down the Peninsula. We have a force to protect the bridges over the Annas and to defend the city, but want cavalry to punish the marauders. Hood's division is expected here this evening. The railroad communication shall be opened at the earliest practicable moment.

### To W. H. F. Lee, Gordonsville

The general detachments of the Yankee cavalry that have been prowling in Goochland and around this city, with the exception of about 500 who escaped down the Peninsula, are from concurring reports believed to have returned toward Louisa Court-House or somewhere thereabouts, perhaps toward the Rapidan.

*Longstreet to Elzey*

. . . I shall remain here [at Petersburg] for the present, to try and prevent this place falling into the hands of the enemy. Some of my troops marched 34 miles the night before last, and all marched all night and nearly all day and night last night, so they must be somewhat scattered. I will hurry them up as much as possible. Hood is not yet at Ivor.[1]

Send out citizens in all directions, to try and have all roads blocked by which the enemy may effect his retreat. Felling trees thickly, particularly in the streams, may prevent the escape of the enemy.

*To Seddon*

I leave at 7 o'clock this evening for Richmond.[2]

W. H. F. Lee at Gordonsville heard by telegram from Richmond "that the enemy was everywhere."[3]

*May 6.* Stoneman halted for breakfast and rest from 4 to 7 a.m., then resumed the march with great caution. He received no intelligence from the Army of the Potomac. Every few miles he ordered a halt, and had the country in front and on the flanks thoroughly patrolled. He reached Orange Springs between 9 and 10 a.m. and there found Buford awaiting him. Buford came near being cut off. When the head of his column reached the North Anna, which was about daylight, the water was rising rapidly, and before the rear had crossed the river, it was swimming. The rear-guard found it impassable, and crossed on rafts. Rodenbough and Drummond were given up as lost, but rejoined the command safely, the former about 10 a.m., the latter about 12 m.

Stoneman now first heard through negroes that the army, having been repulsed, had withdrawn to the north bank of the Rappahannock, but he did not know how much of such reports to believe. Starting at noon, he made another all-night march. It rained harder, the darkness was blacker, and the roads were muddier, than the night before. There was the same mournful refrain of a whippoorwill, and an occasional shot as if from the same guerilla. At the halts the men and horses were generally sound asleep. Intense quiet would prevail until some luckless fellow would lose his balance and fall to the ground, when the rattling of his saber and accoutrements would wake those about him and subject him to a shower of unfeeling epithets, or some innocent snorer would evoke an outcry of "Put a nose-bag on him," "Buck and gag him," etc. The advance got out of the woods and swamps at Verdiersville on the Orange Plank Road, and shivered there an hour or two, waiting for the rear of the column to close up. When the march

---

[1] Pickett was in rear of Hood.          [2] *W. R.,* 26, p. 1045.
[3] *Ib.,* 39, p. 1098.

was resumed, it was comparatively easy, pleasant, and rapid. The men had no longer to give constant attention to their horses. Many of them took advantage of their freedom from care to go to sleep. A number were led off the road by Confederate scouts, and taken prisoners. An attempt was made thus to mislead and capture the train, but was frustrated by the quartermaster in charge of it. The column passed within sight of the enemy's camp-fires and within sound of his drums, but was not attacked.[1]

Kilpatrick at sundown came upon a body of cavalry in the vicinity of King and Queen Court-House, and advanced to attack it, when he discovered that it was the stray portion of the 12 Ill. under Bronson. The two commands probably bivouacked there together.[2]

Lieutenant Estes and his 10 men in the Dragon Swamp were run down and captured. Refusing to be paroled, they were put under guard and marched off for Richmond.

The first report received in the Federal lines from any part of Stoneman's force was the following dispatch:

Yorktown, May 6.

*Major-General Dix:*

Colonel Davis, of the Twelfth Illinois Cavalry, with the advance of his regiment, has arrived at Gloucester Point, having accomplished fully the orders of General Stoneman. I have sent a cavalry scout up the Richmond road to get information of any of our cavalry which may be coming down. General Stoneman seems not to have been aware that the enemy have all along had troops on this Peninsula. . . .

E. D. KEYES,

Major-General.[3]

The perplexity of the enemy occasioned the following communications:

### Lee to Seddon

. . . Unless some of the cavalry in North Carolina and the south is sent here, it will be impossible to arrest these raids, and they will roam through this entire section of country with little or no molestation.

### Longstreet to Seddon

. . . General Hampton ordered to unite his force with that of Captain Minor and with the main force to hover on the enemy's [Stoneman's] rear with the small, select parties, to block all roads that the enemy can take in retiring, and use every means of detaining the enemy until we may be able to set out a force that may destroy the enemy's column. General W. H. F. Lee and General Pettigrew are ordered to keep out their scouts, and endeavor to intercept the passage back of the enemy's cavalry, and to have all of his roads blocked by felling trees in his way.

[1] *History of the First Maine Cavalry*, by E. P. Tobie, p. 142.
[2] *W. R.*, 39, p. 1084.     [3] *Ib.*, 26, p. 701.

*Seddon to Lee*

. . . General Longstreet reached here last night.  His forces in part were then in Petersburg, resting from long march.  A train with escort and provisions was sent [to you] yesterday.  All possible effort shall be made to keep open the railroad and supply you.

It would appear from the last two sentences that railroad communication between Fredericksburg and Richmond was reëstablished yesterday, the 5th, having been interrupted during part of the 3d, the 4th, and part of the 5th, say two days.  That this line was open at any rate on the 6th is shown by the following message telegraphed to-day by Colonel Bradley T. Johnson at Hanover Junction to General Elzey at Richmond:

Train has taken my forage to Fredericksburg. Please send me forage for 70 horses on next train.

*May 7.*  As Stoneman's cavalry left the Orange Plank Road, heading for Raccoon Ford, the 2 U. S. Cavalry was detached to Germanna Ford, to guard that crossing against any enemy that might threaten the column.  There the first reliable information was obtained to the effect that the Army of the Potomac had recrossed the Rappahannock.  Stoneman's advance crossed the Rapidan at Raccoon Ford about 2 a.m., and the rear about daylight.

Lieutenant E. V. Sumner, Jr., aide-de-camp of General Stoneman with 10 of the best men and horses of the regular brigade, was detached to find the commanding general of the Army of the Potomac, and deliver to him a written report from General Stoneman.  Skirting the left bank of the Rapidan, and keeping off the road as much as possible, he reached Germanna Ford without seeing any one.  He entered the ford with his party, intending to cross, and hoping to find the Army of the Potomac on the right side and victorious, when, sitting on his horse in the stream and scanning the landscape about him with the hawk-like glance that a soldier acquires in reconnoitering, he caught sight of a small white object that looked like a handkerchief, waving at him from a window in a house that he had passed.  Taking a couple of men and riding back, he found, where he had been looking, a lady, who, though a Virginian, was in sympathy with the North.  She warned him not to go any further in the direction that he had taken, stating that the Confederates had an outpost just beyond the ford.  He promptly withdrew from the ford, and, on a little reflection, decided to heed this warning and take a longer but safer route.  He accordingly took up the march with his escort in the direction of Kelley's Ford.  Coming suddenly upon an outpost of the enemy, he rushed past it, firing into it.  In a few moments a mounted party was in hot pursuit, and it was a race between him and the enemy for the ford, perhaps 8 miles off.  He succeeded, by turning on the foremost of his pursuers, in dismounting several of them, and just before dark reached his goal with all his men. But on this day it was not a ford. The Rappahannock was swimming, full to the banks, and about 200 yards wide. Giving his men the choice between following him and being captured, he plunged into the stream and started across alone. His men, with the exception of two or three who hid in the bushes and afterward joined Stoneman, were soon in the enemy's hands. His pursuers, on reaching the water's edge, commenced firing at him. Being deep in the water by the side of his swimming horse, he made a difficult target, and the Confederate fire was distracted by that of a strong Federal picket on the opposite side of the river. Neither horse nor rider was hit. Wet and chilled as he was, and urged to rest and recuperate, he started at once on the last stretch of his journey, a distance of about 22 miles. Reaching the headquarters camp, he guided his horse into the maze of tents and headed him toward that of the commanding general. The animal kept the direction, and did not stop until his nose rubbed against the front pole of the general's fly. The rider was unconscious. It was 11 o'clock at night. The apparition of this equestrian statue caused sufficient excitement to bring out the adjutant-general, who, inspecting it, exclaimed: "Why, this is Lieutenant Sumner of Stoneman's staff." There was no reply. He was gently lifted from his horse, carried into an adjoining tent, stripped and rubbed, under the direction of a surgeon, rolled in warm blankets, and left to rest, which he did by sleeping until noon of the following day. In the meantime papers found in his boot were delivered to General Hooker.[1]

Stoneman's main column on the north side of the Rapidan took a good rest. The horses were unsaddled and fed what little forage there was. The men were permitted to build fires and cook what meager rations they had. About 10 a.m. the march was resumed, and the whole command went on to Kelley's Ford, where it arrived about 9 p.m. The night being too dark to attempt a passage, the troops rested until morning near the ford. Here it was learned that the army was back in its old camps about Falmouth.

About as Stoneman started out from Raccoon Ford, Kilpatrick with his regiment, after a 50-mile march, arrived at Gloucester Point. Since leaving Stoneman he and Davis had marched about 200 miles in less than five days.

The following dispatch went to Washington:

Yorktown, Va., May 7, 1863.

Hon. E. M. Stanton, Secretary of War:

Colonel Kilpatrick, with the Harris Light Cavalry and Twelfth Illinois Cavalry, have just arrived at Gloucester Point, having accomplished the object of their mission fully and most gallantly. . . .

RUFUS KING,
Brigadier-General.[2]

---

[1] Manuscript of General Sumner.          [2] W. R., 26, p. 706.

This morning General Dix and General Keyes moved up the Pamunkey River with about 5000 infantry, 2 batteries of artillery, and a battalion of 100 cavalry, to West Point, and established a post there. The cavalry under Major Hall was pushed on at once to White House, where it destroyed the railroad bridge across the Pamunkey. On its way back it met the Confederate column escorting Lieutenant Estes and his men to prison. A short, sharp action, and the escort and the prisoners changed places. Lieutenant Estes and his men escorted their late escort to Gloucester Point.

Lee sent off the following communications:

### To Seddon

. . . It is probably Stoneman, on his way to Rappahannock. General Stuart with Fitz Lee's brigade will endeavor to strike them.

### To President Davis

I hardly think it necessary to state to your Excellency that unless we can increase the cavalry attached to this army we shall constantly be subject to aggressive expeditions of the enemy similar to those experienced in the last ten days. . . . If I could get two divisions of cavalry, I should feel as if we ought to resist the three of the enemy. . . .

*May 8.* As soon as it was light enough to see, Stoneman's cavalry proceeded to cross the Rappahannock at Kelley's Ford. The only craft available was a flat-bottomed boat, or scow. This was used to transport the ammunition-chests of the artillery. The pieces and caissons were drawn over the bottom of the river, the horses swimming. One piece after another was pulled out by its eight horses as they gained their footing on the north bank—its muzzle running like a water-main. The troopers and cannoneers swam their horses sitting in the saddle.[1] The emaciated animals could hardly stem the swift current. There was but one exit for them on the north side wide enough for two to land and ascend the bank together. Every one felt that the enemy was not far off and might come up yelling and shooting at any moment. This feeling grew stronger as the remnant still to cross grew less. Stoneman remained nevertheless on the south bank until almost the entire command had left it, when he took to the boat, and went over among the last. The only losses were one man and five or six horses. The crossing was completed about dark, when the march was continued to Bealeton Station.

Lieutenant-Colonel Austin, Stoneman's commissary, who crossed the Rappahannock with the head of the column, rode on to Falmouth. The informal report which he rendered of Stoneman's operation was received rather coldly. Hooker was apparently not pleased. Butterfield intimated that Stoneman had not done what he set out to do. He remarked: "From your account, I don't see but that you are ready to

---

[1] There were not more than twenty yards to swim (W. R., 39, p. 1063).

start out on another expedition right away.'' Austin, somewhat nettled, retorted: ''Perhaps, sir, your long experience with infantry has unfitted you to form a fair estimate of the work of cavalry,'' or words to that effect.

Longstreet wrote to Seddon:

All our reports represent the enemy's main cavalry force returning to the Rappahannock by the same or nearly the same route as that they came [by]. I fear that no effort has been made by our forces or citizens to obstruct his routes.

The Cavalry Corps remained over the 9th at Bealeton, receiving supplies from Alexandria. On the 10th, leaving a squadron to picket the railroad from Rappahannock Station to Cedar Run, it marched to Deep Run; and on the 11th, leaving the Reserve Brigade, Buford's Regulars, to guard the Rappahannock from the railroad to Falmouth, it returned to its old camp with the Army of the Potomac.[1]

The projected movement of Stuart with Fitzhugh Lee's brigade against Stoneman was not made. It seems that the Confederates had no suspicion of the faithful and efficient guidance that was furnished the Federal cavalry by negroes, and no exact information as to its movements. Stoneman's passage of the river was not known to them for several days after it was effected. As late as the 11th Lee wrote to Stuart: ''Hood is at Frederickshall. . . . I hope between you two you may scatter Stoneman.''

Kilpatrick remained at Gloucester Point, resting and recuperating, until the 30th of May. He then marched with his own regiment and the 8 Ill. through Gloucester Court-House and the Dragon Swamp to Saluda and thence to Urbana on the Rappahannock, taking some prisoners and destroying a considerable amount of property. He crossed at Urbana with his command on transports sent to meet him, and proceeded to Falmouth, where he reported to Hooker on the 3d of June.

## COMMENTS

Stoneman must be held responsible for Averell's not rejoining him from the vicinity of Rapidan Station. His order of April 30 admits of the interpretation by which Averell accounts for his continued separation from him; and Averell could not refuse or fail to obey an order from Stoneman, though it contravened a prior order of Hooker's. He was bound to obey the last order that he received; and he carried out Stoneman's orders as he understood them. But it must be said that a general of cavalry, taking Stoneman's orders in connection with Hooker's of April 12, should not have misunderstood them as Averell did. Averell contented himself between April 29 and May 2 with advancing

[1] W. R., 39, p. 1063.

from Kelley's Ford to Rapidan Station, a distance of 28 miles, without inflicting any appreciable injury upon his opponent, whom he outnumbered more than three to one. On this matter Hooker expressed himself to the Adjutant-General, U. S. Army, as follows:

. . . It is no excuse or justification of his course that he received instructions from General Stoneman in conflict with my own, and it was his duty to know that neither of them afforded an excuse for his culpable indifference and inactivity. If he disregarded all instructions it was his duty to do something. If the enemy did not come to him, he should have gone to the enemy. . . . It is unnecessary for me to add that this army will never be able to accomplish its mission under commanders who not only disregard their instructions, but at the same time display so little zeal and devotion in the performance of their duties. I could excuse General Averell in his disobedience if I could anywhere discover in his operations a desire to find and engage the enemy. I have no disposition to prefer charges against him, and in detaching him from this army my object has been to prevent an active and powerful column from being paralyzed in its future operations by his presence.[1]

Neither Stoneman nor Averell seems to have caught the spirit of the orders he received. Hooker is but just when he remarks before the Committee on the Conduct of the War: "It is charitable to suppose that Generals Stoneman and Averell did not read their orders, and determined to carry on operations in conformity with their own views and inclinations."[2]

Instead of being scattered to raid, Stoneman's troopers should have been used in a body to beat the road to Fredericksburg for the retreating Confederate army. Possibly Stoneman's tactics are attributable to his physical condition. Throughout this campaign he was a sufferer from hemorrhoids, the cavalryman's complaint. He could not sit in a saddle without pain, and so was physically unfit to be in active service. It is not improbable that this circumstance determined his adoption of a plan that would exempt him for a day or two from riding.

The damage done by the Federal cavalry to the railroads was easily repaired. Traffic was not interrupted for more than two days. Stores were destroyed in considerable quantity, but their loss did not seriously affect the Confederate commissariat. The question may be asked: What would have been the strategic effect, had Lee's army been defeated, of the damage done by Stoneman to the Confederate communications? If the pursuit had been prompt and vigorous, and Stoneman had got his scattered regiments to operate against the front and flanks of the retreating army,—neither of which suppositions seems, in the light of events, altogether plausible,—it would have been a serious embarrassment, but not necessarily a fatal check, to the enemy. Stoneman

[1] W. R., 39, pp. 1072, 1073.     [2] Rep. of Com., IV, 140.

claims in his report that "all the road bridges across the South Anna and several across the North Anna were completely destroyed, placing a ditch fordable only in a very few places between the enemy and Richmond." Admitting that this was the case, it is not improbable that these "very few places" would have been found and utilized, and that Lee would have got away from Hooker as he got away from McClellan after Antietam, and was to get away from Meade after Gettysburg.

Nearly all the transportation of Lee's army was collected at Guiney's Station, 18 miles from Chancellorsville, with little or no guard, and might have been destroyed by one third of Stoneman's force. The destruction of the few days' supplies that Lee had on hand, together with that of his transportation, would have proved a heavy, if not a decisive, blow to him. The absence of the Federal cavalry from the front and flanks of the army was, or should have been, severely felt by Hooker, while Lee's plans were not disarranged by its presence in his rear.[1]

Stoneman's cavalry had indeed a share in deterring the enemy from following the defeated Army of the Potomac across the Rappahannock, but it might better have prevented that army from being defeated. It gained from its operations hardihood, instruction, and *morale,* but these acquisitions, together with the damage which it inflicted upon the enemy, directly and indirectly, materially and morally, were hardly an offset to the loss which it sustained in horse-flesh. About 1000 of Stoneman's horses were abandoned. Most of these were replaced by brood-mares and work-horses—not suitable for cavalry—and mules. A number of men, who could not be remounted, were left behind to fall into the enemy's hands. On the 13th of May Stoneman reported the portion of the force brought back with him that was then fit for duty in the field as about 2000—less than 50 per cent. of the total. On the 27th of May Pleasonton, who had succeeded Stoneman in command of the Cavalry Corps, reported the number of serviceable cavalry horses present in the corps as 4677. The trimonthly return for May 31 gives the number of enlisted cavalrymen present for duty as 9626. Thus about 50 per cent. of the force was dismounted.[2]

[1] *Chancellorsville,* by Hotchkiss and Allan, p. 108.
[2] See also Ingalls to Meigs, *W. R.,* 40, p. 547.

# CHAPTER XXIX

OPERATIONS OF INDEPENDENT CAVALRY (CONTINUED)

## Jones and Imboden

ON the 20th of April Imboden marched from Shenandoah Mountain (Map 1, sheet B) with about 1825 men, and on the 21st was reën-forced at Hightown to about 3365, of whom about 700 were mounted. His column was accompanied by a wagon-train carrying 13 days' rations of flour and 30 days' of salt. He relied upon the country for meat. W. E. Jones marched from Lacy Spring on the 21st. Such men and horses as were unfit for a hard campaign he left near Harrisburg to hold the Valley. These troops were to keep up communication with Fitzhugh Lee at Sperryville. The force which Jones took with him consisted mainly of cavalry, but comprised some infantry and artillery, a pack-train, and a wagon-train. It numbered about 3500 men. According to the original plan, approved by General Lee, these two columns were to strike the railroad at the same time, Imboden's at Grafton and Jones' at Oakland. But they were hardly in motion when Jones received a letter from Imboden informing him that when Jones reached Oakland Imboden would be at Beverly. It was too late to rearrange matters, and the movement proceeded on this new plan.[1] Jones had intended by the original plan, and perhaps still hoped, to accomplish such destruction on the Baltimore and Ohio Railroad that for six months at least no troops might pass over it.[2] That the Federals were not taken unawares appears from the following dispatch of 3:30 p.m., the 21st, from Schenck to Halleck:

Many circumstances now tend to indicate that the rebels are preparing to make some movement in force in Western Virginia. General Milroy telegraphed to me yesterday that, except some small scattering parties, the enemy had fallen back with all troops as far as Harrisburg. In a dispatch to-day he says:

"From information received, which I deem reliable, the baggage of [Stonewall] Jackson's army and some artillery and ordnance stores arrived at Staunton some ten days since."

On the 23d Imboden reached Huttonsville, having marched 70 miles in four days, most of the time in a drenching rain, which made the

---

[1] W. R., 39, p. 119.
[2] History of the Laurel Brigade, by W. N. McDonald, p. 117.

roads very difficult.[1]  Jones marched on Moorefield, which the Federals
had left unoccupied. He intended to cross the south branch of the Potomac at that point, but before he reached it the stream was so swollen
by the downpour that he abandoned the idea. He reached Moorefield
on the 23d. The unfavorable weather and bad condition of the roads
made these first three days exceedingly arduous.[2]

*April 24.* Imboden reached and attacked Beverly, garrisoned by
about 900 men with 2 pieces of artillery under Colonel Latham. From
a point 25 miles north of Beverly, he wrote to General Samuel Jones:

Had three hours' fight [with] the enemy on the heights in rear of Beverly
to-day. Drove him from the town; cut his retreat on Buckhannon; hurried
[harried?] him till dark toward Philippi. Renew the pursuit in the morning.
Casualties small on both sides. Enemy set fire to the town in his retreat, and
burned a large part of it. Enemy's loss of stores considerable. Our captures
of wagons and mules valuable.[3]

Roberts at Buckhannon reported the affair to Halleck, stating:

. . . Colonel Latham [commanding at Beverly] has retreated on the road to
Philippi. The enemy interposed cavalry and artillery in the road to this place,
and prevented his falling back [on this place]. Reënforcements should be thrown
into Grafton without delay, or the enemy will reach the Baltimore and Ohio Railroad, and do great damage. The roads in this region are impassable.

He received the following answer sent at 8 p.m.:

Collect your forces, defend the railroad, and drive the enemy back. You are
strong enough to do it if you try. Do not call for reënforcements from here. You
have no need of them, and we have none to give you, if you had. I do not understand how the roads there are impassable to you when by your account they are
passable enough to the enemy. If you can not drive the enemy out, we will seek
some one who can.

Roberts replied at 9:40 p.m.:

. . . I have collected my forces from Sutton [Suttonville] and Bulltown into
this place, to repel the enemy. Colonel Latham, with half of my command, has
allowed himself to be surprised, and has been compelled to retreat in the direction
of Philippi, where he can not reach me. The enemy has five regiments of cavalry.
I have but four companies [of cavalry]. The roads the enemy has passed over
are mountain roads. Those I must move over are in the valley, and I have never
seen any in so impassable a condition. I shall fail in nothing that is possible.

General Jones, to increase his mobility, sent back from Moorefield to
the Valley his infantry, artillery, and wagon-train, thus reducing his
column to cavalry, mounted infantry, and a pack-train.

[1] *W. R.,* 39, pp. 90–106.      [2] *Ib.,* 39, p. 116.      [3] *Ib.,* 39, p. 97.

After making a detour he reached Petersburg, where the river was found to be still dangerously high. Men with weak horses were not forced to attempt the ford, and a few here turned back. A number of citizens of the neighborhood who were familiar with the crossing, having provided themselves with long poles, boldly rode out into the river, and took stations at regular intervals along the ford. They constantly warned the troopers to keep their horses' heads up-stream, and when a horse would start down, would tap him on the neck with a pole, and thus help keep him in the ford. One man and two horses were drowned.[1] Descending the river from Petersburg, Jones camped nearly opposite Moorefield.

*April 25.* Imboden spent the day in resting and reconnoitering and trying to open communication with W. E. Jones, who according to the plan should have been at Oakland. Neither Imboden nor Jones had heard from the other. Roberts, at Buckhannon, sent the following dispatches to Kelley at Harper's Ferry, the first one at 3 p.m.:

1

The troops that reach Grafton should force a march to Philippi, where Colonel Latham attempted to retreat [from Beverly]. I don't know whether he succeeded or not, but a rapid movement on Philippi may save him.

2

Just heard from Colonel Latham. He was near Philippi. Had a running fight of eight hours. Proposes to join me, if possible, to-morrow night.

After leaving Petersburg, Jones' route lay through Greenland Gap. Contrary to his expectations, he learned that this point was occupied. The Federal force consisted of portions of two companies (G, 23 Ill., Captain Martin Wallace; and A, 14 W. Va., Captain Jacob Smith), numbering together 86 men.[2] The position could have been turned, but the consequent delay might have endangered the success of the general plan. Accordingly, Jones decided to force it. The Federals took shelter in a log church and two log houses, and repulsed the repeated assaults of the raiders, who numbered, according to Captain Wallace, 3100 men,[3] and according to a Confederate writer and participant in the affair, 3500.[4] The defenders would not yield until the assailants had succeeded in setting fire to the church, in which the main force of the defence was stationed. By this action the Confederates were detained four hours, and prevented from making important captures at their next objective point. The fight gave them 4 wagons and 1 ambulance,

[1] *History of the Laurel Brigade*, by W. N. McDonald, pp. 118–120; W. R., 39, p. 116.

[2] W. R., 39, pp. 108, 109.

[3] *Ib.*, 39, p. 110.

[4] *Forty Years of Active Service*, by C. T. O'Ferral, p. 58.

encumbered them with 75 or 80 prisoners, and cost them 42 men in killed and wounded.[1] Fortunately for them, they had delayed the assault until near dark. This saved them from a much heavier loss.

The stubborn resistance of the Federals greatly enraged the Confederates. Some insisted that the prisoners should be killed, but General Jones, like the officer and gentleman that he was, replied: "They fought like brave men and did their duty. They shall receive honorable treatment."[2]

Proceeding on a night march, he detached Colonel Harman with the 12 Va. Cavalry, Brown's Maryland battalion of cavalry, and McNeill's company of Partisan Rangers, to burn the bridge of the Baltimore and Ohio Railroad at Oakland, in the southwestern corner of Maryland, and march thence by way of Kingwood and Morgantown to rejoin the main column; and a squadron of the 11 Va. Cavalry under Captain McDonald to Altamont, 12 miles east of Oakland, to burn some small bridges there and follow Colonel Harman. With the remainder of his force he went on toward Rowlesburg. At 12 p.m. he was still on the march. It was a freezing cold night. Many men, wet to the skin, suffered severely. These operations occasioned the following correspondence:

### Schenck to Halleck, April 25, 12 m.

The rebel Jones appears to have left the Valley to go in the direction of Moorefield, perhaps to coöperate with Imboden and [W. L.] Jackson,[3] but more likely to threaten the railroad at New Creek, or some point this side. Elliott's brigade has been sent from Winchester, toward Moorefield, to reconnoiter. I must draw troops westward from Winchester and Harper's Ferry. Will you have General Stahel, with his cavalry, look out toward the Blue Ridge and the Valley, while my forces are thus partially drawn off?[4] . . .

*April 26.* Imboden camped between Philippi and Buckhannon, about 12 miles from each place, and sent all his cavalry to seize and hold the bridge across Buckhannon River near its mouth, intending to cross there. He had not yet heard from W. E. Jones. In a conference which he held with his colonels, it was judged by all that Jones had failed to reach, or interrupt, communications on the Baltimore and Ohio Railroad; that Imboden's command was exposed to attack, and its safety required that it should fall back to a position where escape would be possible, if it were overpowered. It was accordingly decided to move back on the morrow. Latham, falling back from Beverly, joined Rob-

---

[1] Jones reported that for lack of transportation he destroyed 90 Enfield rifles. According to Wallace's report the defenders threw these arms into the flames to save them from the enemy (*W. R.*, 39, pp. 110, 114, 117).

[2] *History of the Laurel Brigade,* by Captain W. N. McDonald, pp. 121–123.

[3] Included in Imboden's command.

[4] This movement of Stahel's was made on the 27th.

erts at Buckhannon.  Roberts ordered the commanders at Big Birch, Suttonville, and Bulltown to send all wagons and supplies that could be removed by way of Weston to Clarksburg, and with the troops to join him by forced marches at Buckhannon.

Jones arrived at the Cheat River, near Rowlesburg, about 2 p.m. With three regiments of cavalry, dismounted, say 1000 men, he attacked the railroad at Rowlesburg, defended by about 250 men, and was repulsed.  It was near sundown.  His command, after thirty-six hours of forced marching, was without forage.  He had difficulty in procuring food for his men.  Rumors reached him of Federal columns advancing from different directions.  The country people were unfriendly and frequently in the mountain passes fired into his column.  His detachments were beyond recall.  He had not heard from Imboden, and could not abandon him.  To renew his attack on the railroad he regarded as hopeless.  He therefore deemed it best to pass on, leaving the railroad bridge and trestlework unharmed, and the garrison at Rowlesburg in his rear.  After a few hours of night marching he found a scanty supply of forage and went into camp, 6 miles east of Evansville.  Harman reached Oakland at 11 a.m., surprised, captured, and paroled a company of infantry stationed there, destroyed two railroad bridges, and proceeded toward Kingwood.  Halting at the Cheat River, he burned the bridge, and bivouacked for the night.  McDonald was behind him, destroying the railroad.

*April 27.*  Imboden marched back to-day to Roaring Run, withdrawing his cavalry from the Buckhannon Bridge.  The road was so bad that it took from 5 a.m. until 2 p.m. to make 2 miles, and the command did not reach camp until after dark.  Roberts was joined at Buckhannon by the detachments already mentioned, which gave him an effective force of 2800 men.[1]

Jones moved to Evansville, where corn was secured for the horses and meat for the men.  Fearing that news would travel rapidly along the railroad, he threw a force into Independence, and had it destroy the bridge at that place.  In the hope of establishing communication with Imboden, he wrote to him:

. . . I have come here to feed men and horses, and wait for news and junction with Harman, when I will make my way to you.  My movements, as a matter of course, will be controlled by circumstances. . . .[2]

The whole command crossed the railroad about dark, and proceeded northward to look up Harman.  About midnight, finding forage, and having heard of Harman, it went into camp near Independence.

[1] 2500 infantry, 200 cavalry, 100 artillery (4 pieces) (*W. R.*, 39, p. 91).
[2] *Ib.*, 39, p. 105.

Harman marched to Morgantown. Several hundred citizens, who had armed themselves and collected here, prepared to offer resistance, when summoned, surrendered unconditionally, depositing their arms in the court-house, and retired to their homes.[1] A portion of Harman's force remained in this place, with the Confederate flag flying over it, for about two hours. While no resistance was made, no sympathy was shown him by the inhabitants. The best efforts of his gallant followers to propitiate the ladies were of no avail. When induced to sing or play they gave the "Star-Spangled Banner," or "Hooker is Our Leader," or the Union version of "Maryland, My Maryland," or some other expression of decidedly Union sentiment.

On receipt of the news from Morgantown the court-house bell at Uniontown, Pa.,[2] was rung, and intense excitement prevailed. The specie of its bank was removed to Pittsburg. The latter place itself was somewhat disturbed. Wheeling was filled with excitement. The mills were stopped, and picked citizens proceeded to form a home guard. A large amount of its specie was shipped also to Pittsburg.

From Morgantown Harman proceeded toward Independence, and camped about 7 miles from that place.

Jones' movements so scared the telegraph operator at Grafton that he destroyed his instruments and left. A Colonel Wilkinson coöperated with the enemy by having a bridge burned near Bridgeport and the track torn up, to prevent the enemy from coming to him by rail.[3]

At 11:30 p.m. Schenck telegraphed him:

. . . You are evidently in a causeless panic. . . . Your burning of the bridge at Bridgeport is disgraceful.

I sincerely hope Mulligan is, as you suppose, at Grafton, where you ought to have been. . . .[4]

Colonel Mulligan, falling back from Philippi, where he had gone to cover Latham's retreat, reached Grafton with two regiments of infantry and a battery of artillery.[5]

Roberts received from Wilkinson a telegram that Grafton was captured, and that he was preparing to evacuate Clarksburg in two hours. He replied that he would reach Clarksburg the following day at noon, and directed him "to hold on, if possible, but if compelled to retreat, to run the railroad stock and supplies to Parkersburg, destroy such as could not be secured, and to fall back to Parkersburg or Weston."[6]

At 4 p.m. Roberts, with the troops at Buckhannon, took up the march for Clarksburg.

*April 28.* Imboden marched to within 4 miles of Buckhannon, hav-

---

[1] *W. R.*, 39, pp. 126, 134.
[2] North of the map.
[3] *W. R.*, 40, p. 296.
[4] *Ib.*, 40, p. 298.
[5] *Ib.*, 39, pp. 91, 112.
[6] *Ib.*, 39, pp. 91, 92.

ing heard that the enemy had abandoned that place.  Roberts with his command reached Clarksburg.

Harman took up the march at 2 a.m. for Independence.  W. E. Jones, proceeding northward, met Harman at daylight and learned from him that the expeditions to Oakland and Altamont had been successful. With his whole command, except the squadron under McDonald, he proceeded to Morgantown, crossed the Monongahela at that point, and rested.  In the course of the day he was joined by McDonald.  Judging that he had gone as far north as was safe, he decided to turn southward and look up Imboden.  He resumed his march at dark, but went into camp a short distance outside of Fairmont.

How these operations were viewed and met by the Federals is indicated in part by the following dispatches of this day:

### Halleck to Schenck

You should concentrate your forces on the rear of Jones' raid, so as to cut off his return. . . . This raid is unquestionably made to divert our attention from the Rappahannock and Suffolk.[1]  If Roberts [at Clarksburg] and Kelley [at New Creek][2] will act promptly, they can cut Jones completely off.  It is believed that his entire force is not over 3000.

### Schenck to Halleck, 2:30 p.m., received 4:40 p.m.

I have Mulligan at Grafton. . . . The whole rebel force that has been on the line of the railroad I do not believe exceeds 1500, but all cavalry. . . . I hope to intercept enemy's retreat.  It is difficult, though, to catch cavalry with infantry. . . . They have got up unnecessary panic at Wheeling, Pittsburg, and Parkersburg.

J. W. Garrett, President of the Baltimore and Ohio Railroad, telegraphed to-day from Baltimore to the company:

. . . But one train of empty cars was stopped, which we have recovered.  One bridge only was destroyed west of Oakland, which we are reconstructing.  We have strong working forces at all points, and expect to reopen through to-morrow. No passenger or freight trains have been disturbed upon our entire line.

*April 29.*  Imboden marched to Buckhannon, 4 miles, and spent the rest of the day resting and gathering supplies.  His horses were breaking down in great numbers.  Some were dying from overwork and lack of nourishment.  Grain was very scarce and had to be procured in small quantities, sometimes less than a bushel at a house.  He employed a considerable portion of his cavalry in collecting cattle and sending them to the rear, paying for everything at the rates that were current before he arrived in the country.  This gave general satisfac-

[1] The raid was not made with such intention.
[2] In general control of the troops on the railroad.

tion, Confederate money being freely accepted.[1] He received his first information from W. E. Jones in the form of the latter's dispatch of the 27th. He also heard that the enemy was massing his troops at Janelew, a village about midway between Buckhannon and Clarksburg, and fortifying his position.

Jones attacked Fairmont, which was defended by 400 men, carried the place, and destroyed the bridge, an iron structure which it had taken two years to build. The result of his day's work was the destruction of 4 railroad bridges, and the capture of 1 piece of artillery, 300 small arms, 260 men, and many horses.

At 9:20 a.m. Roberts at Clarksburg telegraphed to Schenck at Baltimore:

Arrived myself last night [from Buckhannon], men and horses, all exhausted by three days' and nights' forced march. Can do nothing with them for twenty-four hours or more. . . . Jones is now at Fairmont, probably 2000 strong. . . . We must keep this [place] and the supplies here. . . . If General Cox [at Cincinnati] can send 4000 or 5000 men to Parkersburg, it should be done, and the enemy captured or defeated. . . .

Schenck telegraphed to Halleck at 11:30: "Bridge at Fairmont is safe," and on receipt, at 1:10 p.m., of the dispatch of 9:20 a.m. from Roberts: "I do not credit the report of Jones and his 2000 at Fairmont." But at 11 p.m. he added that he had just received the following dispatch from Roberts at Clarksburg:

Fairmont is taken, and the bridge at that place burned, and the piers blown up.

In the meantime Halleck telegraphed:

*To Schenck, 3:05 p.m.*

The enemy's raid is variously estimated at from 1500 to 4000. You have 45,000 under your command. If you can not concentrate enough to meet the enemy, it does not argue well for your military dispositions.

According to his consolidated morning report Schenck's command numbered on the 30th of April 34,297 present for duty.[2]

Burnside, under orders from Halleck, collected all the troops that could be spared from his department, and shipped them up the Ohio to Parkersburg to coöperate with Schenck's forces. He also arranged with the naval authorities for sending a couple of gunboats up the river.

Governor Curtin of Pennsylvania telegraphed to Stanton:

It is reported to me that the rebels have taken Morgantown in force. Please say if you have any information, and if force will be sent on, if true. We have no force in the state, and you could send troops before we could organize any.[3]

---

[1] *W. R.*, 39, p. 102.        [2] *Ib.*, 40, pp. 321, 322.
[3] *The Army of the Potomac from 1861 to 1863*, by S. L. French.

Lincoln telegraphed the same day to Curtin:

I do not think the people of Pennsylvania should be uneasy about invasion. Doubtless a small force of the enemy is flourishing about in the northern part of Virginia on the "scewhorn" principle, on purpose to divert us in another quarter. I believe it is nothing more. We think we have adequate force close after them.[1]

A dispatch of similar import was sent by Stanton.[2]

*April 30.* Imboden spent the day at Buckhannon, collecting corn and cattle. W. E. Jones marched on Clarksburg. This place contained, according to Schenck, "about 4500 troops of all arms," and according to Roberts, who commanded the troops, "2600 effective men, with 10 pieces of artillery."[3] Learning of its occupation and not feeling strong enough to attack it, Jones turned on Bridgeport, and there captured 46 men and a few horses, and destroyed a bridge, making, with the one destroyed by Wilkinson, two bridges destroyed at Bridgeport. He camped about dark a short distance out of that place on the road to Philippi.

*May 1.* Imboden spent another day at Buckhannon foraging and constructing a raft on which to cross the river. He sent a regiment of cavalry to Weston, which found that place evacuated and stores collected there destroyed, but confirmed the report that the enemy was at Janelew. Fearing that Jones had been cut off, and meaning to look him up, he issued orders to move early in the morning toward Philippi.

Jones reached Philippi about noon. He now further lightened his column by sending off his led horses to the Shenandoah Valley. He had received no "certain intelligence" of Imboden, but understanding, probably from the people of the country, that he was at Buckhannon, he proceeded on a night march toward that place.

While Jones was turning the position of Clarksburg the Federals continued to think that he was marching on it. At 2:30 p.m. Halleck received the following dispatches:

*From Cipher Correspondent at Parkersburg*

. . . Enemy captured company cavalry 4 miles east of Clarksburg, and are now represented as surrounding the town. Attack momentarily expected.

*Kelley to Schenck, 1:30 p.m.*

General Kenly [from Harper's Ferry] has just arrived at Grafton; [he] will push right on to Clarksburg by rail as far as he can with safety, then debark and march by turnpike. I will order him to attack and raise the siege [of Clarksburg] at once. . . . Everything looks well now. The enemy have completely surrounded Roberts, but had not attempted to attack him up to last advices.

---

[1] *The Army of the Potomac from 1861 to 1863,* by S. L. French.
[2] *W. R.,* 40, p. 300.          [3] *Ib.,* 40, pp. 348, 376.

While this imaginary siege was being raised Mulligan was to march from Grafton to Philippi and cut off the retreat of the besiegers in that direction. But he was not to move until Kelley heard "something definite" from Roberts,[1] and Roberts, for lack of cavalry, could get no information of a definite character. Kelley telegraphed to Roberts:

. . . What is your latest news of the enemy? Don't let him escape you if it can possibly be prevented. Communicate fully with me.

He received the following reply:

. . . Jones' force passed my left through Bridgeport to-day. It is . . . evidently trying to form a junction with Imboden's. . . . They intend, after joining their forces, to attack this place. . . .

. . . General Kenly has just reached Bridgeport with his command, and will join me before morning.

. . . I have no cavalry that can do any service. The forces of Milroy should be thrown in toward Franklin, to cut off Jones' retreat. Scammon's forces [at Charleston, W. Va.] should be drawn round toward Summerville and Lewisburg, to prevent retreat in that direction.

As a consequence of this call for cavalry the 12 Pa. was ordered by Milroy to take the cars westward from Martinsburg at 6 p.m.

Schenck telegraphed to Curtin, Governor of Pennsylvania:

All I want is some coöperation from the direction of Pennsylvania and the Ohio River, to beat and capture the enemy, if he does not escape by Clarksburg at once.

The enemy was escaping, not by Clarksburg, but by Bridgeport. There was some coöperation coming from the Ohio, but none from Pennsylvania. At 4:25 p.m. Governor Curtin telegraphed to President Lincoln that he was in hourly receipt of dispatches from the western part of his state, that the people of West Virginia were calling for aid from the Pennsylvania militia, and that he should like to have the President's opinion as to the propriety of his complying with such requests. Receiving no reply, he telegraphed later:

. . . I have dispatches stating that the Union forces have been repulsed and are falling back into Pennsylvania. If it is your pleasure that I should call out the militia, immediate arrangements should be made for their transportation and subsistence. . . .

The President replied:

The whole disposable force at Baltimore and elsewhere in reach have already been sent after the enemy that alarms you.

The worst thing the enemy could do for himself would be to weaken himself

---

[1] Preceding dispatch.

before [in front of] Hooker, and therefore it is safe to believe that he is not doing it, and the best he could do for himself would be to get us so scared as to bring part of Hooker's force away, and that is just what he is trying to do.

It is evident from these and previous communications that both Lincoln and Stanton had misjudged the purpose of Lee's raiding columns. There was no thought of a diversion in Lee's immediate front, of drawing troops away from the Army of the Potomac. Lee did think that the raids would draw Milroy from the Shenandoah Valley, but this he considered as a means of opening that country to Confederate foraging, and not as a weakening of Hooker. The great object of the raiders was not to draw Federal forces after them, but to destroy the railroad and collect supplies and recruits.[1]

Among the wild rumors that perplexed the Federal authorities to-day was one that the Confederate force was estimated at 20,000, and was under the command of Stonewall Jackson.[2]

*May 2.* A few miles from Buckhannon, Jones, coming from Philippi, received the first certain intelligence of General Imboden, and on arriving found him ready to move to Weston. Both officers had lost so many men that they hardly had more between them than each one had at the beginning.[3] That they had not struck the railroad simultaneously as had been planned was attributed by Jones to the fact that Imboden encumbered his column with wagons. Jones says in his report:[4]

Knowing the difficulty of moving wagons over mountain roads in early spring, I stipulated with General Imboden that no such impediment should clog his movements after leaving Huttonsville. I was surprised to find a train of 70 wagons at Buckhannon. Had our original plan [Jones'] been carried out, I feel confident northwestern Virginia could have been cleared to the Ohio.

No such consummation could now be hoped for. The whole command, under Jones as senior officer, took up the march for Weston; Imboden marching directly on that point, and Jones by the road to Clarksburg and by-roads, flanking Imboden on the right. Imboden covered about one half, and Jones about one third, of the distance to Weston, and camped for the night.

The Baltimore and Ohio Railroad was now free from the enemy and in working order, except at the bridge destroyed by Wilkinson near Bridgeport.

[1] Lee to Jones, April 26, *ante.*

[2] Curtin to Stanton, *W. R.,* 40, p. 347.

[3] Imboden reports a loss of 200 men by desertion (*W. R.,* 39, p. 102). Jones had given to all his men who desired it permission to go home.

[4] *W. R.,* 39, p. 119.

Schenck telegraphed to Scammon at Charleston, W. Va.:

. . . [W. E.] Jones retreating rapidly by way of Philippi.

. . . . . . . . . .

Roberts and Kelley [Kenly] will pursue south from Clarksburg. You should send whatever force you can to Summerville. . . .

And Lincoln to Curtin:

. . . I really do not see the justification for incurring the trouble and expense of calling out the militia. . . . Our forces are exactly between the enemy and Pennsylvania.

Did Lincoln know that the Federal forces were doing their best to gain the enemy's rear, and thus put the enemy between themselves and Pennsylvania?

*May 3.* Imboden reached Weston and went into camp. Jones camped *en route* to that point.

Roberts, who was to pursue from Clarksburg, telegraphed to Schenck:

No additional information of the enemy. . . . The Twelfth Pennsylvania Cavalry, 320 strong, reaches me to-day, broken down.

No means of transportation gotten here yet. It will be several days before I can do anything but protect railroad.

The transportation had all been removed from Clarksburg by Wilkinson before Roberts arrived there. Roberts had sent for it and was waiting for its return.

*May 4.* W. E. Jones rejoined Imboden at Weston. Here the forces rested until the 6th of May, by which time the campaign of Chancellorsville was decided. Their subsequent operations may be described in a few words. Imboden moved southward through Bulltown, Suttonville, and Big Birch—all of which places he found evacuated—to Summerville, where he arrived on the 13th of May. Jones took his command northward, and struck the railroad at West Union and Cairo. He destroyed two bridges at the former place, and three at the latter. From Cairo he moved to Oil Town, where he arrived on the 9th, and burned a quantity of oil estimated at 150,000 barrels. Turning southward, he proceeded by way of Glenville and Suttonville to Summerville. He arrived there with a portion of his command and united with Imboden on the 13th. The remainder of his command joined him on the 14th, after which Jones and Imboden marched together eastward for some distance, and separated to go to their respective camps.

Their joint operation can not be said to have been a success. They did more damage to the Baltimore and Ohio Railroad than Stoneman did to the railroads in Virginia, but the military effect of it was even less than Stoneman's brief interruption of Lee's communication with Richmond.  They were greatly disappointed in the number of recruits obtained.  The Secessionists were rather incensed than pleased by the treatment that they received from their raiding visitors.  The property seized was taken from these people perhaps more than from Unionists, for the reason that the latter were active in hiding their property, while the Secessionists, trusting to the consideration of their friends, took no such precaution.  The raiders had little regard for persons whose only aid was their sympathy.  A rich Secessionist, who rode into Fairmont on a fine horse, told General Jones how much he was doing to help the Southern cause.  The general interrupted him by a requisition for his horse.  In answer to his protestations on the score of his loyalty, he was told that he ought cheerfully to give his horse for the cause that he loved so well.

The best that General Lee could say of Jones' and Imboden's operations may be gathered from his indorsements of June 15 on their reports:

The expedition under General Jones appears to have been conducted with commendable skill and vigor, and was productive of beneficial results.  The injury inflicted on the enemy was serious, and he will doubtless be induced to keep troops to guard the railroad who might be otherwise employed against us.  General Jones displayed sagacity and boldness in his plans, and was well supported by the courage and fortitude of his officers and men.[1]

Although the expedition under General Imboden failed to accomplish all the results intended, it nevertheless rendered valuable service in the collection of stores and in making the enemy uneasy for his communications with the west. The men and officers deserve much credit for the fortitude and endurance exhibited under the hardships and difficulties of the march, which interfered so seriously with the success of the enterprise.[2]

The Federal defence depended upon anticipating the enemy at his points of attack or at points commanding his line of retreat.  For lack of cavalry it could not undertake to follow or harass him.  What cavalry it had might perhaps have been used to better advantage than it was in observing and reporting the enemy's movements.  At any rate, the failure of the defence to intercept either of the enemy's columns was the natural consequence of its imperfect information.  The defence of Greenland Gap stands out as the finest thing of the whole operation, and seems really deserving of the much-abused characterization of heroic.

[1] W. R., 39, p. 121.

[2] Ib., 39, p. 105.  For some interesting details of the operation, the reader is referred to The Comanches, a History of White's Battalion, Virginia Cavalry, Laurel Brigade, Hampton Division, A. N. V., by F. M. Myers, late Captain Company A, 35 Va. Cavalry.

# CHAPTER XXX

## LOSSES IN THE OPPOSING ARMIES.  COMMENTS

THE losses in killed, wounded, and missing which the campaign entailed upon the Army of the Potomac are given in the following table:

| ORGANIZATION | AGGREGATE PRESENT FOR DUTY EQUIPPED | KILLED AND WOUNDED | | KILLED, WOUNDED, AND MISSING | |
|---|---|---|---|---|---|
| | | NUMBER | PER CENT. | NUMBER | PER CENT. |
| General headquarters, cavalry escort . . . . . . . . | 60 | 0 | 0 | 0 | 0 |
| I    Corps . . . . . . . . | 16,908 | 245 | 1 | 299 | 2 |
| II   Corps . . . . . . . . | 16,893 | 1,193 | 7 | 1,925 | 11 |
| III  Corps . . . . . . . . | 18,721 | 3,023 | 16 | 4,119 | 22 |
| V    Corps . . . . . . . . | 15,824 | 541 | 3 | 700 | 4 |
| VI   Corps . . . . . . . . | 23,667 | 3,145 | 13 | 4,610 | 19 |
| XI   Corps . . . . . . . . | 12,977 | 1,618 | 12 | 2,412 | 19 |
| XII  Corps . . . . . . . . | 13,450 | 1,703 | 13 | 2,824 | 21 |
| General Artillery Reserve . . | 1,610 | 0 | 0 | 0 | 0 |
| Cavalry Corps { Active force . | 9,060 [1] | 81 | 1 | 389 | 4 |
| Cavalry Corps { Depot force . | 2,481 [2] | 0 | 0 | 0 | 0 |
| Provost Guard . . . . . . | 2,217 | 0 | 0 | 0 | 0 |
| Army of the Potomac . . . | 133,868 | 11,549 | 9 | 17,278 [3] | 13 |

The percentages express the ratios of casualties to *Present for Duty Equipped*.  The casualties among non-combatants were insignificant in number.  There were no losses reported in the General Artillery Reserve or Provost Guard of the army.  Two men were reported wounded on signal duty.[4]  The VI and XII Corps reported 3 killed and wounded, and 1 captured or missing, in their respective provost guards.[5]  Berry's old division had 2 men wounded in the ambulance detachment.[6]

The portion of the II Corps that fought under Couch at Chancellors-

---

[1] Pleasonton, 1020; Averell, 3520; Stoneman, 4320 (including horse artillery in each case), and 200 artillerymen, who, with 10 pieces of horse artillery, were in battery at Banks' Ford.

[2] Guarding camps and communications north of Rappahannock.

[3] One casualty was reported in General Hooker's staff and 8 in the Engineer Brigade. These casualties, not included in the table, make the grand aggregate 17,287 (*W. R.*, 39, pp. 173, 216, 192).

[4] *Ib.*, 39, p. 223.

[5] *Ib.*, 39, pp. 183, 189.

[6] *Ib.*, 39, p. 451.

ville lost in killed and wounded 10 per cent. and in killed, wounded, and missing, 16 per cent.

It will be observed that the loss, in proportion to strength, sustained by the XI Corps, on which fell the first heavy blow—intended to be the decisive blow—of the campaign, was exceeded by that of the III and XII Corps and equaled by that of the VI Corps, and that the largest loss in proportion to strength was sustained by the III Corps.

Averell lost at Rapidan Station $\frac{4}{10}$ of 1 per cent. in killed and wounded, and 1 per cent. in killed, wounded, and missing. Pleasonton lost in the march to Chancellorsville and subsequent operations 7 per cent. in killed and wounded, and 20 per cent. in killed, wounded, and missing. Stoneman lost in his immediate command, or raiding column, $\frac{2}{10}$ of 1 per cent. in killed and wounded, and 3 per cent. in killed, wounded, and missing.

The foregoing figures are compiled for the greater part from the monthly return for April, and the returns of casualties for the campaign.[1]

The Confederate records do not give the casualties as fully as the Federal. They contain a report of killed and wounded by the medical director, which, however, does not include the losses of the General Artillery Reserve, of the horse artillery, or of W. H. F. Lee's brigade of cavalry.[2] These omissions may be repaired, at least in part, by reference to the reports of Generals Pendleton and other commanders.[3] Where the losses in killed and wounded are reported by the organization commanders their numbers are generally larger than in the report of the surgeon-general. There is no official statement of the losses of the Army of Northern Virginia in missing. Many of the commanders failed to report such losses. McLaws of the I Corps gives the number for his division.[4] Anderson of the I, and Rodes and Early of the II, Corps give the numbers for their infantry.[5] Pendleton gives the number for the General Artillery Reserve.[6] These statements and reports of other commanders furnish a basis for estimating the number for the army.[7] The Century Company gives this as 1708.[8] General E. P. Alexander gives it as 2196.[9] The official records show 2528 missing, reported or accounted for as such.[10] Doubleday gives his estimate as 2753.[11] Immediately after the campaign Colonel Hofmann, the Federal commissary-general of prisoners, commenced making arrangements for the transportation and accommodation of about 3000 prisoners.[12]

[1] W. R., 40, p. 320, and 39, pp. 172–192.

[2] Ib., 39, pp. 806–809.

[3] Ib., 39, pp. 816, 1050, 1098, 1076 (17th line from bottom).

[4] Ib., 39, p. 829.

[5] Ib., 39, pp. 854 (see also 864), 947, 949, 1002.          [6] Ib., 39, p. 816.

[7] Ib., 39, pp. 822, 1048, 1051, 1098.

[8] B. and L., III, 238.

[9] Memoirs of a Confederate, p. 361.

[10] This is the result of the author's own examination of the published documents.

[11] Chancellorsville and Gettysburg, p. 71.

[12] W. R., 118, pp. 552, 557, 560, 563.

Captain Candler, writing home on the 7th of May, gives the number of prisoners as from 3000 to 4000.[1] In a bombastic order published to his army at the close of the campaign, which will be presented later, Hooker claims 5000. The Confederate missing, including those who escaped capture, may safely be estimated as 3000.

The casualties of the Army of Northern Virginia may now be tabulated as follows. The killed and wounded are generally those reported by the medical director. The killed, wounded, and missing are partly reported by commanders and partly computed by the author.

| ORGANIZATION | AGGREGATE EFFECTIVE | KILLED AND WOUNDED | | KILLED, WOUNDED, AND MISSING | |
|---|---|---|---|---|---|
| | | NUMBER | PER CENT. | NUMBER | PER CENT. |
| 1 Div., Anderson . . . . . | 8,370 | 1,189 | 14 | 1,445 | 17 |
| 2 " McLaws . . . . . . | 8,665 | 1,395 | 16 | 1,775 | 20 |
| Corps Artillery . . . . . | 720 | 52 | 7 | 106 | 15 |
| I Corps . . . . . . . | 17,755 | 2,636 | 14 | 3,326 | 19 |
| 1 Div., A. P. Hill . . . . . | 11,751 | 2,616 | 23 | 2,940 | 26 |
| 2 " Rodes . . . . . . | 10,063 | 2,228 | 22 | 2,937 | 29 |
| 3 " Early . . . . . . | 8,596 | 846 | 10 | 1,346 | 16 |
| 4 " Colston . . . . . | 6,989 | 1,870 [2] | 27 | 2,078 | 30 |
| Corps Artillery . . . . . | 800 | 69 | 9 | 80 | 10 |
| II Corps . . . . . . . | 38,199 | 7,629 [3] | 18 | 9,381 | 25 |
| General Artillery Reserve . . | 480 | 3 | 1 | 3 | 1 |
| Cavalry . . . . . . . . | 2,500 | 25 | 1 | 111 | 4 |
| Army of Northern Virginia . | 60,892 | 10,293 [3] | 17 | 12,821 [3] | 22 |

With respect to non-combatants the Confederates report 1 killed in the signal corps attached to Jackson's headquarters, and 2 wounded in the pioneer corps of Colston's division. In artillery the Federals reported a loss of 14 pieces[4] and the Confederates a loss of 8.[5] But the Confederates claim only 13[6] and the Federals only 7[7] as captured. The Federals lost 17 colors, the Confederates 15.[8] The closeness of the fighting is attested further by the casualties among the general officers. The Federals lost Berry killed and Whipple mortally wounded. The Confederates lost Paxton killed, and Jackson, who died of pneumonia superinduced upon the effects of his wounds. The other wounded generals were, on the side of the Federals, Mott and Devens, and on the

[1] Manuscript.

[2] Including 2 artillerymen. Loss reported as "inconsiderable" (W. R., 39, p. 1044).

[3] Not including 5 casualties at headquarters II Corps.

[4] Hunt's report, W. R., 39, p. 253.

[5] Pendleton's report, ib., 39, p. 816. Lieu-

tenant-Colonel Baldwin, Chief of Ordnance, Army of Northern Virginia, reported a loss of 10 pieces (ib., 40, p. 795).

[6] Lee's report, ib., 40, p. 804.

[7] Hooker's Order No. 49, ib., 40, p. 171.

[8] Ib., 39, pp. 804, 171, and ib., 40, p. 594.

side of the Confederates, A. P. Hill, Heth, McGowan, Hoke, and Nicholls. The general officers numbered in the Army of the Potomac 70 and in the Army of Northern Virginia 40. Hence the Federals lost in killed or wounded 1 general in 18, or, counting Hooker, who was not reported, 1 in 14; and the Confederates 1 in 6. The Federals lost one general captured (General Hays).[1] General Sedgwick reports the capture of a general officer, but does not mention his name.[2] The report must be a mistake. There is no Confederate general identified as captured at Fredericksburg.

An important tactical lesson that may be learned from this campaign is the advantage of rapid or timely deployment, of being properly formed for attack before undertaking it, and the error of piecemeal or dribbling assaults. Sedgwick's failure at Salem Church was due to his attacking before his forces had come up and deployed. His leading division gained some advantage, but, not being supported, was driven back with heavy loss. Stuart's attack of Berry's lines was on the same order. What would have been the effect of Jackson's attack if it had been made as Sedgwick's was at Salem Church? Perhaps not so complete a failure, but certainly not the stunning blow that Jackson's was.

Referring to his situation on the 3d and 4th, Hooker said in a private letter:

With Lee in my front and Jackson on my flank, I was unwilling to attempt to force my way through Lee, especially as the roads through the forests would only enable me to present my columns with narrow fronts, which the enemy would cut down as fast as they were exposed. I knew that I could do this, and I gave the enemy credit for being able to do as much as I could, but no more. Had Sedgwick come up on Lee's rear, the latter would have found himself between two armies, and would doubtless have followed Jackson's flank movement, which I desired, as that would throw the enemy off the short road to Richmond and our troops on it.[3]

Hooker could not have cut down the heads of the enemy's columns because the enemy would not have presented them to him. The forests did not prevent the Confederates as they did the Federals from deploying off the roads and marching in line. The Confederates moved through the Wilderness in every direction and in every kind of formation. They were better woodsmen than the Federals, and better acquainted with the terrain, or better supplied with guides. They were hardier, tougher men. They cared less if they tore their clothes or scratched their hands and faces. Not but that the Federal soldiers would follow their officers, and when so led did follow them, through

---

[1] This officer was erroneously reported as wounded (*W. R.*, 39, pp. 177, 376, and *ib.*, 118, pp. 570, 571, 618).

[2] *Ib.*, 39, p. 561.

[3] General Hooker to Colonel Samuel Ross, *B. and L.*, III, 223.

the thickets. The Confederate movements were better connected and better covered than the Federal.

Hooker was asked by the Committee on the Conduct of the War what he thought would have been the result had Sedgwick carried out his orders vigorously. He replied: "My impression was that Lee would have been compelled to move out on the same road that Jackson had moved on, and pass over to my right."[1] Such a statement does not sound like the remark in Van Alen's dispatch of the 2d to Sedgwick: "You will probably fall upon the rear of the forces commanded by General Lee, and between you and the major-general commanding, he expects to use him up." With such apparent indecision on Hooker's part, it is hard to conjecture what he would have done had Sedgwick succeeded in striking Lee in rear. General Warren was asked by the Committee: "What would have been the effect of an attack by General Sedgwick in conjunction with the main army on the enemy's lines . . . ?" He discreetly answered: "I think we ought to have destroyed Lee's army. But it would depend a great deal upon how hard the other [Hooker's] part of the army fought. . . . If he [Sedgwick] had got over there, and the other part had fought as they ought to have done, I think we should have pretty nearly destroyed General Lee's army. I do not believe that if General Sedgwick had done all that he could, and there had not been harder fighting at the other end of the line, we would have succeeded."[2]

Hooker contented himself with holding his line as a bridge-head. True, if he had moved to join Sedgwick both he and Sedgwick might have been caught between the fords and driven against, if not into, the river. But if Hooker, with the mass of the army, could not safely undertake to join Sedgwick when Sedgwick was moving to join him, it was hardly to be expected that Sedgwick, with a single corps, would succeed in joining Hooker. If Hooker was not to move, Sedgwick's movement should have been directed up the north bank of the Rappahannock and over United States Ford, instead of across country from Fredericksburg, or the I Corps (Reynolds') should have been left with Sedgwick, who would then have had about 40,000 men instead of about 25,000. The I Corps, be it remembered, was taken from Sedgwick, and yet was not actively engaged at Chancellorsville.

Hooker's irresolution in this campaign was only partially due to the injury which he received at the Chancellor House. It was exhibited, as has been shown, long before he sustained that injury, and would in all probability have lasted through the campaign had he not been injured at all.[3]

---

[1] *Rep. of Com.*, IV, 145.
[2] *Ib.*, 47, 48.
[3] A couple of months later, when Hooker had crossed the Rappahannock with the Army of the Potomac in the campaign of Gettysburg, he was asked by General

Before the campaign it appeared from reports and returns that the best corps in the Army of the Potomac was the XI and the poorest the II.[1]   After the campaign it appeared from performance on the march and in action that the best, if there was any best, was the II and the poorest the XI.   Military efficiency can not be reliably estimated without reckoning with the tactical judgment and ability of the commanding general.

On the 6th of May Lieutenant Ropes wrote home: "Everywhere we hear of the shameful cowardice of the XI Corps"; and on the 10th Major Rusling wrote: "The army all did well except the Eleventh Corps.   That broke and ran discreditably.   'I fights mit Sigel' is played out.   Tell S. that his Dutchmen can't begin to stand up against the fury and rush of Americans, even if they are Rebels!''

For the rout of the XI Corps no one was ever officially held to account.   General Schurz in concluding his report of the battle said: "Being charged with such an enormous responsibility as the failure of a campaign involves, it would seem to me that every commander in this corps has a right to a fair investigation of his conduct and of the circumstances surrounding him and his command on that occasion.   I would therefore most respectfully and most urgently ask permission to publish this report."[2]

To this request, it seems, no attention was paid.   While the report was in Hooker's hands, Schurz wrote through regular channels to the Secretary of War asking permission to publish it, and, as an alternative, that a court of inquiry be convened to investigate the circumstances surrounding his command on the 2d of May, and the causes of its defeat.[3]   Howard forwarded this communication without remark. Hooker indorsed it: "I hope to be able to transmit all the reports of the recent battles, and meanwhile I cannot approve of the publication of an isolated report."   Schurz was consequently informed by the Adjutant-General of the Army that it was contrary to orders to publish the reports of battles except through the proper official channels.   He thereupon requested that his report be published when it should reach the War Department through "the proper channel," and repeated his request for a court of inquiry, should his report not be published.   His letter was indorsed by Howard on the 30th of May as follows:

With reference to the court of inquiry asked for, I recommend that the request be granted.   I do not know of any charges against General Schurz from an official

Doubleday: "Hooker, what was the matter with you at Chancellorsville? Some say you were injured by a shell, and others that you were drunk; now tell us what it was." Hooker answered frankly and good-naturedly: "Doubleday, I was not hurt by a shell, and I was not drunk. For once I lost confidence in Hooker, and that is all there is to it" (Manuscript letter of Major E. P. Halstead, U. S. Volunteers, April 19, 1903). See also *History of the Army of the Potomac*, by J. H. Stine, p. 368.

[1] See figures of efficiency of the several corps, *Appendix 3*.

[2] *W. R.*, 39, p. 658.

[3] *Ib.*, 39, pp. 658, 659.

quarter, but I do not shrink from a thorough investigation of all the circumstances connected with the disaster of May 3.

It was forwarded by Hooker without remark, and returned by Halleck on the 4th of June indorsed: "Publication of partial reports not approved till the General commanding has time to make his report." General Hooker never made his report, and General Schurz never had his court of inquiry.

General Howard forwarded to Hooker on the 21st of May a *List of German Troops in the Eleventh Army Corps,* from which it would appear that the Germans in the corps numbered but 5282, or about half the corps present for duty.[1]  But the list does not indicate how the count was taken nor what was understood or meant by "German Troops."  A veteran of the XI Corps writes on this point as follows: "There were 15 of these so-called foreign regiments in the corps, 11 of which were exclusively German, and numbered about 4500 men; the other four regiments were of mixed nationalities, and numbered some 2500 men. . . . Probably ⅗ of the command were foreign-born."[2] There can hardly be a reasonable doubt that the corps was composed mainly of men of German parentage, but it is preposterous to ascribe its *débandade* on the 2d of May to that fact.  Such a disaster would have happened to any body of troops situated as the XI Corps was when Jackson struck it.  But other men might have comported themselves with more dignity, or less ignominy, even while running for their lives.  On this point General Francis A. Walker, who fought through the Civil War, says:

I never saw an American so frightened as to lose his senses, though I have seen thousands of the natives of Columbia leave one battle-field or another in the most dastardly manner.  But if an American is mean enough to abandon the line, it is always done coolly and collectedly.  Indeed, he will exhibit a degree of engineering skill in getting out of a fight under cover which would do credit to a member of the topographical staff.[3]

It should be observed that the XI Corps was commanded by an American; that the compatriots of the Old Dessauer, of Frederick the Great, of von Blücher and von Moltke, who belonged to the corps, were more or less the product of American influences.  They were American Germans, or, as they are more commonly and properly called, German-Americans.  Their courage can hardly be impugned without reflecting to some extent upon the people among whom they had lived as citizens, and many of them been born and bred.

[1] *W. R.,* 39, p. 660.
[2] Captain Hartwell Osborn, *Papers of Illinois Commandery, Military Order Loyal Legion,* IV, 174.
[3] *History of the Second Army Corps,* by F. A. Walker, p. 229, foot-note.

They were not typical Americans, but neither were they typical Germans. An appreciable proportion of our German population comes to our country to escape from military service, and for this reason is not representative of the military population of Germany. This consideration is necessary to understanding how a people who lead the world in the art and science of war, who have produced a host of commanders of the highest order, and have a long and glorious military history, should have furnished our country some of its poorest soldiers. Whether a man who abandons his colors preserves or loses his self-control, he is equally lost to the firing line. His deportment is of military moment only in so far as it influences other men. To that extent the American's deliberation is ordinarily to be preferred to the German-American's precipitation, but the sight of entire regiments of Americans marching off the field under the command of their officers might be hardly less demoralizing to onlooking troops than a panic in a foreign contingent.

Let us consider the reasons which Hooker has given for his repassage of the Rappahannock:

*The rout of the XI Corps.*

This occurred on the 2d. He was stronger in men and in position after the 2d than he was before. At no time during the campaign was he better situated for gaining a decisive victory than he was on the 3d.

*His army had none of its trains of supplies with it.*

There were ample supplies along the north bank of the river ready to be hauled to the troops.

Major J. F. Huntington, the gallant commander of the batteries at Hazel Grove on the evening of May 2, says in a paper read before the Military Historical Society of Massachusetts:

I think (if we can imagine Grant allowing his army to be placed where Hooker's was at noon on that day (Sunday) )that he would have made his soldiers fry their boots, if there was nothing else to eat, before he would have recrossed the river.

The army had at least five days' supplies in its trains;[1] its depots were not 15 miles away; and there was an abundance of transportation on its lines of communication.[2] Ingalls says in his report to the quartermaster-general:

[1] Ingalls says six or eight (*W. R.*, 40, p. 545).

[2] Ingalls says: "To show what was our custom on the eve of battle with regard to our trains, I take the liberty to inclose a copy of my report of our arrangements during the Chancellorsville campaign, here-with, marked B. This report and its accompanying papers now in your office will give you full and valuable information" (*W. R.*, 27, p. 103). The inclosure referred to has disappeared from the files of the War Department. J. B. Jr.

. . . no difficulty was experienced by our department in bringing forward all [the subsistence] that was required. At no time did I feel that there could be any failure to supply the army on either side of the Rappahannock.[1]

Lieutenant-Colonel Woods, chief commissary of subsistence of the III Corps, says:

. . . many commands were obliged to throw away the rations they had received; and during the eight days there were upon an average thirteen days' rations issued. This extraordinary demand was, of course, not anticipated, and the labors of the commissaries were proportionately increased; but during all the time, the troops, so far as I have been able to ascertain, were fully supplied with food.[2]

Lieutenant-Colonel Tolles, chief quartermaster of the VI Corps, says:

As fast as supplies were exhausted, they were replenished from the depots at Falmouth, so that when the movement was completed, the quartermaster's department was as well prepared for a march as at the beginning.[3]

*A heavy rain and consequent rise of the Rappahannock threatened to sever his communications.*

This rain did not set in until about 4 p.m. on the 5th; Hooker's decision was formed and announced to the army before there was any sign of rain. "The order to retire was given 12 hours before any rain, and during a cloudless sky."[4]

*The nature of the country prevented his forcing the enemy's lines in his front.*

That might have been an excuse for not undertaking offensive operations, but could not justify his withdrawing across the river.

*He wanted to get his army together and adopt a plan which would allow of his directing the movements of the several corps himself.*

His errors were largely due to his interfering with his corps commanders, and not allowing them to do what their own judgment dictated. Had he not interfered with Slocum on the 30th, Banks' Ford would probably have been opened on that day. It is questionable whether on the 1st his right wing could have beaten Jackson's force, but had he not, against the judgment of his corps commanders, compelled it to return to Chancellorsville, it would at least have taken up and held a better position than the one to which he withdrew it. But Hooker's desire to have his troops under his own eye was due not so much to distrust of his corps commanders as to his realization of a serious mental defect of his own. He had not the imagination neces-

---

[1] *W. R.*, 40, p. 546.  [2] *Ib.*, 39, p. 399.  [3] *Ib.*, 40, p. 554.
[4] *Campaigns of the Army of the Potomac*, by William Swinton, p. 307.

sary to keep before his mind the changing positions of troops out of his sight. His mental vision was practically limited by his physical vision, and he had apparently no training or faculty for making war on a map.

*In an advance from United States Ford failure would involve disaster, while in an advance from Franklin's Crossing it would not.*

How Hooker deduced or conceived this idea is a mystery. It would seem that no one has presented satisfactory grounds for it, and it may be dismissed as unreasonable.

Butterfield gave as one of the reasons for recrossing the Rappahannock that the terms of enlistment of the 38 New York regiments had expired or were about to expire.[1] Hooker did not attempt to justify his withdrawal on that ground, nor on the other ground advanced by Butterfield, that in case of a successful offensive by the Army of the Potomac the Confederates would fall back on Richmond, and grow stronger as they did so. In the course of the conference held at Hooker's headquarters on the 7th, Hooker said to Halleck in the presence of the President that notwithstanding the losses of the battle of Chancellorsville and the discharge of troops whose services were about to expire, he would have left about 100,000 men, which was all he could employ to advantage.[2]

No greater mistake was made during the campaign than Hooker's final one of recrossing the Rappahannock. Lee was about to play into his hands by attacking him on his own ground; the condition on which his plan of operation was based was at last to be realized, when he weakly retired from the contest. Had he been in defensive position on the south side of the river on the morning of the 6th, he would in all probability have gained a victory that would have made the campaign of Gettysburg impossible, and might have anticipated the surrender of Appomattox.

Lee made a brilliant use of interior lines. On the 2d of May he attacked the larger Federal fraction under Hooker; on the 4th, the smaller one under Sedgwick. He would on the 2d as well as on the 4th have turned first upon the smaller, which was in each case the nearer one, but for the strength of the Federal position of Stafford Heights, which made it impossible to inflict a crushing blow upon it. On the 4th of May Hooker had fallen back from his commanding position, dispirited by the events of the last two days, and Sedgwick was away from the cover of Stafford Heights, and, what was more important, in possession of the Confederate position at Fredericksburg, and of Banks' Ford, by which Hooker might reënforce or join him. Lee was under the impression, too, that Sedgwick was stronger than he really was. To dislodge

---

[1] *Rep. of Com.*, IV, 77; letter to Lincoln, May 5, 11 a.m.
[2] Halleck to Stanton, *W. R.*, 40, p. 505.

Sedgwick was now of immediate and paramount importance. "In all history," says a British military writer, "there is not recorded a campaign which exemplifies more fully the preponderance of skilful direction over superior numbers than this week's fighting in the forest of Virginia." [1] Longstreet comments on Lee's conduct of the campaign as follows:

Chancellorsville is usually accepted as General Lee's most brilliant achievement, and considered as an independent affair, it was certainly grand. As I had no part in its active conduct, it is only apropos to this writing to consider the plan of battle as projected some four months previous, i.e., to stand behind our intrenched lines and await the return of my troops from Suffolk.

Under that plan General Lee would have had time to strengthen and improve his trenches, while Hooker was intrenching at Chancellorsville.

He [Lee] had interior lines for defence, while his adversary was divided by two crossings of the river, which made Lee's 60,000 for defence about equal to the 113,000 under General Hooker. By the time that the divisions of Pickett and Hood could have joined General Lee, General Hooker would have found that he must march to attack or make a retreat without battle. It seems probable that under the original plan the battle would have given fruits worthy of a general engagement. The Confederates would then have had opportunity, and have been in condition, to so follow Hooker as to have compelled his retirement to Washington, and that advantage might have drawn Grant from Vicksburg; whereas General Lee was actually so crippled by his victory that he was a full month restoring his army to condition to take the field.

To these strictures it may be replied that neither Lee nor Longstreet expected such inaction on the part of the enemy as Hooker manifested in this campaign. What might have been the result if, with Lee on the passive defensive and Longstreet marching to join him, Hooker had struck out vigorously on interior lines against these separate fractions? The strategy which Lee put in practice would seem to have been more in accordance with the fundamental principles of war, and a safer precedent for commanders situated as he was, than that which his illustrious lieutenant would have had him adopt.

In the art of writing and interpreting orders and dispatches the Confederates showed themselves superior to the Federals. The Confederate documents were generally shorter and more to the point than those of the Federals. A number of the latter were misunderstood. Suffice it to refer here only to Hooker's orders to Sedgwick for his demonstration and pursuit, and for his retention of a position south of the Rappahannock, to his order to Butterfield relative to Gibbon's passage of that river at Banks' Ford, and to Stoneman's order to Averell respecting the latter's movements. It may be noted, on the other hand, that Lee's important order of 3 a.m. on the 3d to Stuart required expla-

[1] *The Crisis of the Confederacy,* by Cecil Battine, Captain 15th Hussars, p. 95.

nation. With this exception, however, there does not seem to have been an instance of a Confederate written order that admitted of misunderstanding. The Confederate orders that appear to have been misunderstood were generally verbal; for instance, Lee's of the 2d to Early, and Stuart's of the 3d to Archer and McGowan. How many failures and disappointments in garrison and in the field may be avoided by the observance of the simple lesson to be drawn from this fact! Field orders as now understood were unknown in either army. Had they been generally used, the work of historians of the war would be immeasurably easier than it is.

The orders in which certain commanders reviewed their operations for the inspiration or encouragement of their troops may now receive attention:

Headqrs. Army of Northern Virginia, May 7, 1863.

General Orders, No. 59:

With heartfelt gratification, the general commanding expresses to the army his sense of the heroic conduct displayed by officers and men during the arduous operations in which they have just been engaged. Under trying vicissitudes of heat and storm, you attacked the enemy, strongly intrenched in the depths of a tangled wilderness, and again on the hills of Fredericksburg, 15 miles distant, and by the valor that has triumphed on so many fields, forced him once more to seek safety beyond the Rappahannock. While this glorious victory entitles you to the praise and gratitude of the nation, we are especially called upon to return our grateful thanks to the only Giver of victory, for the signal deliverance He has wrought. It is therefore earnestly recommended that the troops unite, on Sunday next, in ascribing to the Lord of Hosts the glory due unto His name.

Let us not forget, in our rejoicing, the brave soldiers who have fallen in defence of their country; and while we mourn their loss, let us resolve to emulate their noble example.

The army and the country alike lament the absence for a time of one to whose bravery, energy, and skill they are so much indebted for success.

The following letter from the President of the Confederate States is communicated to the army as an expression of his appreciation of their success:

"[*General Lee:*]

"I have received your dispatch, and reverently unite with you in giving praise to God for the success with which He has crowned our arms.

"In the name of the people, I offer my cordial thanks to yourself and the troops under your command for this addition to the unprecedented series of great victories which your army has achieved.

"The universal rejoicing produced by this happy result will be mingled with a general regret for the good and the brave who are numbered among the killed and the wounded."

R. E. LEE,
General.

Headquarters Army of the Potomac,
Camp near Falmouth, May 6, 1863.

General Orders, No. 49:

The major-general commanding tenders to this army his congratulations on its achievements of the last seven days. If it has not accomplished all that was expected, the reasons are well known to the army. It is sufficient to say they were of a character not to be foreseen or prevented by human sagacity or resource.

In withdrawing from the south bank of the Rappahannock before delivering a general battle to our adversaries, the army has given renewed evidence of its confidence in itself and its fidelity to the principles it represents. In fighting at a disadvantage we would have been recreant to our trust, to ourselves, our cause, and our country.

Profoundly loyal, and conscious of its strength, the Army of the Potomac will give or decline battle whenever its interests or honor may command. It will also be the guardian of its own history and its own fame.

By our celerity and secrecy of movement, our advance and passage of the rivers were undisputed, and, on our withdrawal, not a rebel ventured to follow.

The events of the last week may swell with pride the heart of every officer and soldier of this army. We have added new luster to its former renown. We have made long marches, crossed rivers, surprised the enemy in his intrenchments; and whenever we have fought, we have inflicted heavier blows than those we have received.

We have taken from the enemy 5000 prisoners [and] fifteen colors; captured and brought off seven pieces of artillery; placed *hors de combat* 18,000 of his chosen troops; destroyed his depots filled with vast amounts of stores; deranged his communications; captured prisoners within the fortifications of his capital; and filled his country with fear and consternation.

We have no other regret than that caused by the loss of our brave companions; and in this we are consoled by the conviction that they have fallen in the holiest cause ever submitted to the arbitrament of battle.

By command of Major-General HOOKER:

S. WILLIAMS,

Assistant Adjutant-General. [1]


Headqrs. Eleventh Army Corps, May 10, 1863.

General Orders, No. 9:

As your commanding General, I cannot fail to notice a feeling of depression on the part of a portion of this corps. Some obloquy has been cast upon us on account of the affair of Saturday, May 2.

I believe that such a disaster might have happened to any other corps of this Army, and do not distrust my command. Every officer who failed to do his duty by not keeping his men together, and not rallying them when broken, is conscious of it, and must profit by the past.

I confidently believe that every honorable officer and every brave man earnestly desires an opportunity to advance against the enemy, and demonstrate to

[1] *W. R.*, 39, p. 171.

the army and to the country that we are not wanting in principle or patriotism. Your energy, sustained and directed under the Divine blessing, shall yet place the Eleventh Corps ahead of them all.

O. O. HOWARD,
Major-General Commanding.[1]

On the 13th Hooker wrote to the President:

Is it asking too much to inquire your opinion of my Orders, No. 49? If so, do not answer me. Jackson is dead, and Mr. Lee beats McClellan in his untruthful bulletins.

What reply, if any, the President vouchsafed to this inquiry and remark is not known, but at 1 p.m. he telegraphed to Hooker: "If it will not interfere with the service, nor personally incommode you, please come up and see me this evening." Hooker replied at 3 p.m.: "Will see you at 8 o'clock this evening."

It is presumable that the interview took place, and that Hooker went away from it enlightened as to Lincoln's opinion of the order in question, and his views on other matters of greater importance.

The navy was not required to act the important part which had been projected for it, but it responded with characteristic zeal and efficiency to the calls made upon it for assistance; and the good will entertained toward it by the Army of the Potomac was repeatedly demonstrated. On the 15th of May Lieutenant-Commander Magaw wrote to Commodore Harwood: "I beg to call your attention to the uniform courtesy and kindness which my division of the Potomac Flotilla has received at the hands of the Army officers and others, heads of their respective departments at their posts." After particularizing the incidents referred to, he said: "I respectfully suggest that some acknowledgment be made to the above-mentioned gentlemen either by yourself or the department. Everything that we have ever asked for has been done with cheerfulness and with remarkable promptitude." In forwarding this letter on the 19th to the Secretary of the Navy, Commodore Harwood remarked: "Truly appreciating the importance of a cordial understanding between the two services, I take pleasure in forwarding to the department this evidence of the satisfactory relation between the Army of the Potomac and the flotilla." On the 8th of June he wrote to Lieutenant-Commander Magaw: "You will please give to the military officers named in your letter my warm thanks for their courtesy to those under my command, and my assurance that it will afford me great pleasure to reciprocate in every way in my power their good feeling."[2]

When Halleck returned to Washington, the President, the Secretary

[1] W. R., 39, p. 631.
[2] Naval W. R., Series I, Vol. V, pp. 271, 272.

of War, and himself held a conference, and concluded "that both the check at Chancellorsville and the retreat were inexcusable, and that Hooker must not be intrusted with the conduct of another battle. Halleck had brought a message from Hooker to the effect that, as he had never sought the command, he could resign it without embarrassment, and would be only too happy to do so, if he could have the command of his old division, and so keep in active service."[1] But as he was appointed by political selection, so on political grounds he was temporarily retained with a view to relieving without disgracing him. In the meantime the command was offered to Couch, who declined it. "Neither his health, always delicate, nor his retiring disposition qualified him for such a post of responsibility."[2] But unwilling to make another campaign under Hooker, he asked to be relieved from duty with the Army of the Potomac, and his request was complied with.

On the 29th of May General Ingalls, in compliance with a request of the Quartermaster-General of the Army, forwarded a report of the operations of the quartermaster's department, inclosing reports of corps quartermasters. These documents throw much light on the logistics of this campaign. The principal conclusions to which they seem to have led may be summarized as follows:

1. *The troops were overloaded.* Many carried both overcoat and blanket. It was intended that either should be taken without the other. Forty rounds of ammunition were deemed sufficient for the soldier to carry on his person in the future.

2. *The knapsack was an unnecessary incumbrance, and should be replaced by the blanket roll.* About 25 per cent. of the knapsacks were lost—thrown away on the march or in action; or laid aside to go into action, and not recovered. In parts of the army the loss in knapsacks was considerably greater. In the V Corps it was about 30 per cent., and in the XI and XII about 50 per cent. The loss in blankets, shelter tents, haversacks, etc., was correspondingly great. General Rodes says in his report: " . . . the enemy abandoned such a large number of knapsacks in retreating to his works that when this division began its homeward march in the rain it was thoroughly equipped with oilcloths and shelter tents of the best quality."[3]

3. *The pack-mule system could not be relied on for long marches with heavy wagons.* Pack-mules should be made auxiliary to wagons for short distances over rough country, where roads are few or bad—the wagons to be moved as far to the front as is safe or practicable, the pack-mules then to be packed with ammunition and necessary forage, and pushed on after the troops to follow them everywhere.

[1] *B. and L.,* III, 241.
[2] *General Hancock,* by F. A. Walker, pp. 92, 93.
[3] *W. R.,* 39, p. 945.

4. *The pack-trains should be organized independently of the wagon-trains.* In this campaign the mules for the pack-trains were detached from the ammunition and supply trains, reducing the teams of the latter to 4 mules. The pack-mules and packers were green and inexperienced. About two thirds of the pack-mules were rendered unserviceable by careless or unskilful packing, causing sore backs.

5. *In the cavalry the horses were overloaded.* Each trooper carried on his horse about 3 days' subsistence and short forage, 40 rounds of carbine, and 20 rounds of pistol ammunition. The load of the horse, without the trooper, must have weighed about 110 pounds, and with trooper—equipped as he was with carbine, saber, and pistol—at least 270 pounds.

6. *The system of cavalry remount was defective.* It was remedied after the campaign of Gettysburg by the formation of a branch of the War Department called the Cavalry Bureau, which was given charge of "the organization and equipment of the cavalry forces of the Army, and of the provision for the mounts and remounts of the same."

Hooker's measures for resuming the offensive were not carried into effect. The armies did not move until Lee initiated the campaign of Gettysburg. The pickets on the opposite banks of the river, while not so intimate as before the campaign, conversed with each other, bandying jokes like old acquaintances, as many of them were. To the taunt: "Where is Joe Hooker now?" the grim reply was: "Gone to the funeral of Stonewall Jackson."

The interval of two months between the battles of Chancellorsville and Gettysburg was for the South—notwithstanding the irreparable loss it sustained in the death of Jackson—the brightest period of the Civil War. But its brightness was that of a false and treacherous light. The overconfidence born of the victory of Chancellorsville carried the Army of Northern Virginia against the impregnable front of the Federal lines at Gettysburg; and it was the victory of Gettysburg that sustained the Army of the Potomac in its desperate wrestling in the Wilderness, and in gaining the point of vantage from which it finally started on the arduous, decisive, and fateful race to Appomattox.

# APPENDIX 1

COMPOSITION AND DISPOSITION OF THE POTOMAC FLOTILLA [1]

**1 DIVISION, UNDER LIEUTENANT-COMMANDER MAGAW**
*Steamers:*
In Rappahannock River (*Anacostia* and *Dragon*) . . . . . . . . . . 2
Off Aquia Creek (*Freeborn*) . . . . . . . . . . . . . . 1
At Piney Point [2] (dispatch-boat *Ella*) . . . . . . . . . . . . 1

   *Sailing-vessels* (mortar schooners) :
Off Aquia Creek (*T. A. Ward*) . . . . . . . . . . . . . 1
At Alexandria, Va. (*Dan Smith, Adolph Hugel*) . . . . . . . . . 2

**2 DIVISION, UNDER LIEUTENANT-COMMANDER MCCREA**
*Steamers:*
Store-ship, not available for other use . . . . . . . . . . . . 1
Convoy of General Hooker's supplies (*Reliance, Jacob Bell*) . . . . . . 2
Other serviceable steamer (*Eureka*) . . . . . . . . . . . . 1

   *Sailing-vessels* (mortar schooners) :
Including 1 tender at Piney Point and 1 guard-vessel . . . . . . . . . 5

**UNDERGOING REPAIRS AT THE NAVY YARD**
   Steamers (*Satellite, Currituck, Resolute*) . . . . . . . . . . . . 3

**WITH ACTING REAR-ADMIRAL LEE**
*Steamers:*
Disabled (*Teaser, Cœur de Lion*) . . . . . . . . . . . . . . 2
Serviceable (*Yankee, Primrose*) . . . . . . . . . . . . . . 2
       Total . . . . . . . . . . . . . . . . . . . . 23

# APPENDIX 2

Special Orders, No. 77 :
   9. There being now 2000 pack-saddles for issue at Aquia Creek, they will be distributed as follows, and corps commanders will at once cause requisitions to be made for the number apportioned to them, viz.: First Corps, 329; Third Corps, 361; Fifth Corps, 328; Sixth Corps, 450; Eleventh Corps, 275; Twelfth Corps, 257.
   Of these pack-saddles, two will be distributed to each regiment to carry the

---

[1] *Naval W. R.*, Series I, Vol. V, p. 260.
[2] Marked on map *Piney Ft.*

shelter tents, with which officers will be provided, and extra rations for officers. The remainder will be devoted to the transportation of ammunition, the average amount of which, to be carried in each pack-saddle, will be two and a half boxes;[1] the stronger and larger animals to carry three boxes, and the lighter ones two boxes.

Waterproof pouches will be used to protect the ammunition in rainy weather.[2] Drill for a few hours each day in packing and unpacking will be instituted, without delay, to familiarize the men and animals to the use of the pack-saddles.

The animals for the ammunition-pack, if there are none extra on hand, will be taken from the ammunition-wagons, in which case the wagons and harness will be turned in to the quartermaster's department.

## APPENDIX 3

On the basis of the inspection reports the following order was issued with a view to promoting emulation and efficiency throughout the army:

Headquarters Army of the Potomac,
Camp near Falmouth, Va., March 3, 1863.

General Orders, No. 18:
.        .        .        .        .        .        .        .        .

V. The inspection reports of the following regiments and batteries give evidences of the necessity of strong exertions on the part of every officer and member of the command to bring them up to a proper state of discipline and efficiency. No further leave of absence or furloughs will be granted to these commands, and all officers absent therefrom must be recalled and their leaves revoked:

*Regiments*—12, 21, 23, 26, 34, 35, 42, 59, 60, 78, 88, 104, 105,[3] 107, 149 New York; 29, 68, 69, 124, 125, 132, 136, 155 Pennsylvania; 27 Indiana; 32 Massachusetts Volunteers.

*Batteries*—B, 1 New York, *Pettit's;* 10 New York, *Bruen's;* 11 New York, [*von*] *Puttkammer's;* C, 1 New York, *Barnes';* B, 1 Maryland, *Snow's;* A, 1 New Jersey, *Hexamer's;* C, 1 Pennsylvania, *McCarthy's;* D, 1 Pennsylvania, *Hall's;*[4] 12 Ohio, *Johnson's;* 3 Pennsylvania, *Hampton's;* and C, 1 New York Battalion, *Langner's.*[5]
.        .        .        .        .        .        .        .        .

VI. The following regiments and battalions appearing from the inspection reports to have earned high commendation from inspecting officers, it is left to the discretion of the corps commander, having regard to the efficiency of the command, to increase the leaves of absence and furloughs to these commands for the 15 days following the receipt of this order to 3 instead of 2 enlisted

---

[1] A box held 1000.

[2] The metallic-case cartridge had not yet come into general use. A few of the kind known as the Burnside cartridge were in service, but the common cartridge was cased in paper and was not waterproof.

[3] Consolidated with the 104 N. Y., March 20, 1863 (*W. R.*, 39, p. 278).

[4] Consolidated before the commencement of active operations with Company C, 1 Pa., Captain McCarthy.

[5] This organization appears in the statement of the organization of the Army of the Potomac for January 31 (*W. R.*, 40, p. 16), but not in that for May 1–6 (*ib.*, 39, pp. 156–170). It was presumably detached.

men for every 100 present for duty and 3 officers instead of 2, as provided in General Orders, No. 3, January 30, 1863, from headquarters Army of the Potomac, viz.:

*Regiments*—1, 2, and 20 Massachusetts; 10 and 19 Maine; 5 and 10 [1] New York; 5 New Jersey; 111 Pennsylvania; 3 Wisconsin; and 1 Minnesota Volunteers.

*Batteries*—5 Maine, *Leppien's;* A, 1 Rhode Island, *Arnold's;* B, 1 Rhode Island, *Hazard's;* K, 4 United States, *Seeley's;* D, 1 New York, *Osborn's;* E, 1 Rhode Island, *Randolph's;* D, 5 United States, *Hazlett's;* C, 1 Massachusetts, *Martin's;* A, 1 Massachusetts, *McCartney's;* 3 New York, *Harn's;* 2 New York, *Blume's;* K, 1 United States, *Graham's;* 5 New York, *Taft's;* B, 1 Connecticut, *Brooker's.*

By referring all the regiments and batteries to their respective corps, balancing the proficient against the deficient, calculating for each corps the ratio of the result to the total number of regiments and batteries in the corps, and reducing the scale of comparison thus obtained to positive numbers, we get the order of instruction and discipline indicated in the following table:

| CORPS | FIGURE OF INSTRUCTION AND DISCIPLINE |
|---|---|
| 1.   XI Corps (Sigel) . . . . . . . . . . . . . . . . . . . . | 105 |
| 2.   V    "    (Meade)  . . . . . . . . . . . . . . . . . . | 96 |
| 3.   III   "    (Sickles)  . . . . . . . . . . . . . . . . . | 94 |
| 4.   VI   "    (Sedgwick)  . . . . . . . . . . . . . . . . | 93 |
| 5.   XII   "    (Slocum) . . . . . . . . . . . . . . . . . | 61 |
| 6.   I    "    (Reynolds)  . . . . . . . . . . . . . . . . | 14 |
| 7.   II    "    (Couch)   . . . . . . . . . . . . . . . . . | 1 |

This showing, be it observed, rests upon inspections, not of corps, but of regiments and batteries. They were poor criterions of tactical efficiency, especially of the larger units (corps and divisions). Regarding the XI Corps, an officer wrote in a private letter under date of March 1, 1863:

Sigel's corps is, or seems to be, composed wholly of Germans. They are disgracefully undisciplined. . . . Sigel's and Slocum's [corps] are very near each other, but there is little communication between them. Sigel is pretty generally regarded as a humbug by the Army of the Potomac. His men are marauders, and are not believed in as fighters.

## APPENDIX 4

### *February 7*

XII. The flag designating the headquarters of army corps will be as follows: A blue swallowtail flag, with white Maltese cross in center of field; the numerical designation of the corps in red figures in the center of the cross.

The chief quartermaster will furnish the flags, on proper requisition, to commanders of army corps.

### *March 21*

For the purpose of ready recognition of corps and divisions in this army, and to prevent injustice by reports of straggling and misconduct through mistake as

[1] See note 5, p. 490.

to its organization, the chief quartermaster will furnish without delay the following badges, to be worn by the officers and enlisted men of all the regiments of the various corps mentioned. They will be securely fastened upon the center of the top of the cap.

Inspecting officers will at all inspections see that these badges are worn as designated:

| | |
|---|---|
| First Corps, a sphere . . . . | First Division, red; Second, white; Third, blue. |
| Second Corps, trefoil . . . . | First Division, red; Second, white; Third, blue. |
| Third Corps, lozenge . . . . | First Division, red; Second, white; Third, blue. |
| Fifth Corps, Maltese cross . . | First Division, red; Second, white; Third, blue. |
| Sixth Corps, cross . . . . . | First Division, red; Second, white; Third, blue. (Light Division, green.) |
| Eleventh Corps, crescent . . . | First Division, red; Second, white; Third, blue. |
| Twelfth Corps, star . . . . . | First Division, red; Second, white; Third, blue. |

The sizes and colors will be according to pattern.[1]

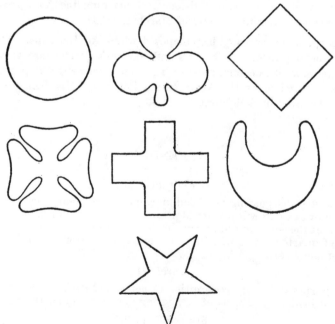

[1] As printed, the badges are one-half size.

## APPENDIX 5

The following table shows the ratio of sick in the several army corps on the 28th of March: [1]

| CORPS | | SICK PER 1000 |
|---|---|---|
| 1. | VI Corps (Sedgwick) . . . . . . . . . . . . . . . . . | 46 |
| 2. | XII " (Slocum) . . . . . . . . . . . . . . . . | 53 |
| 3. | V " (Meade) . . . . . . . . . . . . . . . . . | 61 |
| 4. | XI " (Sigel) . . . . . . . . . . . . . . . . . | 69 |
| 5. | III " (Sickles) . . . . . . . . . . . . . . . . | 76 |
| 6. | II " (Couch) . . . . . . . . . . . . . . . . . | 85 |
| 7. | I " (Reynolds) . . . . . . . . . . . . . . . . | 90 |

Letterman says in a letter to Hooker dated April 4, from which the foregoing data are taken: [2]

The paper marked A [3] shows the whole number of sick in this army to be on the 28th of March ultimo 10,777. The corps exhibiting the greatest ratio of sick are those in which there is the greatest number of new regiments. Thus, the First Corps, having a ratio of 90.02 per 1000, has, according to the data in this office, eighteen new and twenty-one old regiments.

The Sixth Corps, with a ratio of 46.16 per 1000, has only four new regiments and thirty old regiments. The ratio of sick for the whole army is 67.64 per 1000.

. . .

Numerous reports made to this office refer to the general improvement in the health, tone, and vigor of those who are not reported sick; an improvement which figures will not exhibit, but which is apparent to officers whose attention is directed to the health of the men. [4]

The foregoing table of health exhibits roughly the length of service, or experience, of the several corps. As an approximate figure of experience let us take the number of well men per 1000 as shown in this table. We have now for each corps a numerical expression, or factor, (1) of desertion, (2) of instruction and discipline, (3) of sickness, and (4) of experience. By multiplying the factor of instruction and discipline by that of experience, and dividing the result by the product of the factors of sickness and desertion, we get what may be called a figure of efficiency. Doing this for each corps will enable us to arrange the several corps in an order of efficiency as follows:

| CORPS | | FIGURE OF EFFICIENCY |
|---|---|---|
| 1. | XI Corps (Sigel) . . . . . . . . . . . . . . . . | 32.94 |
| 2. | V " (Meade) . . . . . . . . . . . . . . . . | 16.23 |
| 3. | VI " (Sedgwick) . . . . . . . . . . . . . . . . | 15.70 |
| 4. | III " (Sickles) . . . . . . . . . . . . . . . . | 9.60 |
| 5. | XII " (Slocum) . . . . . . . . . . . . . . . . | 9.01 |
| 6. | I " (Reynolds) . . . . . . . . . . . . . . . . | 1.32 |
| 7. | II " (Couch) . . . . . . . . . . . . . . . . | 0.12 |

[1] W. R., 40, p. 240.

[2] This letter is published without date in W. R., 40, p. 239, and without list in Letterman's *Medical Recollections*, pp. 109–111.

[3] Omitted.

[4] Butterfield testified before the Committee on the Conduct of the War that the ratio of sickness was decreased from about 10 per cent. to below 5 per cent. (*Rep. of Com.*, IV, 74). According to Letterman, the ratio of sickness at the end of April was under 4½ per cent. (*Medical Recollections*, p. 112).

## APPENDIX 6

Under date of January 30, Hooker wrote to Halleck:

By General Orders, No. 61, War Department, 1862, leaves of absence cannot be granted in the field, except to prevent death or permanent disability. This rule never has been strictly regarded in this army . . . and I have thought proper to issue the inclosed order. I believe by it much desertion will be stopped, and a more contented feeling pervade the army. . . .

I. No leaves will exceed fifteen days.

II. Leaves to commanders of corps, divisions, and cavalry brigades will only be granted upon approval at these headquarters. One brigade commander only in a corps to be on leave at one time.

III. Not more than one field officer of a regiment to be absent on leave at one time, where the full complement of field officers are present. . . .

IV. Not more than two line officers to be given leave from any regiment at the same time; not more than one from any battery or detachment.

V. Leaves [are] not to exceed ten days, except to residents of the following states, when it [sic] may be given for fifteen days; viz.: Maine, New Hampshire, and Vermont; Ohio, Michigan, and the States west of these last named.

VI. Furloughs to enlisted men must in no case exceed two for every 100 men present for duty in the regiment, battery, or detachment. . . .

VII. In case of the failure of any officer or soldier to return before their [sic] leave expires, leaves will not be granted to others from the same commands until their return. . . .

VIII. A return from each regiment, battery, and detachment will be forwarded to these headquarters within eight days from the date of this order, showing the number of officers and men absent from duty from any cause whatever. . . .

Halleck replied February 30:

. . . In no case will commanders of grand divisions, army corps, etc., be allowed to grant leaves. The number of applications sent to the War Department, approved by such officers, shows a recklessness and carelessness exceedingly reprehensible, for if one third so approved were granted, the efficiency of the army would be completely destroyed. All leaves to officers to visit Washington without the consent of the War Department are deemed null and void, and hereafter all general officers who come here on leave not properly granted will be dismissed. The mere passage through the city, when that is the shortest or only line of travel, is not considered visiting, but any officer who remains here twenty-four hours without authority will be arrested.

In the face of these instructions Hooker, on the 7th, issued an order authorizing corps commanders to grant leaves and furloughs.

Things were going on swimmingly under this order when the following correspondence took place:

*Halleck to Hooker, February 27, 3 p.m.*

The authority given to you to grant leaves of absence cannot be delegated by you to commanders of corps. Leaves not signed by your orders are null.

*Hooker to Kelton, Assistant Adjutant-General, March 3*

. . . the authority to exercise this power, under well-defined restrictions, was conferred upon corps commanders, and I have never heard of its having been abused by them. If officers holding these high positions cannot be intrusted with this duty, it seems to me that they should be replaced by others who can.

The delay incident to applications for leave will be appreciated when you are informed that my camp is nearly 100 miles in circumference, and, if acted on immediately on their receipt at these headquarters, would, in the majority of cases, delay the departure of the applicant eight-and-forty hours. . . .

### Halleck to Hooker, March 5

. . . As many officers presented themselves here in Washington with leaves from commanders of army corps, I applied to the Secretary to ascertain if such authority had been granted. He replied that he had conferred that authority only on you, and that it would not be given to commanders of army corps. . . . Last reports show that 9692 officers are now absent from their commands. It is the determination of the War Department to diminish this number by retaining to itself the power to grant leaves and by refusing them except in the most urgent cases.

The *War Records* contain no reply to this dispatch, nor any order of Hooker's revoking his permission to corps commanders to grant leaves of absence. It would seem that he was sustained by the President.

### APPENDIX 7

On the 31st of January Lee wrote to General H. B. Kershaw in regard to a proposed formation of a "battalion of honor":

. . . The proper selection of the men and officers for such a battalion would be exceedingly difficult, and even were it organized, it would be more difficult still to fill properly vacancies which might occur in its ranks. The fact is, General, we have now an army of brave men. The formation of a battalion of honor would reward a few and leave many equally brave and equally faithful unnoticed, and perhaps with the feeling that an improper distinction had been made between themselves and their comrades.

Again, a battalion of honor would be a distinct order created among us, and such orders have generally been considered inconsistent with the spirit of our institutions. The Congress of the Confederate States, appreciating the difficulties of properly rewarding meritorious conduct in the army, and of inciting a spirit of emulation of deeds of gallantry, proposes the plan embodied in General Orders, No. 93, Act No. 27, of the Adjutant and Inspector General, at Richmond. By this act the President is authorized to bestow medals on such officers as shall be conspicuous for courage and good conduct on the field of battle; also to confer a badge of distinction upon one private or non-commissioned officer of each company after every signal victory he shall have assisted to achieve. This soldier to be indicated by a majority of the votes of his company. If the award fall upon a deceased soldier, the badge will be given to his widow, or to such relative as the President may adjudge entitled to receive it. This plan meets the difficulty in question in some measure.[1]

Hooker wrote to Army Headquarters, Washington, on the 2d of February:

General Orders, No. 19, February 22, 1862, provide for the inscription, upon the colors of all regiments and batteries in the service of the United States, [of]

[1] For an instance of this plan carried out, see General Orders, No. 131, Adjutant and Inspector General's Office, Richmond, Va., October 3, 1863 (*W. R.*, 39, p. 1052).

the names of the battles in which they have borne a meritorious part. Most, if not all, the regiments and batteries now in the service with this army are entitled to distinction. Boards have been organized, and have reported upon the claims for these honorable inscriptions. There are no records at the [these] headquarters of these proceedings, but I am reliably informed that the recommendations of the boards have been forwarded to the headquarters of this army, although they are not now here. . . .

If these records are on file at the headquarters of the Army or of the War Department, I trust they may receive prompt and immediate action. . . .

Following is Kelton's reply:

. . . The only report transmitted to these headquarters was from the board instituted in the Fifth Corps. It was approved by the general-in-chief and submitted to the Secretary of War December 23, 1862.[1]

It does not appear that any further action was taken on Hooker's letter of the 2d of February, but, of their own accord, regiments and batteries put the names of battles in which they were engaged on their colors, which led to great abuse.[2]

In the Confederate army a regular method had been instituted by the following order from the War Department, July 23, 1862:

1. It will be the duty of the commanding generals of separate armies to cause to be entered, in some conspicuous place on the standards of regiments, battalions, and separately organized squadrons of their commands, the names of the several battles in which their regiments, battalions, and separate squadrons have been actually engaged.[3]

## APPENDIX 8

### Couch to Williams,[4] February 21

I telegraphed you last evening that the pickets had reported that sixteen pieces of artillery and eleven pontoons were seen passing through Fredericksburg down the river. The information did not get to me until twenty-four hours or more after the movement was observed—as stupid a thing as ever occurred in military history. It is but a specimen of how military duties are done by a great many officers in my corps. Higher officers spend their time in reading newspapers or books, playing cards or the politician, drinking whisky, and grumbling. Of course this charge does not include all by a long way, for it contains some of the finest officers that ever drew sword, from major-general down.

Upon a personal investigation, I find that the movement of pontoons and artillery was seen by so many that nobody reported the fact. The general officer of the day was Colonel Frank, one of our most sterling officers.

[1] *Rep. of Com.*, IV, 191.

[2] General Meade, when subsequently in command of the Army of the Potomac, sought to remedy this abuse by the appointment of boards whose investigations and conclusions are embodied in General Orders, No. 10, Headquarters Army of the Potomac, 1865.

[3] The present regulations of the U. S. Army, issued in 1908, contain no provision for keeping the memories of battles fresh in the soldiers' minds.

[4] Adjutant-General, Army of the Potomac.

### Williams to Couch, February 21

In reply to your communication just received, Major-General Hooker directs me to say that it is a most extraordinary report. The general can not think you expect him to bring your officers to a sense of their duty. He trusts that you will have no delay in bringing the officer who neglected his duty to trial and punishment. It is of the utmost importance to him to know if the enemy have any pontoons [1] and, if so, how many and where they are. He desires that you should communicate to him without delay all reliable information you can obtain upon this point.

### Couch to Williams, February 22

. . . The men I questioned yesterday were not positive that pontoons were seen, but thought they were.[1] As for the artillery, one man counted thirty-two 6-horse carriages that he supposed were artillery, but could not see the guns. In my letter I did not intend for the major-general commanding to understand that I wished to throw off the responsibility of disciplining my command, but rather for him to be informed as to the difficulties in the way of duty—as, for instance, this most unwarrantable neglect of duty occurred under the best picket officer I have, and as good a one as I ever knew, and, too, at a time when we were endeavoring to perfect our picket system, and thought we were successful.

Among the measures taken in the opposing armies for their protection against spies was the issuing of the following orders:

Camp near Falmouth, Va., February 13, 1863.

*Brig. Gen. M. R. Patrick,*
Provost-Marshal-General:

The commanding general directs that all trading establishments, peddlers, etc., within the lines of this army, except regularly authorized and appointed sutlers, be broken up, and the parties, with their goods, be sent outside our lines to the rear by to-morrow night; that notice be served upon them (and copies to department provost-marshals) that if found within our lines after twenty-four hours, their goods, wares, and horses will be confiscated,—one half to the hospitals of the corps within which they may be arrested or found, the balance to the general hospitals at Aquia, Belle Plain, and Windmill Point.

Very respectfully, etc.,

S. Williams,

Assistant Adjutant-General.

Hdqrs. Army of Northern Virginia, February 16, 1863.

I. The presence of citizens in the camps or within the lines of the army, unless authorized, is forbidden. Persons coming into the lines on special business must make it known to the provost-marshal. Citizens properly vouched for will be allowed to visit within the lines of the army with passports signed by division commanders. Loyal citizens who reside within the lines will obtain permanent passports from the division commanders near them.

II. Corps commanders will take steps to enroll all citizens within the army who are not exempt from military duty, and assign them to such regions as they may select. They will cause the immediate arrest of all unauthorized persons wandering about the various camps and depots. If they can give a satisfactory account of themselves these persons will be liberated and sent out of the lines. . . .

[1] There is no reference to these pontoons in the Confederate records; nor is there, so far as the author can learn, any mention of them elsewhere. They were undoubtedly an optical illusion or a fiction of the imagination.

On the 7th of March Hooker wrote to Lee:

As, in two instances of late, communications have been sent under flags of truce to subordinate officers of my command, I respectfully state that I have directed that, until further orders, no communication coming from your lines be received unless the same be addressed to myself, and under existing circumstances [as long as the armies are in their present position] delivered in front of Fredericksburg.

## APPENDIX 9

### Lee to Davis, February 16

The concentration of a large force of the enemy at Aquia Creek, with other indications, renders it probable that a general movement is in progress. I learn from Baltimore that all transports of every description are ordered from there to Aquia, and deserters report that their army is going to Tennessee or North Carolina; I think more probably the latter.

### Seddon to Lee, February 17

An officer of the Signal Corps . . . reports as certain that about 20,000 men have been landed and are encamped at Newport News. . . . In addition to these troops at Newport News 8000 or 10,000 were reported . . . to have been sent to Suffolk. . . . I am inclined to think the enemy's movements too serious for a feint or a diversion, and that Hooker really designs withdrawing from the Rappahannock and changing his whole plan. . . .

From the foregoing numbers Lee concluded that two corps must have gone from the Army of the Potomac.

### Lee to Seddon, February 17

Reports . . . state that a third corps of General Hooker's army was embarking on the 15th instant, and circumstances they give indicate a continuance of the movement.

### To Davis, February 18

. . . it appears that the Federal Army under General Hooker is abandoning its present position between the Rappahannock and the Potomac. The greater portion which has so far left has descended the Potomac. . . . Accurate information ought to be obtained of the enemy's movements and intentions in Hampton Roads, and it should be ascertained whether he is preparing to reëmbark his troops for the more southern port, or place them in camp, or advance them to Suffolk or into North Carolina.

### To his daughter Agnes, February 21

General Hooker is obliged to do something: I do not know what it will be.[1]

[1] *Memoirs of R. E. Lee*, by A. L. Long, p. 244.

## APPENDIX 10

### Lee to Seddon, March 27

. . . The troops of this portion of the army have for some time been confined to reduced rations, consisting of 18 ounces of flour, 4 ounces of bacon of indifferent quality, with occasional supplies of rice, sugar, or molasses. The men are cheerful, and I receive but few complaints; still I do not think it is enough to continue them in health and vigor, and I fear they will be unable to endure the hardships of the approaching campaign. Symptoms of scurvy are appearing among them, and to supply the place of vegetables each regiment is directed to send a daily detail to gather sassafras buds, wild onions, garlic, lambs' quarters, and poke sprouts, but for so large an army the supply obtained is very small. . . .

### Lee to his troops, April 5

The commanding general again calls the attention of officers and soldiers of the army to the importance of aiding the farmers of the country in raising their crops by abstaining from destruction of fences and avoiding injury to fields of growing grain. The failure of the crops in districts occupied by the army will detract from our supplies, and render a large population heretofore contributing to our support dependent upon other portions of the country. The fortitude of citizens in districts which have suffered from our presence and the inroads of the enemy appeal[s] to the sympathy of their defenders.

The women who have devoted themselves to the care of our sick and wounded claim protection. The contracted limits of cultivated country render it more difficult to procure subsistence, and self-preservation requires that protection and every aid be given to the production of the necessities of life.

## APPENDIX 11

### ARTILLERY OF THE ARMY OF NORTHERN VIRGINIA

#### I Corps

|  | NUMBER OF PIECES |
|---|---|
| **1 DIVISION (Anderson)[1]** | |
| *Hardaway's battalion* | |
| 1. Grandy's battery | 4 |
| 2. Lewis' battery [2] | 4 |
| 3. Maurin's battery [3] | 4 |
| 4. Moore's battery | 4 |
| | 16 |
| **2 DIVISION (McLaws)** | |
| *Cabell's battalion* [4] | |
| 1. Carlton's battery | 4 |
| 2. Fraser's battery | 4 |
| 3. McCarthy's battery | 4 |
| 4. Manly's battery | 4 |
| | 16 |
| *Carried forward,* | 32 |

[1] Commanded also by Garnett.  [2] Commanded by Penick.
[3] This battery was in depot at Guiney's Station throughout the campaign.
[4] Commanded also by Hamilton.

ARTILLERY OF THE ARMY OF NORTHERN VIRGINIA—*Continued*

NUMBER OF
PIECES

Brought forward, 32

ARTILLERY RESERVE (Corps Artillery)[1]

*Alexander's battalion*[2]

1. Eubank's battery[3] . . . . . . . . . . . . . 4
2. Jordan's battery . . . . . . . . . . . . . . 4
3. Moody's battery . . . . . . . . . . . . . . 4
4. Parker's battery . . . . . . . . . . . . . . 4
5. Rhett's battery . . . . . . . . . . . . . . 4
6. Woolfolk's battery . . . . . . . . . . . . . 4

24

*Walton's battalion* (Washington Artillery)

7. Squires' battery (1 company) . . . . . . . . . 2
8. Richardson's battery[4] (2 company) . . . . . . . 4
9. Miller's battery (3 company) . . . . . . . . . 2
10. Eshleman's battery[4] (4 company) . . . . . . . 4

12[4]

## II Corps (Jackson)

1 DIVISION (A. P. Hill)

*Walker's battalion*[5]

1. Brunson's battery . . . . . . . . . . . . . 4
2. Crenshaw's battery[6] . . . . . . . . . . . . 4
3. Davidson's battery . . . . . . . . . . . . . 4
4. McGraw's battery . . . . . . . . . . . . . 4
5. Marye's battery . . . . . . . . . . . . . . 4

20

2 DIVISION (Rodes)

*Carter's battalion*

1. Reese's battery . . . . . . . . . . . . . . 4
2. Carter's battery . . . . . . . . . . . . . . 6
3. Fry's battery . . . . . . . . . . . . . . . 4
4. Page's battery . . . . . . . . . . . . . . 6

20

3 DIVISION (Early)

*Andrews' battalion*

1. Brown's battery . . . . . . . . . . . . . . 4
2. Carpenter's battery . . . . . . . . . . . . . 4
3. Dement's battery . . . . . . . . . . . . . 4
4. Raine's battery . . . . . . . . . . . . . . 4

16

Carried forward, 124

[1] There seems to have been no chief of artillery present with this portion of the corps, and no commander for its artillery reserve, except Pendleton, chief of artillery of the army. During the active operations Alexander's battalion was detached from the reserve.

[2] Commanded also by Huger.

[3] Commanded by C. B. Taylor.

[4] One piece of Richardson's battery and 1 of Eshleman's were absent throughout the campaign, probably in depot at Chesterfield (Map 1, sheet A).

[5] Commanded also by Pegram.

[6] Commanded by Chamberlayne.

ARTILLERY OF THE ARMY OF NORTHERN VIRGINIA—*Continued*

NUMBER OF
PIECES

*Brought forward,*    124

**4 DIVISION** (Colston)

*Jones' battalion*

1. Carrington's battery . . . . . . . . . . . . . 4
2. Garber's battery [1] . . . . . . . . . . . . . 4
3. Tanner's battery [2] . . . . . . . . . . . . . 4
4. Thompson's battery . . . . . . . . . . . . . 4

16

ARTILLERY RESERVE (Crutchfield) [3]

*Brown's battalion* [4]

1. Brooke's battery . . . . . . . . . . . . . . 4
2. Dance's battery . . . . . . . . . . . . . . 4
3. Graham's battery . . . . . . . . . . . . . 4
4. Hupp's battery . . . . . . . . . . . . . . 4
5. Smith's battery . . . . . . . . . . . . . . 4
6. Watson's battery . . . . . . . . . . . . . 4

24

*McIntosh's battalion*

7. Hurt's battery . . . . . . . . . . . . . . 4
8. Johnson's battery . . . . . . . . . . . . . 4
9. Lusk's battery . . . . . . . . . . . . . . 4
10. Wooding's battery . . . . . . . . . . . . . 4

16

*General Artillery Reserve* (Pendleton)

*Cutts' battalion*

1. Patterson's battery . . . . . . . . . . . . . 4
2. Ross' battery . . . . . . . . . . . . . . . 4
3. Wingfield's battery . . . . . . . . . . . . . 4

12

*Nelson's battalion*

4. Kirkpatrick's battery . . . . . . . . . . . . 4
5. Massie's battery . . . . . . . . . . . . . . 4
6. Milledge's battery . . . . . . . . . . . . . 4

12

*Cavalry Division* (Horse Artillery) (Beckham)

1. Moorman's battery . . . . . . . . . . . . . 4
2. Breathed's battery . . . . . . . . . . . . . 4
3. McGregor's battery . . . . . . . . . . . . . 4
4. Hart's battery . . . . . . . . . . . . . . . 4

16

Total . . . . . . . . . . . . . . . . . . . 220 [5]

[1] Commanded also by Fultz.

[2] The name is also given in the *War Records* as *Latimer,* but see *W. R.,* 40, p. 729.

[3] Commanded also by Walker and by J. T. Brown. The artillery "on the field" was at that time commanded by Alexander (*W. R.,* 39, pp. 822, 824, 938).

[4] Commanded also by Watson and by Dance.

[5] Including Maurin's battery (3. 1. I), 1 piece of Richardson's (8. I), and 1 of Eshleman's (10. I), total 6 pieces, absent throughout the campaign.

## ARTILLERY OF THE ARMY OF THE POTOMAC

### I Corps (Reynolds)

NUMBER OF
PIECES

1 DIVISION (Wadsworth)
  1. Edgell's battery . . . . A, 1 N. H. . . . . . . 6
  2. Reynolds' battery . . . . L, 1 N. Y. . . . . . . 6
  3. Stewart's battery . . . . B, 4 U. S. . . . . . . 6

2 DIVISION (Robinson)
  1. Hall's battery . . . . . B, Me. light (2d) . . . 6
  2. Leppien's battery [1] . . . E, Me. light (5th) . . . 5
  3. Thompson's battery . . . C, 4 Pa. . . . . . . 4
  4. Ransom's battery . . . . C, 5 U. S. . . . . . . 6

3 DIVISION (Doubleday)
  1. Cooper's battery . . . . B, 1 Pa. . . . . . . 4
  2. Ricketts' battery . . . . F, 1 Pa. . . . . . . 4
  3. Amsden's battery . . . . G, 1 Pa. . . . . . . 4

51

### II Corps (Couch)

1 DIVISION (Hancock)
  1. Pettit's battery . . . . . B, 1 N. Y. . . . . . . . 6
  2. Thomas' battery . . . . C, 4 U. S. . . . . . . 6

2 DIVISION (Gibbon)
  1. Arnold's battery . . . . A, 1 R. I. . . . . . . 6
  2. Hazard's battery [2] . . . . B, 1 R. I. . . . . . . 6

3 DIVISION (French)
  1. Ames' battery . . . . . G, 1 N. Y. . . . . . . 6
  2. Adams' battery . . . . . G, 1 R. I. . . . . . . 6

Artillery Reserve (Kirby)
  1. Kirby's battery . . . . . I, 1 U. S. . . . . . . 6
  2. Cushing's battery . . . . A, 4 U. S. . . . . . . 6

48

### III Corps (Sickles)

1 DIVISION (Birney)
  1. Clark's battery [3] . . . . B, 1 N. J. . . . . . . 6
  2. Randolph's battery [4] . . . E, 1 R. I. . . . . . . 6
  3. Livingston's battery [5] . . F, K, 3 U. S. . . . . . 6

2 DIVISION (Berry)
  1. Osborn's battery [6] . . . . B, 1 N. Y. . . . . . . 6
  2. Smith's battery [7] . . . . 4 N. Y. . . . . . . . 6
  3. Dimick's battery . . . . H, 1 U. S. . . . . . . 6
  4. Seeley's battery . . . . K, 4 U. S. . . . . . . 6

3 DIVISION (Whipple)
  1. Bruen's battery [8] . . . . 10 N. Y. . . . . . . . 6
  2. von Puttkammer's battery [9] 11 N. Y. . . . . . . . 6
  3. Huntington's battery . . . H, 1 Ohio . . . . . . 6

60

*Carried forward,* 159

[1] Commanded also by Lieutenant Kirby and by Lieutenant Stevens.
[2] Commanded by Lieutenant Brown.
[3] Commanded by Lieutenant Sims.
[4] Commanded by Lieutenant Jastram.
[5] Commanded by Lieutenant Turnbull.

Formed by the consolidation of two depleted batteries.
[6] Commanded by Lieutenant Winslow.
[7] Commanded by Lieutenant McLean.
[8] Commanded by Lieutenant Lewis.
[9] Commanded also by Lieutenant Burton.

NUMBER OF
PIECES

*Brought forward,* 159

### V Corps (Meade)

**1 DIVISION (Griffin)**
1. Martin's battery . . . . C, Mass. . . . . . . 6
2. Phillips' battery . . . . E, Mass. . . . . . . 6
3. Waterman's battery . . . C, 1 R. I. . . . . . . 6
4. Hazlett's battery . . . . D, 5 U. S. . . . . . 6

**2 DIVISION (Sykes)**
1. Gibbs' battery . . . . . L, 1 Ohio . . . . . . 6
2. Weed's battery [1] . . . . I, 5 U. S. . . . . . . 4

**3 DIVISION (Humphreys)**
1. Barnes' battery . . . . . C, 1 N. Y. . . . . . . 4
2. Randol's battery [2] . . . . E, G, 1 U. S. . . . . 4

42

### VI Corps (Sedgwick)

**1 DIVISION (Brooks)**
1. McCartney's battery . . . A, Mass. . . . . . . 6
2. Hexamer's battery [3] . . . A, N. J. . . . . . . 6
3. Rigby's battery . . . . . A, 1 Md. . . . . . . 6
4. Williston's battery . . . D, 2 U. S. . . . . . . 6

**2 DIVISION (Howe)**
1. Cowan's battery . . . . 1 N. Y. . . . . . . 6
2. Martin's battery . . . . F, 5 U. S. . . . . . . 6

**3 DIVISION (Newton)**
1. McCarthy's battery [4] . . . C, D, 1 Pa. . . . . . 6
2. Butler's battery . . . . G, 2 U. S. . . . . . . 6

**4 DIVISION (Burnham)**
Harn's battery . . . . . . 3 N. Y. . . . . . . 6

54

### XI Corps (Howard)

**1 DIVISION (Devens)**
Dieckmann's battery . . . . 13 N. Y. . . . . . . 6
**2 DIVISION (von Steinwehr)**
Wiedrich's battery . . . . I, 1 N. Y. . . . . . . 6
**3 DIVISION (Schurz)**
Dilger's battery . . . . . I, 1 Ohio . . . . . . 6

*Artillery Reserve* (Schirmer)
1. Jahn's battery . . . . . 2 N. Y. . . . . . . 6
2. De Beck's battery . . . . K, 1 Ohio . . . . . . 6
3. Hill's battery . . . . . C, 1 W. Va. . . . . . 6

36

*Carried forward,* 291

[1] Commanded by Lieutenant Watson.
[2] Formed by the consolidation of two depleted batteries.
[3] Commanded by Lieutenant Parsons.
[4] Formed by the consolidation of two depleted batteries.

ARTILLERY OF THE ARMY OF THE POTOMAC—*Continued*

NUMBER OF
PIECES

Brought forward,    291

### XII Corps (Slocum)

1 DIVISION (Williams)
  1. Fitzhugh's battery[1] . . . K, 1 N. Y. . . . . . . 4
  2. Winegar's battery[2] . . . M, 1 N. Y. . . . . . 6
  3. Best's battery[3] . . . . . F, 4 U. S. . . . . . . 6

2 DIVISION (Geary)
  1. Knap's battery[4] . . . . E, Pa. . . . . . . . 6
  2. Hampton's battery[5] . . . F, Pa. . . . . . . . 6

28

### General Artillery Reserve (Graham)[6]

  1. Brooker's battery . . . . B, 1 Conn. . . . . . 4
  2. Pratt's battery . . . . . M, 1 Conn. . . . . . 4
  3. Taft's battery . . . . . 5 N. Y. . . . . . . 4
  4. Hart's battery . . . . . 15 N. Y. . . . . . . 6
  5. von Blücher's battery . . 29 N. Y. . . . . . . 4
  6. Voegelee's battery . . . 30 N. Y. . . . . . . 6
  7. Kusserow's battery[7] . . . 32 N. Y. . . . . . . 6
  8. Graham's battery[8] . . . K, 1 U. S. . . . . . . 6
  9. Meinell's battery . . . . C, 3 U. S. . . . . . 6
  10. Miller's battery . . . . G, 4 U. S. . . . . . . 6
  11. Kinzie's battery . . . K, 5 U. S. . . . . . . 4

56

### Cavalry Corps (Stoneman)

1 DIVISION (Pleasonton)
  Martin's battery . . . . . 6 N. Y. . . . . . . 6
2 DIVISION (Averell)
  Tidball's battery . . . . . A, 2 U. S. . . . . . . 6

ARTILLERY RESERVE (Horse Artillery) (Robertson)
  1. Robertson's battery[9] . . . B, L, 2 U. S. . . . . . 6
  2. Pennington's battery[10] . . M, 2 U. S. . . . . . 6
  3. Elder's battery . . . . . E, 4 U. S. . . . . . . 4

28

### Provost Guard (Patrick)

  1. Snow's battery . . . . . B, Md. ⎱
  2. Johnson's battery . . . . 12 Ohio ⎰ . . . . . . 10    10

Total . . . . . . . . . .    413

---

[1] Commanded by Lieutenant Bailey.
[2] Commanded also by Lieutenant Woodbury.
[3] Commanded by Lieutenant Crosby.
[4] Commanded by Lieutenant Atwell.
[5] Commanded also by Lieutenant Fleming.

[6] Later Tyler.
[7] Commanded by Lieutenant Gaston.
[8] Commanded by Lieutenant Thomas, Jr.
[9] Commanded by Lieutenant Vincent. Formed by the consolidation of two depleted batteries.
[10] Commanded by Lieutenant Clarke.

## APPENDIX 12

### TABLES OF DAILY LOSSES

These tables, while based upon the official records of the war, are in a measure conjectural.

#### Army of the Potomac [1]

| ORGANIZATION | Before May 2 [2] | May 2 | May 3 | After May 3 [3] |
|---|---|---|---|---|
| I Corps .................... | 55 | 109 | 97 | 38 |
| II  " ................... | 3 | 68 | 1,835 | 19 |
| III  " ................... | 4 | 311 | 3,767 | 37 |
| V  " ................... | 232 | 2 | 458 | 8 |
| VI  " ................... | 15 | 5 | 3,490 | 1,100 |
| XI  " ................... | 0 | 2,411 | 0 | 1 |
| XII  " ................... | 49 | 306 | 2,466 | 3 |
| Cav. {Stoneman, including} Averell ... | 42 | 26 | 0 | 121 |
| {Pleasonton ............ | 63 | 136 | 0 | 1 |
| Army of the Potomac ...... | 463 | 3,374 | 12,113 | 1,328 |

#### Army of Northern Virginia [4]

| ORGANIZATION | Before May 2 | May 2 | May 3 | After May 3 |
|---|---|---|---|---|
| 1 Division, I Corps ........... | 66 | 5 | 1,291 | 83 |
| 2  "  I  " ........... | 18 | 38 | 1,719 | 0 |
| Corps Artillery .............. | 0 | 0 | 106 | 0 |
| I Corps ................. | 84 | 43 | 3,116 | 83 |
| 1 Division, II Corps .......... | 0 | 174 | 2,766 | 0 |
| 2  "  II  " ........... | 12 | 709 | 2,213 | 3 |
| 3  "  II  " ........... | 0 | 0 | 0 | 1,346 |
| 4  "  II  " ........... | 0 | 230 | 1,825 | 23 |
| Corps Artillery .............. | 0 | 0 | 80 | 0 |
| II Corps ............... | 12 | 1,113 | 6,884 | 1,372 |
| General Artillery Reserve ...... | 0 | 0 | 3 | 0 |
| Cavalry Division .............. | 94 | 17 | 0 | 0 |
| Army of Northern Virginia. | 190 | 1,173 | 10,003 | 1,455 |

## APPENDIX 13

### EFFECTIVE STRENGTH ACCORDING TO REPORTS

Where the figures in the reports appear to include enlisted men only, the officers have been added on the basis of 1 to every 20 men. The mark + indicates that the number which it follows is less, and the mark — that it is greater, than

[1] Without counting 1 on Hooker's staff and 8 in Engineer Brigade.
[2] With few exceptions, May 1.
[3] With few exceptions, May 4.
[4] Not including 5 casualties at headquarters II Corps.

the true number.  The mark ± indicates that the number which it follows is greater or less than the true number.

### Federal

| ORGANIZATION | April 27 | April 28 | April 29 | April 30 | May 1 | May 2 | May 3 | May 4 |
|---|---|---|---|---|---|---|---|---|
| I Corps .............. | .... | 17,000 ± | .... | .... | .... | .... | .... | .... |
| 4. O.—1. 3. II ......... | .... | .... | .... | .... | .... | .... | 372 | .... |
| 105 Pa.—1. 1. III ..... | .... | 357 | .... | .... | .... | .... | .... | .... |
| 114 Pa.—1. 1. III ..... | .... | .... | .... | .... | .... | .... | 420 | .... |
| 141 Pa.—1. 1. III ..... | .... | 484 | .... | .... | .... | .... | 441 | .... |
| 72 N. Y.—2. 2. III .... | .... | .... | .... | .... | .... | .... | 440 | .... |
| 120 N. Y.—2. 2. III ... | .... | .... | .... | .... | .... | .... | 481 | .... |
| 5 N. J.—2. 2. III ...... | .... | .... | .... | .... | .... | .... | 320 | .... |
| 8 N. J.—2. 2. III ...... | .... | .... | .... | .... | .... | .... | 271 | .... |
| $\frac{3}{\text{III}}$ ............... | .... | 3,500 | .... | .... | .... | .... | .... | .... |
| 12 N. H.—2. 3. III .... | .... | .... | .... | .... | .... | .... | 558 | .... |
| 4 U. S.—1. 2. V. ...... | 220 | .... | .... | .... | .... | .... | .... | .... |
| 10 U. S.—2. 2. V ...... | .... | .... | .... | .... | 108 | .... | .... | .... |
| 17 U. S.—2. 2. V ...... | 331 | .... | .... | .... | .... | .... | .... | .... |
| $\frac{3}{\text{V}}$ ............... | 3,684 [1] | .... | .... | .... | .... | .... | .... | .... |
| $\frac{1}{3.\text{V}}$ ............... | 1,711 | .... | .... | .... | .... | .... | .... | .... |
| $\frac{2}{3.\text{V}}$ ............... | 1,973 | .... | .... | .... | .... | .... | .... | .... |
| 3 N. J.—1. 1. VI ...... | 349 | .... | .... | .... | .... | .... | .... | .... |
| $\frac{2}{1.\text{VI}}$ ............... | .... | .... | .... | .... | .... | .... | 1,500 | .... |
| 121 N. Y.—2. 1. VI .... | .... | .... | .... | .... | .... | .... | 453 | .... |
| $\frac{2}{\text{VI}}$ ............... | .... | .... | .... | .... | .... | .... | .... | 6,000 |
| $\frac{1}{\text{XI}}$ ............... | .... | .... | .... | .... | .... | 4,200 ± | .... | .... |
| $\frac{1}{1.\text{XI}}$ ............... | .... | .... | .... | .... | .... | 1,470 ± | .... | .... |
| 17 Conn.—2. 1. XI .... | .... | .... | .... | .... | .... | 517 | .... | .... |
| 25 O.—2. 1. XI ....... | .... | .... | .... | .... | .... | 349 | .... | .... |
| 55 O.—2. 1. XI ....... | 471 | .... | .... | .... | .... | .... | .... | .... |
| $\frac{2}{2.\text{XI}}$ ............... | .... | .... | .... | .... | .... | 1,575 ± | .... | .... |
| $\frac{2}{\text{XI}}$ ............... | .... | .... | .... | .... | .... | 4,143 ± | .... | .... |
| XII Corps .............. | .... | .... | .... | .... | 9,610 ± | .... | .... | .... |
| $\frac{1}{\text{XII}}$ ............... | .... | .... | .... | .... | 5,700 | .... | 5,000 | .... |
| 5 Conn.—1. 1. XII .... | 481 | .... | .... | .... | .... | .... | .... | .... |
| 66 O.—1. 2. XII ...... | .... | .... | .... | .... | .... | 362 | .... | .... |
| 78 N. Y.—3. 2. XII .... | .... | .... | .... | .... | 322 | .... | .... | .... |
| 137 N. Y.—3. 2. XII ... | .... | .... | .... | .... | .... | .... | 563 | .... |
| 149 N. Y.—3. 2. XII ... | .... | .... | .... | .... | .... | .... | 503 | .... |

### Confederate

| ORGANIZATION | April 27 | April 28 | April 29 | April 30 | May 1 | May 2 | May 3 | May 4 |
|---|---|---|---|---|---|---|---|---|
| 22 Va.—1. 1. II ....... | .... | .... | .... | .... | .... | .... | 107 | .... |
| 40 Va.—1. 1. II ....... | .... | .... | .... | .... | .... | .... | 217 [2] | .... |
| 1 S. Ca.—3. 1. II ...... | .... | .... | .... | .... | .... | .... | 315 | .... |
| 13 S. Ca.—3. 1. II ..... | .... | .... | .... | .... | .... | .... | 315 | .... |
| 33 N. Ca.—4. 1. II .... | .... | .... | .... | .... | 504 | 504 − | .... | .... |
| 45 Ga.—6. 1. II ....... | .... | .... | .... | .... | .... | 375 | 350 | .... |
| 49 Ga.—6. 1. II ....... | .... | .... | 398 | .... | .... | .... | 280 | .... |
| $\frac{5}{1.\text{II}}$ ............... | .... | .... | .... | .... | .... | .... | 1,400 | .... |
| 1 Tenn.—5. 1. II ...... | .... | .... | .... | .... | .... | .... | 262 | .... |
| $\frac{2}{\text{II}}$ ............... | .... | .... | .... | .... | 8,551 | .... | .... | .... |
| $\frac{1}{2.\text{II}}$ ............... | .... | .... | .... | .... | 1,895 | .... | .... | .... |
| $\frac{2}{2.\text{II}}$ ............... | .... | .... | .... | .... | 1,622 | 1,594 | .... | .... |
| $\frac{3}{2.\text{II}}$ ............... | .... | .... | .... | .... | 1,795 | .... | .... | .... |
| $\frac{4}{2.\text{II}}$ ............... | .... | .... | .... | .... | 1,730 | .... | .... | .... |

[1] Infantry only.     [2] After about an hour's fighting.

## Confederate (continued)

| ORGANIZATION | April 27 | April 28 | April 29 | April 30 | May 1 | May 2 | May 3 | May 4 |
|---|---|---|---|---|---|---|---|---|
| $\frac{5}{2}$ II ................. | .... | .... | .... | .... | 1,509 | .... | .... | .... |
| 6 Ala.—1. 2. II ....... | .... | .... | .... | .... | .... | .... | 473 | .... |
| 12 Ala.—1. 2. II ...... | .... | .... | .... | .... | .... | 330 | .... | .... |
| 12 N. Ca.—3. 2. II .... | .... | .... | .... | .... | .... | .... | 225 | .... |
| 23 N. Ca.—3. 2. II .... | .... | .... | .... | .... | .... | .... | 430 | .... |
| $\frac{4}{1}$ II ................. | .... | .... | .... | .... | .... | 6,000 + | .... | .... |
| 4 Va.—1. 4. II ........ | .... | .... | .... | .... | .... | .... | 355 | .... |
| 27 Va.—1. 4. II ....... | .... | .... | .... | .... | .... | .... | 185 | .... |
| 48 Va.—2. 4. II ....... | .... | .... | .... | .... | .... | 345 | .... | .... |
| $\frac{3}{4}$ II ................. | .... | .... | 2,125 | .... | .... | .... | 325 ± [1] | .... |
| 23 Va.—3. 4. II ....... | .... | .... | .... | .... | .... | .... | 70 | .... |
| 1 La.—3. 4. II ........ | .... | .... | .... | .... | .... | 131 ± | .... | .... |
| 2 La.—3. 4. II ........ | .... | .... | .... | .... | .... | .... | 129 [2] | .... |

# APPENDIX 14

## Williams to Stoneman, April 22

### 1

. . . it is expected that you are again prepared for a forward movement, so far as regards your stores. The commanding general, therefore, directs that you proceed across the river to-morrow morning, if the fords are practicable. The general does not look for one moment's delay in your advance from any cause that human effort can obviate, and directs me to add that his army is awaiting your movements.

### 2

The major-general commanding is of the opinion that you are encamped in the immediate vicinity of your depot of supplies, and that you will spare no labor to put your command in a state of the utmost efficiency, while you hold it in readiness to move at the earliest practicable moment. He also directs that you improve the opportunity to keep yourself advised of the condition of the water on the fords; also of the force of the enemy to guard the fords, and also mature your plans for an advance when the signal is given. Determine at what ford you will cross, at what hour, and the lines you will advance on to accomplish your mission. The line of the enemy's pickets, being extended, must be a weak one, and if attacked at break of day, will easily be broken. If you desire, vigorous demonstrations can be made by the infantry and artillery at Kelley's Ford at any hour, which, as before, will tend to draw the enemy in that direction. If necessary, a still larger force can be sent to that point; but as it will require the best part of two days for them to reach there from this camp, it may not be in season. If the detachment you dispatched [dispatch] to look into Culpeper and Gordonsville should find them held by an infantry force too numerous to engage, let them pass around those places. After you break through the enemy's advanced lines, you will find no force in the direction of Richmond, that city itself being without a sufficient force to keep out your own command, should you advance on it. This, however, is not expected. Major-General Keyes has a command at Gloucester Point and also at Fort Magruder. Wise is in his front

---

[1] After battle. Loss in killed, wounded, and missing (since April 29), 670. Stragglers, etc., 1130.

[2] After battle. Loss in killed, wounded, and missing (May 2 and 3), about 135.

with a small force.  *After crossing the Rapidan the major-general suggests that you subdivide your command, and let them take different routes, and have some point of meeting on your line of general operations.  These detachments can dash off to the right and left, and inflict a vast deal of mischief, and at the same time bewilder the enemy as to the course and intentions of the main body.*[1]  It seems to him that these should move without artillery, and if necessary to strike a railroad or effect a surprise, make long marches at night.  You have sent so many animals to the rear, the general hopes that you will be able to pack ammunition for your batteries and leave your wagons behind.  All vehicles will only embarrass your operations.  In his opinion two pieces of artillery to a division should be all that you attempt to move with.  Of this you must be the judge. You have officers and men in your command who have been over much of this country in which you are operating; make use of them.  The experiences of your march up the river will doubtless satisfy you of what can be accomplished by celerity.  Remember that you are turning the rivers, which the enemy, to follow you, must swim, should they become swollen.  Cross them, however, as low down as possible, as that will shorten your marches.  Let the officers and men selected to destroy bridges, etc., be efficient, and let their work be done thoroughly.

Should you be out of forage and food, you will find them at the farm-houses between the rivers flowing into the Potomac, as that country north of York River, low down, has hitherto completely escaped drainage by the army.  I am instructed to inform you that the general regrets that up to this time you have made no mention of Colonel Davis' disaster the third day out from here.[2]  He requests that you will keep him fully and correctly advised of all your operations. He also requires that you will inform him, without delay, of the probable hour you will be able to resume your march.  In marching you must require your men to keep together as much as in an Indian country.  Send any officer to the rear who does not keep his command in hand.  You will lose every man and horse who separates from his command.

## APPENDIX 15

### *Butterfield to Hooker*

Sedgwick asks if column to move on Telegraph road simultaneously with advance on Bowling Green road is to be portion of his present command.  One portion of your letter directs him to move his whole force on Bowling Green road.  I presumed that contingency of moving forces on the two roads was the division of the forces of the enemy.  Am I right?[3]

### *To Sedgwick*

. . . the general commanding has gone to Chancellorsville.  Sickles' (Third) Corps was ordered to move to that point before he wrote your letter of instructions.  From this I judge it [the column to move on Telegraph Road] was to be a portion of your present command.  I will send your letter to him by an orderly with a copy of this reply and may get telegraphic answer.

---

[1] The italics are mine.  J. B. Jr.

[2] Loss of a number of officers and men captured and drowned in recrossing the Rappahannock on the 15th.

[3] The instructions furnished Sedgwick by Hooker's adjutant-general on the 27th suggested that the pursuit be made in two columns, one on the Telegraph Road and one on the Bowling Green Road, whether the enemy retreated in two columns or in one. Those instructions also indicated that both of the pursuing columns were to consist of portions of Sedgwick's command.

## APPENDIX 16

FEDERAL ARTILLERY BETWEEN CHANCELLORSVILLE AND UNITED STATES FORD
AFTER 12 M. MAY 3

### *In Position*

*Randol*—Three batteries of Griffin's division $\left(\frac{3.\ 2.\ 4}{1.\ \mathrm{V}}\right)$; the two batteries of Humphreys' division—*total* 5 batteries, numbering 26 pieces.

*Weed*—Amsden's battery of Doubleday's division; Ames' of French's division; Kirby's of the corps artillery of the II Corps; Seeley's of Berry's (now Carr's) division, except one section; Lewis' and von Puttkammer's of Whipple's division; both batteries of Sykes' division; Bailey's of Williams' division; a section of Waterman's battery of Griffin's division—*total* 9 batteries and one section, numbering 48 pieces.

*Wainwright*—Two groups: Stewart's battery of Wadsworth's division, and Hall's and Ransom's of Robinson's division, 18 pieces; Wiedrich's battery of von Steinwehr's division minus 2 pieces lost, and Atwell's of Geary's division, 10 pieces—*total* 5 batteries, numbering 28 pieces.

*Grand total in position:* 20 batteries, numbering 102 pieces;[1] or, including 4 pieces of Waterman's battery, about midway between Randol's and Weed's masses, 106 pieces.

### *In Reserve*

Though given by corps, the batteries were not thus grouped.

*I Corps*—Edgell's and Reynolds' batteries of Wadsworth's division; Leppien's and Thompson's of Robinson's division; Cooper's and Ricketts' of Doubleday's division—*total* 6 batteries, numbering 29 pieces.

*II Corps*—Pettit's and Thomas' of Hancock's division; Arnold's of Gibbon's division; Cushing's of the corps artillery of the II Corps—*total* 4 batteries, numbering 24 pieces.

*III Corps*—The 3 batteries of Birney's division minus 1 piece of Jastram's lost; Winslow's, McLean's, and Dimick's batteries, and a section of Seeley's battery, of Berry's division; Huntington's battery of Whipple's division minus 3 pieces lost—*total* 7 batteries and one section, numbering 40 pieces.

---

[1] Hunt includes in Weed's mass Martin's battery (F), 5 U. S., representing it as of 4 guns. This was a 6-gun battery belonging to Howe's division of the VI Corps, with which it remained throughout the campaign (*W. R.*, 39, pp. 250, 613, 614). He ignores Watson's battery (2. V), which is entitled to the place he gives to Martin's (*ib.*, pp. 513, 544). His report is based on what he found at 10 p.m. By this time Seeley's and von Puttkammer's batteries (included above) were replaced by Edgell's (1. I) and Ricketts' (3. I). Weed gives the number of guns in his mass as 56, but he does not specify the batteries, nor is he clear as to the time to which he refers. He probably counted guns which were held in reserve (*ib.*, p. 512). Hunt gives the number of guns under Wainwright as 32, but he includes Reynolds' 6-gun battery (1. I), which was not put in line until the 4th, and allows Atwell's battery (2. XII) only 4 pieces. It had 6 in position (*ib.*, pp. 251, 259, 771).

*XI Corps*—Dilger's battery of Schurz's division minus 1 piece lost; the 3 batteries of the corps artillery of the XI Corps—*total* 4 batteries, numbering 23 pieces.

*XII Corps*—Winegar's and Crosby's batteries of Williams' division and Hampton's of Geary's division—*total* 3 batteries, numbering 18 pieces.

*Cavalry Brigade*—Martin's battery of 6 pieces.

*Grand total in reserve:* 25 batteries, numbering 140 pieces.

## APPENDIX 17

### *Pleasonton to Gibbon*

#### 1

Your note of this date [May 5] is received.[1]  I am not authorized to detach any part of the cavalry to other commands without orders from headquarters Army of the Potomac, but I am positively ordered to obtain all the cavalry I can to carry out my instructions.

#### *2, 3 p.m.*

*General:*

I am here [near Phillips House] acting under the direct orders of Major-General Hooker, and am in communication with him.  I will do all I can to assist you, but my own plans cannot be interfered with.  I have a regiment of cavalry at Falmouth guarding the river, but I cannot say at what moment circumstances may induce me to withdraw it to some more important point.  My line now extends from Rappahannock Station to below Fredericksburg some 10 or 12 miles, besides to the rear as far as Dumfries.  Up to this time the reports are quiet from the right and rear.  If the rebels have a pontoon train, they will try to use it below to-night.  I will do my best to keep you informed of events.

#### [*Indorsement addressed to Butterfield*]

For the information of General Williams [Hooker's adjutant-general] I should like to be informed whether I am in command of the forces in this vicinity for the defence of the river.  One thing is certain, if I am, two persons cannot command the troops.

JOHN GIBBON,
Brigadier-General.

### *Gibbon to Butterfield, 3:20 p.m.*

General Pleasonton claims to be here [at Phillips House] under the direct orders of General Hooker, with certain plans to carry out.  Please inform me whether I am responsible for the defence of this part of the river, and whether I have command of all the troops in the vicinity.

### *Williams, Adjutant-General, to Gibbon, 4:10 p.m.*

Your note of this date with reference to General Pleasonton's command received.  I know nothing of the instructions General Pleasonton has received, but will at once refer the subject to the major-general commanding for his decision thereon.

[1] Not found.  J. B. Jr.

*To Butterfield, 4:45 p.m.*

There appears to be some conflict of jurisdiction between Generals Gibbon and Pleasonton. The former thinks he has under his instructions command of all the troops in this vicinity, and the latter considers that his orders give him exclusive control, so far as the cavalry is concerned. Please let me know the decision of the commanding general in the matter.

An examination of the records of the Army of the Potomac fails to discover any answer to this request. The question may have been settled without correspondence.[1]

[1] Statement of Mr. J. W. Kirkley, Army Board of Publication.

# BIBLIOGRAPHY

Abraham Lincoln, by Nicolay and Hay
Abraham Lincoln, by W. H. Ward
Across the Continent with the 5 Cavalry, by G. F. Price
Annals of the Sixth Pennsylvania Cavalry, by S. L. Gracey
Appletons' Cyclopædia of American Biography
Autobiography of Oliver Otis Howard
Battle of Kelley's Ford, by J. B. Cooke
Battles and Leaders of the Civil War. The Century Company
Battles in Culpeper County, Virginia, by D. A. Grimsley
Berdan's U. S. Sharpshooters, by C. A. Stevens
Biographical Memorial of General Daniel Butterfield, A, edited by Julia L. Butterfield
Camp and Field Life of the 5 N. Y. Volunteer Infantry, Duryea Zouaves, by Alfred Davenport
Camp Fires of the Twenty-third [N. Y.], by Pound Sterling
Campaigns of Stuart's Cavalry, by H. B. McClellan
Campaigns of the Army of the Potomac, by William Swinton
Census of 1860, Miscellaneous Statistics
Chancellorsville, by Hotchkiss and Allan
Chancellorsville, by J. W. de Peyster
Chancellorsville and Gettysburg, by Abner Doubleday
Charge of the Eighth Pennsylvania Cavalry at Chancellorsville, by Pennock Huey
Confederate Military History
E. M. Stanton, by F. A. Fowler
Following the Greek Cross, by T. W. Hyde
Forty Years of Active Service, by C. T. O'Ferral
Four Years with the Army of the Potomac, by R. G. de Trobriand
From Manassas to Appomattox, by James Longstreet
General Hancock, by F. A. Walker
General Lee, by Fitzhugh Lee
General Meade, by I. R. Pennypacker
Glimpses of the Nation's Struggle, 2d Series
Hard Tack and Coffee, by J. D. Billings
Historic Records of the 5 N. Y. Cavalry, by L. N. Boudrye
Historical Sketch of the Hundred and Eighteenth Regiment Pennsylvania Volunteers, by H. T. Peck
Histories of the Several Regiments and Battalions from North Carolina in the Great War, 1861–1865, by W. Clark
History and Roster of Maryland Volunteers, by Commissioners
History of a Cavalry Company (A, 4 Pa.), by William Hyndman
History of Battery B, First New Jersey Artillery, by Michael Hanifen
History of Battery B, First Rhode Island Light Artillery, by J. H. Rhodes
History of Battery E, First Rhode Island Light Artillery, by George Lewis
History of McGowan's Brigade, by J. F. J. Caldwell
History of Pennsylvania Volunteers, by S. P. Bates
History of the Army of the Potomac, by J. H. Stine
History of the Bucktails, by O. K. Thomson and W. R. Ranch
History of the Civil War in America, by the Comte de Paris

History of the Corn Exchange Regiment [118 Pa.], by the Survivors' Association
History of the Fifth Regiment New Hampshire Volunteers, by William Child
History of the First Maine Cavalry, 1861–1865, by E. P. Tobie
History of the First Regiment Delaware Volunteers, by W. P. Seville
History of the First Regiment Pennsylvania Reserve Cavalry, by W. P. Lloyd
History of the First- Tenth- Twenty-ninth Maine Regiment, by J. M. Gould
History of the Hundred and Fiftieth Regiment Pennsylvania Volunteers, by Thomas Chamberlin
History of the Laurel Brigade, by W. N. McDonald
History of the Nineteenth Regiment Massachusetts Volunteer Infantry, by Committee
History of the Ninety-third Regiment New York Volunteer Infantry, by D. H. King, A. J. Gibbs, and J. H. Northupp
History of the Ninth Massachusetts Volunteer Infantry, by D. G. Macnamara
History of the Ninth New York Cavalry, by N. Cheney
History of the Ninth Virginia Cavalry, by R. and T. Beale
History of the Philadelphia Brigade, by C. H. Banes
History of the Second Army Corps, by F. A. Walker
History of the Second Regiment of N. H. Volunteer Infantry, by M. A. Haynes
History of the Sixth New York Cavalry, by Committee
History of the Tenth Regiment of Cavalry, New York State Volunteers, by N. D. Preston
History of the Third Pennsylvania Cavalry, by Committee
History of the Twelfth Massachusetts Volunteers, by B. F. Cook
History of the Twentieth Massachusetts, by G. A. Bruce
History of the Twenty-eighth Regiment New York State Volunteers, by C. W. Boyce
History of the Twenty-second Massachusetts Infantry, by J. L. Parker
History of the Twenty-seventh Indiana Volunteer Infantry, by a Member of Company C
History of the Twenty-seventh Regiment N. Y. Volunteers, by C. B. Fairchild
History of the United States from the Compromise of 1850, by James Ford Rhodes
History of the U. S. Secret Service, by L. C. Baker
John Watts de Peyster, by Frank Allaben
Johnny Reb and Billy Yank, by Alexander Hunter
Lee's Last Campaign, with an Accurate History of Stonewall Jackson's Last Wound, by J. C. Gorman
Life and Campaigns of Lieut.-Gen. Thomas J. Jackson, by R. L. Dabney
Life and Letters of R. E. Lee, Soldier and Man, by J. W. Jones
Life of General G. G. Meade, by R. M. Bache
Life of Stonewall Jackson, by a Virginian
Lincoln in the Telegraph Office, by D. H. Bates
Maine in the War for the Union, by W. E. S. Whitman and C. H. True
Major-General Hiram G. Berry, by E. K. Gould
Marginalia, by "Personne"

*Medical Recollections of the Army of the Potomac,* by Jonathan Letterman

*Memoir and Memorials of Brigadier-General E. F. Paxton,* by his son J. G. Paxton

*Memoirs of Henry Villard*

*Memoirs of John Adams Dix,* compiled by his son Morgan Dix

*Memoirs of Robert E. Lee,* by A. L. Long

*Memoirs of the Confederate War,* by H. von Borcke

*Memoirs of William Nelson Pendleton, D.D.,* by his daughter Susan P. Lee

*Memorial of Lieutenant Franklin Butler Crosby, 4 U. S. Artillery*

*Men and Things I Saw in Civil War Days,* by J. F. Rusling

*Military Memoirs of a Confederate,* by E. P. Alexander

*Military Miscellanies,* by J. B. Fry

*Mosby's Men,* by J. H. Alexander

*Mosby's Rangers,* by J. J. Williamson

*Mosby's War Reminiscences and Stuart's Cavalry Campaigns,* by J. S. Mosby

*New York in the War of the Rebellion,* by F. Phisterer

*Obituary of J. W. de Peyster,* by "Anchor"

*Official Records of the Union and Confederate Navies in the War of the Rebellion,* by Prof. E. K. Rawson, U. S. Navy

*Ohio in the War,* by Whitelaw Reid

*Papers of the Military Historical Society of Massachusetts*

*Papers of the Southern Historical Society*

*Partisan Life with Colonel J. S. Mosby,* by Major John Scott

*Personal Recollections of Abraham Lincoln and the Civil War,* by J. R. Gilmore

*Poems of American Patriotism,* chosen by J. Brander Matthews

*Recollections of a Private,* by W. L. Goss

*Recollections of Half a Century,* by A. K. McClure

*Reminiscences of a Mosby Guerilla,* by J. W. Munson

*Reminiscences of Carl Schurz*

*Reminiscences of General Herman Haupt*

*Reminiscences of Service in the First Rhode Island Cavalry,* by G. N. Bliss

*Report of the Joint Committee on the Conduct of*

*the War at the Second Session, Thirty-eighth Congress*

*Sabres and Spurs,* by Frederic Denison

*Slocum and his Men,* by Committee

*Stonewall Jackson and the American Civil War,* by G. F. R. Henderson

*Stories of our Soldiers,* collected from the Boston *Journal*

*The Army of the Potomac from 1861 to 1863,* by S. L. French

*The Army of the United States,* edited by T. F. Rodenbough and W. L. Haskin

*The Battles of Chancellorsville and Gettysburg,* by A. H. Nelson

*The Campaign of Chancellorsville,* by T. A. Dodge

*The Comanches, a History of White's Battalion, Virginia Cavalry, Laurel Brigade, Hampton Division, A. N. V.,* by F. M. Myers

*The Crisis of the Confederacy,* by Cecil Battine

*The Fifth Army Corps,* by W. H. Powell

*The Richmond Howitzers in the War,* by a Member of the Company

*The Signal Corps in the War of the Rebellion,* by J. W. Brown

*The Three Years' Service of the Thirty-third Massachusetts Infantry Regiment,* by A. B. Underwood

*The Volunteer's Manual,* by W. Simmers and P. Bachschmied

*The War of the Rebellion: a Compilation of the Official Records of the Union and Confederate Armies,* by Lieutenant-Colonel R. N. Scott and others

*Three Years in the Army,* by C. E. Davis, Jr.

*Three Years in the Army of the Potomac,* by H. N. Blake

*Three Years in the Federal Cavalry,* by Willard Glazier

*Trials and Triumphs,* by Hartwell Osborn

*Two Days of War,* by H. E. Tremain

*War Papers of the Military Order of the Loyal Legion of the U. S.,* Commanderies of: Illinois, Massachusetts, Michigan, New York, Ohio, Wisconsin

*War Talks in Kansas*

*War Talks of Confederate Veterans,* by G. S. Bernard

*Washington in Lincoln's Time,* by Noah Brooks

*Wisconsin in the War of the Rebellion,* by W. de Love

# INDEX

# INDEX

Besides the abbreviations given on page xiv and others in common use for the states of the Union, the following forms are here used:

adj.= adjutant; adm.= admiral; adv.= advocate; art'y = artillery; assist.= assistant; bat'y = battery; C = Confederate; c.= corps; capt.= captain; cav.= cavalry; ch.= church; C. H.= Court-House; Ch'ville = Chancellorsville; com.= commanding; com'r = commander; comm'y = commissary; corp'l = corporal; dep't = department; eng.= engineer; F = Federal; f'd = ford; Fred'b'g = Fredericksburg; gen.= general; H.= House; headq.= headquarters; hosp.= hospital; inf.= infantry; insp.= inspector; lieut.= lieutenant; maj.= major; med. = medical; mil.= military; n.= foot-note; north'n = northern; northw'n = northwestern; off.= officer; ordn.= ordnance; q.m.= quartermaster; Rapp'k = Rappahannock; reg't = regiment; r. r. = railroad; sec.= secretary; sta.= station; surg.= surgeon; tav.= tavern; tel.= telegraph; transp.= transportation; west'n = western; wil'ness = wilderness

## A

Abercrombie, Brig.-gen. J. J. **F**, cited 440 n.

Acts of Congress: **C**, 85, 87, 127; **F**, 22 n., 35 n., 48

Adams, Capt. G. W. **C**, com. bat'y (3. II), 502

Adams, Capt. R. H. T. **C**, signal off., 323

Adams, Sergeant C. E. **C**, cited 226 n.

Adjutant-general, army of North'n Va. See *Taylor, Maj. W. E.*

Adjutant-general, army of Potomac. See *Williams, Brig.-gen. Seth*

Adjutant-general, U. S. army. See *Thomas, Brig.-gen. Lorenzo*

Agents of **C** government, 3

Aides, army of North'n Va., 14

Aides, army of Potomac, 11

Albright, Col. Charles **F** (3. 3. II), com. brig., 302, 303, 314, 353

Alexander, E. P. **C**, brig.-gen., xiii; col. com. art'y (I), 133 n., 500; at Zion Ch., 215; *May 1*, 245, 248, 252; *May 2*, 273, 274, 319; *May 3*, 341, 348 n., 397, 399, 401; *May 4*, 415; *May 5*, 426; *May 6*, 431, 432; 501 n.

Alexander, Lieut.-col. A. J. **F**, writes to Averell, 227, 228

Alexandria, 29

Allabach, Col. P. H. **F** (2. 3. V), com. brig., 26, 256, 371

Allen, Col. T. S. (5 Wisc.), 391

Alsop, H., combat at, 225–227

Ambulance corps, 21

Ambulances: **C**, 120, 232, 274; **F**, 128, 174, 175, 178, 183, 219; *May 1*, 244, 262; *May 2*, 302; *May 3*, 373, 400; *May 4*, 412; *May 5*, 422, 425

Ames, Lieut. Nelson **F**, com. bat'y (3. II), 502, 509

Ames, Sergeant J. F. **F**, 79, 80

Ammunition, supply and transp. of, 48, 120, 142, 174, 176, 186, 231, 232, 274, 289, 310, 313; *May 3*, 358, 367, 375–377, 402; *May 4*, 414; *May 7*, 437; kinds of, 22, 23, 490 n.; on Stoneman's raid, 441

Amsden, Capt. F. P. **F**, com. bat'y (3. I), 502, 266, 509

Amusements, 33

*Anacostia* **F**, steamer, 154, 489

Anderson, Adna **F**, eng. of r. r. construction, 12

Anderson, Maj.-gen. R. H. **C** (1. I), com. div., 19, 132, 208 n., 209; retires from Ch'ville, 213, 214; at Zion Ch., 214, 215, 220, 222, 233; 218 n.; *May 1*, 242, 248, 262, 265; *May 2*, 273, 281, 299; *May 3*, 367, 378, 405; *May 4*, 406, 407, 410, 413; *May 5*, 426; orders for, 209, 281; writes to Mahone, 115

Andrews, Lieut.-col. R. S. **C**, com. art'y (3. II), 133, 500, 268 n., 387, 408

Aquia Creek Sta., r. r. to, 29; depot at, *ib.*

Archer, Brig.-gen. J. J. **C** (5. 1. II), 133; *May 2*, 282, 284, 292, 298, 299, 316; *May 3*, 340, 346, 347, 348, 354, 367

Armament. See *Artillery, Cavalry, Infantry, Partisan Rangers*

Army corps **C**, 21:

I, 19; on Stafford Heights, 32; 56, 135; art'y of, 499, 500; strength of, 132, 134. Losses, 475, 505

II, 19; on Stafford Heights, 32; 56; order for marching, 120; moves up Rapp'k, 207; *May 1*, 238, 262; *May 2*, 273, 280, 281, 289, 298; *May 3*, 340, 346; *May 4*, 406, 416; art'y of, 500, 501; strength of, 133, 134. Losses, 475, 505

See *Divisions* **C**

Army corps **F**, 21; flags, 47, 491; badges, 47, 48, 491, 492:

I, 18, 21; desertions from, 36; reviewed, 130; hosp. of, 132; strength of reg'ts, 138 n.; trains of, see *Trains* **F**; instructions for, 178; in motion, 190; 231, 233; *May 1*, 265; *May 2*, 271, 303, 306, 307, 308; *May 3*, 342; instruction of, 491; sick, 493; efficiency, *ib.*; art'y of, 502; strength of, 136, 506. Losses, 473, 505

II, 18; desertions from, 36; 39; reported embarked, 53; 111; reviewed, 129; hosp. of, 132; strength of reg'ts, 138 n.; ordered to march, 173, 174; trains of, see *Trains* **F**; at U. S. F'd, 186, 203, 219; at Chandler's, 224; *May 1*, 240; *May 2*, 314; instruction of, 491; sick, 493; efficiency, *ib.*; art'y of, 502; strength of, 136, 225, 260. Losses, 473, 474, 505

III, 18; desertions from, 36; 39; in skirmish at Hartwood Ch., 62; visited by President, 129; hosp. of, 132; strength of reg'ts, 138 n.; 173; trains of, see *Trains* **F**; instructions for, 178; reviewed, 179; under Sedgwick, 184; in motion, 190; 200, 212, 216; ordered to U. S. F'd, 229; on to Ch'ville, 231; *May 1*, 260; *May 2*, 293, 294, 301, 303; *May 3*, 350; instruction of, 491; sick, 493; efficiency, *ib.*; art'y of, 502; strength of, 136. Losses, 473, 474, 505

V, 11, 18; desertions from, 36; 39; reviewed, 129; hosp. of, 132; strength of reg'ts, 138 n.; ordered to march, 173; 174, 175; trains of, see *Trains* **F**; orders for, 190; at Kelley's F'd, 190, 195; cav. for, 187, 194; on to Rapidan, 195, 197; at Rapidan, 199 n.; at Ch'ville, 219, 222, 223; *May 1*, 240, 241, 243; *May 5*, 420; *May 6*, 429; instruction of, 491; sick, 493; efficiency, *ib.*; art'y of, 503; strength of, 136, 225, 260. Losses, 473, 505

VI, 18; desertions from, 36; 39; reviewed, 129; hosp. of, 132; strength of reg'ts, 138 n.; trains of, see *Trains* **F**; instructions for, 178, 190, 191; in motion, 190; 231; *May 1*, 265; *May 2*, 329–335; *May 3*, 382–401; *May 4*, 413, 414, 415; *May 5*, 421; *May 6*, 431; instruction of, 491; sick, 493; efficiency, *ib.*; art'y of, 503; strength of, 136. Losses, 473, 474, 505

IX, 8, 18; transferred, 53, 55 n.; 54, 114; strength of, 55 n.

XI, 18; desertions, 36, 39; command of, 42, 83; 111; visited by President, 130; hosp. of, 132; strength of reg'ts, 138 n.; ordered to march, 173, 174, 175; trains of, see *Trains* **F**; instructions for, 184; at Kelley's F'd, 187, 188, 195, 202; on to Rapidan, *ib.*, 197; at Rapidan, 198; 218; at Dowdall's Tav., 221, 222, 223, 227; *May 1*, 239, 240, 243, 249; *May 2*, 276, 283, 286, 296, 302, 303, 304, 305, 306, 308, 309, 310, 311, 325; *May 3*, 343; German troops in, 478–480, 491; instruction of, 491; sick, 493;